A Stanley Gibbons checklist
of the stamps of Great Britain

Collect **British** *Stamps*

69th Edition

2018

Stanley Gibbons Limited
London and Ringwood

By Appointment to
Her Majesty The Queen
Philatelists
Stanley Gibbons Ltd
London

Published by Stanley Gibbons Ltd
Editorial, Publications Sales Offices
and Distribution Centre:
7 Parkside, Christchurch Road, Ringwood,
Hants BH24 3SH

© Stanley Gibbons Ltd 2017

British Library Cataloguing in
Publication Data.
A catalogue record for this book is available
from the British Library.

Errors and omissions excepted. The colour
reproduction of stamps is only as accurate as
the printing process will allow.

ISBN-10: 1-911304-10-0
ISBN-13: 978-1-911304-10-4

Item No. R0289-18

Printed by Latimer Trend, Plymouth

Contents

The 2018 Edition

COLLECT BRITISH STAMPS has been the standard guide for collectors of Great Britain ever since the first edition was published in September 1967.

It provides a straightforward, easy-to-use work of reference, with every stamp design illustrated in colour and clear, uncomplicated listings ideally suited to the newer collector, while at the same time providing a handy checklist for the more advanced philatelist – small wonder that over four million copies have been sold to collectors around the world.

Collect British Stamps appears in the autumn of each year: for a more detailed listing, the *Great Britain Concise Catalogue* is published in the spring, incorporating many additional features and is ideal for the collector who needs more information about GB stamps.

Scope. Collect British Stamps comprises:

- All stamps with different watermark (wmk) or perforation (perf).
- Visible plate numbers on Victorian issues.
- Graphite-lined and phosphor issues, including variations in the numbers of phosphor bands.
- First Day Covers for Definitives from 1936, Regionals and all Special Issues.
- Presentation, Gift and Souvenir Packs.
- Post Office Yearbooks and year packs.
- Regional issues and War Occupation stamps of Guernsey and Jersey.
- Postage Due and Official Stamps.
- Post Office Picture Cards (PHQ cards).
- Commemorative gutter pairs and 'Traffic Light' gutter pairs listed as mint sets.
- Royal Mail Postage Labels priced as sets and on P.O. First Day Cover.
- Royal Mail Post & Go Stamps
- The introduction includes a full design index for commemorative issues, a Great Britain collector's glossary and articles giving helpful advice on a range of collecting topics

Stamps of the independent postal administrations of Guernsey, Isle of Man and Jersey are contained in *Collect Channel Islands and Isle of Man Stamps*.

New for this edition

- A thorough review of all prices has been carried out, with a number of increases since the 2016 edition
- Issues for 2017 have been added and the listings of earlier issues carefully checked and updated
- Post & Go stamps fully updated with the help of John M Deering

Layout

Stamps are set out chronologically by date of issue. In the catalogue lists the first numeral is the Stanley Gibbons catalogue number; the black (boldface) numeral alongside is the type number referring to the respective illustration. A blank in this column implies that the number immediately above is repeated. The denomination and colour of the stamp are then shown. Before February 1971 British currency was:

£1 = 20s One pound = twenty shillings and

1s = 12d One shilling = twelve pence.

Upon decimalisation this became:

£1 = 100p

One pound = one hundred (new) pence.

The catalogue list then shows two price columns. The left-hand is for unused stamps and the right-hand for used. Corresponding small boxes are provided in which collectors may wish to check off the items in their collection. Our method of indicating prices is: Numerals for pence, e.g. 10 denotes 10p (10 pence). Numerals for pounds and pence, e.g. 4·25 denotes £4·25 (4 pounds and 25 pence). For £100 and above, prices are in whole pounds and so include the £ sign and omit the zeros for pence.

Colour illustrations

The colour illustrations of stamps are intended as a guide only; they may differ in shade from the originals.

Size of illustrations

To comply with Post Office regulations stamp illustrations are three-quarters linear size. Separate illustrations of surcharges, overprints and watermarks are actual size.

Prices

The prices quoted in this catalogue are the estimated selling prices of Stanley Gibbons Ltd at the time of publication. They are *unless it is specifically stated otherwise*, for examples in fine condition for the issue concerned. Superb examples are worth more; those of a lower quality considerably less. For more details on catalogue prices, see page xxxvi

The unused prices for stamps of Queen Victoria to King George V are for lightly hinged examples. Unused prices for King Edward VIII to Queen Elizabeth II are for unmounted mint (though when not available unmounted, mounted stamps are often supplied at a lower price). Prices for used stamps refer to fine postally used examples, for issues from about 1850 with a fine circular or oval dated cancellation. For further guidance on condition, see 'The Stanley Gibbons Guide to Stamp Pricing on page xxxvi. All prices are subject to change without prior notice and we give no guarantee to supply all stamps priced, since it is not possible to keep every catalogued item in stock. Commemorative issues may only be available in complete sets.

In the price columns:

　† = Does not exist.

(—) or blank = Exists, or may exist, but price cannot be quoted.

　* = Not normally issued (the so-called 'Abnormals' of 1862–80).

Minimum price

The minimum price quoted is 10 pence. For individual stamps prices between 10 pence and 95 pence are provided as a guide for catalogue users. The lowest price *charged* for individual stamps or sets purchased from Stanley Gibbons is £1.

Perforations

The 'perforation' is the number of holes in a length of 2 cm, as measured by the Gibbons Instanta gauge. The stamp is viewed against a dark background with the transparent gauge put on top of it. Perforations are quoted to the nearest half. Stamps without perforation are termed 'imperforate'. From 1992 certain stamps occur with a large elliptical (oval) hole inserted in each line of vertical perforations. The £10 definitive, No. 1658, is unique in having two such holes in the horizontal perforations.

Elliptical perforations

Se-tenant combinations

Se-tenant means 'joined together'. Some sets include stamps of different design arranged se-tenant as blocks or strips and these are often collected unsevered as issued. Where such combinations exist the stamps are priced both mint and used, as singles or complete sets. The set price refers to the unsevered combination plus singles of any other values in the set.

First day covers

Prices for first day covers are for complete sets used on plain covers (Nos. 430/8, 453/60, 462/78b, 485/90, and 503/12) or on special covers (Nos. 461, 479/84, 491/502 and 513 onwards), the stamps of which are cancelled with ordinary operational postmarks (1924–1962) or by the standard 'First Day of Issue' postmarks (1963 onwards). The British Post Office did not provide 'First Day' treatment for every definitive issued after 1963. Where the stamps in a set were issued on different days, prices are for a cover from each day.

Presentation Packs

Special packs comprising slip-in cards with printed information inside a protective covering, were introduced for the 1964 Shakespeare issue. Collectors packs, containing commemoratives from the preceding twelve months, were issued from 1967. Some packs with text in German from 1968–69, exist as does a Japanese version of the pack for Nos. 916/17. Yearbooks, hardbound and illustrated in colour within a slip cover, joined the product range in 1984.

It should be noted that prices given for presentation packs are for items as originally sold, including any additional inserts such as questionaire forms and publicity material.

PHQ cards

Since 1973 the Post Office has produced a series of picture cards, which can be sent through the post as postcards. Each card shows an enlarged colour reproduction of a current British stamp, either of one or more values from a set or of all values. Cards are priced here in fine mint condition for sets complete as issued. The Post Office gives each card a 'PHQ' serial number, hence the term. The cards are usually on sale shortly before the date of issue of the stamps, but there is no officially designated 'first day'. Used prices are for cards franked with the stamp depicted, on the obverse or reverse; the stamp being cancelled with an official postmark for first day of issue. For 1973–76 issues cards with stamps on the obverse are worth about 25% more than the prices quoted.

Gutter pair

Gutter pairs

Almost all modern Great Britain commemoratives are produced in sheets containing two panes of stamps separated by a blank horizontal or vertical margin known as a gutter. This feature first made its appearance on some supplies of the 1972 Royal Silver Wedding 3p, and marked the introduction of Harrison & Sons' new "Jumelle" stamp-printing press. There are advantages for both the printer and the Post Office in such a layout which has now been used for nearly all commemorative issues since 1974. The term "gutter pair" is used for a pair of stamps separated by part of the blank gutter margin. We do not list gutter pairs for self-adhesive stamps since, although the production format is the same, the stamps are separated by die-cutting.

Most printers include some form of colour check device on the sheet margins, in addition to the cylinder or plate numbers. Harrison & Sons used round "dabs" or spots of colour, resembling traffic lights. For the period from the 1972 Royal Silver Wedding until the end of 1979 these colour dabs appeared in the gutter margin. Gutter pairs showing these "traffic lights" are worth considerably more than the normal version. From the 2004 Entente Cordiale set, Walsall reintroduced traffic lights in the gutters of certain sets. Where these extend over more than one section of gutter margin on any stamp they are priced as blocks rather than pairs.

Traffic light gutter pair

No Value Indicated Stamps

From 22 August 1989 various definitive and special stamps appeared inscribed "2nd", "1st" or "E" instead of a face value. These were sold at the current minimum rates for these services which were as follows:

Inland Postage Rate	2nd Class	1st Class
5 September 1988	14p.	19p.
2 October 1989	15p.	20p.
17 September 1990	17p.	22p.
16 September 1991	18p.	24p.
1 November 1993	19p.	25p.
8 July 1996	20p.	26p.
26 April 1999	19p.	26p.
17 April 2000	19p.	27p.
8 May 2003	20p.	28p.
1 April 2004	21p.	28p.
7 April 2005	21p.	30p.

Inland Postage Rate	2nd Class	1st Class
3 April 2006	23p.	32p.
2 April 2007	24p.	34p.
7 April 2008	27p.	36p.
6 April 2009	30p.	39p.
6 April 2010	32p.	41p.
4 April 2011	36p.	46p.
30 April 2012	50p.	60p.
31 March 2014	53p.	62p.
30 March 2015	54p.	63p.
29 March 2016	55p.	64p.
27 March 2017	56p.	65p.

European Airmail Rate	
26 April 1999	30p.
25 October 1999	34p.
27 April 2000	36p.
2 July 2001	37p.
27 March 2003	38p.
1 April 2004	40p.

From June 2004, European Airmail rate stamps reverted to showing a face value.

From 21 August 2006 "Large" letters were charged at a higher rate following the introduction of "Pricing in Proportion". Rates as follows:

Inland Postage Rate	2nd Class Large	1st Class Large
21 August 2006	37p.	44p.
2 April 2007	40p.	48p.
7 April 2008	42p.	52p.
6 April 2009	47p.	61p.
6 April 2010	51p.	66p.
4 April 2011	58p.	75p.
30 April 2012	69p.	90p.
31 March 2014	73p.	93p.
30 March 2015	74p	95p
29 March 2016	75p.	96p.
27 March 2017	76p.	98p.

Catalogue numbers used

This checklist uses the same catalogue numbers as other current Stanley Gibbons catalogues.

Latest issue date for stamps recorded in this edition is 14 December 2017.

> We regret we do not give opinions as to the genuineness of stamps, nor do we identify stamps or number them by our Catalogue

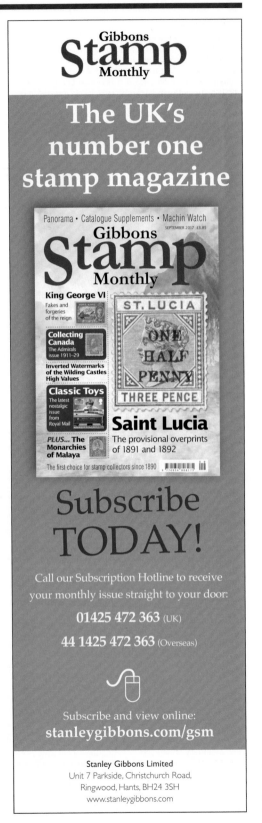

This index gives an easy reference to the inscriptions and designs of the Special Stamps 1953 to December 2017. Where a complete set shares an inscription or type of design, then only the catalogue number of the first stamp is given in addition to separate entries for stamps depicting popular thematic subjects. Paintings, inventions, etc., are indexed under the name of the artist or inventor, where this is shown on the stamp.

Miniature Sheet Design Index

Stanley Gibbons receives, on a regular basis, enquiries concerning the allocation of SG Numbers to some of individual stamps included in Miniature Sheets. Stamps which are available from more than one source, usually from counter sheets in addition to the Miniature sheet, are allocated numbers.

From this flow of enquiries a decision was made, as part of the review of the design index, to include a new section identifying all the Miniature Sheets issued for GB. These are listed numerically by SG Number, alphabetically by title of sheet and finally (alphabetically) by the individual stamps printed within the MS.

In future editions of the catalogue the induvial stamp listing will be expanded to include more detailed identification by thematic elements.

Numerically by SG Number

Luxury Hingeless Albums

The Stanley Gibbons Luxury Hingeless album range offers the ultimate in quality, convenience and style. Handsomely bound in deeply padded navy blue faux leather, each peg-fitting album is richly embossed with the country's national crest on the cover and spine and presented in its own slipcase. Inside, the finest quality 130gsm white leaves (222 x 275mm) have been expertly arranged with spaces for each stamp and clear protective mounts already affixed in place to enable easy insertion of your stamps. Selected illustrations and descriptions for your guidance are also included. Annual supplements are published to help keep your album up to date. These albums follow a simplified system, similar to the Collect British Stamps catalogue.

Great Britain

Stamps of Great Britain 1840-2016, the GB Luxury Hingeless album runs in line with SG Collect British Stamps catalogue.

Vol. 1 Album (1840-1970)	R5284	£170
Vol. 2 Album (1970-1989)	R5285	£170
Vol. 3 Album (1990-1999)	R5290	£170
Vol. 4 Album (2000-2007)	R5295	£170
Vol. 5 Album (2008-2011)	R5331	£170
Vol. 6 Album (2012-2015)	R5333	£170
Vol. 7 Album (2016)	R5671	£90
Volume 1-7 Album Set	R5284(SO)	
	SAVE £210	£900
Vol. 7 Binder	R5671L/RB	£62
Vol. 1 Album (**1952-1989**)	R5546	£190
Vol. 2 Album (**1990-1999**)	R5581	£170
Vol. 3 Album (**2000-2007**)	R5583	£170
Vol. 4 Album (**2008-2011**)	R5618	£170
Vol. 5 Album (**2012-2015**)	R5660	£170
Vol. 6 Album (**2016**)	R5882	£90
Volume 1-6 Album Set	R5546(SO)	
	SAVE £165	£795
GB Headed Leaves	R5402LXRGGB	£15

(per 20) suitable for both the above GB albums

Great Britain Queen Elizabeth II

Covering the stamps of the reign of QEII (1952-2016), the SG LH Great Britain QEII albums are designed to be used in conjunction with the Stanley Gibbons catalogue, Collect British Stamps. The GB QEII comes complete with an Index page as per the standard GB Luxury Hingeless.

Stanley Gibbons Great Britain Standard Album
The standard albums are covered in navy canvas, have peg fittings for ease of inserting leaves and come in luxury slipcases.

Vol. 1 Album (1840-1989)	R5284STSG	£95
Vol. 2 Album (1990-1999)	R5285STSG	£95
Vol. 3 Album (2000-2011)	R5290STSG	£95
Vol. 4 Album (2012-2016)	R5295STSG	£95
Vol. 1-4 Album Set	R5284STSG(SO)	
	SAVE £70	£310

Prices correct at time of printing.

Collecting Stamps – the Basics

It seems reasonable to assume, since you are reading this, that you already collect British stamps – but of course there are many ways of building on any collection and, if you are relatively new to it, we hope that the following will be of some guidance.

Traditionally, stamp collectors were introduced to the hobby with a quantity of world stamps, some still on envelopes and cards, which were then sorted and mounted in an album. In due course, many would decide to concentrate on a single country or group of countries and "specialisation" would begin, based on the experience built up as a "world collector".

More recently, an alternative route has become prevalent, in which, often as a gift, collections may be built on a "standing order" from a philatelic bureau, with stamps or covers arriving automatically, as they are issued, to be mounted in an album or stockbook. Albums are conveniently designed to meet the needs of this type of collection, with an illustrated space in which to mount every stamp.

This type of collection has much to recommend it – but one big disadvantage – it will be exactly the same as thousands of others, built up in the same way.

For this reason, many collectors are now returning to the delights of general collecting while maintaining their existing collections, and finding that the fun they had as children is very easy to recapture!

If you came to the hobby via "the standing order" route and would like to start a second "general collection", here are a few tips and suggestions.

Obtaining your stamps

Children were encouraged to buy – or persuade their parents to buy – the largest packet of stamps they could, as just sorting them into countries would prove enormously useful and interesting. Unfortunately large packets of world stamps are not as easy to obtain as they used to be, but you can still buy existing collections of all sorts at stamp fairs, shops or at auction, prices to suit every pocket. Just sorting and remounting such a collection will prove tremendously exciting.

Sooner or later, of course, you will identify gaps in your collection that you want to fill. It is useful to keep a note of these in a book that you can take with you when you visit a stamp shop or stamp fair – no one can remember everything and it is always annoying to discover that you have just bought a stamp you didn't need!

It is vitally important of course that you keep your "wants" book up-to-date and cross out items as you acquire them.

As well as visiting stamp fairs, you can check out the advertisements in the press; establish a good relationship with a dealer you like and, he will be happy to receive a "wants list" from you. He will then supply you with any items on it he has currently in stock and keep a record of anything else so that he can send it on to you if he gets one. All such items are usually "on approval", so that if you have found them somewhere else, you are not obliged to purchase them.

More expensive items can be purchased at auction. Many of the larger auction houses do not like to sell items of lower value and therefore, in the main, offer more expensive single stamps and covers or complete collections and accumulations.

Other auctions offer single items of lower value and these can be a great way of picking up items you need. Stanley Gibbons Postbid auctions fall into this category, but there are many others and, once again, it is good to identify an auction house which regularly offers the type of material you are looking for and provides a reliable service.

Another method of buying stamps is "kiloware". These are stamps sold by weight and generally assumed to be "unsorted" i.e. no one has been through them before and picked the good ones out. Many collectors enjoy this approach to stamp collecting and they will tell you of the wonderful "finds" they have made – but inevitably you will be left with a vast majority of stamps that you do not want because they duplicate items already in your collection. Charity shops will always be happy to receive them – and they will eventually finish up in someone else's "genuinely unsorted kiloware" – so once again, if this is your kind of collecting, establish a good relationship with a reliable supplier.

"Kiloware" is generally supplied in the form of stamps on paper, torn or cut from envelopes – so this is probably a good point at which to discuss one of the real basics of stamp collecting – soaking stamps off paper.

It is helpful to carry out some rudimentary sorting before you start. Soaking stamps is quite a time-consuming process, so you do not want to waste time on stamps you don't need or don't want, maybe because they are damaged.

Once you have sorted out the stamps you want to soak off, pour some clean water (warm but *not* hot) into a bowl; then float each stamp (face uppermost) on the surface of the water. You can float as many stamps at one time as you have room for.

Leave the stamps for 15 minutes or so to give the water time to soak the gum that is sticking the stamp to the paper. Most stamps can then be gently peeled away. If they do not come away easily do not try to tear them off the paper. Leave them for another five minutes or so and try again.

Providing your hands are clean it's better to handle the stamps with your fingers when peeling off the envelope paper. The paper of stamps is weakened when it is damp and picking them up with tweezers may damage them.

When you have peeled the stamps off the envelope there will probably be some damp gum still on the back of them. Use a soft brush dipped in water to remove this, a paint brush is ideal. Alternatively let the stamp float on the water for a few minutes – the gum will dissolve away. However, do not immerse the stamp in water. For most stamps this would be safe enough but for some it would be dangerous as the ink may run.

Then shake off any excess water and place the stamps face upwards on a sheet of clean kitchen paper towel. This is why it is so important to clean all the gum off. If you do not, your stamps will stick to the paper and you will have to float them off all over again. When all the stamps are laid out cover them with more paper towel then make a kind of sandwich by putting a few sheets of ordinary paper on top.

Place a heavy book on this sandwich. This will flatten the stamps as they dry. After half an hour open up the sandwich and carefully remove the stamps. Spread them out on another piece of clean paper and leave to dry in the air for a little while. When completely dry they are ready for mounting in your album.

Or you can just lay the stamps face down on paper towel and allow them to dry out in the air. If you use this method do not try to speed up the drying by putting the stamps in the sun or close to a hot radiator as they will curl up and you may damage them when you flatten them out to put them in your album.

There are two things which you must be very careful about when floating stamps. Firstly, many old stamps were printed in special inks which run, change colour, or even disappear completely in water. Fewer modern stamps are affected in this way but even so it is best to be safe, so avoid letting water get on the surface of the stamp when you are floating-off. Be careful when floating stamps to keep separate stamps affixed to white and coloured envelopes. Take out any stamp which are stuck to bits of coloured paper and float these separately. Floating can easily make the ink run and so damage your stamps by staining them with unwanted colours.

These days, many countries produce "self-adhesive" stamps and these may not come away from their backing paper at all. If you believe that a stamp may be "self-adhesive", it would be better to leave it on the paper, carefully trimming round it with scissors, making sure you do not cut into the stamp.

Finally, always think twice before tearing a stamp off an envelope. Most old stamps and some modern ones too, if they have interesting postmarks, will be more valuable if left on the envelope. If in doubt always try to ask a more experienced collector's advice.

Choosing an Album and Mounting your stamps

These are two different topics but really need to be considered together, as the way you mount your stamps will depend on the album you choose and your choice of album may depend on the way you wish to mount your stamps. Here are some of the options:

New Age album

Printed Albums

You may be used to an album printed with a space for every stamp, and these may be obtained for larger groups of countries, such as the Stanley Gibbons New Age Album, with spaces for all Commonwealth Queen Elizabeth stamps up to 1962. If this is the sort of collection you hope to build they are fine albums – but as they have a space for every stamp, filling one would be a time-consuming business!

Blank albums

These are made up of blank pages, printed with a faint "quadrille" (tiny squares) which help you lay your stamps out neatly. These give you freedom to lay your collection out as you wish, leaving spaces for stamps you are hoping to obtain, or a neat display of the stamps you have. The former option may mean that you have a lot of gaps on the page, the latter may mean fairly regular rearrangement of your collection – the choice is yours.

Blank albums come in a wide range of prices and binding types, from inexpensive ring binders, through traditional "springbacks" to high quality "peg-fitting" types. Again, the choice is yours.

Stockbooks

In the past, collectors used stockbooks to hold duplicates and stamps awaiting mounting in the main album, but due to their convenience and cost, many collectors are now using stockbooks to house their main collections.

They certainly make it easy to "mount" your stamps – you just slip them into the strips on the pages and you can move them around easily to accommodate new acquisitions too! You can even write notes regarding different stamps or sets and slip those into the strips.

Stock albums

These are loose-leaf stockbooks, which have the added benefit of being able to insert extra pages in the book. Also, because the strips come in a number of formats, they look better than a stockbook layout which is a bit restricting and does not show larger items, such as covers, blocks and miniature sheets, very well.

Mounting your stamps

Before we come on to cover albums, let's return to the matter of mounting your stamps. If you have chosen either the stockbook or stock album option, this is not really an issue as you can just slip your stamps into the strips on the page. If you have opted for a printed or blank album, on the other hand, the question of mounting is important.

The traditional stamp hinge is generally the preferred option for used stamps. Instructions for their use are generally given on the packet, so we will not repeat them here, but we must stress that the key points are to *lightly* moisten the hinge before attaching it to the stamp or album page and *not to try to remove it* until it's dry or you may damage the page – or even more important, the stamp.

For unused stamps that have been previously mounted, stamp hinges are also perfectly acceptable, but for stamps which still have "full original gum" and show no evidence of having been previously hinged, most collectors now favour "hingeless mounts", which allow you to attach the stamp to the page without disturbing the gum (keeping the stamp "unmounted").

For most of the most frequently encountered stamp sizes, cut-to-size mounts are available for immediate use. Less common sizes will have to be cut from bigger strips, but even large blocks and miniature sheets can be mounted in this way.

Although hingeless mounts are gummed, ready for use,

many collectors prefer to use hinges to attach them to the album page as this makes them easier to move around when new stamps are added.

Covers

Many collectors like to include covers in their collections – either "first day" or "souvenir" covers or simply envelopes that show examples of the stamps in use. This is especially desirable in the case of early covers, which might show unusual postmarks or other features.

Universal album

Covers can be mounted on blank pages using gummed photograph corners, but may also be accommodated in purpose-built cover albums. There are even albums, such as the Stanley Gibbons Universal, which are designed to hold stamp and cover pages together (and booklet pages too!).

What else?

So, that's covered the choice of album and the mounting of stamps: What else do you need? This comes under two headings: equipment and information.

Information

You can manage without background information, but it would be a bit like setting out on a journey to somewhere you've never been without a map.

The first thing is a catalogue to tell you what exists and will help you to identify what you have. The Stanley Gibbons catalogue range includes something for every collector from the beginner to the specialist.

Beyond that there are specialist handbooks on just about everything, but many are printed in quite small numbers and, once sold, are unlikely to be reprinted. However, specialist dealers and auction houses can be a useful source of out-of-print literature.

> You should also try to keep up with what is going on in the philatelic world and, again, Stanley Gibbons is able to help, via its monthly magazine, *Gibbons Stamp Monthly*, recently described as "the best magazine for stamp collectors published anywhere". For a free sample copy and subscription details, please write to Stanley Gibbons Publications, *(the address is at the front of this checklist)*.

Of course, as with everything else, much information may also be found on the internet and you will almost certainly find it worth joining the local society in your area, other stamp collectors are always happy to help a newcomer.

Equipment

Again, what you need in the way of equipment will depend largely on what you are collecting, the degree of specialisation you intend to achieve and the type of album you use.

We have already discussed albums and stamp mounts, the only other item every stamp collector must have is a pair of tweezers. All stamps should be handled with tweezers; they ensure that the natural oils in our fingers do not get on to the stamps and, after a bit of practice, they are easier to use than fingers as well. They come in different lengths, with different points and made from different materials (generally stainless steel or gold-plated). Find a style that suits you and stick with it.

From then on the equipment you need is up to you. Most collectors like to have a magnifying glass so they can look at their stamps more closely. Again, they come in a wide range, from the fairly basic, offering 2 or 3× magnification to pocket microscopes giving 30× magnification, and digital microscopes that you can attach to your computer for really detailed examination of your stamps.

Another useful type of magnifier is one that incorporates a millimetre scale – ideal for measuring overprints and other features.

Even a quick look in any catalogue will show that differences in perforation, watermark and colour can make an enormous difference to the price of a stamp. So most collectors like to have the necessary equipment to measure perforations, view watermarks and identify colours and shades.

Fortunately, as far as perforations are concerned, the perforation gauge used by most of the world's top collectors and dealers is accessible to all – it's the Stanley Gibbons Instanta – which measures perforations to a decimal point and is easy to use. There is an electronic perforation measurer which is even easier to use – but it is a bit more expensive than the Instanta.

Watermark detectors also come in a variety of types and a wide range of prices, all of which are effective in their different ways. If you are collecting older stamps, watermarks are generally clearer and can be identified simply by placing the stamps face down on a dark background or watermark tray and, if necessary, adding a few drops of lighter fluid or watermark fluid. The Morley Bright products are an excellent alternative if you do not like using fluids, which many collectors do not.

More modern stamps, especially mint ones are more difficult to sort and for these one of the electric watermark detectors will probably be the answer. The Stanley Gibbons Detectamark and other similar products take a bit of practice to get used to, but are very effective. Their drawback is that they can only handle single stamps and cannot accommodate blocks or sheets. If you are able to, visit a shop where you can see the different products demonstrated and make your choice.

Happily, the standard colour guide for stamp collectors, the Stanley Gibbons Colour Key, is another relatively inexpensive item which will provide years of use. It features 200 different colours and will allow you to tell the difference between "mauve", "purple", "lilac" and "violet" with ease.

Finally and especially if you are collecting the modern stamps of Great Britain at a more specialised level, you will probably want an ultraviolet lamp to identify different papers and phosphor types. Again, these come in a range of designs at different prices, so it is useful to seek the advice of an experienced collector before deciding on the one to buy. If you collect Great Britain stamps, you really need a "short wave" lamp to identify different phosphors, but some lamps incorporate both "long" and "short" wave bulbs, which give them wider potential use.

A lamp with a "hood" or viewing eyepiece is generally to be recommended, firstly because direct exposure to prolonged ultraviolet light is damaging to the eyes, so you should avoid lamps which cause you to see the bulb itself while you are using it. Also, such lamps are more effective in the dark, so anything which shields the stamp being examined from other light sources, including daylight, will improve the effectiveness of the lamp.

The new Stanley Gibbons Ultraviolet lamp, introduced in 2012, offers a broad spectrum light, suitable for detecting all phosphors, while the unique eyepiece makes it suitable for use wherever you are.

Philatelic accessories of all types are available from Stanley Gibbons Publications or at the SG shop in London. The current product guide is available on request. Alternatively, a host of useful information can be found here: www.stanleygibbons.com

Stanley Gibbons Numbers

When Stanley Gibbons published his first stamp catalogue in 1865 the stamps in it were simply listed by country and description. It was not long, however, before there were just too many stamps to be listed in this way and in order to simplify the way in which stamps could be ordered by customers, each was given its unique and individual number.

Nowadays, as each stamp is added to the catalogue in the supplement published in *Gibbons Stamp Monthly*, it is assigned its number; sets being listed according to the date on which they were issued and then by face value within that set. If several stamps of the same value belong to one set, usually issued in the form of a sheet or sheetlet, the numbering starts at the top left-hand stamp and runs down to the stamp at bottom right.

Long definitive series are listed together for the convenience of collectors so this often involves adding new numbers to an existing series. It can also happen that a stamp or set of stamps are discovered which were unknown at the time of issue – these also have to be inserted in their correct chronological sequence.

Easy identification

The Stanley Gibbons number appears in the left-hand column of the stamp listing and should not be confused with the bold number that often appears to its right and refers to its illustration. So, by using the country name and catalogue number, every stamp can be easily identified and, rather than having to order Great Britain 1924 10d. turquoise-blue on Block Cypher watermarked paper, all you have to do is order a Great Britain SG 428 and state whether you want it used or unused.

In order to render them immediately identifiable, certain types of stamps are given a prefix to their catalogue number thus a number prefixed with a "D" is a postage due stamp, while an "O" means it's an official stamp. Some countries' stamps also have a prefix to allow them to be easily identified. Thus, in this catalogue, Scotland stamp numbers are prefixed with an "S" and those for Wales with a "W".

Changes

Once a number has been assigned it is not changed unless absolutely necessary. The reason, for this is that collectors often maintain their "wants lists" using SG numbers, while auction houses around the world quote them in their descriptions, as do books and articles in the philatelic press.

Expertising bodies, including the expert committee of the Royal Philatelic Society London and the British Philatelic Association also quote SG numbers in their certificates, which generally identify scarcer or more valuable stamps, so regular changing of those numbers would render such certificates out-of-date.

Nevertheless, sometimes complete sections of the catalogue, occasionally even complete countries, have to be re-organised, and under such circumstances renumbering does take place – but this is infrequent.

Usually, new stamps added into the middle of listings have a letter suffix. This can occur in two forms. If the stamp is listable in its own right the suffix forms a part of the "main" number in the left-hand column of the listing. Thus, when the Wilding 4½d. and 5d. values with phosphor bands appeared, in 1961 and 1967 respectively, but the 4d. and 6d., both issued in 1960, had already been given the numbers 616 and 617, the 4½d. became 616a and the 5d. was listed as 616b.

Varieties of such "main" stamps, such as errors, booklet panes and watermark varieties are given letter suffixes in a different way, so that the phosphor version of the 1963 6d. Paris Postal Conference stamp (SG 636) has a "p" suffix which appears in the listing itself, to differentiate it from the normal, non-phosphor stamp – so to order one, all you need to ask for is SG 636p.

Sometimes, of course, so many stamps are subsequently added to a listing that the use of suffix letters would just become too complicated and, so far as Great Britain is concerned, this has happened with the decimal Machin series, which are prefixed "X" for the conventionally perforated series, first issued in 1971, and "Y" for the series with elliptical perforations at each side, first issued in 1993. In 2009 a new series with additional security features began to appear and these are listed with a "U" prefix.

Adding new numbers

Thus when new stamps are added to such series – and several are appearing each year – adding new numbers does not have to mean changing those of subsequently issued commemorative issues.

Within the "U" series, new "main" values are initially added with a suffix letter, so the numbers of previously issued stamps do not have to be adjusted with each new catalogue, but every four or five years the complete listing is updated to eliminate the suffix letters and maintain a "clean" listing of numbers. When ordering stamps from these series it is as well to mention which edition of the catalogue you are using as, if your dealer is using a different one, you may not receive what you expect!

The Stanley Gibbons numbering system represents an easy-to-use and universally recognised system of stamp identification. Collectors all over the world use it to keep their collections in order and dealers sort and classify their stocks by it, so its use makes life easier for everyone.

Stanley Gibbons numbers are fully protected by copyright and, while their use is encouraged, they may not be reproduced without the prior permission of Stanley Gibbons Limited.

THE STAMP CENTRE

79 STRAND LONDON WC2R 0DE · WWW.THESTAMPCENTRE.CO.UK
THE ONLY REMAINING INDEPENDENT STAMP DEALER ON THE STRAND

SHOP HOURS MON - SAT 9.30-5.00 - FREEPHONE HOTLINE 0800 975 4581
OVERSEAS CUSTOMERS PLEASE TELEPHONE 00 44 207 836 2341

* COLLECT BRITISH STAMPS READER OFFERS *

A. THE 1841 IMPERFORATE PENNY RED

We will supply 20 different three margin copies of this famous stamp, known the world over for just £39.90 post-free or 40 completely different for just £75 post-free.

B. 1858/70 PENNY RED PLATE NUMBERS

We will supply 40 different stamps in sound used condition. Sort the plates to begin or build your collection & then start searching for the missing ones with this appealing offer for £39.90 post-free.

Welcome to The Stamp Centre, a collectors paradise here in the heart of London, established in 1985 and just twenty five yards across the road from our neighbours at Stanley Gibbons! We send out lists with offers similar to these every few weeks and if you like to receive them, simply call or email; mail@thestampcentre.co.uk

We send out regular Flyer Offers to our customers throughout the year, including our very popular 'Blue List' containing a range of Great Britain material at prices to suit all pockets. Every item on the 'Blue List' is illustrated and with between 450 and 480 items each time, a wide variety of material is included from Queen Victoria to modern. For those who collect stamps of other countries we have our fully illustrated 'Green List' of worldwide items from classics to modern thematics. If you would like either or both of these lists, please write, telephone or email; mail@stamp-centre.co.uk

C. THE 1880/1 INDIGO SET

We offer this popular set of 5 different mid-reign Victorian stamps, SG 164/9 in sound used condition for just £57.50 post-free which represents superb value for money as all our offers.

D. 1867/81 2½D BLUE

There's more plating fun to be had with these! We will supply four different collectable stamps, all with different plate numbers, with a minimum catalogue value of £150 for just £25 post-free.

E. THE GEORGE V DOWNEY HEADS

This is an interesting set of the 10 basic values, SG 322/350. We offer these in sound used condition for £19.95 post-free.

F. THE 1951 FESTIVAL HIGH VALUE SET

We offer this glorious set of 4, lightly mounted mint for just £39.90 post-free.

YOU CAN ALSO CONTACT US AT ANY TIME BY EMAIL - MAIL@THESTAMPCENTRE.CO.UK

G. COMMEMORATIVE COVER STARTER COLLECTION

This fantastic starter collection will provide you with 50 different clean illustrated commemorative FIRST DAY COVERS. What a bargain! Just £49.99 post-free.

H. DEFINITIVE & REGIONAL COVER STARTER COLLECTION

This starter collection will provide you with 50 different clean illustrated Definitive & Regional First Day Covers. Another great offer for just £49.99 post-free.

BUY ITEMS G AND H TOGETHER AND RECEIVE A FREE FIRST DAY COVER ALBUM

I. 1970/81 MACHINS WITH PHOSPHOR BANDS

These stamps are from the complete basic set between SG x841/922. You will receive 83 different mint stamps (not including the ½p side band, available separately) for £75 post-free.

J. 1980s MACHINS ON PHOSPHORISED PAPER

These stamps gradually replaced the banded stamps in offer I. They form a complete series ranging from SG x924/993, a total of 69 different mint stamps for just £39.90 post-free.

K. PRE-DECIMAL REGIONALS COMPLETE MINT SET

This collection of 77 mint stamps includes ALL basic pre-decimal regionals. Save a fortune in show leather and purchase ALL 77 for just £39.90 post-free.

L. DECIMAL REGIONALS COMPLETE MINT SET 1971-1983

The stamps above form part of the complete collection of 99 regional stamps issued between 1971 & 1983 for use in Scotland, Northern Ireland & Wales. The complete set just £39.90 post-free.

TO PURCHASE ANY OF THESE OFFERS CALL FREEPHONE 0800 975 4581 MON-SAT 9-5

PORTISHEAD STAMP AUCTIONS

We have owned this popular public auction for over three years. The number of active participants is steadily increasing and the range of material offered has increased steadily. An active room plus the strength of our mailing list has seen a steady improvement in the number of bidders with each sale and improving results for sellers.

Our auction venue is Gordano School, St. Mary's Road, Portishead, North Somerset, BS20 7QR and catalogues for these sales are available free upon request.

Attend in person or bid postally.

FREE QUARTERLY AUCTION CATALOGUE
available upon request, write, telephone or email
portishead@thestampcentre.co.uk

The Stanley Gibbons Guide to Stamp Pricing

Catalogue editor and lifelong collector, Hugh Jefferies, offers a few tips.

It is a common fallacy that the prices in this catalogue show what a stamp is "worth", should you wish to sell it.

They are, instead, the price at which Stanley Gibbons will sell a fine example of the stamp in question, but that price includes a lot of other factors, as well as the inherent "value" of the stamp itself. There are costs in running any business and these are built into the price of any stamp shown in the catalogue, although the proportion of the price that relates to the stamp and that which relates to "business overheads" will vary from stamp to stamp.

What is true is that the prices shown in this catalogue represent an accurate "guide" to the value of the stamps listed in it. **Stanley Gibbons are now the only major philatelic publisher whose stamp catalogue is also their price list**. Naturally, if the prices are set too high, no one will buy our stamps, if they are too low, we will have difficulty replacing our stocks. It is therefore vitally important to the future of the company that the prices in this catalogue are set as accurately as possible. As a result, a great deal of care is taken over those prices – which is why they are held in such regard by collectors, dealers and stamp auction houses throughout the world.

A very accurate picture

Each year, every price in our annual catalogues is checked and amended if necessary, having regard to the prices being achieved at auction as well as the demands of our customers at 399 Strand and orders coming in via the post, email and our website. Prices are held, increased or reduced according to those factors, giving a very accurate picture of the state of the market for each and every stamp.

Can stamps be purchased for less than the prices quoted in this catalogue? Of course they can. Stanley Gibbons themselves will frequently have stamps in stock at prices lower than "full catalogue". Every business offers discounts and makes "special offers" from time to time and Stanley Gibbons is no different. That apart, however, it should always be remembered that the prices quoted in this catalogue are for stamps in fine condition. Stamps with minor defects, heavy postmarks, slight fading and other flaws will frequently be offered at lower prices, both by Stanley Gibbons and by other dealers and auction houses.

Checking condition

It is very important that, when you are thinking of buying a stamp for your collection, you carefully consider the condition of the item in question. Does it match up to the Stanley Gibbons definition of "Fine"? If it doesn"t, is the price at which it is being offered too high? If you believe that the price is higher that it should be, leave it alone – or if you are really desperate, haggle for a better deal.

The knowledge as to what is "fine" and therefore worthy of "full catalogue" is one that you will gain with experience and will vary from stamp to stamp. Any stamp less than 100 years old should really be perfect in every way, but one can be more forgiving with older issues.

Briefly, here are a few of the things to consider.

* **Gum** – for unused stamps issued after 1936 prices are for unmounted mint – stamps never previously hinged. Modern stamps with hinge marks should be substantially discounted. For earlier stamps, heavy mounts and multiple hinges will also detract from the value, while unused stamps with the gum removed are worth considerably less.

* **Margins** – for imperforate stamps these should be clear on all sides – the design should not be cut into or even touching the edge of the stamp.

* **Perforations** – check that these are complete, that none are missing or short, especially at the stamp corners. Ideally the margin between the stamp design and the perforations should be even and well balanced – known as "well-centred".

* **Paper** – Check that there are no tears or thins to the paper – on the front as well as the back – and that there are no bends or creases. Again, the greater the damage the further away from "full catalogue" the stamp is worth.

* **Postmarks** – these should be clear, clean and should not disfigure the stamp. **The prices for all British stamps issued after 1880 assume used stamps to be cancelled with a clean, clear circular datestamp. Heavy parcel, wavy line or slogan cancellations reduce stamp values significantly.** On the other hand, very lightly cancelled stamps should sometimes be viewed with suspicion. There needs to be enough of the postmark showing to prove that the stamp has really been used!

If the above notes seem complicated, don"t worry. You will soon become adept at viewing every stamp in the light of its condition and deciding what proportion of catalogue you are prepared to pay. If you are not certain, ask the dealer for a guarantee that he will refund your money if you"re not happy with your purchase. All good dealers will be happy to provide this.

So, buy carefully – but, above all, have fun!

It should always be remembered that the prices quoted in this catalogue are for stamps in fine condition.

Adhesive A gummed stamp

Albino A design impression without colour

Aniline A fugitive (water soluble) ink or dye

Bisect Part of a stamp that has been cut in two for separate use; usually during a shortage of stamps

Blind perforation A perforation which has not been punched out

Block A group of four or more unseparated stamps

Bogus A spurious, pretend stamp

Booklet A small book containing "panes" of stamps

Booklet pane A leaf or page of stamps from a booklet

Cachet A commemorative marking, usually applied by rubber stamp

Cancellation Any authorised defacing mark on a stamp

Centre The position of a stamp design within its perforations, e.g. "well-centred" or "off-centre"

Chalk-surfaced paper Stamp paper coated with a chalky solution for security purposes. Attempted removal of the postmark damages the surface of the stamp

Charity stamp One bearing a premium or surcharge for charitable purposes

Classic A country's early stamp issues, mostly up to about 1875; a choice stamp

Coil stamp One from a roll of stamps used in vending machines

Coil join A tab uniting two sections of a roll of stamps

Commemorative A stamp issued to mark a special anniversary or event

Country stamp See Regional

Cover A postally used envelope, letter-sheet or wrapper

Cylinder number Letters/numerals in sheet margins identifying printing cylinders. Normally collected in "Cylinder block" of six stamps. Also see "Plate number"

Die An engraved plate for impressing design etc. on softer metal

Doctor blade A steel blade which removes surplus ink from the printing cylinder in the press – faulty wiping by this blade will cause a "Doctor blade" flaw

Embossing A form of printing in relief, now rarely used

Error A mistake in stamp design, printing or production

Essay A trial stamp design, sometimes differing from the issued stamps

Face value The denomination of a stamp, expressed on its face

Fake A genuine stamp doctored in some way to deceive collectors

First Day Cover A cover bearing stamps postmarked on their day of issue

Flaw A fortuitous blemish on a stamp; a printing fault

Forgery A fraudulent copy of a genuine postage stamp, overprint or postmark

Frama stamps See Machine label

Graphite lines Black vertical lines printed on the back of GB definitives, 1957–1959, for use with automatic letter-sorting equipment. Also see "Phosphor" stamps

Greetings stamp Stamp intended for use on birthday or other greetings mail

Gum Mucilage on the back of adhesive stamps. Not "glue"

Gutter The narrow space between stamps in the sheet permitting perforation

Gutter margin The blank margins dividing a sheet of stamps into panes

Handstamp A postmark or overprint applied by hand

Imperforate Stamps printed and issued without perforations, deliberately or in error

Imprint The name of the printer or issuing authority inscribed on the stamps or in the sheet margins

Imprinted stamps Stamps other than adhesives, printed direct on postal stationery items (postcards, envelopes, etc)

Jubilee line Coloured line found in the sheet margin of British stamps

"Local" A stamp with geographical limits of postal use and validity. These are not normally listed in the Stanley Gibbons catalogues

"Machin" The name given to GB definitives, first issued in 1967, bearing the Queen's head designed by Arnold Machin

Machine label Postage stamp produced by a micro-processor machine after the insertion of coins of the required value, popularly known as Frama stamps

Maltese cross Name given to the cross-shaped cancellation used on the first British stamps

Margin The unprinted edging surrounding or dividing a sheet of stamps. See also "Gutter margin"

Maximum card A picture postcard bearing a stamp and cancellation relevant to the picture on the card

Miniature sheet A small sheet of one or several stamps, usually with decorative margins, issued as a souvenir for collectors

Mint A stamp in its original pristine state, with full gum (if so issued), when it is said to have its "original gum" ("O.G."). "Unmounted mint" stamps have not been hinged. Also see "Unused"

Mulready Envelopes and letter sheets issued by Britain in 1840 with a pictorial motif designed by William Mulready

Non Value Indicator stamp (NVI) A stamp which bears no monetary inscription, but shows the class of postage (1st, 2nd) instead

Obsolete A stamp no longer sold by a post office though it may still be valid for postage

Overprint A printed addition to a stamp. Also see "Surcharge"

Pair Two unseparated stamps, joined as originally issued

Pane A formation or group of stamps within the sheet. Also see "Booklet pane"

Perforations Holes punched between stamps in sheets to enable easy separation

Personalised stamp Stamp with an attached non-postal label bearing an image taken from a personal photograph

Phosphor stamps Stamps overprinted or coated with phosphorescent materials recognised by high technology letter sorting machinery

Plate number Letters/numerals in sheet margins identifying printing plates. Also see "Cylinder number"

Post & Go stamp Illustrated self-adhesive label dispensed from a machine with inkjet printed indicator of the service required. This catalogue only lists Post & Go stamps available from machines within post offices, it does not include those from stamp exhibitions or non-post office establishments.

Postmark Any mark, such as a cancellation, connected with the postal service and found on items transmitted by post

Presentation pack A philatelic souvenir containing a set of stamps and descriptive text

Prestige booklet Stamp booklet devoted to a particular subject or event and containing special panes of stamps with descriptive text printed alongside

Proof A trial impression taken from an original die or printing plate

Regional Name given by collectors to stamps issued by Royal Mail (who term them Country stamps) for use in England, Scotland, Wales or Northern Ireland. Issues were also made for Guernsey and Jersey (until 1969) and the Isle of Man (until 1973)

Seahorse Name given to the high value definitive stamps of King George V

Self-adhesive Gummed stamps (with protective backing) which do not require moistening

Se-tenant Stamps of different design or face value that are joined together

Specimen Sample stamp usually with "specimen" overprinted or perforated on it

Strip Three or more stamps joined in a row

Tête-bêche A stamp inverted in relation to the adjoining stamp in a pair

Traffic lights Collectors' term for the colour check dots found in sheet margins

Unused An uncancelled stamp, not necessarily "mint"

Used A stamp which has been postally used and appropriately postmarked

Used abroad Stamps of one country used and postmarked in another

Used on piece Stamp kept on part of the original cover to preserve the complete postmark

Variety A stamp differing in some detail from the normal issue

Watermark A distinctive device or emblem in stamps, formed by "thinning" of the paper during production. Watermarks illustrated in this catalogue are shown as if viewed through the front of the stamp

"Wilding" The name given to British definitive stamps, first issued in 1952, bearing the Queen's head from a photographic portrait by Dorothy Wilding

Wing margin Wide margin on one side of a stamp caused by central perforation of the sheet gutter margin

For other and fuller definitions, see the Stanley Gibbons book *Philatelic Terms Illustrated* by James Mackay.

How can Stanley Gibbons help you to build your collection?

Our History

Stanley Gibbons started trading in 1856 and we have been at the forefront of stamp collecting for more than 150 years, making us the world's oldest philatelic company. We can help you build your collection in a wide variety of ways – all with the backing of our unrivalled expertise.

When building a collection it helps to know what you have. You can use Collect British Stamps as a checklist to highlight all the items you currently own. You can then easily see where the gaps are that you need to fill.

Visit 399 Strand, London, UK

Our world famous stamp shop is a collector's paradise which aims to keep a full range of Great Britain stamps to sell at current catalogue price - so if there are any changes via a different catalogue, then prices will be adjusted accordingly. As well as stamps, the shop stocks albums, accessories and specialist philatelic books. Plan a visit now!

GB Specialist Department

When purchasing high value items you should definitely contact our specialist department for advice and guarantees on the items purchased. We can explain what to look for and where, and help you plan your future collection.

Auctions and Valuations

Stanley Gibbons Auctions have been running since the 1900's. They offer a range of auctions to suit all levels of collectors and dealers. You can of course also sell your collection or individual rare items through our public auctions and regular postal auctions. You can check out charges with the auction department directly.

Stanley Gibbons Publications

Our catalogues are trusted worldwide as the industry standard To keep up to date with new issues you can follow the additions to this listing in our magazine *Gibbons Stamp Monthly*. This is a must-read for all collectors and dealers. It contains news, views and insights into all things philatelic, from beginner to specialist.

Completing the set

When is it cheaper to complete your collection by buying a whole set rather than item by item? You can use the prices in *Collect British Stamps*, which lists single item values and a complete set value, to check if it is better to buy the odd items missing, or a complete set. Some of the definitive sets can be built up over time. The current definitive set is augmented by the Post Office regularly.

Condition

Condition can make a big difference to the price you can pay for an item (see 'The Stanley Gibbons Guide to Stamp Pricing on p xxxvi). The prices in this catalogue are for items in fine condition. When building your collection you do need to keep condition in mind and always buy the best condition you can find and afford. Collectors are reminded that for issues from 1936 to date, prices in the unused column are for unmounted mint. This means that the condition of the gum is the same as issued from the Post Office. If the gum is disturbed or has had an adhesion it can be classed as mounted. When buying issues prior to 1936 you should always look for the least amount of disturbance and adhesion. You do have to keep in mind the age of the issue when looking at the condition.

When buying philatelic items listed you need to make sure they are in the same condition as issued by the Post Office. This applies to Presentation Packs, were the stamps are issued on a stock card with an information card and held together in a plastic wallet and also to Year Books, which should be in a slip case with a stock card of stamps. The prices quoted are for a complete item in good condition so make sure you check this – and of course that they are complete. You will find some items may appear in different formats (e.g. language cards, different bindings, etc) which will be listed under the normal listing within this catalogue.

Ask the Experts

While you are building your collection, if you need help or guidance, you are welcome to come along to Stanley Gibbons in the Strand and ask for assistance. If you would like to have your collection appraised, you can arrange for a verbal evaluation Monday to Friday 9.00am – 4.30pm. We also provide insurance valuations should you require. Of course this up-to-date catalogue listing can assist with the valuation and may be presented to an insurance agent or company.

See the Stanley Gibbons Contact details: on page xxvii.

UPA UNIQUE REDUCING ESTIMATE SYSTEM
DRIVEN BY YOU

Literally **The** that Every is

Dear Colleague,
For the first time, in this open letter, I'm going to give you the thinking, the 'mindset' if you will, of how and why my stamp auction thrives where others do not...

As many of you will attest. At certain 'peak' times in our auction 'cycle,' I personally answer the telephone to callers. It's a wonderfully enjoyable and rewarding thing for me to do, because, you kindly inform me of your likes and dislikes, about us, and other auctions that you may have dealt with before discovering U P A...

One of the most common 'threads' that I have learnt from You, and from other Dealers and Auctioneers, is simply 'how does U P A do it?' How is it that we have become the largest Stamp Auction in the UK and almost the largest globally? How can we afford to expend more upon advertising worldwide than most dealers sell in a year? Simply put: How can we afford to offer more and charge less – indeed – how can we afford to offer more and charge you no extra w-h-a-t-s-o-e-v-e-r ??

The fundamental reason why is because, unlike others, everything we do is Driven by You.. Over the course of the past 17 years I have discovered that combining this 'bottom-up' thinking with offering **simply MASSIVE Philatelic Choice** – permits us to offer you a Unique Collector-Driven Stamp Auction Experience. Think about it: whilst the rest of our philatelic industry works 'top-down' – issuing diktats, regulation, charges, and fees, and few guarantees – ever increasingly we throw these off encouraged by more and more collectors joining us, who crucially continue to participate in auction after auction... rewarding us by their loyalty, enriching their collections... enabling us, in turn, to reward them.

...So that, when you inform us that You don't like 'X' (extra shipping and insurance charges), and You dislike 'Y' (paying credit card charges) and you positively abhor paying 'Z' – up to 25% buyer's premiums... (particularly when you may realise that you are possibly or probably paying a buyer's premium upon that dealer's own stamps that they are selling to You)... we take that valuable knowledge you've imparted and 'dial' it back into our auction system, not purely for your benefit BUT for our mutual benefit because over the 17 years that U P A has been auctioning I have discovered that if we have enough participating bidders in our auctions we can offer you a **radically superior service and a radically different deal than others**...

1st £55 FREE WINNINGS

Shield Yourself & Save
I SUPPORT NO BP
SUPPORT NO BUYER'S PREMIUM
DRIVEN BY YOU

NO SURCHARGE
MasterCard VISA
DRIVEN BY YOU

NEW ✓
POST-FREE
UPA Loyalty Bonus
DRIVEN BY YOU

Discover the Difference

UNIVERSAL PHILATELIC AUCTIONS
SINCE 1958

Philately Understood

Difference is
thing we Do
Driven by You...

To me it is logical that when you configure your auction to really give collectors what they seek, mixing in a unique reducing-estimate-auction system, blended with hundreds and thousands of simply massive philatelic choice – these are the reasons why more Collectors bid in my U P A auctions than any other auction in the UK and almost all others globally. Consider that each U P A auction adds up to 250 different new bidders when most stamp auctions only have a few hundred bidders TOTAL – the SCALE of Your SUPPORT permits us to 'square' the circle so that, hopefully, we can offer collectors like you *True Philatelic VAL-YOU for Money*...

How can you help? Simply by participating regularly in our auctions permits us to give back, producing the most expensive and the best post-free auction catalogues you may ever receive whilst staying in business. Your continued support is powering our new Loyalty Post-Free System. So, all that I would respectfully ask and encourage you to do – is join the 2,234 different Collectors and Dealers from 51 different countries worldwide, who participated in my last auction U P A #67, creating new philatelic world records of participation and in some cases of realisations... whilst an astonishing 90% of bidders were successful... and those lots that remained unsold carried forward at *ever decreasing estimate and reserve* thereby creating the nucleus of this auction with a 'sprinkling' of more than 8,000 new lots of absolutely extraordinary NEW material... whereby, ultimately collectors like You determine values, not catalogues...

My wife and I, and members of our super Team, wish you Happy Hunting and great Philatelic Fun. With thanks for Your continued support. Please do tell your Philatelic Friends. They'll receive the best Philatelic Thank You for joining us and you'll be rewarded too!

**To Collect
Your NEXT
£20
20,000± lot
Auction
Catalogue
FREE
Request
Yours
NOW**

IT'S SO EASY – START NOW

Andrew McGavin, Managing Director
Universal Philatelic Auctions UPA,

Universal Philatelic Auctions present

TIPS OF THE TRADE
Your Expert Guide to Stamp Collecting

Volume 1

✓How to buy: How to Sell?
✓Catalogue value: common misconceptions
✓How to insure reasonably
✓Which Accessories do you really need?
And Much Much More ...

£55 OFF 1ST UPA STAMP AUCTIONS PURCHASES

£55 OFF: Do You Qualify?
INSIDE: See pages 15/16 →

REQUEST MY 'TIPS
OF THE TRADE'
FREE BOOKLET

UNIVERSAL PHILATELIC AUCTIONS (SG-CBS)
4 The Old Coalyard, West End Northleach, Glos. GL54 3HE UK
Tel: 01451 861111 • Fax: 01451 861297

Guide to Entries

(A) Accession to the Throne

(B) Illustration – Generally all stamps illustrated. To comply with Post Office regulations illustrations are reduced to 75%, with overprints shown actual size.

(C) Illustration or Type Number – These numbers are used to help identify stamps, in the type column.

(D) Date of Issue – When a set of definitive stamps have been issued over several years the Year Date given is for the earliest issue, commemorative sets are set in chronological order.

(E) Phosphor Description – Phosphorised paper is activated by ultraviolet light.

(F) Perforations – The "perforation" is the number of holes in a length of 2cm, as measured by the Stanley Gibbons *Instanta* gauge. From 1992 certain stamps occur with a large elliptical (oval) hole inserted in each line of vertical perforations. From 2009 certain stamps have U-shaped die-cut slits.

(G) Stanley Gibbons Catalogue Number – This is a unique number for each stamp to help the collector identify stamps in the listing. The Stanley Gibbons numbering system is universally recognized as definitive, where insufficient numbers have been left to provide for additional stamps listings, some stamps will have a suffix letter after the catalogue number.

(H) Catalogue Value – Mint/Unused. Prices quoted for pre-1945 stamps are for lightly hinged examples. Prices quoted of unused King Edward VIII to Queen Elizabeth issues are for unmounted mint.

(I) Catalogue Value – Used. Prices generally refer to fine postally used examples.

Prices

Before February 1971 British currency was:

£1 = 20s One pound = twenty shillings *and*
1s = 12d One Shilling = 12 pence

Under decimalisation this became:

£1 = 100p One pound = one hundred (new) pence

Shown in Catalogue as	Explanation
10	10 pence
1.75	£1.75
15.00	£15
£150	£150
£2300	£2300

(J) Face Value – This refers to the value of the stamp and is sold at the Post Office when issued. Some modern stamps do not have their values in figures but instead shown as a letter.

(K) Type Number – Indicates a design type on which stamp is based. These are bold figures found below each illustration. The type numbers are also given in bold in the second column of figures alongside the stamp description to indicate the design of each stamp.

(L) Colour – Colour of stamps (if fewer than four colours, otherwise noted as "multicoloured").

(M) Sets of Stamps – Two or more stamps with a common theme or subject.

(N) First Day Covers – Prices for first day covers are for complete sets used on plain covers or on special covers.

(O) Presentation Packs – Special packs consisting of the issue and slip-in cards with printed information inside a protective covering.

(P) PHQ Cards – Each card shows a large reproduction of a current British stamp.

(Q) Sets of Gutters – The term is used for a pair of stamps separated by part of the blank gutter margin or with Traffic Lights on the gutter margin.

(R) Footnote – Further information on background or key facts on issues.

(S) Other Types of Stamps – Postage Dues, Officials and Regional Issues

(T) Number Prefix – Stamps other than definitives and commemoratives have a prefix letter before the catalogue number.

QUEEN ELIZABETH II

(A) Accession to the Throne ——— 6 February, 1952

(B) Illustration ———

(C) Illustration or Type Number ———

1862 *The Very Hungry Caterpillar* (Eric Carle)   **1526** Butterfly Hat by Dai Rees

E ———

(J) Face Value

Nos. 2589/90, 2591/2, 2593/4 and 2595/6 were printed together, *se-tenant*, as horizontal pairs in sheets of 60(2 panes 6 × 5).

Animal Tales

(D) Date of Issue ——— **2006** (10 Jan.) One side phosphor band (2nd) or two phosphor bands (others). Perf 14½ •———

(E) Phosphor Description

(F) Perforations

				Unused	Used		
2589	**1856**	(2nd) multicoloured		30	35	☐	☐
		a. Horiz pair.					
		Nos. 2589/90		70	70	☐	☐
2590	**1857**	(2nd) multicoloured		30	35	☐	☐
2591	**1858**	(1st) multicoloured		45	50	☐	☐
		a. Horiz pair.					
		Nos. 2591/2		1·50	1·50	☐	☐
2592	**1859**	(1st) multicoloured		45	50	☐	☐
2593	**1860**	42p multicoloured		65	70	☐	☐
		a. Horiz pair.					
		Nos. 2593/4		3·75	3·75	☐	☐
2594	**1861**	42p multicoloured		65	70	☐	☐
2595	**1862**	68p multicoloured		1·00	1·10	☐	☐
		a. Horiz pair.					
		Nos. 2595/6		4·75	4·75	☐	☐
2596	**1863**	68p multicoloured		1·00	1·10	☐	☐
		Set of 8		8·50	8·50	☐	☐
		First Day Cover			8·00		☐
		Presentation Pack		12·00		☐	
		PHQ Cards (*set of 8*)		4·50	12·00	☐	☐
		Set of 4 Gutter Blocks of 4		13·00		☐	
		Set of 4 Traffic Light Gutter Blocks of 8		28·00		☐	

(G) Stanley Gibbons Catalogue Number

(H) Catalogue Value – Unused

(J) Face Value

(K) Type Number

(I) Catalogue Value – Used

(M) Sets

(L) Colour

(O) Special Packs

(N) FDC for Complete Sets

(P) PHQ Cards

(Q) Gutter Combinations

No. 2595 contains two die-cut holes.
A design as No. 2592 but self-adhesive was also issued in sheets of 20 with each stamp accompanied by a *se-tenant* label.

(R) Footnotes

D 1

(S) Postage Due

POSTAGE DUE STAMPS •———

(S) Other Types of Stamps

1968–69 Design size 21½ × 17½ mm. No wmk

(T) Number Prefix

D75	D **1**	4d blue	7·00	6·75	☐	☐
D76		8d red	50	1·00	☐	☐

QUEEN VICTORIA

1837 (20 June)–1901 (22 Jan.)

IDENTIFICATION. In this checklist Victorian stamps are classified firstly according to which printing method was used –line-engraving, embossing or surface-printing.

Corner letters. Numerous stamps also have letters in all four, or just the lower corners. These were an anti-forgery device and the letters differ from stamp to stamp. If present in all four corners the upper pair are the reverse of the lower. Note the importance of these corner letters in the way the checklist is arranged.

Watermarks. Further classification depends on watermarks: these are illustrated in normal position, with stamps priced accordingly.

1 Line-engraved Issues

1 ONE PENNY D

1a TWO PENCE K

1b ONE PENNY

POSTAGE
3 TWO PENCE H
3 White lines added above and below head

2 Small Crown watermark

4 Large Crown watermark

Letters in lower corners

1840 Wmk Small Crown Type **2** Imperforate

2	**1**	1d	black	£12500	£375	☐ ☐
5	**1a**	2d	blue	£38000	£900	☐ ☐

1841

8	**1b**	1d	red-brown	£600	35·00	☐ ☐
14	**3**	2d	blue	£6250	90·00	☐ ☐

1854–57

(i) Wmk Small Crown Type **2** Perf 16

17	**1b**	1d	red-brown	£375	35·00	☐ ☐
19	**3**	2d	blue	£4700	£100	☐ ☐

(ii) Wmk Small Crown Type **2** Perf 14

24	**1b**	1d	red-brown	£675	70·00	☐ ☐
23	**3**	2d	blue	£13000	£225	☐ ☐

(iii) Wmk Large Crown Type **4** Perf 16

26	**1b**	1d	red	£2400	£130	☐ ☐
27	**3**	2d	blue	£18500	£450	☐ ☐

(iv) Wmk Large Crown Type **4** Perf 14

40	**1b**	1d	red	50·00	12·00	☐ ☐
34	**3**	2d	blue	£2850	70·00	☐ ☐

7

5 ONE PENNY

8 THREE

6 TWO PENCE

half penny

9 Watermark extending over three stamps

Letters in all four corners

Plate numbers. Stamps included a 'plate number' in their design and this affects valuation. The cheapest plates are priced here; see complete list of plate numbers overleaf.

1858–70

		(i) Wmk Type **9** Perf 14				
48	**7**	½d	red	£110	30·00	☐ ☐
		(ii) Wmk Large Crown Type **4** Perf 14				
43	**5**	1d	red	27·00	2·75	☐ ☐
51	**8**	1½d	red	£500	75·00	☐ ☐
45	**6**	2d	blue	£350	15·00	☐ ☐

Plate numbers on stamps 1858-70 having letters in all four corners

Showing position of the plate number on the 1d. and 2d. values. (Plate 170 shown)

Showing the plate number (9)

Position of plate Number

HALFPENNY VALUE (SG 48)

48	*Plate 1*	£325	£100	☐ ☐
48	*Plate 3*	£240	55·00	☐ ☐
48	*Plate 4*	£150	50·00	☐ ☐
48	*Plate 5*	£110	30·00	☐ ☐
48	*Plate 6*	£120	30·00	☐ ☐
48	*Plate 8*	£600	£120	☐ ☐
48	*Plate 9*	£6000	£850	☐ ☐
48	*Plate 10*	£130	30·00	☐ ☐
48	*Plate 11*	£120	30·00	☐ ☐
48	*Plate 12*	£120	30·00	☐ ☐
48	*Plate 13*	£120	30·00	☐ ☐
48	*Plate 14*	£120	30·00	☐ ☐
48	*Plate 15*	£175	50·00	☐ ☐
48	*Plate 19*	£300	65·00	☐ ☐
48	*Plate 20*	£350	85·00	☐ ☐

PENNY VALUE (SG 43)

43	*Plate 71*	55·00	4·00	☐ ☐
43	*Plate 72*	60·00	5·00	☐ ☐
43	*Plate 73*	60·00	4·00	☐ ☐
43	*Plate 74*	60·00	2·75	☐ ☐
43	*Plate 76*	55·00	2·75	☐ ☐
43	*Plate 77*	—	£600000	☐
43	*Plate 78*	£130	2·75	☐ ☐
43	*Plate 79*	48·00	2·75	☐ ☐
43	*Plate 80*	65·00	2·75	☐ ☐

THE ICONIC STAMPS OF GREAT BRITAIN

Who knew that the first ever adhesive stamp, the Penny Black, would not only instigate a communications revolution but also a much loved global hobby? It is estimated that there are 60 million stamp collectors worldwide. Stamp collections and the passion for stamp collecting have been passed down from generation to generation and they now form part of our history. But what makes a stamp iconic?

To find out more about these and many other GB stamps, get in touch by contacting our Great Britain Department.

Phone **020 7557 4464** | Email: gb@stanleygibbons.com

PENNY BLACK - GREAT BRITAIN 1840

"SEAHORSE" HIGH VALUES - GREAT BRITAIN 1913

"WILDING" HIGH VALUES - GREAT BRITAIN 1955

£5 ORANGE TELEGRAPHS - GREAT BRITAIN 1877

POSTAL UNION CONGRESS (PUC) £1 - GREAT BRITAIN 1929

"MACHIN" HIGH VALUES - GREAT BRITAIN 1970

STANLEY GIBBONS

LONDON 1856

399 Strand, WC2R 0LX, London
Please phone 020 7557 4464 | Email: gb@stanleygibbons.com
www.stanleygibbons.com

Come and Visit us at 399 Strand

1856   1896   1936   1976   2017

- Get advice from our experienced and knowledgeable staff
- See first hand our superb range of top quality stamps, albums and accessories
- Get insider tips on how to enhance and expand your collection
- Ask for guidance on techniques for care and storage of your stamps and covers
- View our specialist material
- All Stanley Gibbons stamps come with a lifetime guarantee of authenticity from our stamp specialists.

Everything for the stamp collector.

399 Strand opening hours
- Mon-Fri 9am-5.30pm • Sat 9:30am-5.30pm • Sun Closed

For more information visit
stanleygibbons.com

BY APPOINTMENT TO
HER MAJESTY THE QUEEN
PHILATELISTS
STANLEY GIBBONS LTD
LONDON

STANLEY GIBBONS
LONDON 1856

399 Strand, WC2R 0LX, London
Phone: **+44 1425 472 363** | Email: **support@stanleygibbons.com**
www.stanleygibbons.com

43	Plate 81	65·00	3·00	☐ ☐
43	Plate 82	£130	5·00	☐ ☐
43	Plate 83	£155	9·00	☐ ☐
43	Plate 84	80·00	3·00	☐ ☐
43	Plate 85	60·00	4·00	☐ ☐
43	Plate 86	70·00	5·00	☐ ☐
43	Plate 87	48·00	2·75	☐ ☐
43	Plate 88	£190	9·50	☐ ☐
43	Plate 89	60·00	2·75	☐ ☐
43	Plate 90	60·00	2·75	☐ ☐
43	Plate 91	75·00	7·00	☐ ☐
43	Plate 92	55·00	2·75	☐ ☐
43	Plate 93	70·00	2·75	☐ ☐
43	Plate 94	65·00	6·00	☐ ☐
43	Plate 95	60·00	2·75	☐ ☐
43	Plate 96	65·00	2·75	☐ ☐
43	Plate 97	60·00	4·50	☐ ☐
43	Plate 98	70·00	7·00	☐ ☐
43	Plate 99	75·00	6·00	☐ ☐
43	Plate 100	80·00	3·00	☐ ☐
43	Plate 101	80·00	11·00	☐ ☐
43	Plate 102	65·00	2·75	☐ ☐
43	Plate 103	70·00	4·50	☐ ☐
43	Plate 104	£100	6·00	☐ ☐
43	Plate 105	£130	9·00	☐ ☐
43	Plate 106	75·00	2·75	☐ ☐
43	Plate 107	80·00	9·00	☐ ☐
43	Plate 108	£110	3·00	☐ ☐
43	Plate 109	£120	4·50	☐ ☐
43	Plate 110	80·00	11·00	☐ ☐
43	Plate 111	70·00	3·00	☐ ☐
43	Plate 112	90·00	3·00	☐ ☐
43	Plate 113	70·00	15·00	☐ ☐
43	Plate 114	£325	15·00	☐ ☐
43	Plate 115	£130	3·00	☐ ☐
43	Plate 116	£100	11·00	☐ ☐
43	Plate 117	65·00	2·75	☐ ☐
43	Plate 118	70·00	2·75	☐ ☐
43	Plate 119	65·00	2·75	☐ ☐
43	Plate 120	27·00	2·75	☐ ☐
43	Plate 121	60·00	11·00	☐ ☐
43	Plate 122	27·00	2·75	☐ ☐
43	Plate 123	60·00	2·75	☐ ☐
43	Plate 124	42·00	2·75	☐ ☐
43	Plate 125	60·00	2·75	☐ ☐
43	Plate 127	75·00	3·00	☐ ☐
43	Plate 129	60·00	10·00	☐ ☐
43	Plate 130	75·00	3·00	☐ ☐
43	Plate 131	85·00	20·00	☐ ☐
43	Plate 132	£190	27·00	☐ ☐
43	Plate 133	£160	11·00	☐ ☐
43	Plate 134	27·00	2·75	☐ ☐
43	Plate 135	£130	30·00	☐ ☐
43	Plate 136	£130	24·00	☐ ☐
43	Plate 137	42·00	3·00	☐ ☐
43	Plate 138	32·00	2·75	☐ ☐
43	Plate 139	80·00	20·00	☐ ☐
43	Plate 140	32·00	2·75	☐ ☐
43	Plate 141	£160	11·00	☐ ☐
43	Plate 142	95·00	30·00	☐ ☐
43	Plate 143	80·00	17·00	☐ ☐
43	Plate 144	£130	25·00	☐ ☐
43	Plate 145	48·00	3·00	☐ ☐
43	Plate 146	60·00	6·00	☐ ☐
43	Plate 147	70·00	4·00	☐ ☐
43	Plate 148	60·00	4·00	☐ ☐
43	Plate 149	60·00	7·00	☐ ☐
43	Plate 150	27·00	2·75	☐ ☐
43	Plate 151	80·00	11·00	☐ ☐
43	Plate 152	80·00	7·50	☐ ☐
43	Plate 153	£140	11·00	☐ ☐
43	Plate 154	70·00	2·75	☐ ☐
43	Plate 155	70·00	3·00	☐ ☐
43	Plate 156	65·00	2·75	☐ ☐
43	Plate 157	70·00	2·75	☐ ☐
43	Plate 158	48·00	2·75	☐ ☐
43	Plate 159	48·00	2·75	☐ ☐
43	Plate 160	48·00	2·75	☐ ☐
43	Plate 161	80·00	9·00	☐ ☐
43	Plate 162	70·00	9·00	☐ ☐
43	Plate 163	70·00	4·00	☐ ☐
43	Plate 164	70·00	4·00	☐ ☐
43	Plate 165	65·00	2·75	☐ ☐
43	Plate 166	65·00	7·00	☐ ☐
43	Plate 167	65·00	2·75	☐ ☐
43	Plate 168	70·00	10·00	☐ ☐
43	Plate 169	80·00	9·00	☐ ☐
43	Plate 170	55·00	2·75	☐ ☐
43	Plate 171	27·00	2·75	☐ ☐
43	Plate 172	48·00	2·75	☐ ☐
43	Plate 173	95·00	11·00	☐ ☐
43	Plate 174	48·00	2·75	☐ ☐
43	Plate 175	80·00	4·50	☐ ☐
43	Plate 176	80·00	3·00	☐ ☐
43	Plate 177	60·00	2·75	☐ ☐
43	Plate 178	80·00	4·50	☐ ☐
43	Plate 179	70·00	3·00	☐ ☐
43	Plate 180	80·00	6·50	☐ ☐
43	Plate 181	65·00	2·75	☐ ☐
43	Plate 182	£130	6·50	☐ ☐
43	Plate 183	75·00	4·00	☐ ☐
43	Plate 184	48·00	3·00	☐ ☐
43	Plate 185	70·00	4·00	☐ ☐
43	Plate 186	90·00	3·00	☐ ☐
43	Plate 187	70·00	2·75	☐ ☐
43	Plate 188	95·00	12·00	☐ ☐
43	Plate 189	95·00	8·50	☐ ☐
43	Plate 190	70·00	7·00	☐ ☐
43	Plate 191	48·00	9·00	☐ ☐
43	Plate 192	70·00	2·75	☐ ☐
43	Plate 193	48·00	2·75	☐ ☐
43	Plate 194	70·00	10·00	☐ ☐
43	Plate 195	70·00	10·00	☐ ☐
43	Plate 196	70·00	6·50	☐ ☐
43	Plate 197	75·00	11·00	☐ ☐
43	Plate 198	60·00	7·00	☐ ☐
43	Plate 199	75·00	7·00	☐ ☐
43	Plate 200	80·00	2·75	☐ ☐
43	Plate 201	48·00	6·00	☐ ☐
43	Plate 202	80·00	10·00	☐ ☐
43	Plate 203	48·00	20·00	☐ ☐
43	Plate 204	75·00	3·00	☐ ☐
43	Plate 205	75·00	4·00	☐ ☐
43	Plate 206	75·00	11·00	☐ ☐
43	Plate 207	80·00	11·00	☐ ☐
43	Plate 208	75·00	18·00	☐ ☐
43	Plate 209	65·00	10·00	☐ ☐
43	Plate 210	90·00	15·00	☐ ☐
43	Plate 211	95·00	25·00	☐ ☐
43	Plate 212	80·00	13·00	☐ ☐
43	Plate 213	80·00	13·00	☐ ☐
43	Plate 214	90·00	23·00	☐ ☐
43	Plate 215	90·00	23·00	☐ ☐
43	Plate 216	95·00	23·00	☐ ☐
43	Plate 217	95·00	9·00	☐ ☐
43	Plate 218	90·00	10·00	☐ ☐
43	Plate 219	£130	85·00	☐ ☐
43	Plate 220	60·00	9·00	☐ ☐
43	Plate 221	95·00	20·00	☐ ☐
43	Plate 222	£110	50·00	☐ ☐
43	Plate 223	£130	75·00	☐ ☐
43	Plate 224	£165	65·00	☐ ☐
43	Plate 225	£3200	£800	☐ ☐

Plates 69, 70, 75, 77, 126 and 128 were prepared but rejected. No stamps therefore exist, except for a very few from Plate 77 which somehow reached the public. Plate 177 stamps, by accident or design, are sometimes passed off as the rare Plate 77.

THREE-HALFPENNY VALUE (SG 52)

| 52 | Plate (1) | £725 | £110 | ☐☐ |
| 52 | Plate 3 | £500 | 75·00 | ☐☐ |

Plate 1 did not have the plate number in the design. Plate 2 was not completed and no stamps exist.

TWOPENNY VALUE (SG 45)

45	Plate 7	£2000	65·00	☐☐
45	Plate 8	£1850	42·00	☐☐
45	Plate 9	£350	15·00	☐☐
45	Plate 12	£3000	£140	☐☐
46	Plate 13	£375	30·00	☐☐
46	Plate 14	£500	38·00	☐☐
46	Plate 15	£525	38·00	☐☐

Plates 10 and 11 were prepared but rejected.

2 Embossed Issues

Prices are for stamps cut square and with average to fine embossing. Stamps with exceptionally clear embossing are worth more.

12

11

10

13

1847–54 Wmk 13 (6d), no wmk (others) Imperforate

59	12	6d	lilac	£19500	£1000	☐☐
57	11	10d	brown	£11500	£1500	☐☐
54	10	1s	green	£24000	£1000	☐☐

Collectors are reminded that Types **10/12** were also used to print postal stationery. 6d. stamps without watermark and 10d. and 1s. values without 'silk' threads embedded in the paper come from this source and should not be confused with the listed stamps.

---

3 Surface-printed Issues

IDENTIFICATION. Check first whether the design includes corner letters or not, as mentioned for 'Line-engraved Issues'. The checklist is divided up according to whether any letters are small or large, also whether they are white (uncoloured) or printed in the colour of the stamp. Further identification then depends on watermark.

PERFORATION. Except for Nos. 126/9 all the following issues of Queen Victoria are perf 14.

14

15   16   17

18   19   20 Emblems

No corner letters

1855–57

			(i) Wmk Small Garter Type **15**			
62	**14**	4d	red	£8500	£450	☐☐
			(ii) Wmk Medium Garter Type **16**			
65	**14**	4d	red	£13000	£500	☐☐
			(iii) Wmk Large Garter Type **17**			
66a	**14**	4d	red	£1750	£150	☐☐
			(iv) Wmk Emblems Type **20**			
70	**18**	6d	lilac	£1350	£125	☐☐
72	**19**	1s	green	£3250	£350	☐☐

Plate numbers. Stamps Nos. 90/163 should be checked for the 'plate numbers' indicated, as this affects valuation (the cheapest plates are priced here). The mark 'Pl.' shows that several numbers exist, priced in separate list overleaf.

Plate numbers are the small numerals appearing in duplicate in some part of the frame design or adjacent to the lower corner letters (in the 5s value a single numeral above the lower inscription).

21   22   23

24   25

Small white corner letters

1862–64 Wmk Emblems Type **20**, except 4d (Large Garter Type **17**)

76	**21**	3d	red	£2700	£350	☐	☐
80	**22**	4d	red	£2000	£140	☐	☐
84	**23**	6d	lilac	£2250	£140	☐	☐
87	**24**	9d	bistre	£4000	£475	☐	☐
90	**25**	1s	green Pl.	£3200	£300	☐	☐

26

27

28 Hyphen in SIX-PENCE

29

30

31

Large white corner letters

1865–67 Wmk Emblems Type **20** except 4d (Large Garter Type **17**)

92	**26**	3d	red (Plate 4)	£2500	£250	☐	☐
94	**27**	4d	vermilion Pl.	£575	75·00	☐	☐
97	**28**	6d	lilac Pl.	£1200	£140	☐	☐
98	**29**	9d	straw Pl.	£4800	£600	☐	☐
99	**30**	10d	brown (Plate 1)	*	£55000	☐	
101	**31**	1s	green (Plate 4)	£2850	£275	☐	☐

32

33 Spray of Rose

34

1867–80 Wmk Spray of Rose Type **33**

103	**26**	3d	red Pl.	£525	60·00	☐	☐
105	**28**	6d	lilac (with (hyphen) (Plate 6)	£1850	£150	☐	☐
109			6d mauve (without hyphen) Pl.	£700	90·00	☐	☐
111	**29**		9d pale straw (Plate 4)	£2400	£300	☐	☐
112	**30**		10d brown Pl.	£3600	£400	☐	☐
117	**31**		1s green Pl.	£800	45·00	☐	☐
118	**32**		2s blue Pl.	£4200	£225	☐	☐
121			2s brown (Plate 1)	£30000	£4250	☐	☐

1872–73 Wmk Spray of Rose Type **33**

122b	**34**	6d	brown Pl.	£700	65·00	☐	☐
125		6d	grey (Plate 12)	£1900	£300	☐	☐

PLATE NUMBERS ON STAMPS OF 1862–83

Small White Corner Letters (1862–64)

90	*Plate 2*	1s green	£3200	£300	☐	☐
91	*Plate 3*		£35000			

Plate 2 is actually numbered as '1' and Plate 3 as '2' on the stamps.

Large White Corner Letters (1865–83)

103	*Plate 4*	3d red	£1850	£300	☐	☐
103	*Plate 5*		£525	70·00	☐	☐
103	*Plate 6*		£550	70·00	☐	☐
103	*Plate 7*		£650	70·00	☐	☐
103	*Plate 8*		£625	60·00	☐	☐
103	*Plate 9*		£625	70·00	☐	☐
103	*Plate 10*		£875	£150	☐	☐
94	*Plate 7*	4d verm	£650	£130	☐	☐
94	*Plate 8*		£600	90·00	☐	☐
94	*Plate 9*		£600	90·00	☐	☐
94	*Plate 10*		£825	£150	☐	☐
94	*Plate 11*		£625	90·00	☐	☐
94	*Plate 12*		£575	75·00	☐	☐
94	*Plate 13*		£650	75·00	☐	☐
94	*Plate 14*		£775	£110	☐	☐
97	*Plate 5*	6d lilac	£1150	£140	☐	☐
97	*Plate 6*		£3800	£275	☐	☐
109	*Plate 8*	6d mauve	£800	£140	☐	☐
109	*Plate 9*		£700	90·00	☐	☐
109	*Plate 10*		*	£37500	☐	☐
123	*Plate 11*	6d buff	£1100	£125	☐	☐
123	*Plate 12*		£3400	£350	☐	☐
98	*Plate 4*	9d straw	£4800	£600	☐	☐
114	*Plate 1*	10d brown	£3600	£400	☐	☐
114	*Plate 2*		£55000	£17000	☐	☐
117	*Plate 4*	1s green	£975	65·00	☐	☐
117	*Plate 5*		£800	45·00	☐	☐
117	*Plate 6*		£1200	45·00	☐	☐
117	*Plate 7*		£1400	90·00	☐	☐
118	*Plate 1*	2s blue	£4000	£225	☐	☐
118	*Plate 3*		*	£16000	☐	☐
127	*Plate 1*	5s red	£11000	£675	☐	☐
127	*Plate 2*		£18000	£1500	☐	☐

Large Coloured Corner Letters (1873–83)

139	*Plate 1*	2½d mauve	£650	£120	☐	☐
139	*Plate 2*		£650	£120	☐	☐
139	*Plate 3*		£1000	£175	☐	☐
141	*Plate 3*	2½d mauve	£1350	£150	☐	☐
141	*Plate 4*		£525	85·00	☐	☐
141	*Plate 5*		£525	85·00	☐	☐
141	*Plate 6*		£525	85·00	☐	☐
141	*Plate 7*		£525	85·00	☐	☐
141	*Plate 8*		£525	85·00	☐	☐
141	*Plate 9*		£525	85·00	☐	☐
141	*Plate 10*		£550	£100	☐	☐
141	*Plate 11*		£525	85·00	☐	☐
141	*Plate 12*		£525	85·00	☐	☐
141	*Plate 13*		£525	85·00	☐	☐
141	*Plate 14*		£525	85·00	☐	☐
141	*Plate 15*		£525	85·00	☐	☐
141	*Plate 16*		£525	85·00	☐	☐
141	*Plate 17*		£1700	£300	☐	☐
142	*Plate 17*	2½d blue	£575	70·00	☐	☐
142	*Plate 18*		£575	55·00	☐	☐
142	*Plate 19*		£575	55·00	☐	☐
142	*Plate 20*		£575	55·00	☐	☐
157	*Plate 21*	2½d blue	£500	45·00	☐	☐
157	*Plate 22*		£450	45·00	☐	☐
157	*Plate 23*		£450	35·00	☐	☐
143	*Plate 11*	3d red	£450	80·00	☐	☐
143	*Plate 12*		£525	80·00	☐	☐
143	*Plate 14*		£525	80·00	☐	☐
143	*Plate 15*		£450	80·00	☐	☐
143	*Plate 16*		£450	80·00	☐	☐
143	*Plate 17*		£525	80·00	☐	☐
143	*Plate 18*		£525	80·00	☐	☐
143	*Plate 19*		£450	80·00	☐	☐
143	*Plate 20*		£850	£140	☐	☐
158	*Plate 20*	3d red	£900	£150	☐	☐
158	*Plate 21*		£500	£100	☐	☐
152	*Plate 15*	4d verm	£3200	£525	☐	☐
152	*Plate 16*		*	£34000	☐	☐
153	*Plate 15*	4d green	£1600	£325	☐	☐
153	*Plate 16*		£1400	£300	☐	☐

153	*Plate 17*		*	£20000	☐
160	*Plate 17*	4d brown	£475	80·00	☐ ☐
160	*Plate 18*		£450	75·00	☐ ☐
147	*Plate 13*	6d grey	£500	90·00	☐ ☐
147	*Plate 14*		£500	90·00	☐ ☐
147	*Plate 15*		£500	90·00	☐ ☐
147	*Plate 16*		£500	90·00	☐ ☐
147	*Plate 17*		£950	£180	☐ ☐
161	*Plate 17*	6d grey	£425	80·00	☐ ☐
161	*Plate 18*		£400	80·00	☐ ☐
150	*Plate 8*	1s green	£825	£175	☐ ☐
150	*Plate 9*		£825	£175	☐ ☐
150	*Plate 10*		£775	£200	☐ ☐
150	*Plate 11*		£775	£175	☐ ☐
150	*Plate 12*		£650	£160	☐ ☐
150	*Plate 13*		£650	£160	☐ ☐
150	*Plate 14*		*	£40000	☐
163	*Plate 13*	1s brown	£875	£170	☐ ☐
163	*Plate 14*		£750	£170	☐ ☐

 35
 36
 37

 38

 39 Maltese Cross
 40 Large Anchor

1867–83

(i) Wmk Maltese Cross Type **39** Perf 15½ × 15

126	**35**	5s red Pl.	£11000	£675	☐ ☐
128	**36**	10s grey (Plate 1)	£60000	£3200	☐ ☐
129	**37**	£1 brown (Plate 1)	£90000	£4500	☐ ☐

(ii) Wmk Large Anchor Type **40** Perf 14

134	**35**	5s red (Plate 4)	£32000	£4200	☐ ☐
131	**36**	10s grey (Plate 1)	£135000	£5200	☐ ☐
132	**37**	£1 brown (Plate 1)	£175000	£10000	☐ ☐
137	**38**	£5 orange (Plate 1)	£14500	£4750	☐ ☐

 41
 42
 43

 44
 45
 46

 47 Small anchor
 48 Orb
 49 Imperial Crown

Large coloured corner letters

1873–80

		(i) Wmk Small Anchor Type **47**			
139	**41**	2½d mauve Pl.	£650	£120	☐ ☐
		(ii) Wmk Orb Type **48**			
141	**41**	2½d mauve Pl.	£525	85·00	☐ ☐
142		2½d blue Pl.	£575	55·00	☐ ☐
		(iii) Wmk Spray of Rose Type **33**			
143	**42**	3d red Pl.	£450	80·00	☐ ☐
145	**43**	6d pale buff (Plate 13)	*	£25000	☐
147		6d grey Pl.	£500	90·00	☐ ☐
150	**44**	1s green Pl.	£650	£160	☐ ☐
151		1s brown (Plate 13)	£4750	£700	☐ ☐
		(iv) Wmk Large Garter Type **17**			
152	**45**	4d vermilion Pl.	£3200	£525	☐ ☐
153		4d green Pl.	£1400	£300	☐ ☐
154		4d brown (Plate 17)	£2800	£550	☐ ☐
156	**46**	8d orange (Plate 1)	£1850	£350	☐ ☐

$3\overset{.}{\underset{.}{d}}$ $6\overset{.}{\underset{.}{d}}$

(50)   (51)

Surcharges in red

1880–83 Wmk Imperial Crown Type **49**

157	**41**	2½d blue Pl.	£450	35·00	☐ ☐
158	**42**	3d red Pl.	£500	£100	☐ ☐
159		3d on 3d lilac (surch Type 50)	£650	£160	☐ ☐
160	**45**	4d brown Pl.	£450	75·00	☐ ☐
161	**43**	6d grey Pl.	£400	80·00	☐ ☐
162		6d on 6d lilac (surch Type 51)	£675	£150	☐ ☐
163	**44**	1s brown Pl.	£750	£170	☐ ☐

 52
 53
 54

 55
 56

1880–81 Wmk Imperial Crown Type **49**

164	52	½d green	55·00	22·00	☐	☐
166	53	1d brown	35·00	15·00	☐	☐
167	54	1½d brown	£250	60·00	☐	☐
168	55	2d red	£340	£120	☐	☐
169	56	5d indigo	£725	£175	☐	☐

57	**Die** I	**Die** II

1881 Wmk Imperial Crown Type **49**

(a) 14 dots in each corner, Die I

171	57	1d lilac	£225	45·00	☐	☐

(b) 16 dots in each corner, Die II

174	57	1d mauve	2·75	1·70	☐	☐

58	**59**	**60**

Coloured letters in the corners

1883–84 Wmk Anchor Type **40**

178	58	2s6d lilac	£600	£160	☐	☐
181	59	5s red	£975	£250	☐	☐
183	60	10s blue	£2250	£525	☐	☐

61

1884 Wmk 3 Imperial Crowns Type **49**

185	61	£1 brown	£32000	£3000	☐	☐

1888 Wmk 3 Orbs Type **48**

186	61	£1 brown	£72000	£4500	☐	☐

1891 Wmk 3 Imperial Crowns Type **49**

212	61	£1 green	£4000	£800	☐	☐

62	**63**	**64**

65	**66**

1883–84 Wmk Imperial Crown Type **49** (sideways on horiz designs)

187	52	½d blue	35·00	10·00	☐	☐
188	62	1½d lilac	£125	45·00	☐	☐
189	63	2d lilac	£230	80·00	☐	☐
190	64	2½d lilac	95·00	20·00	☐	☐
191	65	3d lilac	£280	£100	☐	☐
192	66	4d dull green	£580	£210	☐	☐

193	62	5d dull green	£580	£210	☐	☐
194	63	6d dull green	£625	£240	☐	☐
195	64	9d dull green	£1250	£480	☐	☐
196	65	1s dull green	£1600	£325	☐	☐

The above prices are for stamps in the true dull green colour. Stamps which have been soaked, causing the colour to run are virtually worthless.

71	**72**	**73**
74	**75**	**76**
77	**78**	**79**
80	**81**	**82**

'Jubilee' Issue

1887–1900 The bicoloured stamps have the value tablets, or the frames including the value tablets, in the second colour. Wmk Imperial Crown Type **49**

197	71	½d vermilion	1·75	1·20	☐	☐
213		½d green*	2·00	2·25	☐	☐
198	72	1½d purple and green	18·00	8·00	☐	☐
200	73	2d green and red	35·00	15·00	☐	☐
201	74	2½d purple on blue	25·00	5·00	☐	☐
202	75	3d purple on yellow	25·00	5·00	☐	☐
205	76	4d green and brown	40·00	18·00	☐	☐
206	77	4½d green and red	11·00	45·00	☐	☐
207a	78	5d purple and blue	42·00	15·00	☐	☐
208	79	6d purple on red	40·00	15·00	☐	☐
209	80	9d purple and blue	75·00	48·00	☐	☐
210	81	10d purple and red	60·00	45·00	☐	☐
211	82	1s green	£275	80·00	☐	☐
214		1s green and red	65·00	£140	☐	☐
Set of 14			£650	£380	☐	☐

*The ½d No. 213 in blue is a colour changeling.

KING EDWARD VII

1901 (22 Jan.)–1910 (6 May)

83   84   85

86   87   88

89   90   91

92   93

94   95   96

97

1902–13 Wmks Imperial Crown Type **49** (½d to 1s), Anchor Type **40** (2s6d to 10s), Three Crowns Type **49** (£1)

(a) Perf 14

215	**83**	½d blue-green	2·00	1·50	☐	☐
217		½d yellow-green	2·00	1·50	☐	☐
219		1d red	2·00	1·50	☐	☐
224	**84**	1½d purple and green	45·00	22·00	☐	☐
291	**85**	2d green and red	28·00	22·00	☐	☐
231	**86**	2½d blue	20·00	12·00	☐	☐
232	**87**	3d purple on yellow	50·00	18·00	☐	☐
238	**88**	4d green and brown	40·00	20·00	☐	☐
240		4d orange	20·00	18·00	☐	☐
294	**89**	5d purple and blue	30·00	22·00	☐	☐
297	**83**	6d purple	30·00	22·00	☐	☐
249	**90**	7d grey	15·00	22·00	☐	☐
307	**91**	9d purple and blue	60·00	60·00	☐	☐
311	**92**	10d purple and red	80·00	60·00	☐	☐
314	**93**	1s green and red	60·00	35·00	☐	☐
260	**94**	2s6d purple	£280	£150	☐	☐
263	**95**	5s red	£450	£220	☐	☐
265	**96**	10s blue	£1000	£500	☐	☐
266	**97**	£1 green	£2000	£825	☐	☐
Set of 15 (to 1s)			£400	£275	☐	☐

(b) Perf 15 × 14

279	**83**	½d green	40·00	45·00	☐	☐
281		1d red	15·00	15·00	☐	☐
283	**86**	2½d blue	22·00	15·00	☐	☐
285	**87**	3d purple on yellow	45·00	15·00	☐	☐
286	**88**	4d orange	30·00	15·00	☐	☐
Set of 5			£130	90·00	☐	☐

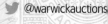

KING GEORGE V

1910 (6 May)–1936 (20 January)

PERFORATION. All the following issues are Perf 15×14 except vertical commemorative stamps which are 14×15, unless otherwise stated.

98 (Hair dark) **99** (Lion unshaded) **100**

1911–12 Wmk Imperial Crown Type 49

322	98	½d green	4·00	4·00	☐	☐
327	99	1d red	4·50	2·50	☐	☐

1912 Wmk Royal Cypher ('Simple') Type 100

335	98	½d green	45·00	40·00	☐	☐
336	99	1d red	30·00	30·00	☐	☐

101 (Hair light) **102** (Lion shaded) **103**

1912 Wmk Imperial Crown Type 49

339	101	½d green	8·00	4·00	☐	☐
341	102	1d red	5·00	2·00	☐	☐

1912 Wmk Royal Cypher ('Simple') Type 100

344	101	½d green	7·00	3·00	☐	☐
345	102	1d red	8·00	4·50	☐	☐

1912 Wmk Royal Cypher ('Multiple') Type 103

346	101	½d green	12·00	8·00	☐	☐
350	102	1d red	18·00	10·00	☐	☐

104 **105** **106**

107 **108**

1912–24 Wmk Royal Cypher Type 100

351	105	½d green	1·00	1·00	☐	☐
357	104	1d red	1·00	1·00	☐	☐
364	105	1½d brown	3·00	1·00	☐	☐
368	106	2d orange	4·00	3·00	☐	☐
371	104	2½d blue	12·00	4·00	☐	☐
375	106	3d violet	8·00	3·00	☐	☐
379		4d grey-green	15·00	2·00	☐	☐

381	107	5d brown	15·00	5·00	☐	☐
385		6d purple	15·00	7·00	☐	☐
		a. Perf 14	90·00	£110	☐	☐
387		7d olive-green	20·00	10·00	☐	☐
390		8d black on yellow	32·00	11·00	☐	☐
392	108	9d black	15·00	6·00	☐	☐
393a		9d olive-green	£110	30·00	☐	☐
394		10d blue	22·00	20·00	☐	☐
395		1s brown	20·00	4·00	☐	☐
Set of 15			£250	95·00		☐

1913 Wmk Royal Cypher ('Multiple') Type 103

397	105	½d green	£150	£180	☐	☐
398	104	1d red	£225	£225	☐	☐

See also Nos. 418/29.

109

110

1913–18 Wmk Single Cypher Type 110 Perf 11×12

414	109	2s6d brown	£160	75·00	☐	☐
416		5s red	£325	£135	☐	☐
417		10s blue	£475	£175	☐	☐
403		£1 green	£3500	£1400	☐	☐
Set of 4			£4000	£1500	☐	☐

T **109**. Background around portrait consists of horizontal lines
See also Nos. 450/2.

111

1924–26 Wmk Block Cypher Type 111

418	105	½d green	1·00	1·00	☐	☐
419	104	1d red	1·00	1·00	☐	☐
420	105	1½d brown	1·00	1·00	☐	☐
421	106	2d orange	2·50	2·50	☐	☐
422	104	2½d blue	5·00	3·00	☐	☐
423	106	3d violet	10·00	2·50	☐	☐
424		4d grey-green	12·00	2·50	☐	☐
425	107	5d brown	20·00	3·00	☐	☐
426a		6d purple	4·00	1·50	☐	☐
427	108	9d olive-green	12·00	3·50	☐	☐
428		10d blue	40·00	40·00	☐	☐
429		1s brown	22·00	3·00	☐	☐
Set of 12			£110	60·00	☐	☐

112

112a

121

122

British Empire Exhibition

1924–25 Wmk **111** Perf 14

(a) 23.4.24. Dated '1924'

430	**112**	1d red	10·00	11·00	☐	☐
431	**112a**	1½d brown	15·00	15·00	☐	☐
First Day Cover				£450	☐	

(b) 9.5.25. Dated '1925'

432	**112**	1d red	15·00	30·00	☐	☐
433	**112a**	1½d brown	40·00	70·00	☐	☐
First Day Cover				£1700	☐	

113

114

115

116 St. George and the Dragon

117

Ninth Universal Postal Union Congress

1929 (10 May)

(a) Wmk **111**

434	**113**	½d green	2·25	2·25	☐	☐
435	**114**	1d red	2·25	2·25	☐	☐
436		1½d brown	2·25	1·75	☐	☐
437	**115**	2½d blue	10·00	10·00	☐	☐

(b) Wmk **117** Perf 12

438	**116**	£1 black	£750	£550	☐	☐
434/7	*Set of 4*		15·00	14·50	☐	☐
434/7	First Day Cover (4 vals.)			£675	☐	
434/8	First Day Cover (5 vals.)			£14000	☐	

118

119

120

1934–36 Wmk **111**

439	**118**	½d green	50	50	☐	☐
440	**119**	1d red	50	50	☐	☐
441	**118**	1½d brown	50	50	☐	☐
442	**120**	2d orange	75	75	☐	☐
443	**119**	2½d blue	1·50	1·25	☐	☐
444	**120**	3d violet	1·50	1·25	☐	☐
445		4d grey-green	2·00	1·25	☐	☐
446	**121**	5d brown	6·50	2·75	☐	☐
447	**122**	9d olive-green	12·00	2·25	☐	☐
448		10d blue	15·00	10·00	☐	☐
449		1s brown	15·00	1·25	☐	☐
Set of 11			50·00	20·00	☐	☐

T **109** (re-engraved). Background around portrait consists of horizontal and diagonal lines

1934 Wmk **110** Perf 11 × 12

450	**109**	2s6d brown	80·00	40·00	☐	☐
451		5s red	£175	85·00	☐	☐
452		10s blue	£350	80·00	☐	☐
Set of 3			£575	£190	☐	☐

123

123a

123b

123c

Silver Jubilee

1935 (7 May) Wmk **111**

453	**123**	½d green	1·00	1·00	☐	☐
454	**123a**	1d red	1·50	2·00	☐	☐
455	**123b**	1½d brown	1·00	1·00	☐	☐
456	**123c**	2½d blue	5·00	6·50	☐	☐
Set of 4			7·50	9·50	☐	☐
First Day Cover				£650	☐	

KING EDWARD VIII

1936 (20 Jan.–10 Dec.)

124   125

1936 Wmk **125**

457	**124**	½d green	30	30
458		1d red	60	50
459		1½d brown	30	30
460		2½d blue	30	85
Set of 4			1·25	1·75

First Day Covers
1 Sept. 1936 Nos. 457, 459/60		£175
14 Sept. 1936 No. 458		£200

Collectors are reminded that for issues from 1936 to date, prices in the unused column are for unmounted mint.

KING GEORGE VI

1936 (11 Dec.)–1952 (6 Feb.)

126 King George VI and Queen Elizabeth   127

Coronation

1937 (13 May) Wmk **127**
461	**126**	1½d brown	30	30
First Day Cover				35·00

128   129   130

King George VI and National Emblems

1937–47 Wmk **127**
462	**128**	½d green	30	25
463		1d scarlet	30	25
464		1½d brown	30	25
465		2d orange	1·20	50
466		2½d blue	40	25
467		3d violet	5·00	1·00
468	**129**	4d green	60	75
469		5d brown	3·50	85
470		6d purple	1·50	60
471	**130**	7d green	5·00	60
472		8d red	7·50	80
473		9d deep green	6·50	1·00
474		10d blue	7·00	1·00
474a		11d plum	3·00	2·75
475		1s brown	9·00	75
Set of 15			45·00	10·00

First Day Covers
10 May 1937	Nos. 462/3, 466	45·00
30 July 1937	No. 464	45·00
31 Jan. 1938	Nos. 465, 467	£100
21 Nov. 1938	Nos. 468/9	65·00
30 Jan. 1939	No. 470	60·00
27 Feb. 1939	Nos. 471/2	85·00
1 May 1939	Nos. 473/4, 475	£500
29 Dec. 1947	No. 474a	55·00

For later printings of the lower values in apparently lighter shades and different colours, see Nos. 485/90 and 503/8.

130a King George VI   131   132

132a   133

1939–48 Wmk **133** Perf 14

476	**130a**	2s6d brown	95·00	8·00	☐ ☐
476b		2s6d green	15·00	1·50	☐ ☐
477	**131**	5s red	20·00	2·00	☐ ☐
478	**132**	10s dark blue	£260	22·00	☐ ☐
478b		10s bright blue	45·00	5·00	☐ ☐
478c	**132a**	£1 brown	25·00	26·00	☐ ☐
Set of 6			£425	60·00	☐ ☐
First Day Covers					
21 Aug. 1939		No. 477		£850	☐
4 Sept. 1939		No. 476		£1800	☐
30 Oct. 1939		No. 478		£3250	☐
9 Mar. 1942		No. 476b		£1750	☐
30 Nov. 1942		No. 478b		£3750	☐
1 Oct. 1948		No. 478c		£325	☐

134 Queen Victoria and
King George VI

**Centenary of
First Adhesive Postage Stamps**

1940 (6 May) Wmk **127** Perf 14½ × 14

479	**134**	½d green	30	75	☐ ☐
480		1d red	1·00	75	☐ ☐
481		1½d brown	50	1·50	☐ ☐
482		2d orange	1·00	75	☐ ☐
483		2½d blue	2·25	50	☐ ☐
484		3d violet	3·00	3·50	☐ ☐
Set of 6			8·75	5·25	☐ ☐
First Day Cover				55·00	☐

Head as Nos. 462–7, but with lighter background

1941–42 Wmk **127**

485	**128**	½d pale green	30	30	☐ ☐
486		1d pale red	30	30	☐ ☐
487		1½d pale brown	60	80	☐ ☐
488		2d pale orange	50	50	☐ ☐
489		2½d light blue	30	30	☐ ☐
490		3d pale violet	2·50	1·00	☐ ☐
Set of 6			3·50	2·75	☐ ☐
First Day Covers					
21 July 1941		No. 489		45·00	☐
11 Aug. 1941		No. 486		22·00	☐
1 Sept. 1941		No. 485		22·00	☐
6 Oct. 1941		No. 488		60·00	☐
3 Nov. 1941		No. 490		£110	☐
28 Sept. 1942		No. 487		55·00	☐

135 Symbols of Peace and
Reconstruction

136 Symbols of Peace and
Reconstruction

Victory

1946 (11 June) Wmk **127**

491	**135**	2½d blue	20	20	☐ ☐
492	**136**	3d violet	20	50	☐ ☐
Set of 2			40	60	☐ ☐
First Day Cover				65·00	☐

137 King George VI and
Queen Elizabeth

138 King George VI and
Queen Elizabeth

Royal Silver Wedding

1948 (26 Apr.) Wmk **127**

493	**137**	2½d blue	35	20	☐ ☐
494	**138**	£1 blue	40·00	40·00	☐ ☐
Set of 2			40·00	40·00	☐ ☐
First Day Cover				£425	☐

1948 (10 May)
Stamps of 1d and 2½d showing seaweed-gathering were on
sale at eight Head Post Offices elsewhere in Great Britain, but
were primarily for use in the Channel Islands and are listed
there (see after Regional Issues).

139 Globe and Laurel Wreath

140 Speed

141 Olympic Symbol

142 Winged Victory

Olympic Games

1948 (29 July) Wmk **127**

495	**139**	2½d blue	50	10	☐ ☐
496	**140**	3d violet	50	50	☐ ☐
497	**141**	6d purple	3·25	1·00	☐ ☐
498	**142**	1s brown	4·50	2·00	☐ ☐
Set of 4			8·00	3·00	☐ ☐
First Day Cover				45·00	☐

143 Two Hemispheres   **144** U.P.U. Monument, Berne

147 HMS *Victory*   **148** White Cliffs of Dover

145 Goddess Concordia, Globe and Points of Compass   **146** Posthorn and Globe

149 St. George and the Dragon   **150** Royal Coat of Arms

75th Anniversary of Universal Postal Union

1949 (10 Oct.) Wmk **127**

499	**143**	2½d blue	25	10	☐	☐
500	**144**	3d violet	25	50	☐	☐
501	**145**	6d purple	50	75	☐	☐
502	**146**	1s brown	1·00	1·25	☐	☐
Set of 4			1·50	2·50	☐	☐
First Day Cover				80·00		☐

4d as No. 468 and others as Nos. 485/9, but colours changed.

1950–51 Wmk **127**

503	**128**	½d pale orange	30	30	☐	☐
504		1d light blue	30	30	☐	☐
505		1½d pale green	65	60	☐	☐
506		2d pale brown	75	40	☐	☐
507		2½d pale red	60	40	☐	☐
508	**129**	4d light blue	2·00	1·75	☐	☐
Set of 6			4·00	3·25	☐	☐
First Day Covers						
2 Oct. 1950 No. 508				£120		☐
3 May 1951 Nos. 503/7				55·00		☐

1951 (3 May) Wmk **133** Perf 11 × 12

509	**147**	2s6d green	7·50	1·00	☐	☐
510	**148**	5s red	35·00	1·00	☐	☐
511	**149**	10s blue	15·00	7·50	☐	☐
512	**150**	£1 brown	45·00	18·00	☐	☐
Set of 4			£100	25·00	☐	☐
First Day Cover				£950		☐

151 Commerce and Prosperity   **152** Festival Symbol

Festival of Britain

1951 (3 May) Wmk **127**

513	**151**	2½d red	20	15	☐	☐
514	**152**	4d blue	30	35	☐	☐
Set of 2			40	40	☐	☐
First Day Cover				38·00		☐

QUEEN ELIZABETH II

6 February, 1952

153 Tudor Crown

 154

 155

163

164

Coronation

1953 (3 June) Wmk **153**

532	**161**	2½d	red	20	25	☐☐
533	**162**	4d	blue	1·10	1·90	☐☐
534	**163**	1s3d	green	5·00	3·00	☐☐
535	**164**	1s6d	blue	10·00	4·75	☐☐
Set of 4				16·00	9·00	☐☐
First Day Cover					80·00	☐

For £1 values as Type **163** see Nos. **MS**2147 and 2380.

165 St. Edward's Crown

166 Carrickfergus Castle
167 Caernarvon Castle

168 Edinburgh Castle
169 Windsor Castle

1955 (1–23 Sept.) Wmk **165** Perf 11 × 12

536	**166**	2s6d	brown	15·00	2·00	☐☐
537	**167**	5s	red	40·00	4·00	☐☐
538	**168**	10s	blue	90·00	14·00	☐☐
539	**169**	£1	black	£140	35·00	☐☐
Set of 4				£250	50·00	☐☐
First Day Cover	(Nos. 538/9) (1 Sept.)				£850	
First Day Cover	(Nos. 536/7) (23 Sept.)				£650	

See also Nos. 595a/8a and 759/62.

1955–58 Wmk **165**

540	**154**	½d	orange	20	15	☐☐
541		1d	blue	30	15	☐☐
542		1½d	green	25	30	☐☐
543		2d	red-brown	25	35	☐☐
543b		2d	light red-brown	30	20	☐☐
544	**155**	2½d	red	30	25	☐☐
545		3d	lilac	40	25	☐☐
546	**156**	4d	blue	1·30	45	☐☐
547	**157**	5d	brown	6·00	6·00	☐☐
548		6d	purple	4·50	1·20	☐☐
549		7d	green	50·00	10·00	☐☐
550	**158**	8d	magenta	7·00	1·30	☐☐
551		9d	bronze-green	20·00	2·75	☐☐
552		10d	blue	20·00	2·75	☐☐
553		11d	plum	1·00	1·10	☐☐
554	**159**	1s	bistre	22·00	65	☐☐
555	**160**	1s3d	green	30·00	1·60	☐☐
556	**159**	1s6d	indigo	23·00	1·60	☐☐
Set of 18				£160	27·00	☐☐

154

155

156

157

158

159

160

1952–54 Wmk **153**

515	**154**	½d	orange	25	15	☐☐
516		1d	ultramarine	30	20	☐☐
517		1½d	green	25	20	☐☐
518		2d	red-brown	30	20	☐☐
519	**155**	2½d	carmine-red	30	15	☐☐
520		3d	deep lilac	1·50	90	☐☐
521	**156**	4d	ultramarine	3·25	1·30	☐☐
		4½d	(See Nos. 577, 594, 609 and 616b)			
522	**157**	5d	brown	1·00	3·50	☐☐
523		6d	reddish purple	4·00	1·00	☐☐
524		7d	bright green	9·50	5·50	☐☐
525	**158**	8d	magenta	1·25	85	☐☐
526		9d	bronze-green	23·00	4·75	☐☐
527		10d	Prussian blue	18·00	4·75	☐☐
528		11d	brown-purple	35·00	15·00	☐☐
529	**159**	1s	bistre-brown	80	50	☐☐
530	**160**	1s3d	green	4·50	3·25	☐☐
531	**159**	1s6d	grey-blue	14·00	3·75	☐☐
Set of 17				£100	40·00	☐☐

First Day Covers

5 Dec. 1952	Nos. 517, 519	28·00	☐
6 July 1953	Nos. 522, 525, 529	60·00	☐
31 Aug. 1953	Nos. 515/16, 518	60·00	☐
2 Nov. 1953	Nos. 521, 530/1	£200	☐
18 Jan. 1954	Nos. 520, 523/4	£125	☐
8 Feb. 1954	Nos. 526/8	£250	☐

See also Nos. 540/56, 561/6, 570/94 and 599/618a and for stamps as Types **154/60** with face values in decimal currency see Nos. 2031/3, 2258/9, **MS**2326, **MS**2367, 2378/9 and 3329.

161

162

MAL 62 MALAYA - A substantial collection of Malaya, Malaysia with Singapore. Contains several hundred unmounted mint and fine used stamps in blocks and singles. Noted: Perak, Selangor, Kedah, Sabah, Perlis, Trengganu, Pulau Pinang, Negri Sembilan, Kelantan, Sarawak, Melaka, Johor, Parhang; with strength in Singapore.Several hundred stamps .... **Price £17.00**

HK 145 HONG KONG - A fine collection of used stamps of Hong Kong. Almost all the stamps pre date the handover to China. Including $ values and popular Chinese New Year Commemoratives. Totally unchecked for catalogue value, over 100 Hong Kong stamps .... **Price £11.00**

CL5 CLEMENT ATTLEE - A scarce political cover commemorating the 70th anniv. of Clement Attlee becoming prime minister. Attlee won a landslide election victory in 1945 bringing the Labour party into power. The scarce cover depicts Clement Attlee in his World War I army uniform. The cover bears the official Royal Mail Attlee commemorative stamp issue with London 26/7/15 postmark. Only 50 of this scarce political cover are known to exist ...... **Price £19.25**

MC.334 - MUSIC - An awesome & valuable collection of music stamps begins with an orchestra of musical instrument stamps. The specialist classical section includes: Mozart, Beethoven, Bach, Tchaikovsky, Verdi, Bartok. Also jazz and popmusic stamps, with Louis Armstrong, Frank Sinatra, Oasis, Marlene Dietrich. With G.B. Royal Mail stamps of Freddy Mercury, The Beatles and Pink Floyd. A multiple of other issues for Rolling Stones, Jimi Hendrix, Michael Jackson, Kylie Minogue, Elvis Presley and many more> Hundreds of stamps - mint and used with several miniature sheets. The best Music collection we have ever seen .... **Price £29.25**

SJ120 MEDICAL - Stamps with specialised lot of Anti-TB and Red Cross stamps. Also Anti-Malaria stamps Red Cross stamps back to the 1940s or earlier up to more recent. With nursing, doctors and all forms of medicine. A most interesting subject rarely offered for sale ideal for anyone with some medical knowledge to form a valuable collection............. **Price £7.00**

G.114 A WORLDWIDE COVERS & FDC'S - Fantastic Accumulation of Commercial & Philatelic covers & FDC's including special pmks, early to modern with Air Mails, Sea Mail, commemorative covers, noted designer signed. Local posts, Islands Post, an unsorted group of about 100 covers............................ **Price £21.00**

Lot K2 GREAT BRITAIN. UNMOUNTED MINT COMMEMORATIVES & DEFINITIVES UNSORTED ACCUMULATION. - Items noted include Traffic Light Gutter Pair Missing Phosphor Error coil strips. Well over 500 stamps, only unmounted mint.. **Price £18.00**

R45 MINIATURE SHEETS - & Souvenir Sheets, various different GB (Exhibition sheets) FOREIGN, odd Brit. Commonwealth. Total of 50+ different (Mainly Foreign) Min sheets.................. **Price £8.00**

NY146 ENTOMOLOGY - One of the most unusual thematic subjects we have ever seen, insects on stamps. Hundreds of them .... **Price £7.00**

SJ53a BARDSEY ISLAND. - (Welsh Local Issue) A superb specialised group of Unmounted Mint (complete sets) Stamps from this small Welsh Island rarely get offered for sale .... **Price £7.00**

NY124 THE THREE KINGS King George V, King ED. VII and King George VI. - A collection of British Colonials. UNMOUNTED MINT STAMPS. In singles and blocks. Approximately 100+ stamps, low price to clear .... **Price £12.00**

FE188 INDIAN FEUDATORY STATES - An interesting reference collection of mainly forgeries of the Indian Feudatory States. Victorian period includes imperforates and stamps printed on various white, coloured and buff papers. Noted: Sirmoor, Charkhari, Duttia, Fardikot, Indore, Rajpipla, Jammu & Kashmir, plus others. Also some stamps unlisted in Stanley Gibbons Catalogue. If genuine the catalogue value would exceed £1000s (Thousands of Pounds) but these are being sold "as is" as forgeries. The collection also includes genuine Indian stamps from Queen Victoria to Geo VI .... **Price £15.00**

BX 486 BOXING - A fine collection of Boxing Stamps Over 80 Stamps in blocks and singles, including champion boxers such as Muhammad Ali. Mainly fine to used, mint noted, with Great Britain Royal Mail 2012 Olympic Games Gold Medal Boxing Stamps .... **Price £9.75**

PM8 THERESA MAY - Official Royal appointment commemorative cover. The cover shows Theresa May being recieved by Her Majesty Queen Elizabeth II, who instructed her to form a Government. The cover bears as official R.M. Buckingham Palace stamp, tried to the cover with a Royal Mail 13/7/16 illustrated Buckingham Palace Postmar. Only 75 of this scarce cover are known to exist .... **Price £26.00**

LU 328 LUNDY ISLAND - A superb collection of unmounted mint British local stamps of Lundy Island in blocks, large multiples and singles + miniature sheet. Starts off with King George VI period."Lundy & Atlantic Coats Air Lines Ltd."Following on to puffin stamps overprinted with 1950s & 1960s stamps on to more recent. With lots of "Puffin" stamps, definitives, commemoratives & Air Mail stamps. Hundreds of unmounted mint Lundy Stamps .... **Price £27.50**

B COM 434 ORNITHOLOGY - A fantastic thematic collection of British Commonwealth BIRDS stamps. Only Unmounted Mint in multiples and single stamps. Several Hundred Brit, Commonwealth Bird Stamps including High Value (£) pound & ($) Dollar stamps in blocks .... **Price £39.00**

GB.51 - GREAT BRITAIN SCARCE FESTIVAL OF BRITAIN COMMEM. Cover. Bearing the Abram Games stamp designer official Royal Mail Commem. Stamp cancelled with iconic Festival of Britain 25/3/14 Postmark. The cover also bears the complete King George VI 1951 Festival stamps with black cachet "G.PO. 1951 Festival of Britain Official Stamp Issue" The edition was limited to only 100 of these important covers................... **Price £11.25**

FA16 -FALKLAND ISLANDS - Scarce Referendum Cover - A rare and unusual cover for the Falkland Islands Referendum. The illustrated Falklands flag cover is inscribed 11/3/2013 Falkland islanders vote on Self Datermination. The cover bears a British Q.E.2. stamp with double penguin postmark dates 11/3/2013 Shetland P.O. It also has a Falkland Is. referendum stamp and Argentine War "Malvinas" ovpt stamp, both tied to the cover with Green Cachet "Falklands Referendum NO to Malvinas. 99.8% vote in favour of remaining with U.K. 11/3/2013" only 50 of rare covers are known to exist .... **Price £18.50**

RA. 8 DESERT RATS WAR COVER - A Sought after British Cover issued for the 70th Anniv. of the Desert Rats Battle for Migliano on 1/12/1944. The cover depicts Migliano and the iconic Desert Rat Emblem, it bears the British Spitfire Commemorative with scarce B.F.P.O 3181 Desert Rats 7th Armoured Brigade Postmark. On the Anniv. Date 1/12/14. Most of this scarce cover are now in specialist collections Recommended at our.................. **Price of £12.50**

HRH. R3 KING RICHARD III - An important historic cover issued for the reburial of Richard III "The Last Plantagenet King of England". The cover depicts King Richard who was buried at Leicester Cathedral 530 years after his death at the battle of Bosworth Field. Only 60 of this scarce covers are in existence. The historic cover bears the British Royal Lion stamp postmarked with the official Royal Mail illustrated "Rest in Peace" Leicester Cathedral Pmk on 26/3/2015. Few available ...Price £16.00

SH. 73 SHETLAND ISLANDS - Impressive cover for "Up-Helly-AA" The Viking Fire festival at Lerwic, when a Viking long boat is set on fire. The cover bears the Shetland Island Local Stamps depicting Vikings and a blazing Viking ship tied to the cover with Hildasay - Shetland Island cachet in blue, in combination with Royal Mail Stamp postmarked with the Celtic "Up-Helly-AA" Lerwic pmk.......................Price £13.25

Alb. 7 ALBANIA - A lovely collection of Albanian stamps, including scarcer older stamps issued for King Zog, unmounted mint. Unusual items noted include 1952 stamps issued by the Albanian Govt, in exile. Also better overprinted stamps. Containing over 100 stamps with blocks and singles mint and used ...Price £15.00

R88A NAZI GERMAN Occupation of World. War II various Croatia Bohemia and Moravia. Occupation of Poland General government (Theresienstadt also Lodz Ghjetto these may not be genuine) plus various other Germany war period Hiijer issues. Mainly genuine unmounted mint/ used ....Price £10.00

M6 PRINCESS DIANA – Worldwide collection Some 1981 Wedding Issues, also Prince William Birth, including scarcer sheetlets, V SCAR CE GUTTER PAIR F.D.C's SIGNED BY THE DESIGNER (stamp designer) also various worldwide 1997 Princess Diana Memoria Issues. The whole collection............Price £13.00

E.32 TIBET Fantastic group printed on rough and thin "Native Type" paper including listed stamps, and some shades and colours which appear not to be listed in Gibbons Catalogue. Included are blocks and singles Due to the crudeness of the printing of this type of Tibet stamps, there is no way we can guarantee any as genuine. If just some of the listed stamps we re genuine the Catalogue Value would be Hundreds of Pounds. We have decided the safest way is to treat them as suspect and possible forgeries. As such we are offering them for sale at the knock down price of only ....Price £13.0

GS 9L GRAF SPEE - The very scarce WWII Commemorative Cover for the 75th Anniv of the scuttling of the pocket battle ship Graf Spee. Captain Hans Langsdorff scuttled the ship in full view of 20,000 onlookers before he shot and killed himself. The cover bears two submarine stamps with B.F.P.O Battle of the River Plate pmk. dated 13 Dec 14., and also the scarce Royal Crown and Lion pmk. Dated 17 Dec 2014 on the Anniv. date It is understood that only 60 of this scarce cover exists .... Price £18.50

SW. 86 SWITZERLAND - A great starter collection to build upon of fine used Swiss mainly Commemorative stamps. 100 + At a different..Price £7.00

NK39 NORTH KOREA - An unusual collection of D.P.R. (North) Korean stamps including controversial and highly political propaganda communist stamps depicting Kim-Jong-Il father of the current leader Kim-Jong-un Includes scarcer blocks, se-tenant and single stamps. Over 100 stamps............ Price £10.75

12 Prince Albert Street, Brighton, Sussex, BN1 1HE
Tel: 01273 326994
Telephone accepted.
Payment by Mastercard or Visa credit cards

We have no e-mail address, please contact us by telephone
Est. 1971 dealing in stamps for over 40 years

170 Scout Badge and 'Rolling Hitch' **171** 'Scouts coming to Britain'

172 Globe within a Compass **173**

World Scout Jubilee Jamboree

1957 (1 Aug.) Wmk **165**

557	**170**	2½d	red	50	50	☐ ☐
558	**171**	4d	blue	75	1·50	☐ ☐
559	**172**	1s3d	green	5·50	4·50	☐ ☐
Set of 3				6·00	5·75	☐ ☐
First Day Cover					28·00	☐

46th Inter Parliamentary Union Conference

1957 (12 Sept.) Wmk **165**

560	**173**	4d	blue	2·00	1·50	☐ ☐
First Day Cover					£150	☐

Graphite-lined and Phosphor Issues

These are used in connection with automatic sorting machinery, originally experimentally at Southampton but now also operating elsewhere. In such areas these stamps were the normal issue, but from mid 1967 all low-value stamps bear phosphor markings.

The graphite lines were printed in black on the back, beneath the gum; two lines per stamp except for the 2d (see below).

½d. to 1½d., 2½d., 3d.   2d.
Graphite-line arrangements
(Stamps viewed from back)

In November 1959, phosphor bands, printed on the front, replaced the graphite. They are wider than the graphite, not easy to see, but show as broad vertical bands at certain angles to the light.

Values representing the rate for printed papers (and second class mail from 1968) have two, three or four bands according to size and format. From 1972 onwards some commemorative stamps were printed with 'all-over' phosphor.

In the small stamps the bands are on each side with the single band at left (except where otherwise stated). In the large-size commemorative stamps the single band may be at left, centre or right varying in different issues. The bands are vertical on both horizontal and vertical designs except where otherwise stated.

See also notes above No. 881.

Graphite-lined issue

1957 (19 Nov.) Two graphite lines on the back, except 2d value, which has one line. Wmk **165**

561	**154**	½d	orange	60	60	☐ ☐
562		1d	blue	80	80	☐ ☐
563		1½d	green	2·00	1·75	☐ ☐
564		2d	light red-brown	2·40	2·40	☐ ☐
565	**155**	2½d	red	8·50	7·00	☐ ☐

566		3d	lilac	1·50	1·50	☐ ☐
Set of 6				15·00	13·00	☐ ☐
First Day Cover					90·00	☐

See also Nos. 587/94.

176 Welsh Dragon **177** Flag and Games Emblem

178 Welsh Dragon

Sixth British Empire and Commonwealth Games, Cardiff

1958 (18 July) Wmk **165**

567	**176**	3d	lilac	20	20	☐ ☐
568	**177**	6d	mauve	60	45	☐ ☐
569	**178**	1s3d	green	2·25	2·50	☐ ☐
Set of 3				2·50	2·75	☐ ☐
First Day Cover					85·00	☐

179 Multiple Crowns

WATERMARK. All the following issues to No. 755 are Watermark **179** (sideways on the vertical commemorative stamps) unless otherwise stated.

1958–65 Wmk **179**

570	**154**	½d	orange	10	10	☐ ☐
571		1d	blue	10	10	☐ ☐
572		1½d	green	10	15	☐ ☐
573		2d	light red-brown	10	10	☐ ☐
574	**155**	2½d	red	10	20	☐ ☐
575		3d	lilac	20	30	☐ ☐
576a	**156**	4d	blue	15	15	☐ ☐
577		4½d	brown	10	25	☐ ☐
578	**157**	5d	brown	30	40	☐ ☐
579		6d	purple	30	25	☐ ☐
580		7d	green	50	45	☐ ☐
581	**158**	8d	magenta	60	40	☐ ☐
582		9d	bronze-green	60	40	☐ ☐
583		10d	blue	1·00	75	☐ ☐
584	**159**	1s	bistre	75	30	☐ ☐
585	**160**	1s3d	green	75	30	☐ ☐
586	**159**	1s6d	indigo	5·00	40	☐ ☐
Set of 17				9·00	4·25	☐ ☐
First Day Cover (No. 577) (9 Feb. 1959)					£250	☐

Graphite-lined issue

1958–59 Two graphite lines on the back, except 2d value, which has one line. Wmk **179**

587Wi	**154**	½d	orange	3·25	4·00	☐ ☐
588		1d	blue	2·00	1·50	☐ ☐
589Wi		1½d	green	75·00	60·00	☐ ☐
590		2d	light red-brown	10·00	3·50	☐ ☐
591	**155**	2½d	red	12·00	10·00	☐ ☐
592		3d	lilac	90	65	☐ ☐
593	**156**	4d	blue	5·50	5·00	☐ ☐

594		4½d brown	6·50	5·00	☐ ☐
Set of 8			£110	70·00	☐ ☐

The prices quoted for Nos. 587 and 589 are for examples with inverted watermark. Stamps with upright watermark are priced at: ½d £9 mint, £9 used and 1½d £90 mint, £80 used.

1959–63 Wmk **179** Perf 11 × 12

595a	**166**	2s6d brown	35	40	☐ ☐
596a	**167**	5s red	1·20	50	☐ ☐
597a	**168**	10s blue	4·50	4·50	☐ ☐
598a	**169**	£1 black	13·00	8·00	☐ ☐
Set of 4			15·00	11·00	☐ ☐

Phosphor-Graphite issue

1959 (18 Nov.) Two phosphor bands on front and two graphite lines on back, except 2d value, which has one band on front and one line on back

(a) Wmk **165**

599	**154**	½d orange	4·50	4·50	☐ ☐
600		1d blue	12·00	12·00	☐ ☐
601		1½d green	5·25	5·25	☐ ☐

(b) Wmk **179**

605	**154**	2d light red-brown (1 band)	6·00	5·00	☐ ☐
606	**155**	2½d red	22·00	18·00	☐ ☐
607		3d lilac	12·00	9·00	☐ ☐
608	**156**	4d blue	20·00	16·00	☐ ☐
609		4½d brown	30·00	20·00	☐ ☐
Set of 8			£100	80·00	☐ ☐

Phosphor issue

1960–67 Two phosphor bands on front, except where otherwise stated. Wmk **179**

610	**154**	½d orange	10	15	☐ ☐
611		1d blue	10	10	☐ ☐
612		1½d green	15	15	☐ ☐
613		2d light red-brown (1 band)	22·00	22·00	☐ ☐
613a		2d light red-brown (2 bands)	10	15	☐ ☐
614	**155**	2½d red (2 bands)	40	30	☐ ☐
614a		2½d red (1 band)	60	75	☐ ☐
615		3d lilac (2 bands)	60	55	☐ ☐
615c		3d lilac (1 side band)	60	55	☐ ☐
615e		3d lilac (1 centre band)	40	45	☐ ☐
616a	**156**	4d blue	25	25	☐ ☐
616b		4½d brown	55	30	☐ ☐
616c	**157**	5d brown	55	35	☐ ☐
617		6d purple	55	30	☐ ☐
617a		7d green	70	50	☐ ☐
617b	**158**	8d magenta	70	45	☐ ☐
617c		9d bronze-green	70	65	☐ ☐
617d		10d blue	1·00	1·00	☐ ☐
617e	**159**	1s bistre	1·00	35	☐ ☐
618	**160**	1s3d green	1·90	2·50	☐ ☐
618a	**159**	1s6d indigo	2·00	2·00	☐ ☐
Set of 17 (one of each value)			10·50	8·00	☐ ☐

No. 615c exists with the phosphor band at the left or right of the stamp.

180 Postboy of 1660

181 Posthorn of 1660

Tercentenary of Establishment of 'General Letter Office'

1960 (7 July)

619	**180**	3d lilac	50	50	☐ ☐
620	**181**	1s3d green	3·75	4·25	☐ ☐
Set of 2			4·00	4·50	☐ ☐
First Day Cover				65·00	☐

182 Conference Emblem

First Anniversary of European Postal and Telecommunications Conference

1960 (19 Sept.)

621	**182**	6d green and purple	2·00	50	☐ ☐
622		1s6d brown and blue	9·50	5·00	☐ ☐
Set of 2			11·00	5·25	☐ ☐
First Day Cover				65·00	☐

183 Thrift Plant

184 'Growth of Savings'   **185** Thrift Plant

Centenary of Post Office Savings Bank

1961 (28 Aug.)

623A	**183**	2½d black and red	25	25	☐ ☐
624A	**184**	3d orange-brown and violet	20	20	☐ ☐
625A	**185**	1s6d red and blue	2·75	3·00	☐ ☐
Set of 3			2·75	3·00	☐ ☐
First Day Cover				75·00	☐

186 C.E.P.T. Emblem   **187** Doves and Emblem

188 Doves and Emblem

European Postal and Telecommunications (C.E.P.T.) Conference, Torquay

1961 (18 Sept.)

626	**186**	2d	orange, pink and brown	15	10	☐ ☐
627	**187**	4d	buff, mauve and ultramarine	15	15	☐ ☐
628	**188**	10d	turquoise, green and blue	25	75	☐ ☐
Set of 3				50	85	☐ ☐
First Day Cover					6·00	☐

189 Hammer Beam Roof, Westminster Hall

190 Palace of Westminster

Seventh Commonwealth Parliamentary Conference

1961 (25 Sept.)

629	**189**	6d	purple and gold	25	25	☐ ☐
630	**190**	1s3d	green and blue	2·50	2·75	☐ ☐
Set of 2				2·75	3·00	☐ ☐
First Day Cover					30·00	☐

191 'Units of Productivity'

192 'National Productivity'

193 'Unified Productivity'

National Productivity Year

1962 (14 Nov.) Wmk **179** (inverted on 2½d and 3d)

631	**191**	2½d	green and red	20	20	☐ ☐
		p.	Phosphor	60	50	☐ ☐
632	**192**	3d	blue and violet	50	25	☐ ☐
		p.	Phosphor	1·50	80	☐ ☐
633	**193**	1s3d	red, blue and green	1·50	1·70	☐ ☐
		p.	Phosphor	35·00	22·00	☐ ☐
Set of 3 (Ordinary)				2·00	1·90	☐ ☐
Set of 3 (Phosphor)				35·00	22·00	☐ ☐
First Day Cover (Ordinary)					55·00	☐
First Day Cover (Phosphor)					£150	☐

194 Campaign Emblem and Family

195 Children of Three Races

Freedom from Hunger

1963 (21 Mar.) Wmk **179** (inverted)

634	**194**	2½d	crimson and pink	25	10	☐ ☐
		p.	Phosphor	3·00	1·20	☐ ☐
635	**195**	1s3d	brown and yellow	1·90	1·90	☐ ☐
		p.	Phosphor	30·00	23·00	☐ ☐
Set of 2 (Ordinary)				2·00	2·00	☐ ☐
Set of 2 (Phosphor)				30·00	23·00	☐ ☐
First Day Cover (Ordinary)					35·00	☐
First Day Cover (Phosphor)					50·00	☐

196 'Paris Conference'

Paris Postal Conference Centenary

1963 (7 May) Wmk **179** (inverted)

636	**196**	6d	green and mauve	50	85	☐ ☐
		p.	Phosphor	6·50	7·00	☐ ☐
First Day Cover (Ordinary)					16·00	☐
First Day Cover (Phosphor)					38·00	☐

197 Posy of Flowers

198 Woodland Life

National Nature Week

1963 (16 May)

637	**197**	3d	multicoloured	15	15	☐ ☐
		p.	Phosphor	60	60	☐ ☐
638	**198**	4½d	multicoloured	35	35	☐ ☐
		p.	Phosphor	3·25	3·25	☐ ☐
Set of 2 (Ordinary)				50	50	☐ ☐
Set of 2 (Phosphor)				3·50	3·50	☐ ☐
First Day Cover (Ordinary)					22·00	☐
First Day Cover (Phosphor)					40·00	☐

199 Rescue at Sea

200 19th-century Lifeboat

201 Lifeboatmen

Ninth International Lifeboat Conference, Edinburgh

1963 (31 May)

639	**199**	2½d	blue, black and red	25	25	☐ ☐
		p.	Phosphor	50	60	☐ ☐
640	**200**	4d	multicoloured	50	50	☐ ☐
		p.	Phosphor	50	60	☐ ☐
641	**201**	1s6d	sepia, yellow and blue	3·00	3·25	☐ ☐
		p.	Phosphor	48·00	28·00	☐ ☐
Set of 3 (Ordinary)				3·25	3·50	☐ ☐
Set of 3 (Phosphor)				48·00	28·00	☐ ☐
First Day Cover (Ordinary)					35·00	☐
First Day Cover (Phosphor)					55·00	☐

202 Red Cross

203

204

Red Cross Centenary Congress

1963 (15 Aug.)

642	**202**	3d	red and lilac	25	25	☐	☐
		p.	Phosphor	1·10	1·00	☐	☐
643	**203**	1s3d	red, blue and grey	3·00	3·00	☐	☐
		p.	Phosphor	35·00	30·00	☐	☐
644	**204**	1s6d	red, blue and bistre	3·00	3·00	☐	☐
		p.	Phosphor	35·00	27·00	☐	☐
Set of 3 (Ordinary)				5·00	5·75	☐	☐
Set of 3 (Phosphor)				65·00	55·00	☐	☐
First Day Cover (Ordinary)					40·00	☐	
First Day Cover (Phosphor)					90·00	☐	

205 'Commonwealth Cable'

Opening of COMPAC (Trans-Pacific Telephone Cable)

1963 (3 Dec.)

645	**205**	1s6d	blue and black	2·75	2·50	☐	☐
		p.	Phosphor	16·00	16·00	☐	☐
First Day Cover (Ordinary)					28·00	☐	
First Day Cover (Phosphor)					40·00	☐	

206 Puck and Bottom
(*A Midsummer Nights Dream*)

207 Feste
(*Twelfth Night*)

208 Balcony Scene
(*Romeo and Juliet*)

209 'Eve of Agincourt'
(*Henry V*)

210 Hamlet contemplating
Yorick's skull (*Hamlet*)
and Queen Elizabeth II

Shakespeare Festival

1964 (23 Apr.) Perf 11 × 12 (2s6d) or 15 × 14 (others)

646	**206**	3d	bistre, black and violet-blue	15	15	☐	☐
		p.	Phosphor	25	30	☐	☐
647	**207**	6d	multicoloured	30	30	☐	☐
		p.	Phosphor	75	1·00	☐	☐
648	**208**	1s3d	multicoloured	75	1·00	☐	☐
		p.	Phosphor	4·00	6·50	☐	☐
649	**209**	1s6d	multicoloured	1·00	1·10	☐	☐
		p.	Phosphor	8·00	8·00	☐	☐
650	**210**	2s6d	deep slate-purple	3·00	3·00	☐	☐
Set of 5 (Ordinary)				4·50	4·50	☐	☐
Set of 4 (Phosphor)				12·00	14·00	☐	☐
First Day Cover (Ordinary)					12·00		
First Day Cover (Phosphor)					17·00		
Presentation Pack (Ordinary)				30·00		☐	

PRESENTATION PACKS were first introduced by the G.P.O. for the Shakespeare Festival issue. The packs include one set of stamps and details of the designs, the designer and the stamp printer. They were issued for almost all later definitive and special issues.

211 Flats near Richmond
Park ('Urban Development')

212 Shipbuilding Yards,
Belfast. ('Industrial Activity')

213 Beddgelert Forest. Park,
Snowdonia ('Forestry')

214 Nuclear Reactor, Dounreay
('Technological Development')

20th International Geographical Congress, London

1964 (1 July)

651	**211**	2½d	multicoloured	10	10	☐	☐
		p.	Phosphor	40	50	☐	☐
652	**212**	4d	multicoloured	30	30	☐	☐
		p.	Phosphor	1·20	1·20	☐	☐
653	**213**	8d	multicoloured	75	85	☐	☐
		p.	Phosphor	2·50	3·50	☐	☐
654	**214**	1s6d	multicoloured	3·50	3·50	☐	☐
		p.	Phosphor	28·00	22·00	☐	☐
Set of 4 (Ordinary)				4·50	4·50	☐	☐
Set of 4 (Phosphor)				30·00	25·00	☐	☐
First Day Cover (Ordinary)					22·00		
First Day Cover (Phosphor)					40·00		
Presentation Pack (Ordinary)				£160		☐	

215 Spring Gentian

216 Dog Rose

217 Honeysuckle

218 Fringed Water Lily

Tenth International Botanical Congress, Edinburgh

1964 (5 Aug.)

655	**215**	3d	violet, blue and green	25	25	☐ ☐
		p.	Phosphor	40	40	☐ ☐
656	**216**	6d	multicoloured	50	50	☐ ☐
		p.	Phosphor	2·50	2·75	☐ ☐
657	**217**	9d	multicoloured	1·70	2·25	☐ ☐
		p.	Phosphor	4·50	4·50	☐ ☐
658	**218**	1s3d	multicoloured	2·50	2·50	☐ ☐
		p.	Phosphor	25·00	20·00	☐ ☐
Set of 4 (Ordinary)				4·50	4·50	☐ ☐
Set of 4 (Phosphor)				30·00	25·00	☐ ☐
First Day Cover (Ordinary)					30·00	☐
First Day Cover (Phosphor)					40·00	☐
Presentation Pack (Ordinary)				£160		☐

219 Forth Road Bridge

220 Forth Road and Railway Bridges

Opening of Forth Road Bridge

1964 (4 Sept.)

659	**219**	3d	black, blue and violet	10	10	☐ ☐
		p.	Phosphor	1·00	1·50	☐ ☐
660	**220**	6d	blackish lilac, blue and red	40	40	☐ ☐
		p.	Phosphor	4·50	4·75	☐ ☐
Set of 2 (Ordinary)				50	50	☐ ☐
Set of 2 (Phosphor)				5·00	5·75	☐ ☐
First Day Cover (Ordinary)					7·00	☐
First Day Cover (Phosphor)					18·00	☐
Presentation Pack (Ordinary)				£450		☐

221 Sir Winston Churchill

221a Sir Winston Churchill

Churchill Commemoration

1965 (8 July)

661	**221**	4d	black and drab	15	10	☐ ☐
		p.	Phosphor	25	25	☐ ☐
662	**221a**	1s3d	black and grey	45	40	☐ ☐
		p.	Phosphor	2·50	3·00	☐ ☐
Set of 2 (Ordinary)				60	50	☐ ☐
Set of 2 (Phosphor)				2·75	3·25	☐ ☐
First Day Cover (Ordinary)					7·00	☐
First Day Cover (Phosphor)					9·00	☐
Presentation Pack (Ordinary)				70·00		☐

222 Simon de Montfort's Seal

223 Parliament Buildings (after engraving by Hollar, 1647)

700th Anniversary of Simon de Montfort's Parliament

1965 (19 July)

663	**222**	6d	green	30	40	☐ ☐
		p.	Phosphor	1·00	1·25	☐ ☐
664	**223**	2s6d	black, grey and drab	80	1·80	☐ ☐
Set of 2 (Ordinary)				1·00	2·00	☐ ☐
First Day Cover (Ordinary)					15·00	☐
First Day Cover (Phosphor)					26·00	☐
Presentation Pack (Ordinary)				85·00		☐

224 Bandsmen and Banner

225 Three Salvationists

Salvation Army Centenary

1965 (9 Aug.)

665	**224**	3d	multicoloured	25	25	☐ ☐
		p.	Phosphor	25	40	☐ ☐
666	**225**	1s6d	multicoloured	1·00	1·50	☐ ☐
		p.	Phosphor	2·50	2·75	☐ ☐
Set of 2 (Ordinary)				1·10	1·60	☐ ☐
Set of 2 (Phosphor)				2·50	3·00	☐ ☐
First Day Cover (Ordinary)					23·00	☐
First Day Cover (Phosphor)					32·00	☐

226 Lister's Carbolic Spray

227 Lister and Chemical Symbols

Centenary of Joseph Lister's Discovery of Antiseptic Surgery

1965 (1 Sept.)

667	**226**	4d	indigo, chestnut and grey	25	15	☐ ☐
		p.	Phosphor	25	25	☐ ☐
668	**227**	1s	black, purple and blue	1·00	1·40	☐ ☐
		p.	Phosphor	2·00	2·50	☐ ☐
Set of 2 (Ordinary)				1·00	1·20	☐ ☐
Set of 2 (Phosphor)				2·00	2·50	☐ ☐
First Day Cover (Ordinary)					12·00	☐
First Day Cover (Phosphor)					15·00	☐

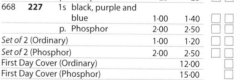
228 Trinidad Carnival Dancers   **229** Canadian Folk Dancers

Commonwealth Arts Festival

1965 (1 Sept.)

669	**228**	6d	black and orange	20	20	☐ ☐
		p.	Phosphor	30	50	☐ ☐
670	**229**	1s6d	black and violet	80	1·10	☐ ☐
		p.	Phosphor	2·50	3·50	☐ ☐
Set of 2 (Ordinary)				1·00	1·20	☐ ☐
Set of 2 (Phosphor)				2·50	3·50	☐ ☐
First Day Cover (Ordinary)					17·00	☐
First Day Cover (Phosphor)					22·00	☐

230 Flight of Supermarine Spitfires

231 Pilot in Hawker Hurricane Mk I

232 Wing-tips of Supermarine Spitfire and Messerschmitt Bf 109

233 Supermarine Spitfires attacking Heinkel He 111H Bomber

234 Supermarine Spitfire attacking Junkers Ju 87B 'Stuka' Dive Bomber

235 Hawker Hurricanes Mk I over Wreck of Dornier Do-17Z Bomber

236 Anti-aircraft Artillery in Action

237 Air Battle over St. Paul's Cathedral

25th Anniversary of Battle of Britain

1965 (13 Sept.)

671	**230**	4d	olive and black	25	25	☐ ☐
	a.		Block of 6.			
			Nos. 671/6	8·00	8·00	☐ ☐
	p.		Phosphor	50	50	☐ ☐
	pa.		Block of 6.			
			Nos. 671p/6p	10·00	12·00	☐ ☐
672	**231**	4d	olive, blackish olive and black	25	25	☐ ☐
	p.		Phosphor	50	50	☐ ☐
673	**232**	4d	multicoloured	25	25	☐ ☐
	p.		Phosphor	50	50	☐ ☐
674	**233**	4d	olive and black	25	25	☐ ☐
	p.		Phosphor	50	50	☐ ☐
675	**234**	4d	olive and black	25	25	☐ ☐
	p.		Phosphor	50	50	☐ ☐
676	**235**	4d	multicoloured	25	25	☐ ☐
	p.		Phosphor	50	50	☐ ☐
677	**236**	9d	violet, orange and purple	1·70	1·70	☐ ☐
	p.		Phosphor	1·70	2·50	☐ ☐
678	**237**	1s3d	multicoloured	1·70	1·70	☐ ☐
	p.		Phosphor	1·70	2·50	☐ ☐
Set of 8 (Ordinary)				10·00	10·00	☐ ☐
Set of 8 (Phosphor)				12·00	14·00	☐ ☐
First Day Cover (Ordinary)					25·00	☐
First Day Cover (Phosphor)					30·00	☐
Presentation Pack (Ordinary)				70·00		☐

Nos. 671/6 were issued together *se-tenant* in blocks of six (3 × 2) within the sheet.

238 Tower and Georgian Buildings

239 Tower and Nash Terrace, Regent's Park

Opening of Post Office Tower

1965 (8 Oct.)

679	**238**	3d	yellow, blue and green	15	15	☐ ☐
	p.		Phosphor	15	15	☐ ☐
680	**239**	1s3d	green and blue	45	45	☐ ☐
	p.		Phosphor	50	50	☐ ☐
Set of 2 (Ordinary)				60	60	☐ ☐
Set of 2 (Phosphor)				65	65	☐ ☐
First Day Cover (Ordinary)					6·50	☐
First Day Cover (Phosphor)					7·00	☐
Presentation Pack (Ordinary)				10·00		☐
Presentation Pack (Phosphor)				10·00		☐

240 U.N. Emblem   **241** I.C.Y. Emblem

20th Anniversary of UNO and International Co-operation Year

1965 (25 Oct.)

681	**240**	3d	black, orange and blue	25	20	☐ ☐
	p.		Phosphor	25	30	☐ ☐
682	**241**	1s6d	black, purple and blue	1·00	80	☐ ☐
	p.		Phosphor	2·75	3·00	☐ ☐
Set of 2 (Ordinary)				1·10	90	☐ ☐
Set of 2 (Phosphor)				2·75	3·00	☐ ☐
First Day Cover (Ordinary)					12·00	☐
First Day Cover (Phosphor)					14·00	☐

242 Telecommunications Network   **243** Radio Waves and Switchboard

I.T.U. Centenary

1965 (15 Nov.)

683	**242**	9d	multicoloured	50	40	☐ ☐
	p.		Phosphor	1·00	75	☐ ☐
684	**243**	1s6d	multicoloured	1·50	1·25	☐ ☐
	p.		Phosphor	4·25	5·25	☐ ☐
Set of 2 (Ordinary)				1·80	1·50	☐ ☐
Set of 2 (Phosphor)				4·75	5·50	☐ ☐
First Day Cover (Ordinary)					17·00	☐
First Day Cover (Phosphor)					20·00	☐

244 Robert Burns (after Skirving chalk drawing) **245** Robert Burns (after Nasmyth portrait)

Burns Commemoration

1966 (25 Jan.)

685	**244**	4d	black, indigo and blue	20	15	☐ ☐
		p.	Phosphor	50	50	☐ ☐
686	**245**	1s3d	black, blue and orange	65	70	☐ ☐
		p.	Phosphor	2·25	2·25	☐ ☐
Set of 2 (Ordinary)				75	75	☐ ☐
Set of 2 (Phosphor)				2·50	2·50	☐ ☐
First Day Cover (Ordinary)					4·00	☐
First Day Cover (Phosphor)					6·00	☐
Presentation Pack (Ordinary)				60·00		☐

246 Westminster Abbey **247** Fan Vaulting, Henry VII Chapel

900th Anniversary of Westminster Abbey

1966 (28 Feb.) Perf 15 × 14 (3d) or 11 × 12 (2s6d)

687	**246**	3d	black, brown and blue	20	20	☐ ☐
		p.	Phosphor	20	25	☐ ☐
688	**247**	2s6d	black	1·00	1·20	☐ ☐
Set of 2				1·00	1·20	☐ ☐
First Day Cover (Ordinary)					6·00	☐
First Day Cover (Phosphor)					14·00	☐
Presentation Pack (Ordinary)				55·00		☐

248 View near Hassocks, Sussex **249** Antrim, Northern Ireland

250 Harlech Castle, Wales **251** Cairngorm Mountains, Scotland

Landscapes

1966 (2 May)

689	**248**	4d	black, yellow-green and blue	10	15	☐ ☐
		p.	Phosphor	10	15	☐ ☐
690	**249**	6d	black, green and blue	15	20	☐ ☐
		p.	Phosphor	15	20	☐ ☐
691	**250**	1s3d	black, yellow and blue	25	35	☐ ☐
		p.	Phosphor	25	35	☐ ☐
692	**251**	1s6d	black, orange and blue	40	35	☐ ☐
		p.	Phosphor	40	40	☐ ☐
Set of 4 (Ordinary)				80	95	☐ ☐
Set of 4 (Phosphor)				80	1·00	☐ ☐

First Day Cover (Ordinary)	7·00	☐
First Day Cover (Phosphor)	8·50	☐

World Cup 1966
252 Players with Ball

253 Goalmouth Mêlée **254** Goalkeeper saving Goal

World Cup Football Championship

1966 (1 June)

693	**252**	4d	multicoloured	10	25	☐ ☐
		p.	Phosphor	10	25	☐ ☐
694	**253**	6d	multicoloured	15	25	☐ ☐
		p.	Phosphor	15	25	☐ ☐
695	**254**	1s3d	multicoloured	50	1·00	☐ ☐
		p.	Phosphor	50	1·00	☐ ☐
Set of 3 (Ordinary)				70	1·25	☐ ☐
Set of 3 (Phosphor)				70	1·25	☐ ☐
First Day Cover (Ordinary)					20·00	☐
First Day Cover (Phosphor)					22·00	☐
Presentation Pack (Ordinary)				20·00		☐

255 Black-headed Gull **256** Blue Tit

257 European Robin **258** Blackbird

British Birds

1966 (8 Aug.)

696	**255**	4d	multicoloured	20	20	☐ ☐
		a.	Block of 4. Nos. 696/9	1·00	2·00	☐ ☐
		p.	Phosphor	20	20	☐ ☐
		pa.	Block of 4. Nos. 696p/9p	1·00	2·00	☐ ☐
697	**256**	4d	multicoloured	20	20	☐ ☐
		p.	Phosphor	20	20	☐ ☐
698	**257**	4d	multicoloured	20	20	☐ ☐
		p.	Phosphor	20	20	☐ ☐
699	**258**	4d	multicoloured	20	20	☐ ☐
		p.	Phosphor	20	20	☐ ☐
Set of 4 (Ordinary)				1·00	2·00	☐ ☐
Set of 4 (Phosphor)				1·00	2·00	☐ ☐
First Day Cover (Ordinary)					8·00	☐
First Day Cover (Phosphor)					8·00	☐
Presentation Pack (Ordinary)				13·00		☐

Nos. 696/9 were issued *se-tenant* in blocks of four within the sheet.

259 Cup Winners

England's World Cup Football Victory

1966 (18 Aug.)

700	**259**	4d	multicoloured	30	30	☐ ☐
First Day Cover					13·00	☐

260 Jodrell Bank Radio Telescope

261 British Motor-cars

262 SR N6 Hovercraft

263 Windscale Reactor

British Technology

1966 (19 Sept.)

701	**260**	4d	black and lemon	15	10	☐ ☐
		p.	Phosphor	10	10	☐ ☐
702	**261**	6d	red, blue and orange	25	20	☐ ☐
		p.	Phosphor	15	25	☐ ☐
703	**262**	1s3d	multicoloured	80	80	☐ ☐
		p.	Phosphor	75	75	☐ ☐
704	**263**	1s6d	multicoloured	1·00	1·00	☐ ☐
		p.	Phosphor	1·00	1·00	☐ ☐
Set of 4 (Ordinary)				2·00	1·90	☐ ☐
Set of 4 (Phosphor)				1·80	1·90	☐ ☐
First Day Cover (Ordinary)					5·00	☐
First Day Cover (Phosphor)					5·00	☐
Presentation Pack (Ordinary)				20·00		☐

264

265

266

267

268

269

270 Norman Ship

271 Norman Horsemen attacking Harold's Troops

900th Anniversary of Battle of Hastings

1966 (14 Oct.) Designs show scenes from Bayeux Tapestry Wmk **179** (sideways on 1s3d)

705	**264**	4d	multicoloured	10	10	☐ ☐
		a.	Strip of 6. Nos. 705/10	1·90	2·25	☐ ☐
		p.	Phosphor	10	10	☐ ☐
		pa.	Strip of 6. Nos. 705p/10p	1·90	2·25	☐ ☐
706	**265**	4d	multicoloured	10	10	☐ ☐
		p.	Phosphor	10	10	☐ ☐
707	**266**	4d	multicoloured	10	10	☐ ☐
		p.	Phosphor	10	10	☐ ☐
708	**267**	4d	multicoloured	10	10	☐ ☐
		p.	Phosphor	10	10	☐ ☐
709	**268**	4d	multicoloured	10	10	☐ ☐
		p.	Phosphor	10	10	☐ ☐
710	**269**	4d	multicoloured	10	10	☐ ☐
		p.	Phosphor	10	10	☐ ☐
711	**270**	6d	multicoloured	25	25	☐ ☐
		p.	Phosphor	25	25	☐ ☐
712	**271**	1s3d	multicoloured	35	1·00	☐ ☐
		p.	Phosphor	35	1·00	☐ ☐
Set of 8 (Ordinary)				2·25	3·00	☐ ☐
Set of 8 (Phosphor)				2·25	3·00	☐ ☐
First Day Cover (Ordinary)					8·00	☐
First Day Cover (Phosphor)					9·00	☐
Presentation Pack (Ordinary)				10·00		☐

Nos. 705/10 show battle scenes, they were issued together *se-tenant* in horizontal strips of six within the sheet.

272 King of the Orient

273 Snowman

Christmas

1966 (1 Dec.) Wmk **179** (upright on 1s6d)

713	**272**	3d	multicoloured	10	25
		p.	Phosphor	10	25
714	**273**	1s6d	multicoloured	30	50
		p.	Phosphor	30	50
Set of 2 (Ordinary)				35	70
Set of 2 (Phosphor)				35	70
First Day Cover (Ordinary)					2·50
First Day Cover (Phosphor)					2·00
Presentation Pack (Ordinary)			12·00		

No. 713p exists with phosphor band at left or right.

274 Sea Freight

275 Air Freight

European Free Trade Association (EFTA)

1967 (20 Feb.)

715	**274**	9d	multicoloured	25	20
		p.	Phosphor	25	20
716	**275**	1s6d	multicoloured	50	45
		p.	Phosphor	25	40
Set of 2 (Ordinary)				60	60
Set of 2 (Phosphor)				60	55
First Day Cover (Ordinary)					3·00
First Day Cover (Phosphor)					3·00
Presentation Pack (Ordinary)			20·00		

276 Hawthorn and Bramble

277 Larger Bindweed and Viper's Bugloss

278 Ox-eye Daisy, Coltsfoot and Buttercup

279 Bluebell, Red Campion and Wood Anemone

280 Dog Violet

281 Primroses

British Wild Flowers

1967 (24 Apr.)

717	**276**	4d	multicoloured	20	20
		a.	Block of 4.		
			Nos. 717/20	80	2·25
		p.	Phosphor	10	15
		pa	Block of 4.		
			Nos. 717p/20p	80	2·00
718	**277**	4d	multicoloured	20	20
		p.	Phosphor	10	15

719	**278**	4d	multicoloured	20	20
		p.	Phosphor	10	15
720	**279**	4d	multicoloured	20	20
		p.	Phosphor	10	15
721	**280**	9d	multicoloured	20	25
		p.	Phosphor	15	25
722	**281**	1s9d	multicoloured	40	55
		p.	Phosphor	40	55
Set of 6 (Ordinary)				1·25	2·75
Set of 6 (Phosphor)				1·25	2·50
First Day Cover (Ordinary)					5·00
First Day Cover (Phosphor)					5·00
Presentation Pack (Ordinary)			14·00		
Presentation Pack (Phosphor)			14·00		

Nos. 717/20 were issued together *se-tenant* in blocks of four within the sheet.

282 (value at left)

282a (value at right)

I   II

Two types of the 2d.

I.   Value spaced away from left side of stamp.

II. Value close to left side from new multi-positive. This results in the portrait appearing in the centre, thus conforming with the other values.

1967 (5 June)–**69** Two phosphor bands, except where otherwise stated. No wmk

723	**282**	½d	orange-brown *(5.2.68)*	30	75
724		1d	light olive (2 bands)		
			(5.2.68)	20	10
725		1d	yellowish olive (1 centre band) *(16.9.68)*	40	55
726		2d	lake-brown (Type I) (2 bands) *(5.2.68)*	20	15
727		2d	lake-brown (Type II) (2 bands) *(1969)*	30	40
728		2d	lake-brown (Type II) (1 centre band) *(27.8.69)*	1·00	1·50
729		3d	violet (1 centre band) *(8.8.67)*	30	10
730		3d	violet (2 bands) *(6.4.68)*	30	45
731		4d	deep sepia (2 bands)	30	30
732		4d	deep olive-brown (1 centre band) *(16.9.68)*	30	30
733		4d	bright vermilion (1 centre band) *(6.1.69)*	20	10
734		4d	vermilion (1 side band) *(6.1.69)*	1·90	2·50
735		5d	blue *(1.7.68)*	20	20
736		6d	purple *(5.2.68)*	50	40
737	**282a**	7d	bright emerald *(1.7.68)*	1·00	1·00
738		8d	bright vermilion *(1.7.68)*	1·25	1·75
739		8d	turquoise-blue *(6.1.69)*	1·00	1·50
740		9d	green *(8.8.67)*	1·00	1·50
741	**282**	10d	drab *(1.7.68)*	1·00	1·25
742		1s	light bluish violet	45	45
743		1s6d	blue and deep blue *(8.8.67)*	50	50
		c.	Phosphorised paper *(10.12.69)*	1·40	1·40
744		1s9d	orange and black	1·00	1·00
Set of 16 (one of each value and colour)				7·00	8·00
Presentation Pack (one of each value)			15·00		
Presentation Pack (German)			£150		

First Day Covers

5 June 1967	Nos. 731, 742, 744	3·50
8 Aug. 1967	Nos. 729, 740, 743	3·50
5 Feb. 1968	Nos. 723/4, 726, 736	3·75
1 July 1968	Nos. 735, 737/8, 741	4·50

No. 734 exists with phosphor band at the left or right.

283 'Master Lambton'
(Sir Thomas Lawrence)

284 'Mares and Foals in a
Landscape' (George Stubbs)

285 'Children Coming Out of
School' (L. S. Lowry)

British Paintings

1967 (10 July) Two phosphor bands. No wmk

748	**283**	4d	multicoloured	10	10
749	**284**	9d	multicoloured	25	25
750	**285**	1s6d	multicoloured	40	50
Set of 3				70	75
First Day Cover					2·50
Presentation Pack				35·00	

286 Gipsy Moth IV

Sir Francis Chichester's World Voyage

1967 (24 July) Three phosphor bands. No wmk

751	**286**	1s9d	multicoloured	45	45
First Day Cover					1·00

287 Radar Screen

288 *Penicillium notatum*

289 Vickers VC-10 Jet Engines

290 Television Equipment

British Discovery and Invention

1967 (19 Sept.) Two phosphor bands (except 4d. three bands).
Wmk **179** (sideways on 1s9d)

752	**287**	4d	yellow, black and		
			vermilion	10	10
753	**288**	1s	multicoloured	35	35
754	**289**	1s6d	multicoloured	45	45
755	**290**	1s9d	multicoloured	50	50
Set of 4				1·20	1·20
First Day Cover					2·00
Presentation Pack				6·00	

NO WATERMARK. All the following issues are on unwatermarked paper unless otherwise stated.

291 'The Adoration
of the Shepherds'
(School of Seville)

292 'Madonna and
Child' (Murillo)

293 'The Adoration of the
Shepherds' (Louis le Nain)

Christmas

1967 Two phosphor bands (except 3d, one phosphor band)

756	**291**	3d	multicoloured *(27 Nov.)*	10	15
757	**292**	4d	multicoloured *(18 Oct.)*	10	15
758	**293**	1s6d	multicoloured *(27 Nov.)*	15	15
Set of 3				30	30
First Day Covers (2)					1·50

Gift Pack 1967

1967 (27 Nov.) Comprises Nos. 715p/22p and 748/58

GP758c	Gift Pack	3·00	

1967–68 No wmk. Perf 11 × 12

759	**166**	2s6d	brown	30	45
760	**167**	5s	red	1·00	1·00
761	**168**	10s	blue	7·75	4·00
762	**169**	£1	black	7·50	4·50
Set of 4				15·00	9·00

294 Tarr Steps, Exmoor

295 Aberfeldy Bridge

296 Menai Bridge

297 M4 Viaduct

British Bridges

1968 (29 Apr.) Two phosphor bands

763	**294**	4d	multicoloured	10	10	☐	☐
764	**295**	9d	multicoloured	15	15	☐	☐
765	**296**	1s6d	multicoloured	25	25	☐	☐
766	**297**	1s9d	multicoloured	30	30	☐	☐
Set of 4				70	70	☐	☐
First Day Cover					1·50	☐	
Presentation Pack			5·00			☐	

298 'TUC' and Trades Unionists

299 Mrs Emmeline Pankhurst. (statue)

300 Sopwith Camel and English Electric Lightning Fighters

301 Captain Cook's *Endeavour* and Signature

British Anniversaries. Events described on stamps

1968 (29 May) Two phosphor bands

767	**298**	4d	multicoloured	10	10	☐	☐
768	**299**	9d	violet, grey and black	15	15	☐	☐
769	**300**	1s	multicoloured	25	30	☐	☐
770	**301**	1s9d	ochre and brown	55	60	☐	☐
Set of 4				1·00	1·00	☐	☐
First Day Cover				5·00		☐	
Presentation Pack			5·00			☐	

302 'Queen Elizabeth I' (Unknown Artist)

303 'Pinkie' (Lawrence)

304 'Ruins of St. Mary Le Port' (John Piper)

305 'The Hay Wain' (John Constable)

British Paintings

1968 (12 Aug.) Two phosphor bands

771	**302**	4d	multicoloured	10	10	☐	☐
772	**303**	1s	multicoloured	10	20	☐	☐
773	**304**	1s6d	multicoloured	20	25	☐	☐
774	**305**	1s9d	multicoloured	25	40	☐	☐
Set of 4				60	85	☐	☐

First Day Cover			2·00	☐
Presentation Pack (P.O. Pack No.1)		6·00		☐
Presentation Pack (German)				
	(P.O. Pack No.1)	19·00		☐

Gift Pack 1968

1968 (16 Sept.) Comprises Nos. 763/74

GP774c	Gift Pack	6·00		☐
GP774d	Gift Pack (German)	80·00		☐

Collectors Pack 1968

1968 (16 Sept.) Comprises Nos. 752/8 and 763/74

CP774e	Collectors Pack	7·00		☐

306 Girl and Boy with Rocking Horse

307 Girl with Doll's House

308 Boy with Train Set

Christmas

1968 (25 Nov.) Two phosphor bands (except 4d, one centre phosphor band)

775	**306**	4d	multicoloured	10	15	☐	☐
776	**307**	9d	multicoloured	15	25	☐	☐
777	**308**	1s6d	multicoloured	15	50	☐	☐
Set of 3				35	80	☐	☐
First Day Cover				1·00		☐	
Presentation Pack (P.O. Pack No.4)			5·00			☐	
Presentation Pack (German)			19·00			☐	

RMS Queen Elizabeth 2

309 *Queen Elizabeth 2*

310 Elizabethan Galleon

311 East Indiaman

312 *Cutty Sark*

SS Great Britain
313 *Great Britain*

RMS Mauretania
314 *Mauretania*

British Ships

1969 (15 Jan.) One horiz phosphor band (5d), two phosphor bands (9d) or two vertical phosphor bands at right (1s)

778	**309**	5d multicoloured	10	15		
779	**310**	9d multicoloured	10	25		
		a. Strip of 3.				
		Nos. 779/81	1·30	1·50		
780	**311**	9d multicoloured	10	25		
781	**312**	9d multicoloured	10	25		
782	**313**	1s multicoloured	40	35		
		a. Pair. Nos. 782/3	1·30	1·50		
783	**314**	1s multicoloured	40	35		
Set of 6			2·40	2·75		
First Day Cover				6·00		
Presentation Pack (P.O. Pack No.5)			6·00			
Presentation Pack (German)						
		(P.O. Pack No.5)	60·00			

The 9d and 1s values were arranged in horizontal strips of three and pairs respectively throughout the sheet.

315 Concorde in Flight   **316** Plan and Elevation Views

317 Concorde's Nose and Tail

First Flight of Concorde

1969 (3 Mar.) Two phosphor bands

784	**315**	4d multicoloured	25	25		
785	**316**	9d multicoloured	55	75		
786	**317**	1s6d deep blue, grey and				
		light blue	75	1·00		
Set of 3			1·00	1·50		
First Day Cover				3·00		
Presentation Pack (P.O. Pack No.6)			12·00			
Presentation Pack (German)			95·00			

318 (See also Type **357**)

1969 (5 Mar.) Perf 12

787	**318**	2s6d brown	35	30		
788		5s lake	1·80	60		
789		10s ultramarine	6·00	7·00		
790		£1 black	3·25	1·50		
Set of 4			10·00	8·50		
First Day Cover				9·50		
Presentation Pack (P.O. Pack No.7)			16·00			
Presentation Pack (German)			80·00			

319 Page from the *Daily Mail*, and Vickers FB-27 Vimy Aircraft   **320** Europa and C.E.P.T. Emblems

321 I.L.O. Emblem   **322** Flags of N.A.T.O. Countries

323 Vickers FB-27 Vimy Aircraft and Globe showing Flight

Anniversaries. Events described on stamps

1969 (2 Apr.) Two phosphor bands

791	**319**	5d multicoloured	10	15		
792	**320**	9d multicoloured	15	25		
793	**321**	1s claret, red and blue	15	25		
794	**322**	1s6d multicoloured	25	50		
795	**323**	1s9d olive, yellow and				
		turquoise-green	60	65		
Set of 5			1·10	1·60		
First Day Cover				4·00		
Presentation Pack (P.O. Pack No.9)			5·00			
Presentation Pack (German)			95·00			

324 Durham Cathedral   **325** York Minster

326 St. Giles' Cathedral, Edinburgh   **327** Canterbury Cathedral

328 St. Paul's Cathedral   **329** Liverpool Metropolitan Cathedral

British Architecture (Cathedrals)

1969 (28 May) Two phosphor bands

796	**324**	5d	multicoloured	10	10	☐ ☐
		a.	Block of 4.				
			Nos. 796/9	1·10	1·25	☐ ☐
797	**325**	5d	multicoloured	10	10	☐ ☐
798	**326**	5d	multicoloured	10	10	☐ ☐
799	**327**	5d	multicoloured	10	10	☐ ☐
800	**328**	9d	multicoloured	25	30	☐ ☐
801	**329**	1s6d	multicoloured	25	35	☐ ☐
Set of 6				1·40	1·70	☐ ☐
First Day Cover					4·00	☐
Presentation Pack (P.O. Pack No.10)			6·00			☐
Presentation Pack (German)			48·00			☐

Nos. 796/9 were issued together *se-tenant* in blocks of four within the sheet.

330 The King's Gate, Caernarvon Castle   **331** The Eagle Tower, Caernarvon Castle   **332** Queen Eleanor's Gate, Caernarvon Castle

333 Celtic Cross, Margam Abbey   **334** Prince Charles

Investiture of H.R.H. The Prince of Wales

1969 (1 July) Two phosphor bands

802	**330**	5d	multicoloured	10	15	☐ ☐
		a.	Strip of 3. Nos. 802/4	50	1·00	☐ ☐
803	**331**	5d	multicoloured	10	15	☐ ☐
804	**332**	5d	multicoloured	10	15	☐ ☐
805	**333**	9d	multicoloured	15	30	☐ ☐
806	**334**	1s	black and gold	15	30	☐ ☐
Set of 5				75	1·40	☐ ☐
First Day Cover					1·70	☐
Presentation Pack (P.O. Pack No.11)			3·00			☐
Presentation Pack (German)			48·00			☐
Presentation Pack (Welsh)			40·00			☐

Nos. 802/4 were printed *se-tenant* in strips of three throughout the sheet.

335 Mahatma Gandhi

Gandhi Centenary Year

1969 (13 Aug.) Two phosphor bands

807	**335**	1s6d	multicoloured	40	30	☐ ☐
First Day Cover					1·00	☐

Collectors Pack 1969

1969 (15 Sept.) Comprises Nos. 775/86 and 791/807

CP807b	Collectors Pack	25·00		☐

336 National Giro   **337** Telecommunications – International Subscriber Dialling

338 Telecommunications – Pulse Code Modulation   **339** Postal Mechanisation – Automatic Sorting

British Post Office Technology

1969 (1 Oct.) Two phosphor bands. Perf 13½ × 14

808	**336**	5d	multicoloured	10	10	☐ ☐
809	**337**	9d	green, blue and black	20	25	☐ ☐
810	**338**	1s	green, lavender and black	20	25	☐ ☐
811	**339**	1s6d	multicoloured	50	50	☐ ☐
Set of 4				90	1·00	☐ ☐
First Day Cover					2·00	☐
Presentation Pack (P.O. Pack No.13)			5·00			☐

340 Herald Angel   **341** The Three Shepherds

342 The Three Kings

Christmas

1969 (26 Nov.) Two phosphor bands (5d, 1s6d) or one centre band (4d)

812	**340**	4d	multicoloured	10	10	☐ ☐
813	**341**	5d	multicoloured	15	15	☐ ☐
814	**342**	1s6d	multicoloured	20	20	☐ ☐
Set of 3				40	40	☐ ☐
First Day Cover					1·00	☐
Presentation Pack (P.O. Pack No.14)			5·00			☐

343 Fife Harling   **344** Cotswold Limestone

345 Welsh Stucco   **346** Ulster Thatch

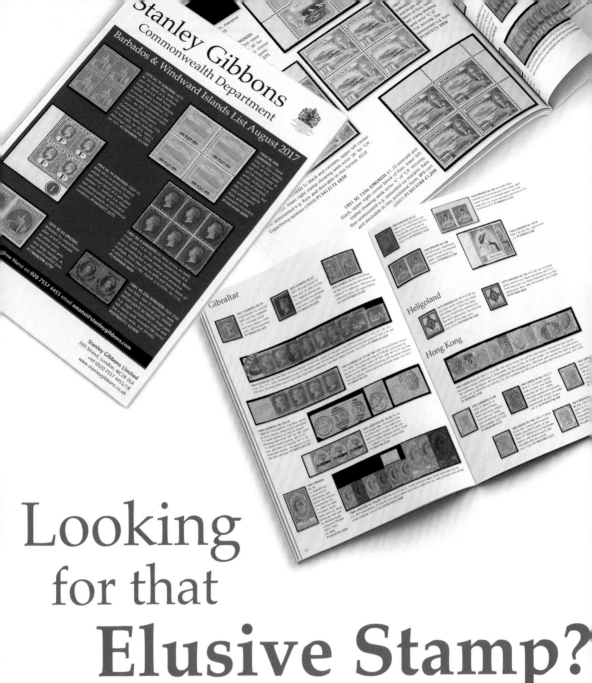

Looking for that **Elusive Stamp?**

British Rural Architecture

1970 (11 Feb.) Two phosphor bands

815	**343**	5d multicoloured	10	10	
816	**344**	9d multicoloured	20	25	
817	**345**	1s multicoloured	25	25	
818	**346**	1s6d multicoloured	30	40	
Set of 4			70	90	
First Day Cover				1·50	
Presentation Pack (P.O. Pack No.15)		6·00			

347 Signing the Declaration of Arbroath

348 Florence Nightingale attending Patients

349 Signing of International Co-operative Alliance

350 Pilgrims and *Mayflower*

351 Sir William Herschel, Francis Baily, Sir John Herschel and Telescope

Anniversaries. Events described on stamps

1970 (1 Apr.) Two phosphor bands

819	**347**	5d multicoloured	10	10	
820	**348**	9d multicoloured	15	15	
821	**349**	1s multicoloured	20	25	
822	**350**	1s6d multicoloured	20	30	
823	**351**	1s9d multicoloured	25	30	
Set of 5			80	1·00	
First Day Cover				2·00	
Presentation Pack (P.O. Pack No.16)		5·00			

352 'Mr Pickwick and Sam' (Pickwick Papers)

353 'Mr and Mrs Micawber' (David Copperfield)

354 'David Copperfield and Betsy Trotwood' (David Copperfield)

355 'Oliver asking for more'(Oliver Twist)

356 'Grasmere' (from engraving by J. Farrington, R.A.)

Literary Anniversaries. Events described on stamps

1970 (3 June) Two phosphor bands

824	**352**	5d multicoloured	10	25	
		a. Block of 4. Nos. 824/7	75	1·50	
825	**353**	5d multicoloured	10	25	
826	**354**	5d multicoloured	10	25	
827	**355**	5d multicoloured	10	25	
828	**356**	1s6d multicoloured	25	50	
Set of 5			90	1·80	
First Day Cover				3·00	
Presentation Pack (P.O. Pack No.17)		6·00			

Nos. 824/7 were issued together *se-tenant* in blocks of four within the sheet.

356a

357 (Value redrawn)

Decimal Currency

1970 (17 June)–**72** 10p and some printings of the 50p were issued on phosphor paper. Perf 12

829	**356a**	10p cerise	50	75	
830		20p olive-green	60	25	
831		50p ultramarine	1·50	40	
831b	**357**	£1 black *(6 Dec. 1972)*	3·50	80	
Set of 4			5·50	2·00	
First Day Cover (Nos. 829/31)				2·75	
First Day Cover (No. 831b)				3·00	
Presentation Pack (P.O Pack No. 18) (Nos. 829/31)			10·00		
Presentation Pack (P.O Pack No. 38) (Nos. 830/1, 790 or 831b)			17·00		

358 Runners

359 Swimmers

360 Cyclists

Ninth British Commonwealth Games, Edinburgh

1970 (15 July) Two phosphor bands. Perf 13½ × 14

832	**358**	5d pink, emerald, greenish yellow and yellow-green	25	25	
833	**359**	1s6d greenish blue, lilac, brown and Prussian blue	50	50	
834	**360**	1s9d yellow-orange, lilac, salmon and red-brown	50	50	
Set of 3			1·10	1·10	
First Day Cover				1·40	
Presentation Pack (P.O. Pack No.19)		5·00			

Collectors Pack 1970

1970 (14 Sept.) Comprises Nos. 808/28 and 832/4

CP834a	Collectors Pack	35·00		☐

5ᵈ Philympia 1970

9ᵈ Philympia 1970

1/6 Philympia 1970

361 1d Black (1840)
362 1s Green (1847)
363 4d Carmine (1855)

1840 first engraved issue — 1847 first embossed issue — 1855 first surface printed issue

'Philympia 70' Stamp Exhibition

1970 (18 Sept.) Two phosphor bands. Perf 14 × 14½

835	**361**	5d	multicoloured	25	10	☐ ☐
836	**362**	9d	multicoloured	25	30	☐ ☐
837	**363**	1s6d	multicoloured	25	45	☐ ☐
Set of 3				70	75	☐ ☐
First Day Cover					1·50	☐
Presentation Pack (P.O. Pack No.21)			5·00			☐

364 Shepherds and Apparition of the Angel

365 Mary, Joseph and Christ. in Manger

366 The Wise Men bearing Gifts

Christmas

1970 (25 Nov.) Two phosphor bands (5d, 1s6d) or one centre phosphor band (4d)

838	**364**	4d	multicoloured	15	10	☐ ☐
839	**365**	5d	multicoloured	15	15	☐ ☐
840	**366**	1s6d	multicoloured	25	30	☐ ☐
Set of 3				50	50	☐ ☐
First Day Cover					1·00	☐
Presentation Pack (P.O. Pack No.22)			5·00			☐

PRINTING PROCESSES

There is a basic distinction between stamps printed by photogravure, later, gravure, and those printed by lithography. Sorting the two is not as difficult as it sounds and with a little experience it should become easy to tell which method of production was employed for a particular stamp.

The tiny dots of the printing screen give uneven edges to the values on gravure stamps (right). Litho values have clean, clear outlines (left).

All you need is a reasonably good glass giving a magnification of × 4 or more (× 10 is even better!).

The image on a gravure stamp is created from a pattern or 'screen', of minute dots which are not evident when looking at the stamp without a glass but show up quite clearly under magnification, especially in the Queen's face and around the margin of the stamp design where it meets the white background of the paper. Now look at the value; here also, what looks to the naked eye like a straight line is in fact made up of rows of tiny little dots.

'Screens' of dots are also used in the production of litho printed stamps but they are only required where the printer is attempting to produce shades and tints as is necessary in the Queen's head portion of the stamp. Where solid colour is used, as in the background of the majority of values, there is no need to resort to a screen of dots and the background is printed as a solid mass of colour. If you look at the margins or the values of stamps produced in this way you will not see any evidence of dots—just a clear clean break between the inked portion of the stamp and the uninked white of the paper.

367   **367a**

Two types of the 3p., 10p. and 26p. (Nos. X930/c, X886/b and X971/b).

I   II

I   II

I   II

Decimal Currency

1971 (15 Feb)–**96**. Type 367

(a) Printed in photogravure by Harrison and Sons (except for some ptgs of Nos. X879 and X913 which were produced by Enschedé) with phosphor bands. Perf 15 × 14

X841	½p turquoise-blue (2 bands)	10	10	☐ ☐
X842	½p turquoise-blue (1 side band)			☐ ☐
	(24.5.72)	55·00	30·00	

X843	½p turquoise-blue (1 centre band) *(14.12.77)*	40	25	☐	☐
X844	1p crimson (2 bands)	10	15	☐	☐
X845	1p crimson (1 centre band) *(14.12.77)*	35	30	☐	☐
X846	1p crimson ('all-over' phosphor) *(10.10.79)*	30	40	☐	☐
X847	1p crimson (1 side band at left) *(20.10.86)*	1·50	1·75	☐	☐
X847Ea	Band at right *(3.3.87)*	4·00	4·25	☐	☐
X848	1½p black (2 bands)	20	30	☐	☐
X849	2p myrtle-green (face value as in T **367**) (2 bands)	15	20	☐	☐
X850	2p myrtle-green (face value as in T **367**) ('all-over' phosphor) *(10.10.79)*	25	30	☐	☐
X851	2½p magenta (1 centre band)	20	15	☐	☐
X852	2½p magenta (1 side band)	1·50	1·75	☐	☐
X853	2½p magenta (2 bands) *(21.5.75)*	80	1·30	☐	☐
X854	2½p rose-red (2 bands) *(26.8.81)*	55	75	☐	☐
X855	3p ultramarine (2 bands)	20	25	☐	☐
X856	3p ultramarine (1 centre band) *(10.9.73)*	15	20	☐	☐
X857	3p bright magenta (Type I) (2 bands) *(1.2.82)*	35	45	☐	☐
X858	3½p olive-grey (2 bands)	25	30	☐	☐
X859	3½p olive-grey (1 centre band) *(24.6.74)*	30	35	☐	☐
X860	3½p purple-brown (1 centre band) *(5.4.83)*	1·40	1·40	☐	☐
X861	4p ochre-brown (2 bands)	40	50	☐	☐
X862	4p greenish blue (2 bands) *(26.8.81)*	2·00	2·50	☐	☐
X863	4p greenish blue (1 centre band) *(3.9.84)*	1·50	1·90	☐	☐
X864	4p greenish blue (1 side band) *(8.1.85)*	3·75	3·75	☐	☐
X865	4½p grey-blue (2 bands) *(24.10.73)*	25	30	☐	☐
X866	5p pale violet (2 bands)	20	20	☐	☐
X867	5p claret (1 centre band) *(20.10.86)*	2·50	2·75	☐	☐
X868	5½p violet (2 bands) *(24.10.73)*	55	65	☐	☐
X869	5½p violet (1 centre band) *(17.3.75)*	25	30	☐	☐
X870	6p light emerald (2 bands)	25	40	☐	☐
X871	6½p greenish blue (2 bands) *(4.9.74)*	70	80	☐	☐
X872	6½p greenish blue (1 centre band) *(24.9.75)*	25	20	☐	☐
X873Ea	6½p greenish blue (1 side band) *(26.1.77)*	1·10	1·40	☐	☐
X874	7p purple-brown (2 bands) *(15.1.75)*	30	35	☐	☐
X875	7p purple-brown (1 centre band) *(13.6.77)*	25	30	☐	☐
X876Ea	7p purple-brown (1 side band) *(13.6.77)*	80	1·00	☐	☐
X877	7½p chestnut (2 bands)	30	40	☐	☐
X878	8p rosine (2 bands) *(24.10.73)*	30	30	☐	☐
X879	8p rosine (1 centre band) *(20.8.79)*	30	30	☐	☐
X880	8p rosine (1 side band) *(28.8.79)*	1·10	1·40	☐	☐
X881	8½p light yellowish green (2 bands) *(24.9.75)*	30	30	☐	☐
X882	9p yellow-orange and black (2 bands)	45	55	☐	☐
X883	9p deep violet (2 bands) *(25.2.76)*	35	30	☐	☐
X884	9½p purple (2 bands) *(25.2.76)*	75	1·00	☐	☐
X885	10p orange-brown and chestnut (2 bands) *(11.8.71)*	35	45	☐	☐
X886	10p orange-brown (Type I) (2 bands) *(25.2.76)*	35	30	☐	☐
	b. Type II *(4.9.84)*	22·00	22·00	☐	☐
X887	10p orange-brown (Type I) ('all-over' phosphor) *(3.10.79)*	35	45	☐	☐
X888	10p orange-brown (Type I) (1 centre band) *(4.2.80)*	35	25	☐	☐
X889	10p orange-brown (Type I) (1 side band) *(4.2.80)*	1·00	1·50	☐	☐
X890	10½p yellow (2 bands) *(25.2.76)*	60	75	☐	☐
X891	10½p blue (2 bands) *(26.4.78)*	80	1·00	☐	☐
X892	11p brown-red (2 bands) *(25.2.76)*	40	40	☐	☐
X893	11½p drab (1 centre band) *(14.1.81)*	40	35	☐	☐
X894	11½p drab (1 side band) *(26.1.81)*	65	80	☐	☐
X895	12p yellowish green (2 bands) *(4.2.80)*	55	65	☐	☐
X896	12p bright emerald (1 centre band) *(29.10.85)*	45	45	☐	☐
X897	12p bright emerald (1 side band) *(14.1.86)*	80	85	☐	☐
X898	12½p light emerald (1 centre band) *(27.1.82)*	45	40	☐	☐
X899	12½p light emerald (1 side band) *(1.2.82)*	70	75	☐	☐
X900	13p pale chestnut (1 centre band) *(28.8.84)*	40	40	☐	☐
X901	13p pale chestnut (1 side band) *(3.9.84)*	65	75	☐	☐
X902	14p grey-blue (2 bands) *(26.1.81)*	1·20	1·40	☐	☐
X903	14p deep blue (1 centre band) *(23.8.88)*	45	50	☐	☐
X904	14p deep blue (1 side band) *(5.9.88)*	4·00	4·00	☐	☐
X905	15p bright blue (1 centre band) *(26.9.89)*	65	65	☐	☐
X906a	15p bright blue (1 side band) *(2.10.89)*	4·25	4·25	☐	☐
X907	15½p pale violet (2 bands) *(1.2.82)*	70	80	☐	☐
X908	16p olive-drab (2 bands) *(5.4.83)*	1·40	1·60	☐	☐
X909	17p grey-blue (2 bands) *(3.9.84)*	60	60	☐	☐
X910	17p deep blue (1 centre band) *(4.9.90)*	80	85	☐	☐
X911Ea	17p deep blue (1 side band) *(4.9.90)*	3·00	3·00	☐	☐
X912	18p deep olive-grey (2 bands) *(20.10.86)*	80	90	☐	☐
X913	18p bright green (1 centre band) *(10.9.91)*	60	60	☐	☐
X914	19p bright orange-red (2 bands) *(5.9.88)*	1·50	1·50	☐	☐
X915	20p dull purple (2 bands) *(25.2.76)*	1·20	1·20	☐	☐
X916	20p brownish black (2 bands) *(2.10.89)*	3·00	3·25	☐	☐
X917	22p bright orange-red (2 bands) *(4.9.90)*	1·60	1·60	☐	☐
X917a	25p rose-red (2 bands) *(6.2.96)*	12·00	12·00	☐	☐
X918	26p rosine (Type I) (2 bands) *(3.3.87)*	15·00	16·00	☐	☐
X919	31p purple (2 bands) *(18.3.86)*	15·00	15·00	☐	☐
X920	34p ochre-brown (2 bands) *(8.1.85)*	9·00	9·50	☐	☐
X921	50p ochre-brown (2 bands) *(2.2.77)*	2·00	75	☐	☐
X922	50p ochre (2 bands) *(20.3.90)*	5·50	6·00	☐	☐

(b) Printed in photogravure by Harrison and Sons on
phosphorised paper. Perf 15 × 14

X924	½p turquoise-blue *(10.12.80)*	20	30
X925	1p crimson *(12.12.79)*	10	15
X926	2p myrtle-green (face value as in T **367**) *(12.12.79)*	15	20
X927	2p deep green (smaller value as in T **367a**) *(26.7.88)*	25	25
X928	2p myrtle-green (smaller value as in T **367a**) *(5.9.88)*	9·00	9·00
X929	2½p rose-red *(14.1.81)*	25	40
X930	3p bright magenta (Type I) *(22.10.80)*	20	25
	c. Type II *(10.10.89)*	1·20	1·50
X931	3½p purple-brown *(30.3.83)*	60	70
X932	4p greenish blue *(30.12.81)*	45	60
X933	4p new blue *(26.7.88)*	20	25
X934	5p pale violet *(10.10.79)*	65	85
X935	5p dull red-brown *(26.7.88)*	25	30
X936	6p yellow-olive *(10.9.91)*	30	40
X937	7p brownish red *(29.10.85)*	1·50	1·75
X938	8½p yellowish green *(24.3.76)*	1·75	2·00
X939	10p orange-brown (Type I) *(11.79)*	35	35
X940	10p dull orange (Type II) *(4.9.90)*	40	35
X941	11p brown-red *(27.8.80)*	2·25	2·25
X942	11½p ochre-brown *(15.8.79)*	65	75
X943	12p yellowish green *(30.1.80)*	45	45
X944	13p olive-grey *(15.8.79)*	1·20	1·20
X945	13½p purple-brown *(30.1.80)*	90	90
X946	14p grey-blue *(14.1.81)*	50	50
X947	15p ultramarine *(15.8.79)*	60	60
X948	15½p pale violet *(14.1.81)*	60	50
X949	16p olive-drab *(30.8.83)*	55	55
X950	16½p pale chestnut *(27.1.82)*	90	1·00
X951	17p light emerald *(30.1.80)*	90	1·00
X952	17p grey-blue *(30.3.83)*	45	45
X953	17½p pale chestnut *(30.1.80)*	1·25	1·25
X954	18p deep violet *(14.1.81)*	1·00	1·10
X955	18p deep olive-grey *(28.8.84)*	75	60
X956	19p bright orange-red *(23.8.88)*	80	60
X957	19½p olive-grey *(27.1.82)*	2·25	2·25
X958	20p dull purple *(10.10.79)*	1·00	75
X959	20p turquoise-green *(23.8.88)*	75	70
X960	20p brownish black *(26.9.89)*	75	75
X961	20½p ultramarine *(30.3.83)*	1·40	1·40
X962	22p blue *(22.10.80)*	1·20	1·20
X963	22p yellow-green *(28.8.84)*	1·00	1·00
X964	22p bright orange-red *(4.9.90)*	90	80
X965	23p brown-red *(30.3.83)*	1·25	1·10
X966	23p bright green *(23.8.88)*	1·60	1·60
X967	24p violet *(28.8.84)*	1·40	1·50
X968	24p Indian red *(26.9.89)*	2·00	2·25
X969	24p chestnut *(10.9.91)*	80	80
X970	25p purple *(14.1.81)*	1·00	1·00
X971	26p rosine (Type I) *(27.1.82)*	1·10	80
	b. Type II *(4.8.87)*	6.50	7·50
X972	26p drab *(4.9.90)*	1·50	1·25
X973	27p chestnut *(23.8.88)*	1·25	1·25
X974	27p violet *(4.9.90)*	1·60	1·60
X975	28p deep violet *(20.3.83)*	1·25	1·25
X976	28p ochre *(23.8.88)*	1·40	1·25
X977	28p deep bluish grey *(10.9.91)*	1·40	1·50
X978	29p ochre-brown *(27.1.82)*	2·00	2·00
X979	29p deep mauve *(26.9.89)*	2·00	2·00
X980	30p deep olive-grey *(26.9.89)*	1·25	1·25
X981	31p purple *(30.8.83)*	1·25	1·25
X982	31p ultramarine *(4.9.90)*	1·60	1·75
X983	32p greenish blue *(23.8.88)*	1·90	1·75
X984	33p light emerald *(4.9.90)*	1·75	1·60
X985	34p ochre-brown *(28.8.84)*	1·75	1·75
X986	34p deep bluish grey *(26.9.89)*	2·00	2·00
X987	34p deep mauve *(10.9.91)*	1·75	1·75
X988	35p sepia *(23.8.88)*	1·60	1·60
X989	35p yellow *(10.9.91)*	1·60	1·60
X990	37p rosine *(26.9.89)*	2·00	1·75
X991	39p bright mauve *(10.9.91)*	1·75	1·75
X991a	50p ochre *(21.1.92)*	5·00	2·00

(c) Printed in photogravure by Harrison and Sons on
ordinary paper. Perf 15 × 14

X992	50p ochre-brown *(21.5.80)*	1·75	70
X993	50p ochre *(13.3.90)*	5·00	2·00
X994	75p grey-black (smaller values as T **367a**) *(26.7.88)*	3·25	1·50

(d) Printed in lithography by John Waddington. Perf 14

X996	4p greenish blue (2 bands) *(30.1.80)*	50	55
X997	4p greenish blue (phosphorised paper) *(11.81)*	45	40
X998	20p dull purple (2 bands) *(21.5.80)*	1·50	1·50
X999	20p dull purple (phosphorised paper) *(11.81)*	1·20	1·20

(e) Printed in lithography by Questa. Perf 14
(Nos. X1000, X1003/4 and X1023) or 15 × 14 (others)

X1000	2p emerald-green (face value as in T **367**) (phosphorised paper) *(21.5.80)*	50	60
	a. Perf 15 × 14 *(10.7.84)*	35	35
X1001	2p bright green and deep green (smaller value as in T **367a**) (phosphorised paper) *(23.2.88)*	1.10	1·25
X1002	4p greenish blue (phosphorised paper) *(13.5.86)*	80	90
X1003	5p light violet (phosphorised paper) *(21.5.80)*	60	75
X1004	5p claret (phosphorised paper) *(27.1.82)*	75	75
	a. Perf 15 × 14 *(21.2.84)*	65	60
X1005	13p pale chestnut (1 centre band) *(9.2.88)*	1·00	1·20
X1006	13p pale chestnut (1 side band) *(9.2.88)*	75	75
X1007	14p deep blue (1 centre band) *(11.10.88)*	2·00	2·00
X1008	17p deep blue (1 centre band) *(19.3.91)*	1·00	1·00
X1009	18p deep olive-grey (phosphorised paper) *(9.2.88)*	1·00	1·10
X1010	18p deep olive-grey (2 bands) *(9.2.88)*	8·00	8·00
X1011	18p bright green (1 centre band) *(27.10.92)*	1·00	1·20
X1012	18p bright green (1 side band at right) *(27.10.92)*	1·80	2·00
X1013	19p bright orange-red (phosphorised paper) *(11.10.88)*	2·20	2·00
X1014	20p dull purple (phosphorised paper) *(13.5.86)*	1·75	1·75
X1015	22p yellow-green (2 bands) *(9.2.88)*	9·00	9·00
X1016	22p bright orange-red (phosphorised paper) *(19.3.91)*	1·00	90

X1017	24p chestnut (phosphorised paper) *(27.10.92)*	90	1·10	☐☐
X1018	24p chestnut (2 bands) *(27.10.92)*	2·25	2·25	☐☐
X1019	33p light emerald (phosphorised paper) *(19.3.91)*	3·00	3·00	☐☐
X1020	33p light emerald (2 bands) *(25.2.92)*	2·00	2·00	☐☐
X1021	34p bistre-brown (2 bands) *(9.2.88)* 8·00	8·00		☐☐
X1022	39p bright mauve (2 bands) *(27.10.92)*	2·50	2·50	☐☐
X1023	75p black (face value as T **367**) (ordinary paper) *(30.1.80)*	3·00	1·50	☐☐
	a. Perf 15 × 14 *(21.2.84)*	4·00	2·25	☐☐
X1024	75p brownish grey and black (smaller value as T **367a**) (ordinary paper) *(23.2.88)*	10·00	10·50	☐☐

(f) Printed in lithography by Walsall. Perf 14

X1050	2p deep green (phosphorised paper) *(9.2.93)*	1·50	1·50	☐☐
X1051	14p deep blue (1 side band) *(9.2.93)*	5·25	5·25	☐☐
X1052	19p bright orange-red (2 bands) *(25.4.89)*	3·00	3·00	☐☐
X1053	24p chestnut (phosphorised paper) *(9.2.93)*	1·40	1·40	☐☐
X1054	29p deep mauve (2 bands) *(2.10.89)*	3·25	3·25	☐☐
X1055	29p deep mauve (phosphorised paper) *(17.4.90)*	4·50	4·50	☐☐
X1056	31p ultramarine (phosphorised paper) *(17.9.90)*	1·50	1·50	☐☐
X1057	33p light emerald (phosphorised paper) *(16.9.91)*	1·75	1·75	☐☐
X1058	39p bright mauve (phosphorised paper) *(16.9.91)*	2·25	2·25	☐☐

Presentation Pack (P.O. Pack No. 26) (contains ½p (X841), 1p (X844), 1½p (X848), 2p (X849), 2½p (X851), 3p (X855), 3½p (X858), 4p (X861), 5p (X866), 6p (X870), 7½p (X877), 9p (X882))   9·50   ☐

Presentation Pack ('Scandinavia 71') (contents as above)   30·00   ☐

Presentation Pack (P.O. Pack No. 37) (contains ½p (X841), 1p (X844), 1½p (X848), 2p (X849), 2½p (X851), 3p (X855 or X856), 3½p (X858 or X859), 4p (X861), 4½p (X865), 5p (X866), 5½p (X868 or X869), 6p (X870), 7½p (X877), 8p (X878), 9p (X882), 10p (X885))   30·00   ☐

Later issues of this pack included the 6½p (X871) or the 6½p (X872) and 7p (X874).

Presentation Pack (P.O. Pack No. 90) (contains ½p (X841), 1p (X844), 1½p (X848), 2p (X849), 2½p (X851), 3p (X856), 5p (X866), 6½p (X872), 7p (X874 or X875), 7½p (X877), 8p (X878), 8½p (X881), 9p (X883), 9½p (X884), 10p (X886), 10½p (X890), 11p (X892), 20p (X915), 50p (X921))   6·00   ☐

Presentation Pack (P.O. Pack No. 129a) (contains 2½p (X929), 3p (X930), 4p (X996), 10½p (X891), 11½p (X893), 11½p (X942), 12p (X943), 13p (X944), 13½p (X945), 14p (X946), 15p (X947), 15½p (X948), 17p (X951), 17½p (X953), 18p (X954), 22p (X962), 25p (X970), 75p (X1023)   20·00   ☐

Presentation Pack (P.O. Pack No. 1) (contains ½p (X924), 1p (X925), 2p (X1000), 3p (X930), 3½p (X931), 4p (X997), 5p (X1004), 10p (X888), 12½p (X898), 16p (X949), 16½p (X950), 17p (X952), 20p (X999), 20½p (X961), 23p

(X965), 26p (X971), 28p (X975), 31p (X981), 50p (X992), 75p (X1023))   40·00   ☐

Presentation Pack (P.O. Pack No. 5) (contains ½p (X924), 1p (X925), 2p (X1000a), 3p (X930), 4p (X997), 5p (X1004a), 10p (X939), 13p (X900), 16p (X949), 17p (X952), 18p (X955), 20p (X999), 22p (X963), 24p (X967), 26p (X971), 28p (X975), 31p (X981), 34p (X985), 50p (X992), 75p (X1023a))   36·00   ☐

Presentation Pack (P.O. Pack No. 9) (contains 1p (X925), 2p (X1000a), 3p (X930), 4p (X997), 5p (X1004a), 7p (X937), 10p (X939), 12p (X896), 13p (X900), 17p (X952), 18p (X955), 20p (X999), 22p (X963), 24p (X967), 26p (X971), 28p (X975), 31p (X981), 34p (X985), 50p (X992), 75p (X1023a))   40·00   ☐

Presentation Pack (P.O. Pack No. 15) (contains 14p (X903), 19p (X956), 20p (X959), 23p (X966), 27p (X973), 28p (X976), 32p (X983), 35p (X988))   12·00   ☐

Presentation Pack (P.O. Pack No. 19) (contains 15p (X905), 20p (X960), 24p (X968), 29p (X979), 30p (X980), 34p (X986), 37p (X990))   10·00   ☐

Presentation Pack (P.O. Pack No. 22) (contains 10p (X940), 17p (X910), 22p (X964), 26p (X972), 27p (X974), 31p (X982), 33p (X984))   9·00   ☐

Presentation Pack (P.O. Pack No. 24) (contains 1p (X925), 2p (X927), 3p (X930), 4p (X933), 5p (X935), 10p (X940), 17p (X910), 20p (X959), 22p (X964), 26p (X972), 27p (X974), 30p (X980), 31p (X982), 32p (X983), 33p (X984), 37p (X990), 50p (X993), 75p (X994))   30·00   ☐

Presentation Pack (P.O. Pack No. 25) (contains 6p (X936), 18p (X913), 24p (X969), 28p (X977), 34p (X987), 35p (X989), 39p (X991))   9·00   ☐

First Day Covers

15 Feb. 1971	½p, 1p, 1½p, 2p, 2½p, 3p, 3½p, 4p, 5p, 6p, 7½p, 9p (Nos. X841, X844, X848/9, X851, X855, X858, X861, X866, X870, X877, X882) (Covers carry 'POSTING DELAYED BY THE POST OFFICE STRIKE 1971' cachet)	2·50	☐
11 Aug. 1971	10p (No. X885)	1·50	☐
24 Oct. 1973	4½p, 5½p, 8p (Nos. X865, X868, X878)	1·50	☐
4 Sept. 1974	6½p (No. X871)	1·50	☐
15 Jan. 1975	7p (No. X874)	1·00	☐
24 Sept. 1975	8½p (No. X881)	1·50	☐
25 Feb. 1976	9p, 9½p, 10p, 10½p, 11p, 20p (Nos. X883/4, X886, X890, X892, X915)	3·50	☐
2 Feb. 1977	50p (No. X921)	1·75	☐
26 Apr. 1978	10½p (No. X891)	1·20	☐
15 Aug. 1979	11½p, 13p, 15p (Nos. X942, X944, X947)	1·75	☐
30 Jan. 1980	4p, 12p, 13½p, 17p, 17½p, 75p (Nos. X996, X943, X945, X951, X953, X1023)	3·25	☐
22 Oct. 1980	3p, 22p (Nos. X930, X962)	1·50	☐
14 Jan. 1981	2½p, 11½p, 14p, 15½p, 18p, 25p (Nos. X929, X893, X946, X948, X954, X970)	2·00	☐
27 Jan. 1982	5p, 12½p, 16½p, 19½p, 26p, 29p (Nos. X1004, X898, X950, X957, X971, X978)	3·50	☐
30 Mar. 1983	3½p, 16p, 17p, 20½p, 23p, 28p, 31p (Nos. X931, X949, X952, X961, X965, X975, X981)	5·00	☐

28 Aug. 1984	13p, 18p, 22p, 24p, 34p (Nos. X900, X955, X963, X967, X985)	3·00	
29 Oct. 1985	7p, 12p (Nos. X937, X896)	3·00	
23 Aug. 1988	14p, 19p, 20p, 23p, 27p, 28p, 32p, 35p (Nos. X903, X956, X959, X966, X973, X976, X983, X988)	6·00	
26 Sept. 1989	15p, 20p, 24p, 29p, 30p, 34p, 37p (Nos. X905, X960, X968, X979/80, X986, X990)	5·00	
4 Sept. 1990	10p, 17p, 22p, 26p, 27p, 31p, 33p (Nos. X940, X910, X964, X972, X974, X982, X984)	5·50	
10 Sept. 1991	6p, 18p, 24p, 28p, 34p, 35p, 39p (Nos. X936, X913, X969, X977, X987, X989, X991)	6·00	

For similar stamps, but with elliptical perforations see Nos. Y1667/1803 in 1993.

PHOSPHOR BANDS. See notes on page 23.

Phosphor bands are applied to the stamps, after the design has been printed, by a separate cylinder. On issues with 'all-over' phosphor the 'band' covers the entire stamp. Parts of the stamp covered by phosphor bands, or the entire surface for 'all-over' phosphor versions, appear matt.

Nos. X847, X852, X864, X873, X876, X880, X889, X894, X897, X899, X901, X906, X911, X1006 and X1012 exist with the phosphor band at the left or right of the stamp.

PHOSPHORISED PAPER. First introduced as an experiment for a limited printing of the 1s6d value (No. 743c) in 1969, this paper has the phosphor, to activate the automatic sorting machinery, added to the paper coating before the stamps were printed. Issues on this paper have a completely shiny surface. Although not adopted after this first trial further experiments on the 8½p in 1976 led to this paper being used for new printings of current values.

368 'A Mountain Road' (T.P. Flanagan)

369 'Deer's Meadow' (Tom Carr)

370 'Slieve na brock' (Colin Middleton)

'Ulster '71' Paintings

1971 (16 June) Two phosphor bands

881	**368**	3p	multicoloured	25	25		
882	**369**	7½p	multicoloured	50	50		
883	**370**	9p	multicoloured	50	50		
Set of 3				1·00	1·00		
First Day Cover					1·80		
Presentation Pack (P.O. Pack No. 26a)				7·50			

371 John Keats (150th Death Anniv)

372 Thomas Gray (Death Bicentenary)

373 Sir Walter Scott (Birth Bicentenary)

Literary Anniversaries. Events described above

1971 (28 July) Two phosphor bands

884	**371**	3p	black, gold and blue	25	10		
885	**372**	5p	black, gold and olive	45	50		
886	**373**	7½p	black, gold and brown	45	45		
Set of 3				1·00	1·00		
First Day Cover					2·00		
Presentation Pack (P.O. Pack No. 32)				7·50			

374 Servicemen and Nurse of 1921   **375** Roman Centurion

376 Rugby Football, 1871

British Anniversaries. Events described on stamps

1971 (25 Aug.) Two phosphor bands

887	**374**	3p	multicoloured	25	25		
888	**375**	7½p	multicoloured	50	50		
889	**376**	9p	multicoloured	50	50		
Set of 3				1·10	1·10		
First Day Cover					2·50		
Presentation Pack (P.O. Pack No. 32A)				7·50			

377 Physical Sciences Building, University College of Wales, Aberystwyth

378 Faraday Building, Southampton University

379 Engineering Department, Leicester University

380 Hexagon Restaurant, Essex University

British Architecture (Modern University Buildings)

1971 (22 Sept.) Two phosphor bands

890	**377**	3p multicoloured	10	10	☐	☐
891	**378**	5p multicoloured	25	20	☐	☐
892	**379**	7½p ochre, black and				
		purple-brown	45	55	☐	☐
893	**380**	9p multicoloured	75	80	☐	☐
Set of 4			1·40	1·50	☐	☐
First Day Cover				2·00		☐
Presentation Pack (P.O. Pack No. 33)			10·00		☐	

Collectors Pack 1971

1971 (29 Sept.) Comprises Nos. 835/40 and 881/93

CP893a	Collectors Pack	50·00	☐	

381 "Dream of the Wise Men"

382 "Adoration of the Magi"

383 "Ride of the Magi"

Christmas

1971 (13 Oct.) Two phosphor bands (3p, 7½p) or one centre phosphor band (2½p)

894	**381**	2½p multicoloured	10	10	☐	☐
895	**382**	3p multicoloured	10	10	☐	☐
896	**383**	7½p multicoloured	55	75	☐	☐
Set of 3			70	85	☐	☐
First Day Cover				2·00		☐
Presentation Pack (P.O. Pack No. 35)			6·00		☐	

384 Sir James Clark Ross

385 Sir Martin Frobisher

386 Henry Hudson

387 Capt. Robert F. Scott

British Polar Explorers

1972 (16 Feb.) Two phosphor bands

897	**384**	3p multicoloured	10	10	☐	☐
898	**385**	5p multicoloured	15	15	☐	☐
899	**386**	7½p multicoloured	45	50	☐	☐
900	**387**	9p multicoloured	70	85	☐	☐
Set of 4			1·20	1·50	☐	☐
First Day Cover				2·50		☐
Presentation Pack (P.O. Pack No. 39)			7·00		☐	

388 Statuette of Tutankhamun

389 19th-century Coastguard

390 Ralph Vaughan Williams and Score

Anniversaries. Events described on stamps

1972 (26 Apr.) Two phosphor bands

901	**388**	3p multicoloured	25	25	☐	☐
902	**389**	7½p multicoloured	50	50	☐	☐
903	**390**	9p multicoloured	50	50	☐	☐
Set of 3			1·10	1·10	☐	☐
First Day Cover				2·25		☐
Presentation Pack (P.O. Pack No. 40)			7·00		☐	

391 St. Andrew's, Greensted - juxta-Ongar, Essex

392 All Saints, Earls Barton, Northants

393 St. Andrew's, Letheringsett, Norfolk

394 St. Andrew's, Helpringham, Lincs

395 St. Mary the Virgin, Huish Episcopi, Somerset

British Architecture (Village Churches)

1972 (21 June) Two phosphor bands

904	**391**	3p multicoloured	10	10	☐	☐
905	**392**	4p multicoloured	10	20	☐	☐
906	**393**	5p multicoloured	15	20	☐	☐
907	**394**	7½p multicoloured	50	75	☐	☐
908	**395**	9p multicoloured	50	80	☐	☐
Set of 5			1·20	1·90	☐	☐
First Day Cover				2·75		☐
Presentation Pack (P.O. Pack No. 41)			10·00		☐	

'Belgica '72' Souvenir Pack

1972 (24 June) Comprises Nos. 894/6 and 904/8

CP908b	Souvenir Pack	10·00	☐

396 Microphones, 1924–69

397 Horn Loudspeaker

398 TV Camera, 1972

399 Oscillator and Spark Transmitter, 1897

Broadcasting Anniversaries.
Events described on stamps

1972 (13 Sept.) Two phosphor bands

909	**396**	3p multicoloured	10	10	☐	☐
910	**397**	5p multicoloured	10	20	☐	☐
911	**398**	7½p multicoloured	45	50	☐	☐
912	**399**	9p multicoloured	50	50	☐	☐
Set of 4			1·00	1·10	☐	☐
First Day Cover				2·75		☐
Presentation Pack (P.O. Pack No. 43)			4·25		☐	

400 Angel holding Trumpet

401 Angel playing Lute

402 Angel playing Harp

Christmas

1972 (18 Oct.) Two phosphor bands (3p, 7½p) or one centre phosphor band (2½p)

913	**400**	2½p multicoloured	10	10	☐	☐
914	**401**	3p multicoloured	10	10	☐	☐
915	**402**	7½p multicoloured	50	45	☐	☐
Set of 3			60	60	☐	☐
First Day Cover				1·50		☐
Presentation Pack (P.O. Pack No. 44)			4·00		☐	

403 Queen Elizabeth II and Prince Philip

404 Europe

Royal Silver Wedding

1972 (20 Nov.) 3p 'all-over' phosphor, 20p without phosphor

916	**403**	3p brownish black, deep blue and silver	40	40	☐	☐
917		20p brownish black, reddish purple and silver	1·20	1·20	☐	☐
Set of 2			1·50	1·50	☐	☐
First Day Cover				2·00		☐
Presentation Pack (P.O. Pack No. 45)			4·00		☐	
Presentation Pack (Japanese)			9·50		☐	
Souvenir Book (P.O. Pack No. 46)			4·00		☐	
Gutter Pair (3p)			1·00		☐	
Traffic Light Gutter Pair (3p)			20·00		☐	

Collectors Pack 1972

1972 (20 Nov.) Comprises Nos. 897/917

CP918a	Collectors Pack	35·00	☐

Britain's Entry into European Communities

1973 (3 Jan.) Two phosphor bands

919	**404**	3p multicoloured	25	25	☐	☐
920		5p multicoloured (blue jigsaw)	25	50	☐	☐
		a. Pair. Nos. 920/1	1·00	1·20	☐	☐
921		5p multicoloured (green jigsaw)	25	50	☐	☐
Set of 3			1·10	1·40	☐	☐
First Day Cover				2·00		☐
Presentation Pack (P.O. Pack No. 48)			3·00		☐	

Nos. 920/1 were issued horizontally se-tenant throughout the sheet.

405 Oak Tree

British Trees (1st Issue)

1973 (28 Feb.) Two phosphor bands

922	**405**	9p multicoloured		35	40	☐ ☐
First Day Cover					1·70	☐
Presentation Pack (P.O. Pack No. 49)			2·75			☐

See also No. 949.

406 David Livingstone

407 H. M. Stanley

408 Sir Francis Drake

409 Sir Walter Raleigh

410 Charles Sturt

British Explorers

1973 (18 Apr.) 'All-over' phosphor

923	**406**	3p multicoloured	40	25	☐ ☐
		a. Pair. Nos. 923/4	80	1·00	☐ ☐
924	**407**	3p multicoloured	40	25	☐ ☐
925	**408**	5p multicoloured	40	50	☐ ☐
926	**409**	7½p multicoloured	40	50	☐ ☐
927	**410**	9p multicoloured	40	75	☐ ☐
Set of 5			1·70	1·70	☐ ☐
First Day Cover				2·50	☐
Presentation Pack (P.O. Pack No. 50)		4·50			☐

Nos. 923/4 were issued horizontally *se-tenant* throughout the sheet.

411   **412**   **413**

County Cricket 1873–1973

1973 (16 May) Designs show sketches of W. G. Grace by Harry Furniss. Queen's head in gold. 'All-over' phosphor

928	**411**	3p black and brown	25	25	☐ ☐
929	**412**	7½p black and green	75	75	☐ ☐
930	**413**	9p black and blue	1·25	1·00	☐ ☐
Set of 3			2·00	1·80	☐ ☐
First Day Cover				2·50	☐
Presentation Pack (P.O. Pack No. 51)		5·00			☐
Souvenir Book			7·00		☐
PHQ Card (No. 928)(1)			70·00	£275	☐ ☐

The PHQ Card did not become available until mid-July. The used price quoted is for an example used in July or August 1973.

414 'Self-portrait'
(Sir Joshua Reynolds)

415 'Self-portrait'
(Sir Henry Raeburn)

416 'Nelly O'Brien'
(Sir Joshua Reynolds)

417 'Rev R. Walker'
(The Skater)'
(Sir Henry Raeburn)

British Paintings. 250th Birth Anniv of Sir Joshua Reynolds and 150th Death Anniv of Sir Henry Raeburn

1973 (4 July) 'All-over' phosphor

931	**414**	3p multicoloured	10	10	☐ ☐
932	**415**	5p multicoloured	30	30	☐ ☐
933	**416**	7½p multicoloured	30	30	☐ ☐
934	**417**	9p multicoloured	60	60	☐ ☐
Set of 4			1·20	1·20	☐ ☐
First Day Cover				2·00	☐
Presentation Pack (P.O. Pack No. 52)		3·25			☐

418 Court Masque Costumes **419** St. Paul's Church, Covent Garden

420 Prince's Lodging, Newmarket **421** Court Masque Stage Scene

400th Anniversary of the Birth of Inigo Jones (architect and designer)

1973 (15 Aug.) 'All-over' phosphor

935	**418**	3p	deep mauve, black and gold	10	25	☐ ☐
		a.	Pair. Nos. 935/6	30	50	☐ ☐
936	**419**	3p	deep brown, black and gold	10	25	☐ ☐
937	**420**	5p	blue, black and gold	35	50	☐ ☐
		a.	Pair. Nos. 937/8	1·00	1·00	☐ ☐
938	**421**	5p	grey-olive, black and gold	35	50	☐ ☐
Set of 4				1·20	1·40	☐ ☐
First Day Cover					2·00	☐
Presentation Pack (P.O. Pack No.53)				3·50		☐
PHQ Card (No. 936) (2)				£200	£200	☐ ☐

The 3p and 5p values were printed horizontally *se-tenant* within the sheet.

422 Palace of Westminster seen from Whitehall **423** Palace of Westminster seen from Millbank

19th Commonwealth Parliamentary Conference

1973 (12 Sept.) 'All-over' phosphor

939	**422**	8p	black, grey and pale buff	45	50	☐ ☐
940	**423**	10p	gold and black	45	40	☐ ☐
Set of 2				80	80	☐ ☐
First Day Cover					1·50	☐
Presentation Pack (P.O. Pack No. 54)				3·00		☐
Souvenir Book (P.O. Pack No. 55)				7·00		☐
PHQ Card (No. 939) (3)				40·00	£150	☐ ☐

424 Princess Anne and Captain Mark Phillips

Royal Wedding

1973 (14 Nov.) 'All-over' phosphor

941	**424**	3½p	violet and silver	25	25	☐ ☐
942		20p	brown and silver	1·00	75	☐ ☐

Set of 2		1·10	90	☐ ☐
First Day Cover			1·50	☐
Presentation Pack (P.O. Pack No. 56)		2·75		☐
PHQ Card (No. 941) (4)		9·00	50·00	☐ ☐
Set of 2 Gutter Pairs		2·75		☐

Set of 2 Traffic Light Gutter Pairs £110 ☐

425

426

427

428

429

430 'Good King Wenceslas, the Page and Peasant'

Christmas

1973 (28 Nov.) One phosphor band (3p) or 'all-over' phosphor (3½p)

943	**425**	3p	multicoloured	20	25	☐ ☐
		a.	Strip of 5. Nos. 943/7	2·25	2·50	☐ ☐
944	**426**	3p	multicoloured	20	25	☐ ☐
945	**427**	3p	multicoloured	20	25	☐ ☐
946	**428**	3p	multicoloured	20	25	☐ ☐
947	**429**	3p	multicoloured	20	25	☐ ☐
948	**430**	3½p	multicoloured	20	25	☐ ☐
Set of 6				2·25	2·50	☐ ☐
First Day Cover					3·00	☐
Presentation Pack (P.O. Pack No. 57)				4·00		☐

The 3p values depict the carol 'Good King Wenceslas' and were printed horizontally *se-tenant* within the sheet.

Collectors Pack 1973

1973 (28 Nov.) Comprises Nos. 919/48

CP948k	Collectors Pack	27·00	☐

431 Horse Chestnut

British Trees (2nd issue)

1974 (27 Feb.) 'All-over' phosphor

949	**431**	10p	multicoloured	40	35	☐ ☐
First Day Cover					1·20	☐
Presentation Pack (P.O. Pack No. 59)				2·50		☐
PHQ Card (5)				£150	£150	☐ ☐
Gutter Pair				1·75		☐

Traffic Light Gutter Pair   65·00   ☐
The pack number is stated to be 58 on the reverse but the
correct number is 59.

432 First. Motor Fire-engine, 1904

433 Prize-winning Fire-engine, 1863

434 First. Steam Fire-engine, 1830

435 Fire-engine, 1766

Bicentenary of the Fire Prevention (Metropolis) Act

1974 (24 Apr.) 'All-over' phosphor

950	**432**	3½p	multicoloured	25	10	☐ ☐
951	**433**	5½p	multicoloured	25	30	☐ ☐
952	**434**	8p	multicoloured	50	50	☐ ☐
953	**435**	10p	multicoloured	50	50	☐ ☐
Set of 4				1·40	1·30	☐ ☐
First Day Cover					3·00	☐
Presentation Pack (P.O. Pack No. 60)				4·00		☐
PHQ Card (No. 950) (6)				£140	£150	☐ ☐
Set of 4 Gutter Pairs				3·00		☐
Set of 4 Traffic Light Gutter Pairs				60·00		☐

436 P & O Packet *Peninsular*, 1888

437 Farman H.F. III Biplane, 1911

438 Airmail-blue Van and Postbox, 1930

439 Imperial Airways Short S.21 Flying Boat *Maia*, 1937

Centenary of Universal Postal Union

1974 (12 June) 'All-over' phosphor

954	**436**	3½p	multicoloured	25	10	☐ ☐
955	**437**	5½p	multicoloured	25	30	☐ ☐
956	**438**	8p	multicoloured	25	35	☐ ☐
957	**439**	10p	multicoloured	50	40	☐ ☐
Set of 4				1·10	1·00	☐ ☐
First Day Cover					2·00	☐
Presentation Pack (P.O. Pack No.64)				4·00		☐
Set of 4 Gutter Pairs				2·50		☐
Set of 4 Traffic Light Gutter Pairs				45·00		☐

440 Robert the Bruce

441 Owain Glyndŵr

442 Henry V

443 The Black Prince

Medieval Warriors

1974 (10 July) 'All-over' phosphor

958	**440**	4½p	multicoloured	25	10	☐ ☐
959	**441**	5½p	multicoloured	25	35	☐ ☐
960	**442**	8p	multicoloured	50	50	☐ ☐
961	**443**	10p	multicoloured	50	50	☐ ☐
Set of 4				1·40	1·30	☐ ☐
First Day Cover					3·00	☐
Presentation Pack (P.O. Pack No. 65)				4·00		☐
PHQ Cards (*set of* 4) (7)				28·00	65·00	☐ ☐
Set of 4 Gutter Pairs				3·00		☐
Set of 4 Traffic Light Gutter Pairs				60·00		☐

444 Churchill in Royal yacht Squadron Uniform

445 Prime Minister, 1940

446 Secretary for War and Air, 1919

447 War Correspondent, South Africa, 1899

Birth Centenary of Sir Winston Churchill

1974 (9 Oct.) Queen's head and inscription in silver. 'All-over' phosphor

962	**444**	4½p	green and blue	20	15	☐ ☐
963	**445**	5½p	grey and black	35	35	☐ ☐
964	**446**	8p	rose and lake	60	50	☐ ☐
965	**447**	10p	stone and brown	60	50	☐ ☐
Set of 4				1·60	1·40	☐ ☐
First Day Cover					2·00	☐
Presentation Pack (P.O. Pack No. 66)				4·00		☐
Souvenir Book				3·00		☐
PHQ Card (No. 963) (8)				6·00	32·00	☐ ☐
Set of 4 Gutter Pairs				4·00		☐
Set of 4 Traffic Light Gutter Pairs				35·00		☐

448 *"Adoration of the Magi"* (York Minister, c 1355)

449 *"The Nativity"* (St. Helen's Church, Norwich, c 1480)

450 *"Virgin and Child"* (Ottery St. Mary Church, c 1350)

451 *"Virgin and Child"* (Worcester Cathedral, c 1224)

Christmas

1974 (27 Nov.) Designs show church roof bosses. One phosphor band (3½p) or 'all-over' phosphor (others)

966	**448**	3½p	multicoloured	10	10	
967	**449**	4½p	multicoloured	10	10	
968	**450**	8p	multicoloured	25	50	
969	**451**	10p	multicoloured	50	50	
Set of 4				85	1·10	
First Day Cover					2·00	
Presentation Pack (P.O. Pack No. 67)				3·00		
Set of 4 Gutter Pairs				2·25		
Set of 4 Traffic Light Gutter Pairs				36·00		

Collectors Pack 1974

1974 (27 Nov.) Comprises Nos. 949/69

CP969a	Collectors Pack	16·00	

452 Invalid in Wheelchair

Health and Handicap Funds

1975 (22 Jan.) 'All-over' phosphor

970	**452**	4½p +1½p azure and blue	25	25	
First Day Cover				1·00	
Gutter Pair			60		
Traffic Light Gutter Pair			2·25		

Turner 1775-1851
453 'Peace – Burial at Sea'

Turner 1775-1851
454 'Snowstorm – Steamer off a Harbour's Mouth'

Turner 1775-1851
455 'The Arsenal, Venice'

Turner 1775-1851
456 'St. Laurent'

Birth Bicentenary of J. M. W. Turner (painter)

1975 (19 Feb.) 'All-over' phosphor

971	**453**	4½p	multicoloured	25	25		
972	**454**	5½p	multicoloured	25	25		
973	**455**	8p	multicoloured	25	50		
974	**456**	10p	multicoloured	50	50		
Set of 4				1·10	1·10		
First Day Cover					1·50		
Presentation Pack (P.O. Pack No. 69)				3·00			
PHQ Card (No. 972) (9)				30·00	34·00		
Set of 4 Gutter Pairs				2·25			
Set of 4 Traffic Light Gutter Pairs				8·00			

457 Charlotte Square, Edinburgh

458 The Rows, Chester

459 Royal Observatory, Greenwich

460 St. George's Chapel, Windsor

461 National Theatre, London

European Architectural Heritage Year

1975 (23 Apr.) 'All-over' phosphor

975	**457**	7p	multicoloured	15	15		
		a.	Pair. Nos. 975/6	90	1·00		
976	**458**	7p	multicoloured	15	15		
977	**459**	8p	multicoloured	40	30		
978	**460**	10p	multicoloured	40	30		
979	**461**	12p	multicoloured	40	35		
Set of 5				1·90	1·70		
First Day Cover					2·50		
Presentation Pack (P.O. Pack No.70)				3·00			
PHQ Cards (Nos. 975/7) (10)				11·00	40·00		
Set of 5 Gutter Pairs				4·00			
Set of 5 Traffic Light Gutter Pairs				22·00			

Nos. 975/6 were printed horizontally *se-tenant* throughout the sheet.

462 Sailing Dinghies

463 Racing Keel Boats

464 Cruising Yachts

465 Multihulls

Sailing

1975 (11 June) 'All-over' phosphor

980	**462**	7p	multicoloured	25	20		
981	**463**	8p	multicoloured	35	40		
982	**464**	10p	multicoloured	35	45		
983	**465**	12p	multicoloured	50	50		
Set of 4				1·30	1·40		
First Day Cover					2·00		
Presentation Pack (P.O. Pack No. 71)				2·50			
PHQ Card (No. 981) (11)				5·75	30·00		
Set of 4 Gutter Pairs				2·75			
Set of 4 Traffic Light Gutter Pairs				25·00			

1825 Stockton and Darlington Railway
466 Stephenson's *Locomotion*, 1825

1876 North British Railway Drummond
467 *Abbotsford*, 1876

1923 Great Western Railway Castle Class
468 *Caerphilly Castle*, 1923

1975 British Rail Inter-City Service HST
469 High Speed Train, 1975

150th Anniversary of Public Railways

1975 (13 Aug.) 'All-over' phosphor

984	**466**	7p	multicoloured	25	25		
985	**467**	8p	multicoloured	50	50		
986	**468**	10p	multicoloured	50	50		
987	**469**	12p	multicoloured	40	50		
Set of 4				1·50	1·50		
First Day Cover					2·50		
Presentation Pack (P.O. Pack No. 72)				4·00			
Souvenir Book (P.O. Pack No. 73)				4·00			
PHQ Cards (*set of* 4) (12)				70·00	70·00		
Set of 4 Gutter Pairs				3·25			
Set of 4 Traffic Light Gutter Pairs				12·00			

470 Palace of Westminster

62nd Inter-Parliamentary Union Conference

1975 (3 Sept.) 'All-over' phosphor

988	**470**	12p	multicoloured	50	40		
First Day Cover					80		
Presentation Pack (P.O. Pack No. 74)				1·80			
Gutter Pair				1·10			
Traffic Light Gutter Pair				3·00			

471 Emma and
Mr Woodhouse (*Emma*)

472 Catherine Morland
(*Northanger Abbey*)

473 Mr Darcy (*Pride
and Prejudice*)

474 Mary and Henry
Crawford (*Mansfield Park*)

Birth Bicentenary of Jane Austen (novelist)

1975 (22 Oct.) 'All-over' phosphor

989	**471**	8½p	multicoloured	25	20		
990	**472**	10p	multicoloured	45	45		
991	**473**	11p	multicoloured	45	45		
992	**474**	13p	multicoloured	50	50		
Set of 4				1·50	1·40		
First Day Cover					2·50		
Presentation Pack (P.O. Pack No. 75)				5·00			
PHQ Cards (*set of* 4) (13)				24·00	42·00		
Set of 4 Gutter Pairs				3·25			
Set of 4 Traffic Light Gutter Pairs				7·00			

475 Angels with Harp and Lute

476 Angel with Mandolin

477 Angel with Horn

478 Angel with Trumpet

Christmas

1975 (26 Nov.) One phosphor band (6½p), phosphor-inked (8½p) (background) or 'all-over' phosphor (others)

993	**475**	6½p	multicoloured	25	25		
994	**476**	8½p	multicoloured	25	40		
995	**477**	11p	multicoloured	50	45		
996	**478**	13p	multicoloured	50	45		
Set of 4				1·40	1·40		
First Day Cover					1·80		
Presentation Pack (P.O. Pack No. 76)				3·00			
Set of 4 Gutter Pairs				3·00			
Set of 4 Traffic Light Gutter Pairs				9·00			

Collectors Pack 1975

1975 (26 Nov.) Comprises Nos. 970/96
CP996a Collectors Pack   9·00   ☐

479 Housewife

480 Policeman

481 District Nurse

482 Industrialist

Telephone Centenary

1976 (10 Mar.) 'All-over' phosphor

997	**479**	8½p multicoloured	25	20	☐	☐
998	**480**	10p multicoloured	40	40	☐	☐
999	**481**	11p multicoloured	50	50	☐	☐
1000	**482**	13p multicoloured	60	60	☐	☐
Set of 4			1·60	1·60	☐	☐
First Day Cover				2·00		☐
Presentation Pack (P.O. Pack No. 78)			3·00		☐	
Set of 4 Gutter Pairs			3·25		☐	
Set of 4 Traffic Light Gutter Pairs			9·00		☐	

483 Hewing Coal
(Thomas Hepburn)

484 Machinery
(Robert Owen)

485 Chimney Cleaning
(Lord Shaftesbury)

486 Hands clutching Prison Bars
(Elizabeth Fry)

Social Reformers

1976 (28 Apr.) 'All-over' phosphor

1001	**483**	8½p multicoloured	25	20	☐	☐
1002	**484**	10p multicoloured	40	40	☐	☐
1003	**485**	11p black, slate-grey and drab	50	50	☐	☐
1004	**486**	13p slate-grey, black and green	60	60	☐	☐
Set of 4			1·60	1·60	☐	☐
First Day Cover				2·00		☐
Presentation Pack (P.O. Pack No. 79)			2·75		☐	
PHQ Card (No. 1001) (14)			6·00	20·00	☐	☐
Set of 4 Gutter Pairs			3·25		☐	
Set of 4 Traffic Light Gutter Pairs			9·00		☐	

The Bicentennial
of American
Independence
1776-1976

487 Benjamin Franklin
(bust. by Jean-Jacques Caffieri)

Bicentenary of American Revolution

1976 (2 June) 'All-over' phosphor

1005	**487**	11p multicoloured	50	50	☐	☐
First Day Cover				1·50		☐
Presentation Pack (P.O. Pack No. 80)			1·50		☐	
PHQ Card (15)			5·00	20·00	☐	☐
Gutter Pair			1·20		☐	
Traffic Light Gutter Pair			2·50		☐	

488 'Elizabeth of Glamis'

489 'Grandpa Dickson'

490 'Rosa Mundi'

491 'Sweet Briar'

Centenary of Royal National Rose Society

1976 (30 June) 'All-over' phosphor

1006	**488**	8½p multicoloured	15	10	☐	☐
1007	**489**	10p multicoloured	40	40	☐	☐
1008	**490**	11p multicoloured	50	50	☐	☐
1009	**491**	13p multicoloured	65	65	☐	☐
Set of 4			1·50	1·50	☐	☐
First Day Cover				2·00		☐
Presentation Pack (P.O. Pack No. 81)			3·00		☐	
PHQ Cards (*set of* 4) (16)			30·00	38·00	☐	☐
Set of 4 Gutter Pairs			3·25		☐	
Set of 4 Traffic Light Gutter Pairs			10·00		☐	

492 Archdruid

493 Morris Dancing

494 Scots Piper

495 Welsh Harpist

British Cultural Traditions

1976 (4 Aug.) 'All-over' phosphor

1010	**492**	8½p	multicoloured	25	20	
1011	**493**	10p	multicoloured	40	40	
1012	**494**	11p	multicoloured	45	45	
1013	**495**	13p	multicoloured	60	60	
Set of 4				1·50	1·50	
First Day Cover					2·00	
Presentation Pack (P.O. Pack No. 82)				2·50		
PHQ Cards (*set of* 4) (17)				18·00	30·00	
Set of 4 Gutter Pairs				3·25		
Set of 4 Traffic Light Gutter Pairs				12·00		

496 *The Canterbury Tales* — William Caxton 1476 — 8½p

497 *The Tretyse of Love* — William Caxton 1476 — 10p

498 *Game and Playe of Chesse* — William Caxton 1476 — 11p

499 *Early Printing Press* — William Caxton 1476 — 13p

500th Anniversary of British Printing

1976 (29 Sept.) 'All-over' phosphor

1014	**496**	8½p	black, blue and gold	25	20	
1015	**497**	10p	black, olive-green and gold	40	40	
1016	**498**	11p	black, grey and gold	45	45	
1017	**499**	13p	brown, ochre and gold	60	60	
Set of 4				1·50	1·50	
First Day Cover					2·00	
Presentation Pack (P.O. Pack No. 83)				2·75		
PHQ Cards (*set of* 4) (18)				10·00	28·00	
Set of 4 Gutter Pairs				3·25		
Set of 4 Traffic Light Gutter Pairs				7·00		

500 Virgin and Child

501 Angel with Crown

502 Angel appearing to Shepherds

503 The Three Kings

Christmas

1976 (24 Nov.) Designs show English medieval embroidery. One phosphor band (6½p) or 'all-over' phosphor (others)

1018	**500**	6½p	multicoloured	25	25	
1019	**501**	8½p	multicoloured	35	25	
1020	**502**	11p	multicoloured	40	45	
1021	**503**	13p	multicoloured	45	50	
Set of 4				1·30	1·30	
First Day Cover					1·80	
Presentation Pack (P.O. Pack No. 87)				2·75		
PHQ Cards (*set of* 4) (19)				4·50	26·00	
Set of 4 Gutter Pairs				2·75		
Set of 4 Traffic Light Gutter Pairs				7·00		

Collectors Pack 1976

1976 (24 Nov.) Comprises Nos. 997/1021

CP1021a	Collectors Pack	13·50	

504 Lawn Tennis

505 Table Tennis

506 Squash

507 Badminton

Racket Sports

1977 (12 Jan.) Phosphorised paper

1022	**504**	8½p	multicoloured	25	20	
1023	**505**	10p	multicoloured	40	40	
1024	**506**	11p	multicoloured	45	40	
1025	**507**	13p	multicoloured	45	50	
Set of 4				1·40	1·40	
First Day Cover					2·00	
Presentation Pack (P.O. Pack No. 89)				3·00		
PHQ Cards (*set of* 4) (20)				8·00	24·00	
Set of 4 Gutter Pairs				3·00		
Set of 4 Traffic Light Gutter Pairs				7·50		

508

1977 (2 Feb.)–**87** Type **508** Ordinary paper

1026	£1	bright yellow-green and blackish olive	3·00	25	☐ ☐
1026b	£1·30	pale drab and deep greenish blue *(3.8.83)*	5·50	6·00	☐ ☐
1026c	£1·33	pale mauve and grey-black *(28.8.84)*	7·50	8·00	☐ ☐
1026d	£1·41	pale drab and deep greenish blue *(17.9.85)*	8·50	8·50	☐ ☐
1026e	£1·50	pale mauve and grey-black *(2.9.86)*	6·00	5·00	☐ ☐
1026f	£1·60	pale drab and deep greenish blue *(15.9.87)*	6·50	7·00	☐ ☐
1027	£2	light emerald and purple-brown	9·00	50	☐ ☐
1028	£5	salmon and chalky blue	22·00	3·00	☐ ☐

Set of 8	60·00	32·00 ☐ ☐
Presentation pack (P.O. Pack No. 91) (small size) (Nos. 1026, 1027/8)	48·00	☐
Presentation Pack (P.O. Pack No 13 (large size)) (Nos. 1026, 1027/8)	£180	☐
Presentation Pack (P.O. Pack No. 14) (No. 1026f)	22·00	☐
Set of 8 Gutter Pairs	£140	☐
Set of 8 Traffic Light Gutter Pairs	£170	☐

First Day Covers
2 Feb. 1977	Nos. 1026, 1027/8	14·00	☐
3 Aug. 1983	No. 1026b	7·00	☐
28th Aug. 1984	No. 1026c	8·50	☐
17 Sept. 1985	No. 1026d	9·50	☐
2 Sept. 1986	No. 1026e	7·00	☐
15 Sept. 1987	No. 1026f	9·00	☐

509 Steroids — Conformational Analysis

8½**p**

510 Vitamin C — Synthesis

10ᵖ

511 Starch — Chromatography **11**ᵖ

512 Salt — Crystallography **13**ᵖ

Centenary of Royal Institute of Chemistry

1977 (2 Mar.) 'All-over' phosphor
1029	**509**	8½p	multicoloured	25	20 ☐ ☐
1030	**510**	10p	multicoloured	45	45 ☐ ☐
1031	**511**	11p	multicoloured	45	45 ☐ ☐
1032	**512**	13p	multicoloured	45	45 ☐ ☐
Set of 4				1·40	1·40 ☐ ☐

First Day Cover		1·80	☐
Presentation Pack (P.O. Pack No. 92)	3·00		☐
PHQ Cards (*set of* 4) (21)	8·00	18·00	☐ ☐
Set of 4 Gutter Pairs	3·00		☐
Set of 4 Traffic Light Gutter Pairs	7·00		☐

513

Silver Jubilee

1977 (11 May–15 June) 'All-over' phosphor
1033	**513**	8½p	multicoloured	25	25 ☐ ☐
1034		9p	multicoloured *(15 June)*	25	25 ☐ ☐
1035		10p	multicoloured	25	25 ☐ ☐
1036		11p	multicoloured	50	50 ☐ ☐
1037		13p	multicoloured	50	50 ☐ ☐
Set of 5				1·60	1·60 ☐ ☐

First Day Covers (2)		2·50	☐
Presentation Pack (ex 9p) (P.O. Pack No. 94)	2·00		☐
Souvenir Book (ex 9p) (P.O. Pack No. 93)	3·00		☐
PHQ Cards (*set of* 5) (22)	14·00	20·00	☐ ☐
Set of 5 Gutter Pairs	3·50		☐
Set of 5 Traffic Light Gutter Pairs	6·00		☐

13p

517 'Gathering of Nations'

Commonwealth Heads of Government Meeting, London

1977 (8 June) 'All-over' phosphor
1038	**517**	13p	black, deep green, rose and silver	50	50 ☐ ☐

First Day Cover		1·30	☐
Presentation Pack (P.O. Pack No. 95)	1·50		☐
PHQ Card (23)	5·00	6·00	☐ ☐
Gutter Pair	1·10		☐
Traffic Light Gutter Pair	1·50		☐

9ᵖ **9**ᵖ **9**ᵖ

518 Hedgehog *Erinaceus europaeus* **519** Brown Hare *Lepus capensis* **520** Red Squirrel *Sciurus vulgaris*

521 Otter   **522** Badger

British Wildlife

1977 (5 Oct.) 'All-over' phosphor

1039	**518**	9p multicoloured	25	20	☐	☐
		a. Strip of 5. Nos.1039/43	1·50	1·80	☐	☐
1040	**519**	9p multicoloured	25	25	☐	☐
1041	**520**	9p multicoloured	25	25	☐	☐
1042	**521**	9p multicoloured	25	25	☐	☐
1043	**522**	9p multicoloured	25	25	☐	☐
Set of 5			1·50	1·80	☐	☐
First Day Cover				3·00	☐	
Presentation Pack (P.O. Pack No. 96)			2·50		☐	
PHQ Cards (*set of* 5) (25)			3·00	7·00	☐	☐
Set of 10 Gutter Strip			3·25		☐	
Set of 10 Traffic Light Gutter Strip			5·00		☐	

Nos. 1039/43 were printed together, *se-tenant*, throughout the sheet.

523 'Three French Hens, Two Turtle Doves and a Partridge in a Pear Tree'   **524** 'Six Geese a laying, Five Gold Rings, Four Colly Birds'

525 'Eight Maids a-milking, Seven Swans a-swimming'   **526** 'Ten Pipers piping, Nine Drummers drumming'

527 'Twelve Lords a-leaping, Eleven Ladies Dancing'   **528** 'A Partridge in a Pear Tree'

Christmas

1977 (23 Nov.) One centre phosphor band (7p) or 'all-over' phosphor (9p)

1044	**523**	7p multicoloured	20	15	☐	☐
		a. Strip of 5. Nos. 1044/8	1·50	1·50	☐	☐
1045	**524**	7p multicoloured	20	15	☐	☐
1046	**525**	7p multicoloured	20	15	☐	☐
1047	**526**	7p multicoloured	20	15	☐	☐
1048	**527**	7p multicoloured	20	15	☐	☐
1049	**528**	9p multicoloured	35	30	☐	☐
Set of 6			1·60	1·60	☐	☐

First Day Cover		2·25		☐
Presentation Pack (P.O. Pack No. 97)	2·25		☐	
PHQ Cards (*set of* 6) (26)	3·00	6·00	☐	☐
Set of 6 Gutter Pairs	3·25		☐	
Set of 6 Traffic Light Gutter Pairs	5·50		☐	

Nos. 1044/9 depict the carol 'The Twelve Days of Christmas'. Nos. 1044/8 were printed horizontally *se-tenant* throughout the sheet.

Collectors Pack 1977

1977 (23 Nov.) Comprises Nos. 1022/5, 1029/49

CP1049b	Collectors Pack	9·00	☐

529 Oil — North Sea Production Platform   **530** Coal — Modern Pithead

531 Natural Gas — Flame Rising from Sea   **532** Electricity — Nuclear Power Station and Uranium Atom

Energy Resources

1978 (25 Jan.) 'All-over' phosphor

1050	**529**	9p multicoloured	25	25	☐	☐
1051	**530**	10½p multicoloured	25	25	☐	☐
1052	**531**	11p multicoloured	50	50	☐	☐
1053	**532**	13p multicoloured	50	50	☐	☐
Set of 4			1·40	1·40	☐	☐
First Day Cover				1·80	☐	
Presentation Pack (P.O. Pack No. 99)			2·00		☐	
PHQ Cards (*set of* 4) (27)			3·00	6·00	☐	☐
Set of 4 Gutter Pairs			3·00		☐	
Set of 4 Traffic Light Gutter Pairs			4·50		☐	

533 Tower of London   **534** Holyroodhouse

535 Caernarvon Castle   **536** Hampton Court Palace

British Architecture (Historic Buildings)

1978 (1 Mar.) 'All-over' phosphor

1054	**533**	9p	multicoloured	25	20	☐ ☐
1055	**534**	10½p	multicoloured	25	40	☐ ☐
1056	**535**	11p	multicoloured	60	40	☐ ☐
1057	**536**	13p	multicoloured	60	40	☐ ☐
Set of 4				1·50	1·50	☐ ☐
First Day Cover					1·80	☐ ☐
Presentation Pack (P.O. Pack No. 100)				2·00		☐
PHQ Cards (set of 4) (28)				3·00	6·00	☐ ☐
Set of 4 Gutter Pairs				3·25		☐
Set of 4 Traffic Light Gutter Pairs				4·50		☐
MS1058 121×90 mm. Nos. 1054/7				1·50	1·75	☐ ☐
First Day Cover					2·25	☐

No. **MS**1058 was sold at 53½p, the premium being used for the London 1980 Stamp Exhibition.

537 State Coach

538 St. Edward's Crown

539 The Sovereign's Orb

540 Imperial State Crown

25th Anniversary of Coronation

1978 (31 May) 'All-over' phosphor

1059	**537**	9p	gold and blue	35	25	☐ ☐
1060	**538**	10½p	gold and red	45	45	☐ ☐
1061	**539**	11p	gold and green	45	45	☐ ☐
1062	**540**	13p	gold and violet	50	50	☐ ☐
Set of 4				1·60	1·50	☐ ☐
First Day Cover					2·00	☐
Presentation Pack (P.O. Pack No. 101)				2·00		☐
Souvenir Book				3·00		
PHQ Cards (set of 4) (29)				3·00	6·00	☐ ☐
Set of 4 Gutter Pairs				3·25		☐
Set of 4 Traffic Light Gutter Pairs				4·25		☐

541 Shire Horse

542 Shetland Pony

543 Welsh Pony

544 Thoroughbred

Horses

1978 (5 July) 'All-over' phosphor

1063	**541**	9p	multicoloured	20	10	☐ ☐
1064	**542**	10½p	multicoloured	35	40	☐ ☐
1065	**543**	11p	multicoloured	35	45	☐ ☐
1066	**544**	13p	multicoloured	45	50	☐ ☐
Set of 4				1·20	1·30	☐ ☐
First Day Cover					1·80	☐
Presentation Pack (P.O. Pack No. 102)				1·80		☐
PHQ Cards (set of 4) (30)				2·25	5·75	☐ ☐
Set of 4 Gutter Pairs				3·00		☐
Set of 4 Traffic Light Gutter Pairs				4·50		☐

545 Penny-farthing and 1884 Safety Bicycle

546 1920 Touring Bicycles

547 Modern Small-wheel Bicycles

548 1978 Road-racers

Centenaries of Cyclists Touring Club and British Cycling Federation

1978 (2 Aug.) 'All-over' phosphor

1067	**545**	9p	multicoloured	25	20	☐ ☐
1068	**546**	10½p	multicoloured	35	40	☐ ☐
1069	**547**	11p	multicoloured	40	40	☐ ☐
1070	**548**	13p	multicoloured	50	50	☐ ☐
Set of 4				1·30	1·40	☐ ☐
First Day Cover					1·80	☐
Presentation Pack (P.O. Pack No. 103)				1·80		☐
PHQ Cards (set of 4) (31)				2·25	5·00	☐ ☐
Set of 4 Gutter Pairs				2·75		☐
Set of 4 Traffic Light Gutter Pairs				4·50		☐

549 Singing Carols round the Christmas Tree

550 The Waits

551 18th-Century Carol Singers

552 'The Boar's Head Carol'

Christmas

1978 (22 Nov.) One centre phosphor band (7p) or 'all-over' phosphor (others)

1071	**549**	7p	multicoloured	25	25	☐ ☐
1072	**550**	9p	multicoloured	25	25	☐ ☐
1073	**551**	11p	multicoloured	50	50	☐ ☐
1074	**552**	13p	multicoloured	50	50	☐ ☐

Set of 4		1·40	1·40	☐ ☐
First Day Cover			1·80	☐
Presentation Pack (P.O. Pack No. 104)		1·80		☐
PHQ Cards (set of 4) (32)		2·25	5·00	☐ ☐
Set of 4 Gutter Pairs		3·00		☐
Set of 4 Traffic Light Gutter Pairs		4·25		☐

Collectors Pack 1978

1978 (22 Nov.) Comprises Nos. 1050/7, 1059/74

CP1074a	Collectors Pack	10·00	☐

553 Old English Sheepdog
554 Welsh Springer Spaniel

555 West. Highland Terrier
556 Irish Setter

Dogs

1979 (7 Feb.) 'All-over' phosphor

1075	**553**	9p	multicoloured	25	20	☐ ☐
1076	**554**	10½p	multicoloured	40	40	☐ ☐
1077	**555**	11p	multicoloured	40	40	☐ ☐
1078	**556**	13p	multicoloured	40	50	☐ ☐
Set of 4				1·30	1·30	☐ ☐
First Day Cover					1·80	☐
Presentation Pack (P.O. Pack No. 106)				1·80		☐
PHQ Cards (set of 4) (33)				2·50	5·00	☐ ☐
Set of 4 Gutter Pairs				2·75		☐
Set of 4 Traffic Light Gutter Pairs				4·25		☐

557 Primrose
558 Daffodil

559 Bluebell
560 Snowdrop

Spring Wild Flowers

1979 (21 Mar.) 'All-over' phosphor

1079	**557**	9p	multicoloured	25	20	☐ ☐
1080	**558**	10½p	multicoloured	25	45	☐ ☐
1081	**559**	11p	multicoloured	50	45	☐ ☐
1082	**560**	13p	multicoloured	50	40	☐ ☐

Set of 4		1·40	1·40	☐ ☐
First Day Cover			1·80	☐
Presentation Pack (P.O. Pack No. 107)		1·80		☐
PHQ Cards (set of 4) (34)		2·50	4·50	☐ ☐
Set of 4 Gutter Pairs		3·00		☐
Set of 4 Traffic Light Gutter Pairs		4·25		☐

561
562
563
564

First Direct Elections to European Assembly

1979 (9 May) Phosphorised paper

1083	**561**	9p	multicoloured	25	20	☐ ☐
1084	**562**	10½p	multicoloured	35	35	☐ ☐
1085	**563**	11p	multicoloured	40	40	☐ ☐
1086	**564**	13p	multicoloured	45	40	☐ ☐
Set of 4				1·30	1·30	☐ ☐
First Day Cover					1·80	☐
Presentation Pack (P.O. Pack No. 108)				1·80		☐
PHQ Cards (set of 4) (35)				2·25	4·50	☐ ☐
Set of 4 Gutter Pairs				2·75		☐
Set of 4 Traffic Light Gutter Pairs				4·25		☐

Nos. 1083/6 show hands placing the flags of the member nations into ballot boxes.

565 'Saddling "Mahmoud" for the Derby, 1936' (Sir Alfred Munnings)
566 'The Liverpool Great National Steeple Chase, 1839' (aquatint by F. C.Turner)

567 'The First. Spring Meeting, Newmarket, 1793' (J.N. Sartorius)
568 'Racing at Dorsett Ferry, Windsor, 1684' (Francis Barlow)

Horseracing Paintings and Bicentenary of The Derby (9p)

1979 (6 June) 'All-over' phosphor

1087	**565**	9p	multicoloured	25	25	☐ ☐
1088	**566**	10½p	multicoloured	25	25	☐ ☐
1089	**567**	11p	multicoloured	50	50	☐ ☐
1090	**568**	13p	multicoloured	50	50	☐ ☐
Set of 4				1·40	1·40	☐ ☐
First Day Cover					1·80	☐
Presentation Pack (P.O. Pack No. 109)				1·80		☐
PHQ Cards (set of 4) (36)				2·25	4·50	☐ ☐

Set of 4 Gutter Pairs	3·00		☐
Set of 4 Traffic Light Gutter Pairs	4·25		☐

569 *The Tale of Peter Rabbit (Beatrix Potter)*

570 *The Wind in the Willows (Kenneth Grahame)*

571 *Winnie-the-Pooh (A.A. Milne)*

572 *Alice's Adventures in Wonderland (Lewis Carroll)*

International Year of the Child

1979 (11 July) 'All-over' phosphor

1091	**569**	9p	multicoloured	30	25	☐	☐
1092	**570**	10½p	multicoloured	35	35	☐	☐
1093	**571**	11p	multicoloured	40	40	☐	☐
1094	**572**	13p	multicoloured	60	60	☐	☐
Set of 4				1·50	1·50	☐	☐
First Day Cover					2·00	☐	
Presentation Pack (P.O. Pack No. 110)				1·80		☐	
PHQ Cards (set of 4) (37)				2·50	4·50	☐	☐
Set of 4 Gutter Pairs				3·50		☐	
Set of 4 Traffic Light Gutter Pairs				4·25		☐	

Nos. 1091/4 depict original illustrations from the four books.

573 *Sir Rowland Hill, 1795-1879*

574 *General Post, c 1839*

575 *London Post, c 1839*

576 *Uniform Postage, 1840*

Death Centenary of Sir Rowland Hill (postal reformer)

1979 (22 Aug.–24 Oct.) 'All-over' phosphor

1095	**573**	10p	multicoloured	25	20	☐	☐
1096	**574**	11½p	multicoloured	25	35	☐	☐
1097	**575**	13p	multicoloured	50	45	☐	☐
1098	**576**	15p	multicoloured	75	50	☐	☐
Set of 4				1·60	1·40	☐	☐
First Day Cover					2·00	☐	
Presentation Pack (P.O. Pack No. 111)				2·50		☐	
PHQ Cards (set of 4) (38)				2·25	4·25	☐	☐
Set of 4 Gutter Pairs				3·25		☐	
Set of 4 Traffic Light Gutter Pairs				4·25		☐	
MS1099 89 × 121 mm. Nos. 1095/8				1·30	1·50	☐	☐
First Day Cover (24.10.79)					1·70		☐

No. **MS**1099 was sold at 59½p, the premium being used for the London 1980 Stamp Exhibition.

577 *Policeman on the Beat*

578 *Policeman directing Traffic*

579 *Mounted Policewoman*

580 *River Patrol Boat*

150th Anniversary of Metropolitan Police

1979 (26 Sept.) Phosphorised paper

1100	**577**	10p	multicoloured	30	20	☐	☐
1101	**578**	11½p	multicoloured	35	35	☐	☐
1102	**579**	13p	multicoloured	40	55	☐	☐
1103	**580**	15p	multicoloured	60	55	☐	☐
Set of 4				1·50	1·50	☐	☐
First Day Cover					2·00		☐
Presentation Pack (P.O. Pack No. 112)				1·80		☐	
PHQ Cards (set of 4) (39)				2·25	4·25	☐	☐
Set of 4 Gutter Pairs				3·25		☐	
Set of 4 Traffic Light Gutter Pairs				4·25		☐	

581 *The Three Kings*

582 *Angel appearing to the Shepherds*

583 *The Nativity*

584 *Mary and Joseph travelling to Bethlehem*

585 The Annunciation

590 *Rocket* approaching Moorish Arch, Liverpool
591 First. and Second Class Carriages passing through Olive Mount Cutting

Christmas

1979 (21 Nov.) One centre phosphor band (8p) or phosphorised paper (others)

1104	**581**	8p	multicoloured	25	20	☐☐
1105	**582**	10p	multicoloured	25	25	☐☐
1106	**583**	11½p	multicoloured	25	35	☐☐
1107	**584**	13p	multicoloured	50	50	☐☐
1108	**585**	15p	multicoloured	50	50	☐☐
Set of 5				1·60	1·60	☐☐
First Day Cover					2·00	☐
Presentation Pack (P.O. Pack No. 113)				2·00		☐
PHQ Cards (*set of 5*) (40)				2·50	4·25	☐☐
Set of 5 Gutter Pairs				3·50		☐
Set of 5 Traffic Light Gutter Pairs				4·50		☐

592 Third Class Carriage and Sheep Truck crossing Chat Moss
593 Horsebox and Carriage Truck near Bridgewater Canal

Collectors Pack 1979

1979 (21 Nov.) Comprises Nos. 1075/98, 1100/8

CP1108a	Collectors Pack	12·00	☐

594 Goods Truck and Mailcoach at Manchester

150th Anniversary of Liverpool and Manchester Railway

1980 (12 Mar.) Phosphorised paper

1113	**590**	12p	multicoloured	20	15	☐☐
			a. Strip of 5. Nos. 1113/17	1·80	1·80	☐☐
1114	**591**	12p	multicoloured	20	15	☐☐
1115	**592**	12p	multicoloured	20	15	☐☐
1116	**593**	12p	multicoloured	20	15	☐☐
1117	**594**	12p	multicoloured	20	15	☐☐
Set of 5				1·80	1·80	☐☐
First Day Cover					2·25	☐
Presentation Pack (P.O. Pack No. 116)				2·25		☐
PHQ Cards (*set of 5*) (42)				3·25	4·50	☐☐
Gutter block of 10				3·75		☐

Nos. 1113/7 were printed together, *se-tenant*, in horizontal strips of five throughout the sheet.

586 Common Kingfisher

587 Dipper

588 Moorhen

589 Yellow Wagtails

Centenary of Wild Bird Protection Act

1980 (16 Jan.) Phosphorised paper

1109	**586**	10p	multicoloured	20	10	☐☐
1110	**587**	11½p	multicoloured	40	35	☐☐
1111	**588**	13p	multicoloured	50	55	☐☐
1112	**589**	15p	multicoloured	50	55	☐☐
Set of 4				1·50	1·40	☐☐
First Day Cover					2·00	☐
Presentation Pack (P.O. Pack No. 115)				2·25		☐
PHQ Cards (*set of 4*) (41)				2·25	4·50	☐☐
Set of 4 Gutter Pairs				3·50		☐

INTERNATIONAL STAMP EXHIBITION
595 Montage of London Buildings

'London 1980' International Stamp Exhibition

1980 (9 Apr.–7 May) Phosphorised paper. Perf 14½ × 14

1118	**595**	50p	agate	1·50	1·50	☐☐
First Day Cover					2·00	☐
Presentation Pack (P.O. Pack No. 117)				1·80		☐
PHQ Card (43)				1·00	3·00	☐☐
Gutter Pair				3·25		☐

MS1119 90 × 123 mm. No. 1118   1·50   1·80 ☐ ☐
First Day Cover *(7.5.80)*   2·00   ☐

No. **MS**1119 was sold at 75p, the premium being used for the exhibition.

10½ᵖ Buckingham Palace   12ᵖ The Albert Memorial   13½ᵖ Royal Opera House

596 Buckingham Palace   **597** The Albert Memorial   **598** Royal Opera House

15ᵖ Hampton Court   17½ᵖ Kensington Palace

599 Hampton Court   **600** Kensington Palace

London Landmarks

1980 (7 May) Phosphorised paper

1120	**596**	10½p	multicoloured	25	10	☐ ☐
1121	**597**	12p	multicoloured	25	15	☐ ☐
1122	**598**	13½p	multicoloured	40	50	☐ ☐
1123	**599**	15p	multicoloured	50	75	☐ ☐
1124	**600**	17½p	multicoloured	75	75	☐ ☐
Set of 5				2·00	2·00	☐ ☐
First Day Cover					2·50	☐
Presentation Pack (P.O. Pack No. 118)				2·00		☐
PHQ Cards (*set of* 5) (43)				2·25	3·00	☐ ☐
Set of 5 Gutter Pairs				4·25		☐

12ᵖ   13½ᵖ

601 Charlotte Brontë *(Jane Eyre)*   **602** George Eliot *(The Mill on the Floss)*

15ᵖ   17½ᵖ

603 Emily Brontë *(Wuthering Heights)*   **604** Mrs Gaskell *(North and South)*

Famous Authoresses

1980 (9 July) Phosphorised paper

1125	**601**	12p	multicoloured	35	20	☐ ☐
1126	**602**	13½p	multicoloured	40	45	☐ ☐
1127	**603**	15p	multicoloured	40	45	☐ ☐
1128	**604**	17½p	multicoloured	50	50	☐ ☐
Set of 4				1·50	1·50	☐ ☐
First Day Cover					2·00	☐
Presentation Pack (P.O. Pack No. 119)				1·80		☐

PHQ Cards (*set of* 4) (44)   2·50   3·00 ☐ ☐
Set of 4 Gutter Pairs   3·75   ☐

Nos. 1125/8 show authoresses and scenes from their novels. Nos. 1125/6 also include the 'Europa' C.E.P.T. emblem.

605 Queen Elizabeth the Queen Mother

80th Birthday of Queen Elizabeth the Queen Mother

1980 (4 Aug.) Phosphorised paper

1129	**605**	12p	multicoloured	30	50	☐ ☐
First Day Cover					1·50	☐
PHQ Card (45)				1·00	2·00	☐ ☐
Gutter Pair				1·00		☐

12ᵖ   13½ᵖ

606 Sir Henry Wood   **607** Sir Thomas Beecham

15ᵖ   17½ᵖ

608 Sir Malcolm Sargent   **609** Sir John Barbirolli

British Conductors

1980 (10 Sept.) Phosphorised paper

1130	**606**	12p	multicoloured	30	10	☐ ☐
1131	**607**	13½p	multicoloured	45	40	☐ ☐
1132	**608**	15p	multicoloured	50	55	☐ ☐
1133	**609**	17½p	multicoloured	50	55	☐ ☐
Set of 4				1·60	1·50	☐ ☐
First Day Cover					2·00	☐
Presentation Pack (P.O. Pack No. 120)				1·80		☐
PHQ Cards (*set of* 4) (46)				2·25	3·75	☐ ☐
Set of 4 Gutter Pairs				3·75		☐

610 Running

611 Rugby

612 Boxing

613 Cricket

Sports Centenaries

1980 (10 Oct.) Phosphorised paper. Perf 14 × 14½

1134	**610**	12p	multicoloured	25	20		
1135	**611**	13½p	multicoloured	50	50		
1136	**612**	15p	multicoloured	50	45		
1137	**613**	17½p	multicoloured	50	50		
Set of 4				1·60	1·50		
First Day Cover					2·00		
Presentation Pack (P.O. Pack No. 121)				1·75			
PHQ Cards (*set of* 4) (47)				2·25	3·75		
Set of 4 Gutter Pairs				3·75			

Centenaries:—12p Amateur Athletics Association; 13½p Welsh Rugby Union; 15p Amateur Boxing Association; 17½p First England v Australia Test Match.

614 Christmas Tree

615 Candles

616 Apples and Mistletoe

617 Crown, Chains and Bell

618 Holly

Christmas

1980 (19 Nov.) One centre phosphor band (10p) or phosphorised paper (others)

1138	**614**	10p	multicoloured	20	10		
1139	**615**	12p	multicoloured	20	20		
1140	**616**	13½p	multicoloured	40	40		
1141	**617**	15p	multicoloured	55	50		
1142	**618**	17½p	multicoloured	55	50		
Set of 5				1·80	1·50		
First Day Cover					2·00		
Presentation Pack (P.O. Pack No. 122)				2·00			
PHQ Cards (*set of* 5) (48)				2·25	4·00		
Set of 5 Gutter Pairs				4·50			

Collectors Pack 1980

1980 (19 Nov.) Comprises Nos. 1109/18, 1120/42

CP1142a	Collectors Pack	15·00	

619 St. Valentine's Day

620 Morris Dancers

621 Lammastide

622 Medieval Mummers

Folklore

1981 (6 Feb.) Phosphorised paper

1143	**619**	14p	multicoloured	25	25		
1144	**620**	18p	multicoloured	50	50		
1145	**621**	22p	multicoloured	75	80		
1146	**622**	25p	multicoloured	1·00	1·10		
Set of 4				2·25	2·40		
First Day Cover					2·50		
Presentation Pack (P.O. Pack No. 124)				2·50			
PHQ Cards (*set of* 4) (49)				2·25	3·25		
Set of 4 Gutter Pairs				4·50			

Nos. 1143/4 also include the 'Europa' C.E.P.T. emblem.

623 Blind Man with Guide Dog

624 Hands spelling 'Deaf' in Sign Language

625 Disabled Man in Wheelchair

626 Disabled Artist. painting with Foot

International Year of the Disabled

1981 (25 Mar.) Phosphorised paper

1147	**623**	14p multicoloured	50	25	☐	☐
1148	**624**	18p multicoloured	50	50	☐	☐
1149	**625**	22p multicoloured	75	85	☐	☐
1150	**626**	25p multicoloured	1·00	1·00	☐	☐
Set of 4			2·50	2·40	☐	☐
First Day Cover				3·00	☐	☐
Presentation Pack (P.O. Pack No. 125)			2·75		☐	
PHQ Cards (*set of* 4) (50)			2·25	3·25	☐	☐
Set of 4 Gutter Pairs			5·25		☐	

627 *Aglais urticae*

628 *Maculinea arion*

629 *Inachis io*

630 *Carterocephalus palaemon*

Butterflies

1981 (13 May) Phosphorised paper

1151	**627**	14p multicoloured	25	20	☐	☐
1152	**628**	18p multicoloured	75	70	☐	☐
1153	**629**	22p multicoloured	70	85	☐	☐
1154	**630**	25p multicoloured	75	85	☐	☐
Set of 4			2·25	2·40	☐	☐
First Day Cover				3·00	☐	
Presentation Pack (P.O. Pack No. 126)			2·50		☐	
PHQ Cards (*set of* 4) (51)			2·25	6·00	☐	☐
Set of 4 Gutter Pairs			4·75		☐	

631 Glenfinnan, Scotland

632 Derwentwater, England

633 Stackpole Head, Wales

634 Giant's Causeway, N. Ireland

635 St. Kilda, Scotland

50th Anniversary of National Trust for Scotland (British landscapes)

1981 (24 June) Phosphorised paper

1155	**631**	14p multicoloured	15	25	☐	☐
1156	**632**	18p multicoloured	45	50	☐	☐
1157	**633**	20p multicoloured	70	75	☐	☐
1158	**634**	22p multicoloured	75	1·00	☐	☐
1159	**635**	25p multicoloured	90	1·00	☐	☐
Set of 5			2·60	3·00	☐	☐
First Day Cover				3·50		☐
Presentation Pack (P.O. Pack No. 127)			3·00		☐	
PHQ Cards (*set of* 5) (52)			2·50	5·00	☐	☐
Set of 5 Gutter Pairs			5·50		☐	

636 Prince Charles and Lady Diana Spencer

Royal Wedding

1981 (22 July) Phosphorised paper

1160	**636**	14p multicoloured	75	25	☐	☐
1161		25p multicoloured	1·50	1·50	☐	☐
Set of 2			2·00	1·50	☐	☐
First Day Cover				2·75		☐
Presentation Pack (P.O. Pack No. 127a)			3·00		☐	
Souvenir Book			3·00		☐	
PHQ Cards (*set of* 2) (53)			1·50	5·00	☐	☐
Set of 2 Gutter Pairs			4·25		☐	

637 'Expeditions'

638 'Skills'

639 'Service'

640 'Recreation'

25th Anniversary of Duke of Edinburgh's Award Scheme

1981 (12 Aug.) Phosphorised paper. Perf 14

1162	**637**	14p multicoloured	25	20	☐	☐
1163	**638**	18p multicoloured	45	50	☐	☐
1164	**639**	22p multicoloured	80	80	☐	☐
1165	**640**	25p multicoloured	90	1·00	☐	☐

Set of 4		2·25	2·40	☐	☐
First Day Cover			3·00		☐
Presentation Pack (P.O. Pack No. 128)		2·50			☐
PHQ Cards (set of 4) (54)		2·50	4·50	☐	☐
Set of 4 Gutter Pairs		5·00			☐

641 Cockle-dredging from
Lindsey II

642 Hauling Trawl Net

643 Lobster Potting

644 Hoisting Seine Net

Fishing Industry

1981 (23 Sept.) Phosphorised paper

1166	**641**	14p	multicoloured	25	25	☐ ☐
1167	**642**	18p	multicoloured	50	50	☐ ☐
1168	**643**	22p	multicoloured	85	85	☐ ☐
1169	**644**	25p	multicoloured	85	85	☐ ☐
Set of 4				2·25	2·25	☐ ☐
First Day Cover					2·75	☐
Presentation Pack (P.O. Pack No. 129)				2·50		☐
PHQ Cards (set of 4) (55)				2·25	4·50	☐ ☐
Set of 4 Gutter Pairs				5·00		☐

Nos. 1166/9 were issued on the occasion of the centenary of Royal National Mission to Deep Sea Fishermen.

645 Father Christmas

646 Jesus Christ

647 Flying Angel

648 Joseph and Mary arriving at Bethlehem

649 Three Kings approaching Bethlehem

Christmas. Children's Pictures

1981 (18 Nov.) One phosphor band (11½p) or phosphorised paper (others)

1170	**645**	11½p	multicoloured	25	20	☐ ☐
1171	**646**	14p	multicoloured	35	20	☐ ☐
1172	**647**	18p	multicoloured	50	60	☐ ☐
1173	**648**	22p	multicoloured	75	75	☐ ☐
1174	**649**	25p	multicoloured	85	85	☐ ☐
Set of 5				2·50	2·40	☐ ☐
First Day Cover					3·00	☐
Presentation Pack (P.O. Pack No. 130)				3·00		☐
PHQ Cards (set of 5) (56)				2·25	5·50	☐ ☐
Set of 5 Gutter Pairs				5·25		☐

Collectors Pack 1981

1981 (18 Nov.) Comprises Nos. 1143/74

CP1174a	Collectors Pack	19·00	☐

650 Charles Darwin and Giant Tortoises

651 Darwin and Marine Iguanas

652 Darwin, Cactus Ground Finch and Large Ground Finch

653 Darwin and Prehistoric Skulls

Death Centenary of Charles Darwin

1982 (10 Feb.) Phosphorised paper

1175	**650**	15½p	multicoloured	50	20	☐ ☐
1176	**651**	19½p	multicoloured	50	60	☐ ☐
1177	**652**	26p	multicoloured	75	85	☐ ☐
1178	**653**	29p	multicoloured	95	90	☐ ☐
Set of 4				2·50	2·40	☐ ☐
First Day Cover					3·00	☐
Presentation Pack (P.O. Pack No. 132)				3·00		☐
PHQ Cards (set of 4) (57)				2·50	6·00	☐ ☐
Set of 4 Gutter Pairs				5·25		☐

654 Boys' Brigade

655 Girls' Brigade

656 Boy Scout Movement

657 Girl Guide Movement

Youth Organizations

1982 (24 Mar.) Phosphorised paper

1179	**654**	15½p	multicoloured	25	15	☐ ☐
1180	**655**	19½p	multicoloured	50	50	☐ ☐
1181	**656**	26p	multicoloured	85	85	☐ ☐
1182	**657**	29p	multicoloured	1·00	1·10	☐ ☐
Set of 4				2·40	2·40	☐ ☐
First Day Cover					3·00	☐
Presentation Pack (P.O. Pack No. 133)				3·00		☐
PHQ Cards (*set of 4*) (58)				2·50	6·00	☐ ☐
Set of 4 Gutter Pairs				5·25		

Nos. 1179/82 were issued on the occasion of the 75th anniversary of the Boy Scout Movement, the 125th birth anniversary of Lord Baden-Powell and the centenary of the Boys' Brigade (1983).

658 Ballerina

659 Harlequin

660 Hamlet

661 Opera Singer

Europa. British Theatre

1982 (28 Apr.) Phosphorised paper

1183	**658**	15½p	multicoloured	25	15	☐ ☐
1184	**659**	19½p	multicoloured	50	50	☐ ☐
1185	**660**	26p	multicoloured	85	1·00	☐ ☐
1186	**661**	29p	multicoloured	1·25	1·25	☐ ☐
Set of 4				2·40	2·40	☐ ☐
First Day Cover					3·00	☐
Presentation Pack (P.O. Pack No. 134)				3·00		☐
PHQ Cards (*set of 4*) (59)				2·50	6·00	☐ ☐
Set of 4 Gutter Pairs				5·25		☐

662 Henry VIII and *Mary Rose*

663 Admiral Blake and *Triumph*

664 Lord Nelson and HMS *Victory*

665 Lord Fisher and HMS *Dreadnought*

666 Viscount Cunningham and HMS *Warspite*

Maritime Heritage

1982 (16 June) Phosphorised paper

1187	**662**	15½p	multicoloured	35	25	☐ ☐
1188	**663**	19½p	multicoloured	50	50	☐ ☐
1189	**664**	24p	multicoloured	75	85	☐ ☐
1190	**665**	26p	multicoloured	75	85	☐ ☐
1191	**666**	29p	multicoloured	1·00	1·00	☐ ☐
Set of 5				3·00	3·25	☐ ☐
First Day Cover					4·00	☐
Presentation Pack (P.O. Pack No. 136)				3·50		☐
PHQ Cards (*set of 5*) (60)				2·50	6·00	☐ ☐
Set of 5 Gutter Pairs				6·50		☐

667 'Strawberry Thief' (William Morris)

668 Untitled (Steiner and Co)

669 'Cherry Orchard' (Paul Nash)

670 'Chevron' (Andrew Foster)

British Textiles

1982 (23 July) Phosphorised paper

1192	**667**	15½p multicoloured	25	25	☐	☐
1193	**668**	19½p multicoloured	75	75	☐	☐
1194	**669**	26p multicoloured	75	1·00	☐	☐
1195	**670**	29p multicoloured	1·00	1·25	☐	☐
Set of 4			2·50	2·75	☐	☐
First Day Cover				3·25		☐
Presentation Pack (P.O. Pack No. 137)			3·00		☐	
PHQ Cards (*set of* 4) (61)			2·50	6·00	☐	☐
Set of 4 Gutter Pairs			5·50		☐	

Nos 1192/5 were issued on the occasion of the 250th birth anniversary of Sir Richard Arkwright (inventor of spinning machine).

671 Development of Communications

672 Modern Technological Aids

Information Technology

1982 (8 Sept.) Phosphorised paper. Perf 14 × 15

1196	**671**	15½p multicoloured	50	25	☐	☐
1197	**672**	26p multicoloured	75	1·00	☐	☐
Set of 2			1·10	1·10	☐	☐
First Day Cover				1·75		☐
Presentation Pack (P.O. Pack No. 138)			2·00		☐	
PHQ Cards (*set of* 2) (62)			2·00	5·25	☐	☐
Set of 2 Gutter Pairs			2·75		☐	

673 Austin 'Seven' and 'Metro'

675 Jaguar 'SS1' and 'XJ6'

676 Rolls-Royce 'Silver Ghost' and 'Silver Spirit'

British Motor Industry

1982 (13 Oct.) Phosphorised paper. Perf 14½ × 14

1198	**673**	15½p multicoloured	50	25	☐	☐
1199	**674**	19½p multicoloured	75	75	☐	☐
1200	**675**	26p multicoloured	75	75	☐	☐
1201	**676**	29p multicoloured	1·00	1·00	☐	☐
Set of 4			2·75	2·75	☐	☐
First Day Cover				3·00		☐
Presentation Pack (P.O. Pack No. 139)			3·25		☐	
PHQ Cards (*set of* 4) (63)			2·50	6·00	☐	☐
Set of 4 Gutter Pairs			5·50		☐	

677 'While Shepherds Watched'

678 'The Holly and the Ivy'

679 'I Saw Three Ships'

680 'We Three Kings'

681 'Good King Wenceslas'

Christmas. Carols

1982 (17 Nov.) One phosphor band (12½p) or phosphorised paper (others)

1202	**677**	12½p multicoloured	30	30	☐	☐
1203	**678**	15½p multicoloured	50	30	☐	☐
1204	**679**	19½p multicoloured	65	75	☐	☐
1205	**680**	26p multicoloured	75	90	☐	☐
1206	**681**	29p multicoloured	1·00	1·00	☐	☐
Set of 5			3·00	3·00	☐	☐
First Day Cover				3·25		☐
Presentation Pack (P.O. Pack No. 140)			3·50		☐	
PHQ Cards (*set of* 5) (64)			2·50	6·00	☐	☐
Set of 5 Gutter Pairs			6·50		☐	

Collectors Pack 1982

1982 (17 Nov.) Comprises Nos. 1175/1206

CP1206a	Collectors Pack	22·00		☐

682 Atlantic Salmon

683 Northern Pike

684 Brown Trout

685 Eurasian Perch

British River Fish

1983 (26 Jan.) Phosphorised paper

1207	**682**	15½p multicoloured	30	35	☐	☐
1208	**683**	19½p multicoloured	60	60	☐	☐
1209	**684**	26p multicoloured	75	85	☐	☐
1210	**685**	29p multicoloured	1·00	1·10	☐	☐
Set of 4			2·50	2·50	☐	☐

First Day Cover		3·00	☐
Presentation Pack (P.O. Pack No. 142)	3·00		☐
PHQ Cards (set of 4) (65)	3·00	7·00	☐ ☐
Set of 4 Gutter Pairs	5·50		☐

686 Tropical Island

687 Desert

688 Temperate Farmland

689 Mountain Range

Commonwealth Day. Geographical Regions

1983 (9 Mar.) Phosphorised paper

1211	686	15½p	multicoloured	40	30	☐	☐
1212	687	19½p	multicoloured	75	75	☐	☐
1213	688	26p	multicoloured	75	75	☐	☐
1214	689	29p	multicoloured	1·00	1·00	☐	☐
Set of 4				2·50	2·50	☐	☐
First Day Cover					3·00	☐	
Presentation Pack (P.O. Pack No. 143)				3·00		☐	
PHQ Cards (set of 4) (66)				2·50	6·50	☐	☐
Set of 4 Gutter Pairs				5·50		☐	

690 Humber Bridge

691 Thames Flood Barrier

692 *Iolair* (oilfield emergency support vessel)

Europa. Engineering Achievements

1983 (25 May) Phosphorised paper

1215	690	16p	multicoloured	50	40	☐	☐
1216	691	20½p	multicoloured	1·00	1·00	☐	☐
1217	692	28p	multicoloured	1·00	1·00	☐	☐
Set of 3				2·25	2·00	☐	☐
First Day Cover					2·50	☐	
Presentation Pack (P.O. Pack No. 144)				3·00		☐	
PHQ Cards (set of 3) (67)				2·50	5·75	☐	☐
Set of 3 Gutter Pairs				5·00		☐	

693 Musketeer and Pikeman, The Royal Scots (1633)

694 Fusilier and Ensign, The Royal Welch Fusiliers (mid-18th-century)

695 Riflemen, 95th Rifles (The Royal Green Jackets) (1805)

696 Sergeant (khaki service uniform) and Guardsman full dress), The Irish Guards (1900).

697 Paratroopers, The Parachute Regiment (1983)

British Army Uniforms

1983 (6 July) Phosphorised paper

1218	693	16p	multicoloured	50	30	☐	☐
1219	694	20½p	multicoloured	50	60	☐	☐
1220	695	26p	multicoloured	75	90	☐	☐
1221	696	28p	multicoloured	75	90	☐	☐
1222	697	31p	multicoloured	75	85	☐	☐
Set of 5				3·00	3·25	☐	☐
First Day Cover					3·75	☐	
Presentation Pack (P.O. Pack No. 145)				3·50		☐	
PHQ Cards (set of 5) (68)				3·50	6·50	☐	☐
Set of 5 Gutter Pairs				6·50		☐	

Nos. 1218/22 were issued on the occasion of the 350th anniversary of The Royal Scots, the senior line regiment of the British Army.

698 20th-Century Garden, Sissinghurst

699 19th-Century Garden, Biddulph Grange

18TH CENTURY GARDEN
BLENHEIM
700 18th-Century
Garden, Blenheim

17TH CENTURY GARDEN
PITMEDDEN
701 17th-Century
Garden, Pitmedden

British Gardens

1983 (24 Aug.) Phosphorised paper. Perf 14

1223	**698**	16p	multicoloured	50	30	☐	☐
1224	**699**	20½p	multicoloured	50	55	☐	☐
1225	**700**	28p	multicoloured	75	1·00	☐	☐
1226	**701**	31p	multicoloured	1·00	1·00	☐	☐
Set of 4				2·50	2·50	☐	☐
First Day Cover					3·00	☐	
Presentation Pack (P.O. Pack No. 146)				3·00		☐	
PHQ Cards (*set of 4*) (69)				3·00	6·25	☐	☐
Set of 4 Gutter Pairs				5·50		☐	

702 Merry-go-round

703 Big Wheel, Helter-skelter and
Performing Animals

704 Side-shows

705 Early Produce Fair

British Fairs

1983 (5 Oct.) Phosphorised paper

1227	**702**	16p	multicoloured	35	35	☐	☐
1228	**703**	20½p	multicoloured	75	75	☐	☐
1229	**704**	28p	multicoloured	75	1·00	☐	☐
1230	**705**	31p	multicoloured	1·00	1·00	☐	☐
Set of 4				2·50	2·75	☐	☐
First Day Cover					3·25	☐	
Presentation Pack (P.O. Pack No. 147)				3·00		☐	
PHQ Cards (*set of 4*) (70)				3·00	6·25	☐	☐
Set of 4 Gutter Pairs				5·50		☐	

Nos. 1227/30 were issued to mark the 850th anniversary of
St Bartholomew's Fair, Smithfield, London.

706 'Christmas Post'
(Pillar box)

707 'The Three Kings'
(chimney-pots)

708 'World at Peace'
(Dove and Blackbird)

709 'Light of Christmas'
(street lamp)

710 'Christmas Dove'
(hedge sculpture)

Christmas

1983 (16 Nov.) One phosphor band (12½p) or phosphorised
paper (others)

1231	**706**	12½p	multicoloured	30	30	☐	☐
1232	**707**	16p	multicoloured	50	35	☐	☐
1233	**708**	20½p	multicoloured	75	1·00	☐	☐
1234	**709**	28p	multicoloured	75	1·00	☐	☐
1235	**710**	31p	multicoloured	1·25	1·25	☐	☐
Set of 5				3·25	3·50	☐	☐
First Day Cover					4·00	☐	
Presentation Pack (P.O. Pack No. 148)				3·50		☐	
PHQ Cards (*set of 5*) (71)				3·00	6·25	☐	☐
Set of 5 Gutter Pairs				7·00		☐	

Collectors Pack 1983

1983 (16 Nov.) Comprises Nos. 1207/35

CP1235a	Collectors Pack	25·00	☐

711 Arms of the College
of Arms

712 Arms of King Richard III
(founder)

713 Arms of the Earl
Marshal of England

714 Arms of the City of
London

500th Anniversary of College of Arms

1984 (17 Jan.) Phosphorised paper. Perf 14½

1236	**711**	16p	multicoloured	50	30	☐	☐
1237	**712**	20½p	multicoloured	50	65	☐	☐
1238	**713**	28p	multicoloured	1·00	1·10	☐	☐
1239	**714**	31p	multicoloured	1·25	1·25	☐	☐
Set of 4				3·00	3·00	☐	☐
First Day Cover					3·50	☐	
Presentation Pack (P.O. Pack No. 150)				3·25		☐	

PHQ Cards (set of 4) (72)	3·00	6·50	☐ ☐
Set of 4 Gutter Pairs		6·50	☐

16ᴾ Highland Cow
715 Highland Cow

20½ᴾ Chillingham Wild Bull
716 Chillingham Wild Bull

26ᴾ Hereford Bull
717 Hereford Bull

28ᴾ Welsh Black Bull
718 Welsh Black Bull

31ᴾ Irish Moiled Cow
719 Irish Moiled Cow

British Cattle

1984 (6 Mar.) Phosphorised paper

1240	**715**	16p	multicoloured	35	30	☐ ☐
1241	**716**	20½p	multicoloured	60	60	☐ ☐
1242	**717**	26p	multicoloured	80	80	☐ ☐
1243	**718**	28p	multicoloured	90	90	☐ ☐
1244	**719**	31p	multicoloured	1·00	1·20	☐ ☐
Set of 5				3·50	3·50	☐ ☐
First Day Cover					4·00	☐
Presentation Pack (P.O. Pack No.151)			4·00			☐
PHQ Cards (set of 5) (73)			3·00	6·50		☐ ☐
Set of 5 Gutter Pairs			7·25			☐

Nos. 1240/4 marked the centenary of the Highland Cattle Society and the bicentenary of the Royal Highland and Agricultural Society of Scotland.

16ᴾ
720 Festival Hall, Liverpool

20½ᴾ
721 Milburngate Shopping Centre, Durham

28ᴾ
722 Bush House, Bristol

31ᴾ
723 Commercial Street Housing Scheme, Perth

Urban Renewal

1984 (10 Apr.) Phosphorised paper

1245	**720**	16p	multicoloured	35	35	☐ ☐
1246	**721**	20½p	multicoloured	50	60	☐ ☐
1247	**722**	28p	multicoloured	1·25	1·25	☐ ☐
1248	**723**	31p	multicoloured	1·25	1·25	☐ ☐
Set of 4				3·00	3·00	☐ ☐
First Day Cover					3·50	☐
Presentation Pack (P.O. Pack No.152)			3·50			☐
PHQ Cards (set of 4) (74)			3·00	6·25		☐ ☐
Set of 4 Gutter Pairs			6·50			☐

Nos. 1245/8 marked the opening of the International Gardens Festival, Liverpool, and the 150th anniversaries of the Royal Institute of British Architects and the Chartered Institute of Building.

724 C.E.P.T. 25th Anniversary Logo
725 Abduction of Europa

Europa. 25th Anniversary of C.E.P.T. and 2nd European Parliamentary Elections

1984 (15 May) Phosphorised paper

1249	**724**	16p	greenish slate, deep blue and gold	60	50	☐ ☐
		a.	Horiz pair. Nos. 1249/50	1·50	1·50	☐ ☐
1250	**725**	16p	greenish slate, deep blue, black and gold	60	50	☐ ☐
1251	**724**	20½p	Venetian red, deep magenta and gold	70	40	☐ ☐
		a.	Horiz pair. Nos. 1251/2	2·50	2·50	☐ ☐
1252	**725**	20½p	Venetian red, deep magenta, black and gold	70	40	☐ ☐
Set of 4				3·50	3·50	☐ ☐
First Day Cover					4·00	☐
Presentation Pack (P.O. Pack No. 153)			4·00			☐
PHQ Cards (set of 4) (75)			3·00	6·25		☐ ☐
Set of 2 Gutter Blocks of 4			7·50			☐

Nos. 1249/50 and 1251/2 were each printed together, se-tenant, in horizontal pairs throughout the sheets.

726 Lancaster House

London Economic Summit Conference

1984 (5 June) Phosphorised paper

1253	**726**	31p	multicoloured	1·25	1·25	☐ ☐
First Day Cover					2·25	☐
PHQ Card (76)			1·00	3·50		☐ ☐
Gutter Pair			2·75			☐

727 View of Earth from 'Apollo 11'

728 Navigational Chart of English Channel

729 Greenwich Observatory

730 Sir George Airey's Transit Telescope

Centenary of Greenwich Meridian

1984 (26 June) Phosphorised paper. Perf 14 × 14½

1254	**727**	16p multicoloured	50	35		
1255	**728**	20½p multicoloured	75	80		
1256	**729**	28p multicoloured	1·00	1·00		
1257	**730**	31p multicoloured	1·00	1·10		
Set of 4			3·00	3·00		
First Day Cover				3·50		
Presentation Pack (P.O. Pack No. 154)			3·50			
PHQ Cards (set of 4) (77)			3·00	6·25		
Set of 4 Gutter Pairs			6·50			

731 Bath Mail Coach, 1784

732 Attack on Exeter Mail, 1816

733 Norwich Mail in Thunderstorm, 1827

734 Holyhead and Liverpool Mails leaving London, 1828

735 Edinburgh Mail Snowbound, 1831

Bicentenary of First Mail Coach Run, Bath and Bristol to London

1984 (31 July) Phosphorised paper

1258	**731**	16p multicoloured	40	35		
		a. Horiz strip of 5. Nos. 1258/62	2·50	2·75		
1259	**732**	16p multicoloured	40	35		
1260	**733**	16p multicoloured	40	35		
1261	**734**	16p multicoloured	40	35		
1262	**735**	16p multicoloured	40	35		
Set of 5			2·50	2·75		
First Day Cover				3·25		
Presentation Pack (P.O. Pack No. 155)			3·00			
Souvenir Book			7·50			
PHQ Cards (set of 5) (78)			3·00	6·50		
Gutter Block of 10			6·00			

Nos. 1285/62 were printed together, *se-tenant*, in horizontal strips of five throughout the sheet.

736 Nigerian Clinic

737 Violinist and Acropolis, Athens

738 Building Project, Sri Lanka

739 British Council Library

50th Anniversary of The British Council

1984 (25 Sept.) Phosphorised paper

1263	**736**	17p multicoloured	50	35		
1264	**737**	22p multicoloured	85	1·00		
1265	**738**	31p multicoloured	85	1·00		
1266	**739**	34p multicoloured	1·00	1·00		
Set of 4			3·00	3·00		
First Day Cover				3·50		
Presentation Pack (P.O. Pack No. 156)			3·25			
PHQ Cards (set of 4) (79)			3·00	6·25		
Set of 4 Gutter Pairs			6·50			

740 The Holy Family

741 Arrival in Bethlehem

742 Shepherd and Lamb

743 Virgin and Child

744 Offering of Frankincense

Christmas

1984 (20 Nov.) One phosphor band (13p) or phosphorised paper (others)

1267	**740**	13p	multicoloured	30	30	☐ ☐
1268	**741**	17p	multicoloured	50	50	☐ ☐
1269	**742**	22p	multicoloured	75	75	☐ ☐
1270	**743**	31p	multicoloured	1·00	1·00	☐ ☐
1271	**744**	34p	multicoloured	1·00	1·00	☐ ☐
Set of 5				3·25	3·25	☐ ☐
First Day Cover					3·75	☐
Presentation Pack (P.O. Pack No. 157)				3·75		☐
PHQ Cards (*set of* 5) (80)				3·00	6·25	☐ ☐
Set of 5 Gutter Pairs				7·00		☐

Collectors Pack 1984

1984 (20 Nov.) Comprises Nos. 1236/71

CP1271a	Collectors Pack	38·00	☐

Post Office Yearbook

1984 Comprises Nos. 1236/71 in hardbound book with slip case

YB1271a	Yearbook	85·00	☐

745 'Flying Scotsman'

746 'Golden Arrow'

747 'Cheltenham Flyer'

748 'Royal Scot'

749 'Cornish Riviera'

Famous Trains

1985 (22 Jan.) Phosphorised paper

1272	**745**	17p	multicoloured	75	35	☐ ☐
1273	**746**	22p	multicoloured	75	1·00	☐ ☐
1274	**747**	29p	multicoloured	1·00	1·25	☐ ☐
1275	**748**	31p	multicoloured	1·25	1·50	☐ ☐
1276	**749**	34p	multicoloured	2·50	2·50	☐ ☐
Set of 5				5·75	6·00	☐ ☐
First Day Cover					6·50	☐
Presentation Pack (P.O. Pack No. 159)				6·00		☐
PHQ Cards (*set of* 5) (81)				6·00	15·00	☐ ☐
Set of 5 Gutter Pairs				13·00		☐

Nos. 1272/6 were issued on the occasion of the 150th anniversary of the Great Western Railway Company.

750 *Bombus terrestris* (Bee)
Buff Tailed Bumble Bee

751 *Coccinella septempunctata* (ladybird)
Seven Spotted Ladybird

752 *Decticus verrucivorus* (bush-cricket)
Wart-Biter Bush-Cricket

753 *Lucanus cervus* (stag beetle)
Stag Beetle

754 *Anax imperator* (dragonfly)
Emperor Dragonfly

Insects

1985 (12 Mar.) Phosphorised paper

1277	**750**	17p	multicoloured	40	35	☐ ☐
1278	**751**	22p	multicoloured	60	60	☐ ☐
1279	**752**	29p	multicoloured	85	90	☐ ☐
1280	**753**	31p	multicoloured	1·00	1·00	☐ ☐
1281	**754**	34p	multicoloured	1·00	90	☐ ☐
Set of 5				3·25	3·50	☐ ☐
First Day Cover					4·00	☐
Presentation Pack (P.O. Pack No. 160)				4·50		☐
PHQ Cards (*set of* 5) (82)				3·00	7·50	☐ ☐
Set of 5 Gutter Pairs				7·00		☐

Nos. 1277/81 were issued on the occasion of the centenaries of the Royal Entomological Society of London's Royal Charter and of the Selborne Society.

SEVENTEEN·PENCE
WATER·MUSIC
George Frideric Handel
755 'Water Music', by Handel

TWENTY·TWO·PENCE
THE·PLANETS·SUITE
Gustav Holst
756 'The Planets', by Holst

THIRTY·ONE·PENCE
THE·FIRST·CUCKOO
Frederick Delius
757 'The First Cuckoo', by Delius

SEA·PICTURES
Edward Elgar
THIRTY·FOUR·PENCE
758 'Sea Pictures', by Elgar

Europa. European Music Year

1985 (14 May) Phosphorised paper. Perf 14½

1282	**755**	17p multicoloured	55	40	☐	☐
1283	**756**	22p multicoloured	1·00	1·00	☐	☐
1284	**757**	31p multicoloured	1·50	1·25	☐	☐
1285	**758**	34p multicoloured	1·50	1·25	☐	☐
Set of 4			4·00	3·50	☐	☐
First Day Cover				4·00		☐
Presentation Pack (P.O. Pack No. 161)			4·75		☐	
PHQ Cards (set of 4) (83)			3·00	6·50	☐	☐
Set of 4 Gutter Pairs			8·50		☐	

Nos. 1282/5 were issued on the occasion of the 300th birth anniversary of Handel.

759 R.N.L.I. Lifeboat and Signal Flags

760 Beachy Head Lighthouse and Chart

761 'Marecs A' Communications Satellite and Dish Aerials

762 Buoys

Safety at Sea

1985 (18 June) Phosphorised paper. Perf 14

1286	**759**	17p multicoloured	40	40	☐	☐
1287	**760**	22p multicoloured	60	75	☐	☐
1288	**761**	31p multicoloured	1·00	1·00	☐	☐
1289	**762**	34p multicoloured	1·50	1·25	☐	☐
Set of 4			3·00	3·25	☐	☐
First Day Cover				3·75		☐
Presentation Pack (P.O. Pack No. 162)			3·75		☐	
PHQ Cards (set of 4) (84)			3·00	6·50	☐	☐
Set of 4 Gutter Pairs			7·00		☐	

Nos. 1286/9 were issued to mark the bicentenary of the unimmersible lifeboat and the 50th anniversary of Radar.

763 Datapost Motorcyclist, City of London

764 Rural Postbus

765 Parcel Delivery in Winter

766 Town Letter Delivery

350 Years of Royal Mail Public Postal Service

1985 (30 July) Phosphorised paper

1290	**763**	17p multicoloured	50	40	☐	☐
1291	**764**	22p multicoloured	75	70	☐	☐
1292	**765**	31p multicoloured	1·00	1·00	☐	☐
1293	**766**	34p multicoloured	1·50	1·50	☐	☐
Set of 4			3·00	3·25	☐	☐
First Day Cover				3·75		☐
Presentation Pack (P.O. Pack No. 163)			3·75		☐	
PHQ Cards (set of 4) (85)			3·00	6·50	☐	☐
Set of 4 Gutter Pairs			6·50		☐	

767 King Arthur and Merlin

768 The Lady of the Lake

769 Queen Guinevere and Sir Lancelot

770 Sir Galahad

Arthurian Legends

1985 (3 Sept.) Phosphorised paper

1294	**767**	17p multicoloured	50	40	☐	☐
1295	**768**	22p multicoloured	75	75	☐	☐
1296	**769**	31p multicoloured	1·25	1·25	☐	☐
1297	**770**	34p multicoloured	1·25	1·25	☐	☐
Set of 4			3·50	3·25	☐	☐
First Day Cover				3·75		☐
Presentation Pack (P.O. Pack No.164)			4·00		☐	
PHQ Cards (set of 4) (86)			3·00	6·50	☐	☐
Set of 4 Gutter Pairs			7·50		☐	

Nos. 1294/7 were issued to mark the 500th anniversary of the printing of Sir Thomas Malory's *Morte d'Arthur*.

771 Peter Sellers (from photo by Bill Brandt)

772 David Niven (from photo by Cornell Lucas)

773 Charlie Chaplin (from photo by Lord Snowdon)

774 Vivien Leigh (from photo by Angus McBean)

775 Alfred Hitchcock
(from photo by Howard Coster)

British Film Year

1985 (8 Oct.) Phosphorised paper. Perf 14½

1298	**771**	17p multicoloured	45	40	☐	☐
1299	**772**	22p multicoloured	60	75	☐	☐
1300	**773**	29p multicoloured	1·00	1·25	☐	☐
1301	**774**	31p multicoloured	1·10	1·50	☐	☐
1302	**775**	34p multicoloured	1·40	1·50	☐	☐
Set of 5			4·00	4·75	☐	☐
First Day Cover				5·50		☐
Presentation Pack (P.O. Pack No. 165)			5·50		☐	
Souvenir Book			11·50		☐	
PHQ Cards (*set of* 5) (87)			3·00	10·00	☐	☐
Set of 5 Gutter Pairs			9·00		☐	

The souvenir book is a 24-page ullustrated booklet with a set of stamps in a sachet attached to the front cover

776 Principal Boy

777 Genie

778 Dame

779 Good Fairy

780 Pantomime Cat

Christmas. Pantomime Characters

1985 (19 Nov.) One phosphor band (12p) or phosphorised paper (others)

1303	**776**	12p multicoloured	50	30	☐	☐
1304	**777**	17p multicoloured	50	40	☐	☐
1305	**778**	22p multicoloured	75	1·10	☐	☐
1306	**779**	31p multicoloured	1·25	1·40	☐	☐
1307	**780**	34p multicoloured	1·25	1·40	☐	☐
Set of 5			4·00	4·25	☐	☐
First Day Cover				4·75		☐
Presentation Pack (P.O. Pack No. 166)			4·25		☐	
PHQ Cards (*set of* 5) (88)			3·00	6·50	☐	☐
Set of 5 Gutter Pairs			8·50		☐	

Collectors Pack 1985

1985 (19 Nov.) Comprises Nos. 1272/1307

CP1307a	Collectors Pack	35·00	☐

Post Office Yearbook

1985 Comprises Nos. 1272/1307 in hardbound book with slip case

YB1307a	Yearbook	75·00	☐

17 PENCE · INDUSTRY YEAR 1986 · **781** Light Bulb and North Sea Oil Drilling Rig (Energy)

22 PENCE · INDUSTRY YEAR 1986 · **782** Thermometer and Pharmaceutical Laboratory (Health)

31 PENCE · INDUSTRY YEAR 1986 · **783** Garden Hoe and Steel Works (Steel)

34 PENCE · INDUSTRY YEAR 1986 · **784** Loaf of Bread and Cornfield (Agriculture)

Industry Year

1986 (14 Jan.) Phosphorised paper. Perf 14½ × 14

1308	**781**	17p multicoloured	75	40	☐	☐
1309	**782**	22p multicoloured	50	75	☐	☐
1310	**783**	31p multicoloured	1·25	1·40	☐	☐
1311	**784**	34p multicoloured	1·25	1·40	☐	☐
Set of 4			3·50	3·50	☐	☐
First Day Cover				4·00		☐
Presentation Pack (P.O. Pack No. 168)			3·75		☐	
PHQ Cards (*set of* 4) (89)			3·50	6·50	☐	☐
Set of 4 Gutter Pairs			7·50		☐	

785 Dr Edmond Halley as Comet

786 Giotto Spacecraft approaching Comet

787 'Twice in a Lifetime'

788 Comet orbiting Sun and Planets

Appearance of Halley's Comet

1986 (18 Feb.) Phosphorised paper

1312	**785**	17p multicoloured	50	40	☐	☐
1313	**786**	22p multicoloured	75	75	☐	☐
1314	**787**	31p multicoloured	1·25	1·25	☐	☐
1315	**788**	34p multicoloured	1·25	1·40	☐	☐
Set of 4			3·50	3·50	☐	☐
First Day Cover				4·00		☐
Presentation Pack (P.O. Pack No. 168)*			3·75		☐	
PHQ Cards (*set of* 4) (90)			3·50	6·50	☐	☐
Set of 4 Gutter Pairs			7·50		☐	

*The presentation pack was incorrectly numbered "168".

Sixtieth Birthday 17p Sixtieth Birthday 17p

789 Queen Elizabeth II in 1928, 1942 and 1952 **790** Queen Elizabeth II in 1958, 1973 and 1982

60th Birthday of Queen Elizabeth II

1986 (21 Apr.) Phosphorised paper

1316	**789**	17p multicoloured	60	50	☐	☐
	a.	Horiz pair.				
		Nos. 1316/17	1·50	1·50	☐	☐
1317	**790**	17p multicoloured	60	50	☐	☐
1318	**789**	34p multicoloured	1·25	1·25	☐	☐
	a.	Horiz pair.				
		Nos. 1318/19	3·00	4·00	☐	☐
1319	**790**	34p multicoloured	1·25	1·25	☐	☐
Set of 4			4·50	5·00	☐	☐
First Day Cover				5·50		☐
Presentation Pack (P.O. Pack No. 170)			5·50		☐	
Souvenir Book			8·50		☐	
PHQ Cards (*set of* 4) (91)			5·00	6·50	☐	☐
Set of 2 Gutter Blocks of 4			9·50		☐	

Nos. 1316/17 and 1318/19 were each printed together, *se-tenant*, in horizontal pairs throughout the sheets.

The souvenir book is a special booklet, fully illustrated and containing a complete set of stamps.

791 Barn Owl

792 Pine Marten

793 Wild Cat

794 Natterjack Toad

Europa. Nature Conservation. Endangered Species

1986 (20 May) Phosphorised paper. Perf 14½ × 14

1320	**791**	17p multicoloured	40	45	☐	☐
1321	**792**	22p multicoloured	80	1·00	☐	☐
1322	**793**	31p multicoloured	1·50	1·25	☐	☐
1323	**794**	34p multicoloured	1·65	1·40	☐	☐
Set of 4			4·00	3·75	☐	☐
First Day Cover				4·25		☐
Presentation Pack (P.O. Pack No. 171)			4·50		☐	
PHQ Cards (*set of* 4) (92)			3·50	6·50	☐	☐
Set of 4 Gutter Pairs			8·50		☐	

795 Peasants Working in Fields

796 Freemen working at Town Trades

797 Knight and Retainers

798 Lord at Banquet

900th Anniversary of Domesday Book

1986 (17 June) Phosphorised paper

1324	**795**	17p multicoloured	40	45	☐	☐
1325	**796**	22p multicoloured	85	85	☐	☐
1326	**797**	31p multicoloured	1·25	1·40	☐	☐
1327	**798**	34p multicoloured	1·25	1·40	☐	☐
Set of 4			3·50	3·75	☐	☐
First Day Cover				4·25		☐
Presentation Pack (P.O. Pack No. 172)			4·00		☐	
PHQ Cards (*set of* 4) (93)			3·50	6·50	☐	☐
Set of 4 Gutter Pairs			7·50		☐	

799 Athletics

800 Rowing

801 Weightlifting

802 Rifle-shooting

803 Hockey

Thirteenth Commonwealth Games, Edinburgh (Nos. 1328/31) and World Men's Hockey Cup, London (No. 1332)

1986 (15 July) Phosphorised paper

1328	**799**	17p multicoloured	40	45	☐	☐
1329	**800**	22p multicoloured	55	75	☐	☐
1330	**801**	29p multicoloured	75	1·00	☐	☐
1331	**802**	31p multicoloured	1·50	1·75	☐	☐
1332	**803**	34p multicoloured	1·75	1·75	☐	☐
Set of 5			4·00	4·50	☐	☐
First Day Cover				5·00		☐
Presentation Pack (P.O. Pack No. 173)			4·50		☐	
PHQ Cards (*set of* 5) (94)			3·50	7·50	☐	☐

Set of 5 Gutter Pairs   8·75   ☐
No. 1332 also marked the centenary of the Hockey Association.

804 Prince Andrew
and Miss Sarah Ferguson

805 Prince Andrew
and Miss Sarah Ferguson

Royal Wedding

1986 (22 July) One side band (12p) or phosphorised paper
(17p)

1333	**804**	12p multicoloured	50	45	☐ ☐
1334	**805**	17p multicoloured	1·00	1·25	☐ ☐
Set of 2			1·50	1·50	☐ ☐
First Day Cover				2·00	☐
Presentation Pack (P.O. Pack No. 174)			1·75		☐
PHQ Cards (*set of* 2) (95)			2·25	5·00	☐ ☐
Set of 2 Gutter Pairs			3·25		☐

806 Stylised Cross on
Ballot Paper

32nd Commonwealth Parliamentary Conference, London

1986 (19 Aug.) Phosphorised paper. Perf 14 × 14½

1335	**806**	34p multicoloured	1·25	1·25	☐ ☐
First Day Cover				1·75	☐
PHQ Card (96)			1·00	3·00	☐ ☐
Gutter Pair			2·75		☐

807 Lord Dowding and
Hawker Hurricane I

808 Lord Tedder and
Hawker Typhoon 1B

809 Lord Trenchard and
de Havilland D.H.9A

810 Sir Arthur Harris and
Avro Lancaster

811 Lord Portal and de
Havilland DH.98 Mosquito

History of the Royal Air Force

1986 (16th Sept.) Phosphorised paper. Perf 14½ × 14

1336	**807**	17p multicoloured	50	45	☐ ☐
1337	**808**	22p multicoloured	75	95	☐ ☐
1338	**809**	29p multicoloured	1·25	1·25	☐ ☐
1339	**810**	31p multicoloured	1·75	1·60	☐ ☐
1340	**811**	34p multicoloured	1·75	1·90	☐ ☐
Set of 5			5·00	5·50	☐ ☐
First Day Cover				6·00	☐
Presentation Pack (P.O. Pack No. 175)			5·50		☐
PHQ Cards (*set of* 5) (97)			4·50	10·00	☐ ☐
Set of 5 Gutter Pairs			12·00		☐

Nos. 1336/40 were issued to celebrate the 50th anniversary of
the first R.A.F. Commands.

812 The Glastonbury Thorn

813 The Tanad Valley Plygain

814 The Hebrides Tribute

815 The Dewsbury Church Knell

816 The Hereford Boy Bishop

Christmas. Folk Customs

1986 (18 Nov.–2 Dec.) One phosphor band (12p, 13p) or
phosphorised paper (others)

1341	**812**	12p multicoloured *(2 Dec.)*	50	50	☐ ☐
1342		13p multicoloured	30	40	☐ ☐
1343	**813**	18p multicoloured	50	50	☐ ☐
1344	**814**	22p multicoloured	1·00	1·00	☐ ☐
1345	**815**	31p multicoloured	1·25	1·00	☐ ☐
1346	**816**	34p multicoloured	1·25	1·10	☐ ☐
Set of 6			4·25	4·00	☐ ☐
First Day Covers (2)				4·50	☐
Presentation Pack (Nos. 1342/6)					
		(P.O. Pack No. 176)	5·00		☐
PHQ Cards (*set of* 5) (Nos. 1342/6) (98)			3·50	6·50	☐ ☐
Set of 6 Gutter Pairs			9·00		☐

Collectors Pack 1986

1986 (18 Nov.) Comprises Nos. 1308/40, 1342/6
CP1346a   Collectors Pack   38·00   ☐

Post Office Yearbook

1986 Comprises Nos. 1308/40, 1342/6 in hardbound book with slip case
YB1346a   Yearbook   70·00   ☐

817 North American
Blanket Flower

818 Globe Thistle

819 Echeveria

820 Autumn Crocus

Flower Photographs by Alfred Lammer

1987 (20 Jan.) Phosphorised paper. Perf 14½ × 14

1347	**817**	18p	multicoloured	40	40	☐ ☐
1348	**818**	22p	multicoloured	70	85	☐ ☐
1349	**819**	31p	multicoloured	1·10	1·25	☐ ☐
1350	**820**	34p	multicoloured	1·10	1·25	☐ ☐
Set of 4				3·25	3·50	☐ ☐
First Day Cover					4·00	☐
Presentation Pack (P.O. Pack No. 178)				4·00		☐
PHQ Cards (set of 4) (99)				3·00	7·00	☐ ☐
Set of 4 Gutter Pairs				7·50		☐

821 The Principia
Mathematica

822 Motion of Bodies
in Ellipses

823 Optick Treatise

824 The System of
the World

300th Anniversary of The Principia Mathematica by Sir Isaac Newton

1987 (24 Mar.) Phosphorised paper

1351	**821**	18p	multicoloured	50	40	☐ ☐
1352	**822**	22p	multicoloured	75	75	☐ ☐
1353	**823**	31p	multicoloured	1·25	1·50	☐ ☐
1354	**824**	34p	multicoloured	1·25	1·25	☐ ☐
Set of 4				3·50	3·50	☐ ☐
First Day Cover					4·00	☐
Presentation Pack (P.O. Pack No. 179)				4·00		☐
PHQ Cards (set of 4) (100)				3·00	6·50	☐ ☐
Set of 4 Gutter Pairs				8·00		☐

825 Willis Faber and Dumas Building, **826** Pompidou Centre, Paris
Ipswich

827 Staatsgalerie, Stuttgart   **828** European Investment Bank,
Luxembourg

Europa. British Architects in Europe

1987 (12 May) Phosphorised paper

1355	**825**	18p	multicoloured	50	40	☐ ☐
1356	**826**	22p	multicoloured	75	75	☐ ☐
1357	**827**	31p	multicoloured	1·25	1·25	☐ ☐
1358	**828**	34p	multicoloured	1·25	1·25	☐ ☐
Set of 4				3·50	3·50	☐ ☐
First Day Cover					4·00	☐
Presentation Pack (P.O. Pack No. 180)				4·00		☐
PHQ Cards (set of 4) (101)				3·00	6·50	☐ ☐
Set of 4 Gutter Pairs				8·00		☐

829 Brigade Members   **830** Bandaging Blitz
with Ashford Litter, 1887   Victim, 1940

831 Volunteer with   **832** Transport of Transplant
fainting Girl, 1965   Organ by Air Wing, 1987

Centenary of St John Ambulance Brigade

1987 (16 June) Phosphorised paper. Perf 14 × 14½

1359	**829**	18p multicoloured	40	45	
1360	**830**	22p multicoloured	60	75	
1361	**831**	31p multicoloured	1·25	1·25	
1362	**832**	34p multicoloured	1·25	1·25	
Set of 4			3·25	3·50	
First Day Cover				4·00	
Presentation Pack (P.O. Pack No. 181)			4·00		
PHQ Cards (*set of* 4) (102)			3·00	6·50	
Set of 4 Gutter Pairs			8·00		

833 Arms of the Lord Lyon King of Arms

834 Scottish Heraldic Banner of Prince Charles

835 Arms of Royal Scottish Academy of Painting, Sculpture and Architecture

836 Arms of Royal Society of Edinburgh

300th Anniversary of Revival of Order of the Thistle

1987 (21 July) Phosphorised paper. Perf 14½

1363	**833**	18p multicoloured	50	40	
1364	**834**	22p multicoloured	75	90	
1365	**835**	31p multicoloured	1·40	1·40	
1366	**836**	34p multicoloured	1·50	1·40	
Set of 4			3·75	3·75	
First Day Cover				4·25	
Presentation Pack (P.O. Pack No.182)			4·00		
PHQ Cards (*set of* 4) (103)			3·00	6·50	
Set of 4 Gutter Pairs			8·00		

837 Crystal Palace, 'Monarch of the Glen' (Landseer) and Grace Darling

838 Great Eastern, Beeton's Book of Household Management and Prince Albert

839 Albert Memorial, Ballot Box and Disraeli

840 Diamond Jubilee Emblem, Morse Key and Newspaper Placard for Relief of Mafeking

150th Anniversary of Queen Victoria's Accession

1987 (8 Sept.) Phosphorised paper

1367	**837**	18p multicoloured	50	45	
1368	**838**	22p multicoloured	80	75	
1369	**839**	31p multicoloured	1·25	1·50	
1370	**840**	34p multicoloured	1·35	1·60	
Set of 4			3·50	4·00	
First Day Cover				4·50	
Presentation Pack (P.O. Pack No. 183)			4·25		
PHQ Cards (*set of* 4) (104)			3·00	6·50	
Set of 4 Gutter Pairs			7·50		

841 Pot by Bernard Leach

842 Pot by Elizabeth Fritsch

843 Pot by Lucie Rie

844 Pot by Hans Coper

Studio Pottery

1987 (13 Oct.) Phosphorised paper. Perf 14½ × 14

1371	**841**	18p multicoloured	50	40	
1372	**842**	26p multicoloured	70	75	
1373	**843**	31p multicoloured	1·25	1·25	
1374	**844**	34p multicoloured	1·40	1·50	
Set of 4			3·50	3·50	
First Day Cover				4·00	
Presentation Pack (P.O. Pack No. 184)			4·00		
PHQ Cards (*set of* 4) (105)			3·00	6·50	
Set of 4 Gutter Pairs			7·50		

Nos. 1371/4 also mark the birth centenary of Bernard Leach, the potter.

845 Decorating the Christmas Tree

846 Waiting for Father Christmas

847 Sleeping Child and Father Christmas in Sleigh

848 Child reading

849 Child playing Flute and Snowman

Christmas

1987 (17 Nov.) One phosphor band (13p) or phosphorised paper (others)

1375	**845**	13p multicoloured	30	30	☐ ☐
1376	**846**	18p multicoloured	40	40	☐ ☐
1377	**847**	26p multicoloured	80	1·00	☐ ☐
1378	**848**	31p multicoloured	1·10	1·25	☐ ☐
1379	**849**	34p multicoloured	1·25	1·50	☐ ☐
Set of 5			3·50	4·00	☐ ☐
First Day Cover				4·50	☐
Presentation Pack (P.O. Pack No. 185)			4·00		☐
PHQ Cards (*set of 5*) (106)			3·00	6·50	☐ ☐
Set of 5 Gutter Pairs			7·50		☐

Collectors Pack 1987

1987 (17 Nov.) Comprises Nos. 1347/79

CP1379a	Collectors Pack	38·00	☐

Post Office Yearbook

1987 Comprises Nos. 1347/79 in hardbound book with slip case

YB1379a	Yearbook	35·00	☐

850 Short-spined Seascorpion ('Bull-rout') (Jonathan Couch)

851 Yellow Waterlily (Major Joshua Swatkin)

852 Whistling ('Bewick's') Swan (Edward Lear)

853 *Morchella esculenta* (James Sowerby)

Bicentenary of Linnean Society. Archive Illustrations

1988 (19 Jan.) Phosphorised paper

1380	**850**	18p multicoloured	55	35	☐ ☐
1381	**851**	26p multicoloured	85	1·00	☐ ☐
1382	**852**	31p multicoloured	1·10	1·25	☐ ☐
1383	**853**	34p multicoloured	1·25	1·40	☐ ☐
Set of 4			3·25	3·50	☐ ☐
First Day Cover				4·00	☐
Presentation Pack (P.O. Pack No.187)			4·00		☐
PHQ Cards (*set of 4*) (107)			3·00	6·50	☐ ☐
Set of 4 Gutter Pairs			8·00		☐

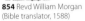

854 Revd William Morgan (Bible translator, 1588)

855 William Salesbury (New Testament translator, 1567)

856 Bishop Richard Davies (New Testament translator, 1567)

857 Bishop Richard Parry (editor of Revised Welsh Bible, 1620)

400th Anniversary of Welsh Bible

1988 (1 Mar.) Phosphorised paper. Perf 14½ × 14

1384	**854**	18p multicoloured	40	40	☐ ☐
1385	**855**	26p multicoloured	70	95	☐ ☐
1386	**856**	31p multicoloured	1·25	1·25	☐ ☐
1387	**857**	34p multicoloured	1·40	1·25	☐ ☐
Set of 4			3·25	3·50	☐ ☐
First Day Cover				4·00	☐
Presentation Pack (P.O. Pack No. 188)			4·00		☐
PHQ Cards (*set of 4*) (108)			3·00	6·50	☐ ☐
Set of 4 Gutter Pairs			8·00		☐

858 Gymnastics (Centenary of British Amateur Gymnastics Association)

859 Downhill Skiing (Ski Club of Great Britain)

860 Tennis (Centenary of Lawn Tennis Association)

861 Football (Centenary of Football League)

Sports Organizations

1988 (22 Mar.) Phosphorised paper. Perf 14½

1388	**858**	18p multicoloured	40	40	☐ ☐
1389	**859**	26p multicoloured	70	80	☐ ☐
1390	**860**	31p multicoloured	1·10	1·25	☐ ☐
1391	**861**	34p multicoloured	1·25	1·25	☐ ☐
Set of 4			3·25	3·25	☐ ☐
First Day Cover				3·75	☐
Presentation Pack (P.O. Pack No. 189)			4·00		☐
PHQ Cards (*set of 4*) (109)			2·50	6·00	☐ ☐
Set of 4 Gutter Pairs			8·00		☐

862 *Mallard* and Mailbags on Pick-up Arms

863 Loading Transatlantic Mail on Liner *Queen Elizabeth*

864 Glasgow Tram No. 1173 and Pillar Box

865 Imperial Airways Handley Page H.P.45 *Horatius* and Airmail Van

Europa. Transport and Mail Services in 1930's

1988 (10 May) Phosphorised paper

1392	**862**	18p	multicoloured	50	35	
1393	**863**	26p	multicoloured	1·00	1·00	
1394	**864**	31p	multicoloured	1·25	1·25	
1395	**865**	34p	multicoloured	1·60	1·50	
Set of 4				4·00	3·75	
First Day Cover					4·25	
Presentation Pack (P.O. Pack No.190)				4·25		
PHQ Cards (*set of* 4) (110)				2·25	6·00	
Set of 4 Gutter Pairs				9·00		

866 Early Settler and Sailing Clipper

867 Queen Elizabeth II with British and Australian Parliament Buildings

868 W. G. Grace (cricketer) and Tennis Racquet

869 Shakespeare, John Lennon (entertainer) and Sydney Landmarks

Bicentenary of Australian Settlement

1988 (21 June) Phosphorised paper. Perf 14½

1396	**866**	18p	multicoloured	40	50	
		a.	Horiz pair.			
			Nos. 1396/7	1·25	1·50	
1397	**867**	18p	multicoloured	40	50	
1398	**868**	34p	multicoloured	1·00	1·25	
		a.	Horiz pair.			
			Nos. 1398/9	2·50	3·00	
1399	**869**	34p	multicoloured	1·00	1·25	
Set of 4				3·50	4·00	
First Day Cover					4·50	
Presentation Pack (P.O. Pack No. 191)				4·00		
Souvenir Book				15·00		
PHQ Cards (*set of* 4) (111)				2·25	6·00	
Set of 2 Gutter Blocks of 4				8·25		

Nos. 1396/7 and 1398/9 were each printed together, *se-tenant*, in horizontal pairs throughout the sheets, each pair showing a background design of the Australian flag.

Stamps in similar designs were also issued by Australia. These are included in the Souvenir Book.

870 Spanish Galeasse off The Lizard

871 English Fleet leaving Plymouth

872 Engagement off Isle of Wight

873 Attack of English Fire-ships, Calais

874 Armada in Storm, North Sea

400th Anniversary of Spanish Armada

1988 (19 July) Phosphorised paper

1400	**870**	18p	multicoloured	45	50	
		a.	Horiz strip of 5.			
			Nos. 1400/4	3·00	3·00	
1401	**871**	18p	multicoloured	45	50	
1402	**872**	18p	multicoloured	45	50	
1403	**873**	18p	multicoloured	45	50	
1404	**874**	18p	multicoloured	45	50	
Set of 5				3·00	3·00	
First Day Cover					3·75	
Presentation Pack (P.O. Pack No.192)				3·75		
PHQ Cards (*set of* 5) (112)				2·75	7·00	
Gutter Block of 10				8·00		

Nos. 1400/4 were printed together, *se-tenant*, in horizontal strips of five throughout the sheet, forming a composite design.

875 'The Owl and the pussy-cat'

876 'Edward Lear as a Bird' (self-portrait)

877 'Cat' (from alphabet book)

878 'There was a Young Lady whose Bonnet...' (limerick)

Death Centenary of Edward Lear (artist and author)

1988 (6–27 Sept.) Phosphorised paper

1405	**875**	19p	black, pale cream and carmine	65	40	☐ ☐
1406	**876**	27p	black, pale cream and yellow	1·00	1·00	☐ ☐
1407	**877**	32p	black, pale cream and emerald	1·25	1·40	☐ ☐
1408	**878**	35p	black, pale cream and blue	1·40	1·40	☐ ☐
Set of 4				4·00	3·75	☐ ☐
First Day Cover					4·25	☐
Presentation Pack (P.O. Pack No. 193)				4·25		☐
PHQ Cards (*set of* 4) (113)				2·25	6·00	☐ ☐
Set of 4 Gutter Pairs				9·00		☐
MS1409 122 × 90 mm. Nos. 1405/8				7·00	8·50	☐ ☐
First Day Cover (27.9.88)					8·50	☐

No. **MS**1409 was sold at £1·35, the premium being used for the 'Stamp World London 90' International Stamp Exhibition.

879 Carrickfergus Castle

880 Caernarfon Castle

881 Edinburgh Castle

882 Windsor Castle

1988 (18 Oct.) Ordinary paper

1410	**879**	£1	deep green	4·25	60	☐ ☐
1411	**880**	£1·50	maroon	4·50	1·25	☐ ☐
1412	**881**	£2	indigo	8·00	1·50	☐ ☐
1413	**882**	£5	deep brown	21·00	5·50	☐ ☐
Set of 4				35·00	8·00	☐ ☐
First Day Cover					35·00	☐
Presentation Pack (P.O. Pack No. 18)				36·00		☐
Set of 4 Gutter pairs				80·00		☐

For similar designs, but with silhouette of Queen's head see Nos. 1611/14 and 1993/6.

883 Journey to Bethlehem

884 Shepherds and Star

885 Three Wise Men

886 Nativity

887 The Annunciation

Christmas

1988 (15 Nov.) One phosphor band (14p) or phosphorised paper (others)

1414	**883**	14p	multicoloured	45	35	☐ ☐
1415	**884**	19p	multicoloured	50	50	☐ ☐
1416	**885**	27p	multicoloured	90	1·00	☐ ☐
1417	**886**	32p	multicoloured	1·10	1·25	☐ ☐
1418	**887**	35p	multicoloured	1·40	1·25	☐ ☐
Set of 5				4·00	3·75	☐ ☐
First Day Cover					4·25	☐
Presentation Pack (P.O. Pack No. 194)				4·50		☐
PHQ Cards (*set of* 5) (114)				3·00	6·00	☐ ☐
Set of 5 Gutter Pairs				9·50		☐

Collectors Pack 1988

1988 (15 Nov.) Comprises Nos. 1380/1408, 1414/18

CP1418a	Collectors Pack		35·00	☐

Post Office Yearbook

1988 Comprises Nos. 1380/1404, **MS**1409, 1414/18 in hardbound book with slip case

YB1418a	Yearbook		38·00	☐

888 Atlantic Puffin

889 Avocet

890 Oystercatcher

891 Northern Gannet

Centenary of Royal Society for the Protection of Birds

1989 (17 Jan.) Phosphorised paper

1419	**888**	19p	multicoloured	35	40	☐ ☐
1420	**889**	27p	multicoloured	1·25	1·25	☐ ☐
1421	**890**	32p	multicoloured	1·25	1·25	☐ ☐
1422	**891**	35p	multicoloured	1·25	1·25	☐ ☐
Set of 4				3·50	3·50	☐ ☐
First Day Cover					4·00	☐
Presentation Pack (P.O. Pack No. 196)				4·00		☐
PHQ Cards (*set of* 4) (115)				3·00	7·00	☐ ☐
Set of 4 Gutter Pairs				8·50		☐

892 Rose

893 Cupid

894 Yachts

895 Fruit

896 Teddy Bear

Greetings. Booklet Stamps

1989 (31 Jan.) Phosphorised paper

1423	**892**	19p	multicoloured	3·00	3·00	☐	☐
		a.	Booklet pane.				
			Nos. 1423/7 × 2	50·00		☐	
		b.	Horiz strip of 5.				
			Nos. 1423/7	25·00	25·00	☐	☐
1424	**893**	19p	multicoloured	3·00	3·00	☐	☐
1425	**894**	19p	multicoloured	3·00	3·00	☐	☐
1426	**895**	19p	multicoloured	3·00	3·00	☐	☐
1427	**896**	19p	multicoloured	3·00	3·00	☐	☐
Set of 5				25·00	25·00	☐	☐
First Day Cover					25·00	☐	

Nos. 1423/7 were printed together, *se-tenant*, in horizontal strips of five, two such strips forming the booklet pane with twelve half stamp-size labels.

897 Fruit and Vegetables

898 Meat Products

899 Dairy Produce

900 Cereal Products

Food and Farming Year

1989 (7 Mar.) Phosphorised paper. Perf 14 × 14½

1428	**897**	19p	multicoloured	45	50	☐	☐
1429	**898**	27p	multicoloured	90	85	☐	☐
1430	**899**	32p	multicoloured	1·25	1·40	☐	☐
1431	**900**	35p	multicoloured	1·40	1·50	☐	☐
Set of 4				3·50	3·50	☐	☐

First Day Cover			4·00	☐
Presentation Pack (P.O. Pack No. 197)	4·00			☐
PHQ Cards (*set of* 4) (116)		2·25	6·50	☐ ☐
Set of 4 Gutter Pairs		8·50		☐

901 Mortar Board (150th Anniv of Public Education in England)

902 Cross on Ballot Paper (3rd Direct Elections to European Parliament)

903 Posthorn (26th Postal, Telegraph and Telephone International Congress, Brighton)

904 Globe (Inter - Parliamentry Union Centenary Conference, London)

Anniversaries

1989 (11 Apr.) Phosphorised paper. Perf 14 × 14½

1432	**901**	19p	multicoloured	60	60	☐	☐
		a.	Horiz pair.				
			Nos. 1432/3	1·50	1·50	☐	☐
1433	**902**	19p	multicoloured	60	60	☐	☐
1434	**903**	35p	multicoloured	1·00	1·00	☐	☐
		a.	Horiz pair.				
			Nos. 1434/5	2·50	2·50	☐	☐
1435	**904**	35p	multicoloured	1·00	1·00	☐	☐
Set of 4				3·50	3·50	☐	☐
First Day Cover					4·50	☐	
Presentation Pack (P.O. Pack No. 198)			4·00			☐	
PHQ Cards (*set of* 4) (117)			2·25	6·50		☐ ☐	
Set of 2 Gutter Strips of 4			8·00			☐	

Nos. 1432/3 and 1434/5 were each printed together, *se-tenant*, in horizontal pairs throughout the sheets.

905 Toy Train and Aeroplanes

906 Building Bricks

907 Dice and Board Games

908 Toy Robot, Boat and Doll's House

Europa. Games and Toys

1989 (16 May) Phosphorised paper

1436	**905**	19p multicoloured	65	50	
1437	**906**	27p multicoloured	95	1·00	
1438	**907**	32p multicoloured	1·40	1·25	
1439	**908**	35p multicoloured	1·50	1·25	
Set of 4			4·00	3·75	
First Day Cover				4·25	
Presentation Pack (P.O. Pack No. 199)			4·25		
PHQ Cards (set of 4) (118)			2·25	6·50	
Set of 4 Gutter Pairs			9·00		

909 Ironbridge, Shropshire

910 Tin Mine, St Agnes Head, Cornwall

911 Cotton Mills, New Lanark, Strathclyde

912 Pontcysyllite Aqueduct, Clwyd

912a

Industrial Archaeology

1989 (4–25 July) Phosphorised paper

1440	**909**	19p multicoloured	60	15	
1441	**910**	27p multicoloured	1·00	1·10	
1442	**911**	32p multicoloured	1·10	1·25	
1443	**912**	35p multicoloured	1·25	1·50	
Set of 4			3·50	4·00	
First Day Cover				4·50	
Presentation Pack (P.O. Pack No. 200)			4·00		
PHQ Cards (set of 4) (119)			2·25	6·50	
Set of 4 Gutter Pairs			8·50		
MS1444 122×90 mm. **912a** As Nos. 1440/3 but designs horizontal			6·00	6·50	
First Day Cover (25.7.89)				7·00	

No. **MS**1444 was sold at £1·40, the premium being used for the 'Stamp World London 90' International Stamp Exhibition.

913 **914**

Booklet Stamps

1989 (22 Aug.)–**92**

(a) Printed in photogravure by Harrison and Sons. Perf 15×14

1445	**913**	(2nd)	bright blue (1 centre band)	1·25	1·50	
1446		(2nd)	bright blue (1 side band) (20.3.90)	3·50	3·75	
1447	**914**	(1st)	brownish black (phosphorised paper)	1·75	1·50	
1448		(1st)	brownish black (2 bands) (20.3.90)	3·75	3·75	

(b) Printed in lithography by Walsall. Perf 14

1449	**913**	(2nd)	bright blue (1 centre band)	1·00	1·00	
1450	**914**	(1st)	blackish brown (2 bands)	2·50	2·75	

(c) Printed in lithography by Questa. Perf 15×14

1451	**913**	(2nd)	bright blue (1 centre band) (19.9.89)	1·00	1·00	
1451a		(2nd)	bright blue (1 side band) (25.2.92)	3·25	3·25	
1452	**914**	(1st)	brownish black (phosphorised paper) (19.9.89)	2·50	2·75	
First Day Cover (Nos. 1445, 1447)					6·00	

For similar stamps showing changed colours see Nos. 1511/16, for those with elliptical perforations Nos. 1664/71 and for self-adhesive versions Nos. 2039/40, 2295, U2941/2, U2945, U2948, U3001/2 and U3271.

No. 1451a exists with the phosphor band at the left or right of the stamp.

915 Snowflake (×10)

916 Calliphora erythrocephala (fly) (×5)

917 Blood Cells (×500)

918 Microchip (×600)

150th Anniversary of Royal Microscopical Society

1989 (5 Sept.) Phosphorised paper. Perf 14½×14

1453	**915**	19p multicoloured	45	45	
1454	**916**	27p multicoloured	95	1·00	
1455	**917**	32p multicoloured	1·10	1·25	
1456	**918**	35p multicoloured	1·25	1·25	
Set of 4			3·50	3·75	

First Day Cover		4·25		☐
Presentation Pack (P.O. Pack No. 201)	4·00			☐
PHQ Cards (set of 4) (120)		2·25	6·50	☐ ☐
Set of 4 Gutter Pairs		8·50		☐

919 Royal Mail Coach

920 Escort of Blues and Royals

921 Lord Mayor's Coach

922 Coach Team passing St Paul's

923 Blues and Royals Drum Horse

Lord Mayor's Show, London

1989 (17 Oct.) Phosphorised paper

1457	**919**	20p	multicoloured	45	50	☐ ☐
			a. Horiz strip of 5. Nos. 1457/61	3·00	3·00	☐ ☐
1458	**920**	20p	multicoloured	45	50	☐ ☐
1459	**921**	20p	multicoloured	45	50	☐ ☐
1460	**922**	20p	multicoloured	45	50	☐ ☐
1461	**923**	20p	multicoloured	45	50	☐ ☐
Set of 5				3·00	3·00	☐ ☐
First Day Cover					3·50	☐
Presentation Pack (P.O. Pack No. 202)				3·50		☐
PHQ Cards (set of 5) (121)				3·00	6·50	☐ ☐
Gutter Strip of 10				8·00		☐

Nos. 1457/61 commemorate the 800th anniversary of the installation of the first Lord Mayor of London.

Nos. 1457/61 were printed together, *se-tenant*, in horizontal strips of five throughout the sheet, forming a composite design. See also No. 2957.

924 14th-century Peasants from Stained-glass Window

925 Arches and Roundels, West Front

926 Octagon Tower

927 Arcade from West Transept

928 Triple Arch from West Front

Christmas. 800th Anniversary of Ely Cathedral

1989 (14 Nov.) One phosphor band (Nos. 1462/3) or phosphorised paper (others)

1462	**924**	15p	gold, silver and blue	40	40	☐ ☐
1463	**925**	15p	+1p gold, silver and blue	50	40	☐ ☐
1464	**926**	20p	+1p gold, silver and rosine	65	80	☐ ☐
1465	**927**	34p	+1p gold, silver and emerald	1·25	1·75	☐ ☐
1466	**928**	37p	+1p gold, silver and yellow-olive	1·40	1·90	☐ ☐
Set of 5				3·75	4·75	☐ ☐
First Day Cover					5·50	☐
Presentation Pack (P.O. Pack No. 203)				4·50		☐
PHQ Cards (set of 5) (122)				3·00	6·00	☐ ☐
Set of 5 Gutter Pairs				8·50		☐

Collectors Pack 1989

1989 (14 Nov.) Comprises Nos. 1419/22, 1428/43 and 1453/66

CP1466a	Collectors Pack	38·00	☐

Post Office Yearbook

1989 (14 Nov.) Comprises Nos. 1419/22, 1428/44 and 1453/66 in hardback book with slip case

YB1466a	Yearbook	42·00	☐

929 Queen Victoria
and Queen Elizabeth II

150th Anniversary of the Penny Black

1990 (10 Jan.–17 Apr.)

(a) Printed in photogravure by Harrison and Sons (Nos. 1468, 1470, 1472 from booklets only). Perf 15 × 14

1467	**929**	15p	bright blue (1 centre band)	80	80	☐ ☐
1468		15p	bright blue (1 side band) *(30.1.90)*	4·00	4·00	☐ ☐
1469		20p	brownish black and cream (phosphorised paper)	1·00	1·00	☐ ☐
1470		20p	brownish black and cream (2 bands) *(30.1.90)*	3·50	3·50	☐ ☐
1471		29p	deep mauve (phosphorised paper)	1·75	1·75	☐ ☐
1472		29p	deep mauve (2 bands) *(20.3.90)*	9·00	9·00	☐ ☐
1473		34p	deep bluish grey (phosphorised paper)	2·00	2·00	☐ ☐
1474		37p	rosine (phosphorised paper)	2·25	2·25	☐ ☐
Set of 5 (Nos. 1467, 1469, 1471, 1473/4)				7·00	7·00	☐ ☐
First Day Cover (Nos. 1467, 1469, 1471, 1473/4)					7·00	☐
Presentation Pack (Nos. 1467, 1469, 1471, 1473/4) (P.O. Pack No. 21)				9·00		☐

(b) Litho Walsall (booklets). Perf 14 (30 Jan.)

1475	**929**	15p	bright blue (1 centre band) *(30.1.90)*	1·50	1·75	☐ ☐
1476		20p	brownish black and cream (phosphorised paper) *(30.1.90)*	1·75	1·90	☐ ☐

(c) Litho Questa (booklets). Perf 15 × 14 (17 Apr.)

1477	**929**	15p	bright blue (1 centre band) *(17.4.90)*	2·50	2·75	☐ ☐
1478		20p	brownish black (phosphorised paper) *(17.4.90)*	2·75	3·00	☐ ☐

No. 1468 exists with the phosphor band at the left or right of the stamp.
For Type **929** redrawn with "1st" face value see Nos. 2133 and 2956.

1840·RSPCA·1990
930 Kitten

1840·RSPCA·1990
931 Rabbit

1840·RSPCA·1990
932 Duckling

1840·RSPCA·1990
933 Puppy

150th Anniversary of Royal Society for Prevention of Cruelty to Animals

1990 (23 Jan.) Phosphorised paper. Perf 14 × 14½

1479	**930**	20p	multicoloured	75	50	☐ ☐
1480	**931**	29p	multicoloured	1·25	1·25	☐ ☐
1481	**932**	34p	multicoloured	1·25	1·50	☐ ☐
1482	**933**	37p	multicoloured	1·50	1·50	☐ ☐
Set of 4				4·50	4·25	☐ ☐
First Day Cover					4·75	☐
Presentation Pack (P.O. Pack No. 205)				4·75		☐
PHQ Cards (*set* of 4) (123)				3·00	7·50	☐ ☐
Set of 4 Gutter Pairs				9·50		☐

934 Teddy Bear

935 Dennis the Menace

936 Punch

937 Cheshire Cat

938 The Man in the Moon

939 The Laughing Policeman

940 Clown

941 Mona Lisa

942 Queen of Hearts

943 Stan Laurel (comedian)

Greetings 'Smiles'. Booklet Stamps

1990 (6 Feb.) Two phosphor bands

1483	**934**	20p	multicoloured	2·25	2·40	☐ ☐
		a.	Booklet pane.			
			Nos. 1483/92	30·00	26·00	☐ ☐
1484	**935**	20p	multicoloured	2·25	2·40	☐ ☐
1485	**936**	20p	multicoloured	2·25	2·40	☐ ☐
1486	**937**	20p	multicoloured	2·25	2·40	☐ ☐
1487	**938**	20p	multicoloured	2·25	2·40	☐ ☐
1488	**939**	20p	multicoloured	2·25	2·40	☐ ☐
1489	**940**	20p	multicoloured	2·25	2·40	☐ ☐
1490	**941**	20p	multicoloured	2·25	2·40	☐ ☐
1491	**942**	20p	multicoloured	2·25	2·40	☐ ☐
1492	**943**	20p	gold and grey-black	2·25	2·40	☐ ☐
Set of 10				30·00	26·00	☐ ☐
First Day Cover					28·00	☐

Nos. 1483/92 were printed together, *se-tenant*, in booklet panes of ten.

For these designs with the face value expressed as '1st' see Nos. 1550/9.

> **SET PRICES.** Please note that set prices for booklet greetings stamps are for complete panes. Sets of single stamps are worth considerably less.

944 Alexandra Palace ('Stamp World London 90' Exhibition)

945 Glasgow School of Art

946 British Philatelic Bureau, Edinburgh

947 Templeton Carpet Factory, Glasgow

Europa (Nos. 1493 and 1495) and 'Glasgow 1990 European City of Culture' (Nos. 1494 and 1496)

1990 (6 Mar.) Phosphorised paper

1493	**944**	20p	multicoloured	50	40	☐ ☐
1494	**945**	20p	multicoloured	50	40	☐ ☐
1495	**946**	29p	multicoloured	1·25	1·75	☐ ☐
1496	**947**	37p	multicoloured	1·50	1·75	☐ ☐
Set of 4				3·50	4·00	☐ ☐
First Day Cover					4·25	☐
Presentation Pack (P.O. Pack No. 206)				4·25		☐
PHQ Cards (set of 4) (124)				3·00	6·00	☐ ☐
Set of 4 Gutter Pairs				8·00		☐

948 Export Achievement Award

949 Technological Achievement Award

25th Anniversary of Queen's Awards for Export and Technology

1990 (10 Apr.) Phosphorised paper. Perf 14 × 14½

1497	**948**	20p	multicoloured	50	60	☐ ☐
		a.	Horiz pair.			
			Nos. 1497/8	1·40	1·60	☐ ☐
1498	**949**	20p	multicoloured	50	60	☐ ☐
1499	**948**	37p	multicoloured	1·25	1·25	☐ ☐
		a.	Horiz pair.			
			Nos. 1499/1500	3·00	3·00	☐ ☐
1500	**949**	37p	multicoloured	1·25	1·25	☐ ☐
Set of 4				4·00	4·25	☐ ☐
First Day Cover					4·75	☐
Presentation Pack (P.O. Pack No. 207)				4·50		☐
PHQ Cards (set of 4) (125)				3·00	6·00	☐ ☐
Set of 2 Gutter Strips of 4				8·50		☐

Nos. 1497/8 and 1499/1500 were each printed together, *se-tenant*, in horizontal pairs throughout the sheets.

949a

'Stamp World London 90' International Stamp Exhibition, London. Minature sheet

1990 (3 May) Sheet 122 × 90 mm. Phosphorised paper

MS1501	**949a**	20p	brownish black and cream	5·50	5·50	☐ ☐
First Day Cover					5·75	☐
Souvenir Book (Nos. 1467, 1469, 1471, 1473/4 and **MS**1501)				20·00		☐

No. **MS**1501 was sold at £1, the premium being used for the exhibition.

KEW GARDENS 1840-1990
950 Cycad and Sir
Joseph Banks Building

KEW GARDENS 1840-1990
951 Stone Pine and Princess
of Wales Conservatory

KEW GARDENS 1840-1990
952 Willow Tree and
Palm House

KEW GARDENS 1840-1990
953 Cedar Tree and
Pagoda

150th Anniversary of Kew Gardens

1990 (5 June) Phosphorised paper

1502	**950**	20p	multicoloured	55	40	☐ ☐
1503	**951**	29p	multicoloured	75	1·00	☐ ☐
1504	**952**	34p	multicoloured	1·25	1·60	☐ ☐
1505	**953**	37p	multicoloured	1·50	1·50	☐ ☐
Set of 4				3·50	4·00	☐ ☐
First Day Cover					4·50	☐
Presentation Pack (P.O. Pack No. 208)				4·00		☐
PHQ Cards (*set of 4*) (126)				3·00	6·00	☐ ☐
Set of 4 Gutter Pairs				8·00		☐

954 Thomas Hardy and Clyffe Clump, Dorset

150th Birth Anniversary of Thomas Hardy (author)

1990 (10 July) Phosphorised paper

1506	**954**	20p	multicoloured	80	75	☐ ☐
First Day Cover					1·50	☐
Presentation Pack (P.O. Pack No. 209)				1·50		☐
PHQ Card (127)				1·00	2·25	☐ ☐
Gutter Pair				1·75		☐

955 Queen Elizabeth
the Queen Mother

956 Queen Elizabeth

957 Elizabeth,
Duchess of York

958 Lady Elizabeth
Bowes-Lyon

90th Birthday of Queen Elizabeth the Queen Mother

1990 (2 Aug.) Phosphorised paper

1507	**955**	20p	multicoloured	95	60	☐ ☐
1508	**956**	29p	silver, indigo and grey-blue	1·40	1·50	☐ ☐
1509	**957**	34p	multicoloured	2·00	2·50	☐ ☐
1510	**958**	37p	silver, sepia and stone	2·25	2·50	☐ ☐
Set of 4				6·00	6·50	☐ ☐
First Day Cover					7·00	☐
Presentation Pack (P.O. Pack No. 210)				7·00		☐
PHQ Cards (*set of 4*) (128)				5·50	8·00	☐ ☐
Set of 4 Gutter Pairs				15·00		☐

For these designs with Queen mother's head and frame in black see Nos. 2280/3.

Booklet Stamps

1990 (7 Aug.)–**92** As Types **913/14**, but colours changed

(a) Photo Harrison. Perf 15 × 14

1511	**913**	(2nd)	deep blue (1 centre band)	1·50	1·50	☐ ☐
1512	**914**	(1st)	bright orange-red (phosphorised paper)	1·50	1·50	☐ ☐

(b) Litho Questa. Perf 15 × 14

1513	**913**	(2nd)	deep blue (1 centre band)	2·50	2·75	☐ ☐
1514	**914**	(1st)	bright orange-red (phosphorised paper)	1·50	1·00	☐ ☐
1514a		(1st)	bright orange-red (2 bands) *(25.2.92)*	3·25	3·25	☐ ☐

(c) Litho Walsall. Perf 14

1515	**913**	(2nd)	deep blue (1 centre band)	1·50	1·20	☐ ☐
1516	**914**	(1st)	bright orange-red (phosphorised paper)	1·20	1·20	☐ ☐
		c.	Perf 13	6·00	6·50	☐ ☐
First Day Cover (Nos. 1515/16)					5·00	☐

For similar stamps with elliptical perforations see Nos. 1664/71.

959 Victoria Cross

960 George Cross

961 Distinguished Service Cross and Distinguished Service Medal

962 Military Cross and Military Medal

963 Distinguished Flying Cross and Distinguished Flying Medal

Gallantry Awards

1990 (11 Sept.) Phosphorised paper

1517	**959**	20p	multicoloured	80	75	☐	☐
1518	**960**	20p	multicoloured	80	75	☐	☐
1519	**961**	20p	multicoloured	80	75	☐	☐
1520	**962**	20p	multicoloured	80	75	☐	☐
1521	**963**	20p	multicoloured	80	75	☐	☐
Set of 5				3·75	3·50	☐	☐
First Day Cover					4·00	☐	
Presentation Pack (P.O. Pack No. 211)				4·00		☐	
PHQ Cards (set of 5) (129)				3·00	8·00	☐	☐
Set of 5 Gutter Pairs				8·50		☐	

For Type **959** with 'all-over' phosphor and perf 14 × 14½ see No. 2666.

964 Armagh Observatory, Jodrell Bank Radio Telescope and La Palma Telescope

965 Newton's Moon and Tides Diagram with Early Telescopes

966 Greenwich Old Observatory and Early Astronomical Equipment

967 Stonehenge, Gyroscope and Navigating by Stars

Astronomy

1990 (16 Oct.) Phosphorised paper. Perf 14 × 14½

1522	**964**	22p	multicoloured	65	50	☐	☐
1523	**965**	26p	multicoloured	1·00	1·10	☐	☐
1524	**966**	31p	multicoloured	1·25	1·40	☐	☐
1525	**967**	37p	multicoloured	1·50	1·40	☐	☐
Set of 4				3·75	4·00	☐	☐
First Day Cover					4·50	☐	
Presentation Pack (P.O. Pack No. 212)				4·50		☐	
PHQ Cards (set of 4) (130)				3·00	7·00	☐	☐
Set of 4 Gutter Pairs				8·50		☐	

Nos. 1522/5 commemorate the centenary of the British

Astronomical Association and the bicentenary of the Armagh Observatory.

968 Building a Snowman

969 Fetching the Christmas Tree

970 Carol Singing

971 Tobogganing

972 Ice-skating

Christmas Scenes

1990 (13 Nov.) One phosphor band (17p) or phosphorised paper (others)

1526	**968**	17p	multicoloured	50	40	☐	☐
1527	**969**	22p	multicoloured	70	50	☐	☐
1528	**970**	26p	multicoloured	70	1·10	☐	☐
1529	**971**	31p	multicoloured	1·25	1·50	☐	☐
1530	**972**	37p	multicoloured	1·25	1·50	☐	☐
Set of 5				4·00	4·50	☐	☐
First Day Cover					5·00	☐	
Presentation Pack (P.O. Pack No. 213)				4·50		☐	
PHQ Cards (set of 5) (131)				3·00	7·00	☐	☐
Set of 5 Gutter Pairs				10·00		☐	

Collectors Pack 1990

1990 (13 Nov.) Comprises Nos. 1479/82, 1493/1510 and 1517/30

CP1530a	Collectors Pack		30·00	☐

Post Office Yearbook

1990 Comprises Nos. 1479/82, 1493/1500, 1502/10 and 1517/30 in hardback book with slip case

YB1530a	Yearbook		45·00	☐

973 'King Charles Spaniel'

974 'A Pointer'

975 'Two Hounds in a Landscape'   976 'A Rough Dog'

977 'Fino and Tiny'

986 Heart-shaped Butterflies   987 Wishing Well and Sixpence

Greetings 'Good Luck' (3rd series). Booklet Stamps

1991 (5 Feb.) Two phosphor bands

1536	978	(1st)	multicoloured	1·25	1·00	☐	☐
		a.	Booklet pane.				
			Nos. 1536/45	15·00	17·00	☐	☐
1537	979	(1st)	multicoloured	1·25	1·00	☐	☐
1538	980	(1st)	multicoloured	1·25	1·00	☐	☐
1539	981	(1st)	multicoloured	1·25	1·00	☐	☐
1540	982	(1st)	multicoloured	1·25	1·00	☐	☐
1541	983	(1st)	multicoloured	1·25	1·00	☐	☐
1542	984	(1st)	multicoloured	1·25	1·00	☐	☐
1543	985	(1st)	multicoloured	1·25	1·00	☐	☐
1544	986	(1st)	multicoloured	1·25	1·00	☐	☐
1545	987	(1st)	multicoloured	1·25	1·00	☐	☐
Set of 10				15·00	17·00		☐
First Day Cover					19·00		☐

Nos. 1536/45 were printed together, *se-tenant*, in booklet panes of ten stamps and 12 half stamp-size labels, the backgrounds of the stamps forming a composite design.

SET PRICES. Please note that set prices for booklet greetings stamps are for complete panes. Sets of single stamps are worth considerably less.

Dogs. Paintings by George Stubbs

1991 (8 Jan.) Phosphorised paper. Perf 14 × 14½

1531	973	22p	multicoloured	50	50	☐ ☐
1532	974	26p	multicoloured	75	1·25	☐ ☐
1533	975	31p	multicoloured	1·00	1·25	☐ ☐
1534	976	33p	multicoloured	1·25	1·25	☐ ☐
1535	977	37p	multicoloured	1·25	1·25	☐ ☐
Set of 5				4·50	5·00	☐ ☐
First Day Cover					5·50	☐
Presentation Pack (P.O. Pack No. 215)				5·00		☐
PHQ Cards (set of 5) (132)				3·50	8·00	☐ ☐
Set of 5 Gutter Pairs				11·00		☐

978 Thrush's Nest   979 Shooting Star and Rainbow

988 Michael Faraday (inventor of electric motor) (Birth Bicentenary)   989 Charles Babbage (computer science pioneer) (Birth Bicentenary)

980 Magpies and Charm Bracelet   981 Black Cat

982 Common Kingfisher with Key   983 Mallard and Frog

990 Radar Sweep of East Anglia (50th Anniv of Discovery by Sir Robert Watson-Watt)   991 Gloster Whittle E28/39 Aircraft over East Anglia (50th Anniv of First Flight of Sir Frank Whittle's Jet Engine)

Scientific Achievements

1991 (5 Mar.) Phosphorised paper

1546	988	22p	multicoloured	60	60	☐ ☐
1547	989	22p	multicoloured	60	60	☐ ☐
1548	990	31p	multicoloured	1·20	1·50	☐ ☐
1549	991	37p	multicoloured	1·40	1·75	☐ ☐
Set of 4				3·50	4·00	☐ ☐
First Day Cover					4·50	☐
Presentation Pack (P.O. Pack No. 216)				4·25		☐

984 Four-leaf Clover in Boot and Match Box   985 Pot of Gold at End of Rainbow

PHQ Cards (set of 4) (133)			3·50	7·00	☐ ☐	
Set of 4 Gutter Pairs			8·50		☐	

992 Teddy Bear

Greetings (4th series) 'Smiles'. Booklet Stamps

1991 (26 Mar.) As Nos. 1483/92, but inscribed '1st' as T **992**. Two phosphor bands. Perf 15 × 14

1550	**992**	(1st)	multicoloured	1·25	1·00	☐ ☐
	a.	Booklet pane.				
		Nos. 1550/9	12·00	13·00	☐ ☐
1551	**935**	(1st)	multicoloured	1·25	1·00	☐ ☐
1552	**936**	(1st)	multicoloured	1·25	1·00	☐ ☐
1553	**937**	(1st)	multicoloured	1·25	1·00	☐ ☐
1554	**938**	(1st)	multicoloured	1·25	1·00	☐ ☐
1555	**939**	(1st)	multicoloured	1·25	1·00	☐ ☐
1556	**940**	(1st)	multicoloured	1·25	1·00	☐ ☐
1557	**941**	(1st)	multicoloured	1·25	1·00	☐ ☐
1558	**942**	(1st)	multicoloured	1·25	1·00	☐ ☐
1559	**943**	(1st)	multicoloured	1·25	1·00	☐ ☐
Set of 10			12·00	13·00	☐ ☐
First Day Cover				14·00	☐

Nos. 1550/9 were originally printed together, *se-tenant*, in booklet panes of ten stamps and 12 half-stamp-size labels.

The stamps were re-issued in sheets of ten, printed in gravure, each with *se-tenant* label on 22 May 2000 in connection with 'customised' stamps available at 'Stamp Show 2000'. The labels show either a pattern of ribbons or a personal photograph.

A similar sheet, but in lithography instead of gravure, and perforated 14½ × 14, appeared on 3 July 2001 with the labels showing either greetings or a personal photograph.

Three further sheets, also in lithography, appeared on 1 October 2002. One contained Nos. 1550/1 each × 10 with greetings labels. Both designs were also available in sheets of 20 with personal photographs.

993 Man looking at Space

994

995 Space looking at Man

996

Europa. Europe in Space

1991 (23 Apr.) Phosphorised paper

1560	**993**	22p	multicoloured	60	60	☐ ☐
	a.	Horiz pair.				
		Nos. 1560/1	1·50	1·50	☐ ☐
1561	**994**	22p	multicoloured	60	60	☐ ☐
1562	**995**	37p	multicoloured	1·25	1·25	☐ ☐
	a.	Horiz pair.				
		Nos. 1562/3	3·50	3·00	☐ ☐
1563	**996**	37p	multicoloured	1·25	1·25	☐ ☐
Set of 4			4·50	4·50	☐ ☐
First Day Cover				5·00	☐
Presentation Pack (P.O. Pack No. 217)			5·00		☐
PHQ Cards (set of 4) (134)			3·00	7·00	☐ ☐
Set of 2 Gutter Strips of 4			9·50		☐

Nos. 1560/1 and 1562/3 were each printed together, *se-tenant*, in horizontal pairs throughout the sheets, each pair forming a composite design.

997 Fencing

998 Hurdling

999 Diving

1000 Rugby

World Student Games, Sheffield (Nos. 1564/6) and World Cup Rugby Championship, London (No. 1567)

1991 (11 June) Phosphorised paper. Perf 14½ × 14

1564	**997**	22p	multicoloured	60	50	☐ ☐
1565	**998**	26p	multicoloured	1·00	1·00	☐ ☐
1566	**999**	31p	multicoloured	1·25	1·25	☐ ☐
1567	**1000**	37p	multicoloured	1·50	1·50	☐ ☐
Set of 4			3·50	3·75	☐ ☐
First Day Cover				4·25	☐
Presentation Pack (P.O. Pack No. 218)			4·50		☐
PHQ Cards (set of 4) (135)			3·00	7·00	☐ ☐
Set of 4 Gutter Pairs			8·00		☐

Rosa Silver Jubilee
1001 'Silver Jubilee'

Rosa Mme Alfred Carrière
1002 'Mme Alfred Carrière'

1003 *Rosa moyesii*

1004 'Harvest Fayre'

1005 'Mutabilis'

9th World Congress of Roses, Belfast

1991 (16 July) Phosphorised paper. Perf 14½ × 14

1568	**1001**	22p multicoloured	50	50		
1569	**1002**	26p multicoloured	75	1·25		
1570	**1003**	31p multicoloured	1·00	1·25		
1571	**1004**	33p multicoloured	1·25	1·50		
1572	**1005**	37p multicoloured	1·50	1·50		
Set of 5			4·50	5·50		
First Day Cover				6·00		
Presentation Pack (P.O. Pack No. 219)			5·00			
PHQ Cards (*set of* 5) (136)			3·00	9·00		
Set of 5 Gutter Pairs			10·00			

1006 Iguanodon

1007 Stegosaurus

1008 Tyrannosaurus

1009 Protoceratops

1010 Triceratops

150th Anniversary of Dinosaurs' Identification by Owen

1991 (20 Aug.) Phosphorised paper. Perf 14½ × 14

1573	**1006**	22p multicoloured	60	50		
1574	**1007**	26p multicoloured	1·10	1·25		
1575	**1008**	31p multicoloured	1·25	1·25		
1576	**1009**	33p multicoloured	1·50	1·50		
1577	**1010**	37p multicoloured	1·60	1·50		
Set of 5			5·75	5·50		
First Day Cover				6·00		
Presentation Pack (P.O. Pack No. 220)			6·00			
PHQ Cards (*set of* 5) (137)			3·00	9·00		
Set of 5 Gutter Pairs			12·00			

1011 Map of 1816

1012 Map of 1906

1013 Map of 1959

1014 Map of 1991

Bicentenary of Ordnance Survey. Maps of Hamstreet, Kent

1991 (17 Sept.) Phosphorised paper. Perf 14½ × 14

1578	**1011**	24p multicoloured	60	50		
1579	**1012**	28p multicoloured	1·00	95		
1580	**1013**	33p multicoloured	1·25	1·40		
1581	**1014**	39p multicoloured	1·50	1·40		
Set of 4			3·50	3·75		
First Day Cover				4·25		
Presentation Pack (P.O. Pack No. 221)			4·50			
PHQ Cards (*set of* 4) (138)			3·00	7·00		
Set of 4 Gutter Pairs			8·50			

1015 Adoration of the Magi

1016 Mary and Baby Jesus in Stable

1017 Holy Family and Angel

1018 The Annunciation

1019 The Flight into Egypt

Christmas. Illuminated Manuscripts from the Bodleian Library, Oxford

1991 (12 Nov.) One phosphor band (18p) or phosphorised paper (others)

1582	**1015**	18p	multicoloured	75	35
1583	**1016**	24p	multicoloured	90	45
1584	**1017**	28p	multicoloured	95	1·25
1585	**1018**	33p	multicoloured	1·10	1·50
1586	**1019**	39p	multicoloured	1·25	1·75
Set of 5				4·50	4·75
First Day Cover					5·50
Presentation Pack (P.O. Pack No. 222)				5·00	
PHQ Cards (set of 5) (139)				3·00	7·50
Set of 5 Gutter Pairs				11·00	

Collectors Pack 1991

1991 (12 Nov.) Comprises Nos. 1531/5, 1546/9 and 1560/86
CP1586a Collectors Pack 32·00

Post Office Yearbook

1991 Comprises Nos. 1531/5, 1546/9 and 1560/86 in hardback book with slip case
YB1586a Yearbook 45·00

1020 Fallow Deer in Scottish Forest

1021 Hare on North Yorkshire Moors

1022 Fox in the Fens

1023 Redwing and Home Counties Village

1024 Welsh Mountain Sheep in Snowdonia

The Four Seasons (1st series). Wintertime

1992 (14 Jan.) One phosphor band (18p) or phosphorised paper (others)

1587	**1020**	18p	multicoloured	55	40
1588	**1021**	24p	multicoloured	75	50
1589	**1022**	28p	multicoloured	1·00	1·25
1590	**1023**	33p	multicoloured	1·25	1·50
1591	**1024**	39p	multicoloured	1·40	1·75
Set of 5				4·50	5·00

First Day Cover		5·50
Presentation Pack (P.O. Pack No. 224)	5·00	
PHQ Cards (set of 5) (140)	3·00	8·00
Set of 5 Gutter Pairs	11·00	

1025 Flower Spray

1026 Double Locket

1027 Key

1028 Model Car and Cigarette Cards

1029 Compass and Map

1030 Pocket Watch

1031 1854 1d. Red Stamp and Pen

1032 Pearl Necklace

1033 Marbles

1034 Bucket, Spade and Starfish

Greetings (5th series) 'Memories'. Booklet Stamps

1992 (28 Jan.) Two phosphor bands

1592	**1025**	(1st)	multicoloured	1·25	1·00
		a.	Booklet pane. Nos. 1592/1601	13·00	13·00
1593	**1026**	(1st)	multicoloured	1·25	1·00
1594	**1027**	(1st)	multicoloured	1·25	1·00
1595	**1028**	(1st)	multicoloured	1·25	1·00
1596	**1029**	(1st)	multicoloured	1·25	1·00
1597	**1030**	(1st)	multicoloured	1·25	1·00
1598	**1031**	(1st)	multicoloured	1·25	1·00
1599	**1032**	(1st)	multicoloured	1·25	1·00
1600	**1033**	(1st)	multicoloured	1·25	1·00
1601	**1034**	(1st)	multicoloured	1·25	1·00
Set of 10				13·00	13·00
First Day Cover					15·00
Presentation Pack (P.O. Pack No. G1)				17·00	

Nos. 1592/1601 were printed together, se-tenant, in booklet panes of ten stamps and 12 half stamp-size labels, the backgrounds of the stamps forming a composite design.

SET PRICES. Please note that set prices for booklet greetings stamps are for complete panes. Sets of single stamps are worth considerably less.

1035 Queen Elizabeth in Coronation Robes and Parliamentary Emblem   **1036** Queen Elizabeth in Garter Robes and Archiepiscopal Arms

1037 Queen Elizabeth with Baby Prince Andrew and Royal Arms   **1038** Queen Elizabeth at Trooping the Colour and Service Emblems

1039 Queen Elizabeth and Commonwealth Emblem

40th Anniversary of Accession

1992 (6 Feb.) Two phosphor bands. Perf 14½ × 14

1602	**1035**	24p	multicoloured	90	90	
		a.	Horiz strip of 5.			
			Nos. 1602/6	6·00	6·50	
1603	**1036**	24p	multicoloured	90	90	
1604	**1037**	24p	multicoloured	90	90	
1605	**1038**	24p	multicoloured	90	90	
1606	**1039**	24p	multicoloured	90	90	
Set of 5				6·00	6·50	
First Day Cover					7·00	
Presentation Pack (P.O. Pack No. 225)				7·00		
PHQ Cards (*set of* 5) (141)				3·00	7·50	
Gutter Block of 10				15·00		

Nos. 1602/6 were printed together, *se-tenant*, in horizontal strips of five throughout the sheet.

1040 Tennyson in 1888 and 'The Beguiling of Merlin' (Sir Edward Burne-Jones)   **1041** Tennyson in 1856 and 'April Love' (Arthur Hughes)

1042 Tennyson in 1864 and 'I am Sick of the Shadows' (John Waterhouse)   **1043** Tennyson as a Young Man and 'Mariana' (Dante Gabriel Rossetti)

Death Centenary of Alfred, Lord Tennyson (poet)

1992 (10 Mar.) Phosphorised paper. Perf 14½ × 14

1607	**1040**	24p	multicoloured	60	50	
1608	**1041**	28p	multicoloured	85	85	
1609	**1042**	33p	multicoloured	1·40	1·60	
1610	**1043**	39p	multicoloured	1·50	1·60	
Set of 4				4·00	4·00	
First Day Cover					4·50	
Presentation Pack (P.O. Pack No. 226)				4·50		
PHQ Cards (*set of* 4) (142)				3·00	7·00	
Set of 4 Gutter Pairs				9·00		

1044 Caernarfon Castle

1992 (24 Mar.)–**95** Designs as Nos. 1410/13, but showing Queen's head in silhouette as T **1044**. Perf 15 × 14 (with one elliptical hole in each vertical side)

1611	**879**	£1	bottle green and gold†	5·50	1·00	
1612	**1044**	£1·50	maroon and gold†	6·00	1·20	
1613	**881**	£2	indigo and gold†	8·00	1·20	
1613a	**1044**	£3	reddish violet and gold† (22.8.95)	19·00	3·00	
1614	**882**	£5	deep brown and gold†	18·00	3·00	
Set of 5				50·00	8·00	
First Day Cover (Nos. 1611/13, 1614)					35·00	
First Day Cover (22.8.95) (No. 1613a)					10·00	
Presentation Pack (P.O. Pack No. 27) (Nos. 1611/13, 1614)				38·00		
Presentation Pack (P.O. Pack No 33) (No. 1613a)				30·00		
PHQ Cards (Nos. 1611/13, 1614) (D2-5)				15·00	35·00	
PHQ Card (No. 1613a) (D8)				10·00	25·00	
Set of 5 Gutter Pairs				£100		

†The Queen's head on these stamps is printed in optically variable ink which changes colour from gold to green when viewed from different angles.

PHQ cards for Nos. 1611/13 and 1614 were not issued until 16 February 1993.

Nos. 1611/14 were printed by Harrison. For stamps with different lettering by Enschedé see Nos. 1410/13 and 1993/6.

1045 British Olympic Association Logo (Olympic Games, Barcelona)

1046 British Paralympic Association Symbol (Paralympics '92, Barcelona)

1052 Musketeer

1053 Standard Bearer

350th Anniversary of the Civil War

1992 (16 June) Phosphorised paper. Perf 14½ × 14

1620	**1050**	24p multicoloured	60	50	☐	☐
1621	**1051**	28p multicoloured	85	85	☐	☐
1622	**1052**	33p multicoloured	1·40	1·50	☐	☐
1623	**1053**	39p multicoloured	1·50	1·75	☐	☐
Set of 4			4·00	4·25	☐	☐
First Day Cover				4·75		☐
Presentation Pack (P.O. Pack No. 228)			4·50		☐	
PHQ Cards (*set of 4*) (144)			3·00	7·00	☐	☐
Set of 4 Gutter Pairs			9·50		☐	

1047 *Santa Maria* (500th Anniv of Discovery of America by Columbus)

1048 *Kaisei* (Japanese cadet brigantine) (Grand Regatta Columbus, 1992)

1054 *The Yeomen of the Guard*

1055 *The Gondoliers*

1049 British Pavilion, 'EXPO 92', Seville

Europa. International Events

1992 (7 Apr.) Phosphorised paper. Perf 14 × 14½

1615	**1045**	24p multicoloured	50	50	☐	☐
		a. Horiz pair.				
		Nos. 1615/16	2·25	1·75	☐	☐
1616	**1046**	24p multicoloured	50	50	☐	☐
1617	**1047**	24p multicoloured	1·00	75	☐	☐
1618	**1048**	39p multicoloured	1·40	1·50	☐	☐
1619	**1049**	39p multicoloured	1·40	1·50	☐	☐
Set of 5			4·50	4·50	☐	☐
First Day Cover				5·00		☐
Presentation Pack (P.O. Pack No. 227)			5·25		☐	
PHQ Cards (*set of 5*) (143)			3·00	7·00	☐	☐
Set of 3 Gutter Pairs and a Gutter						
Strip of 4			11·00		☐	

Nos. 1615/16 were printed together, *se-tenant*, in horizontal pairs throughout the sheet.

1056 *The Mikado*

1057 *The Pirates of Penzance*

1058 *Iolanthe*

1050 Pikeman

1051 Drummer

150th Birth Anniversary of Sir Arthur Sullivan (composer). Gilbert and Sullivan Operas

1992 (21 July) One phosphor band (18p) or phosphorised paper (others). Perf 14½ × 14

1624	**1054**	18p multicoloured	50	40	☐	☐
1625	**1055**	24p multicoloured	80	60	☐	☐
1626	**1056**	28p multicoloured	95	1·00	☐	☐
1627	**1057**	33p multicoloured	1·50	1·60	☐	☐
1628	**1058**	39p multicoloured	1·60	1·60	☐	☐
Set of 5			4·50	4·75	☐	☐
First Day Cover				5·25		☐
Presentation Pack (P.O. Pack No. 229)			5·00		☐	
PHQ Cards (*set of 5*) (145)			3·00	6·25	☐	☐
Set of 5 Gutter Pairs			10·00		☐	

1059 'Acid Rain Kills'

1060 'Ozone Layer'

1061 'Greenhouse Effect'

1062 'Bird of Hope'

Protection of the Environment. Children's Paintings

1992 (15 Sept.) Phosphorised paper. Perf 14 × 14½

1629 **1059**	24p	multicoloured	70	60	
1630 **1060**	28p	multicoloured	1·10	1·25	
1631 **1061**	33p	multicoloured	1·25	1·50	
1632 **1062**	39p	multicoloured	1·40	1·50	
Set of 4			4·00	4·25	
First Day Cover				4·75	
Presentation Pack (P.O. Pack No. 230)			4·50		
PHQ Cards (set of 4) (146)			3·00	6·25	
Set of 4 Gutter Pairs			9·00		

1063 European Star

Single European Market

1992 (13 Oct.) Phosphorised paper

1633 **1063**	24p	multicoloured	1·00	1·00	
First Day Cover				1·50	
Presentation Pack (P.O. Pack No. 231)			1·50		
PHQ Card (147)			1·50	4·00	
Gutter Pair			2·25		

1064 'Angel Gabriel', St. James's, Pangbourne

1065 'Madonna and Child', St. Mary's, Bibury

1066 'King with Gold', Our Lady and St. Peter, Leatherhead

1067 'Shepherds', All Saints, Porthcawl

1068 'Kings with Frankincense and Myrrh', Our Lady and St. Peter, Leatherhead

Christmas. Stained Glass Windows

1992 (10 Nov.) One phosphor band (18p) or phosphorised paper (others)

1634 **1064**	18p	multicoloured	50	30	
1635 **1065**	24p	multicoloured	75	60	
1636 **1066**	28p	multicoloured	1·00	1·10	
1637 **1067**	33p	multicoloured	1·25	1·50	
1638 **1068**	39p	multicoloured	1·25	1·50	
Set of 5			4·25	4·50	
First Day Cover				5·00	
Presentation Pack (P.O. Pack No. 232)			5·00		
PHQ Cards (set of 5) (148)			3·00	7·50	
Set of 5 Gutter Pairs			9·50		

Collectors Pack 1992

1992 (10 Nov.) Comprises Nos. 1587/91, 1602/10 and 1615/38

CP1638a	Collectors Pack	32·00	

Post Office Yearbook

1992 (11 Nov.) Comprises Nos. 1587/91, 1602/10 and 1615/38 in hardback book with slip case

YB1638a	Yearbook	50·00	

1069 Mute Swan Cob and St. Catherine's, Abbotsbury

1070 Cygnet and Decoy

1071 Swans and Cygnet

1072 Eggs in Nest and Tithe Barn, Abbotsbury

1073 Young Swan and the Fleet

600th Anniversary of Abbotsbury Swannery

1993 (19 Jan.) One phosphor band (18p) or phosphorised paper (others)

1639	**1069**	18p	multicoloured	1·25	70	☐	☐
1640	**1070**	24p	multicoloured	1·10	70	☐	☐
1641	**1071**	28p	multicoloured	1·40	2·25	☐	☐
1642	**1072**	33p	multicoloured	1·75	2·50	☐	☐
1643	**1073**	39p	multicoloured	1·90	2·50	☐	☐
Set of 5				6·50	8·00	☐	☐
First Day Cover					8·50		☐
Presentation Pack (P.O. Pack No. 234)				7·00			☐
PHQ Cards (set of 5) (149)				4·25	8·50	☐	☐
Set of 5 Gutter Pairs				15·00			☐

1074 Long John Silver and Parrot (*Treasure Island*)

1075 Tweedledum and Tweedledee (*Alice Through the Looking-Glass*)

1076 William (*William books*)

1077 Mole and Toad (*The Wind in the Willows*)

1078 Teacher and Wilfrid ('*The Bash Street Kids*')

1079 Peter Rabbit and Mrs Rabbit (*The Tale of Peter Rabbit*)

1080 Snowman (*The Snowman*) and Father Christmas (Father Christmas)

1081 The Big Friendly Giant and Sophie (*The BFG*)

1082 Bill Badger and Rupert Bear

1083 Aladdin and the Genie

Greetings (6th series) 'Gift Giving'. Booklet Stamps

1993 (2 Feb.) Two phosphor bands. Perf 15 × 14 (with one elliptical hole in each vertical side)

1644	**1074**	(1st)	multicoloured	1·25	1·00	☐	☐
		a.	Booklet pane. Nos. 1644/53	14·00	12·00	☐	☐
1645	**1075**	(1st)	gold, cream and black	1·25	1·00	☐	☐
1646	**1076**	(1st)	multicoloured	1·25	1·00	☐	☐
1647	**1077**	(1st)	multicoloured	1·25	1·00	☐	☐
1648	**1078**	(1st)	multicoloured	1·25	1·00	☐	☐

1649	**1079**	(1st)	multicoloured	1·25	1·00	☐	☐
1650	**1080**	(1st)	multicoloured	1·25	1·00	☐	☐
1651	**1081**	(1st)	multicoloured	1·25	1·00	☐	☐
1652	**1082**	(1st)	multicoloured	1·25	1·00	☐	☐
1653	**1083**	(1st)	multicoloured	1·25	1·00	☐	☐
Set of 10				14·00	12·00	☐	☐
First Day Cover					13·00		☐
Presentation Pack (P.O. Pack No. G2)				16·00			☐
PHQ Cards (set of 10) (GS1)				16·00	30·00	☐	☐

Nos. 1644/53 were printed together, *se-tenant*, in booklet panes of ten stamps and 20 half stamp-size labels.

SET PRICES. Please note that set prices for booklet greetings stamps are for complete panes. Sets of single stamps are worth considerably less.

1084 Decorated Enamel Dial

1085 Escapement, Remontoire and Fusee

1086 Balance, Spring and Temperature Compensator

1087 Back of Movement

300th Birth Anniversary of John Harrison (inventor of the marine chronometer). Details of 'H4' Clock

1993 (16 Feb.) Phosphorised paper. Perf 14½ × 14

1654	**1084**	24p	multicoloured	60	60	☐	☐
1655	**1085**	28p	multicoloured	1·00	1·25	☐	☐
1656	**1086**	33p	multicoloured	1·40	1·25	☐	☐
1657	**1087**	39p	multicoloured	1·50	1·50	☐	☐
Set of 4				4·00	4·00	☐	☐
First Day Cover					4·50		☐
Presentation Pack (P.O. Pack No. 235)				4·50			☐
PHQ Cards (set of 4) (150)				4·25	7·00	☐	☐
Set of 4 Gutter Pairs				9·00			☐

1088 Britannia

1993 (2 Mar.) Granite paper. Perf 14 × 14½ (with two elliptical holes in each horizontal side)

1658	**1088**	£10	multicoloured	40·00	12·00	☐	☐
First Day Cover					25·00		☐
Presentation Pack (P.O. Pack No. 29)				45·00			☐
PHQ Card (D1)				8·00	60·00	☐	☐

1089 *Dendrobium hellwigianum*

1090 *Paphiopedilum Maudiae 'Magnifcum'*

1091 *Cymbidium lowianum*

1092 *Vanda Rothschildiana*

1093 *Dendrobium vexillarius var albiviride*

1093a

14th World Orchid Conference, Glasgow

1993 (16 Mar.) One phosphor band (18p) or phosphorised paper (others)

1659	**1089**	18p multicoloured	45	40	☐☐
1660	**1090**	24p multicoloured	75	60	☐☐
1661	**1091**	28p multicoloured	1·00	1·25	☐☐
1662	**1092**	33p multicoloured	1·25	1·50	☐☐
1663	**1093**	39p multicoloured	1·60	1·50	☐☐
Set of 5			4·50	4·75	☐☐
First Day Cover				5·25	☐
Presentation Pack (P.O. Pack No. 236)			5·00		☐
PHQ Cards (*set of 5*) (151)			4·50	7·00	☐☐
Set of 5 Gutter Pairs			10·00		☐

1993 (6 Apr.)–**2017**. As T **913/14** and **1093a**, but Perf 14 (No. 1665) or 15 × 14 (others) (both with one elliptical hole in each vertical side)

(a) Gravure

Harrison (No. 1666), Questa (Nos. 1664a, 1667a), Walsall (No. 1665), Harrison (later De La Rue), Questa or Walsall (No. 1667), Harrison (later De La Rue), Enschedé, Questa or Walsall (Nos. 1664, 1668, 1669) or ISP Walsall (No. 1668s)

1664	**913**	(2nd)	bright blue (1 centre band)		
			(7.9.93)	1·50	1·30	☐☐
	a.	Perf 14 *(1.12.98)*	1·50	1·30	☐☐
1665c		(2nd)	bright blue (1 side band) *(13.10.98)*	2·25	2·25	☐☐
1666	**914**	(1st)	bright orange-red (phosphorised paper)1·80	1·50	☐☐
1667		(1st)	bright orange-red (2 phosphor bands) *(4.4.95)*	1·80	1·30	☐☐
	a.	Perf 14 *(1.12.98)*	2·00	1·80	☐☐
1668		(1st)	gold (2 phosphor bands) *(21.4.97)*	1·60	1·60	☐☐
1668s		(1st)	brownish black (2 phosphor bands) *(5.6.17)*	2·75	2·75	☐☐
1669	**1093a**	(E)	deep blue (2 phosphor bands) *(19.1.99)*	2·00	1·50	☐☐

(b) Litho Questa or Walsall (No. 1670), Questa, Enschedé or Walsall (No. 1671), De La Rue or Walsall (No. 1672)

1670	**913**	(2nd)	bright blue (1 centre band)	1·50	90	☐☐
1671	**914**	(1st)	bright orange-red (2 phosphor bands)	1·80	1·00	☐☐

1672		(1st)	gold (2 phosphor bands) *(8.1.08)*	3·00	3·00	☐☐

First Day Covers

21 Apr. 1997	(1st) (No 1668), and 26p (Y1692)	3·50	☐
19 Jan. 1999	(E) (No 1669)	3·50	☐

Nos. 1664, 1667, 1669 and 1670/1 also come from sheets.

No. 1665 exists with the phosphor band at the left or right of the stamp and was only issued in booklets.

No. 1668 was issued by Harrison in booklets and Walsall in sheets and booklets for the Queen's Golden Wedding on 21 April 1997. The gold colour was later adopted for the (1st) class rate, replacing bright orange-red.

For No. 1668 in presentation pack see Pack No. 38 listed below, No. Y1667 etc.

No. 1668s was issued on 5 June 2017 in the £15·14 50th Anniversary of the Machin Definitive Prestige booklet.

No. 1669 was valid for the basic European airmail rate, initially 30p.

No. 1672 was only issued in £7·40 or £7·15 stamp booklets.

For self-adhesive versions in these colours see Nos. 2039/40 and 2295/8.

II Normal figures of face value

III Open '4' and open lower curve of '5'

1993–2011 As Nos. X841 etc, but perf 14 (No. Y1678) or 15 × 14 (others) (both with one elliptical hole in each vertical side)

(a) Gravure

Enschedé: 20p (Y1684), 29p, 35p (Y1698), 36p, 38p (Y1706), 41p (Y1712), 43p (Y1716)

Harrison: 20p (Y1686), 25p (Y1689), 26p (Y1692), 35p (Y1699), 41p (Y1713), 43p (Y1717)

Walsall: 10p (Y1676), 19p (Y1683), 38p (Y1707), 43p (Y1717)

Enschedé or Harrison (later De La Rue): 4p, 6p, 25p (Y1690), 31p, 39p (Y1708), £1 (Y1743)

Enschedé, or Harrison (later De La Rue Questa or Walsall): 1p, 2p

Enschedé, Harrison (later De La Rue) or Walsall: 5p, 10p. (Y1676), 30p, 37p (Y1703), 42p, 50p (Y1726), 63p

Harrison (later De La Rue) or Questa: 19p (Y1682), 20p (Y1685), 26p (Y1691)

De La Rue or Walsall: 20p (Y1687), 38p (Y1707), 39p (Y1709), 40p (Y1710), 50p (Y1727), 64p, 65p, 68p

De La Rue: 7p, 8p, 9p, 12p, 14p, 15p, 16p, 17p, 22p, 33p, 34p, 35p (Y1700), 37p (Y1704/5), 41p (Y1714), 43p (Y1718), 44p, 45p, 48p, 49p, 56p, 60p, 62p, 67p, 72p, 78p, 81p, 88p, 90p, 97p, £1 (Y1744), £1·46, £1·50, £2, £3, £5

Enschedé or De La Rue: 35p (Y1701), 40p (Y1711), 46p, 47p, 54p

Y1667	**367**	1p crimson (2 bands) *(8.6.93)*	30	25	☐☐
Y1668		2p deep green (2 bands) *(11.4.95)*	30	30	☐☐
Y1669		4p new blue (2 bands) *(14.12.93)*	30	30	☐☐
Y1670		5p dull red-brown (2 bands) (Type II) *(8.6.93)*	30	35	☐☐
Y1671		6p yellow-olive (2 bands) *(27.4.93)*	50	50	☐☐
Y1672		7p grey (2 bands) *(20.4.99)*	2·75	2·75	☐☐
Y1673		7p bright magenta (2 bands) *(1.4.04)*	1·20	1·20	☐☐

Y1674	8p	yellow (2 bands) *(25.4.00)*	35	35
Y1675	9p	yellow-orange (2 bands) *(5.4.05)*	30	20
Y1676	10p	dull orange (2 bands)*(8.6.93)*	35	35
		a. Perf 14 *(13.10.98)*	2·25	2·25
Y1677	12p	greenish blue (2 bands) *(1.8.06)*	1·25	1·40
Y1678	14p	rose-red (2 bands) *(1.8.06)*	75	90
Y1679	15p	bright magenta (2 bands) *(1.4.08)*	70	85
Y1680	16p	pale cerise (2 bands) *(27.3.07)*	70	85
Y1681	17p	brown-olive (2 bands) *(31.3.09)*	1·80	2·00
Y1682	19p	bistre (1 centre band) *(26.10.93)*	40	45
Y1683	19p	bistre (1 side band) *(15.2.00)*	3·00	3·00
Y1684	20p	turquoise-green (2 bands) *(14.12.93)*	80	80
Y1685	20p	bright green (1 centre band) *(25.6.96)*	50	50
Y1686	20p	bright green (1 side band) *(23.9.97)*	3·50	3·50
Y1687	20p	bright green (2 bands) *(20.4.99)*	75	75
Y1688	22p	drab (2 bands) *(31.3.09)*	2·00	2·00
Y1689	25p	rose-red (phosphorised paper) *(26.10.93)*	70	70
Y1690	25p	rose-red (2 bands) *(20.12.94)*	70	70
Y1691	26p	red-brown (2 bands) *(25.6.96)*	70	70
Y1692	26p	gold (2 bands) *(21.4.97)*	90	90
Y1693	29p	grey (2 bands) *(26.10.93)*	1·25	1·25
Y1694	30p	deep olive-grey (2 bands) *(27.7.93)*	90	90
Y1695	31p	deep mauve (2 bands) *(25.6.96)*	1·20	1·20
Y1696	33p	grey-green (2 bands) *(25.4.00)*	1·20	1·20
Y1697	34p	yellow-olive (2 bands) *(6.5.03)*	4·00	4·00
Y1698	35p	yellow (2 bands) *(17.8.93)*	1·50	1·50
Y1699	35p	yellow (phosphorised paper) *(1.11.93)*	10·00	10·00
Y1700	35p	sepia (2 bands) *(1.4.04)*	1·30	1·30
Y1701	35p	yellow-olive (1 centre band) *(5.4.05)*	1·10	1·10
Y1702	36p	bright ultramarine (2 bands) *(26.10.93)*	1·75	1·75
Y1703	37p	bright mauve (2 bands)*(25.6.96)*	1·40	1·40
Y1704	37p	grey-black (2 bands) *(4.7.02)*	1·90	1·90
Y1705	37p	brown-olive (1 centre band) *(28.3.06)*	2·10	2·10
Y1706	38p	rosine (2 bands) *(26.10.93)*	1·50	1·50
Y1707	38p	ultramarine (2 bands) *(20.4.99)*	1·60	1·60
		a. Perf 14 *(15.2.00)*	8·00	8·00
Y1708	39p	bright magenta (2 bands) *(25.6.96)*	1·50	1·50
Y1709	39p	grey (2 bands) *(1.4.04)*	1·60	1·60
Y1710	40p	deep azure (2 bands) *(25.4.00)*	1·40	1·40
Y1711	40p	turquoise-blue (2 bands) *(1.4.04)*	1·00	1·00
Y1712	41p	grey-brown (2 bands) *(26.10.93)*	1·75	1·75
Y1713	41p	drab (phosphorised paper) *(1.11.93)*	10·00	10·00
Y1714	41p	rosine (2 bands) *(25.4.00)*	1·40	1·40
Y1715	42p	deep olive-grey		
		(2 bands) *(4.7.02)*	1·40	1·40
Y1716	43p	deep olive-brown (2 bands) *(25.6.96)*	1·75	1·75
Y1717	43p	sepia (2 bands) *(8.7.96)*	2·50	2·50
		a. Perf 14 *(13.10.98)*	2·75	2·75
Y1718	43p	emerald (2 bands) *(1.4.04)*	1·90	1·90
Y1719	44p	grey-brown (2 bands) *(20.4.99)*	5·00	5·00
Y1720	44p	deep bright blue (2 bands) *(28.3.06)*	1·50	1·50
Y1721	45p	bright mauve (2 bands) *(25.4.00)*	1·50	1·50
Y1722	46p	yellow (2 bands) *(5.4.05)*	1·50	1·50
Y1723	47p	turquoise-green (2 bands) *(4.7.02)*	1·75	1·75
Y1724	48p	bright mauve (2 bands) *(27.3.07)*	1·80	1·80
Y1725	49p	red-brown (2 bands) *(28.3.06)*	2·50	2·50
Y1726	50p	ochre (2 bands) *(14.12.93)*	1·25	1·25
Y1727	50p	grey (2 bands) *(27.3.07)*	1·00	1·00
Y1728	54p	red-brown (Type II) (2 bands) *(27.3.07)*	1·75	1·75
Y1729	56p	yellow-olive (2 bands) *(1.4.08)*	1·90	1·90
Y1730	60p	light emerald (2 bands) *(30.3.10)*	1·50	1·50
Y1731	62p	rosine (2 bands) *(31.3.09)*	2·10	2·10
Y1732	63p	light emerald (2 bands) *(25.6.96)*	2·00	2·00
Y1733	64p	turquoise-green (2 bands) *(20.4.99)*	2·25	2·25
Y1734	65p	greenish blue (2 bands) *(25.4.00)*	2·10	2·10
Y1735	67p	bright mauve (2 bands) *(30.3.10)*	3·00	3·00
Y1736	68p	grey-brown (2 bands) *(4.7.02)*	2·10	2·10
Y1737	72p	rosine (2 bands) *(28.3.06)*	2·25	2·25
Y1738	78p	emerald (2 bands) *(27.3.07)*	1·50	1·50
Y1739	81p	turquoise-green (2 bands) *(1.4.08)*	2·00	2·00
Y1740	88p	bright magenta (2 bands) *(30.3.10)*	2·25	2·25
Y1741	90p	ultramarine (2 bands) *(31.3.09)*	2·25	2·25
Y1742	97p	violet (2 bands) *(30.3.10)*	3·00	3·00
Y1743	£1	bluish violet (2 bands) *(22.8.95)*	2·00	2·00
Y1744	£1	magenta (2 bands) *(5.6.07)*	2·00	2·00
Y1745	£1·46	greenish-blue (2 bands) *(30.3.10)*	5·50	5·50
Y1746	£1·50	brown-red (2 bands) *(1.7.03)*	3·50	3·50
Y1747	£2	deep blue-green (2 bands) *(1.7.03)*	5·00	5·00
Y1748	£3	deep mauve (2 bands) *(1.7.03)*	7·00	7·00
Y1749	£5	azure (2 bands) *(1.7.03)*	12·00	12·00

(b) Litho Cartor (1p (Y1761), 5p (Y1765),10p (Y1767), 16p, 17p, 20p (Y1773), 22p, 50p, 54p, 60p (Y1785), 62p, 67p, 90p, 97p), De La Rue (48p), Cartor, Questa or De La Rue (10p)(Y1767), Questa or Walsall (25p, 35p, 41p), Walsall (37p, 60p (Y1784), 63p), Questa (others), Cartor or De La Rue (5p (Y1762)

Y1760 **367**	1p	lake (2 bands) *(8.7.96)*	80	80
Y1761	1p	reddish purple (2 bands) *(17.9.09)*	2·50	2·50
Y1762	5p	chocolate (2 bands) *(12.2.09)*	3·25	3·25
Y1763	5p	Red-brown (Type II) *(12.2.09)*	3·00	3·00
Y1765	5p	red-brown (2 bands) (Type III) *(7.1.10)*	3·75	3·75

Y1766	6p yellow-olive (2 bands) *(26.7.94)*	12·00	13·00	☐	☐
Y1767	10p dull orange (2 bands) *(25.4.95)*	3·50	3·50	☐	☐
Y1768	10p pale brownish orange *(7.1.10)*	3·50	3·50		
Y1769	16p pale cerise (2 bands) *(13.1.09)*	3·00	3·00	☐	☐
Y1770	17p bistre (2 bands) *(18.8.09)*	2·50	2·50	☐	☐
Y1771	19p bistre (1 side band at left) *(26.7.94)*	2·50	2·50	☐	☐
Y1772	20p bright yellow-green (1 centre band) *(8.7.96)*	2·25	2·25	☐	☐
Y1773	20p light green (2 bands) *(7.1.10)*	3·00	3·00	☐	☐
Y1774	22p olive-brown (2 bands) *(18.8.09)*	4·00	4·00	☐	☐
Y1775	25p red (2 bands) *(1.11.93)*	1·10	1·10	☐	☐
Y1776	26p chestnut (2 bands) *(8.7.96)*	1·00	1·00	☐	☐
Y1777	30p olive-grey (2 bands) *(25.4.95)*	5·50	5·50	☐	☐
Y1778	35p yellow (2 bands) *(1.11.93)*	1·60	1·60	☐	☐
Y1779	37p bright mauve (2 bands) *(8.7.96)*	3·50	3·50	☐	☐
Y1780	41p drab (2 bands) *(1.11.93)*	1·75	1·75	☐	☐
Y1781	48p bright mauve (2 bands) *(12.2.09)*	3·00	3·00	☐	☐
Y1782	50p grey (2 bands) *(13.1.09)*	3·75	3·75	☐	☐
Y1783	54p chestnut (2 bands) (Type III) *(7.1.10)*	3·50	3·50	☐	☐
Y1784	60p dull blue-grey (2 bands) *(9.8.94)*	2·50	2·50	☐	☐
Y1785	60p emerald (2 bands) *(13.5.10)*	6·00	6·00	☐	☐
Y1786	62p rosine (2 bands) *(18.8.09)*	4·00	4·00	☐	☐
Y1787	63p light emerald (2 bands) *(8.7.96)*	3·75	3·75	☐	☐
Y1788	67p bright mauve (2 bands) *(22.3.11)*	7·50	8·00	☐	☐
Y1789	90p bright blue (2 bands) *(17.9.09)*	4·75	4·75	☐	☐
Y1790	97p bluish violet (2 bands) *(22.3.11)*	8·00	8·00	☐	☐

(c) Recess Enschedé or De La Rue

Y1800	**367** £1·50 red *(9.3.99)*	4·00	2·00	☐	☐
Y1801	£2 dull blue *(9.3.99)*	5·00	2·25	☐	☐
Y1802	£3 dull violet *(9.3.99)*	7·00	3·00	☐	☐
Y1803	£5 brown *(9.3.99)*	12·00	5·00	☐	☐
PHQ Card (No. Y1725) (D7)		3·00	15·00	☐	☐

PHQ Cards (Nos. 1664, 1668, Y1667/8, Y1670, Y1675/6, Y1679/80, Y1687, Y1724, Y1727, Y1729, Y1739, Y1744, Y1746/9, 2357a, 2358, 2359, 2652/3)(D30) **15·00** ☐

Presentation Pack (P.O. Pack No. 30) (contains 19p (Y1682), 25p (Y1689), 29p (Y1693), 36p (Y1702), 38p (Y1706), 41p (Y1712)) **7·00** ☐

Presentation Pack (P.O. Pack No. 34) (contains 1p (Y1667), 2p (Y1668), 4p (Y1669), 5p (Y1670), 6p (Y1671), 10p (Y1676), 19p (Y1682), 20p (Y1684), 25p (Y1690), 29p (Y1693), 30p (Y1694), 35p (Y1698), 36p (Y1702), 38p (Y1706), 41p (Y1712), 50p (Y1726), 60p (Y1730), £1 (Y1743)) **35·00** ☐

Presentation Pack (P.O. Pack No. 35) (contains 20p (Y1685), 26p (Y1691), 31p (Y1695), 37p (Y1703), 39p (Y1708), 43p (Y1716), 63p (Y1732)) **9·50** ☐

Presentation Pack (P.O. Pack No. 38) (contains 1st (Y1668), 26p (Y1692)) **7·50** ☐

Presentation Pack (P.O. Pack No. 41) (contains 2nd (Y1664), 1st (Y1667), 1p (Y1667), 2p (Y1668), 4p (Y1669), 5p (Y1670), 6p (Y1671), 10p (Y1676), 20p

(Y1685), 26p (Y1691), 30p (Y1694), 31p (Y1695), 37p (Y1703), 39p (Y1708), 43p (Y1717), 50p (Y1726), 63p (Y1732), £1 (Y1743)) **20·00** ☐

Presentation Pack (P.O. Pack No. 43 or 43A) (contains £1·50 (Y1800), £2 (Y1801), £3 (Y1802), £5 (Y1803)) **55·00** ☐

Presentation Pack (P.O. Pack No. 44) contains 7p (Y1672), 19p (Y1682), 38p (Y1707), 44p (Y1719), 64p (Y1733)) **11·00** ☐

Presentation Pack (P.O. Pack No. 49) (contains 8p (Y1674), 33p (Y1696), 40p (Y1710), 41p (Y1714), 45p (Y1721), 65p (Y1734)) **10·00** ☐

Presentation Pack (P.O. Pack No. 57) (contains 2nd (1664), 1st (1667), E (1669), 1p (1667), 2p (1668), 4p (1669), 5p (1670), 8p (Y1674), 10p (Y1676), 20p (Y1687), 33p (Y1696), 40p (Y1710), 41p (Y1714), 45p (Y1721), 50p (Y1726), 65p (Y1734), £1 (Y1743)) **18·00** ☐

Presentation Pack (P.O. Pack No. 58) (contains 37p (Y1704), 42p (Y1715), 47p (Y1723), 68p (Y1736)) **7·50** ☐

Presentation Pack (P.O. Pack No. 62) (contains £1·50 (Y1746), £2 (Y1747), £3 (Y1748), £5 (Y1749)) **25·00** ☐

Presentation Pack (P.O. Pack No. 67) (contains 7p (No. Y1673), 1st (1668), 35p (Y1700), 39p (Y1709), 40p (Y1711), 43p (Y1718), Worldwide postcard (2357a)) **15·00** ☐

Presentation Pack (P.O. Pack No. 71) (contains 1p (Y1667), 2p (Y1668), 5p (Y1670), 9p (Y1675), 10p (Y1676), 20p (Y1687), 35p (Y1701), 40p (Y1711), 42p (Y1715), 46p (Y1722), 47p (Y1723), 50p (Y1726), 68p (Y1736), £1 (Y1743), 2nd (2039), 1st (2295), Worldwide postcard (2357a), Europe up to 40 grams (2358), Worldwide up to 40 grams (2359)) **60·00** ☐

Presentation Pack (P.O. Pack No. 72) (contains 37p (Y1705), 44p (Y1720), 49p (Y1725), 72p (Y1737)) **12·00** ☐

Presentation Pack (P.O. Pack No.75) (contains 16p (Y1680), 48p (Y1724), 54p (Y1728), 78p (Y1738)) **10·00** ☐

Presentation Pack (P.O. Pack No.77) (contains 1p (Y1667), 2p (Y1668), 5p (Y1670), 10p (Y1676), 14p (Y1678), 16p (Y1679), 20p (Y1687), 46p (Y1722), 48p (Y1724), 50p (Y1727), 54p (Y1728), 78p (Y1738), £1 (Y1744), 2nd (1664), 1st (1668), 2nd Large (2652), 1st Large (2653), Worldwide postcard (2357a), Europe up to 40 grams (2358), Worldwide up to 40 grams (2359)) **45·00** ☐

Presentation Pack (P.O. Pack No.78) (contains 15p (Y1679), 56p (Y1729), 81p (Y1739)) **6·00** ☐

Presentation Pack (P.O. Pack No. 84) (contains 17p (Y1681), 22p (Y1688), 62p (Y1731), 90p (Y1741)) **8·50** ☐

Presentation Pack (P.O. Pack No. 86) (contains 60p (Y1730), 67p (Y1735), 88p (Y1740), 97p (Y1742), £1·46 (Y1745), Europe up to 20 grams (2357b), Worldwide up to 20 grams (2358a), Recorded Signed for 1st (U2981), Recorded Signed for 1st Large (U2982)) **28·00** ☐

Presentation Pack (P.O. Pack No. 88) (contains 1p (Y1667), 2p (Y1668), 5p (Y1670), 9p (Y1675), 10p (Y1676), 20p (Y1687), 50p (Y1727), 60p (Y1730), 67p (Y1735), 88p (Y1740), 97p (Y1742),

£1 (Y1744), £1·46 (Y1745), Worldwide postcard (2357a), Europe up to 20 grams (2357b), Europe up to 40 grams (2358), Worldwide up to 20 grams (2358a), Worldwide up to 40 grams (2359a), 2nd (1664), 1st (1668), 2nd Large (2652), 1st Large (2653), Recorded Signed for 1st (U2981), Recorded Signed for 1st Large (U2982))   55·00   ☐

For P.O. Pack No. 37 see below No. 1977.
For P.O. Pack No. 74 containing Nos. Y1677/8 see below No. 2657.

First Day Covers

26 Oct. 1993	19p, 25p, 29p, 36p, 38p, 41p (Nos. Y1682, Y1689, Y1693, Y1702, Y1706, Y1712)	6·00	☐
9 Aug. 1994	60p (No. Y1784)	4·00	☐
22 Aug. 1995	£1 (No. Y1743)	3·50	☐
25 June 1996	20p, 26p, 31p, 37p, 39p, 43p, 63p (Nos. Y1685, Y1691, Y1695, Y1703, Y1708, Y1716, Y1732)	8·00	☐
9 Mar. 1999	£1·50, £2, £3, £5 (Nos. Y1800/3)	27·00	☐
20 Apr. 1999	7p, 38p, 44p, 64p (Nos. Y1672, Y1707, Y1719, Y1733)	5·00	☐
25 Apr. 2000	8p, 33p, 40p, 41p, 45p, 65p (Nos. Y1674, Y1696, Y1710, Y1714, Y1721, Y1734)	6·00	☐
4 July 2002	37p, 42p, 47p, 68p, (Nos. Y1704, Y1715, Y1723, Y1736)	6·00	☐
6 May 2003	34p (No. Y1697)	2·00	☐
1 July 2003	£1·50, £2, £3, £5 (Nos. Y1746/9)	21·00	☐
1 Apr. 2004	7p, 35p, 39p, 40p, 43p, Worldwide post- card (Nos. Y1673, Y1700, Y1709, Y1711, Y1718, 2357a)	9·00	☐
5 Apr. 2005	9p, 35p, 46p (Nos. Y1675, Y1701, Y1722)	3·00	☐
28 Mar. 2006	37p, 44p, 49p, 72p (Nos. Y1705, Y1720, Y1725, Y1737)	6·00	☐
27 Mar. 2007	16p, 48p, 50p, 54p, 78p (Nos. Y1680, Y1724, Y1727/8, Y1738)	7·50	☐
1 Apr. 2008	15p, 56p, 81p (Nos. Y1679, Y1729, Y1739)	5·50	☐
31 Mar. 2009	17p, 22p, 62p, 90p, (Nos. Y1681, Y1688, Y1731, Y1741)	6·50	☐
30 Mar. 2010	60p, 67p, 88p, 97p, £1·46, Europe up to 20 grams, Worldwide up to 20 grams (Nos. Y1730, 1735, Y1740, Y1742, Y1745, 2357b, 2358a)	16·00	☐

For Nos. Y1677/8 on first day cover see under Nos. 2650/7.
Nos. Y1743/9 are printed in Iriodin ink which gives a shiny effect to the solid part of the background behind the Queen's head.
Nos. Y1699 and Y1713 were only issued in coils and Nos. Y1676, Y1683, Y1678, Y1686, Y1707, Y1717 and Y1660/89 only in booklets.
No. Y1771 exists with the phosphor band at the left or right of the stamp, but Nos. Y1683 and Y1686 exist with band at right only.

For self-adhesive versions of the 42p and 68p see Nos. 2297/8.

1094 'Family Group' (bronze sculpture) (Henry Moore)

1095 'Kew Gardens' (lithograph) (Edward Bawden)

1096 'St Francis and the Birds' (Stanley Spencer)

1097 'Still Life: Odyssey I' (Ben Nicholson)

Europa. Contemporary Art

1993 (11 May) Phosphorised paper. Perf 14 × 14½

1767	**1094**	24p	multicoloured	60	60	☐ ☐
1768	**1095**	28p	multicoloured	90	1·00	☐ ☐
1769	**1096**	33p	multicoloured	1·25	1·40	☐ ☐
1770	**1097**	39p	multicoloured	1·75	1·75	☐ ☐
Set of 4				4·00	4·25	☐
First Day Cover					4·75	☐
Presentation Pack (P.O. Pack No. 237)				4·50		☐
PHQ Cards (set of 4) (152)				4·00	7·00	☐ ☐
Set of 4 Gutter Pairs				9·00		☐

1098 Emperor Claudius (from gold coin)

1099 Emperor Hadrian (bronze head)

1100 Goddess Roma (from gemstone)

1101 Christ (Hinton St. Mary mosaic)

Roman Britain

1993 (15 June) Phosphorised paper with two phosphor bands. Perf 14 × 14½

1771	**1098**	24p	multicoloured	60	50	☐ ☐
1772	**1099**	28p	multicoloured	90	1·00	☐ ☐
1773	**1100**	33p	multicoloured	1·30	1·50	☐ ☐
1774	**1101**	39p	multicoloured	1·50	1·60	☐ ☐
Set of 4				4·00	4·25	☐
First Day Cover					4·75	☐
Presentation Pack (P.O. Pack No. 238)				4·50		☐
PHQ Cards (set of 4) (153)				4·25	7·00	☐ ☐
Set of 4 Gutter Pairs				9·00		☐

1102 *Midland Maid* and other Narrow Boats, Grand Junction Canal

1103 *Yorkshire Maid* and other Humber Keels, Stainforth and Keadby Canal

1104 *Valley Princess* and other Horse-drawn Barges, Brecknock and Abergavenny Canal

1105 Steam Barges including *Pride of Scotland* and Fishing Boats, Crinan Canal

Inland Waterways

1993 (20 July) Two phosphor bands. Perf 14½ × 14

1775	**1102**	24p multicoloured	50	50	☐	☐
1776	**1103**	28p multicoloured	1·00	1·00	☐	☐
1777	**1104**	33p multicoloured	1·25	1·25	☐	☐
1778	**1105**	39p multicoloured	1·50	1·40	☐	☐
Set of 4			3·75	3·75	☐	☐
First Day Cover				4·25	☐	
Presentation Pack (P.O. Pack No. 239)			4·50		☐	
PHQ Cards (*set of* 4) (154)			4·25	7·00	☐	☐
Set of 4 Gutter Pairs			8·50		☐	

Nos. 1775/8 commemorate the bicentenaries of the Acts of Parliament authorising the canals depicted.

1106 Horse Chestnut

1107 Blackberry

1108 Hazel

1109 Rowan

1110 Pear

The Four Seasons. (2nd series) Autumn.
Fruits and Leaves

1993 (14 Sept.) One phosphor band (18p) or phosphorised paper (others)

1779	**1106**	18p multicoloured	50	30	☐	☐
1780	**1107**	24p multicoloured	75	50	☐	☐
1781	**1108**	28p multicoloured	1·10	1·25	☐	☐
1782	**1109**	33p multicoloured	1·40	1·50	☐	☐
1783	**1110**	39p multicoloured	1·50	1·50	☐	☐
Set of 5			4·75	4·50	☐	☐

First Day Cover		5·00	☐
Presentation Pack (P.O. Pack No. 240)	5·00		☐
PHQ Cards (*set of* 5) (155)	4·50	7·00	☐ ☐
Set of 5 Gutter Pairs		10·50	☐

SHERLOCK HOLMES & DR WATSON
"THE REIGATE SQUIRE"
1111 *The Reigate Squire*

SHERLOCK HOLMES & SIR HENRY
"THE HOUND OF THE BASKERVILLES"
1112 *The Hound of the Baskervilles*

SHERLOCK HOLMES & LESTRADE
"THE SIX NAPOLEONS"
1113 *The Six Napoleons*

SHERLOCK HOLMES & MYCROFT
"THE GREEK INTERPRETER"
1114 *The Greek Interpreter*

SHERLOCK HOLMES & MORIARTY
"THE FINAL PROBLEM"
1115 *The Final Problem*

Sherlock Holmes.
Centenary of the Publication of The Final Problem

1993 (12 Oct.) Phosphorised paper. Perf 14 × 14½

1784	**1111**	24p multicoloured	50	60	☐	☐
		a. Horiz strip of 5.				
		Nos. 1784/8	5·00	5·25	☐	☐
1785	**1112**	24p multicoloured	50	60	☐	☐
1786	**1113**	24p multicoloured	50	60	☐	☐
1787	**1114**	24p multicoloured	50	60	☐	☐
1788	**1115**	24p multicoloured	50	60	☐	☐
Set of 5			5·00	5·25	☐	☐
First Day Cover				5·75	☐	
Presentation Pack (P.O. Pack No. 241)			5·50		☐	
PHQ Cards (*set of* 5) (156)			4·50	10·00	☐	☐
Gutter Strip of 10			11·00		☐	

Nos. 1784/8 were printed together, *se-tenant*, in horizontal strips of five throughout the sheet.

1116

Self-adhesive Booklet Stamp

1993 (19 Oct.) Litho Walsall. Two phosphor bands. Die-cut perf 14 × 15 (with one elliptical hole in each vertical side)

1789 **1116** (1st) orange-red	2·50	2·75	☐ ☐
First Day Cover		5·50	☐
Presentation Pack (booklet pane of 20) (P.O. Pack No. 29)	28·00		☐
PHQ Card (D6)	4·00	8·00	☐ ☐

For similar 2nd and 1st designs printed in gravure by Enschedé see Nos. 1976/7.

1117 Bob Cratchit and Tiny Tim   **1118** Mr and Mrs Fezziwig

1119 Scrooge   **1120** The Prize Turkey

1121 Mr Scrooge's Nephew

Christmas.
150th Anniversary of Publication of A Christmas Carol

1993 (9 Nov.) One phosphor band (19p) or phosphorised paper (others)

1790 **1117**	19p	multicoloured	60	40	☐ ☐
1791 **1118**	25p	multicoloured	90	60	☐ ☐
1792 **1119**	30p	multicoloured	1·25	1·50	☐ ☐
1793 **1120**	35p	multicoloured	1·40	1·60	☐ ☐
1794 **1121**	41p	multicoloured	1·40	1·60	☐ ☐
Set of 5			4·50	5·25	☐ ☐
First Day Cover				5·75	☐
Presentation Pack (P.O. Pack No. 242)			5·00		☐
PHQ Cards (*set of 5*) (157)			4·50	8·00	☐ ☐
Set of 5 Gutter Pairs			10·00		☐

Collectors Pack 1993

1993 (9 Nov.) Comprises Nos. 1639/43, 1654/7, 1659/63, 1767/88 and 1790/4

CP1794a	Collectors Pack	45·00	☐

Post Office Yearbook

1993 (9 Nov.) Comprises Nos. 1639/43, 1654/7, 1659/63, 1767/88 and 1790/4 in hardback book with slip case

YB1794a	Yearbook	85·00	☐

1122 Class 5 No. 44957 and Class B1 No. 61342 on West Highland Line   **1123** Class A1 No. 60149 *Amadis* at Kings Cross

1124 Class 4 No. 43000 on Turntable at Blythe North   **1125** Class 4 No. 42455 near Wigan Central

1126 Castle Class No. 7002 *Devizes Castle* on Bridge crossing Worcester and Birmingham Canal

The Age of Steam. Railway Photographs by Colin Gifford

1994 (18 Jan.) One phosphor band (19p) or phosphorised paper with two bands (others). Perf 14½

1795 **1122**	19p	deep blue-green, grey-black and black	55	45	☐ ☐
1796 **1123**	25p	slate-lilac, grey-black and black	90	95	☐ ☐
1797 **1124**	30p	lake-brown, grey-black and black	1·40	1·50	☐ ☐
1798 **1125**	35p	deep claret, grey-black and black	1·75	1·80	☐ ☐
1799 **1126**	41p	indigo, grey-black and black	1·80	1·90	☐ ☐
Set of 5			6·00	6·00	☐ ☐
First Day Cover				6·50	☐
Presentation Pack (P.O. Pack No. 244)			6·50		☐
PHQ Cards (*set of 5*) (158)			5·75	17·00	☐ ☐
Set of 5 Gutter Pairs			12·00		☐

1127 Dan Dare and the Mekon   **1128** The Three Bears

1129 Rupert Bear   **1130** Alice (*Alice in Wonderland*)

1131 Noggin and the Ice Dragon

1132 Peter Rabbit posting Letter

1133 Red Riding Hood and Wolf

1134 Orlando the Marmalade Cat

1135 Biggles

1136 Paddington Bear on Station

Greetings Stamps. 'Messages' (7th series).
Booklet Stamps

1994 (1 Feb.) Two phosphor bands. Perf 15 × 14 (with one elliptical hole in each vertical side)

1800 **1127**	(1st)	multicoloured	1·25	1·00
	a.	Booklet pane. Nos. 1800/9	15·00	15·00
1801 **1128**	(1st)	multicoloured	1·25	1·00
1802 **1129**	(1st)	multicoloured	1·25	1·00
1803 **1130**	(1st)	gold, bistre-yellow and black	1·25	1·00
1804 **1131**	(1st)	multicoloured	1·25	1·00
1805 **1132**	(1st)	multicoloured	1·25	1·00
1806 **1133**	(1st)	multicoloured	1·25	1·00
1807 **1134**	(1st)	multicoloured	1·25	1·00
1808 **1135**	(1st)	multicoloured	1·25	1·00
1809 **1136**	(1st)	multicoloured	1·25	1·00
Set of 10			15·00	15·00
First Day Cover				16·00
Presentation Pack (P.O. Pack No. G3)			18·00	
PHQ Cards (*set of* 10) (GS2)			16·00	30·00

Nos. 1800/9 were printed together, *se-tenant*, in booklet panes of ten stamps and 20 half stamp-size labels.

SET PRICES. Please note that set prices for booklet greetings stamps are for complete panes. Sets of single stamps are worth considerably less.

1137 Castell Y Waun (Chirk Castle), Clwyd, Wales

1138 Ben Arkle, Sutherland, Scotland

1139 Mourne Mountains, County Down, Northern Ireland

1140 Dersingham, Norfolk, England

Dolwyddelan, Gwynedd, Cymru / Wales

1141 Dolwyddelan, Gwynedd, Wales

25th Anniversary of Investiture of the Prince of Wales.
Paintings by Prince Charles

1994 (1 Mar.) One phosphor band (19p) or phosphorised paper (others)

1810 **1137**	19p	multicoloured	55	40
1811 **1138**	25p	multicoloured	1·00	60
1812 **1139**	30p	multicoloured	1·10	1·50
1813 **1140**	35p	multicoloured	1·40	1·75
1814 **1141**	41p	multicoloured	1·50	1·75
Set of 5			5·00	5·50
First Day Cover				6·00
Presentation Pack (P.O. Pack No. 245)			5·50	
PHQ Cards (*set of* 5) (159)			5·75	11·50
Set of 5 Gutter Pairs			11·00	

1142 Bather at Blackpool

1143 'Where's my Little Lad?'

1144 'Wish You were Here!'

1145 Punch and Judy Show

1146 'The Tower Crane' Machine

Centenary of Picture Postcards

1994 (12 Apr.) One side band (19p) or two phosphor bands (others). Perf 14 × 14½

1815 **1142**	19p	multicoloured	60	40
1816 **1143**	25p	multicoloured	90	60
1817 **1144**	30p	multicoloured	1·10	1·50
1818 **1145**	35p	multicoloured	1·40	1·75
1819 **1146**	41p	multicoloured	1·50	1·75
Set of 5			5·00	5·50
First Day Cover				6·00
Presentation Pack (P.O. Pack No. 246)			5·50	
PHQ Cards (*set of* 5) (160)			5·75	11·50
Set of 5 Gutter Pairs			11·00	

1147 British Lion and French Cockerel over Tunnel

1148 Symbolic Hands over Train

Opening of Channel Tunnel

1994 (3 May) Phosphorised paper. Perf 14 × 14½

1820	**1147**	25p	multicoloured	75	60
	a.	Horiz pair.			
		Nos. 1820/1	2·00	2·00	
1821	**1148**	25p	multicoloured	75	60
1822	**1147**	41p	multicoloured	1·00	1·00
	a.	Horiz pair.			
		Nos. 1822/3	3·25	2·50	
1823	**1148**	41p	multicoloured	1·00	1·00
Set of 4				4·50	4·75
First Day Cover					5·25
First Day Covers (2) (UK and					
French stamps)				20·00	
Presentation Pack (P.O. Pack No. 247)			5·00		
Presentation Pack (UK and					
French stamps)				25·00	
Souvenir Book				50·00	
PHQ Cards (*set of* 4) (161)			5·75	9·00	

Stamps in similar designs were also issued by France and these are included in the joint Presentation Pack and Souvenir Book.

Nos. 1820/1 and 1822/3 were printed together, *se-tenant*, in horizontal pairs throughout the sheets.

1149 Groundcrew replacing Smoke Canisters on Douglas Boston of 88 Sqn

1150 H.M.S. *Warspite* (battleship) shelling Enemy Positions

1151 Commandos Landing on Gold Beach

1152 Infantry regrouping on Sword Beach

1153 Tank and Infantry advancing, Ouistreham

50th Anniversary of D-Day

1994 (6 June) Two phosphor bands. Perf 14½ × 14

1824	**1149**	25p	multicoloured	60	60
	a.	Horiz strip of 5.			
		Nos. 1824/8	4·25	5·00	
1825	**1150**	25p	multicoloured	60	60
1826	**1151**	25p	multicoloured	60	60
1827	**1152**	25p	multicoloured	60	60
1828	**1153**	25p	multicoloured	60	60
Set of 5				4·25	5·00
First Day Cover					5·50
Presentation Pack (P.O. Pack No. 248)			5·50		
PHQ Cards (*set of* 5) (162)			5·00	11·50	
Gutter Block of 10				11·00	

Nos. 1824/8 were printed together, *se-tenant*, in horizontal strips of five throughout the sheet.

1154 The Old Course, St Andrews

1155 The 18th Hole, Muirfield

1156 The 15th Hole ('Luckyslap'), Carnoustie

1157 The 8th Hole ('The Postage Stamp'), Royal Troon

1158 The 9th Hole, Turnberry

Scottish Golf Courses

1994 (5 July) One phosphor band (19p) or phosphorised paper (others). Perf 14½ × 14

1829	**1154**	19p	multicoloured	50	40
1830	**1155**	25p	multicoloured	75	60
1831	**1156**	30p	multicoloured	1·10	1·40
1832	**1157**	35p	multicoloured	1·25	1·40
1833	**1158**	41p	multicoloured	1·40	1·40
Set of 5				4·50	4·75

First Day Cover	5·25	☐
Presentation Pack (P.O. Pack No. 249)	5·00	☐
PHQ Cards (*set of 5*) (163)	5·75	11·50 ☐ ☐
Set of 5 Gutter Pairs	10·00	☐

Nos. 1829/33 commemorate the 250th anniversary of golf's first set of rules produced by the Honourable Company of Edinburgh Golfers.

1159 Royal Welsh Show, Llanelwedd

1160 All England Tennis Championships, Wimbledon

1161 Cowes Week

1162 Test Match, Lord's

1163 Braemar Gathering

The Four Seasons (3rd series). Summertime. Events

1994 (2 Aug.) One phosphor band (19p) or phosphorised paper (others)

1834 **1159**	19p multicoloured	50	40	☐ ☐
1835 **1160**	25p multicoloured	75	60	☐ ☐
1836 **1161**	30p multicoloured	1·10	1·25	☐ ☐
1837 **1162**	35p multicoloured	1·25	1·60	☐ ☐
1838 **1163**	41p multicoloured	1·40	1·60	☐ ☐
Set of 5		4·50	5·00	☐ ☐
First Day Cover			5·50	
Presentation Pack (P.O. Pack No. 250)		5·00		☐
PHQ Cards (*set of 5*) (164)		5·75	11·50	☐ ☐
Set of 5 Gutter Pairs		10·00		☐

1164 Ultrasonic Imaging

1165 Scanning Electron Microscopy

1166 Magnetic Resonance Imaging

1167 Computed Tomography

Europa. Medical Discoveries

1994 (27 Sept.) Phosphorised paper. Perf 14 × 14½

1839 **1164**	25p multicoloured	75	60	☐ ☐
1840 **1165**	30p multicoloured	1·00	1·25	☐ ☐
1841 **1166**	35p multicoloured	1·50	1·75	☐ ☐
1842 **1167**	41p multicoloured	1·75	1·75	☐ ☐
Set of 4		4·50	4·75	☐ ☐
First Day Cover			5·25	
Presentation Pack (P.O. Pack No. 251)		5·00		☐
PHQ Cards (*set of 4*) (165)		5·75	10·00	☐ ☐
Set of 4 Gutter Pairs		10·00		☐

1168 Virgin Mary and Joseph

1169 Three Wise Men

1170 Virgin and Child

1171 Shepherds

1172 Angels

Christmas. Children's Nativity Plays

1994 (1 Nov.) One phosphor band (19p) or phosphorised paper (others)

1843 **1168**	19p multicoloured	50	40	☐ ☐
1844 **1169**	25p multicoloured	75	60	☐ ☐
1845 **1170**	30p multicoloured	1·00	1·50	☐ ☐
1846 **1171**	35p multicoloured	1·25	1·50	☐ ☐
1847 **1172**	41p multicoloured	1·50	1·75	☐ ☐
Set of 5		4·50	5·25	☐ ☐
First Day Cover			5·75	
Presentation Pack (P.O. Pack No. 252)		5·00		☐
PHQ Cards (*set of 5*) (166)		5·75	11·50	☐ ☐
Set of 5 Gutter Pairs		10·50		☐

Year Pack 1994

1994 (14 Nov.) Comprises Nos. 1795/1847

CP1847a Year Pack	48·00	☐

Post Office Yearbook

1994 (14 Nov.) Comprises Nos. 1795/9 and 1810/47 in hardback book with slip case

YB1847a Yearbook	50·00	☐

19

25

1173 Sophie (black cat)

1174 Puskas (Siamese) and Tigger (tabby)

30

35

1175 Chloe (ginger cat)

1176 Kikko (tortoiseshell) and Rosie (Abyssinian)

41

1177 Fred (black and white cat)

Cats

1995 (17 Jan.) One phosphor band (19p) or two phosphor bands (others). Perf 14½ × 14

1848	**1173**	19p	multicoloured	75	40	☐ ☐
1849	**1174**	25p	multicoloured	75	60	☐ ☐
1850	**1175**	30p	multicoloured	1·00	1·50	☐ ☐
1851	**1176**	35p	multicoloured	1·25	1·50	☐ ☐
1852	**1177**	41p	multicoloured	1·50	1·50	☐ ☐
Set of 5				4·75	5·00	☐ ☐
First Day Cover					5·50	☐
Presentation Pack (P.O. Pack No. 254)				5·50		☐
PHQ Cards (set of 5) (167)				6·00	11·50	☐ ☐
Set of 5 Gutter Pairs				11·00		☐

1178 Dandelions

1179 Sweet Chestnut Leaves

1180 Garlic Leaves

1181 Hazel Leaves

1182 Spring Grass

The Four Seasons (4th series). Springtime. Plant Sculptures by Andy Goldsworthy

1995 (14 Mar.) One phosphor band (19p) or two phosphor bands (others)

1853	**1178**	19p	multicoloured	75	40	☐ ☐
1854	**1179**	25p	multicoloured	75	60	☐ ☐
1855	**1180**	30p	multicoloured	1·00	1·50	☐ ☐
1856	**1181**	35p	multicoloured	1·25	1·50	☐ ☐
1857	**1182**	41p	multicoloured	1·50	1·75	☐ ☐
Set of 5				4·75	5·25	☐ ☐
First Day Cover					5·75	☐
Presentation Pack (P.O. Pack No. 255)				5·50		☐
PHQ Cards (set of 5) (168)				6·00	11·50	☐ ☐
Set of 5 Gutter Pairs				11·00		☐

1183 'La Danse à la Campagne' (Renoir)

1184 'Troilus and Criseyde' (Peter Brookes)

1185 'The Kiss' (Rodin)

1186 'Girls on the Town' (Beryl Cook)

1187 'Jazz' (Andrew Mockett)

1188 'Girls performing a Kathal Dance' (Aurangzeb period)

1189 'Alice Keppel with her Daughter' (Alice Hughes)

1190 'Children Playing' (L. S. Lowry)

1191 'Circus Clowns' (Emily Firmin and Justin Mitchell)

1192 Decoration from 'All the Love Poems of Shakespeare' (Eric Gill)

Greetings. (8th series) 'Greetings in Art'. Booklet stamps

1995 (21 Mar.) Two phosphor bands. Perf 14½ × 14 (with one elliptical hole in each vertical side)

1858	**1183**	(1st)	multicoloured	1·25	1·00	☐ ☐
		a.	Booklet pane. Nos. 1858/67	14·00	11·00	
1859	**1184**	(1st)	multicoloured	1·25	1·00	☐ ☐
1860	**1185**	(1st)	multicoloured	1·25	1·00	☐ ☐
1861	**1186**	(1st)	multicoloured	1·25	1·00	☐ ☐

1862	**1187**	(1st)	multicoloured	1·25	1·00	☐ ☐
1863	**1188**	(1st)	multicoloured	1·25	1·00	☐ ☐
1864	**1189**	(1st)	purple-brown and silver	1·25	1·00	☐ ☐
1865	**1190**	(1st)	multicoloured	1·25	1·00	☐ ☐
1866	**1191**	(1st)	multicoloured	1·25	1·00	☐ ☐
1867	**1192**	(1st)	black, greenish yellow and silver	1·25	1·00	☐ ☐
Set of 10				14·00	14·00	☐ ☐
First Day Cover					15·00	☐
Presentation Pack (P.O. Pack No. G4)				15·00		☐
PHQ Cards (*set of 10*) (GS3)				16·00	30·00	☐ ☐

Nos. 1858/67 were printed together, *se-tenant*, in booklet panes of ten stamps and 20 half stamp-size labels.

The National Trust *Celebrating 100 Years* **19**
1193 Fireplace Decoration, Attingham Park, Shropshire

The National Trust *Protecting Land* **25**
1194 Oak Seedling

The National Trust *Conserving Art* **30**
1195 Carved Table Leg, Attingham Park

The National Trust *Saving Coast* **35**
1196 St. David's Head, Dyfed, Wales

The National Trust *Repairing Buildings* **41**
1197 Elizabethan Window, Little Moreton Hall, Cheshire

Centenary of The National Trust

1995 (11 Apr.) One phosphor band (19p), two phosphor bands (25p, 35p) or phosphorised paper (30p, 41p)

1868	**1193**	19p	multicoloured	60	40	☐ ☐
1869	**1194**	25p	multicoloured	80	60	☐ ☐
1870	**1195**	30p	multicoloured	1·00	1·50	☐ ☐
1871	**1196**	35p	multicoloured	1·25	1·50	☐ ☐
1872	**1197**	41p	multicoloured	1·40	1·75	☐ ☐
Set of 5				4·50	5·25	☐ ☐
First Day Cover					5·75	☐
Presentation Pack (P.O. Pack No. 256)				5·00		☐
PHQ Cards (*set of 5*) (169)				6·00	11·50	☐ ☐
Set of 5 Gutter Pairs				10·50		☐

1198 British Troops and French Civilians celebrating

1199 Symbolic Hands and Red Cross

1200 St. Paul's Cathedral and Searchlights

1201 Symbolic Hand releasing Peace Dove

1202 Symbolic Hands

Europa. Peace and Freedom

1995 (2 May) One phosphor band (Nos. 1873/4) or two phosphor bands (others). Perf 14½ × 14

1873	**1198**	19p	silver, bistre-brown and grey-black	70	50	☐ ☐
1874	**1199**	19p	multicoloured	70	50	☐ ☐
1875	**1200**	25p	silver, blue and grey-black	1·00	1·00	☐ ☐
1876	**1201**	25p	multicoloured	1·00	1·00	☐ ☐
1877	**1202**	30p	multicoloured	1·25	2·25	☐ ☐
Set of 5				4·25	4·75	☐ ☐
First Day Cover					5·25	☐
Presentation Pack (P.O. Pack No. 257)				5·00		☐
PHQ Cards (*set of 5*) (170)				6·00	11·50	☐ ☐
Set of 5 Gutter Pairs				10·50		☐

Nos. 1873 and 1875 commemorate the 50th anniversary of the end of the Second World War, No. 1874 the 125th anniversary of the British Red Cross Society and Nos. 1876/7 the 50th anniversary of the United Nations.

Nos. 1876/7 include the 'EUROPA' emblem.

For Type **1200** with the face value expressed as '1st' see No. **MS**2547.

1203 The Time Machine

1204 The First Men in the Moon

1205 *The War of the Worlds*

1206 *The Shape of Things to Come*

Science Fiction. Novels by H. G. Wells

1995 (6 June) Two phosphor bands. Perf 14½ × 14

1878	**1203**	25p	multicoloured	75	60	☐ ☐
1879	**1204**	30p	multicoloured	1·25	1·50	☐ ☐
1880	**1205**	35p	multicoloured	1·25	1·60	☐ ☐
1881	**1206**	41p	multicoloured	1·50	1·60	☐ ☐
Set of 4				4·25	4·75	☐ ☐
First Day Cover					5·25	☐
Presentation Pack (P.O. Pack No. 258)				5·00		☐
PHQ Cards (*set of 4*) (171)				6·00	11·50	☐ ☐
Set of 4 Gutter Pairs				10·00		☐

Nos. 1878/81 commemorate the centenary of publication of Wells's *The Time Machine*.

1207 The Swan, 1595

1208 The Rose, 1592

1209 The Globe, 1599

1210 The Hope, 1613

1211 The Globe, 1614

Reconstruction of Shakespeare's Globe Theatre

1995 (8 Aug.) Two phosphor bands. Perf 14½

1882	**1207**	25p	multicoloured	60	60	☐ ☐
		a.	Horiz strip of 5.			
			Nos. 1882/6	4·50	4·75	☐ ☐
1883	**1208**	25p	multicoloured	60	60	☐ ☐
1884	**1209**	25p	multicoloured	60	60	☐ ☐
1885	**1210**	25p	multicoloured	60	60	☐ ☐
1886	**1211**	25p	multicoloured	60	60	☐ ☐
Set of 5				4·50	4·75	☐ ☐
First Day Cover					5·50	☐
Presentation Pack (P.O. Pack No. 259)				5·00		☐

PHQ Cards (*set of 5*) (172)		6·00	11·50	☐ ☐
Gutter Strip of 10			10·50	☐

Nos. 1882/6 were printed together, *se-tenant*, in horizontal strips of five throughout the sheet, the backgrounds forming a composite design.

1212 Sir Rowland Hill and Uniform Penny Postage Petition

1213 Hill and Penny Black

1214 Guglielmo Marconi and Early Wireless

1215 Marconi and Sinking of *Titanic* (liner)

Pioneers of Communications

1995 (5 Sept.) One phosphor band (19p) or phosphorised paper (others). Perf 14½ × 14

1887	**1212**	19p	silver, red and black	75	40	☐ ☐
1888	**1213**	25p	silver, brown and black	1·00	60	☐ ☐
1889	**1214**	41p	silver, grey-green and black	1·50	1·75	☐ ☐
1890	**1215**	60p	silver, deep ultramarine and black	1·75	2·25	☐ ☐
Set of 4				4·50	4·50	☐ ☐
First Day Cover					5·00	☐
Presentation Pack (P.O. Pack No. 260)				5·00		☐
PHQ Cards (*set of 4*) (173)				5·75	11·50	☐ ☐
Set of 4 Gutter Pairs				10·00		☐

Nos. 1887/8 mark the birth bicentenary of Sir Rowland Hill and Nos. 1889/90 the centenary of the first radio transmissions.

1216 Harold Wagstaff

1217 Gus Risman

1218 Jim Sullivan

1219 Billy Batten

BRIAN BEVAN
RUGBY LEAGUE 1895-1995
1220 Brian Bevan

Centenary of Rugby League

1995 (3 Oct.) One phosphor band (19p) or two phosphor bands (others). Perf 14 × 14½

1891	**1216**	19p	multicoloured	75	40	☐ ☐
1892	**1217**	25p	multicoloured	75	60	☐ ☐
1893	**1218**	30p	multicoloured	1·00	1·50	☐ ☐
1894	**1219**	35p	multicoloured	1·00	1·60	☐ ☐
1895	**1220**	41p	multicoloured	1·50	1·60	☐ ☐
Set of 5				4·75	5·25	☐ ☐
First Day Cover					5·75	☐
Presentation Pack (P.O. Pack No. 261)				5·50		☐
PHQ Cards (*set of* 5) (174)				6·00	11·50	☐ ☐
Set of 5 Gutter Pairs				11·00		☐

1221 European Robin in Mouth of Pillar Box

1222 European Robin on Railings and Holly

1223 European Robin on Snow-covered Milk Bottles

1224 European Robin on Road Sign

1225 European Robin on Door Knob and Christmas Wreath

Christmas. Christmas Robins

1995 (30 Oct.) One phosphor band (19p) or two phosphor bands (others)

1896	**1221**	19p	multicoloured	60	40	☐ ☐
1897	**1222**	25p	multicoloured	85	60	☐ ☐
1898	**1223**	30p	multicoloured	1·25	1·50	☐ ☐
1899	**1224**	41p	multicoloured	1·60	1·75	☐ ☐
1900	**1225**	60p	multicoloured	1·75	1·90	☐ ☐
Set of 5				5·50	6·00	☐ ☐
First Day Cover					6·50	☐
Presentation Pack (P.O. Pack No. 262)				6·00		☐
PHQ Cards (*set of* 5) (175)				6·00	11·50	☐ ☐
Set of 5 Gutter Pairs				12·00		☐

The 19p value was re-issued on 3 October 2000 and 9 October 2001 in sheets of 20 each with *se-tenant* label, in connection with 'customised' stamps available from the Philatelic Bureau. The labels show either Christmas greetings or a personal photograph.

Year Pack 1995

1995 (30 Oct.) Comprises Nos. 1848/1900
CP1900a	Year Pack	48·00	☐

Post Office Yearbook

1995 (30 Oct.) Comprises Nos. 1848/57 and 1868/1900 in hardback book with slip case
YB1900a	Yearbook	50·00	☐

1226 Opening Lines of 'To a Mouse' and Fieldmouse

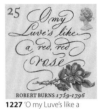

1227 'O my Luve's like a red, red rose' and Wild Rose

1228 'Scots, wha hae wi Wallace bled' and Sir William Wallace

1229 'Auld Lang Syne' and Highland Dancers

Death Bicentenary of Robert Burns (Scottish poet)

1996 (25 Jan.) One phosphor band (19p) or two phosphor bands (others). Perf 14½

1901	**1226**	19p	cream, bistre-brown and black	75	40	☐ ☐
1902	**1227**	25p	multicoloured	1·00	60	☐ ☐
1903	**1228**	41p	multicoloured	1·50	2·00	☐ ☐
1904	**1229**	60p	multicoloured	1·75	2·50	☐ ☐
Set of 4				4·50	5·00	☐ ☐
First Day Cover					5·50	☐
Presentation Pack (P.O. Pack No. 264)				5·00		☐
PHQ Cards (*set of* 4) (176)				6·00	11·50	☐ ☐
Set of 4 Gutter Pairs				10·50		☐

1230 'MORE! LOVE' (Mel Calman)

1231 'Sincerely' (Charles Barsotti)

1232 'Do you have something for the HUMAN CONDITION?' (Mel Calman)

1233 'MENTAL FLOSS' (Leo Cullum)

1234 '4.55 P.M.'
(Charles Barsotti)

1235 'Dear lottery prize
winner' (Larry)

1236 'I'm writing to you
because...' (Mel Calman)

1237 'FETCH THIS, FETCH THAT'
(Charles Barsotti)

1238 'My day starts before
I'm ready for it' (Mel Calman)

1239 'THE CHEQUE IN THE POST'
(Jack Ziegler)

Greetings (9th series) 'Cartoons'. Booklet Stamps

1996 (26 Feb.–11 Nov.) '2' phosphor. Perf 14½ × 14 (with one
elliptical hole in each vertical side)

1905 **1230**	(1st)	black and bright mauve	1·25	75	☐ ☐
	a.	Booklet pane. Nos. 1905/14	14·00	11·00	☐ ☐
	p.	Two phosphor bands	3·00	2·50	☐ ☐
	pa.	Booklet pane. Nos. 1905p/14p (11.11.96)	45·00	45·00	☐ ☐
1906 **1231**	(1st)	black and blue-green	1·25	75	☐ ☐
	p.	Two phosphor bands	3·00	2·50	☐ ☐
1907 **1232**	(1st)	black and new blue	1·25	75	☐ ☐
	p.	Two phosphor bands	3·00	2·50	☐ ☐
1908 **1233**	(1st)	black and bright violet	1·25	75	☐ ☐
	p.	Two phosphor bands	3·00	2·50	☐ ☐
1909 **1234**	(1st)	black and vermilion	1·25	75	☐ ☐
	p.	Two phosphor bands	3·00	2·50	☐ ☐
1910 **1235**	(1st)	black and new blue	1·25	75	☐ ☐
	p.	Two phosphor bands	3·00	2·50	☐ ☐
1911 **1236**	(1st)	black and vermilion	1·25	75	☐ ☐
	p.	Two phosphor bands	3·00	2·50	☐ ☐
1912 **1237**	(1st)	black and bright violet	1·25	75	☐ ☐
	p.	Two phosphor bands	3·00	2·50	☐ ☐
1913 **1238**	(1st)	black and blue-green	1·25	75	☐ ☐
	p.	Two phosphor bands	3·00	2·50	☐ ☐
1914 **1239**	(1st)	black and bright mauve	1·25	75	☐ ☐
	p.	Two phosphor bands	3·00	2·50	☐ ☐
Set of 10 (Nos. 1905/14)			14·00	11·00	☐ ☐
Set of 10 (Nos. 1905p/14p)			45·00	45·00	☐ ☐
First Day Cover (Nos. 1905/14)				12·00	☐
Presentation Pack (Nos. 1905/14) (P.O. Pack No. G5)			16·00		☐
PHQ Cards (set of 10) (GS4)			16·00	30·00	☐ ☐

Nos. 1905/14 were printed together, *se-tenant*, in booklet
panes of ten stamps and 20 half stamp-size labels.

Nos. 1905/14 were re-issued on 18 December 2001 in sheets
of ten, each stamp with a *se-tenant* label showing cartoon
titles. They were again issued on 29 July 2003 in sheets of 20
containing two of each design, each stamp accompanied by
a half stamp size label showing a crossword grid or personal
photograph. Such sheets are perforated without elliptical holes.

SET PRICES. Please note that set prices for booklet greetings
stamps are for complete panes. Sets of single stamps are
worth considerably less.

1240 'Muscovy Duck'

1241 'Lapwing'

1242 'White-fronted Goose'

1243 'Bittern'

1244 'Whooper Swan'

50th Anniversary of the Wildfowl and Wetlands Trust.
Bird Paintings by C. F. Tunnicliffe

1996 (12 Mar.) One phosphor band (19p) or phosphorised
paper (others). Perf 14 × 14½

1915 **1240**	19p multicoloured	70	40	☐ ☐
1916 **1241**	25p multicoloured	90	60	☐ ☐
1917 **1242**	30p multicoloured	1·00	1·25	☐ ☐
1918 **1243**	35p multicoloured	1·10	1·50	☐ ☐
1919 **1244**	41p multicoloured	1·50	1·60	☐ ☐
Set of 5		4·75	4·75	☐ ☐
First Day Cover			5·50	☐
Presentation Pack (P.O. Pack No. 265)		5·50		☐
PHQ Cards (set of 5) (177)		6·00	11·50	☐ ☐
Set of 5 Gutter Pairs		10·50		☐

1245 The Odeon, Harrogate

1246 Laurence Olivier and Vivien
Leigh in Lady Hamilton (film)

1247 Old Cinema Ticket

1248 Pathé News Still

1249 Cinema Sign,
The Odeon, Manchester

Centenary of Cinema

1996 (16 Apr.) One phosphor band (19p) or two phosphor bands (others). Perf 14 × 14½

1920	**1245**	19p	multicoloured	50	40	☐ ☐
1921	**1246**	25p	multicoloured	70	60	☐ ☐
1922	**1247**	30p	multicoloured	1·00	1·75	☐ ☐
1923	**1248**	35p	black, red and silver	1·25	2·00	☐ ☐
1924	**1249**	41p	multicoloured	1·50	2·25	☐ ☐
Set of 5				4·75	6·25	☐ ☐
First Day Cover					7·00	☐
Presentation Pack (P.O. Pack No. 266)				5·50		☐
PHQ Cards (set of 5) (178)				6·00	11·50	☐ ☐
Set of 5 Gutter Pairs				11·00		☐

1250 Dixie Dean

1251 Bobby Moore

1252 Duncan Edwards

1253 Billy Wright

1254 Danny Blanchflower

European Football Championship

1996 (14 May) One phosphor band (19p) or two phosphor bands (others). Perf 14½ × 14

1925	**1250**	19p	multicoloured	50	40	☐ ☐
1926	**1251**	25p	multicoloured	75	60	☐ ☐
1927	**1252**	35p	multicoloured	1·25	1·75	☐ ☐
1928	**1253**	41p	multicoloured	1·50	1·75	☐ ☐
1929	**1254**	60p	multicoloured	1·75	2·00	☐ ☐
Set of 5				5·50	6·00	☐ ☐

First Day Cover		6·50	☐
Presentation Pack (P.O. Pack No. 267)	6·00		☐
PHQ Cards (set of 5) (179)	6·00	11·50	☐ ☐
Set of 5 Gutter Pairs	12·00		☐

1255 Athlete on Starting Blocks

1256 Throwing the Javelin

1257 Basketball

1258 Swimming

1259 Athlete celebrating and Olympic Rings

Olympic and Paralympic Games, Atlanta

1996 (9 July) Two phosphor bands. Perf 14½ × 14

1930	**1255**	26p	multicoloured	60	70	☐ ☐
		a.	Horiz strip of 5.			
			Nos. 1930/4	4·50	4·50	☐ ☐
1931	**1256**	26p	multicoloured	60	70	☐ ☐
1932	**1257**	26p	multicoloured	60	70	☐ ☐
1933	**1258**	26p	multicoloured	60	70	☐ ☐
1934	**1259**	26p	multicoloured	60	70	☐ ☐
Set of 5				4·50	4·50	☐ ☐
First Day Cover					5·00	☐
Presentation Pack (P.O. Pack No. 268)				5·00		☐
PHQ Cards (set of 5) (180)				6·00	11·50	☐ ☐
Gutter Strip of 10				10·00		☐

Nos. 1930/4 were printed together, se-tenant, in horizontal strips of five throughout the sheet.

For these designs with the face value expressed as '1st' see **MS**2554.

1260 Prof. Dorothy Hodgkin (scientist)

1261 Dame Margot Fonteyn (ballerina)

1262 Dame Elisabeth Frink (sculptress)

1263 Dame Daphne du Maurier (novelist)

1264 Dame Marea Hartman
(sports administrator)

Europa. Famous Women

1996 (6 Aug.) One phosphor band (20p) or two phosphor bands (others). Perf 14½

1935	**1260**	20p	dull blue-green, brownish grey and black	60	50	☐ ☐
1936	**1261**	26p	dull mauve, brownish grey and black	75	60	☐ ☐
1937	**1262**	31p	bronze, brownish grey and black	1·10	1·10	☐ ☐
1938	**1263**	37p	silver, brownish grey and black	1·25	1·40	☐ ☐
1939	**1264**	43p	gold, brownish grey and black	1·50	1·50	☐ ☐
Set of 5				4·75	4·50	☐ ☐
First Day Cover					5·00	☐
Presentation Pack (P.O. Pack No. 269)				5·50		☐
PHQ Cards (set of 5) (181)				6·00	11·50	☐ ☐
Set of 5 Gutter Pairs				11·00		☐

Nos. 1936/7 include the 'EUROPA' emblem.

1265 Muffin the Mule   **1266** Sooty

1267 Stingray   **1268** The Clangers

1269 Dangermouse

50th Anniversary of Children's Television

1996 (3 Sept.)–**97** One phosphor band (20p) or two phosphor bands (others). Perf 14½ × 14

1940	**1265**	20p	multicoloured	55	30	☐ ☐
			a. Perf 15 × 14 (23.9.97)	2·00	2·00	☐ ☐
1941	**1266**	26p	multicoloured	80	40	☐ ☐
1942	**1267**	31p	multicoloured	1·00	1·50	☐ ☐
1943	**1268**	37p	multicoloured	1·40	1·75	☐ ☐
1944	**1269**	43p	multicoloured	1·60	2·00	☐ ☐
Set of 5				4·75	5·50	☐ ☐
First Day Cover					6·00	☐
Presentation Pack (P.O. Pack No. 270)				5·50		☐

PHQ Cards (set of 5) (182)		6·00	11·50	☐ ☐
Set of 5 Gutter Pairs		10·50		☐

No. 1940a was only issued in the £6·15 'Celebrating 75 years of the BBC' stamp booklet, No. DX19.

1270 Triumph TR3

1271 MG TD

1272 Austin-Healey 100

1273 Jaguar XK120

1274 Morgan Plus 4

Classic Sports Cars

1996 (1 Oct.) One phosphor band (20p) or two phosphor bands (others). Perf 14½

1945	**1270**	20p	multicoloured	55	40	☐ ☐
1946	**1271**	26p	multicoloured	1·10	50	☐ ☐
1947	**1272**	37p	multicoloured	1·40	1·90	☐ ☐
1948	**1273**	43p	multicoloured	1·60	1·90	☐ ☐
1949	**1274**	63p	multicoloured	1·75	2·00	☐ ☐
Set of 5				5·75	6·00	☐ ☐
First Day Cover					6·50	☐
Presentation Pack (P.O. Pack No. 271)				6·50		☐
PHQ Cards (set of 5) (183)				6·00	11·50	☐ ☐
Set of 5 Gutter Pairs				13·00		☐

1275 The Three Kings

1276 The Annunciation

1277 The Journey to Bethlehem

1278 The Nativity

1279 The Shepherds

Christmas. Biblical Scenes

1996 (28 Oct.) One phosphor band (2nd) or two phosphor bands (others)

1950	**1275**	(2nd)	multicoloured	75	60	☐☐
1951	**1276**	(1st)	multicoloured	1·00	70	☐☐
1952	**1277**	31p	multicoloured	1·25	1·75	☐☐
1953	**1278**	43p	multicoloured	1·25	1·75	☐☐
1954	**1279**	63p	multicoloured	1·50	2·00	☐☐
Set of 5				5·50	6·00	☐☐
First Day Cover					6·50	☐
Presentation Pack (P.O. Pack No. 272)				6·00		☐
PHQ Cards (*set of* 5) (184)				6·00	11·50	☐☐
Set of 5 Gutter Pairs				12·50		☐

Year Pack 1996

1996 (28 Oct.) Comprises Nos. 1901/54

CP1954a	Year Pack	55·00	☐

Post Office Yearbook

1996 (28 Oct.) Comprises Nos. 1901/4 and 1915/54 in hardback book with slip case

YB1954a	Yearbook	55·00	☐

1280 *Gentiana acaulis* (Georg Ehret)

1281 *Magnolia grandiflora* (Ehret)

1282 *Camellia japonica* (Alfred Chandler)

1283 *Tulipa* (Ehret)

1284 *Fuchsia* 'Princess of Wales' (Augusta Sowerby)

1285 *Tulipa gesneriana* (Ehret)

1286 *Gazania splendens* (Charlotte Sowerby)

1287 *Iris latifolia* (Ehret)

1288 *Hippeastrum rutilum* (Pierre-Joseph Redoute)

1289 *Passiflora coerulea* (Ehret)

Greetings Stamps (10th series)
19th-century Flower Paintings. Booklet Stamps

1997 (6 Jan.) Two phosphor bands. Perf 14½×14 (with one elliptical hole in each vertical side)

1955	**1280**	(1st)	multicoloured	1·25	1·00	☐☐
		a.	Booklet pane. Nos. 1955/64	14·00	14·00	☐☐
1956	**1281**	(1st)	multicoloured	1·25	1·00	☐☐
1957	**1282**	(1st)	multicoloured	1·25	1·00	☐☐
1958	**1283**	(1st)	multicoloured	1·25	1·00	☐☐
1959	**1284**	(1st)	multicoloured	1·25	1·00	☐☐
1960	**1285**	(1st)	multicoloured	1·25	1·00	☐☐
1961	**1286**	(1st)	multicoloured	1·25	1·00	☐☐
1962	**1287**	(1st)	multicoloured	1·25	1·00	☐☐
1963	**1288**	(1st)	multicoloured	1·25	1·00	☐☐
1964	**1289**	(1st)	multicoloured	1·25	1·00	☐☐
Set of 10				14·00	14·00	☐☐
First Day Cover					15·00	☐
Presentation Pack (P.O. Pack No. G6)				16·00		☐
PHQ Cards (*set of* 10) (GS5)				16·00	30·00	☐☐

Nos. 1955/64 were printed together, *se-tenant*, in booklet panes of ten stamps and 20 half stamp-size labels.

Nos. 1955/64 were re-issued on 21 January 2003 in *se-tenant* sheets of 20, each accompanied by a label showing flowers or personal photograph. Such sheets are perforated without elliptical holes.

For Types **1280, 1283** and **1287** perf 15×14 see Nos. 2463/5. For Types **1283** and **1287** printed in photogravure and perf 14, see Nos. 2942/3.

1290 'King Henry VIII'

1291 'Catherine of Aragon'

1292 'Anne Boleyn'

1293 'Jane Seymour'

1294 'Anne of Cleves'   **1295** 'Catherine Howard'   **1296** 'Catherine Parr'

450th Death Anniversary of King Henry VIII

1997 (21 Jan.) Two phosphor bands. Perf 15 (No. 1965) or 14×15 (others)

1965 **1290**	26p multicoloured	60	60	
1966 **1291**	26p multicoloured	60	60	
	a. Horiz strip of 6.			
	Nos. 1966/71	8·00	8·50	
1967 **1292**	26p multicoloured	60	60	
1968 **1293**	26p multicoloured	60	60	
1969 **1294**	26p multicoloured	60	60	
1970 **1295**	26p multicoloured	60	60	
1971 **1296**	26p multicoloured	60	60	
Set of 7		8·50	9·00	
First Day Cover			9·50	
Presentation Pack (P.O. Pack No. 274)		10·00		
PHQ Cards (*set of 7*) (185)		10·00	18·00	
Gutter Pair and Gutter Block of 12		18·00		

Nos. 1966/71 were printed together, *se-tenant*, in horizontal strips of six throughout the sheet.

1297 St. Columba in Boat   **1298** St. Columba on Iona

1299 St. Augustine with King Ethelbert   **1300** St. Augustine with Model of Cathedral

Religious Anniversaries

1997 (11 Mar.) Two phosphor bands. Perf 14½

1972 **1297**	26p multicoloured	75	60	
1973 **1298**	37p multicoloured	1·10	1·50	
1974 **1299**	43p multicoloured	1·50	1·50	
1975 **1300**	63p multicoloured	2·00	2·10	
Set of 4		4·75	5·25	
First Day Cover			5·75	
Presentation Pack (P.O. Pack No. 275)		5·25		
PHQ Cards (*set of 4*) (186)		5·75	11·50	
Set of 4 Gutter Pairs		11·50		

Nos. 1972/3 commemorate the 1400th death anniversary of St Columba and Nos. 1974/5 the 1400th anniversary of the arrival of St Augustine of Canterbury in Kent.

1301   **1302**

Self-adhesive Coil Stamps

1997 (18 Mar.) Gravure Enschedé. One centre phosphor band (2nd) or two phosphor bands (1st). Perf 14×15 die-cut (with one elliptical hole in each vertical side)

1976 **1301** (2nd)	bright blue	2·50	2·50	
1977 **1302** (1st)	bright orange-red	2·75	2·75	
Set of 2		5·00	5·00	
First Day Cover			5·50	
Presentation Pack (P.O. Pack No. 37)		7·00		

Nos. 1976/7, which were priced at 20p and 26p, were each sold in rolls of 100 with the stamps separate on the backing paper.

Machin stamps printed in gold were issued on 21 April 1997 for the Royal Golden Wedding. These are listed as definitives under Nos. 1668 (1st) and Y1692 26p.

Nos. 1978/9 are vacant

1303 Dracula   **1304** Frankenstein

1305 Dr Jekyll and Mr Hyde   **1306** The Hound of the Baskervilles

Europa. Tales and Legends. Horror Stories

1997 (13 May) Two phosphor bands. Perf 14×15

1980 **1303**	26p multicoloured	1·00	60	
1981 **1304**	31p multicoloured	1·10	1·50	
1982 **1305**	37p multicoloured	1·30	1·75	
1983 **1306**	43p multicoloured	2·00	1·95	
Set of 4		5·00	5·50	
First Day Cover			6·00	
Presentation Pack (P.O. Pack No. 276)		5·50		
PHQ Cards (*set of 4*) (187)		5·75	11·50	
Set of 4 Gutter Pairs		11·50		

Nos. 1980/3 commemorate the birth bicentenary of Mary Shelley (creator of Frankenstein) with the 26p and 31p values incorporating the 'EUROPA' emblem.

1307 Reginald Mitchell and Supermarine Spitfire IIA

1308 Roy Chadwick and Avro Lancaster I

1309 Ronald Bishop and de Havilland Mosquito B XVI

1310 George Carter and Gloster Meteor T7

1311 Sir Sidney Camm and Hawker Hunter FGA9

British Aircraft Designers

1997 (10 June) One phosphor band (20p) or two phosphor bands (others)

1984	**1307**	20p	multicoloured	75	50	☐ ☐
1985	**1308**	26p	multicoloured	1·10	1·25	☐ ☐
1986	**1309**	37p	multicoloured	1·40	1·25	☐ ☐
1987	**1310**	43p	multicoloured	1·50	1·60	☐ ☐
1988	**1311**	63p	multicoloured	2·00	2·00	☐ ☐
Set of 5				6·00	6·00	☐ ☐
First Day Cover					6·50	☐
Presentation Pack (P.O. Pack No. 277)				6·50		☐
PHQ Cards (set of 5) (188)				6·00	13·00	☐ ☐
Set of 5 Gutter Pairs				14·00		☐

For Type **1307** printed in lithography and perf 14, see No. 2868.

1312 Carriage Horse and Coachman

1313 Lifeguards Horse and Trooper

1314 Household Cavalry Drum Horse and Drummer

1315 Duke of Edinburgh's Horse and Groom

50th Anniversary of the British Horse Society 'All The Queen's Horses'.

1997 (8 July) One phosphor band (20p) or two phosphor bands (others). Perf 14½

1989	**1312**	20p	multicoloured	80	45	☐ ☐
1990	**1313**	26p	multicoloured	1·10	1·50	☐ ☐
1991	**1314**	43p	multicoloured	1·50	1·50	☐ ☐
1992	**1315**	63p	multicoloured	2·00	2·00	☐ ☐
Set of 4				5·00	5·25	☐ ☐
First Day Cover					5·75	☐
Presentation Pack (P.O. Pack No. 278)				5·50		☐
PHQ Cards (set of 4) (189)				5·75	11·50	☐ ☐
Set of 4 Gutter Pairs				12·00		☐

1315a Caernarfon Castle

CASTLE
Harrison printing (Nos. 1611/14)

CASTLE
Enschedé printing (Nos. 1993/6)

Differences between Harrison and Enschedé printings:

Harrison – 'C' has top serif and tail of letter points to right. 'A' has flat top. 'S' has top and bottom serifs.

Enschedé – 'C' has no top serif and tail of letter points upwards. 'A' has pointed top. 'S' has no serifs.

1997 (29 July) Designs as Nos. 1611/14 with Queen's head in silhouette as T **1044**, but re-engraved as above. Perf 15 × 14 (with one elliptical hole in each vertical side)

1993	**1315a**	£1·50	deep claret and gold†	12·00	6·00	☐ ☐
1994	**881**	£2	indigo and gold†	14·00	2·25	☐ ☐
1995	**1044**	£3	violet and gold†	30·00	3·50	☐ ☐
1996	**882**	£5	deep brown and gold†	35·00	10·00	☐ ☐
Set of 4				80·00	18·00	☐ ☐
Set of 4 Gutter Pairs				£175		☐
Presentation Pack (P.O Pack No. 40)				£150		☐

† The Queen's head on these stamps is printed in optically variable ink which changes colour from gold to green when viewed from different angles. See also Nos. 1410/13.

1316 Haroldswick, Shetland

1317 Painswick, Gloucestershire

1318 Beddgelert, Gwynedd

1319 Ballyroney, County Down

Sub-Post Offices

1997 (12 Aug.) One phosphor band (20p) or two phosphor bands (others). Perf 14½

1997	**1316**	20p	multicoloured	75	50	☐ ☐
1998	**1317**	26p	multicoloured	1·00	1·00	☐ ☐
1999	**1318**	43p	multicoloured	1·50	1·50	☐ ☐
2000	**1319**	63p	multicoloured	2·25	2·25	☐ ☐
Set of 4				5·50	5·00	☐ ☐
First Day Cover					5·75	☐
Presentation Pack (P.O. Pack No. 279)				6·00		☐
PHQ Cards (*set of* 4) (190)				5·75	11·50	☐ ☐
Set of 4 Gutter Pairs				12·00		☐

Nos. 1997/2000 also mark the centenary of the National Federation of Sub-Postmasters.

Enid Blyton's *Noddy*
1320 'Noddy'

Enid Blyton's *Famous Five*
1321 'Famous Five'

Enid Blyton's *Secret Seven*
1322 'Secret Seven'

Enid Blyton's *Faraway Tree*
1323 'Faraway Tree'

Enid Blyton's *Malory Towers*
1324 'Malory Towers'

Birth Centenary of Enid Blyton (children's author)

1997 (9 Sept.) One phosphor band (20p) or two phosphor bands (others). Perf 14×14½

2001	**1320**	20p	multicoloured	50	45	☐ ☐
2002	**1321**	26p	multicoloured	1·00	1·25	☐ ☐
2003	**1322**	37p	multicoloured	1·25	1·25	☐ ☐
2004	**1323**	43p	multicoloured	1·50	2·00	☐ ☐
2005	**1324**	63p	multicoloured	1·75	2·00	☐ ☐
Set of 5				5·50	6·00	☐ ☐
First Day Cover					6·50	☐
Presentation Pack (P.O. Pack No. 280)				6·00		☐
PHQ Cards (*set of* 5) (191)				6·00	13·00	☐ ☐
Set of 5 Gutter Pairs				12·00		☐

1325 Children and Father Christmas pulling Cracker

1326 Father Christmas with Traditional Cracker

1327 Father Christmas riding Cracker

1328 Father Christmas on Snowball

1329 Father Christmas and Chimney

Christmas. 150th Anniversary of the Christmas Cracker

1997 (27 Oct.) One phosphor band (2nd) or two phosphor bands (others)

2006	**1325**	(2nd)	multicoloured	1·00	40	☐ ☐
2007	**1326**	(1st)	multicoloured	1·25	60	☐ ☐
2008	**1327**	31p	multicoloured	1·00	1·50	☐ ☐
2009	**1328**	43p	multicoloured	1·25	1·75	☐ ☐
2010	**1329**	63p	multicoloured	1·60	2·00	☐ ☐
Set of 5				5·50	5·75	☐ ☐
First Day Cover					6·50	☐
Presentation Pack (P.O. Pack No. 282)				6·00		☐
PHQ Cards (*set of* 5) (192)				6·00	13·00	☐ ☐
Set of 5 Gutter Pairs				12·00		☐

The 1st value was re-issued on 3 October 2000 and 9 October 2001, in sheets of ten in photogravure, each stamp with a *se-tenant* label, in connection with 'customised' service available from the Philatelic Bureau. On 1 October 2002 in sheet size of 20 in lithography the 1st value was again issued but perforated 14½×14. The labels show either Christmas greetings or a personal photograph.

1330 Wedding Photograph, 1947

1331 Queen Elizabeth II and Prince Philip, 1997

Royal Golden Wedding

1997 (13 Nov.) One phosphor band (20p) or two phosphor bands (others). Perf 15

2011	**1330**	20p	gold, yellow-brown and grey-black	85	45	☐ ☐
2012	**1331**	26p	multicoloured	1·10	70	☐ ☐
2013	**1330**	43p	gold, bluish green and grey-black	1·90	2·25	☐ ☐
2014	**1331**	63p	multicoloured	2·50	3·00	☐ ☐
Set of 4				5·75	5·75	☐ ☐

First Day Cover		7·00		☐
Presentation Pack (P.O. Pack No. 281)	6·25			☐
Souvenir Book (contains Nos. 1668, 1989/92 and 2011/14)		50·00		☐
PHQ Cards (*set of* 4) (192)		5·75	11·50	☐ ☐
Set of 4 Gutter Pairs		12·00		☐

Year Pack 1997

1997 (13 Nov.) Comprises Nos. 1965/75, 1980/92 and 1997/2014

| CP2014a | Year Pack | 55·00 | ☐ |

Post Office Yearbook

1997 (13 Nov.) Comprises Nos. 1965/75, 1980/92 and 1997/2014 in hardback book with slip case

| YB2014a | Yearbook | 50·00 | ☐ |

20 **ENDANGERED SPECIES**
Common dormouse
Muscardinus avellanarius
1332 Common Doormouse

26 **ENDANGERED SPECIES**
Lady's slipper orchid
Cypripedium calceolus
1333 Lady's Slipper Orchid

31 **ENDANGERED SPECIES**
Song thrush
Turdus philomelos
1334 Song Thrush

37 **ENDANGERED SPECIES**
Shining ram's-horn snail
Segmentina nitida
1335 Shining Ram's-horn Snail

43 **ENDANGERED SPECIES**
Mole cricket
Gryllotalpa gryllotalpa
1336 Mole Cricket

63 **ENDANGERED SPECIES**
Devil's bolete
Boletus satanas
1337 Devil's Bolete

Endangered Species

1998 (20 Jan.) One side phosphor band (20p) or two phosphor bands (others). Perf 14 × 14½

2015	**1332**	20p	multicoloured	60	40	☐ ☐
2016	**1333**	26p	multicoloured	75	40	☐ ☐
2017	**1334**	31p	multicoloured	1·00	2·00	☐ ☐
2018	**1335**	37p	multicoloured	1·25	1·25	☐ ☐
2019	**1336**	43p	multicoloured	1·40	1·75	☐ ☐
2020	**1337**	63p	multicoloured	1·90	2·25	☐ ☐
Set of 6				6·25	7·50	☐
First Day Cover					8·00	☐
Presentation Pack (P.O. Pack No. 284)			6·75			☐
PHQ Cards (*Set of* 6) (194)			6·00	14·00		☐ ☐
Set of 6 Gutter Pairs			14·00			☐

1338 Diana, Princess of Wales (photo by Lord Snowdon)

1339 At British Lung Foundation Function, April 1997 (photo by John Stillwell)

1340 Wearing Tiara, 1991 (photo by Lord Snowdon)

1341 On Visit to Birmingham, October 1995 (photo by Tim Graham)

1342 In Evening Dress, 1987 (photo by Terence Donovan)

Diana, Princess of Wales Commemoration

1998 (3 Feb.) Two phosphor bands

2021	**1338**	26p	multicoloured	50	50	☐ ☐
		a.	Horiz strip of 5. Nos. 2021/5	4·50	4·50	☐ ☐
2022	**1339**	26p	multicoloured	50	50	☐ ☐
2023	**1340**	26p	multicoloured	50	50	☐ ☐
2024	**1341**	26p	multicoloured	50	50	☐ ☐
2025	**1342**	26p	multicoloured	50	50	☐ ☐
Set of 5				4·50	4·50	☐ ☐
First Day Cover					5·00	☐
Presentation Pack (Unnumbered)			16·00			☐
Presentation Pack (Welsh)			70·00			☐
Gutter Strip of 10			10·00			☐

Nos. 2021/5 were printed together, *se-tenant*, in horizontal strips of 5 throughout the sheet.

1343 Lion of England and Griffin of Edward III

1344 Falcon of Plantagenet and Bull of Clarence

1345 Lion of Mortimer and Yale of Beaufort

1346 Greyhound of Richmond and Dragon of Wales

1347 Unicorn of Scotland and Horse of Hanover

650th Anniversary of the Order of the Garter.
The Queen's Beasts

1998 (24 Feb.) Two phosphor bands

2026	**1343**	26p multicoloured	90	90	☐ ☐
		a. Horiz strip of 5.			
		Nos. 2026/30	4·50	4·50	☐ ☐
2027	**1344**	26p multicoloured	90	90	☐ ☐
2028	**1345**	26p multicoloured	90	90	☐ ☐
2029	**1346**	26p multicoloured	90	90	☐ ☐
2030	**1347**	26p multicoloured	90	90	☐ ☐
Set of 5			4·50	4·50	☐ ☐
First Day Cover				5·25	☐
Presentation Pack (P.O. Pack No. 285)			5·00		☐
PHQ Cards (*set of* 5) (195)			6·00	13·00	☐ ☐
Gutter Block of 10			10·00		☐

Nos. 2026/30 were printed together, *se-tenant*, in horizontal strips of five throughout the sheet.
The phosphor bands on Nos. 2026/30 are only half the height of the stamps and do not cover the silver parts of the designs.

1348

Wilding definitives. The Definitive Portrait.
Booklet Stamps

1998 (10 Mar.) Design as T **157** (issued 1952–54), but with face values in decimal currency as T **1348**. One side phosphor band (20p) or two phosphor bands (others). Perf 14 (with one elliptical hole in each vertical side)

2031	**1348**	20p light green	70	75	☐ ☐
2032		26p red-brown	1·00	1·10	☐ ☐
2033		37p light purple	2·75	2·75	☐ ☐
Set of 3			4·00	4·00	☐ ☐
First Day Cover				7·00	☐

Nos. 2031/3 were only issued in the £7·49 'The Definitive Portrait' booklet, No. DX20.

For further Wilding designs in decimal currency see Nos. 2258/9, **MS**2326, **MS**2367, 2378/80 and 3329.

1349 St. John's Point Lighthouse, County Down

1350 Smalls Lighthouse, Pembrokeshire

1351 Needles Rock Lighthouse, Isle of Wight, *c* 1900

1352 Bell Rock Lighthouse, Arbroath, mid-19th-century

1353 Eddystone Lighthouse, Plymouth, 1698

Lighthouses

1998 (24 Mar.) One side phosphor band (20p) or two phosphor bands (others). Perf 14½ × 14

2034	**1349**	20p multicoloured	50	40	☐ ☐
2035	**1350**	26p multicoloured	75	50	☐ ☐
2036	**1351**	37p multicoloured	1·10	1·50	☐ ☐
2037	**1352**	43p multicoloured	1·50	1·75	☐ ☐
2038	**1353**	63p multicoloured	2·10	2·50	☐ ☐
Set of 5			5·50	6·00	☐ ☐
First Day Cover				6·50	☐
Presentation Pack (P.O. Pack No. 286)			6·00		☐
PHQ Cards (*set of* 5) (196)			6·00	13·00	☐ ☐
Set of 5 Gutter Pairs			13·00		☐

Nos. 2034/8 commemorate the 300th anniversary of the first Eddystone Lighthouse and the final year of manned lighthouses.

Self-adhesive stamps

1998 (6 Apr.–22 June) Gravure Enschedé, Questa or Walsall. Designs as T **913/14**. One centre phosphor band (2nd) or two phosphor bands (1st). Perf 15 × 14 die-cut (with one elliptical hole in each vertical side)

2039	(2nd)	bright blue	1·20	80	☐ ☐
		b. Perf 14½ × 14			
		die-cut (22.6.98)	£300		☐
2040	(1st)	bright orange-red	1·50	1·50	☐ ☐
		b. Perf 14½ × 14			
		die-cut (22.6.98)	£300		☐
Set of 2			2·50	2·50	☐ ☐

Nos. 2039/40 were initially priced at 20p and 26p, and were available in coils of 200 (Enschedé), sheets of 100 (Enschedé, Questa or Walsall) or self-adhesive booklets (Questa or Walsall). See also Nos. 2295/8.

1354 Tommy Cooper **1355** Eric Morecambe
1356 Joyce Grenfell **1357** Les Dawson
1358 Peter Cook

Comedians

1998 (23 Apr.) One phosphor band (20p) or two phosphor bands (others). Perf 14½ × 14

2041	**1354**	20p multicoloured	50	50	☐ ☐
2042	**1355**	26p multicoloured	75	85	☐ ☐
2043	**1356**	37p multicoloured	1·25	1·25	☐ ☐
2044	**1357**	43p multicoloured	1·50	1·50	☐ ☐
2045	**1358**	63p multicoloured	1·75	2·10	☐ ☐
Set of 5			5·25	5·50	☐ ☐
First Day Cover				6·00	☐
Presentation Pack (P.O. Pack No. 287)			6·00		☐
PHQ Cards (*set of* 5) (197)			6·00	13·00	☐ ☐
Set of 5 Gutter Pairs			13·50		

1359 Hands forming Heart

1360 Adult and Child holding Hands

1361 Hands forming Cradle

1362 Hands taking Pulse

50th Anniversary of National Health Service

1998 (23 June) One side phosphor band (20p) or two phosphor bands (others). Perf 14 × 14½

2046	**1359**	20p multicoloured	50	50	☐ ☐
2047	**1360**	26p multicoloured	90	90	☐ ☐
2048	**1361**	43p multicoloured	1·50	1·50	☐ ☐
2049	**1362**	63p multicoloured	2·10	2·10	☐ ☐
Set of 4			4·50	4·50	☐ ☐
First Day Cover				5·00	☐
Presentation Pack (P.O. Pack No. 288)			5·50		☐
PHQ Cards (*set of* 4) (198)			5·75	11·50	☐ ☐
Set of 4 Gutter Pairs			11·00		☐

1363 'The Hobbit' (J.R.R. Tolkien)

1364 'The Lion, The Witch and the Wardrobe' (C. S. Lewis)

1365 'The Phoenix and the Carpet' (E. Nesbit)

1366 'The Borrowers' (Mary Norton)

1367 'Through the Looking Glass' (Lewis Carroll)

Famous Children's Fantasy Novels

1998 (21 July) One phosphor band (20p) or two phosphor bands (others)

2050	**1363**	20p multicoloured	50	50	☐ ☐
2051	**1364**	26p multicoloured	75	75	☐ ☐
2052	**1365**	37p multicoloured	1·25	1·50	☐ ☐
2053	**1366**	43p multicoloured	1·50	1·50	☐ ☐
2054	**1367**	63p multicoloured	2·10	2·00	☐ ☐
Set of 5			5·75	5·75	☐ ☐
First Day Cover				6·50	☐
Presentation Pack (P.O. Pack No. 289)			6·50		☐
PHQ Cards (*set of* 5) (199)			6·00	13·00	☐ ☐
Set of 5 Gutter Pairs			13·00		☐

Nos. 2050/4 commemorate the birth centenary of C. S. Lewis and the death centenary of Lewis Carroll.

1368 Woman in Yellow Feathered Costume

1369 Woman in Blue Costume and Headdress

1370 Group of Children in White and Gold Robes

1371 Child in 'Tree' Costume

Europa. Festivals. Notting Hill Carnival

1998 (25 Aug.) One centre phosphor band (20p) or two phosphor bands (others). Perf 14 × 14½

2055	**1368**	20p multicoloured	75	45	☐ ☐
2056	**1369**	26p multicoloured	95	55	☐ ☐
2057	**1370**	43p multicoloured	1·50	2·00	☐ ☐
2058	**1371**	63p multicoloured	2·00	2·75	☐ ☐
Set of 4			4·75	5·25	☐ ☐
First Day Cover				5·75	☐
Presentation Pack (P.O. Pack No. 290)			5·25		☐
PHQ Cards (*set of* 4) (200)			5·75	11·50	☐ ☐
Set of 4 Gutter Pairs			11·50		☐

Nos. 2055/6 include the 'EUROPA' emblem.

1372 Sir Malcolm Campbell's 'Bluebird', 1925

1373 Sir Henry Segrave's Sunbeam, 1926

1374 John G. Parry Thomas's Babs, 1926   **1375** John R. Cobb's Railton Mobil Special, 1947

1376 Donald Campbell's 'Bluebird' CN7, 1964

British Land Speed Record Holders

1998 (29 Sept.–13 Oct.) One phosphor band (20p) or two phosphor bands (others). Perf 15 × 14

2059 **1372**	20p multicoloured (centre band)	50	30		
	a. Perf 14½ × 13½ (side band) *(13.10.98)*	1·40	1·20		
2060 **1373**	26p multicoloured	75	45		
2061 **1374**	30p multicoloured	1·25	1·50		
2062 **1375**	43p multicoloured	1·50	1·60		
2063 **1376**	63p multicoloured	2·00	2·40		
Set of 5		5·50	5·75		
First Day Cover			6·50		
Presentation Pack (P.O. Pack No. 291)		6·25			
PHQ Cards (*set of* 5) (201)		6·00	13·00		
Set of 5 Gutter Pairs		13·00			

No. 2059a, which occurs with the phosphor band at the left or right of the stamp, was only issued in the £6·16 "Breaking Barriers" booklet, No. DX21. There are minor differences of design between No. 2059 and No. 2059a, which also omits the copyright symbol and date.

Nos. 2059/63 commemorate the 50th death anniversary of Sir Malcolm Campbell.

1377 Angel with Hands raised in Blessing   **1378** Angel praying

1379 Angel playing Flute   **1380** Angel playing Lute

1381 Angel praying

Christmas. Angels

1998 (2 Nov.) One phosphor band (20p) or two phosphor bands (others)

2064 **1377**	20p multicoloured	50	50		
2065 **1378**	26p multicoloured	75	60		
2066 **1379**	30p multicoloured	1·25	1·50		
2067 **1380**	43p multicoloured	1·50	1·60		
2068 **1381**	63p multicoloured	2·00	2·25		
Set of 5		5·75	5·75		
First Day Cover			6·50		
Presentation Pack (P.O. Pack No. 292)		6·50			
PHQ Cards (*set of* 5) (202)		6·00	13·00		
Set of 5 Gutter Pairs		12·50			

Year Pack 1998

1998 (2 Nov.) Comprises Nos. 2015/30, 2034/8 and 2041/68

CP2068a	Year Pack	65·00	

Post Office Yearbook

1998 (2 Nov.) Comprises Nos. 2015/30, 2034/8 and 2041/68 in hardback book with slip case

YB2068a	Yearbook	60·00	

1382 Greenwich Meridian and Clock (John Harrison's Chronometer)   **1383** Industrial Worker and Blast Furnace (James Watt's discovery of steam power)

1384 Early Photos of Leaves (Henry Fox-Talbot's photographic experiments)   **1385** Computer inside Human Head (Alan Turing's work on computers)

Millennium Series. The Inventors' Tale

1999 (12 Jan.–21 Sept.) One centre phosphor band (20p) or two phosphor bands (others). Perf 14 × 14½

2069 **1382**	20p multicoloured	75	70		
2070 **1383**	26p multicoloured	95	1·00		
2071 **1384**	43p multicoloured	1·50	1·60		
2072 **1385**	63p multicoloured	2·25	2·40		
	a. Perf 13½ × 14 *(21.9.99.)*	3·50	3·50		
Set of 4		5·25	5·25		
First Day Cover			8·00		
Presentation Pack (P.O. Pack No. 294)		7·50			
PHQ Cards (*set of* 4) (203)		6·00	13·00		
Set of 4 Gutter Pairs		12·00			

No. 2072a was only issued in the £6·99 "World Changers" booklet, No. DX23.

1386 Airliner hugging
Globe (International air travel)

1387 Woman on Bicycle
(Development of the bicycle)

1388 Victorian Railway
Station (Growth of public transport)

1389 Captain Cook and
Maori (Captain James Cook's voyages)

Millennium Series. The Travellers' Tale

1999 (2 Feb.) One centre phosphor band (20p) or two phosphor
bands (others). Perf 14 × 14½

2073 **1386**	20p	multicoloured	75	70
2074 **1387**	26p	multicoloured	95	1·00
2075 **1388**	43p	grey-black, stone and bronze	1·50	1·60
2076 **1389**	63p	multicoloured	2·25	2·40
Set of 4			5·25	5·25
First Day Cover				7·00
Presentation Pack (P.O. Pack No. 295)			7·50	
PHQ Cards (*set of* 4) (204)			6·00	13·00
Set of 4 Gutter Pairs			12·00	

1390

'Profile on Print'. Booklet Stamps

1999 (16 Feb.)

(a) Embossed and litho Walsall. Self-adhesive.
Die-cut perf 14 × 15
2077 **1390** (1st) grey (face value)
(Queen's head in
colourless relief)
(phosphor background
around head)   3·00   2·75

(b) Recess Enschedé. Perf 14 × 14½
2078 **1390** (1st) grey-black
(2 phosphor bands)   3·00   2·75

(c) Typo Harrison. Perf 14 × 15
2079 **1390** (1st) black
(2 phosphor bands)   3·00   2·75
Set of 3   8·00   7·50
Nos. 2077/9 were only issued in £7·54 the 'Profile on Print'
stamp booklet No. DX22.

1391 Vaccinating Child
(pattern in cow markings) (Jenner's
development of smallpox vaccine)

1392 Patient on Trolley
(nursing care)

1393 Penicillin Mould
(Fleming's discovery of Penicillin)

1394 Sculpture of Test-tube Baby
(development of in vitro fertilization)

Millennium Series. The Patients' Tale

1999 (2 Mar.) One centre phosphor band (20p) or two
phosphor bands (others). Perf 13½ × 14

2080 **1391**	20p	multicoloured	75	70
2081 **1392**	26p	multicoloured	95	1·00
2082 **1393**	43p	multicoloured	1·50	1·60
2083 **1394**	63p	multicoloured	2·25	2·40
Set of 4			5·25	5·25
First Day Cover				7·00
Presentation Pack (P.O. Pack No. 296)			7·50	
PHQ Cards (*set of* 4) (205)			6·00	13·00
Set of 4 Gutter Pairs			12·00	

1395 Dove and Norman
Settler (medieval migration
to Scotland)

1396 Pilgrim Fathers and
Red Indian (17th-century migration
to America)

1397 Sailing Ship and
Aspects of Settlement
(19th-century migration
to Australia)

1398 Hummingbird and
Superimposed Stylised
Face (20th-century
migration to Great Britain)

Millennium Series. The Settlers' Tale

1999 (6 Apr.) One centre phosphor band (20p) or two phosphor
bands (others). Perf 14 × 14½

2084 **1395**	20p	multicoloured	75	70
2085 **1396**	26p	multicoloured	95	1·00
2086 **1397**	43p	multicoloured	2·00	1·75
2087 **1398**	63p	multicoloured	3·00	3·00
Set of 4			5·75	5·75

First Day Cover		7·00		☐	
Presentation Pack (P.O. Pack No. 297)	7·50			☐	
PHQ Cards (set of 4) (206)	8·50	13·00		☐	☐
Set of 4 Gutter Pairs	12·00			☐	

1399 Woven Threads (woollen industry)

1400 Salts Mill, Saltaire (worsted cloth industry)

1401 Hull on Slipway (shipbuilding)

1402 Lloyd's Building (City of London finance centre)

Millennium Series. The Workers' Tale

1999 (4 May) One centre phosphor band (19p) or two phosphor bands (others). Perf 14 × 14½

2088	**1399**	19p multicoloured	75	70	☐	☐
2089	**1400**	26p multicoloured	95	1·00	☐	☐
2090	**1401**	44p multicoloured	1·75	1·60	☐	☐
2091	**1402**	64p multicoloured	2·25	2·40	☐	☐
Set of 4			5·25	5·25	☐	☐
First Day Cover				7·00	☐	
Presentation Pack (P.O. Pack No. 298)			7·50		☐	
PHQ Cards (set of 4) (207)			8·50	13·00	☐	☐
Set of 4 Gutter Pairs			12·00		☐	

1403 Freddie Mercury (lead singer of Queen) ('Popular Music')

1404 Bobby Moore with World Cup, 1966 ('Sport')

1405 Dalek from Dr Who (science-fiction series) ('Television')

1406 Charlie Chaplin (film star) ('Cinema')

Millennium Series. The Entertainers' Tale

1999 (1 June) One centre phosphor band (19p) or two phosphor bands (others). Perf 14 × 14½

2092	**1403**	19p multicoloured	75	70	☐	☐
2093	**1404**	26p multicoloured	95	1·00	☐	☐
2094	**1405**	44p multicoloured	1·50	1·60	☐	☐

2095	**1406**	64p multicoloured	2·25	2·40	☐	☐
Set of 4			5·25	5·25	☐	☐
First Day Cover				7·00		☐
Presentation Pack (P.O. Pack No. 299)			7·50		☐	
PHQ Cards (set of 4) (208)			8·50	13·00	☐	☐
Set of 4 Gutter Pairs			12·00		☐	

1407 Prince Edward and Miss Sophie Rhys-Jones (from photos by John Swannell)

1408 Prince Edward and Miss Sophie Rhys-Jones (from photos by John Swannell)

Royal Wedding

1999 (15 June) Two phosphor bands

2096	**1407**	26p multicoloured	85	85	☐	☐
2097	**1408**	64p multicoloured	2·50	2·50	☐	☐
Set of 2			3·00	3·00	☐	☐
First Day Cover				4·00		☐
Presentation Pack (P.O. Pack No. M01)			4·00		☐	
PHQ Cards (set of 2) (PSM1)			8·50	6·75	☐	☐
Set of 2 Gutter Pairs			7·00		☐	

1409 Suffragette behind Prison Window ('Equal Rights for Women')

1410 Water Tap ('Right to Health')

1411 Generations of School Children ('Right to Education')

1412 'MAGNA CARTA' ('Human Rights')

Millennium Series. The Citizens' Tale

1999 (6 July) One centre phosphor band (19p) or two phosphor bands (others). Perf 14 × 14½

2098	**1409**	19p multicoloured	75	70	☐	☐
2099	**1410**	26p multicoloured	95	1·00	☐	☐
2100	**1411**	44p multicoloured	1·75	1·60	☐	☐
2101	**1412**	64p multicoloured	2·50	2·40	☐	☐
Set of 4			5·75	5·25	☐	☐
First Day Cover				7·00		☐
Presentation Pack (P.O. Pack No. 300)			7·50		☐	
PHQ Cards (set of 4) (209)			8·50	13·00	☐	☐
Set of 4 Gutter Pairs			12·00		☐	

1413 Molecular Structures ('DNA decoding')

1414 Galapagos Finch and Fossilized Skeleton ('Darwin's theory of evolution')

1415 Rotation of Polarized Light by Magnetism (Faraday's work on electricity)

1416 Saturn (development of astronomical telescopes)

Millennium Series. The Scientists' Tale

1999 (3 Aug.–21 Sept.) One centre phosphor band (19p) or two phosphor bands (others). Perf 13½ × 14 (19p, 64p) or 14 × 14½ (26p, 44p)

2102	**1413**	19p	multicoloured	75	70	☐ ☐
2103	**1414**	26p	multicoloured	1·50	1·00	☐ ☐
		b.	Perf 14½ × 14			
			(21.9.99)	2·50	2·50	☐ ☐
2104	**1415**	44p	multicoloured	1·50	1·60	☐ ☐
		a.	Perf 14½ × 14			
			(21.9.99)	2·75	2·75	☐ ☐
2105	**1416**	64p	multicoloured	2·25	2·40	☐ ☐
Set of 4				5·25	5·25	☐ ☐
First Day Cover					7·00	☐
Presentation Pack (P.O. Pack No. 301)				7·50		☐
PHQ Cards (*set of* 4) (210)				8·50	13·00	☐ ☐
Set of 4 Gutter Pairs				12·00		☐

Nos. 2103b and 2104a were only issued in the £6·99 'World Changers' booklet, No. DX23.

1416a

Solar Eclipse miniature sheet

1999 (11 Aug.) Sheet 89 × 121 mm. Two phosphor bands. Perf 14 × 14½

MS2106	**1416a**	64p × 4 multicoloured	22·00	22·00	☐ ☐
First Day Cover				24·00	☐

1417 Upland Landscape (Strip farming)

1418 Horse-drawn Rotary Seed Drill (Mechanical farming)

1419 Man peeling Potato (Food imports)

1420 Aerial View of Combine Harvester (Satellite agriculture)

Millennium Series. The Farmers' Tale

1999 (7 Sept.) One centre phosphor band (19p) or two phosphor bands (others). Perf 14 × 14½

2107	**1417**	19p	multicoloured	75	70	☐ ☐
2108	**1418**	26p	multicoloured	95	1·00	☐ ☐
2109	**1419**	44p	multicoloured	2·00	1·60	☐ ☐
2110	**1420**	64p	multicoloured	2·50	2·40	☐ ☐
Set of 4				5·75	5·25	☐ ☐
First Day Cover					7·00	☐
Presentation Pack (P.O. Pack No. 302)				7·50		☐
PHQ Cards (*set of* 4) (211)				8·50	13·00	☐ ☐
Set of 4 Gutter Pairs				13·00		☐

No. 2107 includes the 'EUROPA' emblem.

1421 Robert the Bruce (Battle of Bannockburn, 1314)

1422 Cavalier and Horse (English Civil War)

1423 War Graves Cemetery, The Somme (World Wars)

1424 Soldiers with Boy (Peace-keeping)

Millennium Series. The Soldiers' Tale

1999 (5 Oct.) One centre phosphor band (19p) or two phosphor bands (others). Perf 14 × 14½

2111	**1421**	19p	black, stone and silver	75	70	☐ ☐
2112	**1422**	26p	multicoloured	95	1·00	☐ ☐

2113	**1423**	44p grey-black, black and silver	2·00	1·60	☐	☐
2114	**1424**	64p multicoloured	2·50	2·40	☐	☐
Set of 4			5·75	5·25	☐	☐
First Day Cover				7·00	☐	
Presentation Pack (P.O. Pack No. 303)			7·50		☐	
PHQ Cards (set of 4) (212)			8·50	13·00	☐	☐
Set of 4 Gutter Pairs			12·00		☐	

The presentation pack was numbered '302' in error.

1425 'Hark the herald angels sing' and Hymn book (John Wesley)

1426 King James I and Bible (Authorised Version of Bible)

1427 St. Andrews Cathedral, Fife ('Pilgrimage')

1428 Nativity ('First Christmas')

Millennium Series. The Christians' Tale

1999 (2 Nov.) One centre phosphor band (19p) or two phosphor bands (others). Perf 14 × 14½

2115	**1425**	19p multicoloured	75	70	☐	☐
2116	**1426**	26p multicoloured	95	1·00	☐	☐
2117	**1427**	44p multicoloured	1·50	1·60	☐	☐
2118	**1428**	64p multicoloured	2·25	2·40	☐	☐
Set of 4			5·25	5·25	☐	☐
First Day Cover				7·00	☐	
Presentation Pack (P.O. Pack No. 304)			7·50		☐	
PHQ Cards (set of 4) (213)			8·50	13·00	☐	☐
Set of 4 Gutter Pairs			12·00		☐	

1429 'World of the Stage' (Allen Jones)

1430 'World of Music' (Bridget Riley)

1431 'World of Literature' (Lisa Milroy)

1432 'New Worlds' (Sir Howard Hodgkin)

Millennium Series. The Artists' Tale

1999 (7 Dec.) One centre phosphor band (19p) or two phosphor bands (others). Perf 14 × 14½

2119	**1429**	19p multicoloured	75	70	☐	☐
2120	**1430**	26p multicoloured	95	1·00	☐	☐
2121	**1431**	44p multicoloured	1·50	1·60	☐	☐
2122	**1432**	64p multicoloured	2·25	2·40	☐	☐
Set of 4			5·25	5·25	☐	☐
First Day Cover				7·00	☐	
Presentation Pack (P.O. Pack No. 305)			7·50		☐	
PHQ Cards (set of 4) (214)			8·50	13·00	☐	☐
Set of 4 Gutter Pairs			12·00		☐	

Year Pack 1999

1999 (7 Dec.) Comprises Nos. 2069/76, 2080/2105 and 2107/22

CP2122a	Year Pack	90.00	☐

Post Office Yearbook

1999 (7 Dec.) Comprises Nos. 2069/76, 2080/2105 and 2107/22 in hardback book with slip case

YB2122a	Yearbook	90.00	☐

1433a

Millennium Series. 'Millennium Timekeeper' Minature Sheet

1999 (14 Dec.) Sheet 120 × 89 mm. Multicoloured. Two phosphor bands. Perf 14 × 14½

MS2123	**1433a**	64p Clock face and map of North America; 64p Clock face and map of Asia; 64p Clock face and map of Middle East; 64p Clock face and map of Europe	20·00	20·00	☐	☐
First Day Cover				21·00	☐	
Presentation Pack (P.O. Pack No. M02)			22·00		☐	
PHQ Cards (set of 5) (PSM02)			11·00	24·00	☐	☐

No. **MS**2123 also exists overprinted 'EARLS COURT, LONDON 22–28 MAY 2000 THE STAMP SHOW 2000' from Exhibition Premium Passes, costing £10, available from 1 March 2000.

The five PHQ cards show the four individual stamps and the complete miniature sheet.

1437 Queen Elizabeth II

New Millennium

2000 (6 Jan–23 May.) Photo De La Rue, Questa or Walsall (No. 2124); Questa or Walsall (No. 2124d). Two phosphor bands. Perf 15 × 14 (with one elliptical hole in each vertical side)

2124 **1437**	(1st) olive-brown	1·50	1·00	☐ ☐
	d. Perf 14 *(23 May)*	1·50	1·00	☐ ☐
First Day Cover			3·00	☐
Presentation Pack (P.O. Pack No. 48)		9·00		
PHQ Card *(23 May)* (D16)		5·00	16·00	☐ ☐

No. 2124 comes from sheets or stamp booklets and No. 2124d from booklets only.

1438 Barn Owl (World Owl Trust, Muncaster)

1439 Night Sky (National Space Science Centre, Leicester)

1440 River Goyt and Textile Mills (Torrs Walkaway, New Mills)

1441 Cape Gannets (Seabird Centre, North Berwick)

Millennium Projects (1st series). 'Above and Beyond'

2000 (18 Jan.–26 May) One centre phosphor band (19p) or two phosphor bands (others). Perf 14 × 14½ (1st, 44p) or 13½ × 14 (others)

2125 **1438**	19p multicoloured	1·25	70	☐ ☐
2126 **1439**	26p multicoloured	95	1·00	☐ ☐
2126a	(1st) multicoloured			
	(26 May)	5·25	4·50	☐ ☐
2127 **1440**	44p multicoloured	1·75	1·75	☐ ☐
2128 **1441**	64p multicoloured	2·75	2·75	☐ ☐
Set of 4 (ex No. 2126a)		6·00	6·00	☐ ☐
First Day Cover			7·00	☐
Presentation Pack (P.O. Pack No. 307)		7·00		☐
PHQ Cards *(set of* 4) (215)		8·50	13·00	☐ ☐
Set of 4 Gutter Pairs		13·00		☐

No. 2126a was only issued in the £2·70 Millennium booklet, No. HBA3, and, on 24 Sept 2002 in the £6·83 'Across the Universe' booklet, No. DX29.

1442 Millennium Beacon (Beacons across the Land)

1443 Garratt Steam Locomotive No. 143 pulling Train (Rheilffordd Eryri, Welsh Highland Railway)

1444 Lightning (Dynamic Earth Centre, Edinburgh)

1445 Multicoloured Lights (Lighting Croydon's Skyline)

Millennium Projects (2nd series). 'Fire and Light'

2000 (1 Feb.) One centre phosphor band (19p) or two phosphor bands (others). Perf 14 × 14½

2129 **1442**	19p multicoloured	75	70	☐ ☐
2130 **1443**	26p multicoloured	1·25	1·00	☐ ☐
2131 **1444**	44p multicoloured	1·50	1·50	☐ ☐
2132 **1445**	64p multicoloured	2·25	2·50	☐ ☐
Set of 4		5·50	5·50	☐ ☐
First Day Cover			7·00	☐
Presentation Pack (P.O. Pack No. 308)		7·00		☐
PHQ Cards *(set of* 4) (216)		8·50	13·00	☐ ☐
Set of 4 Gutter Pairs		13·00		☐

1446 Queen Victoria and Queen Elizabeth II

Booklet Stamps

2000 (15 Feb.) - **17** Design T **929**, but redrawn with '1st' face value as T **1446**. Two phosphor bands. Perf 14 (No. 2133) or Perf 14½ × 14 (both with one elliptical hole in each vertical side)

2133 **1446**	20p brownish black			
	and cream *(5.6.17)*	2·75	2·75	☐ ☐
2133a	(1st) brownish black			
	and cream	2·75	2·75	☐ ☐
First Day Cover (2133a)			4·00	☐

No. 2133 comes from the £15·14 50th Anniversary of the Machin Prestige booklet, No. DY21, issued on 5 June 2017. No. 2133a was only issued in the £7·50 'Special by Design' booklet. See also No. 2956

1447 Beach Pebbles (Turning the Tide, Durham Coast)

1448 Frog's Legs and Water Lilies (National Pondlife Centre, Merseyside)

1449 Cliff Boardwalk (Parc Ardfordirol, Llanelli Coast)

1450 Reflections in Water (Portsmouth Harbour Development)

Millennium Projects (3rd series). 'Water and Coast'

2000 (7 Mar.) One centre phosphor band (19p) or two phosphor bands (others). Perf 14 × 14½

2134	**1447**	19p multicoloured	75	70	☐	☐
2135	**1448**	26p multicoloured	1·25	1·00	☐	☐
2136	**1449**	44p black, grey and silver	1·50	1·50	☐	☐
2137	**1450**	64p multicoloured	2·25	2·50	☐	☐
Set of 4			5·50	5·50	☐	☐
First Day Cover				7·00		☐
Presentation Pack (P.O. Pack No. 309)			7·00		☐	
PHQ Cards (*set of* 4) (217)			8·50	13·00	☐	☐
Set of 4 Gutter Pairs			13·00		☐	

1451 Reed Beds, River Braid (ECOS, Ballymena)

1452 South American Leaf-cutter Ants ('Web of Life' Exhibition, London Zoo)

1453 Solar Sensors (Earth Centre, Doncaster)

1454 Hydroponic Leaves (Project SUZY, Teesside)

Millennium Projects (4th series). 'Life and Earth'

2000 (4 Apr.) One centre phosphor band (2nd) or two phosphor bands (others). Perf 14 × 14½

2138	**1451**	(2nd) multicoloured	1·00	70	☐	☐
2139	**1452**	(1st) multicoloured	1·25	1·00	☐	☐
2140	**1453**	44p multicoloured	1·50	1·50	☐	☐
2141	**1454**	64p multicoloured	2·25	1·50	☐	☐
Set of 4			5·75	5·50	☐	☐
First Day Cover				7·00		☐
Presentation Pack (P.O. Pack No. 310)			7·00		☐	
PHQ Cards (*set of* 4) (218)			8·50	13·00	☐	☐
Set of 4 Gutter Pairs			13·00		☐	

1455 Pottery Glaze (Ceramic Museum, Stoke-on-Trent)

1456 Bankside Galleries (Tate Modern, London)

1457 Road Marking (Cycle Network Artworks)

1458 People of Salford (Lowry Centre, Salford)

Millennium Projects (5th series). 'Art and Craft'

2000 (2 May) One centre phosphor band (2nd) or two phosphor bands (others). Perf 14 × 14½

2142	**1455**	(2nd) multicoloured	1·00	70	☐	☐
2143	**1456**	(1st) multicoloured	1·25	1·00	☐	☐
2144	**1457**	45p multicoloured	1·50	1·50	☐	☐
2145	**1458**	65p multicoloured	2·25	2·50	☐	☐
Set of 4			5·75	5·50	☐	☐
First Day Cover				7·00		☐
Presentation Pack (P.O. Pack No. 311)			7·50		☐	
PHQ Cards (*set of* 4) (219)			8·50	13·00	☐	☐
Set of 4 Gutter Pairs			13·00		☐	

1459

'Stamp Show 2000' International Stamp Exhibition, (1st issue) London. Jeffrey Matthews Colour Palette Minature Sheet

2000 (22 May) Sheet, 124 × 70 mm, containing stamps as T **367** with two labels. Phosphorised paper. Perf 15 × 14 (with one elliptical hole in each vertical side)

MS2146	**1459**	4p new blue; 5p dull red-brown; 6p yellow-olive; 10p dull orange; 31p deep mauve; 39p deep bright magenta; 64p turqoise-green; £1 bluish violet	30·00	30·00	☐ ☐
First Day Cover				30·00	☐
Exhibition Card (wallet, sold at £4·99, containing one mint sheet and one cancelled on postcard)			60·00		☐

The £1 value is printed in Iriodin ink which gives a shiny effect to the solid part of the background behind the Queen's head.

1459a

'Stamp Show 2000' International Stamp Exhibition, (2nd issue) London. 'Her Majesty's Stamps' Miniature Sheet

2000 (23 May) Sheet 121 × 89 mm. Phosphorised paper. Perf 15 × 14 (with one elliptical hole in each vertical side of stamps as T **1437**)

MS2147	**1459a**	(1st) olive-brown (Type **1437**) × 4; £1 slate-green (as Type **163**)	21·00	21·00	☐ ☐

First Day Cover		22·00	
Presentation Pack (P.O. Pack No. M03)		80·00	
PHQ Cards (set of 2) (PSM03)	16·00	34·00	

The £1 value is an adaptation of the 1953 Coronation 1s3d stamp. It is shown on one of the PHQ cards with the other depicting the complete miniature sheet.

See also No. 2380 for T **163** from £7·46 stamp booklet.

1460 Children playing (Millenium Greens Project)

1461 Millennium Bridge, Gateshead

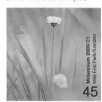

1462 Daisies (Mile End Park, London)

1463 African Hut and Thatched Cottage ('On the Meridian Line' Project)

Millennium Projects (6th series). 'People and Places'

2000 (6 June) One centre phosphor band (2nd) or two phosphor bands (others). Perf 14 × 14½

2148	**1460**	(2nd)	multicoloured	1·00	70	
2149	**1461**	(1st)	multicoloured	1·25	1·00	
2150	**1462**	45p	multicoloured	1·50	1·50	
2151	**1463**	65p	multicoloured	2·25	2·50	
Set of 4				5·75	5·50	
First Day Cover					7·00	
Presentation Pack (P.O. Pack No. 312)				7·50		
PHQ Cards (set of 4) (220)				8·50	13·00	
Set of 4 Gutter Pairs				13·00		

1464 Raising the Stone (Strangford Stone, Killyleagh)

1465 Horse's Hooves (Trans Pennine Trail, Derbyshire)

1466 Cyclist (Kingdom of Fife Cycle Ways, Scotland)

1467 Bluebell Wood (Groundwork's 'Changing Places' Project)

Millennium Projects (7th series). 'Stone and Soil'

2000 (4 July) One centre phosphor band (2nd) or two phosphor bands (others). Perf 14 × 14½

2152	**1464**	(2nd)	brownish black, grey-black and silver	1·00	70	
2153	**1465**	(1st)	multicoloured	1·25	1·00	

2154	**1466**	45p	multicoloured	1·50	1·75	
2155	**1467**	65p	multicoloured	2·50	2·50	
Set of 4				5·75	5·75	
First Day Cover					7·00	
Presentation Pack (P.O. Pack No. 313)				7·50		
PHQ Cards (set of 4) (221)				8·50	13·00	
Set of 4 Gutter Pairs				13·00		

1468 Tree Roots ('Yews for the Millennium' Project)

1469 Sunflower ('Eden' Project, St. Austell)

1470 Sycamore Seeds (Millennium Seed Bank, Wakehurst Place, Surrey)

1471 Forest, Doire Dach ('Forest for Scotland')

Millennium Projects (8th series). 'Tree and Leaf'

2000 (1 Aug.) One centre phosphor band (2nd) or two phosphor bands (others). Perf 14 × 14½

2156	**1468**	(2nd)	multicoloured	1·00	70	
2157	**1469**	(1st)	multicoloured	1·25	1·00	
2158	**1470**	45p	multicoloured	1·50	1·60	
2159	**1471**	65p	multicoloured	2·50	2·50	
Set of 4				5·75	5·50	
First Day Cover					7·00	
Presentation Pack (P.O. Pack No. 314)				7·50		
PHQ Cards (set of 4) (222)				8·50	13·00	
Set of 4 Gutter Pairs				13·00		

1472 Queen Elizabeth the Queen Mother

1472a Royal Family on Queen Mother's 100th Birthday (from photo by J. Swannell)

Queen Elizabeth the Queen Mother's 100th Birthday

2000 (4 Aug.) Phosphorised paper plus two phosphor bands.
Perf 14½

2160 **1472**	27p multicoloured	2·50	2·75	☐ ☐

MS2161 121×89 mm. **1472a** 27p
Queen Elizabeth II; 27p Prince
William; 27p Queen Elizabeth the
Queen Mother; 27p Prince Charles 11·00   11·00 ☐ ☐
First Day Cover (**MS**2161)   12·00 ☐
Presentation Pack (**MS**2161)
　　　　　(P.O. Pack No. M04) 38·00   ☐
PHQ Cards (*set of* 5) (PSM04) 11·00   24·00 ☐ ☐
No. 2160 was only issued in the £7·03 "Life of the Century"
booklet No. DX25 and in No. **MS**2161.

The complete miniature sheet is shown on one of the PHQ
cards with the others depicting individual stamps.

1473 Head of *Gigantiops*
destructor (Ant)
(Wildscreen at Bristol)

1474 Gathering Water Lilies
on Broads (Norfolk and
Norwich Project)

1475 X-ray of Hand holding
Computer Mouse (Millennium
Point, Birmingham

1476 Tartan Wool Holder
(Scottish Cultural
Resources Access Network)

Millennium Projects (9th series). 'Mind and Matter'

2000 (5 Sept.) One centre phosphor band (2nd) or two
phosphor bands (others). Perf 14×14½

2162 **1473**	(2nd) multicoloured	1·00	70	☐ ☐
2163 **1474**	(1st) multicoloured	1·25	1·00	☐ ☐
2164 **1475**	45p multicoloured	1·50	1·75	☐ ☐
2165 **1476**	65p multicoloured	2·25	2·50	☐ ☐
Set of 4		5·75	5·75	☐ ☐
First Day Cover			7·00	☐
Presentation Pack (P.O. Pack No. 315)		7·50		☐
PHQ Cards (*set of* 4) (223)		8·50	13·00	☐ ☐
Set of 4 Gutter Pairs		13·00		☐

1477 Acrobatic Performers
(Millennium Dome)

1478 Football Players (Hampden
Park, Glasgow)

1479 Bather (Bath Spa
Project)

1480 Hen's Egg under
Magnification (Centre for Life,
Newcastle)

Millennium Projects (10th series). 'Body and Bone'

2000 (3 Oct.) One centre phosphor band (2nd) or two phosphor
bands (others). Perf 14×14½ (2nd) or 13½×14 (others)

2166 **1477**	(2nd)	black, slate-blue and silver	1·00	70	☐ ☐
2167 **1478**	(1st)	multicoloured	1·25	1·00	☐ ☐
2168 **1479**	45p	multicoloured	1·50	1·50	☐ ☐
2169 **1480**	65p	multicoloured	2·25	2·50	☐ ☐
Set of 4			5·75	5·75	☐ ☐
First Day Cover				7·00	☐
Presentation Pack (P.O. Pack No. 316)			7·50		☐
PHQ Cards (*set of* 4) (224)			8·50	13·00	☐ ☐
Set of 4 Gutter Pairs			13·00		☐

1481 Virgin and Child Stained
Glass Window, St. Edmundsbury
Cathedral (Suffolk Cathedral
Millennium Project)

1482 Floodlit Church of
St. Peter and St. Paul,
Overstowey (Church Floodlighting
Trust)

1483 12th-cent. Latin
Gradual (St. Patrick Centre,
Downpatrick)

1484 Chapter House
Ceiling, York Minster (York
Millennium Mystery Plays)

Millennium Projects (11th series). 'Spirit and Faith'

2000 (7 Nov.) One centre phosphor band (2nd) or two
phosphor bands (others). Perf 14×14½

2170 **1481**	(2nd) multicoloured	1·00	70	☐ ☐
2171 **1482**	(1st) multicoloured	1·25	1·00	☐ ☐
2172 **1483**	45p multicoloured	1·50	1·50	☐ ☐
2173 **1484**	65p multicoloured	2·25	2·50	☐ ☐ *Set*
of 4		5·75	5·50	☐ ☐
First Day Cover			7·00	☐
Presentation Pack (P.O. Pack No. 317)		7·50		☐
PHQ Cards (*set of* 4) (225)		8·50	13·00	☐ ☐
Set of 4 Gutter Pairs		13·00		☐

Post Office Yearbook

2000 (7 Nov.) Comprises Nos. 2125/6, 2127/32, 2134/45,
2148/59 and **MS**2161/77 in hardback book with slip case
YB2177a   Yearbook   £100 ☐
The last two issues in the Millennium Projects Series were

supplied for insertion into the above at a later date.

1485 Church Bells (Ringing in the Millennium)

1486 Eye (Year of the Artist)

1487 Top of Harp (Canolfan Mileniwn, Cardiff)

1488 Figure within Latticework (TS2K Creative Enterprise Centres, London)

Millennium Projects (12th series). 'Sound and Vision'

2000 (5 Dec.) One centre phosphor band (2nd) or two phosphor bands (others). Perf 14 × 14½

2174	**1485**	(2nd)	multicoloured	1·00	70	☐ ☐
2175	**1486**	(1st)	multicoloured	1·25	1·00	☐ ☐
2176	**1487**	45p	multicoloured	1·50	1·50	☐ ☐
2177	**1488**	65p	multicoloured	2·25	2·50	☐ ☐
Set of 4				5·75	5·50	☐ ☐
First Day Cover					7·00	☐
Presentation Pack (P.O. Pack No. 318)				7·50		☐
PHQ Cards (*set of* 4) (226)				8·50	13·00	☐ ☐
Set of 4 Gutter Pairs				13·00		☐

Year Pack 2000

2000 (5 Dec.) Comprises Nos. 2125/6, 2127/32, 2134/45, 2148/59 and **MS**2161/77

CP2177a	Year Pack	£100	☐

1489 'Flower' ('Nurture Children')

1490 'Tiger' ('Listen to Children')

1491 'Owl' ('Teach Children')

1492 'Butterfly' ('Ensure Children's Freedom')

New Millennium. Rights of the Child.
Face Paintings

2001 (16 Jan.) One centre phosphor band (2nd) or two phosphor bands (others). Perf 14 × 14½

2178	**1489**	(2nd)	multicoloured	1·00	75	☐ ☐
2179	**1490**	(1st)	multicoloured	1·25	1·10	☐ ☐

2180	**1491**	45p	multicoloured	1·60	1·75	☐ ☐
2181	**1492**	65p	multicoloured	2·40	2·50	☐ ☐
Set of 4				5·75	5·75	☐ ☐
First Day Cover					7·00	☐
Presentation Pack (P.O. Pack No. 319)				7·50		☐
PHQ Cards (*set of* 4) (227)				7·50	10·00	☐ ☐
Set of 4 Gutter Pairs				13·00		☐

1493 'Love'

1494 'THANKS'

1495 'abc' (New Baby)

1496 'WELCOME'

1497 'Cheers'

Greetings Stamps (1st series) 'Occasions'

2001 (6 Feb.–13 Feb.) Two phosphor bands. Perf 14½ × 14

2182	**1493**	(1st)	multicoloured	1·30	1·30	☐ ☐
2183	**1494**	(1st)	multicoloured	1·30	1·30	☐ ☐
2184	**1495**	(1st)	multicoloured	1·30	1·30	☐ ☐
2185	**1496**	(1st)	multicoloured	1·30	1·30	☐ ☐
2186	**1497**	(1st)	multicoloured	1·30	1·30	☐ ☐
Set of 5				6·00	6·00	☐ ☐
First Day Cover					7·50	☐
Presentation Pack *(13 Feb.)*						
(P.O. Pack No. M05)				10·00		☐
PHQ Cards (*set of* 5) (PSM05)				8·50	11·00	☐ ☐
Set of 5 Gutter Pairs				13·00		☐

The silver-grey backgrounds are printed in Iriodin ink which gives a shiny effect.

Further packs of Nos. 2182/6 were sold from 3 July 2001. These comprised the listed stamps in blocks of ten (from sheets) with an insert describing the occasion (*Price* £10 *per pack*).

Nos. 2182/6 were printed in gravure. They were subsequently re-issued on 1 May, as sheets of 20, printed in lithography instead of gravure with each stamp accompanied by a half stamp-size label showing either postal symbols or a personal photograph.

1498 Dog and Owner on Bench

1499 Dog in Bath

1500 Boxer at Dog Show

1501 Cat in Handbag

1502 Cat on Gate

1503 Dog in Car

1504 Cat at Window

1505 Dog behind Fence

1506 Cat watching Bird

1507 Cat in Washbasin

Cats and Dogs

2001 (13 Feb.) Self-adhesive. Two phosphor bands. Die-cut
perf 15×14

2187	**1498**	(1st)	black, grey and silver	1·25	1·00	☐ ☐
		a.	Sheetlet.			
			Nos. 2187/96	15·00	15·00	☐ ☐
		b.	Booklet pane.			
			Nos.2187/96 plus			
			Nos. 2040×2	30·00		☐
2188	**1499**	(1st)	black, grey and silver	1·25	1·00	☐ ☐
2189	**1500**	(1st)	black, grey and silver	1·25	1·00	☐ ☐
2190	**1501**	(1st)	black, grey and silver	1·25	1·00	☐ ☐
2191	**1502**	(1st)	black, grey and silver	1·25	1·00	☐ ☐
2192	**1503**	(1st)	black, grey and silver	1·25	1·00	☐ ☐
2193	**1504**	(1st)	black, grey and silver	1·25	1·00	☐ ☐
2194	**1505**	(1st)	black, grey and silver	1·25	1·00	☐ ☐
2195	**1506**	(1st)	black, grey and silver	1·25	1·00	☐ ☐
2196	**1507**	(1st)	black, grey and silver	1·25	1·00	☐ ☐
Set of 10				15·00	15·00	☐ ☐
First Day Cover					16·00	☐
Presentation Pack (P.O. Pack No. 320)				20·00		☐
PHQ Cards (*set of* 10) (228)				14·00	30·00	☐ ☐

Nos. 2187/96 were printed together in sheetlets of ten
(5×2), with the surplus self-adhesive paper around each
stamp retained. They were also issued in £3·24 booklets, the
booklet pane has vertical roulettes between rows 2/3 and 4/5.

1508 'RAIN'

1509 'FAIR'

1510 'STORMY'

1511 'VERY DRY'

The Weather

2001 (13 Mar.) One side phosphor band (19p) or two phosphor
bands (others). Perf 14½

2197	**1508**	19p	multicoloured	70	75	☐ ☐
2198	**1509**	27p	multicoloured	85	1·00	☐ ☐
2199	**1510**	45p	multicoloured	1·50	1·50	☐ ☐
2200	**1511**	65p	multicoloured	2·40	2·50	☐ ☐
Set of 4				5·00	5·50	☐ ☐
First Day Cover					7·00	☐
Presentation Pack (P.O. Pack No. 321)				14·00		☐
Set of 4 Gutter Pairs				12·00		☐
MS2201 105×105 mm.						
	Nos. 2197/2200			18·00	18·00	☐ ☐
First Day Cover					19·00	☐
PHQ Cards (*set of* 5) (229)				8·50	20·00	☐ ☐

Nos. 2197/2200 show the four quadrants of a barometer dial
which are combined on the miniature sheet.

The reddish violet on both the 27p and the miniature sheet
is printed in thermochromic ink which changes from reddish
violet to light blue when exposed to heat.

The PHQ cards depict the four values and the miniature
sheet.

1512 Vanguard Class Submarine, 1992

1513 Swiftsure Class Submarine, 1973

1514 Unity Class Submarine, 1939

1515 'Holland' Type Submarine, 1901

1516 White Ensign

1517 Union Jack

1518 Jolly Roger flown by HMS *Proteus* (submarine)

1519 Flag of Chief of Defence Staff

Centenary of the Royal Navy Submarine Service

2001 (10 Apr.–22 Oct.) One centre phosphor band (2nd) or two phosphor bands (others).

(a) Submarines. Ordinary gum. Perf 15 × 14

2202	**1512**	(2nd)	multicoloured	1·00	75	☐ ☐
		a.	Perf 15½ × 15			
			(22 Oct.)	3·75	3·00	☐ ☐
2203	**1513**	(1st)	multicoloured	1·25	90	☐ ☐
		a.	Perf 15½ × 15*(22 Oct.)*	3·75	3·00	☐ ☐
2204	**1514**	45p	multicoloured	1·75	1·60	☐ ☐
		a.	Perf 15½ × 15			
			(22 Oct.)	3·75	3·00	☐ ☐
2205	**1515**	65p	multicoloured	2·40	2·50	☐ ☐
		a.	Perf 15½ × 15			
			(22 Oct.)	3·75	3·00	☐ ☐
Set of 4				5·75	5·25	☐ ☐
First Day Cover					7·00	☐
Presentation Pack (P.O. Pack No. 322)				20·00		☐
PHQ Cards (*set of 4*) (230)				7·50	12·00	☐ ☐
Set of 4 Gutter Pairs				13·00		☐

(b) Flags. Sheet 92 × 97 mm. Ordinary gum. Perf 14½

MS2206	**1516**	(1st)	multicoloured;			
	1517	(1st)	multicoloured; **1518**			
	(1st)	multicoloured; **1519**	(1st)			
	multicoloured *(22 Oct.)*			9·00	9·00	☐ ☐
First Day Cover					11·00	☐
Presentation Pack (P.O. Pack No. M06)				30·00		☐
PHQ Cards (*set of 5*) (PSM07)				12·00	15·00	☐ ☐

(c) Self-adhesive. Die-cut perf 15½ × 14 (No. 2207) or 14½ (others)

2207	**1513**	(1st)	multicoloured			
			(17 Apr.)	50·00	40·00	☐ ☐
2208	**1516**	(1st)	multicoloured			
			(22 Oct.)	15·00	15·00	☐ ☐
2209	**1518**	(1st)	multicoloured			
			(22 Oct.)	15·00	15·00	☐ ☐

Nos. 2202a/5a were only issued in the £6·76 "Unseen and Unheard" booklet No. DX27.

The five PHQ cards depict the four designs and the complete miniature sheet, **MS**2206.

Nos. 2207/9 only come from two different £1·62 booklets.

Type **1516** was re-issued on 21 June 2005 in sheets of 20, printed in lithography instead of gravure, with half stamp-size *se-tenant* labels showing signal flags.

Designs as Type **1517** were issued on 27 July 2004 in sheets of 20 printed in lithography instead of gravure with each vertical row of stamps alternated with half stamp-size labels. See also Nos. 2581, 2805 and 2970.

1520 Leyland X2 Open-top, London General B Type, Leyland Titan TD1 and AEC Regent 1

1521 AEC Regent 1, Daimler COG5, Utility Guy Arab Mk II and AEC Regent III RT Type

1522 AEC Regent III RT Type, Bristol KSW5G Open-Top, AEC Routemaster and Bristol Lodekka FSF6G

1523 Bristol Lodekka FSF6G, Leyland Titan PD3/4, Leyland Atlantean PDR1/1 and Daimler Fleetline CRG6LX-33

1524 Daimler Fleetline CRG6LX-33, MCW Metrobus DR102/43, Leyland Olympian ONLXB/1R and Dennis Trident

150th Anniversary of First Double-decker Bus

2001 (15 May) 'All-over' phosphor. Perf 14½ × 14

2210	**1520**	(1st)	multicoloured	1·25	1·00	☐ ☐
		a.	Horiz strip of 5.			
			Nos. 2210/14	7·00	7·00	☐ ☐
2211	**1521**	(1st)	multicoloured	1·25	1·00	☐ ☐
2212	**1522**	(1st)	multicoloured	1·25	1·00	☐ ☐
2213	**1523**	(1st)	multicoloured	1·25	1·00	☐ ☐
2214	**1524**	(1st)	multicoloured	1·25	1·00	☐ ☐
Set of 5				7·00	7·00	☐ ☐
First Day Cover					8·00	☐
Presentation Pack (P.O. Pack No. 323)				10·00		☐
PHQ Cards (*set of 6*) (231)				14·00	16·00	☐ ☐
Gutter Strip of 10				15·00		☐
MS2215 120 × 105 mm. Nos. 2210/14				10·50	12·50	☐ ☐
First Day Cover					15·00	☐

Nos. 2210/4 were printed together, *se-tenant*, in horizontal strips of five throughout the sheet. The illustrations of the first bus on No. 2210 and the last bus on No. 2214 continue onto the sheet margins.

In No. **MS**2215 the illustrations of the AEC Regent III RT Type and the Daimler Fleetline CRG6LX-33 appear twice.

The six PHQ cards show the stamps and the miniature sheet.

1525 Toque Hat by Pip Hackett

1526 Butterfly Hat by Dai Rees

1527 Top Hat by Stephen Jones

1528 Spiral Hat by Philip Treacy

Fashion Hats

2001 (19 June) 'All-over' phosphor. Perf 14½

2216	**1525**	(1st)	multicoloured	1·25	90	☐ ☐
2217	**1526**	(E)	multicoloured	1·50	1·25	☐ ☐
2218	**1527**	45p	multicoloured	1·60	1·60	☐ ☐
2219	**1528**	65p	multicoloured	2·50	2·50	☐ ☐
Set of 4				6·00	5·50	☐ ☐
First Day Cover					6·50	☐
Presentation Pack (P.O. Pack No. 324)				7·50		☐
PHQ Cards (*set of 4*) (232)				8·50	14·00	☐ ☐
Set of 4 Gutter Pairs				13·00		☐

1529 Common Frog

1530 Great Diving Beetle

1531 Three-spined Stickleback

1532 Southern Hawker Dragonfly

Europa. Pond Life

2001 (10 July) Two phosphor bands

2220	**1529**	(1st)	multicoloured	1·25	1·00	☐ ☐
2221	**1530**	(E)	multicoloured	1·50	1·25	☐ ☐
2222	**1531**	45p	multicoloured	1·50	1·50	☐ ☐
2223	**1532**	65p	multicoloured	2·00	2·25	☐ ☐
Set of 4				6·00	5·75	☐ ☐
First Day Cover					7·50	☐
Presentation Pack (P.O. Pack No. 325)				7·50		☐
PHQ Cards (*set of* 4) (233)				8·50	14·00	☐ ☐
Set of 4 Gutter Pairs				13·00		

The 1st and E values incorporate the 'EUROPA' emblem.

The bluish silver on all four values is in Iriodin ink and was used as a background for those parts of the design below the water line.

1533 Policeman

1534 Clown

1535 Mr. Punch

1536 Judy

1537 Beadle

1538 Crocodile

Punch and Judy Show Puppets

2001 (4 Sept.) Two phosphor bands

		(a) Ordinary gum. Perf 14 × 15				
2224	**1533**	(1st)	multicoloured	1·25	1·00	☐ ☐
		a. Horiz strip of 6.				
		Nos. 2224/9		6·50	6·50	☐ ☐
2225	**1534**	(1st)	multicoloured	1·25	1·00	☐ ☐
2226	**1535**	(1st)	multicoloured	1·25	1·00	☐ ☐
2227	**1536**	(1st)	multicoloured	1·25	1·00	☐ ☐
2228	**1537**	(1st)	multicoloured	1·25	1·00	☐ ☐
2229	**1538**	(1st)	multicoloured	1·25	1·00	☐ ☐
Set of 6				6·50	6·50	☐ ☐
First Day Cover					7·00	☐
Presentation Pack (P.O. Pack No. 326)				7·00		☐
PHQ Cards (*set of* 6) (234)				8·50	18·00	☐ ☐
Gutter Block of 12				14·00		☐

		(b) Self-adhesive. Die-cut perf 14 × 15½				
2230	**1535**	(1st)	multicoloured	17·00	17·00	☐ ☐
2231	**1536**	(1st)	multicoloured	17·00	17·00	☐ ☐

Nos. 2230/1 were only issued in £1·62 stamp booklets.

Nos. 2224/9 were printed together, *se-tenant*, in horizontal strips of six throughout the sheet.

CHEMISTRY
Nobel Prize 100th Anniversary
1539 Carbon 60 Molecule (Chemistry)

ECONOMIC SCIENCES
Nobel Prize 100th Anniversary
1540 Globe (Economic Sciences)

PEACE
Nobel Prize 100th Anniversary
1541 Embossed Dove (Peace)

PHYSIOLOGY OR MEDICINE
Nobel Prize 100th Anniversary
1542 Crosses (Physiology or Medicine)

LITERATURE
Nobel Prize 100th Anniversary
1543 Poem 'The Addressing of Cats' by T.S. Eliot in Open Book (Literature)

PHYSICS
Nobel Prize 100th Anniversary
1544 Hologram of Boron Molecule (Physics)

Centenary of Nobel Prizes

2001 (2 Oct.) One side phosphor band (2nd) or phosphor frame (others). Perf 14½

2232	**1539**	(2nd)	black, silver and grey-black	1·00	80	☐ ☐
2233	**1540**	(1st)	multicoloured	1·50	1·00	☐ ☐
2234	**1541**	(E)	black, silver and bright green	1·50	1·50	☐ ☐
2235	**1542**	40p	multicoloured	2·00	1·50	☐ ☐
2236	**1543**	45p	multicoloured	3·00	2·00	☐ ☐
2237	**1544**	65p	black and silver	5·00	2·50	☐ ☐
Set of 6				12·00	8·00	☐ ☐
First Day Cover					9·00	☐

Presentation Pack (P.O. Pack No. 327)	40·00		☐
PHQ Cards (set of 6) (235)	10·00	14·00	☐ ☐
Set of 6 Gutter Pairs	25·00		☐

The grey-black on No. 2232 is printed in thermochromic ink which temporarily changes to pale grey when exposed to heat.

The centre of No. 2235 is coated with a eucalyptus scent.

1545 Robins with Snowman

1546 Robins on Bird Table

1547 Robins skating on Bird Bath

1548 Robins with Christmas Pudding

1549 Robins in Paper Chain Nest

Christmas. Robins

2001 (6 Nov.) Self-adhesive. One centre phosphor band (2nd) or two phosphor bands (others). Die-cut perf 14½

2238	**1545**	(2nd)	multicoloured	1·00	80	☐ ☐
2239	**1546**	(1st)	multicoloured	1·25	1·00	☐ ☐
2240	**1547**	(E)	multicoloured	1·50	1·50	☐ ☐
2241	**1548**	45p	multicoloured	2·00	2·00	☐ ☐
2242	**1549**	65p	multicoloured	3·00	3·00	☐ ☐
Set of 5				7·50	7·50	☐
First Day Cover					8·50	☐
Presentation Pack (P.O. Pack No. 328)				8·00		☐
PHQ Cards (set of 5) (236)				11·00	16·00	☐ ☐

The 1st value was re-issued on 30 September 2003, in sheets of 20, in lithography instead of gravure, each stamp se-tenant with a Christmas label or a personal photograph. The sheet contained die-cut perforated stamps and labels.

The 2nd and 1st class stamps were issued again on 1 November 2005 in sheets of 20 containing ten 1st class and ten 2nd class stamps, each stamp accompanied by a se-tenant label showing a snowman.

Year Pack 2001

2001 (6 Nov.) Comprises Nos. 2178/2200, 2202/**MS**2206, 2210/14, 2216/29 and 2232/42

CP2242a	Year Pack	£110	☐

Post Office Yearbook

2001 (6 Nov.) Comprises Nos. 2178/96, **MS**2201/6, **MS**2215/29 and 2232/42 in hardback book with slip case

YB2242a	Yearbook	£110	☐

1550 'How the Whale got his Throat'

1551 'How the Camel got his Hump'

1552 'How the Rhinoceros got his Skin'

1553 'How the Leopard got his Spots'

1554 'The Elephant's Child'

1555 'The Sing-Song of Old Man Kangaroo'

1556 'The Beginning of the Armadillos'

1557 'The Crab that played with the Sea'

1558 'The Cat that walked by Himself'

1559 'The Butterfly that stamped'

Centenary of Publication of Rudyard Kipling's Just So Stories

2002 (15 Jan.) Self-adhesive. Two phosphor bands. Die-cut perf 15 × 14

2243	**1550**	(1st)	multicoloured	1·25	1·00	☐ ☐
		a.	Sheetlet.			
			Nos. 2243/52	14·00	11·00	☐ ☐
2244	**1551**	(1st)	multicoloured	1·25	1·00	☐ ☐
2245	**1552**	(1st)	multicoloured	1·25	1·00	☐ ☐
2246	**1553**	(1st)	multicoloured	1·25	1·00	☐ ☐
2247	**1554**	(1st)	multicoloured	1·25	1·00	☐ ☐
2248	**1555**	(1st)	multicoloured	1·25	1·00	☐ ☐
2249	**1556**	(1st)	multicoloured	1·25	1·00	☐ ☐
2250	**1557**	(1st)	multicoloured	1·25	1·00	☐ ☐
2251	**1558**	(1st)	multicoloured	1·25	1·00	☐ ☐
2252	**1559**	(1st)	multicoloured	1·25	1·00	☐ ☐
Set of 10				14·00	11·00	☐ ☐
First Day Cover					12·00	☐
Presentation Pack (P.O. Pack No. 330)				16·00		☐
PHQ Cards (set of 10) (237)				10·00	28·00	☐ ☐

Nos. 2243/52 were printed together in sheetlets of ten (5 × 2), with the surplus self-adhesive paper around each stamp retained.

1560 Queen Elizabeth II,
1952 (Dorothy Wilding)

1561 Queen Elizabeth II,
1968 (Cecil Beaton)

1562 Queen Elizabeth II,
1978 (Lord Snowdon)

1563 Queen Elizabeth II,
1984 (Yousef Karsh)

1564 Queen Elizabeth II,
1996 (Tim Graham)

1565

Golden Jubilee. Studio portraits of Queen Elizabeth II by photographers named

2002 (6 Feb.) One centre phosphor band (2nd) or two phosphor bands (others). W **1565** (sideways). Perf 14½ × 14

2253	**1560**	(2nd)	multicoloured	1·00	80	☐ ☐
2254	**1561**	(1st)	multicoloured	1·25	90	☐ ☐
2255	**1562**	(E)	multicoloured	1·50	1·50	☐ ☐
2256	**1563**	45p	multicoloured	1·75	2·00	☐ ☐
2257	**1564**	65p	multicoloured	2·75	3·00	☐ ☐
Set of 5				7·50	7·50	☐ ☐
First Day Cover					8·50	☐
Presentation Pack (P.O. Pack No. 331)				9·00		☐
PHQ Cards (set of 5) (238)				4·50	14·00	☐ ☐
Set of 5 Gutter Pairs				16·00		☐

Nos. 2253/7 were also issued with watermark upright, in the £7·29 'A Gracious Accession' booklet, No DX28.

1566

Booklet Stamps

2002 (6 Feb.) Designs as 1952-54 issue, but with service indicator as T **1566**. One centre phosphor band (2nd) or two phosphor bands (1st). W **1565**. Uncoated paper. Perf 15 × 14 (with one elliptical hole in each vertical side)

2258	**1566**	(2nd)	carmine-red	1·60	1·60	☐ ☐
2259	**154**	(1st)	green	2·00	2·00	☐ ☐
Set of 2				3·25	3·25	☐ ☐
First Day Cover					10·00	☐

Nos. 2258/9 were only issued in the £7·29 'The Gracious Accession' stamp booklet, No. DX18.

For other Wilding designs with decimal face vace values, see Nos. 2031/3, **MS**2326, **MS**2367, 2378/80 and 3329.

1567 Rabbits ('a new baby')

1568 'LOVE'

1569 Aircraft Sky-writing 'hello'

1570 Bear pulling Potted Topiary Tree (Moving Home)

1571 Flowers ('best wishes')

Greetings Stamps 'Occasions'

2002 (5 Mar.)-**03** Two phosphor bands

(a) Litho. Ordinary gum. Perf 15 × 14

2260	**1567**	(1st)	multicoloured	1·50	1·10	☐ ☐
2261	**1568**	(1st)	multicoloured	1·50	1·10	☐ ☐
2262	**1569**	(1st)	multicoloured	1·50	1·10	☐ ☐
2263	**1570**	(1st)	multicoloured	1·50	1·10	☐ ☐
2264	**1571**	(1st)	multicoloured	1·50	1·10	☐ ☐
Set of 5				6·50	5·00	☐ ☐
First Day Cover					6·00	☐
Presentation Pack (P.O. Pack No. M07)				7·50		☐
PHQ Cards (set of 5) (PSM08)				4·50	14·00	☐ ☐
Set of 5 Gutter Pairs				13·00		☐

(b) Photo. Self-adhesive. Die-cut perf 15 × 14

2264a	**1569**	(1st)	multicoloured *(4.3.03)*	6·00	6·00	☐ ☐

Nos. 2260/4 were re-issued on 23 April 2002 in sheets of 20 perforated 14, either of one design or se-tenant, with each stamp accompanied by a half stamp-size label showing either greetings or a personal photograph.

No. 2262 was also issued in sheets of 20 with *se-tenant* labels in connection with the Hong Kong Stamp Expo on 30 January 2004. It was issued in sheets of 20 perforated 14 with *se-tenant* labels on 21 April 2005 for Pacific Explorer 2005 World Stamp Expo, on 25 May 2006 for Washington 2006 International Stamp Exhibition, on 14 November 2006 for Belgica 2006 International Stamp Exhibition, on 5 August 2008 for Beijing 2008 Olympic Expo, on 3 August 2009 for Thaipex 09 Stamp Exhibition, on 21 October 2009 for Italia 2009 International Stamp Exhibition and on 4 December 2009 for MonacoPhil International Stamp Exhibition.

No. 2264a was only issued in £1·62 stamp booklets in which the surplus self-adhesive paper around each stamp was removed.

1572 Studland Bay, Dorset

1573 Luskentyre, South Harris

1574 Cliffs, Dover, Kent

1575 Padstow Harbour, Cornwall

1576 Broadstairs, Kent

1577 St. Abb's Head, Scottish Borders

1578 Dunster Beach, Somerset

1579 Newquay Beach, Cornwall

1580 Portrush, County Antrim

1581 Sand-spit, Conwy

British Coastlines

2002 (19 Mar.) Two phosphor bands. Perf 14½

2265	**1572**	27p	multicoloured	80	70	
		a.	Block of 10.			
			Nos. 2265/74	8·75	8·75	
2266	**1573**	27p	multicoloured	80	70	
2267	**1574**	27p	multicoloured	80	70	
2268	**1575**	27p	multicoloured	80	70	
2269	**1576**	27p	multicoloured	80	70	
2270	**1577**	27p	multicoloured	80	70	
2271	**1578**	27p	multicoloured	80	70	
2272	**1579**	27p	multicoloured	80	70	
2273	**1580**	27p	multicoloured	80	70	
2274	**1581**	27p	multicoloured	80	70	
Set of 10				8·75	8·75	
First Day Cover					10·00	
Presentation Pack (P.O. Pack No. 332)				10·50		
PHQ Cards (*set of* 10) (239)				9·25	28·00	
Gutter Block of 20				19·00		

Nos. 2265/74 were printed together, *se-tenant*, in blocks of ten (5 × 2) throughout the sheet.

1582 Slack Wire Act

1583 Lion Tamer

1584 Trick Tri-cyclists

1585 Krazy Kar

1586 Equestrienne

Europa. Circus

2002 (10 Apr.) One centre phosphor band (2nd) or two phosphor bands (others). Perf 14½

2275	**1582**	(2nd)	multicoloured	1·00	80	
2276	**1583**	(1st)	multicoloured	1·25	1·00	
2277	**1584**	(E)	multicoloured	1·50	1·25	
2278	**1585**	45p	multicoloured	1·75	1·50	
2279	**1586**	65p	multicoloured	2·75	2·25	
Set of 5				6·50	6·25	
First Day Cover					7·00	
Presentation Pack (P.O. Pack No. 333)				7·50		
PHQ Cards (*set of* 5) (240)				4·50	14·00	
Set of 5 Gutter Pairs				14·00		

The 1st and E values incorporate the "EUROPA" emblem.

Due to the funeral of the Queen Mother, the actual issue of Nos. 2275/9 was delayed from 9 April which is the date that appears on first day covers.

1587 Queen Elizabeth
the Queen Mother

Queen Elizabeth the Queen Mother Commemoration

2002 (25 Apr.) Vert designs as T **955/8** with changed face values and showing both the Queen's head and frame in black as in T **1587**. Two phosphor bands. Perf 14 × 15

2280	**1587**	(1st)	multicoloured	1·25	85	
2281	**956**	(E)	black and indigo	1·50	1·10	
2282	**957**	45p	multicoloured	1·50	1·50	
2283	**958**	65p	black, stone & sepia	2·00	2·25	
Set of 4				5·50	5·50	
First Day Cover					7·00	
Presentation Pack (P.O. Pack No. M08)				7·00		
Set of 4 Gutter Pairs				13·00		

1588 Airbus A340-600 (2002)   **1589** Concorde (1976)

1590 Trident (1964)   **1591** VC 10 (1964)

1592 Comet (1952)

50th Anniversary of Passenger Jet Aviation. Airliners

2002 (2 May) One centre phosphor band (2nd) or two phosphor bands (others). Perf 14½

(a) Photo De La Rue. Ordinary gum

2284	**1588**	(2nd)	multicoloured	1·00	70	☐ ☐
2285	**1589**	(1st)	multicoloured	1·25	1·00	☐ ☐
2286	**1590**	(E)	multicoloured	1·50	1·50	☐ ☐
2287	**1591**	45p	multicoloured	2·00	2·00	☐ ☐
2288	**1592**	65p	multicoloured	3·00	3·00	☐ ☐
Set of 5				8·00	7·50	☐ ☐
First Day Cover					8·00	☐
Presentation Pack (P.O. Pack No. 334)				10·00		☐
Set of 5 Gutter Pairs				17·00		☐
MS2289 120×105 mm. Nos. 2284/8				12·00	11·00	☐ ☐
First Day Cover					12·00	☐
PHQ Cards (set of 6) (241)				5·25	18·00	☐ ☐

(b) Photo Questa. Self-adhesive

2290	**1589**	(1st)	multicoloured	7·00	7·00	☐ ☐

The complete miniature sheet is shown on one of the PHQ cards with the others depicting individual stamps.

No. 2290 was only issued in £1·62 stamp booklets. For Type **1589** printed by lithography see No. 2897.

1593 Crowned Lion with Shield of St. George

1594 Top Left Quarter of English Flag, and Football   **1595** Top Right Quarter of English Flag, and Football

1596 Bottom Left Quarter of English Flag, and Football   **1597** Bottom Right Quarter of English Flag, and Football

World Cup Football Championship, Japan and Korea

2002 (21 May) Two phosphor bands. Perf 14½ × 14

(a) Ordinary gum

2291	**1593**	(1st)	deep turquoise-blue, scarlet-vermilion and silver	2·50	2·50	☐ ☐
MS2292	145×74 mm. No. 2291; **1594** (1st) multicoloured; **1595** (1st) multicoloured; **1596** (1st) multicoloured; **1597** (1st) multicoloured			7·50	7·50	☐ ☐
First Day Cover (**MS**2292)					8·50	☐
Presentation Pack (**MS**2292) (P.O. Pack No. 335)				8·50		☐
PHQ Cards (set of 6) (242)				5·25	15·00	☐ ☐
Gutter Pair (No. 2291)				6·00		☐

(b) Self-adhesive. Die-cut perf 15 × 14

2293	**1594**	(1st)	multicoloured	6·00	6·00	☐ ☐
2294	**1595**	(1st)	multicoloured	6·00	6·00	☐ ☐

The complete miniature sheet is shown on one of the PHQ cards with the others depicting individual stamps from **MS**2292 and No. 2291.

Nos. 2293/4 were only issued in £1·62 stamp booklets.

Stamps as Type **1597** were also issued in sheets of 20, se-tenant with half stamp-sized labels, printed in lithography instead of gravure. The labels show either match scenes or personal photographs.

Stamps as Type **1593** but with 'WORLD CUP 2002' inscription omitted were issued on 17 May 2007 in sheets of 20 with se-tenant labels showing scenes from Wembley Stadium.

Self-adhesive Stamps

2002 (5 June–4 July) Self-adhesive. Photo Questa, Walsall, De La Rue or Enschedé (No. 2295) or Walsall (others). Two phosphor bands. Perf 15×14 die-cut (with one elliptical hole in each vertical side)

2295	**914**	(1st)	gold	1·50	1·00	☐ ☐
2296	**1093a**	(E)	deep blue (4 July)	2·50	2·50	☐ ☐
2297	**367a**	42p	deep olive-grey (4 July)	3·75	3·75	☐ ☐
2298		68p	grey-brown (4 July)	4·25	4·25	☐ ☐
Set of 4				11·00	10·50	☐ ☐
PHQ Card (No. 2295) Walsall (27.3.03)(D22)			60	3·50	☐ ☐

Further printings of No. 2295 in sheets of 100 appeared on 4 July 2002 produced by Enschedé and on 18 March 2003 printed by Walsall.

1598 Swimming

1599 Running

1600 Cycling

1601 Long Jumping

1602 Wheelchair Racing

17th Commonwealth Games, Manchester

2002 (16 July) One side phosphor band (2nd) or two phosphor bands (others). Perf 14½

2299	**1598**	(2nd)	multicoloured	1·00	80	☐ ☐
2300	**1599**	(1st)	multicoloured	1·25	1·00	☐ ☐
2301	**1600**	(E)	multicoloured	1·50	1·25	☐ ☐
2302	**1601**	47p	multicoloured	1·50	1·50	☐ ☐
2303	**1602**	68p	multicoloured	2·00	2·25	☐ ☐
Set of 5				6·50	6·00	☐ ☐
First Day Cover					7·00	☐
Presentation Pack (P.O. Pack No. 336)				7·50		☐
PHQ Cards (*set of* 5) (243)				4·75	16·00	☐ ☐
Set of 5 Gutter Pairs				14·00		☐

1603 Tinkerbell

1604 Wendy, John and Michael Darling in front of Big Ben

1605 Crocodile and Alarm Clock

1606 Captain Hook

1607 Peter Pan

150th Anniversary of Great Ormond Street Children's Hospital. Peter Pan by Sir James Barrie

2002 (20 Aug.) One centre phosphor band (2nd) or two phosphor bands (others). Perf 15 × 14

2304	**1603**	(2nd)	multicoloured	1·00	80	☐ ☐
2305	**1604**	(1st)	multicoloured	1·25	1·00	☐ ☐
2306	**1605**	(E)	multicoloured	1·50	1·25	☐ ☐
2307	**1606**	47p	multicoloured	1·50	1·50	☐ ☐
2308	**1607**	68p	multicoloured	2·00	2·25	☐ ☐
Set of 5				6·50	6·00	☐ ☐
First Day Cover					7·00	☐
Presentation Pack (P.O. Pack No. 337)				7·50		☐
PHQ Cards (*set of* 5) (244)				4·75	15·00	☐ ☐
Set of 5 Gutter Pairs				14·00		☐

1608 Millennium Bridge, 2001

1609 Tower Bridge, 1894

1610 Westminster Bridge, 1864

1611 'Blackfriars Bridge, *c* 1800' (William Marlow)

1612 'London Bridge, *c* 1670' (Wenceslaus Hollar)

Bridges of London

2002 (10 Sept.) One centre phosphor band (2nd) or two phosphor bands (others)

(a) Litho. Ordinary gum. Perf 15 × 14						
2309	**1608**	(2nd)	multicoloured	1·00	80	☐ ☐
2310	**1609**	(1st)	multicoloured	1·25	80	☐ ☐
2311	**1610**	(E)	multicoloured	2·00	1·50	☐ ☐
2312	**1611**	47p	multicoloured	2·50	2·00	☐ ☐
2313	**1612**	68p	multicoloured	3·50	3·00	☐ ☐
Set of 5				9·00	7·50	☐ ☐
First Day Cover					8·50	☐
Presentation Pack (P.O. Pack No. 338)				45·00		☐
PHQ Cards (*set of* 5) (245)				4·00	12·00	☐ ☐
Set of 5 Gutter Pairs				20·00		☐

(b) Gravure. Self-adhesive. Die-cut perf 15 × 14
2314 **1609**   (1st) multicoloured   6·00   6·00   ☐ ☐

No. 2314 was only issued in £1·62 stamp booklets.

1613 Galaxies and Nebula

Astronomy

2002 (24 Sept.) Sheet 120×89 mm. Multicoloured. Two phosphor bands. Perf 14½ × 14

MS2315 **1613** (1st) Planetary nebula
     in Aquila; (1st) Seyfert 2 galaxy in
     Pegasus; (1st) Planetary nebula
     in Norma; (1st) Seyfert 2 galaxy in
     Circinus   6·00   6·00   ☐ ☐
First Day Cover   7·00   ☐
Presentation Pack (P.O. Pack No. 339)   20·00   ☐
PHQ Cards (set of 5) (246)   4·75   18·00   ☐ ☐

The five PHQ cards depict the four designs and the complete miniature sheet.

No. **MS**2315 was also issued the £6·83 'Accross the Universe' booklet, No. DX29.

1614 Green Pillar Box,
1857

1615 Horizontal
Aperture Box, 1874

1616 Air Mail Box,
1934

1617 Double
Aperture Box, 1939

1618 Modern Style
Box, 1980

150th Anniversary of the First Pillar Box

2002 (8 Oct.) One centre phosphor band (2nd) or two phosphor bands (others). Perf 14 × 14½
2316 **1614** (2nd) multicoloured   1·00   80   ☐ ☐
2317 **1615** (1st) multicoloured   1·25   1·00   ☐ ☐
2318 **1616** (E)   multicoloured   1·75   1·75   ☐ ☐
2319 **1617** 47p   multicoloured   2·00   2·50   ☐ ☐
2320 **1618** 68p   multicoloured   2·50   3·00   ☐ ☐
Set of 5   7·50   8·00   ☐ ☐

First Day Cover   9·00   ☐
Presentation Pack (P.O. Pack No. 340)   8·00   ☐
PHQ Cards (set of 5) (247)   4·75   16·00   ☐ ☐
Set of 5 Gutter Pairs   16·00   ☐

1619 Blue Spruce Star   **1620** Holly

1621 Ivy   **1622** Mistletoe

1623 Pine Cone

Christmas. Christmas Plants

2002 (5 Nov.) Self-adhesive. One centre phosphor band (2nd) or two phosphor bands (others). Die-cut perf 14½ × 14
2321 **1619** (2nd) multicoloured   1·00   80   ☐ ☐
2322 **1620** (1st) multicoloured   1·25   80   ☐ ☐
2323 **1621** (E)   multicoloured   1·50   1·50   ☐ ☐
2324 **1622** 47p   multicoloured   2·00   1·75   ☐ ☐
2325 **1623** 68p   multicoloured   3·00   2·75   ☐ ☐
Set of 5   8·00   7·00   ☐ ☐
First Day Cover   8·00   ☐ ☐
Presentation Pack (P.O. Pack No. 341)   8·50   ☐
PHQ Cards (set of 5) (248)   4·75   16·00   ☐ ☐

Year Pack 2002

2002 (5 Nov.) Comprises Nos. 2243/57, 2260/4, 2265/88, **MS**2292, 2299/2313 and **MS**2315/25
CP2325a   Year Pack   £110   ☐

Post Office Yearbook

2002 (5 Nov.) Comprises Nos. 2243/57, 2260/4, 2265/88, 2291/2, 2299/2313 and **MS**2315/25 in hardback book with slip case
YB2325a   Yearbook   £100   ☐

The Wilding definitives collection 1 ~ 1952 - 1953

1623a

50th Anniversary of Wilding Definitives (1st series)

2002 (5 Dec.) Sheet, 124×70 mm, containing designs as T **154/5** and **157/60** (1952–54 issue), but with values in decimal currency as T **1348** or with service indicator as T **1566**, printed on pale cream. One centre phosphor band (2nd) or two phosphor bands (others). W **1565**. Perf 15×14 (with one elliptical hole in each vertical side)

MS2326 1p orange-red; 2p ultramarine; 5p red-brown; (2nd) carmine-red; (1st) green; 33p brown; 37p magenta; 47p bistre-brown; 50p green and label showing national emblems

ing national emblems	10·00	10·00
First Day Cover		11·00
Presentation Pack (P.O. Pack No. 59)	65·00	
PHQ Cards (set of 5) (D21)	3·00	12·00

The PHQ cards depict the (2nd), (1st), 33p, 37p and 47p stamps.
  For further Wilding designs with decimal face values, see Nos. 2031/3, 2258/9, **MS**2367 and 2378/80.

1624 Barn Owl landing

1625 Barn Owl with folded Wings and Legs down

1626 Barn Owl with extended Wings and Legs down

1627 Barn Owl in Flight with Wings lowered

1628 Barn Owl in Flight with Wings raised

1629 Kestrel with Wings folded

1630 Kestrel with Wings fully extended upwards

1631 Kestrel with Wings horizontal

1632 Kestrel with Wings partly extended downwards **1633** Kestrel with Wings fully extended downwards

Birds of Prey

2003 (14 Jan.) Phosphor background. Perf 14½

2327	**1624**	(1st)	multicoloured	1·25	1·00
		a.	Block of 10.		
			Nos. 2327/36	14·00	14·00
2328	**1625**	(1st)	multicoloured	1·25	1·00
2329	**1626**	(1st)	multicoloured	1·25	1·00
2330	**1627**	(1st)	multicoloured	1·25	1·00
2331	**1628**	(1st)	multicoloured	1·25	1·00
2332	**1629**	(1st)	multicoloured	1·25	1·00
2333	**1630**	(1st)	multicoloured	1·25	1·00
2334	**1631**	(1st)	multicoloured	1·25	1·00
2335	**1632**	(1st)	multicoloured	1·25	1·00
2336	**1633**	(1st)	multicoloured	1·25	1·00
Set of 10				14·00	14·00
First Day Cover					15·00
Presentation Pack (P.O. Pack No. 343)				15·00	
PHQ Cards (set of 10) (249)				9·25	28·00
Gutter Block of 20				30·00	

Nos. 2327/36 were printed together, se-tenant, in blocks of ten (5×2) throughout the sheet.

1634 'Gold star, See me, Playtime' **1635** 'I♥U, XXXX, S.W.A.L.K.'

1636 'Angel, Poppet, Little terror' **1637** 'Yes, No, Maybe'

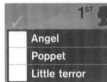

1638 'Oops!, Sorry, Will try harder' **1639** 'I did it!, You did it!, We did it!'

Greetings Stamps 'Occasions' (3rd series)

2003 (4 Feb.) Two phosphor bands. Perf 14½×14

2337	**1634**	(1st)	lemon and new blue	1·25	1·00
		a.	Block of 6.		
			Nos. 2337/42	8·00	6·50
2338	**1635**	(1st)	red and deep ultramarine	1·25	1·00
2339	**1636**	(1st)	purple and bright yellow-green	1·25	1·00
2340	**1637**	(1st)	bright yellow-green and red	1·25	1·00

2341	**1638**	(1st)	deep ultramarine and lemon	1·25	1·00	☐ ☐
2342	**1639**	(1st)	new blue and purple	1·25	1·00	☐ ☐
	Set of 6			8·00	6·50	☐ ☐
	First Day Cover				7·50	☐
	Presentation Pack (P.O. Pack No. M09)			10·00		☐
	PHQ Cards (*set of 6*) (PSM09)			5·25	18·00	☐ ☐
	Gutter Block of 12			17·00		☐

Nos. 2337/42 were printed together, *se-tenant*, in blocks of six (3×2) throughout the sheet.

Nos. 2337/42 were also available in *se-tenant* sheets of 20 containing four examples of Nos. 2338 and 2340 and three of each of the others. The stamps are accompanied by half stamp-size printed labels or a personal photograph.

1640 Completing the Genome Jigsaw

1641 Ape with Moustache and Scientist

1642 DNA Snakes and Ladders

1643 'Animal Scientists'

1644 Genome Crystal Ball

50th Anniversary of Discovery of DNA

2003 (25 Feb.) One centre phosphor band (2nd) or two phosphor bands (others). Perf 14½

2343	**1640**	(2nd)	multicoloured	1·00	80	☐ ☐
2344	**1641**	(1st)	multicoloured	1·25	1·00	☐ ☐
2345	**1642**	(E)	multicoloured	1·50	1·25	☐ ☐
2346	**1643**	47p	multicoloured	1·50	1·50	☐ ☐
2347	**1644**	68p	multicoloured	2·00	2·25	☐ ☐
	Set of 5			6·50	6·00	☐
	First Day Cover				8·00	☐
	Presentation Pack (P.O. Pack No. 344)			9·00		☐
	PHQ Cards (*set of 5*) (250)			4·75	18·00	☐ ☐
	Set of 5 Gutter Pairs			15·00		☐

Nos. 2343/7 were also issued in a £6·99 'Microcosmos' booklet

1645 Strawberry   **1646** Potato

1647 Apple   **1648** Red Pepper

1649 Pear   **1650** Orange

1651 Tomato   **1652** Lemon

1653 Brussels Sprout   **1654** Aubergine

Fruit and Vegetables

2003 (25 Mar.) Self-adhesive. Two phosphor bands. Perf 14½×14 die-cut (without teeth around protruding tops or bottoms of the designs)

2348	**1645**	(1st)	multicoloured	1·25	1·00	☐ ☐
		a.	Sheetlet. Nos. 2348/57 and pane of decorative labels	14·00		☐
2349	**1646**	(1st)	multicoloured	1·25	1·00	☐ ☐
2350	**1647**	(1st)	multicoloured	1·25	1·00	☐ ☐
2351	**1648**	(1st)	multicoloured	1·25	1·00	☐ ☐
2352	**1649**	(1st)	multicoloured	1·25	1·00	☐ ☐
2353	**1650**	(1st)	multicoloured	1·25	1·00	☐ ☐
2354	**1651**	(1st)	multicoloured	1·25	1·00	☐ ☐
2355	**1652**	(1st)	multicoloured	1·25	1·00	☐ ☐
2356	**1653**	(1st)	multicoloured	1·25	1·00	☐ ☐
2357	**1654**	(1st)	multicoloured	1·25	1·00	☐ ☐
	Set of 10			14·00	14·00	☐ ☐
	First Day Cover				15·00	☐
	Presentation Pack (P.O. Pack No. 345)			20·00		☐
	PHQ Cards (*set of 10*) (251)			9·25	25·00	☐ ☐

Nos. 2348/57 were printed together in sheets of ten with the surplus self-adhesive paper around each stamp retained. The stamp pane is accompanied by a similar-sized pane of self-adhesive labels showing ears, eyes, mouths, hats, etc which are intended for the adornment of fruit and vegetables depicted. This pane is separated from the stamps by a line of roulettes.

Nos. 2348/57 were re-issued on 7th March 2006 in sheets of 20 containing two of each of the ten designs, each stamp accompanied by a *se-tenant* speech bubble label. These sheets were printed in lithography instead of gravure, and have stickers showing eyes, hats, etc in the sheet margin.

1655

Overseas Booklet Stamps

2003 (27 Mar.)–**2010** Self-adhesive. Two phosphor bands. Perf 15 × 14 die-cut with one elliptical hole in each vertical side

2357a	(Worldwide postcard) grey-black, rosine and ultramarine *(1.4.04)*	1·75	1·75	
2357b	(Europe up to 20 grams) deep blue-green, new blue and rosine *(30.3.10)*	3·00	3·00	
2358	**1655** (Europe up to 40 grams) new blue and rosine	3·00	3·00	
2358a	(Worldwide up to 20grams) deep mauve, new blue and rosine *(30.3.10)*	3·00	3·00	
2359	(Worldwide up to 40 grams) rosine and new blue	4·25	4·25	
Set of 5		15·00	15·00	
First Day Cover (Nos. 2358, 2359)			8·00	
Presentation Pack (Nos. 2358, 2359) (P.O. Pack No. 60)		9·00		
PHQ Card (No. 2358) (D23)		45	3·50	

Nos. 2358 and 2359 were intended to pay postage on mail up to 40 grams to either Europe (52p) or to foreign destinations outside Europe (£1·12). No. 2357a was intended to pay postcard rate to foreign destinations (43p).

Operationally they were only available in separate booklets of four, initially sold at £2·08, £4·48 and £1·72, with the surplus self-adhesive paper around each stamp removed. Single examples of the stamps were available from philatelic outlets as sets of two or in presentation packs.

Nos. 2357b and 2358a were intended to pay postage on mail up to 20 grams to either Europe (initially 56p, or to foreign destinations outside Europe (90p).

They were only available in separate booklets of four (Nos. MI3 and MJ3) initially sold at £2·24 and £3·60, increasing to £2·40 and £3·88 from 6 April 2010, with the surplus self-adhesive paper around each stamp removed.

For first day covers and presentation packs for Nos. 2357a/b and 2358a and PHQ cards for Nos. 2357a, 2358 and 2359 see below Nos. Y1667/1803.

1656 Amy Johnson (pilot) and Biplane

1657 Members of 1953 Everest Team

1658 Freya Stark (traveller and writer) and Desert

1659 Ernest Shackleton (Antarctic explorer) and Wreck of *Endurance*

1660 Francis Chichester (yachtsman) and *Gipsy Moth IV*

1661 Robert Falcon Scott (Antarctic explorer) and Norwegian Expedition at the Pole

Extreme Endeavours (British Explorers)

2003 (29 Apr.) One centre phosphor band (2nd) or two phosphor bands (others)

		(a) Ordinary gum. Perf 15 × 14½			
2360	**1656**	2nd) multicoloured	1·00	1·00	
2361	**1657**	(1st) multicoloured	1·25	1·00	
2362	**1658**	(E) multicoloured	1·50	1·50	
2363	**1659**	42p multicoloured	1·75	1·75	
2364	**1660**	47p multicoloured	2·00	2·00	
2365	**1661**	68p multicoloured	2·50	2·50	
Set of 6			8·00	8·50	
First Day Cover				10·00	
Presentation Pack (P.O. Pack No. 346)			10·00		
PHQ Cards (*set of 6*) (252)			3·25	14·00	
Set of 6 Gutter Pairs			17·00		

		(b) Self-adhesive. Die-cut perf 14½			
2366	**1657**	(1st) multicoloured	5·00	5·00	

The phosphor bands on Nos. 2361/5 are at the centre and right of each stamp.

No. 2366 was only issued in £1·62 stamp booklets in which the surplus self-adhesive paper around each stamp was removed.

1661a

50th Anniversary of Wilding Definitives (2nd series)

2003 (20 May) Sheet, 124×70 mm, containing designs as T **155/8** and **160** (1952–54 issue), but with values in decimal currency as T **1348** or with service indicator as T **1566**, printed on pale cream. One centre phosphor band (20p) or two phosphor bands (others). W **1565**. P 15×14 (with one elliptical hole in each vertical side).

MS2367 4p deep lilac; 8p ultramarine;
    10p reddish purple; 20p bright
    green; 28p bronze-green; 34p
    brown-purple; (E) chestnut; 42p
    Prussian blue; 68p grey-blue and

label showing national emblems 11·00	12·00	☐ ☐
First Day Cover	13·00	☐
Presentation Pack (P.O. Pack No. 61) 15·00		☐

For further Wilding designs with decimal face values see Nos. 2031/3, 2258/9, **MS**2326 and 2378/80.

1662 Guardsmen in Coronation Procession

1663 East End Children reading Coronation Party Poster

1664 Queen Elizabeth II in Coronation Chair with Bishops of Durham and Bath & Wells

1665 Children in Plymouth working on Royal Montage

1666 Queen Elizabeth II in Coronation Robes (photograph by Cecil Beaton)

1667 Children's Race at East End Street Party

1668 Coronation Coach passing through Marble Arch

1669 Children in Fancy Dress

1670 Coronation Coach outside Buckingham Palace

1671 Children eating at London Street Party

50th Anniversary of Coronation

2003 (2 June) W **1565**. Two phosphor bands. Perf 14½×14

2368 **1662**	(1st)	multicoloured	1·25	1·00	☐ ☐
	a.	Block of 10.			
		Nos. 2368/77	14·00	12·00	☐ ☐
2369 **1663**	(1st)	black and gold	1·25	1·00	☐ ☐
2370 **1664**	(1st)	multicoloured	1·25	1·00	☐ ☐
2371 **1665**	(1st)	black and gold	1·25	1·00	☐ ☐
2372 **1666**	(1st)	multicoloured	1·25	1·00	☐ ☐
2373 **1667**	(1st)	black and gold	1·25	1·00	☐ ☐
2374 **1668**	(1st)	multicoloured	1·25	1·00	☐ ☐
2375 **1669**	(1st)	black and gold	1·25	1·00	☐ ☐
2376 **1670**	(1st)	multicoloured	1·25	1·00	☐ ☐
2377 **1671**	(1st)	black and gold	1·25	1·00	☐ ☐
Set of 10			14·00	12·00	☐ ☐
First Day Cover				13·00	☐
Presentation Pack (P.O. Pack No. 347)			20·00		☐
PHQ Cards (set of 10) (253)			9·25	20·00	☐ ☐
Gutter Block of 20			30·00		☐

Nos. 2368/77 were printed together, se-tenant, as blocks of ten (5×2) in sheets of 60 (2 panes of 30).

No. 2372 does not show the Queen's head in gold as do the other nine designs.

50th Anniversary of Coronation. Booklet Stamps

2003 (2 June) Designs as T **160** (Wilding definitive of 1952) and 163 (Coronation commemorative of 1953), but with values in decimal currency as T **1348**. W **1565**. Two phosphor bands. P 15×14 (with one elliptical hole in each vertical side for Nos. 2378/9)

2378	**160**	47p bistre-brown	5·00	4·00	☐ ☐
2379		68p grey-blue	5·00	4·00	☐ ☐
2380	**163**	£1 deep yellow-green	60·00	55·00	☐ ☐
Set of 3			65·00	60·00	☐ ☐

Nos. 2378/80 were only available in the £7·46 'A Perfect Coronation' stamp booklet, No. DX31. Stamps as Nos. 2378/9, but on pale cream, were also included in the Wilding miniature sheets, Nos. **MS**2326 and **MS**2367. A £1 design as No. 2380, but on phosphorised paper, was previously included in the "Stamp Show 2000" miniature sheet, No. **MS**2147.

For further Wilding designs with decimal face values see Nos. 2031/3, 2258/9, **MS**2326 and **MS**2367.

1672 Prince William in September 2001 (Brendan Beirne)

1673 Prince William in September 2000 (Tim Graham)

1674 Prince William in September 2001 (Camera Press)

1675 Prince William in September 2001 (Tim Graham)

21st Birthday of Prince William of Wales

2003 (17 June) Phosphor backgrounds. Perf 14½

2381	**1672**	28p	multicoloured	1·00	80	☐ ☐
2382	**1673**	(E)	dull mauve, grey-black and light green	2·25	1·50	☐ ☐
2383	**1674**	47p	multicoloured	2·75	2·00	☐ ☐
2384	**1675**	68p	sage-green, black and bright green	4·00	2·50	☐ ☐
Set of 4				9·00	6·00	☐ ☐
First Day Cover					8·00	☐
Presentation Pack (P.O. Pack No. 348)				20·00		☐
PHQ Cards (*set of* 4) (254)				7·50	20·00	☐ ☐
Set of 4 Gutter Pairs				19·00		☐

1676 Loch Assynt, Sutherland

1677 Ben More, Isle of Mull

1678 Rothiemurchus, Cairngorms

1679 Dalveen Pass, Lowther Hills

1680 Glenfinnan Viaduct, Lochaber

1681 Papa Little, Shetland Islands

A British Journey (1st series): Scotland

2003 (15 July) One centre phosphor band (2nd) or two phosphor bands (others). Perf 14½

(a) Ordinary gum

2385	**1676**	(2nd)	multicoloured	1·00	90	☐ ☐
2386	**1677**	(1st)	multicoloured	1·25	1·00	☐ ☐
2387	**1678**	(E)	multicoloured	1·50	1·25	☐ ☐
2388	**1679**	42p	multicoloured	1·25	1·50	☐ ☐
2389	**1680**	47p	multicoloured	1·50	2·00	☐ ☐
2390	**1681**	68p	multicoloured	2·00	2·50	☐ ☐

Set of 6		7·00	8·50	☐ ☐
First Day Cover			10·00	☐
Presentation Pack (P.O. Pack No. 349)		9·50		☐
PHQ Cards (*set of* 6) (255)		3·00	14·00	☐ ☐
Set of 6 Gutter Pairs		15·00		☐

(b) Self-adhesive. Die-cut perf 14½

2391	**1677**	(1st)	multicoloured	6·00	6·00	☐ ☐

No. 2391 was only issued in £1·68 stamp booklets in which the surplus self-adhesive paper around each stamp was removed.

1682 'The Station' (Andrew Davidson)

1683 'Black Swan' (Stanley Chew)

1684 'The Cross Keys' (George Mackenney)

1685 'The Mayflower' (Ralph Ellis)

1686 'The Barley Sheaf' (Joy Cooper)

Europa. British Pub Signs

2003 (12 Aug.) Two phosphor bands. Perf 14 × 14½

2392	**1682**	(1st)	multicoloured	1·25	70	☐ ☐
2393	**1683**	(E)	multicoloured	2·00	2·00	☐ ☐
2394	**1684**	42p	multicoloured	1·50	1·50	☐ ☐
2395	**1685**	47p	multicoloured	1·75	2·00	☐ ☐
2396	**1686**	68p	multicoloured	2·00	2·25	☐ ☐
Set of 5				7·50	8·00	☐ ☐
First Day Cover					9·00	☐
Presentation Pack (P.O. Pack No. 350)				11·00		☐
PHQ Cards (*set of* 5) (256)				3·00	12·00	☐ ☐
Set of 5 Gutter Pairs				16·00		☐

The 1st and E values incorporate the "EUROPA" emblem.

No. 2392 was also issued in the £7·44 'Letters by Night' booklet, No. DX32.

1687 Meccano Constructor Biplane, c. 1931

1688 Wells-Brimtoy Clockwork Double-decker Omnibus, c. 1938

1689 Hornby M1 Clockwork Locomotive and Tender, c. 1948

1690 Dinky Toys Ford Zephyr, c. 1956

1691 Mettoy Friction Drive Space Ship Eagle, c. 1960

Classic Transport Toys

2003 (18 Sept.) Two phosphor bands

(a) Ordinary gum. Perf 14½ × 14

2397	**1687**	(1st)	multicoloured	1·25	70	☐ ☐
2398	**1688**	(E)	multicoloured	1·50	1·25	☐ ☐
2399	**1689**	42p	multicoloured	1·50	1·50	☐ ☐
2400	**1690**	47p	multicoloured	1·75	1·75	☐ ☐
2401	**1691**	68p	multicoloured	2·50	2·50	☐ ☐
Set of 5				7·50	7·00	☐ ☐
First Day Cover					8·50	☐
Presentation Pack (P.O. Pack No. 351)			12·00			☐
PHQ Cards (set of 6) (257)			3·00	14·00		☐ ☐
Set of 5 Gutter Pairs				16·00		☐
MS2402 115 × 105 mm. Nos. 2397/2401			8·00	8·50		☐ ☐
First Day Cover					10·00	☐

(b) Self-adhesive. Die-cut perf 14½ × 14

2403	**1687**	(1st)	multicoloured	6·00	6·00	☐ ☐

The complete miniature sheet is shown on one of the PHQ cards with the others depicting individual stamps.

No. 2403 was only issued in £1·68 stamp booklets in which the surplus self-adhesive paper around each stamp was removed.

1692 Coffin of Denytenamun, Egyptian, c. 900BC

1693 Alexander the Great, Greek, c. 200BC

1694 Sutton Hoo Helmet, Anglo-Saxon, c. AD600

1695 Sculpture of Parvati, South Indian, c. AD1550

1696 Mask of Xiutechuhtli, Mixtec-Aztec, c. AD1500

1697 Hoa Hakananai'a, Easter Island, c. AD1000

250th Anniversary of the British Museum

2003 (7 Oct.) One side phosphor band (2nd), two phosphor bands ((1st), (E), 47p) or phosphor background at left and band at right (42p, 68p). Perf 14 × 14½

2404	**1692**	(2nd)	multicoloured	1·00	70	☐ ☐
2405	**1693**	(1st)	multicoloured	1·25	90	☐ ☐
2406	**1694**	(E)	multicoloured	1·50	1·25	☐ ☐
2407	**1695**	42p	multicoloured	1·50	1·50	☐ ☐
2408	**1696**	47p	multicoloured	2·00	2·00	☐ ☐
2409	**1697**	68p	multicoloured	2·75	2·75	☐ ☐
Set of 6				8·00	8·00	☐ ☐
First Day Cover					10·00	☐
Presentation Pack (P.O. Pack No. 352)			11·00			☐
PHQ Cards (set of 6) (258)			3·00	14·00		☐ ☐
Set of 6 Gutter Pairs				17·00		☐

1698 Ice Spiral

1699 Icicle Star

1700 Wall of Ice Blocks

1701 Ice Ball

1702 Ice Hole

1703 Snow Pyramids

Christmas. Ice Sculptures by Andy Goldsworthy

2003 (4 Nov.) Self-adhesive. One side phosphor band (2nd), 'all-over' phosphor (1st) or two bands (others). Die-cut perf 14½ × 14

2410	**1698**	(2nd)	multicoloured	1·00	70	☐ ☐
2411	**1699**	(1st)	multicoloured	1·25	90	☐ ☐
2412	**1700**	(E)	multicoloured	1·50	1·50	☐ ☐
2413	**1701**	53p	multicoloured	2·00	2·00	☐ ☐
2414	**1702**	68p	multicoloured	2·50	2·50	☐ ☐
2415	**1703**	£1·12	multicoloured	3·00	3·00	☐ ☐
Set of 6				10·00	9·50	☐ ☐
First Day Cover					11·00	☐
Presentation Pack (P.O. Pack No. 353)			12·00			☐
PHQ Cards (set of 6) (259)			4·00	14·00		☐ ☐

The 2nd and 1st class were also issued in separate sheets of 20, each stamp printed in lithography instead of photogravure and accompanied by a half stamp-size *se-tenant* label showing either animals, ice sculptures or a personal photograph.

Year Pack 2003

2003 (4 Nov.) Comprises Nos. 2327/57, 2360/5, 2368/77, 2381/90, 2392/2401 and 2404/15

CP2415a	Year Pack	£120	☐

Post Office Yearbook

2003 (4 Nov.) Comprises Nos. 2327/57, 2360/5, 2368/77, 2381/90, 2392/2401 and 2404/15

YB2415a	Yearbook	£100	☐

1704 Rugby Scenes

England's Victory in Rugby World Cup Championship, Australia. Miniature Sheet

2003 (19 Dec.) Sheet 115×85 mm. Multicoloured. Two phosphor bands. Perf 14

MS2416 **1704** (1st) England flags and fans; (1st) England team standing in circle before match; 68p World Cup trophy; 68p Victorious England players after match	14·00	14·00	☐ ☐	
First Day Cover		15·00	☐	
Presentation Pack (P.O. Pack No. M9B)	18·00		☐	

1705 Dolgoch, Rheilffordd Talyllyn Railway, Gwynedd

1706 CR Class 439, Bo'ness and Kinneil Railway, West Lothian

1707 GCR Class 8K, Leicestershire

1708 GWR Manor Class *Bradley Manor*, Severn Valley Railway, Worcestershire

1709 SR West Country class *Blackmoor Vale*, Bluebell Railway, East Sussex

1710 BR Standard class, Keighley & Worth Valley Railway, Yorkshire

Classic Locomotives

2004 (13 Jan.) One side phosphor band (20p) or two phosphor bands (others). Perf 14½

2417	**1705**	20p	multicoloured	65	65	☐ ☐
2418	**1706**	28p	multicoloured	90	90	☐ ☐
2419	**1707**	(E)	multicoloured	1·20	1·20	☐ ☐
2420	**1708**	42p	multicoloured	1·50	1·50	☐ ☐
2421	**1709**	47p	multicoloured	2·00	2·00	☐ ☐
2422	**1710**	68p	multicoloured	3·00	3·50	☐ ☐
Set of 6				8·00	8·50	☐
First Day Cover					10·00	☐
Presentation Pack (P.O. Pack No. 355)				25·00		☐
PHQ Cards (*set of 7*) (260)				8·50	15·00	☐ ☐
Set of 6 Gutter Pairs				17·00		☐
MS2423 190×67 mm. Nos. 2417/22				25·00	25·00	☐ ☐
First Day Cover					25·00	☐

The seven PHQ cards depict the six stamps and the miniature sheet.

Nos. 2418/20 were also issued in the £7·44 'Letters by Night' booklet, No. DX32.

1711 Postman   1712 Face

1713 Duck   1714 Baby

1715 Aircraft

Greetings Stamps 'Occasions' (4th series)

2004 (3 Feb.) Two phosphor bands. Perf 14½ × 14

2424	**1711**	(1st)	bright mauve and black	1·25	1·00	☐ ☐
		a.	Horiz strip of 5. Nos. 2424/8	7·00	6·00	☐ ☐
2425	**1712**	(1st)	magenta and black	1·25	1·00	☐ ☐
2426	**1713**	(1st)	lemon and black	1·25	1·00	☐ ☐
2427	**1714**	(1st)	pale turquoise-green and black	1·25	1·00	☐ ☐
2428	**1715**	(1st)	bright new blue and black	1·25	1·00	☐ ☐
Set of 5				7·00	6·00	☐ ☐
First Day Cover					7·00	☐
Presentation Pack (P.O. Pack No. M10)				8·00		☐
PHQ Cards (*set of 5*) (PSM10)				4·75	12·00	☐ ☐
Gutter Block of 10				15·00		☐

Nos. 2424/8 were printed together, *se-tenant*, as horizontal strips of five in sheets of 25 (5×5).

Nos. 2424/8 were also issued in sheets of 20 containing the five designs se-tenant with half stamp-size printed message labels. Similar sheets containing either Nos. 2424 and 2428 or Nos. 2425/7 came with personal photographs on the labels.

1716 Map showing
Middle Earth

1717 Forest of Lothlórien
in Spring

1718 Dust-jacket for
The Fellowship of the Ring

1719 Rivendell

1720 The Hall at Bag End

1721 Orthanc

1722 Doors of Durin

1723 Barad-dûr

1724 Minas Tirith

1725 Fangorn Forest

50th Anniversary of Publication of *The Fellowship of the Ring* and *The Two Towers* by J. R. R. Tolkien

2004 (26 Feb.) Two phosphor bands. Perf 14½

2429	**1716**	(1st)	multicoloured	1·25	1·00	☐ ☐
		a.	Block of 10.			
			Nos. 2429/38	14·00	12·00	☐ ☐
2430	**1717**	(1st)	multicoloured	1·25	1·00	☐ ☐
2431	**1718**	(1st)	multicoloured	1·25	1·00	☐ ☐
2432	**1719**	(1st)	multicoloured	1·25	1·00	☐ ☐
2433	**1720**	(1st)	multicoloured	1·25	1·00	☐ ☐
2434	**1721**	(1st)	multicoloured	1·25	1·00	☐ ☐
2435	**1722**	(1st)	multicoloured	1·25	1·00	☐ ☐
2436	**1723**	(1st)	multicoloured	1·25	1·00	☐ ☐
2437	**1724**	(1st)	multicoloured	1·25	1·00	☐ ☐
2438	**1725**	(1st)	multicoloured	1·25	1·00	☐ ☐
Set of 10				14·00	12·00	☐
First Day Cover					13·00	☐

Presentation Pack (P.O. Pack No. 356)	20·00			☐
PHQ Cards (*set of* 10) (261)	9·75	18·00	☐ ☐
Gutter Block of 20	30·00		☐

Nos. 2429/38 were printed together, *se-tenant*, in blocks of ten (5×2) throughout the sheet.

1726 Ely Island, Lower
Lough Erne

1727 Giant's Causeway,
Antrim Coast

1728 Slemish, Antrim Mountains

1729 Banns Road,
Mourne Mountains

1730 Glenelly Valley,
Sperrins

1731 Islandmore,
Strangford Lough

A British Journey (2nd series): Northern Ireland

2004 (16 Mar.) One side phosphor band (2nd) or two phosphor bands (others). Perf 14½

(a) Ordinary gum

2439	**1726**	(2nd)	multicoloured	1·00	75	☐ ☐
2440	**1727**	(1st)	multicoloured	1·25	90	☐ ☐
2441	**1728**	(E)	multicoloured	1·50	1·20	☐ ☐
2442	**1729**	42p	multicoloured	1·30	1·30	☐ ☐
2443	**1730**	47p	multicoloured	1·50	1·50	☐ ☐
2444	**1731**	68p	multicoloured	2·20	2·20	☐ ☐
Set of 6				8·00	7·00	☐ ☐
First Day Cover					9·00	☐
Presentation Pack (P.O. Pack No. 357)			12·00			☐
PHQ Cards (*set of* 6) (262)			5·75	14·00		☐ ☐
Set of 6 Gutter Pairs			17·00			☐

(b) Self-adhesive. Die-cut perf 14½

2445	**1727**	(1st)	multicoloured	6·00	6·00	☐ ☐

No. 2445 was only issued in £1·68 stamp booklets in which the surplus self-adhesive paper around each stamp was removed.

1732 'Lace 1 (trial
proof) 1968' (Sir Terry Frost)

1733 'Coccinelle'
(Sonia Delaunay)

Centenary of the Entente Cordiale. Contemporary Paintings

2004 (6 Apr.) Two phosphor bands. Perf 14 × 14½

2446 **1732**	28p	grey, black and rosine	1·00	85
2447 **1733**	57p	multicoloured	2·25	2·00
Set of 2			3·00	2·75
First Day Cover				3·75
Presentation Pack (P.O. Pack No. 358)			25·00	
Presentation Pack (UK and French				
stamps)			25·00	
PHQ Cards (*set of 2*) (263)			3·50	6·00
Set of 2 Gutter Pairs			7·00	
Set of 2 Traffic Light Gutter Blocks of 4			15·00	

Stamps in similar designs were issued by France and these are included in the joint Presentation Pack.

1734 'RMS Queen Mary 2, 2004' (Edward D. Walker)

1735 'SS Canberra 1961' (David Cobb)

1736 'RMS Queen Mary 1936' (Charles Pears)

1737 'RMS Mauretania, 1907' (Thomas Henry)

1738 'SS City of New York, 1888' (Raphael Monleaon y Torres)

1739 'PS Great Western, 1838' (Joseph Walter)

Ocean Liners

2004 (13 Apr.) Two phosphor bands.

(a) Gravure. Ordinary gum. Perf 14½ × 14

2448 **1734**	(1st)	multicoloured	1·25	90
2449 **1735**	(E)	multicoloured	1·50	1·30
2450 **1736**	42p	multicoloured	1·30	1·30
2451 **1737**	47p	multicoloured	1·50	1·50
2452 **1738**	57p	multicoloured	1·80	1·80
2453 **1739**	68p	multicoloured	2·20	2·20
Set of 6			9·00	9·00
First Day Cover				11·00
Presentation Pack (P.O. Pack No. 359)			11·00	
PHQ Cards (*set of 7*) (264)			6·75	20·00
Set of 6 Gutter Pairs			20·00	
MS2454 114 × 104 mm. Nos. 2448/53			20·00	18·00
First Day Cover				19·00

(b) Self-adhesive. Die-cut perf 14½ × 14

2455 **1734**	(1st)	multicoloured	6·00	6·00

Nos. 2448/55 commemorate the introduction to service of the *Queen Mary 2*.

No. 2455 was only issued in £1·68 stamp booklets in which the surplus self-adhesive paper around each stamp was removed.

The complete miniature sheet is shown on one of the PHQ cards with the others depicting individual stamps. See also No. 2614

For Type **1739** printed in lithography, see No. 2514.

1740 *Dianthus Allwoodii* Group

1741 Dahlia 'Garden Princess'

1742 Clematis 'Arabella'

1743 Miltonia 'French Lake'

1744 Lilium 'Lemon Pixie'

1745 Delphinium 'Clifford Sky'

Bicentenary of the Royal Horticultural Society (1st issue)

2004 (25 May) One side phosphor band (2nd) or 'all-over' phosphor (others). Perf 14½

2456 **1740**	(2nd)	multicoloured	1·00	80
2457 **1741**	(1st)	multicoloured	1·25	1·00
2458 **1742**	(E)	multicoloured	1·50	1·30
2459 **1743**	42p	multicoloured	2·00	2·00
2460 **1744**	47p	multicoloured	2·50	2·50
2461 **1745**	68p	multicoloured	3·50	3·50
Set of 6			11·00	10·00
First Day Cover				12·00
Presentation Pack (P.O. Pack No. 360)			12·00	
PHQ Cards (*set of 7*) (265)			6·75	20·00
Set of 6 Gutter Pairs			23·00	
MS2462 115 × 105 mm. Nos. 2456/61			14·00	14·00
First Day Cover				16·00

The complete miniature sheet is shown on one of the PHQ cards with the others depicting individual stamps.

The 1st class stamp was also issued in sheets of 20, printed in lithography instead of gravure, each stamp accompanied by a *se-tenant* stamp-size label. Nos. 2456/61 were also, issued in the £7·23 'The Glory of the Garden' booklet No. DX33.

Bicentenary of the Royal Horticultural Society (2nd issue). Booklet stamps

2004 (25 May) Designs as Nos. 1955, 1958 and 1962 (1997 Greeting Stamps 19th-century Flower Paintings). Two phosphor bands. Perf 15 × 14 (with one elliptical hole in each vertical side)

2463 **1280**	(1st)	multicoloured	8·00	8·00
2464 **1283**	(1st)	multicoloured	4·00	4·00
2465 **1287**	(1st)	multicoloured	8·00	8·00
Set of 3			18·00	18·00

On Nos. 2463/5 the phosphor bands appear at the left and the centre of each stamp.

Nos. 2463/5 were only issued in the in £7·23 'The Glory of the Garden' booklet, No. DX33.

1746 Barmouth Bridge **1747** Hyddgen, Plynlimon

1748 Brecon Beacons **1749** Pen-pych, Rhondda Valley

1750 Rhewl, Dee Valley **1751** Marloes Sands

A British Journey (3rd series): Wales

2004 (15 June) One centre phosphor band (2nd), 'all-over' phosphor (1st) or two phosphor bands (others)

(a) Ordinary gum. Perf 14½

2466	**1746**	(2nd) multicoloured	1·00	80
2467	**1747**	(1st) multicoloured	1·25	1·00
2468	**1748**	40p multicoloured	1·75	1·50
2469	**1749**	43p multicoloured	2·00	2·00
2470	**1750**	47p multicoloured	2·50	3·00
2471	**1751**	68p multicoloured	3·50	4·00

Set of 6 ... 10·00 / 11·00
First Day Cover ... 12·00
Presentation Pack (P.O. Pack No. 361) 11·00
PHQ Cards (set of 6) (266) 5·75 12·00
Set of 6 Gutter Pairs 22·00

(b) Self-adhesive. Die-cut perf 14½

2472 **1747** (1st) multicoloured 8·00 8·00

The 1st and 40p values include the 'EUROPA' emblem.

No. 2472 was only issued in £1·68 stamp booklets in which the surplus self-adhesive paper around each stamp was removed.

1752 Sir Rowland Hill Award **1753** William Shipley (Founder of Royal Society of Arts)

1754 'RSA' as Typewriter Keys and Shorthand **1755** Chimney Sweep

1756 'Gill Typeface' **1757** 'Zero Waste'

250th Anniversary of the Royal Society of Arts

2004 (10 Aug.) Two phosphor bands. Perf 14

2473	**1752**	(1st) multicoloured	1·25	95
2474	**1753**	40p multicoloured	1·30	1·30
2475	**1754**	43p multicoloured	1·40	1·40
2476	**1755**	47p multicoloured	1·50	1·50
2477	**1756**	57p silver, vermilion and black	2·20	2·20
2478	**1757**	68p silver, vermilion and black	3·00	3·00

Set of 6 ... 10·00 / 10·00
First Day Cover ... 12·00
Presentation Pack (P.O. Pack No. 362) 11·00
PHQ Cards (set of 6) (267) 5·75 14·00
Set of 6 Gutter Pairs 22·00

1758 Pine Marten **1759** Roe Deer

1760 Badger **1761** Yellow-necked Mouse

1762 Wild Cat **1763** Red Squirrel

1764 Stoat **1765** Natterer's Bat

1766 Mole

1767 Fox

Woodland Animals

2004 (16 Sept.) Two phosphor bands. Perf 14½

2479	**1758**	(1st)	multicoloured	1·25	1·00	☐	☐
		a.	Block of 10.				
			Nos. 2479/88	14·00	12·00	☐	☐
2480	**1759**	(1st)	multicoloured	1·25	1·00	☐	☐
2481	**1760**	(1st)	multicoloured	1·25	1·00	☐	☐
2482	**1761**	(1st)	multicoloured	1·25	1·00	☐	☐
2483	**1762**	(1st)	multicoloured	1·25	1·00	☐	☐
2484	**1763**	(1st)	multicoloured	1·25	1·00	☐	☐
2485	**1764**	(1st)	multicoloured	1·25	1·00	☐	☐
2486	**1765**	(1st)	multicoloured	1·25	1·00	☐	☐
2487	**1766**	(1st)	multicoloured	1·25	1·00	☐	☐
2488	**1767**	(1st)	multicoloured	1·25	1·00	☐	☐
Set of 10				14·00	12·00	☐	
First Day Cover					13·00	☐	
Presentation Pack (P.O. Pack No. 363)				16·00		☐	
PHQ Cards (*set of 10*) (268)				9·75	18·00	☐	☐
Gutter Block of 20				30·00		☐	

Nos. 2479/88 were printed together, *se-tenant*, in blocks of ten (5 × 2) throughout the sheet.

For the miniature sheet celebrating the opening of the new Scottish Parliament Building, Ediburgh, issued 5 October 2004, see the Regionals section.

1768 Pte. McNamara,
5th Dragoon Guards,
Heavy Brigade Charge,
Battle of Balaklava

1769 Piper Muir,
42nd Regt of Foot,
Amphibious Assault
on Kerch

1770 Sgt. Maj. Edwards,
Scots Fusilier Guards,
Gallant Action,
Battle of Inkerman

1771 Sgt. Powell,
1st Regt of Foot
Guards, Battles of
Alma and Inkerman

1772 Sgt. Maj. Poole,
Royal Sappers and
Miners, Defensive Line,
Battle of Inkerman

1773 Sgt. Glasgow,
Royal Artillery, Gun
Battery besieged
Sevastopol

150th Anniversary of the Crimean War

2004 (12 Oct.) One centre phosphor band (2nd) or two phosphor bands (others). Perf 14

2489	**1768**	(2nd)	multicoloured	1·00	80	☐	☐
2490	**1769**	(1st)	multicoloured	1·25	1·00	☐	☐
2491	**1770**	40p	multicoloured	2·00	2·00	☐	☐
2492	**1771**	57p	multicoloured	2·50	2·50	☐	☐
2493	**1772**	68p	multicoloured	2·75	3·00	☐	☐
2494	**1773**	£1·12	multicoloured	4·50	5·00	☐	☐
Set of 6				12·00	13·00	☐	
First Day Cover					14·00	☐	
Presentation Pack (P.O. Pack No. 364)				14·00		☐	
PHQ Cards (*set of 6*) (269)				5·75	16·00	☐	☐
Set of 6 Gutter Pairs				25·00		☐	
Set of 6 Traffic Light Pairs				30·00		☐	

Nos. 2489/94 show 'Crimean Heroes' photographs taken in 1856.

1774 Father Christmas
on Snowy Roof

1775 Celebrating the
Sunrise

1776 On Roof in Gale

1777 With Umbrella
in Rain

1778 In Fog on Edge
of Roof with Torch

1779 Sheltering from
Hailstorm behind Chimney

Christmas. Father Christmas

2004 (2 Nov.) One centre phosphor band (2nd) or two phosphor bands (others). Perf 14½ × 14

			(a) Self-adhesive				
2495	**1774**	(2nd)	multicoloured	1·00	80	☐	☐
2496	**1775**	(1st)	multicoloured	1·25	1·00	☐	☐
2497	**1776**	40p	multicoloured	1·30	1·30	☐	☐
2498	**1777**	57p	multicoloured	1·80	1·80	☐	☐
2499	**1778**	68p	multicoloured	2·20	2·20	☐	☐

2500 **1779** £1·12 multicoloured		3·75	3·75	☐	☐
Set of 6		11·00	12·00	☐	☐
First Day Cover			13·50		☐
Presentation Pack (P.O. Pack No. 365)		12·50			☐
PHQ Cards (*set of 7*) (270)		6·75	18·00	☐	☐

(b) Ordinary gum

MS2501 115 × 105 mm.

As Nos. 2495/2500	12·00	13·00	☐	☐
First Day Cover		14·00		☐

The seven PHQ cards depict the six individual stamps and the miniature sheet.

The 2nd and 1st class stamps were also issued in sheets of 20 printed in lithography instead of gravure containing ten 1st class and ten 2nd class stamps, each stamp accompanied by a *se-tenant* stamp-size label showing Father Christmas.

Separate sheets of either 20 1st or 20 2nd class were available with personal photographs.

Year Pack 2004

2004 (2 Nov.) Comprises Nos. 2417/22, 2424/44, 2446/53, 2456/61, 2466/71 and 2473/2500

CP2500a Year Pack	£120		☐

Post Office Yearbook

2004 (2 Nov.) Comprises Nos. 2417/22, 2424/44, 2446/53, 2456/61, 2466/71 and 2473/2500

YB2500a Yearbook	£110		☐

1780 British Saddleback Pigs

1781 Khaki Campbell Ducks

1782 Clydesdale Mare and Foal

1783 Dairy Shorthorn Cattle

1784 Border Collie Dog

1785 Light Sussex Chicks

1786 Suffolk Sheep

1787 Bagot Goat

1788 Norfolk Black Turkeys

1789 Embden Geese

Farm Animals

2005 (11 Jan.) Two phosphor bands. Perf 14½

2502 **1780**	(1st)	multicoloured		1·25	1·00	☐	☐
	a.	Block of 10.					
		Nos. 2502/11		14·00	12·00	☐	☐
2503 **1781**	(1st)	multicoloured		1·25	1·00	☐	☐
2504 **1782**	(1st)	multicoloured		1·25	1·00	☐	☐
2505 **1783**	(1st)	multicoloured		1·25	1·00	☐	☐
2506 **1784**	(1st)	multicoloured		1·25	1·00	☐	☐
2507 **1785**	(1st)	multicoloured		1·25	1·00	☐	☐
2508 **1786**	(1st)	multicoloured		1·25	1·00	☐	☐
2509 **1787**	(1st)	multicoloured		1·25	1·00	☐	☐
2510 **1788**	(1st)	multicoloured		1·25	1·00	☐	☐
2511 **1789**	(1st)	multicoloured		1·25	1·00	☐	☐
Set of 10				14·00	12·00	☐	☐
First Day Cover					13·00		☐
Presentation Pack (P.O. Pack No. 367)				15·00			☐
PHQ Cards (*set of 10*) (271)				9·75	18·00	☐	☐
Gutter Block of 20					30·00		☐
Traffic Light Gutter Block of 20					32·00		☐

Nos. 2502/11 were printed together, *se-tenant*, in blocks of ten (5 × 2) throughout the sheet.

Nos. 2502/11 were also issued in sheets of 20, printed in lithography instead of gravure, containing two of each of the ten designs, arranged in vertical strips of five alternated with printed labels.

1790 Old Harry Rocks, Studland Bay

1791 Wheal Coates, St. Agnes

1792 Start Point, Start Bay

1793 Horton Down, Wiltshire

1794 Chiselcombe, Exmoor

1795 St. James's Stone, Lundy

Stanley Gibbons - the home of stamp collecting since 1856 and today's market leader for all your philatelic needs.

For the best quality in stamps, catalogues, albums and all other accessories log on to our website today and explore our unrivalled range of products all available at the touch of a button.

www.stanleygibbons.com

A British Journey (4th series): South West England

2005 (8 Feb.) One centre phosphor band (2nd) or two phosphor bands (others). Perf 14½

2512	**1790**	(2nd) multicoloured	1·00	80	☐	☐
2513	**1791**	(1st) multicoloured	1·25	90	☐	☐
2514	**1792**	40p multicoloured	1·50	1·75	☐	☐
2515	**1793**	43p multicoloured	1·75	2·00	☐	☐
2516	**1794**	57p multicoloured	2·50	2·50	☐	☐
2517	**1795**	68p multicoloured	3·50	3·00	☐	☐
Set of 6			10·00	10·00	☐	☐
First Day Cover				12·00		☐
Presentation Pack (P.O. Pack No. 368)			11·00		☐	
PHQ Cards (set of 6) (272)			6·00	14·00	☐	☐
Set of 6 Gutter Pairs			21·00			☐

1796 'Mr Rochester'

1797 'Come to Me'

1798 'In the Comfort of her Bonnet'

1799 'La Ligne des Rats'

1800 'Refectory'

1801 'Inspection'

150th Death Anniversary of Charlotte Brontë.
Illustrations of Scenes from 'Jane Eyre' by Paula Rego

2005 (24 Feb.) One centre phosphor band (2nd) or two phosphor bands (others). Perf 14 × 14½

2518	**1796**	(2nd) multicoloured	1·00	80	☐	☐
2519	**1797**	(1st) multicoloured	1·25	1·00	☐	☐
2520	**1798**	40p multicoloured	1·50	1·50	☐	☐
2521	**1799**	57p silver, brownish grey and black	3·00	2·50	☐	☐
2522	**1800**	68p multicoloured	3·75	3·00	☐	☐
2523	**1801**	£1·12 silver, brownish grey and black	4·50	3·50	☐	☐
Set of 6			12·00	11·00	☐	☐
First Day Cover				12·00		☐
Presentation Pack (P.O. Pack No. 369)			13·00		☐	
PHQ Cards (set of 6) (273)			6·00	18·00	☐	☐
Set of 6 Gutter Pairs			25·00			☐
Set of 6 Traffic Light gutter blocks of four			48·00			☐
MS2524 114 × 105 mm. Nos. 2518/23			12·00	11·00	☐	☐
First Day Cover				12·00		☐

The complete miniature sheet is shown on one of the PHQ cards with the others depicting individual stamps.

Nos. 2518/23 were also issued in the £7·43 'The Brontë Sisters' booklet No. DX34.

1802 Spinning Coin

1803 Rabbit out of Hat Trick

1804 Knotted Scarf Trick

1805 Card Trick

1806 Pyramid under Fez Trick

Centenary of the Magic Circle

2005 (15 Mar.) Two phosphor bands. Perf 14½ × 14

2525	**1802**	(1st) multicoloured	1·25	80	☐	☐
2526	**1803**	40p multicoloured	1·00	90	☐	☐
2527	**1804**	47p multicoloured	2·50	2·75	☐	☐
2528	**1805**	68p multicoloured	3·00	3·00	☐	☐
2529	**1806**	£1·12 multicoloured	3·50	3·50	☐	☐
Set of 5			10·00	11·00	☐	☐
First Day Cover				12·00		☐
Presentation Pack (P.O. Pack No. 370)			15·00		☐	
PHQ Cards (set of 5) (274)			5·00	12·00	☐	☐
Set of 5 Gutter Pairs			21·00			☐

Nos. 2525/9 are each printed with instructions for the illusion or trick on the stamp.

No. 2525 can be rubbed with a coin to reveal the 'head' or 'tail' of a coin. The two versions, which appear identical before rubbing, are printed in alternate rows of the sheet, indicated by the letters H and T in the side margins of the sheet.

No. 2525 was also issued in sheets of 20 with se-tenant labels showing magic tricks, printed in lithography instead of gravure.

Nos. 2526 and 2528 each show optical illusions.

The spotted scarf on No. 2527 and the fezzes on No. 2529 are printed in thermochromic inks which fade temporarily when exposed to heat, making the pyramid under the centre fez visible.

1806a

50th Anniversary of First Castles Definitives.
Miniature Sheet

2005 (22 Mar.) Sheet 127×73 mm, printed on pale cream. 'All-over' phosphor. Perf 11×11½
MS2530 **1806a** 50p brownish-black;
50p black; £1 dull vermilion; £1

royal blue	10·00	10·00
First Day Cover		12·00
Presentation Pack (P.O. Pack No. 69)	15·00	
PHQ Cards (*set of* 5) (D28)	5·00	12·00

See also No. 3221

1807 Prince Charles and Mrs Camilla Parker Bowles

Royal Wedding. Miniature Sheet

2005 (9 Apr.) Sheet 85×115 mm. Multicoloured. 'All-over' phosphor. Perf 13½×14
MS2531 **1807** 30p×2 Prince Charles
and Mrs Camilla Parker Bowles
laughing; 68p×2 Prince Charles
and Mrs Camilla Parker Bowles

smiling into camera	8·00	9·00
First Day Cover		10·00
Presentation Pack (P.O. Pack No. M10)	18·00	

1808 Hadrian's Wall, England

1809 Uluru-Kata Tjuta National Park, Australia

1810 Stonehenge, England

1811 Wet Tropics of Queensland, Australia

1812 Blenheim Palace, England

1813 Greater Blue Mountains Area, Australia

1814 Heart of Neolithic Orkney, Scotland

1815 Purnululu National Park, Australia

World Heritage Sites

2005 (21 Apr.) One side phosphor band (2nd) or two phosphor bands (others). Perf 14½

2532	**1808**	(2nd) multicoloured	1·00	80
		a. Horiz pair. Nos. 2532/3	2·00	1·60
2533	**1809**	(2nd) multicoloured	1·00	80
2534	**1810**	(1st) multicoloured	1·25	90
		a. Horiz pair. Nos. 2534/5	2·50	2·00
2535	**1811**	(1st) multicoloured	1·25	90
2536	**1812**	47p multicoloured	1·00	1·00
		a. Horiz pair. Nos. 2536/7	2·00	2·25
2537	**1813**	47p multicoloured	1·00	1·00
2538	**1814**	68p multicoloured	1·50	1·40
		a. Horiz pair. Nos. 2538/9	3·00	3·00
2539	**1815**	68p multicoloured	1·50	1·40
Set of 8			8·50	8·00
First Day Cover				10·00
Presentation Pack (P.O. Pack No. 371)			10·00	
Presentation Pack (UK and Australian stamps)			16·00	
PHQ Cards (*set of* 8) (275)			7·00	16·00
Set of 4 Gutter Strips of 4			20·00	
Set of 4 Traffic Light Gutter Blocks of 8			42·00	

Nos. 2532/3, 2534/5, 2536/7 and 2538/9 were each printed together, *se-tenant*, in horizontal pairs.

Stamps in these designs were also issued by Australia and these are included in the joint Presentation Pack.

1816 Ensign of the Scots Guards, 2002

1817 Queen taking the salute as Colonel-in-Chief of the Grenadier Guards, 1983

1818 Trumpeter of the Household Calvalry, 2004

1819 Welsh Guardsman, 1990s

1820 Queen riding side-saddle, 1972

1821 Queen and Duke of Edinburgh in Carriage, 2004

Trooping the Colour

2005 (7 June) One phosphor band (2nd), two phosphor bands (others). Perf 14½

2540	**1816**	(2nd)	multicoloured	1·00	80	☐ ☐
2541	**1817**	(1st)	multicoloured	1·25	1·00	☐ ☐
2542	**1818**	42p	multicoloured	1·00	1·20	☐ ☐
2543	**1819**	60p	multicoloured	2·00	2·00	☐ ☐
2544	**1820**	68p	multicoloured	2·50	2·50	☐ ☐
2545	**1821**	£1·12	multicoloured	3·50	3·50	☐ ☐
Set of 6				10·00	10·00	☐ ☐
First Day Cover					12·00	☐
Presentation Pack (P.O. Pack No. 372)				14·00		☐
PHQ Cards (set of 6) (276)				5·00	20·00	☐ ☐
Set of 6 Gutter Pairs				21·00		☐
MS2546 115×105 mm. Nos. 2540/5				11·00	11·00	☐ ☐
First Day Cover					12·00	☐

The six PHQ cards show the six stamps and the miniature sheet.

1822

60th Anniversary of End of the Second World War. Miniature Sheet

2005 (5 July) Sheet 115×105 mm containing design as T **1200** (1995 Peace and Freedom) but with service indicator and No. 1664b×5. Two phosphor bands. Perf 15×14 (with one elliptical hole in each vertical side) (1664b) or 14½×14 (T **1200**)

MS2547 **1822** (1st) gold ×5; (1st) silver, blue and grey-black   7·50   7·00   ☐ ☐
First Day Cover   8·00   ☐

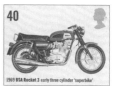

1823 Norton F.1, Road Version of Race Winner (1991)

1824 BSA Rocket 3, Early Three Cylinder 'Superbike' (1969)

1825 Vincent Black Shadow, Fastest Standard Motorcycle (1949)

1826 Triumph Speed Twin, Two Cylinder Innovation (1938)

1827 Brough Superior, Bespoke Luxury Motorcycle (1930)

1828 Royal Enfield, Small Engined Motor Bicycle (1914)

Motorcycles

2005 (19 July) Two phosphor bands. Perf 14×14½

2548	**1823**	(1st)	multicoloured	1·25	1·00	☐ ☐
2549	**1824**	40p	multicoloured	90	1·00	☐ ☐
2550	**1825**	42p	multicoloured	1·25	1·00	☐ ☐
2551	**1826**	47p	multicoloured	1·75	2·00	☐ ☐
2552	**1827**	60p	multicoloured	2·50	2·50	☐ ☐
2553	**1828**	68p	multicoloured	3·00	3·00	☐ ☐
Set of 6				9·00	9·00	☐ ☐
First Day Cover					11·00	☐
Presentation Pack (P.O. Pack No. 373)				13·00		☐
PHQ Cards (set of 6) (277)				5·00	14·00	☐ ☐
Set of 6 Gutter Pairs				19·00		☐

1829

London's Successful Bid for Olympic Games, 2012.
Miniature Sheet

2005 (5 Aug.) Sheet 115×105 mm containing designs as T **1255/9**, but with service indicator. Multicoloured. Two phosphor bands. Perf 14½

MS2554	**1829**	(1st)	Athlete	

celebrating×2; (1st) Throwing the javelin; (1st) Swimming; (1st) Athlete on starting blocks; (1st) Basketball6·50   6·50 ☐ ☐
First Day Cover   8·00   ☐
Presentation Pack (P.O. Pack No. M11)   12·00   ☐

Stamps from **MS**2554 are all inscribed 'London 2012—Host City' and have imprint date '2005'. The design as Type **1259** omits the Olympic rings.

1830 African Woman eating Rice

1831 Indian Woman drinking Tea

1832 Boy eating Sushi

1833 Woman eating Pasta

1834 Woman eating Chips

1835 Teenage Boy eating Apple

Europa. Gastronomy. Changing Tastes in Britain

2005 (23 Aug.) One side phosphor band (2nd) or two phosphor bands (others). Perf 14½

2555	**1830**	(2nd)	multicoloured	1·00	80	☐ ☐
2556	**1831**	(1st)	multicoloured	1·25	1·00	☐ ☐
2557	**1832**	42p	multicoloured	1·30	1·40	☐ ☐
2558	**1833**	47p	multicoloured	1·50	1·60	☐ ☐
2559	**1834**	60p	multicoloured	2·00	1·90	☐ ☐
2560	**1835**	68p	multicoloured	2·50	2·20	☐ ☐

Set of 6   8·00   8·00 ☐ ☐
First Day Cover   10·00   ☐
Presentation Pack (P.O. Pack No. 374)   9·00   ☐
PHQ Cards (set of 6) (278)   5·00   12·00 ☐ ☐
Set of 6 Gutter Pairs   17·00   ☐

The 1st and 42p values include the 'EUROPA' emblem.

1836 'Inspector Morse'

1837 'Emmerdale'

1838 'Rising Damp'

1839 'The Avengers'

1840 'The South Bank Show'

1841 'Who Wants to be a Millionaire'

50th Anniversary of Independent Television.
Classic ITV Programmes

2005 (15 Sept.) One side phosphor band (2nd) or two phosphor bands (others). Perf 14½ × 14

2561	**1836**	(2nd)	multicoloured	1·00	1·00	☐ ☐
2562	**1837**	(1st)	multicoloured	1·25	1·00	☐ ☐
2563	**1838**	42p	multicoloured	1·30	1·40	☐ ☐
2564	**1839**	47p	multicoloured	1·40	1·50	☐ ☐
2565	**1840**	60p	multicoloured	2·00	1·90	☐ ☐
2566	**1841**	68p	multicoloured	2·20	2·20	☐ ☐

Set of 6   8·00   8·00 ☐ ☐
First Day Cover   10·00   ☐
Presentation Pack (P.O. Pack No. 375)   9·00   ☐
PHQ Cards (set of 6) (279)   5·00   12·00 ☐ ☐
Set of 6 Gutter Pairs   17·00   ☐

The 1st class stamps were also issued in sheets of 20 with each stamp accompanied by a half stamp-size se-tenant label.

1842 Gazania Splendens (Charlotte Sowerby)

1842a "LOVE"

'Smilers' (1st series). Booklet stamps

2005 (4 Oct.) Designs as Types 992, 1221, 1286, 1517 and 1568/9 but smaller, 20×23 mm, and inscribed 1st as T **1842**. Self-adhesive. Two phosphor bands. Die-cut perf 15×14.

2567	**1842**	(1st)	multicoloured	2·50	2·50	☐ ☐
			a. Booklet pane.		
			Nos· 2567/72	14·00		☐
2568	**1569**	(1st)	multicoloured	2·50	2·50	☐ ☐
2569	**1842a**	(1st)	multicoloured	2·50	2·50	☐ ☐
2570	**1517**	(1st)	multicoloured	2·50	2·50	☐ ☐
2571	**992**	(1st)	multicoloured	2·50	2·50	☐ ☐
2572	**1221**	(1st)	multicoloured	2·50	2·50	☐ ☐

Set of 6   14·00   14·00 ☐ ☐
First Day Cover   15·00   ☐

Nos. 2567/72 were printed together, se-tenant, in booklet panes of six in which the surplus self-adhesive paper around each stamp was removed.

Nos. 2567/72 were re-issued on 4 July 2006 in sheets of 20 with *se-tenant* labels, printed in lithography instead of gravure.

Nos. 2568/70 were re-issued on 18 January 2008 in sheets of 20 with circular *se-tenant* labels, printed in lithography.

No. 2567 was re-issued on 28 October 2008 in sheets of ten with circular *se-tenant* 'Flower Fairy' labels, printed in lithography.

Stamps as Nos. 2569 and 2572 but perforated with one elliptical hole on each vertical side were issued, together with Nos. 2674 and 2821/3 and four designs from **MS**3024, on 8 May 2010 in sheets of 20 stamps with *se-tenant* greetings labels.

See also No. 2693 and Nos. 2819/24.

1843 Cricket Scenes

England's Ashes Victory. Miniature Sheet

2005 (6 Oct.) Sheet 115 × 90 mm. Multicoloured. Two phosphor bands. Perf 14½ × 14.

MS2573 **1843** (1st) England team with Ashes trophy; (1st) Kevin Pieterson, Michael Vaughan and Andrew Flintoff on opening day of First Test, Lords; 68p Michael Vaughan, Third Test, Old Trafford; 68p Second Test Edgbaston .... 7·50   7·50 ☐ ☐

First Day Cover .... 9·00 ☐

Presentation Pack (P.O. Pack No. M12) ...... 10·00 ☐

1844 *Entrepreante* with dismasted British *Belle Isle*

1845 Nelson wounded on Deck of HMS *Victory*

1846 British Cutter *Entrepreante* attempting to rescue crew of burning French *Achille*

1847 Cutter and HMS *Pickle* (schooner)

1848 British Fleet attacking in two columns

1849 Franco/Spanish Fleet putting to sea from Cadiz

Bicentenary of the Battle of Trafalgar (1st issue). Scenes from 'Panorama of the Battle of Trafalgar' by William Heath

2005 (18 Oct.) Two phosphor bands. Perf 15 × 14½

2574	**1844**	(1st) multicoloured	1·25	1·00	☐	☐
		a. Horiz pair. Nos. 2574/5	2·50	2·25	☐	☐
2575	**1845**	(1st) multicoloured	1·25	1·00	☐	☐
2576	**1846**	42p multicoloured	1·00	1·10	☐	☐
		a. Horiz pair. Nos. 2576/7	2·50	2·75	☐	☐
2577	**1847**	42p multicoloured	1·00	1·10	☐	☐
2578	**1848**	68p multicoloured	1·25	1·50	☐	☐
		a. Horiz pair. Nos. 2578/9	4·00	4·40	☐	☐
2579	**1849**	68p multicoloured	1·25	1·50	☐	☐
Set of 6			8·00	8·50		
First Day Cover				10·00		☐
Presentation Pack (P.O. Pack No. 376)			10·00		☐	
PHQ Cards (*set of* 7) (280)			7·00	20·00	☐	☐
Set of 3 Gutter Strips of 4			18·00			
MS2580 190 × 68 mm. Nos. 2574/9			10·00	11·00	☐	☐
First Day Cover				12·00		☐

Nos. 2574/5, 2576/7 and 2578/9 were each printed together, *se-tenant*, in horizontal pairs throughout the sheets, each pair forming a composite design and were also issued in the £7·26 'Bicentenary of the Battle of Trafalgar' booklet, No. DX35.

The phosphor bands are at just left of centre and at right of each stamp

The seven PHQ cards depict the six individual stamps and the miniature sheet.

Bicentenary of the Battle of Trafalgar (2nd issue). Booklet stamp

2005 (18 Oct.) Design as Type **1516** (White Ensign from 2001 Submarine Centenary). Litho. Two phosphor bands. Perf 14½

2581 **1516** (1st) multicoloured .... 5·00   5·00 ☐ ☐

No. 2581 was only issued in the £7·26 'Bicentenary of the Battle of Trafalgar', No. DX41 £7·40 'Ian Fleming's James Bond', No. DX35 and £7·93 'Royal Navy Uniforms, No. DX47, booklets.

1850 Black Madonna and Child from Haiti

1851 'Madonna and Child' (Marianne Stokes)

1852 'The Virgin Mary
with the Infant Christ'

1853 Choctaw Virgin
Mother and Child
(Fr. John Giuliani)

1858 The Enormous
Crocodile (Roald Dahl)

1859 More About
Paddington (Michael Bond)

1854 'Madonna and
the Infant Jesus'
(from India)

1855 'Come let us
adore Him'
(Dianne Tchumut)

1860 Comic Adventures
of Boots (Satoshi Kitamura)

1861 Alice's Adventures in
Wonderland (Lewis Carroll)

Christmas. Madonna and Child Paintings

2005 (1 Nov.) One side phosphor band (2nd) or two phosphor
bands (others). Perf 14½ × 14

1862 The Very Hungry
Caterpillar (Eric Carle)

1863 Maisy's ABC
(Lucy Cousins)

(a) Self-adhesive

2582	**1850**	(2nd)	multicoloured	1·00	80	☐ ☐
2583	**1851**	(1st)	multicoloured	1·25	1·00	☐ ☐
2584	**1852**	42p	multicoloured	1·30	1·40	☐ ☐
2585	**1853**	60p	multicoloured	1·80	1·90	☐ ☐
2586	**1854**	68p	multicoloured	2·00	2·20	☐ ☐
2587	**1855**	£1·12	multicoloured	3·40	3·60	☐ ☐
Set of 6				9·50	10·00	☐ ☐
First Day Cover					12·00	☐
Presentation Pack (P.O. Pack No. 377)				11·00		☐
PHQ Cards (*set of 7*) (281)				7·00	16·00	☐ ☐

(b) Ordinary gum

MS2588	115×102 mm. As Nos.			
2582/7		10·50	11·00	☐ ☐
First Day Cover			12·00	☐

The seven PHQ cards depict the six individual stamps and the
miniature sheet.

Year Pack

2005 (1 Nov.) Comprises Nos. 2502/23, 2525/9, **MS**2531/45,
2548/53, 2555/66, 2574/9 and 2582/7

CP2587a	Year Pack	£110	☐

Post Office Yearbook

2005 (1 Nov.) Comprises Nos. 2502/23, 2525/9, **MS**2531/45,
2548/53, 2555/66, 2574/9 and 2582/7

YB2587a	Yearbook	95·00	☐

Miniature Sheet Collection

2005 (21 Nov.) Comprises Nos. **MS**2524, **MS**2530/1, **MS**2546/7,
MS2554, **MS**2573, **MS**2580, **MS**2588 and **MS**2588a

Miniature Sheet Collection	75·00	☐

Animal Tales

2006 (10 Jan.) One side phosphor band (2nd) or two phosphor
bands (others). Perf 14½

2589	**1856**	(2nd)	multicoloured	90	75	☐ ☐
		a. Horiz. pair.				
			Nos. 2589/90	1·75	1·60	☐ ☐
2590	**1857**	(2nd)	multicoloured	90	75	☐ ☐
2591	**1858**	(1st)	multicoloured	1·25	1·00	☐ ☐
		a. Horiz. pair.				
			Nos. 2591/2	2·50	2·25	☐ ☐
2592	**1859**	(1st)	multicoloured	1·25	1·00	☐ ☐
2593	**1860**	42p	multicoloured	90	1·10	☐ ☐
		a. Horiz. pair.				
			Nos. 2593/4	4·00	4·00	☐ ☐
2594	**1861**	42p	multicoloured	90	1·10	☐ ☐
2595	**1862**	68p	multicoloured	1·25	1·60	☐ ☐
		a. Horiz. pair.				
			Nos. 2595/6	5·00	5·00	☐ ☐
2596	**1863**	68p	multicoloured	1·25	1·60	☐ ☐
Set of 8				12·00	11·50	☐ ☐
First Day Cover					13·00	☐
Presentation Pack (P.O. Pack No. 379)				13·00		☐
PHQ Cards (*set of 8*) (282)				7·00	16·00	☐ ☐
Set of 4 Gutter Blocks of 4				25·00		☐
Set of 4 Traffic Light Gutter Blocks of 8				50·00		☐

Nos. 2589/90, 2591/2, 2593/4 and 2595/6 were printed
together, *se-tenant*, as horizontal pairs in sheets of 60 (2 panes
6 × 5)

No. 2595 contains two die-cut holes.

A design as No. 2592 but self-adhesive was also issued in
sheets of 20 with each stamp accompanied by a *se-tenant* label.

1856 The Tale of Mr. Jeremy
Fisher (Beatrix Potter)

1857 Kipper (Mick Inkpen)

1864 Carding Mill Valley, Shropshire   **1865** Beachy Head, Sussex

1866 St. Paul's Cathedral, London   **1867** Brancaster, Norfolk

1868 Derwent Edge, Peak District   **1869** Robin Hood's Bay, Yorkshire

1870 Buttermere, Lake District   **1871** Chipping Campden, Cotswolds

1872 St. Boniface Down,
Isle of Wight   **1873** Chamberlain Square,
Birmingham

A British Journey (5th series): England

2006 (7 Feb.) Two phosphor bands. Perf 14½

2597	**1864**	(1st)	multicoloured	1·25	1·00	☐ ☐
		a.	Block of 10.			
			Nos. 2597/2606	14·00	12·00	☐ ☐
2598	**1865**	(1st)	multicoloured	1·25	1·00	☐ ☐
2599	**1866**	(1st)	multicoloured	1·25	1·00	☐ ☐
2600	**1867**	(1st)	multicoloured	1·25	1·00	☐ ☐
2601	**1868**	(1st)	multicoloured	1·25	1·00	☐ ☐
2602	**1869**	(1st)	multicoloured	1·25	1·00	☐ ☐
2603	**1870**	(1st)	multicoloured	1·25	1·00	☐ ☐
2604	**1871**	(1st)	multicoloured	1·25	1·00	☐ ☐
2605	**1872**	(1st)	multicoloured	1·25	1·00	☐ ☐
2606	**1873**	(1st)	multicoloured	1·25	1·00	☐ ☐
Set of 10				14·00	12·00	☐ ☐
First Day Cover					13·00	☐
Presentation Pack (P.O. Pack No. 380)				15·00		☐
PHQ Cards (set of 10) (283)				9·00	18·00	☐ ☐
Gutter Block of 20				30·00		☐

Nos. 2597/2606 were printed together, *se-tenant*, as blocks of ten (5×2) in sheets of 60 (2 panes of 30)

1874 Royal Albert Bridge

1875 Box Tunnel

1876 Paddington Station

1877 PSS *Great Eastern* (paddle-steamer)

1878 Clifton Suspension Bridge Design

1879 Maidenhead Bridge

Birth Bicentenary of Isambard Kingdom Brunel (engineer) (1st issue)

2006 (23 Feb.) Phosphor-coated paper (42p) or two phosphor bands (others). Perf 14×13½

2607	**1874**	(1st)	multicoloured	1·25	80	☐ ☐
2608	**1875**	40p	multicoloured	1·10	1·10	☐ ☐
2609	**1876**	42p	multicoloured	1·10	1·10	☐ ☐
2610	**1877**	47p	multicoloured	1·50	1·50	☐ ☐
2611	**1878**	60p	multicoloured	2·00	1·75	☐ ☐
2612	**1879**	68p	multicoloured	2·50	2·25	☐ ☐
Set of 6				7·50	7·50	☐
First Day Cover					9·00	☐
Presentation Pack (P.O. Pack No. 381)				10·00		☐
PHQ Cards (set of 7) (284)				6·00	14·00	☐ ☐
Set of 6 Gutter Pairs				16·00		☐
MS2613 190×65 mm. Nos. 2607/12				8·50	8·50	☐ ☐
First Day Cover					9·00	☐

The phosphor bands on Nos. 2607/8 and 2610/12 are at just left of centre and at right of each stamp.

The complete miniature sheet is shown on one of the PHQ cards with the others depicting individual stamps.

Nos. 2607/12 were also issued in the £7·40 'Isambard Kingdom Brunel' booklet, No. DX36.

Birth Bicentenary of Isambard Kingdom Brunel (engineer) (2nd issue). Booklet stamp

2006 (23 Feb.) Design as Type **1739** (PS *Great Western* from 2004 Ocean Liners). Litho. Two phosphor bands. Perf 14½ × 14

2614 **1739** 68p multicoloured   12·00   12·50 ☐ ☐

No. 2614 was only issued in the £7·40 'Isambard Kingdom Brunel' stamp booklet, No. DX36.

For the miniature sheet celebrating the opening of the New Welsh Assembly, Cardiff, issued 1 March 2006, see the Regionals section.

1880 Sabre-tooth Cat

1881 Giant Deer

1882 Woolly Rhino

1883 Woolly Mammoth

1884 Cave Bear

Ice Age Animals

2006 (21 Mar.) Two phosphor bands. Perf 14½

2615 **1880**	(1st)	black and silver	1·25	1·00	☐ ☐
2616 **1881**	42p	black and silver	1·00	1·00	☐ ☐
2617 **1882**	47p	black and silver	2·00	2·00	☐ ☐
2618 **1883**	68p	black and silver	2·25	2·25	☐ ☐
2619 **1884**	£1·12	black and silver	3·25	3·25	☐ ☐
Set of 5			8·50	8·50	☐ ☐
First Day Cover				10·00	☐
Presentation Pack (P.O. Pack No. 382)			12·00		☐
PHQ Cards (*set of 5*) (285)			4·00	12·00	☐ ☐
Set of 5 Gutter Pairs			18·00		☐

1885 On Britannia, 1972

1886 At Royal Windsor Horse Show, 1985

1887 At Heathrow Airport, 2001

1888 As Young Princess Elizabeth with Duchess of York, 1931

1889 At State Banquet, Ottawa, 1951

1890 Queen Elizabeth II in 1960

1891 As Princess Elizabeth, 1940

1892 With Duke of Edinburgh, 1951

80th Birthday of Queen Elizabeth II

2006 (18 Apr.) One side phosphor band (No. 2620), one centre phosphor band (No. 2621) or two phosphor bands (others). Perf 14½

2620 **1885**	(2nd)	black, turquoise green and grey	1·00	1·00	☐ ☐
	a.	Horiz pair. Nos. 2620/1	2·25	2·25	☐ ☐
2621 **1886**	(2nd)	black, turquoise-green and grey	1·00	1·00	☐ ☐
2622 **1887**	(1st)	black, turquoise-green and grey	1·25	1·10	☐ ☐
	a.	Horiz pair. Nos. 2622/3	2·50	2·40	☐ ☐
2623 **1888**	(1st)	black, turquoise-green and grey	1·25	1·10	☐ ☐
2624 **1889**	44p	black, turquoise-green and grey	1·00	1·25	☐ ☐
	a.	Horiz pair. Nos. 2624/5	2·75	2·75	☐ ☐
2625 **1890**	44p	black, turquoise-green and grey	1·00	1·25	☐ ☐
2626 **1891**	72p	black, turquoise-green and grey	1·50	2·00	☐ ☐
	a.	Horiz pair. Nos. 2626/7	4·50	4·50	☐ ☐
2627 **1892**	72p	black, turquoise-green and grey	1·50	2·00	☐ ☐
Set of 8			11·00	11·00	☐ ☐
First Day Cover				12·00	☐
Presentation Pack (P.O. Pack No. 383)			12·00		☐
PHQ Cards (*set of 8*) (286)			7·00	16·00	☐ ☐
Set of 4 Gutter Strips of 4			23·00		☐

Nos. 2620/1, 2622/3, 2624/5 and 2626/7 were each printed together, *se-tenant*, as horizontal pairs in sheets of 60 (2 panes 6 × 5)

1893 England (1966)

1894 Italy (1934, 1938, 1982)

1895 Argentina
(1978, 1986)

1896 Germany
(1954, 1974, 1990)

1897 France (1998)

1898 Brazil (1958, 1962,
1970, 1994, 2002)

World Cup Football Championship, Germany.
World Cup Winners

2006 (6 June) Two phosphor bands. Perf 14½

2628 **1893**	(1st)	multicoloured	1·25	1·00
2629 **1894**	42p	multicoloured	1·25	1·10
2630 **1895**	44p	multicoloured	1·25	1·25
2631 **1896**	50p	multicoloured	2·00	2·00
2632 **1897**	64p	multicoloured	3·00	3·00
2633 **1898**	72p	multicoloured	3·50	3·50
Set of 6			11·00	10·50
First Day Cover				12·00
Presentation Pack (P.O. Pack No. 384)			13·00	
PHQ Cards (set of 6) (287)			5·00	12·00
Set of 6 Gutter Pairs			23·00	

The 1st class stamp was also issued in sheets of 20 with each stamp accompanied by a *se-tenant* label showing scenes from the 1966 World Cup final.

1899 30 St. Mary Axe, London

1900 Maggie's Centre, Dundee

1901 Selfridges, Birmingham

1902 Downland Gridshell, Chichester

1903 An Turas, Isle of Tiree

1904 The Deep, Hull

Modern Architecture

2006 (20 June) Two phosphor bands. Perf 14½

2634 **1899**	(1st)	multicoloured	1·25	1·00
2635 **1900**	42p	multicoloured	1·10	1·10
2636 **1901**	44p	multicoloured	1·25	1·25
2637 **1902**	50p	multicoloured	1·75	1·75
2638 **1903**	64p	multicoloured	2·00	2·00
2639 **1904**	72p	multicoloured	2·50	2·50
Set of 6			9·00	8·50
First Day Cover				11·00
Presentation Pack (P.O. Pack No. 385)			11·00	
PHQ Cards (set of 6) (288)			5·00	14·00
Set of 6 Gutter Pairs			20·00	

1905 'Sir Winston Churchill'
(Walter Sickert)

1906 'Sir Joshua Reynolds'
(self-portrait)

1907 'T. S. Eliot'
(Patrick Heron)

1908 'Emmeline Pankhurst'
(Georgina Agnes Brackenbury)

1909 Virginia Woolf (photo by George Charles Beresford)

1910 Bust of Sir Walter Scott (Sir Francis Leggatt Chantry)

1911 'Mary Seacole' (Albert Charles Challen)

1912 'William Shakespeare'
(attrib to John Taylor)

1913 'Dame Cicely Saunders' (Catherine Goodman)

1914 'Charles Darwin' (John Collier)

150th Anniversary of National Portrait Gallery, London

2006 (18 July) Two phosphor bands. Perf 14½

2640 **1905**	(1st)	multicoloured	1·25	1·00
	a.	Block of 10.		
		Nos. 2640/9	14·00	12·00
2641 **1906**	(1st)	multicoloured	1·25	1·00

2642 **1907**	(1st)	multicoloured	1·25	1·00	☐☐
2643 **1908**	(1st)	multicoloured	1·25	1·00	☐☐
2644 **1909**	(1st)	multicoloured	1·25	1·00	☐☐
2645 **1910**	(1st)	multicoloured	1·25	1·00	☐☐
2646 **1911**	(1st)	multicoloured	1·25	1·00	☐☐
2647 **1912**	(1st)	multicoloured	1·25	1·00	☐☐
2648 **1913**	(1st)	multicoloured	1·25	1·00	☐☐
2649 **1914**	(1st)	multicoloured	1·25	1·00	☐☐
Set of 10			14·00	12·00	☐
First Day Cover				13·00	☐
Presentation Pack (P.O. Pack No. 386)			15·00		☐
PHQ Cards (set of 10) (289)			9·00	18·00	☐☐
Gutter Block of 20			28·00		☐
Traffic Light Gutter Block of 20			30·00		☐

Nos. 2640/9 were printed together, *se-tenant*, as blocks of ten (5×2) in sheets of 60 (2 panes of 30)

1915   1916

'Pricing in Proportion'

2006 (1 Aug.–12 Sept.) Perf 15×14 (with one elliptical hole in each vertical side)

(a) Ordinary gum. Gravure De La Rue (No. 2651 also Enschedé or Walsall from prestige booklets)

(i) As T **1915**

2650	(2nd)	bright blue (1 centre band)	1·50	1·10	☐☐
2651	(1st)	gold (2 bands)	1·75	1·20	☐☐

(ii) As T **1916**

2652	(2nd Large)	bright blue (2 bands)	1·50	1·00	☐☐
2653	(1st Large)	gold (2 bands)	2·00	1·00	☐☐

(b) Self-adhesive. Gravure Walsall

(i) As T **1915**

2654	(2nd)	bright blue (1 centre band) *(12 Sept)*	1·50	40	☐☐
2655	(1st)	gold (2 bands) *(12 Sept)*	1·75	50	☐☐

(ii) As T **1916**

2656	(2nd Large)	bright blue (2 bands) *(15 Aug)*	2·50	1·00	☐☐
2657	(1st Large)	gold (2 bands) *(15 Aug)*	2·50	1·00	☐☐
First Day Cover (Nos. Y1676b/c, 2650/3)				5·00	☐
Presentation Pack (Nos. Y1676b/c, 2650/3) (P.O. Pack No. 74)			8·00		☐

No. 2654 was issued in booklets of 12 sold at £2·76.

No. 2655 was available in booklets of six or twelve, sold at £1·92 or £3·84.

Nos. 2656/7 were issued in separate booklets of four, sold at £1·48 or £1·76.

No. 2650/3 were also issued in the £7·66 'The Machin. The Making of a Masterpiece' booklet, No.DX39 and 2651 from the £15.14 50th Anniversary of the Machin Definitive Prestige booklet, DY21, issued 5 June 2017.

All these booklets had the surplus self-adhesive paper around each stamp removed.

For PHQ cards for Nos. 2652/3 see below No. Y1803.

1917

70th Anniversary of the Year of Three Kings. Miniature Sheet

2006 (31 Aug.) Sheet 127×72 mm containing No. Y1748. Multicoloured. Two phosphor bands. Perf 15×14 (with one elliptical hole in each vertical side)

MS2658 **1917**	£3 deep mauve		10·00	10·00	☐☐
First Day Cover				11·00	☐

1918 Corporal Agansing Rai   1919 Boy Seaman Jack Cornwell

1920 Midshipman Charles Lucas   1921 Captain Noel Chavasse

1922 Captain Albert Ball   1923 Captain Charles Upham

150th Anniversary of the Victoria Cross (1st issue)

2006 (21 Sept.) One side phosphor band. Perf 14½×14

2659 **1918**	(1st)	multicoloured	1·25	1·10	☐☐
	a.	Horiz pair. Nos. 2659/60	2·50	2·25	☐☐
2660 **1919**	(1st)	multicoloured	1·25	1·10	☐☐
2661 **1920**	64p	multicoloured	2·00	2·00	☐☐
	a.	Horiz pair. Nos. 2661/2	4·00	4·00	☐☐
2662 **1921**	64p	multicoloured	2·00	2·00	☐☐
2663 **1922**	72p	multicoloured	2·50	2·50	☐☐
	a.	Horiz pair. Nos. 2663/4	5·00	5·00	☐☐
2664 **1923**	72p	multicoloured	2·50	2·50	☐☐
Set of 6			10·00	10·00	☐
First Day Cover				12·00	☐
Presentation Pack (P.O. Pack No. 387)			12·00		☐
Set of 3 Gutter Strips of 4			22·00		☐

MS2665 190×67 mm. No. 2666 and as
    Nos. 2659/64 but 'all-over'
    phosphor   11·00   11·00 ☐☐
First Day Cover   13·00 ☐
PHQ Cards (*set of* 7) (290)   7·00   18·00 ☐☐

Nos. 2659/60, 2661/2 and 2663/4 were each printed together, *se-tenant*, as horizontal pairs in sheets of 60 (2 panes 6×5) and were also issued in the £7·44 'Victoria Cross' booklet, No. DY37.

    The seven PHQ cards depict the six individual stamps and the miniature sheet.

150th Anniversary of the Victoria Cross (2nd issue). Booklet stamp

2006 (21 Sept.) Design as No. 1517 (1990 Gallantry Awards). 'All-over' phosphor. Perf 14×14½

2666 **959** 20p multicoloured   7·00   7·00 ☐☐

No. 2666 was only issued in the £7·44 'Victoria Cross' booklet, No. DX37 and in **MS**2665

1924 Sitar Player and Dancer

1925 Reggae Bass Guitarist and African Drummer

1926 Fiddler and Harpist

1927 Sax Player and Blues Guitarist

1928 Maraca Player and Salsa Dancers

Europa. Integration. Sounds of Britain

2006 (3 Oct.) 'All-over' phosphor. Perf 14½

2667	**1924**	(1st)	multicoloured	1·25	1·05	☐☐
2668	**1925**	42p	multicoloured	1·25	1·25	☐☐
2669	**1926**	50p	multicoloured	1·50	1·50	☐☐
2670	**1927**	72p	multicoloured	2·00	2·00	☐☐
2671	**1928**	£1·19	multicoloured	3·50	3·50	☐☐
Set of 5				8·50	8·50	☐☐
First Day Cover					10·00	☐
Presentation Pack (P.O. Pack No. 388)				10·00		☐
PHQ Cards (*set of* 5) (291)				5·00	13·00	☐☐
Set of 5 Gutter Pairs				19·00		☐
Set of 5 Traffic Light Gutter Blocks of 4			40·00			☐

The 1st class and 50p values include the 'EUROPA' emblem.

1929 'New Baby' (Alison Carmichael)

1930 'Best Wishes' (Alan Kitching)

1931 'THANK YOU' (Alan Kitching)

1932 Balloons (Ivan Chermayeff)

1933 Firework (Kam Tang)

1934 Champagne, Flowers and Butterflies (Olaf Hajek)

'Smilers' (2nd series). Occasions. Booklet stamps

2006 (17 Oct.) Self-adhesive. Two phosphor bands. Die-cut perf 15×14

2672	**1929**	(1st)	chrome-yellow	1·40	1·20	☐☐
		a.	Booklet pane. Nos. 2672/7	9·00	7·00	☐☐
2673	**1930**	(1st)	turquoise-blue	1·40	1·20	☐☐
2674	**1931**	(1st)	scarlet-vermilion, rosine and yellow	1·40	1·20	☐☐
2675	**1932**	(1st)	multicoloured	1·40	1·20	☐☐
2676	**1933**	(1st)	multicoloured	1·40	1·20	☐☐
2677	**1934**	(1st)	multicoloured	1·40	1·20	☐☐
Set of 6				9·00	7·00	☐☐
First Day Cover					8·00	☐
Presentation Pack (P.O. Pack No. M13)			18·00			☐
PHQ Cards (D29)				5·00	12·00	☐☐

Nos. 2672/7 were printed together, *se-tenant*, in booklet panes of six in which the surplus self-adhesive paper around each stamp was removed.

    They were also issued in sheets of 20, containing four of Nos. 2672 and 2677 and three of the other designs, and *se-tenant* labels. Separate sheets of each design were available with personal photographs on the labels.

    Stamps as No. 2672 but perforated with one eliptical hole on each vertical side were issued on 28 October 2008 in sheets of 10 or 20 with circular *se-tenant* Peter Rabbit labels.

    Stamps as Nos. 2674 but perforated with one elliptical hole in each vertical side were issued, together with Nos. 2569, 2572, 2821/3 and four designs from **MS**3024, on 8 May 2010 in sheets of 20 stamps with *se-tenant* greetings labels.

    These generic sheets were all printed in lithography instead of gravure.

1935 Snowman

1936 Father Christmas

1937 Snowman

1938 Father Christmas

1939 Reindeer

1940 Christmas Tree

Christmas. Christmans scenes

2006 (7 Nov.) One centre phosphor band (2nd) or two phosphor bands (others). Perf 15×14

(a) Self-adhesive

2678	**1935**	(2nd) multicoloured	1·00	90	
2679	**1936**	(1st) multicoloured	1·25	1·00	
2680	**1937**	(2nd Large) multicoloured	1·50	1·25	
2681	**1938**	(1st Large) multicoloured	2·00	1·40	
2682	**1939**	72p multicoloured	2·00	2·00	
2683	**1940**	£1·19 multicoloured	3·50	3·50	
Set of 6			10·00	10·00	
First Day Cover				12·00	
Presentation Pack (P.O. Pack No. 389)			12·00		
PHQ Cards (*set of 7*) (292)			6·00	18·00	

(b) Ordinary gum

MS2684 115×102 mm.

As Nos. 2678/83	10·00	10·00	
First Day Cover		12·00	

The seven PHQ cards depict the six individual stamps and the miniature sheet.

The 2nd and 1st class stamps were also issued in sheets of 20 printed in lithography instead of gravure containing ten 1st class and ten 2nd class stamps, each stamp accompanied by a *se-tenant* label. Separate sheets of 20 1st or 20 2nd class were available with personal photographs.

1941 Lest We Forget

'Lest We Forget' (1st series). 90th Anniversary of the Battle of the Somme. Miniature Sheet

2006 (9 Nov.) Sheet 124×71 mm containing new stamp as No. 2883 and designs as Nos. EN17, W109, S120 and NI102. Multicoloured. Two phosphor bands. Perf 14½ (1st) or 15×14 (with one elliptical hole in each vertical side) (72p)

MS2685 **1941** (1st) Poppies on barbed wire stems;			
72p×4	9·00	9·00	
First Day Cover		10·00	
Presentation Pack (P.O. Pack No. 390)	12·00		

No. **MS**2685 (including the Northern Ireland stamp) is printed in gravure.

The 1st class stamp was also issued in sheets of 20 with *se-tenant* labels showing war memorials, and on 6 Nov 2008, in a *se-tenant* strip of three, both issues printed in lithography instead of gravure. See No. 2883.

For the miniature sheet entitled 'Celebrating Scotland', issued 30 November 2006, see the Regionals section.

Year Pack

2006 (9 Nov.) Comprises Nos. 2589/2612, 2615/49, 2659/64, 2667/71, 2678/83 and **MS**2685

CP2685a	Year Pack	£120	

Post Office Yearbook

2006 (9 Nov.) Comprises Nos. 2589/2612, 2615/49, 2659/64, 2667/71, 2678/83 and **MS**2685

YB2685a	Yearbook	£100	

Miniature Sheet Collection

2006 (30 Nov.) Comprises Nos. **MS**2613, **MS**2658, **MS**2665, **MS**2684/5, **MS**S153 and **MS**W143

MS2685a Miniature Sheet Collection	75·00	

1942 'with the beatles'   **1943** 'Sgt Pepper's Lonely Hearts Club Band'

1944 'Help!'   **1945** 'Abbey Road'

1946 'Revolver'   **1947** 'Let It Be'

1948 Beatles Memorabilia

The Beatles. Album Covers (1st issue)

2007 (9 Jan.) Two phosphor bands

(a) Gravure Walsall. Self-adhesive. Die-cut irregular
perf 13½ × 14½

2686	**1942**	(1st)	multicoloured	1·25	1·00	☐ ☐
	a.	Horiz pair. Nos. 2686/72·75				☐
2687	**1943**	(1st)	multicoloured	1·25	1·00	☐ ☐
2688	**1944**	64p	multicoloured	1·90	1·90	☐ ☐
	a.	Horiz pair. Nos. 2688/93·75				☐
2689	**1945**	64p	multicoloured	1·90	1·90	☐ ☐
2690	**1946**	72p	multicoloured	2·00	2·00	☐ ☐
	a.	Horiz pair. Nos. 2690/14·00				☐
2691	**1947**	72p	multicoloured	2·00	2·00	☐ ☐
Set of 6				9·00	9·00	☐ ☐
First Day Cover					11·00	☐
Presentation Pack (Nos. 2686/**MS**92)						
		(P.O. Pack No. 392)		16·00		☐
PHQ Cards (set of 11) (293)				9·00	20·00	☐ ☐

(b) Litho Walsall. Ordinary gum. Two phosphor bands. Perf 14

MS2692 115×89 mm. **1948** (1st) Guitar;
(1st) Yellow Submarine lunch-box
and key-rings; (1st) Record 'Love
Me Do'; (1st) Beatles badges 5·00 5·00 ☐ ☐
First Day Cover 7·00 ☐

Nos. 2686/91 are all die-cut in the shape of a pile of records.

Nos. 2686/7, 2688/9 and 2690/1 were each printed together in sheets of 60 (2 panes of 30), with the two designs alternating horizontally and the surplus backing paper around each stamp removed.

Nos. 2686/92 commemorate the 50th anniversary of the first meeting of Paul McCartney and John Lennon.

The complete miniature sheet is shown on one of the eleven PHQ cards, with the others depicting individual stamps, including those from **MS**2692.

'Smilers' (3rd series). Booklet stamp

2007 (16 Jan.)–**08** As No. 2569. Self-adhesive. Two phosphor bands. Die-cut Perf 15×14 (with one elliptical hole in each vertical side)

2693	(1st)	multicoloured	10·00	10·00	☐ ☐
	a.	Booklet pane.			
		No. 2655×5			
		and No. 2693	15·00		☐
	b.	Booklet pane.			
		No. 2693×2 with two			
		attached labels and			
		No. 2295×4 (15.1.08)	22·00		☐

No. 2693 was issued in stamp booklets in which the surplus backing paper around each stamp was removed.

Nos. 2694/8 are left vacant.

1949 Moon Jellyfish

1950 Common Starfish

1951 Beadlet Anemone

1952 Bass

1953 Thornback Ray

1954 Lesser Octopus

1955 Common Mussels

1956 Grey Seal

1957 Shore Crab

1958 Common Sun Star

Sea Life

2007 (1 Feb.) Two phosphor bands. Perf 14½

2699	**1949**	(1st)	multicoloured	1·25	90	☐ ☐
	a.	Block of 10.				
		Nos. 2699/2708		14·00	12·00	☐ ☐
2700	**1950**	(1st)	multicoloured	1·25	90	☐ ☐
2701	**1951**	(1st)	multicoloured	1·25	90	☐ ☐
2702	**1952**	(1st)	multicoloured	1·25	90	☐ ☐
2703	**1953**	(1st)	multicoloured	1·25	90	☐ ☐
2704	**1954**	(1st)	multicoloured	1·25	90	☐ ☐
2705	**1955**	(1st)	multicoloured	1·25	90	☐ ☐
2706	**1956**	(1st)	multicoloured	1·25	90	☐ ☐
2707	**1957**	(1st)	multicoloured	1·25	90	☐ ☐
2708	**1958**	(1st)	multicoloured	1·25	90	☐ ☐
Set of 10				14·00	12·00	☐ ☐
First Day Cover					13·00	☐
Presentation Pack (P.O. Pack No. 393)				16·00		☐
PHQ Cards (set of 10) (294)				8·00	18·00	☐ ☐
Gutter Block of 20				29·00		☐

Nos. 2699/2708 were printed together, se-tenant, as blocks of ten (5×2) in sheets of 60 (2 panes of 30)

1959 Saturn Nebula C55

1960 Eskimo Nebula C39

1961 Cat's Eye Nebula C6

1962 Helix Nebula C63

1963 Flaming Star
Nebula C31

1964 The Spindle C53

50th Anniversary of 'The Sky at Night'
(TV programme). Nebulae

2007 (13 Feb.) Self-adhesive. Two phosphor bands. Die-cut
perf 14½ × 14

2709	**1959**	(1st)	multicoloured	1·25	90
		a. Horiz pair. Nos. 2709/102·50			
2710	**1960**	(1st)	multicoloured	1·25	90
2711	**1961**	50p	multicoloured	1·50	1·50
		a. Horiz pair. Nos. 2711/123·00			
2712	**1962**	50p	multicoloured	1·50	1·50
2713	**1963**	72p	multicoloured	2·00	2·00
		a. Horiz pair. Nos. 2713/44·00			
2714	**1964**	72p	multicoloured	2·00	2·00
Set of 6				8·50	7·00
First Day Cover					8·00
Presentation Pack (P.O. Pack No. 394)			10·00		
PHQ Cards (set of 6) (295)				4·50	14·00

Nos. 2709/10, 2711/12 and 2713/14 were each printed
together in sheets of 60 (2 panes of 30), with the two designs
alternating horizontally and the surplus backing paper around
each stamp removed.

1965 Iron Bridge
(Thomas Telford)

1966 Steam Locomotive
and Railway Tracks

1967 Map of British Isles
and Australia (telephone)

1968 Camera and
Television (John Logie Baird)

1969 Globe as Web
(email and internet)

1970 Couple with
Suitcases on Moon
(space travel)

World of Invention (1st series)

2007 (1 Mar.) Self-adhesive. Two phosphor bands. Die-cut perf
14½ × 14

2715	**1965**	(1st)	multicoloured	1·25	90
		a. Horiz pair. Nos. 2715/163·00			
2716	**1966**	(1st)	multicoloured	1·25	90
2717	**1967**	64p	multicoloured	1·80	1·80
		a. Horiz pair. Nos. 2717/183·50			
2718	**1968**	64p	multicoloured	1·80	1·80
2719	**1969**	72p	multicoloured	2·00	2·25

		a. Horiz pair. Nos. 2719/204·50			
2720	**1970**	72p	multicoloured	2·00	2·25
Set of 6				10·00	10·00
First Day Cover					12·00
Presentation Pack (P.O. Pack No. 395)			12·00		
PHQ Cards (set of 7) (296)				6·00	16·00

The seven PHQ Cards depict the six individual stamps and
MS2727.

Nos. 2715/16, 2717/18 and 2719/20 were each printed
together in sheets of 60 (2 panes of 30), with the two designs
alternating horizontally and the surplus backing paper around
each stamp removed.

World of Invention (2nd series). Booklet stamps

2007 (1 Mar.) Ordinary gum. Two phosphor bands. Perf
14½ × 14

2721	**1965**	(1st)	multicoloured	1·25	1·25
2722	**1966**	(1st)	multicoloured	1·25	1·25
2723	**1967**	64p	multicoloured	2·50	2·50
2724	**1968**	64p	multicoloured	2·50	2·50
2725	**1969**	72p	multicoloured	4·50	4·50
2726	**1970**	72p	multicoloured	4·50	4·50
Set of 6				15·00	15·00
MS2727 115 × 104 mm. Nos. 2721/6			15·00	15·00	
First Day Cover					16·00

Nos. 2721/6 were only issued in the £7·49 'World of Invention'
booklet and in **MS**2727.

1971 William
Wilberforce and
Anti-Slavery
Poster

1972 Olaudah
Equiano and Map
of Slave Trade
Routes

1973 Granville
Sharp and Slave Ship

1974 Thomas Clarkson
and Diagram of Slave
Ship

1975 Hannah More
and Title Page of
'The Sorrows of
Yamba'

1976 Ignatius
Sancho and
Trade/Business Card

Bicentenary of the Abolition of the Slave Trade

2007 (22 Mar.) Two phosphor bands. Perf 14½

2728	**1971**	(1st)	multicoloured	1·25	90
		a. Horiz pair.			
		Nos. 2728/9	2·50	2·50	
2729	**1972**	(1st)	multicoloured	1·25	90
2730	**1973**	50p	multicoloured	1·50	1·20
		a. Horiz pair.			
		Nos. 2730/1	3·00	3·00	
2731	**1974**	50p	multicoloured	1·50	1·20
2732	**1975**	72p	multicoloured	2·00	1·80
		a. Horiz pair.			
		Nos. 2732/3	4·00	4·00	
2733	**1976**	72p	multicoloured	2·00	1·80
Set of 6				8·50	8·50
First Day Cover					10·00

Presentation Pack (P.O. Pack No. 396)	10·00	
PHQ Cards (set of 6) (297)	4·50	14·00
Set of 3 Gutter Strips of 4	17·00	
Set of 3 Traffic Light Gutter Strips of 4	19·00	

Nos. 2728/9, 2730/1 and 2732/3 were each printed together, se-tenant, in horizontal pairs throughout the sheets.

For the miniature sheet entitled 'Celebrating England', issued 23 April 2007, see Regionals section.

1977 Ice Cream Cone

1978 Sandcastle

1979 Carousel Horse

1980 Beach Huts

1981 Deckchairs

1982 Beach Donkeys

'Beside the Seaside'

2007 (15 May) Two phosphor bands. Perf 14½

2734	**1977**	(1st) multicoloured	1·25	90
2735	**1978**	46p multicoloured	1·40	1·20
2736	**1979**	48p multicoloured	1·40	1·30
2737	**1980**	54p multicoloured	1·60	1·40
2738	**1981**	69p multicoloured	2·00	1·80
2739	**1982**	78p multicoloured	2·25	2·00
Set of 6			9·00	8·00
First Day Cover				9·00
Presentation Pack (P.O. Pack No. 397)			11·00	
PHQ Cards (set of 6) (298)			4·50	14·00
Set of 6 Gutter Pairs			20·00	

For Type **1977**, but self-adhesive , see No. 2848.

1983

New Wembley Stadium, London. Miniature Sheet

2007 (17 May) Sheet 113×103 mm containing design as Type **1593** but with 'WORLD CUP 2002' inscription omitted, and Nos. EN6 and EN18, each×2. One centre band (2nd) or two phosphor bands (others). Perf 14½×14 (1st) or 15×14 (with one elliptical hole in each vertical side) (2nd, 78p)

MS2740 **1983** (1st) As Type **1593**; (2nd) No. EN6×2; 78p No. EN18×2 and one central stamp-size label	8·00	8·00
First Day Cover		9·00

The design as Type **1593** was also issued in sheets of 20 with se-tenant labels showing scenes from Wembley Stadium.

1984 Arnold Machin

1985 1967 4d. Machin

1986

40th Anniversary of the First Machin Definitives. Booklet stamps and Miniature Sheet

2007 (5 June) 'All-over' phosphor (1st) or Two phosphor bands (others) Perf 14½ (1st) or 15×14 (with one elliptical hole in each vertical side) (£1)

2741	**1984**	(1st) multicoloured	4·50	4·50
2742	**1985**	(1st) multicoloured	4·50	4·50
MS2743	127×73 mm. **1986** Nos. 2741/2, Y1743 and Y1744		12·00	12·00
First Day Cover (MS2743)				13·00
Presentation Pack (MS2743) (P.O. Pack No. 398)			14·00	

PHQ Cards (*Set of* 3) (Nos. 2741/
    MS2743) (299)   3·00   14·00   ☐ ☐

Nos. 2741/2 were only issued in the £7·66 'The Machin, the Making of a Masterpiece' booklet, No. DX39, and in **MS**2743.

Stamps as Type **1984** but with phosphor frames were issued in sheets of 20 with *se-tenant* labels showing the 1967–9 Machin definitives.

1987 Stirling Moss in Vanwall 2.5L, 1957

1988 Graham Hill in BRM P57, 1962

1989 Jim Clark in Lotus 25 Climax, 1963

1990 Jackie Stewart in Tyrrell 006/2, 1973

1991 James Hunt in McLaren M23, 1976

1992 Nigel Mansell in Williams FW11, 1986

50th Anniversary of the British Grand Prix, Silverstone. Racing Cars

2007 (3 July) Two phosphor bands. Perf 14½

2744	**1987**	(1st)	multicoloured	1·25	90	☐ ☐
2745	**1988**	(1st)	multicoloured	1·25	90	☐ ☐
2746	**1989**	54p	multicoloured	1·60	1·50	☐ ☐
2747	**1990**	54p	multicoloured	1·60	1·50	☐ ☐
2748	**1991**	78p	multicoloured	2·25	2·00	☐ ☐
2749	**1992**	78p	multicoloured	2·25	2·00	☐ ☐
Set of 6				9·00	8·00	☐ ☐
First Day Cover					10·00	☐
Presentation Pack (P.O. Pack No. 399)			11·00			☐
PHQ Cards (*set of* 6) (300)			4·50	14·00		☐ ☐
Set of 6 Gutter Pairs			19·00			☐

1993 Harry Potter and the Philosopher's Stone

1994 Harry Potter and the Chamber of Secrets

1995 Harry Potter and the prisoner of Azkaban

1996 Harry Potter and the Goblet of Fire

1997 Harry Potter and the Order of the Phoenix

1998 Harry Potter and the Half-Blood Prince

1999 Harry Potter and the Deathly Hallows

2000 Crests of Hogwarts School and its Four Houses

Publication of Final Book in the Harry Potter Series

2007 (17 July)

(a) Book Covers. 'All-over' phosphor. Perf 14½

2750	**1993**	(1st)	multicoloured	1·25	90	☐ ☐
		a.	Horiz strip of 7.			
			Nos. 2750/6	9·00	8·00	☐ ☐
2751	**1994**	(1st)	multicoloured	1·25	90	☐ ☐
2752	**1995**	(1st)	multicoloured	1·25	90	☐ ☐
2753	**1996**	(1st)	multicoloured	1·25	90	☐ ☐
2754	**1997**	(1st)	multicoloured	1·25	90	☐ ☐
2755	**1998**	(1st)	multicoloured	1·25	90	☐ ☐
2756	**1999**	(1st)	multicoloured	1·25	90	☐ ☐
Set of 7				9·00	8·00	☐ ☐
First Day Cover					9·00	☐
Presentation Pack (Nos. 2750)						
	(P.O. Pack No. M16)		17·00			☐
PHQ Cards (*set of* 13) (HP)			11·00	27·00		☐ ☐
Gutter Block of 14			20·00			☐
Traffic Light Gutter Block of 14			22·00			☐

(b) Crests of Hogwarts School and its Four Houses. Multicoloured. Two phosphor bands. Perf 15 × 14

MS2757 123 × 70 mm. **2000** (1st)
    Gryffindor; (1st) Hufflepuff; (1st)
    Hogwarts; (1st) Ravenclaw; (1st)
    Slytherin   6·00   6·00   ☐ ☐
First Day Cover   7·50   ☐

Nos. 2750/6 were printed together, *se-tenant*, as horizontal strips of seven stamps in sheets of 56 (2 panes 7 × 4).

The complete miniature sheet is shown on one of the thirteen PHQ cards with the others depicting the individual stamps including those from **MS**2757.

Stamps as those within **MS**2757 but self-adhesive were issued in sheets of 20 containing the five designs *se-tenant* with labels depicting either magic spells or personal photographs. The magic spells labels are printed in thermochromic ink which fades temporarily when exposed to heat, revealing the meaning of the spells.

2001 Scout and Camp Fire

2002 Scouts Rock climbing

2003 Scout planting Tree

2004 Adult Volunteer teaching Scout Archery

2005 Scouts learning gliding

2006 Scouts from Many Nations

Centenary of Scouting and 21st World Scout Jamboree, Chelmsford, Essex

2007 (26 July) Two phosphor bands. Perf 14½ × 14

2758	**2001**	(1st)	multicoloured	1·25	90
2759	**2002**	46p	multicoloured	1·40	1·20
2760	**2003**	48p	multicoloured	1·40	1·20
2761	**2004**	54p	multicoloured	1·60	1·40
2762	**2005**	69p	multicoloured	2·00	1·80
2763	**2006**	78p	multicoloured	2·25	2·00
Set of 6				9·00	8·00
First Day Cover					10·00
Presentation Pack (P.O. Pack No. 400)			11·00	
PHQ Cards (set of 6) (301)			4·50	14·00
Set of 6 Gutter Pairs			20·00	

The 1st class and 48p values include the 'EUROPA' emblem.

2007 White-tailed Eagle

2008 Bearded Tit

2009 Red Kite

2010 Cirl Bunting

2011 Marsh Harrier

2012 Avocet

2013 Bittern

2014 Dartford Warbler

2015 Corncrake

2016 Peregrine Falcon

'Action for Species' (1st series). Birds

2007 (4 Sept.) Two phosphor bands. Perf 14½

2764	**2007**	(1st)	multicoloured	1·25	90
	a.	Block of 10.			
		Nos. 2764/73		14·00	10·00
2765	**2008**	(1st)	multicoloured	1·25	90
2766	**2009**	(1st)	multicoloured	1·25	90
2767	**2010**	(1st)	multicoloured	1·25	90
2768	**2011**	(1st)	multicoloured	1·25	90
2769	**2012**	(1st)	multicoloured	1·25	90
2770	**2013**	(1st)	multicoloured	1·25	90
2771	**2014**	(1st)	multicoloured	1·25	90
2772	**2015**	(1st)	multicoloured	1·25	90
2773	**2016**	(1st)	multicoloured	1·25	90
Set of 10				14·00	10·00
First Day Cover					11·00
Presentation Pack (P.O. Pack No. 401)			15·00	
PHQ Cards (set of 10) (302)			9·00	18·00
Gutter Block of 20			30·00	

Nos. 2764/73 were printed together, *se-tenant*, in blocks of ten (5 × 2) in sheets of 60 (2 panes of 30).

2017 NCO, Royal Military Police, 1999

2018 Tank Commander, 5th Royal Tank Regiment, 1944

2019 Observer, Royal Field Artillery, 1917

2020 Rifleman, 95th Rifles, 1813

2021 Grenadier, Royal Regiment of Foot of Ireland, 1704

2022 Trooper, Earl of Oxford's Horse, 1661

Military Uniforms (1st series). British Army Uniforms

2007 (20 Sept.) Two phosphor bands. Perf 14½

2774	**2017**	(1st)	multicoloured	1·25	90	☐ ☐
		a.	Horiz strip of 3.			
			Nos. 2774/6	4·00	4·00	☐ ☐
2775	**2018**	(1st)	multicoloured	1·25	90	☐ ☐
2776	**2019**	(1st)	multicoloured	1·25	90	☐ ☐
2777	**2020**	78p	multicoloured	2·00	2·00	☐ ☐
		a.	Horiz strip of 3.			
			Nos. 2777/9	7·00	7·00	☐ ☐
2778	**2021**	78p	multicoloured	2·00	2·00	☐ ☐
2779	**2022**	78p	multicoloured	2·00	2·00	☐ ☐
Set of 6				10·00	10·00	☐ ☐
First Day Cover					11·00	☐
Presentation Pack (P.O. Pack No. 402)				12·00		☐
PHQ Cards (*set of* 6) (303)				4·50	14·00	☐ ☐
Set of 2 Gutter Strips of 6				22·00		☐
Set of 2 Traffic Light Gutter Strips of 6				24·00		☐

Nos. 2774/6 and 2777/9 were each printed together, *se-tenant*, in horizontal strips of three stamps in sheets of 60 (2 panes 6×5) and were also issued in the £7·66 'British Army Uniforms' booklet, No. DX40.

2023 Leaving St. Paul's Cathedral after Thanksgiving Service, 2006

2024 Inspecting King's Troop Royal Horse Artillery, Regents Park, 1997

2025 At Garter Ceremony, Windsor, 1980

2026 At Royal Ascot, 1969

2027 At Premiere of 'The Guns of Navarone', 1961

2028 At Clydebank, 1947

2029 Photographs of the Royal Family

Royal Diamond Wedding Anniversary of Queen Elizabeth II and Duke of Edinburgh

2007 (16 Oct.)

(a) Ordinary gum. Litho Cartor. 'All-over' phosphor. Perf 14½ × 14

2780	**2023**	(1st)	blackish-brown and black	1·25	90	☐ ☐
		a.	Horiz pair. Nos. 2780/1	2·50	2·00	☐ ☐
2781	**2024**	(1st)	blackish-brown and black	1·25	90	☐ ☐
2782	**2025**	54p	blackish-brown and black	1·50	1·40	☐ ☐
		a.	Horiz pair. Nos. 2782/3	3·00	3·00	☐ ☐
2783	**2026**	54p	blackish-brown and black	1·50	1·40	☐ ☐
2784	**2027**	78p	blackish-brown and black	2·25	2·00	☐ ☐
		a.	Horiz pair. Nos. 2784/5	4·50	4·50	☐ ☐
2785	**2028**	78p	blackish-brown and black	2·25	2·00	☐ ☐
Set of 6				9·00	9·00	☐ ☐
First Day Cover					11·00	☐
Presentation Pack (Nos. 2780/**MS**2786)						
		(P.O. Pack No. 403)		17·00		☐
PHQ Cards (*set of* 11) (304)				9·00	27·00	☐ ☐
Set of 3 Gutter Strips of 4				19·00		☐

Nos. 2780/1, 2782/3 and 2784/5 were each printed together, *se-tenant*, in horizontal pairs throughout the sheets.

(b) Self-adhesive. Gravure Walsall. Two phosphor bands. Perf 14½

MS2786	**2029**	115 × 89 mm. (1st) Royal family, Balmoral, 1972; (1st) Queen and Prince Philip, Buckingham Palace, 2007; 69p. Royal family, Windsor Castle, 1965; 78p. Princess Elizabeth, Prince Philip, Prince Charles and Princess Anne, Clarence House, 1951	6·00	6·00	☐ ☐
First Day Cover				7·00	☐

The complete miniature sheet is shown on one of the eleven PHQ cards with the others depicting individual stamps including those from **MS**2786.

2030 'Madonna and Child' (William Dyce), c 1827

2031 'The Madonna of Humility' (Lippo di Dalmasio), c 1390–1400

Christmas (1st issue).
Paintings of the Madonna and Child

2007 (6 Nov.) One centre band (2nd) or two phosphor bands (1st). Self-adhesive. Die-cut perf 15×14 (with one elliptical hole in each vertical side)

2787 **2030** (2nd) multicoloured	1·25	1·00	□ □
2788 **2031** (1st) multicoloured	1·75	1·10	□ □
First Day Cover		4·00	□

2032 Angel playing Trumpet ('PEACE')

2033 Angel playing Lute ('GOODWILL')

2034 Angel playing Trumpet ('PEACE')

2035 Angel playing Lute ('GOODWILL')

2036 Angel playing Flute ('JOY')

2037 Angel playing Tambourine ('GLORY')

Christmas (2nd issue). Angels

2007 (6 Nov.) One centre band (2nd) or two phosphor bands (others). Perf 15×14

(a) Self-adhesive

2789 **2032** (2nd) multicoloured	1·00	80	□ □
2790 **2033** (1st) multicoloured	1·25	90	□ □
2791 **2034** (2nd Large) multicoloured	1·50	1·00	□ □
2792 **2035** (1st Large) multicoloured	2·00	2·00	□ □
2793 **2036** 78p multicoloured	2·25	2·00	□ □
2794 **2037** £1·24 multicoloured	3·75	3·50	□ □
Set of 6	10·00	10·00	□ □
First Day Cover		11·00	□
Presentation Pack (Nos. 2787/94) (P.O. Pack No. 404)	14·00		□
PHQ Cards (set of 9) (305)	8·00	18·00	□ □

(b) Ordinary gum

MS2795 115×102 mm.

As Nos. 2789/94	10·00	10·00	□ □
First Day Cover		11·00	□

The phosphor bands on Nos. 2791/2 are at the centre and right of each stamp.

The PHQ cards depict Nos. 2787/94 and **MS**2795.

The 2nd class, 1st class and 78p stamps were also issued in sheets of 20 printed in lithography instead of gravure containing eight 1st class, eight 2nd class and four 78p stamps, each stamp accompanied by a se-tenant label. Separate sheets of 20 1st, 20 2nd or ten 78p were available with personal photographs.

2038 Lest We Forget

'Lest We Forget' (2nd series). 90th Anniversary of the Battle of Passchendaele. Miniature Sheet

2007 (8 Nov.) Litho. Sheet 124×70 mm containing new stamp as No. 2884 and designs as Nos. EN18, W110, S121 and NI128. Two phosphor bands. Perf 14½ (1st) or 15×14 (with one elliptical hole in each vertical side) (78p)

MS2796 **2038** (1st) Soldiers in poppy flower; 78p.×4	10·00	10·00	□ □
First Day Cover		11·00	□
Presentation Pack (P.O. Pack No. 405)	12·00		□

The 1st class stamp was also issued in sheets of 20 with se-tenant labels showing soldiers and their letters home and, on 6 Nov. 2008 in a se-tenant strip of three, see No. 2884.

Year Pack

2007 (8 Nov.) Comprises Nos. 2686/92, 2699/2720, 2728/39, **MS**2743/94 and **MS**2796

CP2796a Year Pack	£190	□

Post Office Yearbook

2007 (8 Nov.) Comprises Nos. 2686/92, 2699/2720, 2728/39, **MS**2743/94 and **MS**2796

YB2796a Yearbook	£130	□

Miniature Sheet Collection

2007 (8 Nov.) Comprises Nos. **MS**2692, **MS**2727, **MS**2740, **MS**2743, **MS**2757, **MS**2786 and **MS**2795/6

MS2796a Miniature Sheet Collection	75·00	□

2039 Casino Royale

2040 Dr. No

2041 Goldfinger

2042 Diamonds are Forever

2043 *For Your Eyes Only*

2044 *From Russia with Love*

Birth Centenary of Ian Fleming (author of James Bond books) (1st issue). Book Covers

2008 (8 Jan.) Two phosphor bands. Perf 14½ × 14

2797	**2039**	(1st)	multicoloured	1·25	90	☐	☐
2798	**2040**	(1st)	multicoloured	1·25	90	☐	☐
2799	**2041**	54p	multicoloured	1·60	1·40	☐	☐
2800	**2042**	54p	multicoloured	1·60	1·40	☐	☐
2801	**2043**	78p	multicoloured	2·25	2·00	☐	☐
2802	**2044**	78p	multicoloured	2·25	2·00	☐	☐
Set of 6				8·50	8·00	☐	
First Day Cover					9·00	☐	
Presentation Pack (P.O. Pack No. 407)				11·00		☐	
PHQ Cards (*set of 7*) (306)				6·00	20·00	☐	☐
Set of 6 Gutter Pairs				19·00		☐	
MS2803 189 × 68 mm. Nos. 2797/2802				9·00	9·00	☐	☐
First Day Cover					11·00		☐

No. 2797/2802 were also issued in the £7·40 'Ian Fleming's James Bond' booklet No DX41.

The seven PHQ cards depict the individual stamps and **MS**2803.

No. 2804 is vacant.

Birth Centenary of Ian Fleming (author of James Bond books) (2nd issue). Booklet stamps

2008 (8 Jan.) Design as Type **1517** but printed in lithography. Two phosphor bands. Perf 14½

2805	**1517**	(1st)	multicoloured	4·25	4·25	☐	☐

No. 2805 was only issued in the £7·40 'Ian Fleming's James Bond' booklet, No. DX41. For White Ensign stamp from this booklet see No. 2581.

2045 Assistance Dog carrying Letter (Labrador 'Rowan')

2046 Mountain Rescue Dog (Cross-bred 'Merrick')

2047 Police Dog (German Shepherd 'Max')

2048 Customs Dog (Springer Spaniel 'Max')

2049 Sheepdog (Border Collie 'Bob')

2050 Guide Dog (Labrador 'Warwick')

Working Dogs

2008 (5 Feb.) Two phosphor bands. Perf 14½

2806	**2045**	(1st)	multicoloured	1·25	90	☐	☐
2807	**2046**	46p	multicoloured	1·20	1·20	☐	☐
2808	**2047**	48p	multicoloured	1·20	1·20	☐	☐
2809	**2048**	54p	multicoloured	1·40	1·40	☐	☐
2810	**2049**	69p	multicoloured	1·80	1·80	☐	☐
2811	**2050**	78p	multicoloured	2·00	2·00	☐	☐
Set of 6				8·00	8·00	☐	
First Day Cover					10·00	☐	
Presentation Pack (P.O. Pack No. 408)				10·00		☐	
PHQ Cards (*set of 6*) (307)				4·50	14·00	☐	☐
Set of 6 Gutter Pairs				18·00		☐	

The 1st value includes the 'EUROPA' emblem.

2051 Henry IV (1399–1413)

2052 Henry V (1413–1422)

2053 Henry VI (1422–1461 & 1470–1471)

2054 Edward IV (1461–1470 & 1471–1473)

2055 Edward V (1483)

2056 Richard III (1483–1485)

2057 The Age of Lancaster and York

Kings and Queens (1st series). Houses of Lancaster and York

2008 (28 Feb.) Two phosphor bands. Perf 14½

2812	**2051**	(1st)	multicoloured	1·25	90	☐	☐
2813	**2052**	(1st)	multicoloured	1·25	90	☐	☐
2814	**2053**	54p	multicoloured	1·40	1·40	☐	☐
2815	**2054**	54p	multicoloured	1·40	1·40	☐	☐

2816 **2055**	69p	multicoloured	1·80	1·80	☐	☐	
2817 **2056**	69p	multicoloured	1·80	1·80	☐	☐	
Set of 6			8·00	8·00	☐	☐	
First Day Cover				10·00		☐	
Presentation Pack (Nos. 2812/**MS**2818)			17·00				
(P.O. Pack No. 409)					☐		
PHQ Cards (set of 11) (308)			9·00	27·00	☐	☐	
Set of 6 Gutter Pairs			18·00		☐		
Set of 6 Traffic Light Gutter Blocks of 4			38·00		☐		

MS2818 123×70 mm. **2057** (1st)
Owain Glyn Dwr ('Parliament'),
1404; (1st) Henry V's triumph
at Battle of Agincourt, 1415;
78p. Yorkish victory at Battle of
Tewkesbury, 1471; 78p. William
Caxton, first English printer, 1477   7·00   7·00 ☐ ☐

First Day Cover   8·00   ☐

The complete miniature sheet is shown on one of the eleven PHQ cards with the others depicting individual stamps including those from **MS**2818.

'Smilers' (4th series). Booklet stamps

2008 (28 Feb.) Designs as Nos. 2567/8, 2570 and 2675/7. Self-adhesive. Two phosphor bands. Die-cut perf 15×14 (with one elliptical hole in each vertical side)

2819 **1569**	(1st)	multicoloured	8·00	8·00	☐	☐
	a. Booklet pane. Nos.					
	2819/24		42·00		☐	
2820 **1842**	(1st)	multicoloured	8·00	8·00	☐	☐
2821 **1517**	(1st)	multicoloured	8·00	8·00	☐	☐
2822 **1932**	(1st)	multicoloured	8·00	8·00	☐	☐
2823 **1933**	(1st)	multicoloured	8·00	8·00	☐	☐
2824 **1934**	(1st)	multicoloured	8·00	8·00	☐	☐
Set of 6			42·00	42·00	☐	☐

Nos. 2819/24 were issued in £2·04 booklets in which the surplus backing paper around each stamp was removed.

Nos. 2820 and 2822 were reissued on 28 October 2008 in separate sheets of ten or 20 with circular se-tenant labels showing the Almond Blossom fairy (2820), Mr. Men or Noddy (2822).

Nos. 2819, 2820 and 2822 were issued again on 30 April 2009 in separate sheets of ten or 20 with circular se-tenant labels showing Jeremy Fisher (2819), Wild Cherry fairy (2820), Little Miss Sunshine or Big Ears (2822).

No. 2819 was issued in sheets of 20 with se-tenant labels on 8 May 2010 for London 2010 Festival of Stamps, on 28 July 2011 for Philanippon '11 International Stamp Exhibition, Yokohama, on 18 June 2012 for Indonesia 2012 International Stamp Exhibition, Jakarta, on 10 May 2013 for Australia 2013 World Stamp Exhibition, on 2 August 2013 for Bangkok 2013 World Stamp Exhibition on 1 December 2014 for Kuala Lumpur 2014 FIP Exhibition on 13 May 2015 for London 2015 Europhilex International Stamp Exhibition, on 28 May 2016 for New York World Stamp Show and on 24 May 2017 for Finlandia 2017 FIP Exhibition, Tampere.

Nos. 2821 (and Nos. 2822/3) were issued, together with Nos. 2569, 2572, 2674 and four designs from **MS**3024, on 8 May 2010 in sheets of 20 with se-tenant greetings labels.

No. 2821 was issued on 12 February 2011 in sheets of 20 with se-tenant labels for Indipex International Stamp Exhibition.

No. 2821 was issued on 30 March 2011 in sheets of ten with se-tenant labels for the 50th Anniversary of the Jaguar E-type car.

No. 2823 was issued in sheets of 20 with se-tenant labels on 20 January 2012 (Lunar New Year – Year of the Dragon), 7 February 2013 (Lunar New Year – Year of the Snake), 10 December 2013 (Lunar New Year – Year of the Horse), 19 November 2014 (Lunar New Year – Year of the Sheep), 9 November 2015 (Lunar New Year – Year of the Monkey), 15 November 2016 (Lunar New Year – Year of the Rooster) and 16 November 2017 (Lunar New Year – Year of the Dog).

All these sheets were printed in lithography instead of gravure.

For the miniature sheet entitled 'Celebrating Northern Ireland', issued 11 March 2008, see the Regionals section.

2058 Lifeboat, Barra

2059 Lifeboat approaching Dinghy, Appledore

2060 Helicopter Winchman, Portland

2061 Inshore lifeboat, St. Ives

2062 Rescue Helicopter, Lee-on-Solent

2063 Launch of Lifeboat, Dinbych-y-Pysgod, Tenby

Rescue at Sea

2008 (13 Mar.) 'All-over' phosphor. Perf 14½×14*

2825 **2058**	(1st)	multicoloured	1·25	90	☐	☐	
2826 **2059**	46p	multicoloured	1·20	1·20	☐	☐	
2827 **2060**	48p	multicoloured	1·20	1·20	☐	☐	
2828 **2061**	54p	multicoloured	1·40	1·40	☐	☐	
2829 **2062**	69p	multicoloured	1·80	1·80	☐	☐	
2830 **2063**	78p	multicoloured	2·00	2·00	☐	☐	
Set of 6			8·00	8·00	☐	☐	
First Day Cover				10·00		☐	
Presentation Pack (P.O. Pack No. 411)			10·00		☐		
PHQ Cards (set of 6) (309)			4·50	14·00	☐	☐	
Set of 6 Gutter Pairs			18·00		☐		

*Nos. 2825/30 have interrupted perforations along the top and bottom edges of the stamps, the gaps in the perforations forming the three dots and three dashes that spell out 'SOS' in morse code.

2064 Lysandra bellargus (Adonis Blue)

2065 Coenagrion mercuriale (Southern Damselfly)

2066 Formica rufibarbis (Red-barbed Ant)

2067 Pareulype berberata (Barberry Carpet Moth)

2068 *Lucanus cervus*
(Stag Beetle)

2069 *Cryptocephalus coryli*
(Hazel Pot Beetle)

2070 *Gryllus campestris*
(Field Cricket)

2071 *Hesperia comma*
(Silver-Spotted Skipper)

2072 *Pseudepipona herrichii*
(Purbeck Mason Wasp)

2073 *Gnorimus nobilis*
(Noble Chafer)

'Action for Species' (2nd series). Insects

2008 (15 Apr.) Phosphor background. Perf 14½

2831	**2064**	(1st)	multicoloured	1·25	90	☐ ☐
	a.	Block of 10.				
		Nos. 2831/40		14·00	10·00	☐ ☐
2832	**2065**	(1st)	multicoloured	1·25	90	☐ ☐
2833	**2066**	(1st)	multicoloured	1·25	90	☐ ☐
2834	**2067**	(1st)	multicoloured	1·25	90	☐ ☐
2835	**2068**	(1st)	multicoloured	1·25	90	☐ ☐
2836	**2069**	(1st)	multicoloured	1·25	90	☐ ☐
2837	**2070**	(1st)	multicoloured	1·25	90	☐ ☐
2838	**2071**	(1st)	multicoloured	1·25	90	☐ ☐
2839	**2072**	(1st)	multicoloured	1·25	90	☐ ☐
2840	**2073**	(1st)	multicoloured	1·25	90	☐ ☐
Set of 10				14·00	10·00	☐ ☐
First Day Cover					11·00	☐
Presentation Pack (P.O. Pack No. 412)				16·00		☐
PHQ Cards (*set of 10*) (310)				9·00	16·00	☐ ☐
Gutter Block of 20				30·00		☐

Nos. 2831/40 were printed together, *se-tenant*, in blocks of ten (5 × 2) in sheets of 60 (2 panes of 30).

2074 Lichfield Cathedral

2075 Belfast Cathedral

2076 Gloucester Cathedral

2077 St. David's Cathedral

2078 Westminster Cathedral

2079 St. Magnus Cathedral, Kirkwall, Orkney

2080 St. Paul's Cathedral

Cathedrals

2008 (13 May) 'All-over' phosphor. Perf 14½

2841	**2074**	(1st)	multicoloured	1·25	90	☐ ☐
2842	**2075**	48p	multicoloured	1·20	1·20	☐ ☐
2843	**2076**	50p	multicoloured	1·30	1·30	☐ ☐
2844	**2077**	56p	multicoloured	1·40	1·40	☐ ☐
2845	**2078**	72p	multicoloured	1·80	1·80	☐ ☐
2846	**2079**	81p	multicoloured	2·00	2·00	☐ ☐
Set of 6				8·00	8·00	☐
First Day Cover					10·00	☐
Presentation Pack (Nos. 2841/**MS**2847)						
		(P.O. Pack No. 413)		20·00		☐
PHQ Cards (*set of 11*) (311)				9·00	27·00	☐ ☐
Set of 6 Gutter Pairs				17·00		☐
Set of 6 Traffic Light Gutter Pairs				20·00		☐

MS2847 115 × 89 mm. **2080** (1st)
multicoloured; (1st) multicoloured;
81p. multicoloured; 81p.

multicoloured. Perf 14½ × 14	7·00	7·00	☐ ☐
First Day Cover		8·00	☐

No. **MS**2847 commemorates the 300th anniversary of St. Paul's Cathedral.

The complete miniature sheet is shown on one of the eleven PHQ cards with the others depicting individual stamps including those from **MS**2847.

'Beside the Seaside' (2nd series)

2008 (13 May) As Type **1977** but self-adhesive. Two phosphor bands. Die-cut perf 14½

2848	**1977**	(1st)	multicoloured	4·75	4·75	☐ ☐

No. 2848 was only issued in £2·16 booklets.

2081 'Carry on Sergeant'

2082 'Dracula'

2083 'Carry on Cleo'

2084 'The Curse of Frankenstein'

2085 'Carry on Screaming'

2086 'The Mummy'

Posters for Carry On and Hammer Horror Films

2008 (10 June) Two phosphor bands. Perf 14

2849	**2081**	(1st)	multicoloured	1·25	90	
2850	**2082**	48p	multicoloured	1·20	1·20	
2851	**2083**	50p	multicoloured	1·30	1·30	
2852	**2084**	56p	multicoloured	1·40	1·40	
2853	**2085**	72p	multicoloured	1·80	1·80	
2854	**2086**	81p	multicoloured	2·00	2·00	
Set of 6				8·00	8·00	
First Day Cover					10·00	
Presentation Pack (P.O. Pack No. 414)			10·00			
PHQ Cards (*set of* 6) (312)			4·50	13·00		
PHQ Cards ("brick wall" background) and Stamps Set			9·00			
Set of 6 Gutter Pairs			18·00			

Nos. 2849/54 commemorate the 50th anniversary of 'Dracula' and the first Carry On film ('Carry on Sergeant').

2087 Red Arrows, Dartmouth Regatta Airshow, 2006

2088 RAF Falcons Parachute Team, Biggin Hill, 2006

2089 Spectator watching Red Arrows, Farnborough

2090 Prototype Avro Vulcan Bombers and Avro 707s, Farnborough, 1953

2091 Parachutist Robert Wyndham on Wing of Avro 504, 1933

2092 Air Race rounding the Beacon, Hendon, c. 1912

Air Displays

2008 (17 July) Gravure. Two phosphor bands. Perf 14½ × 14

2855	**2087**	(1st)	multicoloured	1·25	90	
2856	**2088**	48p	multicoloured	1·20	1·20	
2857	**2089**	50p	multicoloured	1·30	1·30	

2858	**2090**	56p	multicoloured	1·40	1·40	
2859	**2091**	72p	multicoloured	1·80	1·80	
2860	**2092**	81p	multicoloured	2·00	2·00	
Set of 6				8·00	8·00	
First Day Cover					10·00	
Presentation Pack (P.O. Pack No. 415)			11·00			
PHQ Cards (*set of* 6) (313)			4·50	13·00		
Set of 6 Gutter Pairs			18·00			

The 1st class stamp was also issued in sheets of 20 with *se-tenant* labels and, on 18 September, in booklets, perf 14 both issues printed in lithography instead of gravure. For the booklet stamps, see also No. 2869.

2093 Landmarks of Beijing and London

Handover of Olympic Flag from Beijing to London. Miniature Sheet

2008 (22 Aug.) Sheet 115 × 76 mm. Multicoloured. Phosphorised paper. Perf 14½

MS2861 **2093** (1st) National Stadium, Beijing; (1st) London Eye; (1st) Tower of London; (1st) Corner Tower of the Forbidden City, Beijing	8·00	8·00	
First Day Cover		9·00	
Presentation Pack (P.O. Pack No. M17)	35·00		
PHQ Cards (*set of* 5) (OGH)	4·00	15·00	

The Olympic rings overprinted on **MS**2861 are in silk-screen varnish.

The five PHQ cards show the four individual stamps and the complete miniature sheet.

2094 Drum Major, RAF Central Band, 2007

2095 Helicopter Rescue Winchman, 1984

2096 Hawker Hunter Pilot, 1951

2097 Lancaster Air Gunner, 1944

2098 WAAF Plotter, 1940

2099 Pilot, 1918

Military Uniforms (2nd series). RAF Uniforms

2008 (18 Sept.) Two phosphor bands. Perf 14

2862	**2094**	(1st)	multicoloured	1·25	90	☐	☐
	a.	Horiz strip of 3.					
		Nos. 2862/4		4·00	4·00	☐	☐
2863	**2095**	(1st)	multicoloured	1·25	90	☐	☐
2864	**2096**	(1st)	multicoloured	1·25	90	☐	☐
2865	**2097**	81p	multicoloured	2·00	2·00	☐	☐
	a.	Horiz strip of 3.					
		Nos. 2865/7		7·00	7·00	☐	☐
2866	**2098**	81p	multicoloured	2·00	2·00	☐	☐
2867	**2099**	81p	multicoloured	2·00	2·00	☐	☐
Set of 6				10·00	10·00	☐	☐
First Day Cover					11·00		☐
Presentation Pack (P.O. Pack No. 416)				12·00		☐	
PHQ Cards (set of 6) (314)				5·00	14·00	☐	☐
Set of 2 Gutter Strips of 6				21·00			
Set of 2 Traffic Light Gutter Blocks of 12				42·00			☐

Nos. 2862/4 and 2865/7 were each printed together, se-tenant, in horizontal strips of three stamps in sheets of 60 (2 panes 6×5) and were also issued in the £7·15 'RAF Uniforms, Pilot to Plane' booklet, No. DX42.

'Pilot to Plane'. RAF Uniforms. Booklet stamps

2008 (18 Sept.) Designs as Types **1307** (Spitfire from 1997 British Aircraft Designers) and **2087** (Red Arrows from 2008 Air Displays) but printed in lithography. Two phosphor bands. Perf 14

2868	**1307**	20p	multicoloured	4·00	4·00	☐	☐
2869	**2087**	(1st)	multicoloured	4·00	4·00	☐	☐

Nos. 2868/9 were only available from the £7·15 'RAF Uniforms, Pilot to Plane' booklet, No. DX42.

For the miniature sheet and booklet stamps issued 29 September 2008 to celebrate the 50th Anniversary of the Country Definitives, see the Regional section.

2100 Millicent Garrett Fawcett (suffragist)

2101 Elizabeth Garrett Anderson (physician–women's health)

2102 Marie Stopes (family planning pioneer)

2103 Eleanor Rathbone (family allowance campaigner)

2104 Claudia Jones (civil rights activist)

2105 Barbara Castle (politician–Equal Pay Act)

Women of Distinction

2008 (14 Oct.) 'All-over' phosphor. Perf 14 × 14½

2870	**2100**	(1st)	multicoloured	1·25	90	☐	☐
2871	**2101**	48p	multicoloured	1·20	1·20	☐	☐
2872	**2102**	50p	multicoloured	1·30	1·30	☐	☐
2873	**2103**	56p	multicoloured	1·40	1·40	☐	☐
2874	**2104**	72p	multicoloured	1·80	1·80	☐	☐
2875	**2105**	81p	multicoloured	2·00	2·00	☐	☐
Set of 6				8·00	8·00	☐	☐
First Day Cover					9·00		☐
Presentation Pack (P.O. Pack No. 417)				10·00		☐	
PHQ Cards (set of 6) (315)				4·50	13·00	☐	☐
Set of 6 Gutter Pairs				17·00		☐	

2106 Ugly Sisters from Cinderella

2107 Genie from Aladdin

2108 Ugly Sisters from Cinderella

2109 Captain Hook from Peter Pan

2110 Genie from Aladdin

2111 Wicked Queen from Snow White

Christmas. Pantomimes

2008 (4 Nov.) One centre band (2nd) or two phosphor bands (others). Perf 15 × 14

(a) Self-adhesive

2876	**2106**	(2nd)	multicoloured	1·25	70	☐	☐
2877	**2107**	(1st)	multicoloured	1·40	1·00	☐	☐
2878	**2108**	(2nd Large)	multicoloured	1·75	1·25	☐	☐
2879	**2109**	50p	multicoloured	1·75	1·40	☐	☐
2880	**2110**	(1st Large)	multicoloured	2·40	1·60	☐	☐
2881	**2111**	81p	multicoloured	2·40	2·25	☐	☐
Set of 6				10·00	7·50	☐	☐
First Day Cover					8·50		☐
Presentation Pack (P.O. Pack No. 418)				12·00		☐	
PHQ Cards (set of 7) (316)				6·00	26·00	☐	☐

(b) Ordinary gum

MS2882 114 × 102 mm.

As Nos. 2876/81		10·00	10·00	☐ ☐
First Day Cover			11·00	☐

The phosphor bands on Nos. 2878/9 are at the centre and right of each stamp.

The seven PHQ cards depict the six stamps and **MS**2882.

The 2nd class, 1st class and 81p stamps were also issued in sheets of 20 printed in lithography instead of gravure containing eight 1st class, eight 2nd class and four 81p stamps, each stamp accompanied by a se-tenant label. Separate sheets of 20 1st, 20 2nd, ten 1st or ten 81p were available with personal photographs.

2112 Seven Poppies on Barbed Wire Stems

2113 Soldiers in Poppy Flower

2114 Soldier's Face in Poppy Flower

2115 'Lest We Forget'

'Lest We Forget' (3rd series).
90th Anniversary of the Armistice

2008 (6 Nov.) Phosphor background (No. 2885) or two phosphor bands (others). Perf 14½ (1st) or 15×14 (with one elliptical hole in each vertical side) (81p)

2883	**2112**	(1st)	multicoloured	2·00	90	☐ ☐
		a.	Horiz strip of 3.			
			Nos. 2883/5	6·00	6·00	☐ ☐
2884	**2113**	(1st)	multicoloured	2·00	90	☐ ☐
2885	**2114**	(1st)	multicoloured	2·00	90	☐ ☐
Set of 3				6·00	6·00	☐ ☐
Presentation Pack (Nos. 2883/**MS**2886)						
			(P.O. Pack No. 419)	14·00		☐
PHQ Cards (*set of* 6) (317)				4·75	14·00	☐ ☐
Gutter Strip of 6				13·00		☐
Traffic Light Gutter Block of 12				26·00		☐
MS2886 124×70 mm. **2115** No. 2885						
		and as Nos. EN19, W111, S122 and				
		NI129		12·00	12·00	☐ ☐
First Day Cover					13·00	☐

Nos. 2883/5 were printed together, *se-tenant*, in horizontal strips of three stamps in sheets of 30.

No. **MS**2886 (including the Northern Ireland, Scotland and Wales stamps) is printed in lithography.

The six PHQ cards depict Nos. **MS**2685, **MS**2796 and 2883/**MS**2886.

The 1st class stamp was also issued in sheets of 20 with *se-tenant* labels.

Year Pack

2008 (6 Nov.) Comprises Nos. 2797/2802, 2806/**MS**2818, 2825/**MS**2847, 2849/67, 2870/81, **MS**2886 and **MS**NI152

CP2886a	Year Pack	£140	☐

Post Office Yearbook

2008 (6 Nov.) Comprises Nos. 2797/2802, 2806/**MS**2818, 2825/**MS**2847, 2849/67, 2870/81, **MS**2886 and **MS**N152/3

YB2886a	Yearbook	£125	☐

Miniature Sheet Collection

2008 (6 Nov.) Comprises Nos. **MS**2803, **MS**2818, **MS**2847, **MS**2861, **MS**2882, **MS**2886 and **MS**NI110/11

MS2886a Miniature Sheet Collection 75·00 ☐

2116 Supermarine Spitfire (R. J. Mitchell)

2117 Mini Skirt (Mary Quant)

2118 Mini (Sir Alec Issigonis)

2119 Anglepoise Lamp (George Carwardine)

2120 Concorde (Aérospatiale-BAC)

2121 K2 Telephone Kiosk (Sir Giles Gilbert Scott)

2122 Polypropylene Chair (Robin Day)

2123 Penguin Books (Edward Young)

2124 London Underground Map

2125 Routemaster Bus (design team led by AAM Durrant)

British Design Classics (1st issue)

2009 (13 Jan.) Printed in lithography. Phosphor background.
Perf 14½

2887	**2116**	(1st)	multicoloured	1·25	90	☐	☐
		a.	Block of 10. Nos.				
			2887/96	14·00	12·00	☐	☐
2888	**2117**	(1st)	multicoloured	1·25	90	☐	☐
2889	**2118**	(1st)	multicoloured	1·25	90	☐	☐
2890	**2119**	(1st)	multicoloured	1·25	90	☐	☐
2891	**2120**	(1st)	multicoloured	1·25	90	☐	☐
2892	**2121**	(1st)	multicoloured	1·25	90	☐	☐
2893	**2122**	(1st)	multicoloured	1·25	90	☐	☐
2894	**2123**	(1st)	multicoloured	1·25	90	☐	☐
2895	**2124**	(1st)	multicoloured	1·25	90	☐	☐
2896	**2125**	(1st)	multicoloured	1·25	90	☐	☐
Set of 10				14·00	12·00	☐	☐
First Day Cover					13·00		☐
Presentation Pack (P.O. Pack No. 421)				16·00		☐	
PHQ Cards (*set of* 10) (318)				9·00	20·00	☐	☐
Gutter Block of 20				30·00		☐	

Nos. 2887/96 were printed together, *se-tenant*, in blocks of
ten (2×5) throughout the sheet and also in
the £7·68 'British Design Classics' booklet,
No. DX44.

No. 2889 was also issued in sheets of 20 with *se-tenant* labels,
perforated 14×14½, on 13 January 2009.

No. 2891 was also issued in sheets of 20 with *se-tenant* labels,
perforated 14×14½, issued on 2 March 2009.

No. 2887 was also issued on 15 September 2010 in sheets of
20 with *se-tenant* labels, perforated 14×14½.

British Design Classics (2nd issue). Booklet stamp

2009 (13 Jan.) Design as Type **1589** (Concorde from 2002
Passenger Jet Aviation) but printed in lithography. Two
phosphor bands. Perf 14½

2897	**1589**	(1st)	multicoloured	10·00	10·00	☐	☐

No. 2897 was only issued in the £7·68 'British Design Classics'
booklet, No DX44.

See also Nos. 2911/15b.

For the miniature sheet entitled "Robert Burns 250th
Anniversary", issued on 22 January 2009, see the Regionals
section.

2126 Charles Darwin

2127 Marine Iguana

2128 Finches

2129 Atoll

2130 Bee Orchid

2131 Orang-utan

2132 Fauna and Map of the Galapagos Islands

Birth Bicentenary of Charles Darwin (naturalist and evolutionary theorist) (1st issue)

2009 (12 Feb.) (a) Self-adhesive. Printed in gravure. 'All-over'
phosphor. Perf 14

2898	**2126**	(1st)	multicoloured	1·25	90	☐	☐
2899	**2127**	48p	multicoloured	1·20	1·20	☐	☐
2900	**2128**	50p	multicoloured	1·30	1·30	☐	☐
2901	**2129**	56p	multicoloured	1·40	1·40	☐	☐
2902	**2130**	72p	multicoloured	1·80	1·80	☐	☐
2903	**2131**	81p	multicoloured	2·00	2·00	☐	☐
Set of 6				8·00	8·00	☐	☐
First Day Cover					10·00		☐
Presentation Pack (Nos. 2898/**MS**2904)							
		(P.O. Pack No. 423)		18·00		☐	
PHQ Cards (*set of* 11) (320)				9·00	20·00	☐	☐

(b) Ordinary gum. Printed in lithography.
Two phosphor bands. Perf 14

MS2904 115×89 mm. **2132** (1st) Flightless
Cormorant; (1st) Giant Tortoise and
Cactus Finch; 81p Marine Iguana; 81p
Floreana Mockingbird

			8·00	8·00	☐ ☐
First Day Cover				9·00	☐

Nos. 2898/2903 have 'jigsaw' perforations on the two vertical
sides.

The complete miniature sheet is shown on one of the
eleven PHQ cards with the others depicting individual stamps
including those from **MS**2904.

Birth Bicentenary of Charles Darwin (naturalist) (2nd issue). Booklet stamps

2009 (12 Feb.) Printed in gravure. 'All-over' phosphor. Perf 14

2905	**2126**	(1st)	multicoloured	5·00	6·00	☐	☐
2906	**2127**	48p	multicoloured	6·00	6·50	☐	☐
2907	**2128**	50p	multicoloured	6·50	7·00	☐	☐
2908	**2129**	56p	multicoloured	7·00	8·00	☐	☐
2909	**2130**	72p	multicoloured	7·50	8·50	☐	☐
2910	**2131**	81p	multicoloured	8·00	9·00	☐	☐
Set of 6				36·00	40·00	☐	☐

Nos. 2905/10 were only issued in the £7·75 'Charles Darwin'
booklet, No. DX46. They have 'jigsaw' perforations on both
vertical sides.

2132a

2132b

2132c

2132d

2009 (17 Feb)–**17**. Self-adhesive. Designs as T **367**, T **913/14** or T **2132a/d**. One centre band (U2957, U3001) or two bands (others). U-shaped slits. Die-cut perf 14½ × 14 (with one elliptical hole in each vertical side)

(a) Self-adhesive. As T **367**. Iridescent overprint.
Printed in gravure

U2920	1p	crimson *(3.1.13)*	50	50
U2921	2p	deep green *(3.1.13)*	60	60
U2922	5p	dull red-brown *(3.1.13)*	60	60
U2923	10p	dull orange *(3.1.13)*	70	70
U2924	20p	bright green *(3.1.13)*	80	80
U2911	50p	grey	2·00	2·00
U2925	50p	slate *(3.1.13)*	2·25	2·25
U2926	68p	deep turquoise-green *(29.3.11)*	2·60	2·60
U2927	76p	bright rose *(29.3.11)*	2·70	2·70
U2928	78p	deep mauve *(27.3.13)*	2·40	2·40
U2928a	81p	emerald *(26.3.14)*	2·40	2·40
U2929	87p	yellow-orange *(25.4.12)*	5·50	5·50
U2930	88p	orange-yellow *(27.3.13)*	3·00	3·00
U2930a	97p	bluish-violet *(26.3.14)*	3·25	3·25
U2912	£1	magenta	7·25	7·25
U2932	£1	bistre-brown *(3.1.13)*	3·25	3·25
U2932a	£1·05	grey-olive *(22.6.16)*	2·75	2·75
U2933	£1·10	yellow-olive *(29.3.11)*	3·75	3·75
U2933a	£1·17	orange-red *(21.3.17)*	3·00	3·00
U2934	£1·28	emerald *(25.4.12)*	5·50	5·50
U2934a	£1·33	orange-yellow *(24.3.15)*	3·25	3·25
U2934ab	£1·40	grey-olive *(21.3.17)*	3·25	3·25
U2934b	£1·47	lavender-grey *(26.3.14)*	3·75	3·75
U2913	£1·50	brown-red	3·25	3·25
U2934c	£1·52	bright mauve *(24.3.15)*	3·75	3·75
U2934ca	£1·57	yellow-olive *(21.3.17)*	3·75	3·75
U2935	£1·65	grey-olive *(29.3.11)*	4·75	4·75
U2936	£1·88	dull ultramarine *(27.3.13)*	5·25	5·25
U2937	£1·90	bright mauve *(25.4.12)*	5·75	5·75
U2914	£2	deep blue-green	9·00	9·00
U2939	£2.15	greenish-blue *(26.3.14)*	5·25	5·25
U2940	£2·25	deep violet *(24.3.15)*	5·50	5·50
U2940aa	£2·27	bistre *(21.3.17)*	5·50	5·50
U2940a	£2·45	emerald *(24.3.15)*	6·00	6·00
U2940ab	£2·55	deep rose-red *(23.3.17)*	6·00	6·00
U2915	£3	deep mauve	6·25	6·25
U2940b	£3·15	turquoise-blue *(24.3.15)*	7·50	7·50
U2940c	£3·30	bright magenta *(24.3.15)*	8·00	8·00
U2916	£5	azure	10·50	10·50
Set of 39			£140	£140

First Day Cover (Nos. U2941/4 and U2911/12)	14.00	
First Day Cover (Nos. U2913/16)	30.00	
First Day Cover (Nos. U2926/7, U2933, U2935)	10.50	
First Day Cover (Nos. U2929, U2934, U2937 and U3276)	14·00	
First Day Cover (Nos. U2928, U2930, U2936, U2983a and U2984a)	16·00	
First Day Cover (Nos. U2928a, U2930a, U2934b, and U2939)	17·00	
First Day Cover (Nos. U2934a, U2493c and U2940/c)	40·00	
First Day Cover (Nos. U2932a)	3·00	

First Day Cover (Nos. U2933a, U2934ab, U2934ca and U2940c)	25·00	
First Day Cover (Nos. U3920)	14·00	
Presentation Pack (Nos. U2941/4 and U2911/12) (P.O. Pack No. 82)	10.00	
Presentation Pack (Nos. U2913/16) (P.O. Pack No. 83)	30·00	
Presentation Pack (Nos. U2926/7, U2933, U2935 and U2991/5) (P.O. Pack No. 90)	17.00	
Presentation Pack (Nos. U2929, U2934, U2937, U3271 and U3276) (P.O. Pack No. 94)	13·50	
Presentation Pack (Nos. U2920/5, U2932, U2958a and U2960a (P.O. Pack No. 96)	9·00	
Presentation Pack (Nos. U2928, U2930, U2936, U2983a and U2984a)(P.O. Pack No. 97)18·00		
Presentation Pack (Nos. U2928a, U2930a, U2934b, and U2939 (P.O. Pack No. 99)	14·00	
Presentation Pack (Nos. U4239a, U2934c, and U2940/c) (P.O. Pack No. 101)	35·00	
Presentation Pack (No. U2932a) (P.O. Pack No. 103)	3·00	
Presentation Pack (Nos. U2933a, U2934ab, U2934ca, U2940ab and U2940c) (P.O. Pack No. 106)	22·00	

(b) Self-adhesive. As T **913/14**, T **1916** or T **2132a/d**. Iridescent overprint. Printed in gravure

U2957	(2nd)	bright blue *(1.7.10)*	2·40	2·40
U2958	(1st)	gold *(20.5.10)*	3·50	3·50
U3271	(1st)	slate-blue *(6.2.12)*	2·00	2·00
U2958a	(1st)	vermilion *(3.1.13)*	2·00	2·00
U3744	(1st)	bright lilac *(9.9.15)*	2·00	2·00
U958b	(1st)	bright scarlet *(11.4.17)*	2·00	2·00
U2959	(2nd Large)	bright blue *(26.1.11)*	2·75	2·75
U2960	(1st Large)	gold *(3.11.10)*	3·25	3·25
U3276	(1st Large)	slate-blue *(25.4.12)*	2·75	2·75
U2960a	(1st Large)	vermilion *(3.1.13)*	2·75	2·75
U2960b	(1st Large)	bright scarlet *(11.4.17)*	2·75	2·75
U2981	(Recorded Signed for 1st) bright orange-red and lemon *(17.11.09)*		6·50	6·50
U2983a	(Royal Mail Signed for 1st) bright orange-red and lemon *(27.3.13)*		5·25	5·25
U2982	(Recorded Signed for 1st Large) bright orange-red and lemon *(17.11.09)*		8·00	8·00
U2984a	(Royal Mail Signed for 1st Large) bright orange-red and lemon *(27.3.13)*		6·00	6·00
U2985	(Special Delivery up to 100g) blue and silver *(26.10.10)*		13·50	13·50
U2986	(Special Delivery up to 500g) blue and silver *(26.10.10)*		15·50	15.50

First Day Cover (Nos. U2981/2)	6.75	
First Day Cover (Nos. U2985/6)	30.00	
Presentation Pack (Nos. U2985/6) (P.O. Pack No. 89)	30.00	

(c) Self-adhesive. Designs as T **367**. No iridescent overprint.
Printed in gravure

U2991	1p	crimson *(8.3.11)*	75	75
U2992	2p	deep green *(8.3.11)*	50	50
U2993	5p	dull red-brown *(8.3.11)*	60	60
U2994	10p	dull orange *(8.3.11)*	70	70
U2995	20p	bright green *(8.3.11)*	1·00	1·00
Set of 5			3·25	3·25

First Day Cover (Nos. U2991/5)	3.50	

(d) Ordinary gum. Designs as T **367** and T **913/14**.
Iridescent overprint. Printed in gravure

U3001	(2nd)	bright blue (13.5.10)	4.25	4.25	☐ ☐
U3002	(1st)	gold (13.5.10)	4.50	4.50	☐ ☐
U3003	(1st)	bright scarlet (5.6.17)	2.50	2.50	☐ ☐
U3005	68p	turquoise-green (10.1.12)	4.00	4.00	☐ ☐
U3007	£1	magenta (5.6.17)	3.50	3.50	☐ ☐

(e) Ordinary gum. As T **367** and T **913/14**.
Iridescent overprint. Printed in litho

U3010	1p	crimson (9.5.13)	1·20	1·20	☐ ☐
U3011	2p	deep green (9.5.13)	1·40	1·40	☐ ☐
U3012	5p	red-brown (26.3.13)	1·50	1·50	☐ ☐
U3013	10p	dull orange (26.3.13)	1·50	1·50	☐ ☐
U3014	20p	bright green (26.3.13)	1·60	1·60	☐ ☐
U3014a	(2nd)	bright blue (17.12.15)	2·75	2·75	☐ ☐
U3015	(1st)	gold (9.9.11)	5·00	5·00	☐ ☐
U3016	(1st)	vermilion (9.5.13)	2·40	2·40	☐ ☐
U3016b	(1st)	bright scarlet (15.2.17)	2·40	2·40	☐ ☐
U3747	(1st)	bright lilac (21.4.16)	3·00	3·00	☐ ☐
U3017	50p	slate-blue (19.9.13)	3·00	3·00	☐ ☐
U3019	76p	bright rose (9.9.11)	5·50	5·50	☐ ☐
U3019a	81p	deep turquoise-green (19.2.15)	8·00	8·00	☐ ☐
U3020	87p	yellow-orange (26.3.13)	6·00	6·00	☐ ☐
U3020a	97p	bluish violet (19.2.15)	3·75	3·75	☐ ☐
U3021	£1	sepia (15.4.14)	4·50	4·50	☐ ☐
U3021b	£1·05	grey-olive (28.7.16)	3·00	3·00	☐ ☐
U3022	£1·33	orange yellow (14.5.15)	4·00	4·00	☐ ☐
U3023	£1·40	grey-green (14.12.17)	3·25	3·25	☐ ☐

(f) Ordinary gum. T **3086**. Perf 14 × 15.

U3966	£1	gold (5.6.17)	3·50	3·50	☐ ☐

(g) Ordinary gum. T **3041a**. Iridescent overprint reading '65th ANNIVERSARY of ACCESSION'. Gravure. Perf 14 × 14½.

U3920	£5	ultramarine (5.6.17)	12·00	12·00	☐ ☐
First Day Cover				15.00	☐

No. U2981 originally sold for £1·14, U2982 for £1·36, U2983 for £5.05 and U2984 for £5.50.

No. U2983a was originally sold for £1·55 (£1·70 from 2 April 2013) and U2984a was originally sold for £1·85 (£2 from 2 April 2013).

Nos. U3271 and U3276 have an iridescent overprint reading 'DIAMOND JUBILEE', and Nos. U3744 and U3747 have an iridescent overprint 'LONG TO REIGN OVER US' The others have an iridescent overprint with the words 'ROYAL MAIL' repeated throughout.

Nos. U3003/23 all come from premium booklets as follows:

U3003	£15·14 50th Anniversary the Machin Definitive
U3005	£11·47 Roald Dahl
U3007	£15·14 50th Anniversary the Machin Definitive
U3010	£11·11 Football Heroes, £14·60 Inventive Britain, £13·96 First World War Centenary (2nd issue)
U3011	£11·11 Football Heroes, £13·97 Classic Locomotives, £14·60 Inventive Britain
U3012	£13·77 Dr· Who, £11·11 Football Heroes, £11·19 Merchant Navy, £13·97 Classic Locomotives, £13·96 First World War Centenary (3rd issue), £14·47 Battle of Waterloo Bicentenary, £15·37 Beatrix Potter
U3013	£13·77 Dr· Who, £11·11 Football Heroes, £11·39 Buckingham Palace, £11·30 First World War Centenary (1st issue), Battle of Waterloo Bicentenary, £15·37 Beatrix Potter
U3014	£13·77 Dr· Who, £11·39 Buckingham Palace, First World War Centenary (1st issue)
U3014a	£16·99 Star Wars
U3015	£9·97 Aerial Post Centenary
U3016	£11·11 Football Heroes, £16·99 Star Wars, £15·11 90th Birthday of Queen Elizabeth II
U3747	£15·11 90th Birthday of Queen Elizabeth II
U3017	£11·19 Merchant Navy, £14·47 Battle of Waterloo Bicentenary
U3019	£9·97 Aerial Post Centenary
U3019a	£14·60 Inventive Britain
U3020	£13·77 Dr· Who
U3020a	£14·60 Inventive Britain
U3021	£11·39 Buckingham Palace, £11·30 First World War Centenary (1st issue), £14·47 Battle of Waterloo Bicentenary
U3021b	£15·37 Beatrix Potter
U3022	£13·96 First World War Centenary (2nd issue)
U3023	£15·99 Star Wars. The Making of the Droids, Aliens and Creatures

For presentation pack containing Nos. U2981/2 see after No. Y1803.

Catalogue numbers U2941/4 from P.O. Pack No. 82 and first day cover are for 2nd bright blue, 1st gold, 2nd Large bright blue and 1st Large gold. They differ from the listed Nos. U2957/8 and U2959/60 by having no source or date codes in the iridescent overprint.

Catalogue numbers U2983/4 from P.O. Pack No. 89 and first day cover are for Recorded Signed for 1st and Recorded Signed for 1st Large. They differ from the listed Nos. U2983/4 by having source and date codes in the iridescent overprint.

Variations in the source and date codes incorporated into the iridescent overprint are outside the scope of this catalogue. Please refer to the *Great Britain Concise Catalogue* for further information.

For the miniature sheet entitled 'Celebrating Wales', issued 26 Feb 2009, see the regionals section.

British Design Classics (3rd series). Booklet stamps

2009 (10 Mar.)–**10** Designs as Nos. 2887/9, 2891/2 and 2896. Printed in gravure. Self-adhesive. Phosphor background. Die-cut perf 14½

2911	**2121**	(1st)	multicoloured	4·25	4·25	☐ ☐
2912	**2125**	(1st)	multicoloured	4·25	4·25	☐ ☐
2913	**2118**	(1st)	multicoloured			
			(21.4.09)	4·25	3·00	☐ ☐
2914	**2120**	(1st)	multicoloured			
			(18.8.09)	4·25	3·00	☐ ☐
2915	**2117**	(1st)	multicoloured			
			(17.9.09)	4·25	3·00	☐ ☐
2915b	**2116**	(1st)	multicoloured			
			(15.9.10)	4·25	3·00	☐ ☐
Set of 6				23·00	19·00	☐ ☐

Nos. 2911/15b were only issued in booklets.

2133 Matthew Boulton and Factory (manufacturing)

2134 James Watt and Boulton & Watt Condensing Engine (steam engineering)

2135 Richard Arkwright and Spinning Machine (textiles)

2136 Josiah Wedgwood and Black Basalt Teapot and Vase (ceramics)

2137 George Stephenson and *Locomotion* (railways)

2138 Henry Maudslay and Table Engine (machine making)

2139 James Brindley and Bridgewater Canal Aqueduct (canal engineering)

2140 John McAdam (road building)

Pioneers of the Industrial Revolution

2009 (10 Mar.) 'All-over' phosphor. Perf 14 × 14½

2916	**2133**	(1st)	multicoloured	1·25	90	☐ ☐
	a.	Horiz pair.				
		Nos. 2916/17		2·75	2·75	☐ ☐
2917	**2134**	(1st)	multicoloured	1·25	90	☐ ☐

2918	**2135**	50p	multicoloured	1·30	1·30	☐ ☐
	a.	Horiz pair.				
		Nos. 2918/19		3·00	3·00	☐ ☐
2919	**2136**	50p	multicoloured	1·30	1·30	☐ ☐
2920	**2137**	56p	multicoloured	1·40	1·40	☐ ☐
	a.	Horiz pair.				
		Nos. 2920/1		3·00	3·00	☐ ☐
2921	**2138**	56p	multicoloured	1·40	1·40	☐ ☐
2922	**2139**	72p	multicoloured	1·80	1·80	☐ ☐
	a.	Horiz pair.				
		Nos· 2922/3		4·00	4·00	☐ ☐
2923	**2140**	72p	multicoloured	1·80	1·80	☐ ☐
Set of 8				11·50	11·50	☐ ☐
First Day Cover					13·00	☐
Presentation Pack (P.O. Pack No. 425)				14·00		☐
PHQ Cards (*set of 8*) (321)				6·00	16·00	☐ ☐
Set of 4 Gutter Strips of 4				24·00		☐

Nos. 2916/17, 2918/19, 2920/1 and 2922/3 were each printed together, *se-tenant*, in horizontal pairs throughout the sheets.

2141 Henry VII (1485–1509)

2142 Henry VIII (1509–47)

2143 Edward VI (1547–53)

2144 Lady Jane Grey (1553)

2145 Mary I (1553–8)

2146 Elizabeth I (1558–1603)

2147 The Age of the Tudors

Kings and Queens (2nd series). House of Tudor

2009 (21 Apr.) Two phosphor bands. Perf 14

2924	**2141**	(1st)	multicoloured	1·25	90	☐ ☐
2925	**2142**	(1st)	multicoloured	1·25	90	☐ ☐
2926	**2143**	62p	multicoloured	1·60	1·60	☐ ☐
2927	**2144**	62p	multicoloured	1·60	1·60	☐ ☐
2928	**2145**	81p	multicoloured	2·10	2·10	☐ ☐
2929	**2146**	81p	multicoloured	2·10	2·10	☐ ☐
Set of 6				9·00	9·00	☐ ☐
First Day Cover					10·00	☐
Presentation Pack (Nos. 2924/**MS**2930)						
			(P.O. Pack No. 426)	18·00		☐
PHQ Cards (*set of 11*) (322)				9·00	22·00	☐ ☐
Set of 6 Gutter Pairs				19·00		☐
Set of 6 Traffic Light Gutter Blocks of 4			40·00			☐

MS2930 123 × 70 mm. **2147** (1st) *Mary
Rose* (galleon), 1510; (1st) Field of
Cloth of Gold Royal Conference,
1520; 90p Royal Exchange (centre
of commerce), 1565; 90p Francis
Drake (circumnavigation), 1580   7·00   7·00   ☐ ☐
First Day Cover   8·00   ☐

The complete miniature sheet is shown on one of the 11 PHQ
cards with the others depicting individual stamps including
those from **MS**2930.

2148 *Allium sphaerocephalon*
(Round-headed Leek)

2149 *Luronium natans*
(Floating Water-plantain)

2150 *Cypripedium calceolus*
(Lady's Slipper Orchid)

2151 *Polygala amarella*
(Dwarf Milkwort)

2152 *Saxifraga hirculus*
(Marsh Saxifrage)

2153 *Stachys germanica*
(Downy Woundwort)

2154 *Euphorbia serrulata*
(Upright Spurge)

2155 *Pyrus cordata*
(Plymouth Pear)

2156 *Polygonum
maritimum* (Sea Knotgrass)

2157 *Dianthus armeria*
(Deptford Pink)

2158 Royal Botanic Gardens, Kew

'Action for Species' (3rd series).
Plants and 250th Anniversary of Creation of
Royal Botanic Gardens, Kew (MS2941)

2009 (19 May)

(a) Phosphor background. Perf 14½

2931	**2148**	(1st)	multicoloured	1·25	90	☐ ☐
		a.	Block of 10.			
			Nos. 2931/40	14·00	10·00	☐ ☐
2932	**2149**	(1st)	multicoloured	1·25	90	☐ ☐
2933	**2150**	(1st)	multicoloured	1·25	90	☐ ☐
2934	**2151**	(1st)	multicoloured	1·25	90	☐ ☐
2935	**2152**	(1st)	multicoloured	1·25	90	☐ ☐
2936	**2153**	(1st)	multicoloured	1·25	90	☐ ☐
2937	**2154**	(1st)	multicoloured	1·25	90	☐ ☐
2938	**2155**	(1st)	multicoloured	1·25	90	☐ ☐
2939	**2156**	(1st)	multicoloured	1·25	90	☐ ☐
2940	**2157**	(1st)	multicoloured	1·25	90	☐ ☐
Set of 10				14·00	10·00	☐ ☐
First Day Cover					12·00	☐
Presentation Pack (Nos. 2931/**MS**2941)						
		(P.O. Pack No. 427)		22·00		☐
PHQ Cards (*set of* 15) (323)				12·00	30·00	☐ ☐
Gutter Block of 10				16·00		☐

Nos. 2931/40 were printed together, *se-tenant*, in blocks of ten
(5 × 2) throughout the sheet.

(b) Two phosphor bands. Perf 14 × 14½

MS2941   115 × 89   mm.   **2158**   (1st)
Palm House, Kew Gardens; (1st)
Millennium Seed Bank, Wakehurst
Place; 90p Pagoda, Kew Gardens;
90p Sackler Crossing, Kew Gardens 7·00   7·00   ☐ ☐
First Day Cover   8·00   ☐

The complete miniature sheet is shown on one of the 15 PHQ
cards with the others depicting individual stamps including
those from **MS**2941.

50th Anniversary of National Association of Flower
Arrangement Societies. Booklet stamps

2009 (21 May) Designs as Nos. 1958 and 1962 (1997 Greetings
Stamps 19th-century Flower Paintings) but printed in gravure.
Self-adhesive. Two phosphor bands. Die-cut perf 14 (with one
elliptical hole in each vert side)

2942	**1287**	(1st)	multicoloured	4·00	4·00	☐ ☐
2943	**1283**	(1st)	multicoloured	4·00	4·00	☐ ☐

Nos. 2942/3 were only issued in £2·34 stamp booklets.

2159 Dragon

2160 Unicorn

2161 Giant

2162 Pixie

2163 Mermaid

2164 Fairy

Mythical Creatures

2009 (16 June) 'All-over' phosphor. Perf 14½

2944	**2159**	(1st)	multicoloured	1·25	90	☐ ☐
2945	**2160**	(1st)	multicoloured	1·25	90	☐ ☐
2946	**2161**	62p	multicoloured	1·60	1·60	☐ ☐
2947	**2162**	62p	multicoloured	1·60	1·60	☐ ☐
2948	**2163**	90p	multicoloured	2·25	2·25	☐ ☐
2949	**2164**	90p	multicoloured	2·25	2·25	☐ ☐
Set of 6				9·00	9·00	☐ ☐
First Day Cover					10·00	☐
Presentation Pack (P.O. Pack No. 428)			11·00			☐
PHQ Cards (set of 6) (324)			5·00	12·00		☐ ☐
Set of 6 Gutter Pairs			19·00			☐

2165 George V
Type B Wall Letter
Box, 1933–6

2167 Victorian
Lamp Letter Box, 1896

2166 Edward VII
Ludlow Letter Box,
1901–10

2168 Elizabeth II Type A
Wall Letter Box, 1962–3

2169 Post Boxes

Post Boxes

2009 (18 Aug.) 'All-over' phosphor. Perf 14

2950	**2165**	(1st)	multicoloured	1·75	1·75	☐ ☐
2951	**2166**	56p	multicoloured	2·50	2·50	☐ ☐
2952	**2167**	81p	multicoloured	3·00	3·00	☐ ☐
2953	**2168**	90p	multicoloured	4·00	4·00	☐ ☐
Set of 4				10·00	10·00	☐ ☐
MS2954 **2169** 145 × 74 mm.						
Nos. 2950/3				11·00	11·00	☐ ☐
First Day Cover					12·00	☐
Presentation Pack (P.O. Pack No. 430)			12·00			☐
PHQ Cards (set of 5) (325)			4·00	12·00		☐ ☐

Nos. 2950/3 were only issued in the £8·18 'Treasures of the Archive' booklet, No. DX46, and in **MS**2954.

The five PHQ cards show the four individual stamps and the miniature sheet.

Type **2165** was also issued in sheets of 20 with *se-tenant* labels showing post boxes.

'Treasures of the Archive' (1st series). Booklet stamps

2009 (18 Aug.) Designs as Type **929** (1990 150th anniversary of the Penny Black) and **1446** (with redrawn 1st face value). Printed in lithography. Two phosphor bands. Perf 14½ × 14 (with one elliptical hole in each vertical side)

2955	**929**	20p	brownish-black and grey-brown	3·50	3·50	☐ ☐
2956	**1446**	(1st)	brownish-black and grey-brown	3·50	3·50	☐ ☐

Nos. 2955/6 were only issued in the £8·18 'Treasures of the Archive' stamp booklet No. DX46.

'Treasures of the Archive' (2nd series). Booklet stamps

2009 (18 Aug.) Design as Type **919** (1989 Lord Mayor's Show) but printed in lithography. 'All-over' phosphor. Perf 14

2957	**919**	20p	multicoloured	4·50	4·50	☐ ☐

No. 2957 was only issued in the £8·18 'Treasures of the Archive' stamp booklets, No. DX46

2170 Firefighting

2171 Chemical Fire

56

2172 Emergency Rescue

62

2173 Flood Rescue

81

2174 Search and Rescue

90

2175 Fire Safety

Fire and Rescue Service

2009 (1 Sept.) 'All-over' phosphor. Perf 14 × 14½

2958	**2170**	(1st) multicoloured	1·25	90
2959	**2171**	54p multicoloured	1·40	1·40
2960	**2172**	56p multicoloured	1·40	1·40
2961	**2173**	62p multicoloured	1·60	1·60
2962	**2174**	81p multicoloured	2·00	2·00
2963	**2175**	90p multicoloured	2·25	2·25
Set of 6			10·00	10·00
First Day Cover				11·00
Presentation Pack (P.O. Pack No. 429)			12·00	
PHQ Cards (set of 6) (326)			5·00	12·00
Set of 6 Gutter Pairs			21·00	

2176 Flight Deck Officer, 2009

2177 Captain, 1941

2178 Second Officer WRNS, 1918

2179 Able Seaman, 1880

2180 Royal Marine, 1805

2181 Admiral, 1795

Military Uniforms (3rd series). Royal Navy Uniforms

2009 (17 Sept.) Phosphor background. Perf 14

2964	**2176**	(1st) multicoloured	1·25	90
		a. Horiz strip of 3.		
		Nos. 2964/6	4·00	4·00
2965	**2177**	(1st) multicoloured	1·25	90
2966	**2178**	(1st) multicoloured	1·25	90
2967	**2179**	90p multicoloured	2·25	2·25
		a. Horiz strip of 3.		
		Nos. 2967/9	7·00	7·00

2968	**2180**	90p multicoloured	2·25	2·25
2969	**2181**	90p multicoloured	2·25	2·25
Set of 6			10·00	10·00
First Day Cover				11·00
Presentation Pack (P.O. Pack No. 431)			12·00	
PHQ Cards (set of 6) (327)			5·00	12·00
Set of 2 Gutter Strips of 6			21·00	
Set of 2 Traffic Light Gutter Blocks of 12			42·00	

Nos. 2964/6 and 2967/9 were each printed together, *se-tenant*, in horizontal strips of three stamps in sheets of 60 (2 panes 6 × 5) and in the £7·93 'Royal Navy Uniforms' booklet, No. DX47.

Royal Navy Uniforms. Booklet stamp

2009 (17 Sept.) Design as Type **1518** (Jolly Roger flag from 2001 Submarine Centenary) but printed in lithography. Two phosphor bands. Perf 14½

2970	**1518**	(1st) multicoloured	5·00	5·00

No. 2970 was only issued in the £7·93 'Royal Navy Uniforms' stamp booklet, No DX47.

2182 Fred Perry 1909–1995 (lawn tennis champion)

2183 Henry Purcell 1659–95 (composer and musician)

2184 Sir Matt Busby 1909–94 (footballer and football manager)

2185 William Gladstone 1809–98 (statesman and Prime Minister)

2186 Mary Wollstonecraft 1759–97 (pioneering feminist)

2187 Sir Arthur Conan Doyle 1859–1930 (writer and creator of Sherlock Holmes)

2188 Donald Campbell 1921–67 (water speed record broken 1959)

2189 Judy Fryd 1909–2000 (campaigner and founder of MENCAP)

2190 Samuel Johnson 1709–84 (lexicographer, critic and poet)

2191 Sir Martin Ryle 1918–84 (radio survey of the Universe 1959)

2198 Paralympic Games Dressage

2199 Badminton

2200 Weightlifting

2201 Basketball

Eminent Britons

2009 (8 Oct.) Phosphor background. Perf 14½

2971	**2182**	(1st)	multicoloured	1·25	90	☐ ☐
		a.	Horiz strip of 5.			
			Nos. 2971/5	7·00	7·00	☐ ☐
2972	**2183**	(1st)	multicoloured	1·25	90	☐ ☐
2973	**2184**	(1st)	multicoloured	1·25	90	☐ ☐
2974	**2185**	(1st)	multicoloured	1·25	90	☐ ☐
2975	**2186**	(1st)	multicoloured	1·25	90	☐ ☐
2976	**2187**	(1st)	multicoloured	1·25	90	☐ ☐
		a.	Horiz strip of 5.			
			Nos. 2976/80	7·00	7·00	☐ ☐
2977	**2188**	(1st)	multicoloured	1·25	90	☐ ☐
2978	**2189**	(1st)	multicoloured	1·25	90	☐ ☐
2979	**2190**	(1st)	multicoloured	1·25	90	☐ ☐
2980	**2191**	(1st)	multicoloured	1·25	90	☐ ☐
Set of 10				13·00	13·00	☐
First Day Cover					14·00	☐
Presentation Pack (P.O. Pack No. 432)				15·00		☐
PHQ Cards (*set of* 10) (328)				9·00	20·00	☐ ☐
Set of 2 Gutter Strips of 10				28·00		☐

Nos. 2971/5 and 2976/80 were each printed together, *se-tenant*, in horizontal strips of five stamps throughout the sheets. No. 2980 includes the 'EUROPA' emblem.

2192 Canoe Slalom

2193 Paralympic Games Archery

2194 Athletics: Track

2195 Diving

2196 Paralympic Games Boccia

2197 Judo

Olympic and Paralympic Games, London (2012)
(1st series)

2009 (22 Oct.) 'All-over' phosphor. Perf 14½

2981	**2192**	(1st)	multicoloured	1·25	90	☐ ☐
		a.	Horiz strip of 5.			
			Nos. 2981/5	7·00	7·00	☐ ☐
2982	**2193**	(1st)	multicoloured	1·25	90	☐ ☐
2983	**2194**	(1st)	multicoloured	1·25	90	☐ ☐
2984	**2195**	(1st)	multicoloured	1·25	90	☐ ☐
2985	**2196**	(1st)	multicoloured	1·25	90	☐ ☐
2986	**2197**	(1st)	multicoloured	1·25	90	☐ ☐
		a.	Horiz strip of 5.			
			Nos. 2986/90	7·00	7·00	☐ ☐
2987	**2198**	(1st)	multicoloured	1·25	90	☐ ☐
2988	**2199**	(1st)	multicoloured	1·25	90	☐ ☐
2989	**2200**	(1st)	multicoloured	1·25	90	☐ ☐
2990	**2201**	(1st)	multicoloured	1·25	90	☐ ☐
Set of 10				13·00	13·00	☐
First Day Cover					14·00	☐
Presentation Pack (P.O. Pack No. M18)				15·00		☐
PHQ Cards (*set of* 10) (OXPG1)				9·00	20·00	☐ ☐
Set of 2 Gutter Strips of 10				27·00		☐

Nos. 2981/5 and 2986/90 were each printed together, *se-tenant*, in horizontal strips of five stamps throughout the sheets and were also issued on 27 July 2011, in a sheetlet containing all 30 stamps in the series. See **MS**3204a.

See also Nos. 3020/3.

2202 Angel playing Lute (William Morris), Church of St. James, Staveley, Kendal, Cumbria

2203 Madonna and Child (Henry Holiday), Church of Ormesby St. Michael, Great Yarmouth, Norfolk

2204 Angel playing Lute (William Morris), Church of St. James, Staveley, Kendal, Cumbria

2205 Joseph (Henry Holiday), Parish Church of St. Michael, Minehead, Somerset

2206 Madonna and Child (Henry Holiday), Church of Ormesby St. Michael, Ormesby, Great Yarmouth, Norfolk

2207 Wise Man (Sir Edward Burne-Jones), Church of St. Mary the Virgin, Rye, East Sussex

2208 Shepherd (Henry Holiday),
St. Mary's Church, Upavon, Wiltshire

Christmas. Stained Glass windows

2009 (3 Nov.) Gravure. One centre band (2nd) or two phosphor bands (others). Perf 14½ × 14 (with one elliptical hole in each vert side)

(a) Self-adhesive

2991	**2202**	(2nd)	multicoloured	1·00	60	
2992	**2203**	(1st)	multicoloured	1·25	85	
2993	**2204**	(2nd Large) multicoloured	1·50	1·10	
2994	**2205**	56p	multicoloured	1·40	1·40	
2995	**2206**	(1st Large) multicoloured	2·00	1·25	
2996	**2207**	90p	multicoloured	2·25	2·25	
2997	**2208**	£1·35	multicoloured	3·50	3·00	
Set of 7				12·00	11·00	
First Day Cover					12·00	
Presentation Pack (P.O. Pack No. 433)			14·00		
PHQ Cards (set of 8) (328)			6·00	16·00	

(b) Ordinary gum

MS2998 115×102 mm. As Nos. 2991/71	12·00	11·00	
First Day Cover			12·00	

The eight PHQ cards show the seven individual stamps and the miniature sheet.

The 2nd class, 1st class, 56p and 90p stamps were also issued in sheets of 20 containing eight 2nd class, eight 1st class, two 56p and two 90p stamps, each stamp accompanied by a *se-tenant* label. Separate sheets of 20 2nd, 20 1st, ten 1st, ten 56p and ten 90p were available with personal photographs.

All these sheets wer printed in lithography instead of gravure.

For the 2nd class stamp printed in lithography with ordinary gum see No. 3186a.

Year Pack

2009 (3 Nov.) Comprises Nos. 2887/96, 2898/**MS**2904, 2916/**MS**2941, 2944/9, **MS**2954, 2958/69, 2971/97, **MS**S157 and **MS**W147

CP2998a	Year Pack	£120	

Post Office Yearbook

2009 (3 Nov.) Comprises Nos. 2887/96, 2898/**MS**2904, 2916/**MS**2941, 2944/9, **MS**2954, 2958/69, 2971/97, **MS**S157 and **MS**W147

YB2998a	Yearbook	£130	

Miniature Sheet Collection

2009 (3 Nov.) Comprises Nos. **MS**2904, **MS**2930, **MS**2941, **MS**2954, **MS**2998, **MS**S157 and **MS**W147

MS2998a Miniature Sheet Collection	70·00	

2209 *The Division Bell* (Pink Floyd)

2210 *A Rush of Blood to the Head* (Coldplay)

2211 *Parklife* (Blur)

2212 *Power Corruption and Lies* (New Order)

2213 *Let It Bleed* (Rolling Stones)

2214 *London Calling* (The Clash)

2215 *Tubular Bells* (Mike Oldfield)

2216 *IV* (Led Zeppelin)

2217 *Screamadelica* (Primal Scream)

2218 *The Rise and Fall of Ziggy Stardust and the Spiders from Mars* (David Bowie)

Classic Album Covers (1st issue)

2010 (7 Jan.) 'All-over' phosphor. Self-adhesive. Gravure De La Rue. Die-cut perf 14½ (interrupted)

2999	**2209**	(1st)	multicoloured	1·25	90	
		a.	Horiz strip of 5. Nos. 2999/3003	7·00		
3000	**2210**	(1st)	multicoloured	1·25	90	
3001	**2211**	(1st)	multicoloured	1·25	90	
3002	**2212**	(1st)	multicoloured	1·25	90	
3003	**2213**	(1st)	multicoloured	1·25	90	
3004	**2214**	(1st)	multicoloured	1·25	90	
		a.	Horiz strip of 5. Nos. 3004/8	7·00		
3005	**2215**	(1st)	multicoloured	1·25	90	
3006	**2216**	(1st)	multicoloured	1·25	90	
3007	**2217**	(1st)	multicoloured	1·25	90	
3008	**2218**	(1st)	multicoloured	1·25	90	
Set of 10				13·00	13·00	
First Day Cover					14·00	
Presentation Pack (P.O. Pack No. 435)			15·00		
PHQ Cards (set of 10) (330)			9·00	22·00	

Nos. 2999/3003 and 3004/8 were each printed together as horizontal strips of five stamps in sheets of 50 (2 panes of 25)

Classic Album Covers (2nd issue)

2010 (7 Jan.) 'All-over' phosphor. Litho Cartor. Perf 14½ (interrupted)

3009	**2213**	(1st)	multicoloured	2·40	2·40	
3010	**2216**	(1st)	multicoloured	2·40	2·40	
3011	**2218**	(1st)	multicoloured	2·40	2·40	
3012	**2212**	(1st)	multicoloured	2·40	2·40	

3013	**2217**	(1st)	multicoloured	2·40	2·40	☐ ☐
3014	**2209**	(1st)	multicoloured	2·40	2·40	☐ ☐
3015	**2215**	(1st)	multicoloured	2·40	2·40	☐ ☐
3016	**2214**	(1st)	multicoloured	2·40	2·40	☐ ☐
3017	**2211**	(1st)	multicoloured	2·40	2·40	☐ ☐
3018	**2210**	(1st)	multicoloured	2·40	2·40	☐ ☐
Set of 10				22·00	22·00	☐ ☐
MS3019	223×189 mm.					
		As Nos. 3009/18		35·00	35·00	☐ ☐
First Day Cover					32·00	☐

Nos. 3009/18 were only issued in the £8·06 'Classic Album Covers', No. DX48, and **MS**3019.

The right-hand edges of Nos. 2999/3018 and the miniature sheet **MS**3019 are all cut around in an imperforate section to show the vinyl disc protruding from the open edge of the album cover. Stamps from the miniature sheet have a white background, while those from the booklet have a brown background containing descriptive texts.

A miniature sheet containing No. 3014×10 *The Division Bell* (Pink Floyd) was issued on 6 March 2010 and sold for £4·75 per sheet.

Olympic and Paralympic Games, London (2012) (2nd series). Booklet stamps

2010 (7 Jan.–25 Feb.) Designs as Nos. 2982/3, 2986 and 2990 but printed in photogravure. Self-adhesive. 'All-over' phosphor. Die-cut perf 14½

3020	**2197**	(1st)	multicoloured	4·75	4·75	☐ ☐
3021	**2193**	(1st)	multicoloured	4·75	4·75	☐ ☐
3022	**2194**	(1st)	multicoloured			
			(25 Feb)	4·75	4·75	☐ ☐
3023	**2201**	(1st)	multicoloured			
			(25 Feb)	4·75	4·75	☐ ☐
Set of 4				17·00	17·00	☐ ☐

Nos. 3020/1 and 3022/3 were only issued in separate booklets, each originally sold for £2·34.

2219

Business and Consumer Smilers Miniature Sheet

2010 (26 Jan.) Sheet 124×71 mm. Multicoloured. Two phosphor bands. Perf 14½×14 (with one elliptical hole in each vertical side)

MS3024 **2219** (1st) Propeller driven aircraft; (1st) Vintage sports roadster; (1st) Recreation of crown seal; (1st) Birthday cake; (1st) Steam locomotive; (1st) Ocean liner; (1st) Six poppies on barbed wire stems; (1st) Birthday present; (Europe up to 20 grams) Bird carrying envelope; (Worldwide up to 20 grams) 'Hello' in aeroplane vapour trail	17·00	17·00 ☐ ☐
First Day Cover		19·00 ☐
Presentation Pack (P.O. Pack No. M19)	19·00	☐
PHQ Cards (*set of 11*) (D31)	9·00	22·00 ☐ ☐

MS3024 was sold for £4·58.

The eleven PHQ cards show the ten individual stamps and the complete miniature sheet.

Stamps in designs as within **MS**3024 but self-adhesive were available printed together, *se-tenant*, in sheets of 20 containing two of each design with greetings labels.

The (1st) birthday cake, (1st) birthday present, Europe and Worldwide designs were also available in separate sheets with personal photographs.

A stamp as the crown seal design in **MS**3024 but self-adhesive was issued on 15 September 2011 in sheets of 20 with postmark labels for the 350th Anniversary of the Postmark.

The other 1st class designs were for the business customised service.

Stamps as the 1st Birthday cake (×4), 1st Birthday present (×4), Europe Bird carrying envelope (×2) and Worldwide 'Hello' in aeroplane vapour trail (×2) designs but self-adhesive were issued, together with Nos. 2569, 2572, 2674 and 2821/3 on 8 May 2010 in sheets of 20 stamps with *se-tenant* greetings labels.

For the self-adhesive (1st) six poppies stamp, see No. 3414.

2220 Girlguiding UK

Centenary of Girlguiding. Miniature Sheet

2010 (2 Feb.) Sheet 190×67 mm. Multicoloured. Phosphor background. Perf 14×14½

MS3025 **2220** (1st) Rainbows; 56p Brownies; 81p Guides; 90p Senior Section members	8·00	7·00 ☐ ☐
First Day Cover		8·00 ☐
Presentation Pack (P.O. Pack No. 436)	12·00	☐
PHQ Cards (*set of 5*) (331)	4·00	10·00 ☐ ☐

The five PHQ cards show the four individual stamps and the complete miniature sheet.

2221 Sir Robert Boyle (chemistry)

2222 Sir Isaac Newton (optics)

2223 Benjamin Franklin (electricity)

2224 Edward Jenner (pioneer of smallpox vaccination)

2225 Charles Babbage (computing)

2226 Alfred Russel Wallace (theory of evolution)

2227 Joseph Lister (antiseptic surgery)

2228 Ernest Rutherford (atomic structure)

2229 Dorothy Hodgkin (crystallography)

2230 Sir Nicholas Shackleton (earth sciences)

350th Anniversary of the Royal Society

2010 (25 Feb.) 'All-over' phosphor. Perf 14½

3026	**2221**	(1st)	multicoloured	1·25	90	☐ ☐
	a.	Block of 10.				
		Nos. 3026/35		15·00	13·00	☐ ☐
3027	2222	(1st)	multicoloured	1·25	90	☐ ☐
3028	**2223**	(1st)	multicoloured	1·25	90	☐ ☐
3029	**2224**	(1st)	multicoloured	1·25	90	☐ ☐
3030	**2225**	(1st)	multicoloured	1·25	90	☐ ☐
3031	**2226**	(1st)	multicoloured	1·25	90	☐ ☐
3032	**2227**	(1st)	multicoloured	1·25	90	☐ ☐
3033	**2228**	(1st)	multicoloured	1·25	90	☐ ☐
3034	**2229**	(1st)	multicoloured	1·25	90	☐ ☐
3035	**2230**	(1st)	multicoloured	1·25	90	☐ ☐
Set of 10				15·00	13·00	☐
First Day Cover					14·00	☐
Presentation Pack (P.O. Pack No. 437)				17·00		☐
PHQ Cards (set of 10) (332)				9·00	20·00	☐ ☐
Gutter Block of 20				32·00		☐

Nos. 3026/35 were printed together, *se-tenant*, as blocks of ten (5 × 2) in sheets of 60 (2 panes of 30) and were also issued in the £7·72 '350th Anniversary of the Royal Society' booklet, No. DX49.

2231 "Pixie" (mastiff cross)

2232 "Button"

2233 "Herbie" (mongrel)

2234 "Mr. Tumnus"

2235 "Tafka" (border collie)

2236 "Boris" (bulldog cross)

2237 "Casey" (lurcher) **2238** "Tigger"

2239 "Leonard" (Jack Russell cross)

2240 "Tia" (terrier cross)

150th Anniversary of Battersea Dogs and Cats Home

2010 (11 Mar.) Phosphor background. Perf 14½

3036	**2231**	(1st)	multicoloured	1·25	90	☐ ☐
	a.	Block of 10.				
		Nos. 3036/45		15·00	13·00	☐ ☐
3037	2232	(1st)	multicoloured	1·25	90	☐ ☐
3038	**2233**	(1st)	multicoloured	1·25	90	☐ ☐
3039	**2234**	(1st)	multicoloured	1·25	90	☐ ☐
3040	**2235**	(1st)	multicoloured	1·25	90	☐ ☐
3041	**2236**	(1st)	multicoloured	1·25	90	☐ ☐
3042	**2237**	(1st)	multicoloured	1·25	90	☐ ☐
3043	**2238**	(1st)	multicoloured	1·25	90	☐ ☐
3044	**2239**	(1st)	multicoloured	1·25	90	☐ ☐
3045	**2240**	(1st)	multicoloured	1·25	90	☐ ☐
Set of 10				15·00	13·00	☐ ☐
First Day Cover					14·00	☐
Presentation Pack (P.O. Pack No. 438)				17·00		☐
PHQ Cards (set of 10) (333)				9·00	20·00	☐ ☐
Gutter Block of 20				32·00		☐

Nos. 3036/45 were printed together, *se-tenant*, as blocks of ten (5 × 2) in sheets of 60 (2 panes of 30) .

2241 James I (1406–37) **2242** James II (1437–60) **2243** James III (1460–88)

2244 James IV
(1488–1513)

2245 James V
(1513–42)

2246 Mary
(1542–67)

2247 James VI (1567–1625)

2248 The Age of the Stewarts

Kings and Queens (3rd series). House of Stewart

2010 (23 Mar.) Two phosphor bands. Perf 14

3046	**2241**	(1st)	multicoloured	1·25	90	☐ ☐
3047	**2242**	(1st)	multicoloured	1·25	90	☐ ☐
3048	**2243**	(1st)	multicoloured	1·25	90	☐ ☐
3049	**2244**	62p	multicoloured	1·60	1·60	☐ ☐
3050	**2245**	62p	multicoloured	1·60	1·60	☐ ☐
3051	**2246**	81p	multicoloured	2·00	2·00	☐ ☐
3052	**2247**	81p	multicoloured	2·00	2·00	☐ ☐
Set of 7				10·00	10·00	☐
First Day Cover					11·00	☐
Presentation Pack (Nos. 3046/**MS**3053						
		(P.O. Pack No. 439)		18·00		☐
PHQ Cards (*set of* 12) (334)				10·00	24·00	☐ ☐
Set of 7 Gutter Pairs				21·00		☐
Set of 7 Traffic Light Gutter Blocks of 4				42·00		☐

MS3053 123×70 mm. **2248** (1st) Foundation of the University of St. Andrews, 1413; (1st) Foundation of the College of Surgeons, Edinburgh, 1505; 81p Foundation of Court of Session, 1532; 81p John Knox (Reformation, 1559)   6·50   6·50   ☐ ☐

First Day Cover   7·50   ☐

The complete miniature sheet is shown on one of the 12 PHQ cards with the others depicting individual stamps including those from **MS**3053.

2249 Humpback Whale
(*Megaptera novaeangliae*)

2250 Wildcat
(*Felis silvestris*)

2251 Brown Long-eared
Bat (*Plecotus auritus*)

2252 Polecat
(*Mustela putorius*)

2253 Sperm Whale
(*Physeter macrocephalus*)

2254 Water Vole
(*Arvicola terrestris*)

2255 Greater Horseshoe
Bat (*Rhinolophus
ferrumequinum*)

2256 Otter (*Lutra lutra*)

2257 Dormouse
(*Muscardinus avellanarius*)

2258 Hedgehog
(*Erinaceus europaeus*)

'Action for Species' (4th series). Mammals.

2010 (13 Apr.) 'All-over' phosphor. Perf 14½

3054	**2249**	(1st)	multicoloured	1·25	1·00	☐ ☐
	a.	Block of 10.				
		Nos. 3054/63		14·00	12·00	☐ ☐
3055	2250	(1st)	multicoloured	1·25	1·00	☐ ☐
3056	2251	(1st)	multicoloured	1·25	1·00	☐ ☐
3057	2252	(1st)	multicoloured	1·25	1·00	☐ ☐
3058	2253	(1st)	multicoloured	1·25	1·00	☐ ☐
3059	2254	(1st)	multicoloured	1·25	1·00	☐ ☐
3060	2255	(1st)	multicoloured	1·25	1·00	☐ ☐
3061	2256	(1st)	multicoloured	1·25	1·00	☐ ☐
3062	2257	(1st)	multicoloured	1·25	1·00	☐ ☐
3063	2258	(1st)	multicoloured	1·25	1·00	☐ ☐
Set of 10				14·00	12·00	☐ ☐
First Day Cover					13·00	☐
Presentation Pack (P.O. Pack No. 440)				16·00		☐

PHQ Cards (*set of* 10) (335)   9·00   20·00 ☐ ☐
Gutter Block of 20   30·00   ☐
Nos. 3054/63 were printed together, *se-tenant*, as blocks of ten
(5 × 2) in sheets of 60 (2 panes of 30)
See also Nos. 3095/6.

No. 3064, and T **2259** are vacant.

2260 King George V and Queen Elizabeth II (1st); Two portraits of King George V (£1)

London 2010 Festival of Stamps (1st issue) and Centenary of Accession of King George V

2010 (6 May) 'All-over' phosphor. Perf 14½ × 14. Sheet 141 × 74 mm
MS3065 **2260** (1st) rosine; £1 blackish
brown, grey-brown and silver   4·50   4·50 ☐ ☐
First Day Cover   5·50   ☐

A miniature sheet as No. **MS**3065 but inscr 'BUSINESS DESIGN CENTRE, LONDON 8–15 MAY 2010' along the top right margin was only available at London 2010 Festival of Stamps. (*Price £15*)

The eight PHQ cards depict the individual stamps from **MS**3065 and **MS**3072 and the complete miniature sheets.

2261 King George V and Queen Elizabeth II

2262 1924 British Empire Exhibition 1½d. Brown Stamp

2263 1924 British Empire Exhibition 1d. Scarlet Stamp

2264 Two Portraits of King George V

2265 1913 £1 Green 'Sea Horses' Design Stamp

2266 1913 10s. Blue 'Sea Horses' Design Stamp

LONDON 2010 FESTIVAL OF STAMPS

2267

London 2010 Festival of Stamps (2nd issue) and Centenary of Accession of King George V

2010 (6-8 May) Litho (Nos. 3066 and 3069) or recess and litho. 'All-over' phosphor. Perf 14½ × 14

3066	**2261**	(1st)	rosine (*6 May*)	1·75	1·50	☐ ☐
3067	**2262**	(1st)	multicoloured (*8 May*)	1·75	1·50	☐ ☐
3068	**2263**	(1st)	multicoloured (*8 May*)	1·75	1·50	☐ ☐
3069	**2264**	£1	blackish brown, grey-brown and silver (*8 May*)	3·00	3·00	☐ ☐
3070	**2265**	£1	multicoloured (*8 May*)	3·00	3·00	☐ ☐
3071	**2266**	£1	multicoloured (*8 May*)	3·00	3·00	☐ ☐
Set of 6				**13·00**	12·00	☐ ☐
Gutter Pair (No. 3066)				3·50		☐
MS3072	115 × 90	mm.	**2267**			
Nos. 3067/8 and 3070/1 (*8 May*)				10·00	10·00	☐ ☐
First Day Cover (**MS**3072)					13·00	☐
Presentation Pack (**MS**3065 and **MS**3072) (P.O. Pack No. 441)				14·00		☐
PHQ Cards (*set of* 8) (336)				7·00	17·00	☐ ☐

No. 3066 was issued as a sheet stamp on 6 May 2010.
Nos. 3066/71 all come from the £11·15 '1910-1936, King George V' stamp booklet, No. DX50 issued on 8 May 2010.
Nos. 3066 and 3069 also come from miniature sheet **MS**3065, issued on 6 May 2010.
Nos. 3067/8 and 3070/1 also come from **MS**3072, issued on 8 May 2010.
For presentation pack and PHQ cards for No. **MS**3072 see under **MS**3065.

2268

London 2010 Festival of Stamps (3rd issue).
Jeffery Matthews Colour Palette. Miniature Sheet

2010 (8 May) Sheet, 104×95 mm, containing stamps as T **367** with a label. Two phosphor bands. Perf 15 × 14 (with one elliptical hole in each vertical side)

MS3073 **2268** 1p reddish purple; 2p deep grey-green; 5p reddish-brown; 9p bright orange; 10p orange; 20p light green; 60p emerald; 67p bright mauve; 88p bright magenta; 97p bluish violet; £1·46 turquoise-blue	30·00	30·00	
First Day Cover		32·00	

2269 Winston Churchill

2270 Land Girl

2271 Home Guard

2272 Evacuees

2273 Air Raid Wardens

2274 Woman working in Factory

2275 Royal Broadcast by Princess Elizabeth and Princess Margaret

2276 Fire Service

'Britain Alone' (1st issue)

2010 (13 May) 'All-over' phosphor. Perf 14½

3074	**2269**	(1st)	pale stone, pale bistre and black	1·25	1·00
3075	**2270**	(1st)	pale stone, pale bistre and black	1·25	1·00
3076	**2271**	60p	pale stone, pale bistre and black	1·50	1·50
3077	**2272**	60p	pale stone, pale bistre and black	1·50	1·50
3078	**2273**	67p	pale stone, pale bistre and black	1·70	1·70
3079	**2274**	67p	pale stone, pale bistre and black	1·70	1·70
3080	**2275**	97p	pale stone, pale bistre and black	2·40	2·40
3081	**2276**	97p	pale stone, pale bistre and black	2·40	2·40
Set of 8				12·00	12·00
First Day Cover					13·00
Presentation Pack (Nos. 3074/81 and **MS**3086) (P.O. Pack No. 442)				25·00	
PHQ Cards (*set of* 13) (337)				11·00	29·00
Set of 8 Gutter Pairs				25·00	

Nos. 3074/81 were also issued in the £9·76 'Britain Alone' booklet, No. DX51.

The 13 PHQ cards depict Nos. 3074/85 and the complete miniature sheet **MS**3086.

2277 Evacuation of British Soldiers from Dunkirk

2278 Vessels from Upper Thames Patrol in 'Operation Little Ships'

2279 Rescued Soldiers on Board Royal Navy Destroyer, Dover

2280 Steamship and Other Boat loaded with Troops

2281 Evacuation of British Troops from Dunkirk, 1940

'Britain Alone' (2nd issue)

2010 (13 May) 'All-over' phosphor. Perf 14½

3082	**2277**	(1st)	pale stone, pale bistre and black	2·00	2·00	
3083	**2278**	60p	pale stone, pale bistre and black	3·00	3·00	
3084	**2279**	88p	pale stone, pale bistre and black	4·00	4·00	
3085	**2280**	97p	pale stone, pale bistre and black	4·00	4·00	
3082/85 Set of 4				12·00	12·00	

MS3086 115×89 mm. **2281**
Nos. 3082/5   7·50   7·50

First Day Cover (**MS**3086)   8·50

Nos. 3082/5 were only issued in the £9·76 'Britain Alone' booklet, No. DX51 and in **MS**3086.

2282 James I (1603–25)

2283 Charles I (1625–49)

2284 Charles II (1660–85)

2285 James II (1685–8)

2286 William III (1689–1702)

2287 Mary II (1689–94)

2288 Anne (1702–14)

2289 The Age of the Stuarts

Kings and Queens (4th series). House of Stuart

2010 (15 June) Two phosphor bands. Perf 14

3087	**2282**	(1st)	multicoloured	1·25	1·00	
3088	**2283**	(1st)	multicoloured	1·25	1·00	
3089	**2284**	60p	multicoloured	1·50	1·50	
3090	**2285**	60p	multicoloured	1·50	1·50	
3091	**2286**	67p	multicoloured	1·70	1·70	
3092	**2287**	67p	multicoloured	1·70	1·70	
3093	**2288**	88p	multicoloured	2·25	2·25	
Set of 7				10·00	10·00	

First Day Cover   11·00
Presentation Pack (Nos. 3087/**MS**3094)
(P.O. Pack No. 443)   19·00
PHQ Cards (set of 12) (338)   10·00   24·00
Set of 7 Gutter Pairs   21·00
Set of 7 Traffic Light Gutter Blocks of 4   42·00

MS3094 123×70 mm. **2289** (1st)
William Harvey (discovery of blood circulation, 1628); 60p Civil War Battle of Naseby, 1645; 88p John Milton (Paradise Lost, 1667); 97p Castle Howard (John Vanbrugh, 1712)   7·50   7·50

First Day Cover   8·50

The complete miniature sheet is shown on one of the 12 PHQ cards with the others depicting individual stamps including those from **MS**3094.

Mammals. Booklet stamps

2010 (15 June) Designs as Nos. 3061 and 3063 but printed in gravure. Self-adhesive. 'All-over' phosphor. Die-cut perf 14½

3095	**2256**	(1st)	multicoloured	5·75	6·00
3096	**2258**	(1st)	multicoloured	5·75	6·00

Nos. 3095/6 were only issued in stamp booklets, originally sold for £2·46.

2290 Paralympic Games: Rowing

2291 Shooting

2292 Modern Pentathlon

2293 Taekwondo

2294 Cycling

2295 Paralympic Games: Table Tennis

2296 Hockey

2297 Football

2298 Paralympic Games: Goalball   **2299** Boxing

Olympic and Paralympic Games, London (2012) (3rd series)

2010 (27 July) 'All-over' phosphor. Perf 14½

3097	**2290**	(1st)	multicoloured	1·25	1·00	☐ ☐
		a.	Horiz strip of 5. Nos. 3097/3101	6·25	5·50	☐ ☐
3098	2291	(1st)	multicoloured	1·25	1·00	☐ ☐
3099	**2292**	(1st)	multicoloured	1·25	1·00	☐ ☐
3100	**2293**	(1st)	multicoloured	1·25	1·00	☐ ☐
3101	**2294**	(1st)	multicoloured	1·25	1·00	☐ ☐
3102	**2295**	(1st)	multicoloured	1·25	1·00	☐ ☐
		a.	Horiz strip of 5. Nos. 3102/6	6·25	5·50	☐ ☐
3103	2296	(1st)	multicoloured	1·25	1·00	☐ ☐
3104	**2297**	(1st)	multicoloured	1·25	1·00	☐ ☐
3105	**2298**	(1st)	multicoloured	1·25	1·00	☐ ☐
3106	**2299**	(1st)	multicoloured	1·25	1·00	☐ ☐
Set of 10				12·00	10·00	☐
First Day Cover					11·00	☐
Presentation Pack (P.O. Pack No. 444)				13·00		☐
PHQ Cards (set of 10) (339)				9·00	20·00	☐ ☐
Set of 2 Gutter Strips of 10				25·00		☐

Nos. 3097/3101 and 3102/6 were each printed together, se-tenant, in horizontal strips of five stamps in sheets of 50 (2 panes 5 × 5) and were also issued on 27 July 2011 in a miniature sheet containing all 30 stamps in the series. See **MS**3204a.

Olympic and Paralympic Games, London (2012) (4th series). Booklet stamps

2010 (27 July–12 Oct.) Designs as Nos. 3097, 3101/2 and 3104 but printed in gravure. Self-adhesive. 'All-over' phosphor. Die-cut perf 14½

3107	**2290**	(1st)	multicoloured	3·75	3·25	☐ ☐
3108	**2295**	(1st)	multicoloured	3·75	3·25	☐ ☐
3108a	**2297**	(1st)	multicoloured			
		(12 Oct)		3·75	3·25	☐ ☐
3108b	**2294**	(1st)	multicoloured			

		(12 Oct)	3·75	3·25	☐ ☐
Set of 4			13·00	12·00	☐ ☐

Nos. 3107/8 and 3108a/b were only issued in two separate stamp booklets each originally sold for £2·46.

2300 LMS Coronation Class Locomotive, Euston Station, 1938

2301 BR Class 9F Locomotive *Evening Star*, Midsomer Norton, 1962

2302 GWR King Class Locomotive *King William IV*, near Teignmouth, 1935

2303 LNER Class A1 Locomotive *Royal Lancer*, 1929

2304 SR King Arthur Class Locomotive *Sir Mador de la Porte*, Bournemouth Central Station, 1935–9

2305 LMS NCC Class WT No. 2, Larne Harbour, c. 1947

Great British Railways

2010 (19 Aug.) 'All-over' phosphor. Perf 14

3109	**2300**	(1st)	gold, bluish grey and black	1·25	1·00	☐ ☐
3110	**2301**	(1st)	gold, bluish grey and black	1·25	1·00	☐ ☐
3111	**2302**	67p	gold, bluish grey and black	1·70	1·70	☐ ☐
3112	**2303**	67p	gold, bluish grey and black	1·70	1·70	☐ ☐
3113	**2304**	97p	gold, bluish grey and black	2·50	2·50	☐ ☐
3114	**2305**	97p	gold, bluish grey and black	2·50	2·50	☐ ☐
Set of 6				10·00	10·00	☐ ☐
First Day Cover					11·00	☐
Presentation Pack (P.O. Pack No. 445)				12·00		☐
PHQ Cards (set of 6) (340)				5·00	12·00	☐ ☐
Set of 6 Gutter Pairs				21·00		☐

2306 Heart-regulating Beta Blockers (Sir James Black, 1962)

2307 Antibiotic Properties of Penicillin (Sir Alexander Fleming, 1928)

2308 Total Hip Replacement Operation (Sir John Charnley, 1962)

2309 Artificial Lens Implant Surgery (Sir Harold Ridley, 1949)

2310 Malaria Parasite transmitted by Mosquitoes (proved by Sir Ronald Ross, 1897)

2311 Computed Tomography Scanner (Sir Godfrey Hounsfield, 1971)

Medical Breakthroughs

2010 (16 Sept.) 'All-over' phosphor. Perf 14 × 14½

3115	**2306**	(1st)	multicoloured	1·25	1·00	☐ ☐
3116	**2307**	58p	multicoloured	1·50	1·50	☐ ☐
3117	**2308**	60p	multicoloured	1·50	1·50	☐ ☐
3118	**2309**	67p	multicoloured	1·70	1·70	☐ ☐
3119	**2310**	88p	multicoloured	2·25	2·25	☐ ☐
3120	**2311**	97p	multicoloured	2·50	2·50	☐ ☐
Set of 6				9·50	9·50	☐
First Day Cover					11·00	☐
Presentation Pack (P.O. Pack No. 446)				11·00		☐
PHQ Cards (*set of 6*) (341)				5·00	12·50	☐ ☐
Set of 6 Gutter Pairs				20·00		☐

See also No. 3153.

2312 Winnie the Pooh and Christopher Robin (*Now we are Six*)

2313 Winnie the Pooh and Piglet (*The House at Pooh Corner*)

2314 Winnie the Pooh and Rabbit (*Winnie the Pooh*)

2315 Winnie the Pooh and Eeyore (*Winnie the Pooh*)

2316 Winnie the Pooh and Friends (*Winnie the Pooh*)

2317 Winnie the Pooh and Tigger (*The House at Pooh Corner*)

2318 Winnie the Pooh

Europa. Children's Books. Winnie the Pooh by A. A. Milne. Book Illustrations by E. H. Shepard

2010 (12 Oct.) 'All-over' phosphor. Perf 14 × 14½

3121	**2312**	(1st)	yellow-brown, pale stone and black	1·25	1·00	☐ ☐
3122	**2313**	58p	yellow-brown, pale stone and black	1·40	1·40	☐ ☐
3123	**2314**	60p	yellow-brown, pale stone and black	1·50	1·50	☐ ☐
3124	**2315**	67p	yellow-brown, pale stone and black	1·70	1·70	☐ ☐
3125	**2316**	88p	yellow-brown, pale stone and black	2·25	2·25	☐ ☐
3126	**2317**	97p	yellow-brown, pale stone and black	2·40	2·40	☐ ☐
Set of 6				9·50	9·50	☐ ☐
First Day Cover					11·00	☐
Presentation Pack (Nos. 3121/**MS**3127) (P.O. Pack No. 447)				19·00		☐
PHQ Cards (*set of 11*) (342)				9·00	22·00	☐ ☐
Set of 6 Gutter Pairs				20·00		☐

MS3127 115 × 89 mm. **2318** (1st) Winnie the Pooh and Christopher Robin (from *Now we are Six*); 60p Christopher Robin reads to Winnie the Pooh (from *Winnie the Pooh*); 88p Winnie the Pooh and Christopher Robin sailing in umbrella (from *Winnie the Pooh*); 97p Christopher Robin (putting on wellingtons) and Pooh (from *Winnie the Pooh*). Perf 14½

		7·50	7·50	☐ ☐
First Day Cover			8·50	☐

The 1st class value includes the 'EUROPA' emblem.

Stamps from **MS**3127 show lines from poem 'We Too' by A. A. Milne: 'Wherever I am, there's always Pooh' (1st); "There's always Pooh and Me. Whatever I do, he wants to do" (60p); "Where are you going to-day?" says Pooh: "Well that's very odd 'cos I was too" (88p); "Let's go together," says Pooh, says he. "Let's go together," says Pooh (97p).

The eleven PHQ cards show the six stamps, the four individual stamps within **MS**3127 and the complete miniature sheet.

2319 Wallace and Gromit carol singing

2320 Gromit posting Christmas Cards

2321 Wallace and Gromit carol singing

2322 Wallace and Gromit decorating Christmas Tree

2323 Gromit posting Christmas Cards

2324 Gromit carrying Christmas Pudding

2325 Gromit putting on Bone-themed Pullover

2326 Joe 90

2327 Captain Scarlet

2328 Thunderbird 2 (Thunderbirds)

2329 Stingray

2330 Fireball XL5

2331 Supercar

2332 Thunderbird 4; Thunderbird 3; Thunderbird 2; Thunderbird 1

Christmas with Wallace and Gromit

2010 (2 Nov.) One centre band (3128) or two phosphor bands (others). Perf 14½×14 (with one elliptical hole in each vert side)

(a) Self-adhesive

3128	**2319**	(2nd) multicoloured	1·00	75		
3129	**2320**	(1st) multicoloured	1·25	1·00		
3130	**2321**	(2nd Large) multicoloured	1·50	1·50		
3131	**2322**	60p multicoloured	1·50	1·50		
3132	**2323**	(1st Large) multicoloured	2·00	2·00		
3133	**2324**	97p multicoloured	2·40	2·40		
3134	**2325**	£1·46 multicoloured	3·50	3·50		
Set of 7			**12·00**	11·00		
First Day Cover				12·00		
Presentation Pack (P.O. Pack No. 448)			14·00			
PHQ Cards (set of 8) (343)			6·00	17·00		

(b) Ordinary gum

MS3135	115×102 mm. As Nos. 3128/3412·00	12·00			
First Day Cover		13·00			

The eight PHQ cards show the seven individual stamps and the miniature sheet.

The 2nd class, 1st class, 60p and 97p stamps were also issued together in sheets of 20 containing eight 2nd class, eight 1st class, two 60p and two 97p stamps, each stamps accompanied by a *se-tenant* label. Separate sheets of 20 2nd, 20 1st, ten 1st, ten 60p and ten 97p were available with personal photographs on the labels. All these sheets were printed in lithography instead of gravure.

Year Pack

2010 (2 Nov.) Comprises Nos. 2999/3008, **MS**3025/63, **MS**3065, **MS**3072, 3074/81, **MS**3086/94, 3097/3106 and 3109/34

CP3135a	Year Pack	£145	

Post Office Yearbook

2010 (2 Nov.) Comprises Nos. 2999/3008, **MS**3025/63, **MS**3065, **MS**3072, 3074/81, **MS**3086/94, 3097/3106 and 3109/34

YB3135a	Yearbook	£140	

Miniature Sheet Collection

2010 (2 Nov.) Comprises Nos. **MS**3024, **MS**3025, **MS**3053, **MS**3065, **MS**3072, **MS**3086, **MS**3094, **MS**3127 and **MS**3135

MS3135a Miniature Sheet Collection   60·00

'F.A.B. The Genius of Gerry Anderson' (producer of TV programmes)

2011 (11 Jan.) 'All-over' phosphor

(a) Litho. Ordinary gum. Perf 14

3136	**2326**	(1st) multicoloured	1·25	1·00		
		a. Horiz strip of 3.				
		Nos. 3136/8	4·00	4·00		
3137	**2327**	(1st) multicoloured	1·25	1·00		
3138	**2328**	97p multicoloured	1·25	1·00		
3139	**2329**	97p multicoloured	2·40	2·40		
		a. Horiz strip of 3.				
		Nos. 3139/41	8·00	8·00		
3140	**2330**	97p multicoloured	2·40	2·40		
3141	**2331**	97p multicoloured	2·40	2·40		
Set of 6			11·00	11·00		
First Day Cover				12·00		
Presentation Pack (P.O. Pack No. 450)			19·00			
PHQ Cards (set of 11) (344)			9·00	22·00		
Set of 2 Gutter Strips of 6			23·00			

(b) Microlenticular. 'All-over' phosphor Perf 14

MS3142 116×89 mm. **2332** 41p			
Thunderbird 4, 60p Thunderbird 3,			
88p Thunderbird 2, 97p Thunderbird			
1 multicoloured	8·00	8·00	
First Day Cover		9·00	

(c) Self-adhesive. As No. 3138 but printed
in gravure. Die-cut perf 14

3143 **2328** (1st) multicoloured   3·50   3·50   ☐ ☐

Nos. 3136/8 and 3139/41 were each printed together,
se-tenant, as horizontal strips of three stamps in sheets of 60
(2 panes 6×5).

The stamps within **MS**3142 use microlenticular technology
to show each vehicle's launch sequences when the miniature
sheet is tilted.

No. 3143 was only issued in booklets originally sold for £1·46.

2333 Classic Locomotives of England

Classic Locomotives (1st series). England Miniature Sheet

2011 (1 Feb.) Sheet 180×74 mm. Multicoloured. 'All-over'
phosphor. Perf 14

MS3144 **2333** (1st) BR Dean Goods
No. 2532; 60p Peckett R2 *Thor*;
88p Lancashire and Yorkshire
Railway 1093 No. 1100; 97p
BR WD No. 90662   7·50   7·50   ☐ ☐
First Day Cover   8·50   ☐
Presentation Pack (P.O. Pack No. 451) 8·00   ☐
PHQ Cards (*set of 5*) (345)   4·00   10·00   ☐ ☐

The five PHQ cards show the four individual stamps and the
complete miniature sheet.

See also No. 3215.

2334 *Oliver*

2335 *Blood Brothers*

2336 *We Will Rock You*

2337 *Spamalot*

2338 *Rocky Horror Show*

2339 *Me and My Girl*

2340 *Return to the Forbidden Planet*

2341 *Billy Elliot*

Musicals

2011 (24 Feb.) 'All-over' phosphor. Perf 14

3145 **2334**	(1st)	multicoloured	1·25	1·00	☐ ☐
3146 **2335**	(1st)	multicoloured	1·25	1·00	☐ ☐
3147 **2336**	(1st)	multicoloured	1·25	1·00	☐ ☐
3148 **2337**	(1st)	multicoloured	1·25	1·00	☐ ☐
3149 **2338**	97p	multicoloured	2·40	2·40	☐ ☐
3150 **2339**	97p	multicoloured	2·40	2·40	☐ ☐
3151 **2340**	97p	multicoloured	2·40	2·40	☐ ☐
3152 **2341**	97p	multicoloured	2·40	2·40	☐ ☐
Set of 8			13·00	13·00	☐
First Day Cover				14·00	☐
Presentation Pack (P.O. Pack No. 452)			15·00		☐
PHQ Cards (*set of 8*) (346)			6·00	17·00	☐ ☐
Set of 8 Gutter Pairs			27·00		☐
Set of 8 Traffic Light Gutter Pairs			29·00		☐

50th Anniversary of the British Heart Foundation. Booklet stamp

2011 (24 Feb.) Design as No. 3115 but printed in gravure. Self-
adhesive. 'All-over' phosphor. Die-cut perf 14×14½

3153 **2306** (1st) multicoloured   3·00   3·00   ☐ ☐

No. 3153 was only issued in booklets originally sold for £2·46.

2342 Rincewind (Terry Pratchett's *Discworld*)

2343 Nanny Ogg (Terry Pratchett's *Discworld*)

2344 Michael Gambon as Dumbledore (J. K. Rowling's Harry Potter)

2345 Ralph Fiennes as Lord Voldemort (J. K. Rowling's Harry Potter)

2346 Merlin (Arthurian Legend)

2347 Morgan Le Fay (Arthurian Legend)

2348 Aslan (C. S. Lewis's Narnia)

2349 Tilda Swinton as The White Witch (C. S. Lewis's Narnia)

Magical Realms

2011 (8 Mar.-2 Dec.) 'All-over' phosphor. Perf 14½

3154	**2342**	(1st)	multicoloured	1·25	1·00	☐ ☐
		a.	Vert pair.			
			Nos. 3154/5	2·60	2·60	☐ ☐
3155	**2343**	(1st)	multicoloured	1·25	1·00	☐ ☐
3156	**2344**	(1st)	multicoloured	1·25	1·00	☐ ☐
		a.	Vert pair.			
			Nos. 3156/7	2·60	2·60	☐ ☐
3157	**2345**	(1st)	multicoloured	1·25	1·00	☐ ☐
3158	**2346**	60p	multicoloured	1·50	1·50	☐ ☐
		a.	Vert pair.			
			Nos. 3158/9	3·25	3·25	☐ ☐
3159	**2347**	60p	multicoloured	1·50	1·50	☐ ☐
3160	**2348**	97p	multicoloured	2·40	2·40	☐ ☐
		a.	Vert pair.			
			Nos. 3160/1	5·00	5·00	☐ ☐
3161	**2349**	97p	multicoloured	2·40	2·40	☐ ☐
Set of 8				12·00	12·00	☐
First Day Cover					13·00	☐
Presentation Pack (P.O. Pack No. 453)				14·00		☐
Presentation Pack ('Heroes and Villains'						
	containing Nos. 3156/7,					
	each × 5) (2 Dec)			15·00		☐
PHQ Cards (set of 8) (347)				6·00	18·00	☐ ☐
Set of 4 Gutter Strips of 4				25·00		☐

Nos. 3154/5, 3156/7, 3158/9 and 3160/1 were each printed together, se-tenant, as vertical pairs in sheets of 60 (2 panes 5×6).

2350 African Elephant

2351 Mountain Gorilla

2352 Siberian Tiger

2353 Polar Bear

2354 Amur Leopard

2355 Iberian Lynx

2356 Red Panda

2357 Black Rhinoceros

2358 African Wild Dog

2359 Golden Lion Tamarin

2360 Wildlife of the Amazon Rainforest

50th Anniversary of the WWF

2011 (22 Mar.) 'All-over' phosphor. Perf 14 (**MS**3172) or 14½ (others)

3162	**2350**	(1st)	multicoloured	1·25	1·00	☐ ☐
		a.	Horiz strip of 5.			
			Nos. 3162/6	7·00	7·00	☐ ☐
3163	**2351**	(1st)	multicoloured	1·25	1·00	☐ ☐
3164	**2352**	(1st)	multicoloured	1·25	1·00	☐ ☐
3165	**2353**	(1st)	multicoloured	1·25	1·00	☐ ☐
3166	**2354**	(1st)	multicoloured	1·25	1·00	☐ ☐
3167	**2355**	(1st)	multicoloured	1·25	1·00	☐ ☐
		a.	Horiz strip of 5.			
			Nos. 3167/71	7·00	7·00	☐ ☐
3168	**2356**	(1st)	multicoloured	1·25	1·00	☐ ☐
3169	**2357**	(1st)	multicoloured	1·25	1·00	☐ ☐
3170	**2358**	(1st)	multicoloured	1·25	1·00	☐ ☐
3171	**2359**	(1st)	multicoloured	1·25	1·00	☐ ☐
Set of 10				12·50	12·50	☐ ☐
First Day Cover					14·00	☐
Presentation Pack (Nos. 3162/**MS**3172)						
		(P.O. Pack No. 454)		22·00		☐
PHQ Cards (set of 15) (348)				12·00	30·00	☐ ☐
Set of 2 Gutter Strips of 10				26·00		☐
MS3172 115×89 mm. **2360** (1st) Spider						
	Monkey; 60p Hyacinth Macaw;					
	88p Poison Dart Frog; 97p Jaguar			7·50	7·50	☐ ☐
First Day Cover					8·50	☐

Nos. 3162/6 and 3167/71 were each printed together, se-tenant, as horizontal strips of five stamps in sheets of 50 (2 panes 5×5) and were also issued in the £9·05 '50th Anniversary of the WWF' booklet, No. DX52.

The 1st class value from **MS**3172 includes the 'EUROPA' emblem.

2361 David Tennant as Hamlet, 2008

2362 Antony Sher as Prospero, The Tempest, 2009

2363 Chuk Iwuji as Henry VI, 2006

2364 Paul Schofield as King Lear, 1962

2365 Sara Kestelman as Titania, *A Midsummer Night's Dream*, 1970

2366 Ian McKellen and Francesca Annis as Romeo and Juliet, 1976

2367 The Four Theatres of the Royal Shakespeare Company, Stratford-upon-Avon

50th Anniversary of the Royal Shakespeare Company

2011 (12 Apr.) 'All-over' phosphor

(a) Gravure Walsall. Perf 14½

3173	**2361**	(1st)	black, brownish black and bright scarlet	1·25	1·00	☐ ☐
3174	**2362**	66p	black, brownish black and bright scarlet	1·70	1·70	☐ ☐
3175	**2363**	68p	black, brownish black and bright scarlet	1·70	1·70	☐ ☐
3176	**2364**	76p	black, brownish black and bright scarlet	1·90	1·90	☐ ☐
3177	**2365**	£1	black, brownish black and bright scarlet	2·50	2·50	☐ ☐
3178	**2366**	£1·10	black, brownish black and bright scarlet	2·75	2·75	☐ ☐
Set of 6				10·50	10·50	☐ ☐
First Day Cover					12·00	☐
Presentation Pack (Nos. 3173/**MS**3179) (P.O. Pack No. 455)				19·00		☐
PHQ Cards (*set of* 11) (349)				9·00	20·00	☐ ☐
Set of 6 Gutter Pairs				22·00		☐

(b) Litho Cartor. Multicoloured. Perf 14

MS3179 115×89 mm. **2367** (1st) Janet Suzman as Ophelia, *Hamlet*, 1965, Royal Shakespeare Theatre; 68p Patrick Stewart in *Antony and Cleopatra*, 2006, Swan Theatre; 76p Geoffrey Streatfeild in *Henry V*, 2007, The Courtyard Theatre; £1 Judy Dench as Lady Macbeth, 1976, The Other Place   7·50   7·50   ☐ ☐

First Day Cover   8·50   ☐

The eleven PHQ cards show the six stamps, the four individual stamps within **MS**3179 and the complete miniature sheet.

2368 Prince William and Miss Catherine Middleton

Royal Wedding. Official Engagement Portraits by Mario Testino. Miniature Sheet

2011 (21 Apr.) Sheet 115×89 mm. Multicoloured. 'All-over' phosphor. Perf 14½×14

MS3180 **2368** (1st)×2 Prince William and Miss Catherine Middleton embracing; £1·10×2 Formal portrait of Prince William and Miss Catherine Middleton in Council Chamber, St. James's Palace	8·50	8·50	☐ ☐
First Day Cover		9·50	☐
Presentation Pack (P.O. Pack No. M20)	13·00		☐
Commemorative Document	15·00		☐

2369 Cray (fabric print by William Morris), 1884

2370 Cherries (detail from panel by Philip Webb), 1867

2371 Seaweed (wallpaper pattern by John Henry Dearle), 1901

2372 Peony (ceramic tile design by Kate Faulkner), 1877

2373 Acanthus (tile by William Morris and William De Morgan), 1876

2374 The Merchant's Daughter (detail of stained glass window by Edward Burne-Jones), 1864

150th Anniversary of Morris and Company (designers and manufacturers of textiles, wallpaper and furniture) (1st issue)

2011 (5 May) 'All-over' phosphor. Perf 14 × 14½

3181	**2369**	(1st)	multicoloured	1·00	1·00
3182	**2370**	(1st)	multicoloured	1·25	1·00
3183	**2371**	76p.	multicoloured	1·90	1·90
3184	**2372**	76p.	multicoloured	1·90	1·90
3185	**2373**	£1·10	multicoloured	2·75	2·75
3186	**2374**	£1·10	multicoloured	2·75	2·75
Set of 6				11·00	11·00
First Day Cover					12·00
Presentation Pack (P.O. Pack No. 456)				12·00	
PHQ Cards (set of 6) (350)				5·00	14·00
Set of 6 Gutter Pairs				23·00	

Nos. 3181/6 were also issued in the £9·99 'Morris & Co' booklet, No. DY1.

150th Anniversary of Morris and Company (2nd issue)

2011 (5 May) Design as Type **2202** (2009 Christmas stained-glass windows). One centre band. Perf 14½ × 14 (with one elliptical hole in each vert side)

3186a **2202** (2nd) multicoloured   3·00   3·00

No. 3186a was only issued in the £9·99 'Morris & Co' stamp booklet, No. DY1.

2375 Thomas the Tank Engine

2376 James the Red Engine

2377 Percy the Small Engine

2378 Daisy (diesel railcar)

2379 Toby the Tram Engine

2380 Gordon the Big Engine

2381 Book Illustrations by John T. Kenny (76p.) or C. Reginald Dalby (others)

2382 "Goodbye, Bertie," called
Thomas (from *Tank Engine Thomas Again*)

Thomas the Tank Engine

2011 (14 June) 'All-over' phosphor

(a) Ordinary gum. Perf 14 (**MS**3193) or 14½ × 14 (others)

3187	**2375**	(1st)	multicoloured	1·25	1·00
3188	**2376**	66p	multicoloured	1·70	1·70
3189	**2377**	68p	multicoloured	1·70	1·70
3190	**2378**	76p	multicoloured	1·90	1·90
3191	**2379**	£1	multicoloured	2·50	2·50
3192	**2380**	£1·10	multicoloured	2·75	2·75
Set of 6				11·00	11·00
First Day Cover					12·00
Presentation Pack (Nos. 3187/**MS**3193)					
		(P.O. Pack No. 457)		20·00	
PHQ Cards (set of 11) (351)				9·00	20·00
Set of 6 Gutter Pairs				23·00	

MS3193 115 × 89 mm. **2381** "Goodbye, Bertie," called Thomas (from *Tank Engine Thomas Again*) (1st); James was more dirty than hurt (from *Toby the Tram Engine*) (68p); "Yes Sir," Percy shivered miserably (from *The Eight Famous Engines*) (76p); They told Henry, "We shall leave you there for always" (from *The Three Railway Engines*) (£1)   7·50   7·50

First Day Cover   8·50

(b) Self-adhesive. Die-cut perf 14
3194 **2382** (1st) multicoloured   4·00   4·00

The 11 PHQ Cards show the six stamps, the four individual stamps within **MS**3193 and the complete miniature sheet.

Nos. 3187/92 show scenes from TV series *Thomas and Friends*, and Nos. **MS**3193/3194 book illustrations from *The Railway Series*.

No. 3194 was only issued in stamp booklets originally sold for £2·76.

2383 Paralympic Games: Sailing

2384 Athletics: Field

2385 Volleyball

2386 Wheelchair Rugby

2387 Wrestling

2388 Wheelchair Tennis

2389 Fencing

2390 Gymnastics

2391 Triathlon

2392 Handball

Olympic and Paralympic Games, London (2012) (5th series)

2011 (27 July) 'All-over' phosphor. Perf 14½

3195	**2383**	(1st)	multicoloured	1·25	1·00	
		a.	Horiz strip of 5.			
			Nos. 3195/9	6·25	5·50	
3196	**2384**	(1st)	multicoloured	1·25	1·00	
3197	**2385**	(1st)	multicoloured	1·25	1·00	
3198	**2386**	(1st)	multicoloured	1·25	1·00	
3199	**2387**	(1st)	multicoloured	1·25	1·00	
3200	**2388**	(1st)	multicoloured	1·25	1·00	
		a.	Horiz strip of 5.			
			Nos. 3200/4	6·25	5·50	
3201	**2389**	(1st)	multicoloured	1·25	1·00	
3202	**2390**	(1st)	multicoloured	1·25	1·00	
3203	**2391**	(1st)	multicoloured	1·25	1·00	
3204	**2392**	(1st)	multicoloured	1·25	1·00	
Set of 10				12·00	10·00	

First Day Cover		11·00
Presentation Pack (P.O. Pack No. 458)	14·00	
PHQ Cards (*set of* 10) (352)	9·00	20·00
Set of 2 Gutter Strips of 10	25·00	

MS3204a 210×300 mm. Nos. 2981/90, 3097/3106 and 3195/3204   60·00   65·00

Nos. 3195/9 and 3200/4 were each printed together, *se-tenant*, in horizontal strips of five stamps in sheets of 50 (2 panes 5×5) and in **MS**3204a.

Olympic and Paralympic Games (2012) (6th series)

2011 (27 July) Booklet stamps. Designs as Nos. 3195, 3198 and 3201/2. Self-adhesive. 'All-over' phosphor. Die-cut perf 14½×14

3205	**2386**	(1st)	multicoloured	3·75	3·50
3206	**2383**	(1st)	multicoloured	3·75	3·50
3206a	**2390**	(1st)	multicoloured	3·75	3·50
3206b	**2389**	(1st)	multicoloured	3·75	3·50

Nos. 3205/6 and 3206a/b were only issued in two separate stamp booklets originally sold for £2·76.

2393 The Sovereign's Sceptre with Cross

2394 St. Edward's Crown

2395 Rod and Sceptre with Doves

2396 Queen Mary's Crown

2397 The Sovereign's Orb

2398 Jewelled Sword of Offering

2399 Imperial State Crown

2400 Coronation Spoon

Crown Jewels

2011 (23 Aug.) Phosphor background. Perf 14 × 14½

3207	**2393**	(1st)	multicoloured	1·25	1·00	☐ ☐
3208	**2394**	(1st)	multicoloured	1·25	1·00	☐ ☐
3209	**2395**	68p	multicoloured	1·70	1·70	☐ ☐
3210	**2396**	68p	multicoloured	1·70	1·70	☐ ☐
3211	**2397**	76p	multicoloured	1·90	1·90	☐ ☐
3212	**2398**	76p	multicoloured	1·90	1·90	☐ ☐
3213	**2399**	£1·10	multicoloured	2·75	2·75	☐ ☐
3214	**2400**	£1·10	multicoloured	2·75	2·75	☐ ☐
Set of 8				14·00	14·00	☐
First Day Cover					15·00	☐
Presentation Pack (P.O. Pack No. 459)				16·00		☐
PHQ Cards (*set of* 8) (353)				7·00	21·00	☐ ☐
Set of 8 Gutter Pairs				29·00		☐

2401 BR Dean Goods Locomotive
No. 2532, 1951

Classic Locomotives. Booklet stamps

2011 (23 Aug.) Design as 1st class stamp within **MS**3144 but printed in gravure. Self-adhesive. 'All-over' phosphor. Die-cut perf 14

3215	**2401**	(1st)	black and gold	5·00	5·00	☐ ☐

No. 3215 was only issued in stamp booklets originally sold for £2·76.

2402 Pilot Gustav Hamel receiving mailbag

2403 Gustav Hamel in cockpit

2404 Pilot Clement Greswell and Blériot monoplane

2405 Delivery of first airmail to Postmaster General at Windsor

2406 First United Kingdom Aerial Post, 9 September 1911

Centenary of First United Kingdom Aerial Post (1st issue)

2011 (9 Sept.) 'All-over' phosphor. Perf 14

3216	**2402**	(1st)	purple-black and pale grey-lilac	1·25	1·10	☐ ☐
3217	**2403**	68p	brownish black and stone	1·70	1·70	☐ ☐
3218	**2404**	£1	deep sepia and pale grey-brown	2·50	2·50	☐ ☐
3219	**2405**	£1·10	black and pale grey	2·75	2·75	☐ ☐
Set of 4				7·50	7·50	☐ ☐
MS3220	**2406**	146×74 mm. Nos. 3216/19		7·50	7·50	☐ ☐
First Day Cover					9·00	☐
Presentation Pack (P.O. Pack No. 460)				9·00		☐
PHQ Cards (*set of* 5) (354)				4·50	10·00	☐ ☐

Nos. 3216/19 were only issued in the £9·97 'First United Kingdom Aerial Post' stamp booklet, No. DY2.
The five PHQ cards show the four individual stamps and the complete miniature sheet.

2407 Windsor Castle

Centenary of First United Kingdom Aerial Post (2nd issue)

2011 (9 Sept.) Recess and Litho. Perf 11 × 11½

3221	**2407**	50p	black on cream	5·00	5·00	☐ ☐

No. 3221 was only issued in the £9·99 'First United Kingdom Aerial Post' stamp booklet, No. DY2.

2408

Birth Centenary of Arnold Machin (sculptor). Miniature Sheet

2011 (14 Sept.) Sheet 124×71 mm containing stamps as No. U3002. Two phosphor bands. Perf 14½ × 14 (with one elliptical hole in each vertical side)

MS3222	**2408**	(1st) gold × 10	15·00	15·00	☐ ☐
First Day Cover				16·00	☐

2409 George I
(1714–27)

2410 George II
(1727–60)

2411 George III
(1760–1820)

2412 George IV
(1820–30)

2413 William IV
(1830–7)

2414 Victoria
(1837–1901)

2415 The Age of the Hanoverians

Kings and Queens (5th series). House of Hanover

2011 (15 Sept.) Two phosphor bands. Perf 14

3223	**2409**	(1st)	multicoloured	1·25	1·10	☐☐
3224	**2410**	(1st)	multicoloured	1·25	1·10	☐☐
3225	**2411**	76p	multicoloured	1·90	1·90	☐☐
3226	**2412**	76p	multicoloured	1·90	1·90	☐☐
3227	**2413**	£1·10	multicoloured	2·75	2·75	☐☐
3228	**2414**	£1·10	multicoloured	2·75	2·75	☐☐
Set of 6				11·00	11·00	☐
First Day Cover					13·00	☐

Presentation Pack (Nos. 3223/**MS**3229)

(P.O. Pack No. 461) 20·00 ☐

PHQ Cards (*set of* 11) (355)	9·00	20·00	☐☐
Set of 6 Gutter Pairs		23·00	☐
Set of 6 Traffic Light Gutter Blocks of 4	48·00		☐

MS3229 123×70 mm. **2415** (1st)
Robert Walpole (first Prime
Minister), 1721; 68p Ceiling by
Robert Adam, Kedleston Hall, 1763;
76p Penny Black (uniform postage),
1840; £1 Queen Victoria (Diamond
Jubilee), 1897

7·50 7·50 ☐☐

First Day Cover 8·50 ☐

The complete miniature sheet is shown on one of the 11 PHQ
cards with the others depicting individual stamps, including
those from **MS**3229.

2416 Angel of the North

2417 Blackpool Tower

2418 Carrick-a-Rede,
Co. Antrim

2419 Downing Street

2420 Edinburgh Castle

2421 Forth Railway Bridge

2422 Glastonbury Tor

2423 Harlech Castle

2424 Ironbridge

2425 Jodrell Bank

2426 Kursaal, Southend,
Essex

2427 Lindisfarne Priory

UK A-Z (1st series). Famous Landmarks A-L

2011 (13 Oct.) 'All-over' phosphor. Perf 14½

3230	**2416**	(1st)	multicoloured	1·40	1·25	☐☐
		a.	Horiz strip of 6.			
			Nos. 3230/35	8·00	7·00	☐☐
3231	**2417**	(1st)	multicoloured	1·40	1·25	☐☐
3232	**2418**	(1st)	multicoloured	1·40	1·25	☐☐
3233	**2419**	(1st)	multicoloured	1·40	1·25	☐☐
3234	**2420**	(1st)	multicoloured	1·40	1·25	☐☐
3235	**2421**	(1st)	multicoloured	1·40	1·25	☐☐
3236	**2422**	(1st)	multicoloured	1·40	1·25	☐☐
		a.	Horiz strip of 6.			
			Nos. 3236/41	8·00	7·00	☐☐
3237	**2423**	(1st)	multicoloured	1·40	1·25	☐☐
3238	**2424**	(1st)	multicoloured	1·40	1·25	☐☐
3239	**2425**	(1st)	multicoloured	1·40	1·25	☐☐
3240	**2426**	(1st)	multicoloured	1·40	1·25	☐☐
3241	**2427**	(1st)	multicoloured	1·40	1·25	☐☐
Set of 12				16·00	13·00	☐☐
First Day Covers (2)					14·00	☐

Presentation Pack (P.O. Pack No. 462)	18·00		☐
PHQ Cards (set of 12) (356)	10·00	20·00	☐ ☐
Set of 2 Gutter Strips of 12	32·00		☐
Set of 2 Traffic Light Gutter Strips of 24	60·00		☐

Nos. 3230/35 and 3236/41 were each printed together, se-tenant, as horizontal strips of six stamps in sheets of 60 (2 panes of 30) and were also issued on 10 April 2012 in a sheet containing all 26 stamps. See MS3308.

2428 Joseph visited by the Angel (Matthew 1:21)

2429 Madonna and Child (Matthew 1:23)

2430 Joseph visited by the Angel (Matthew 1:21)

2431 Madonna and Child (Matthew 1:23)

2432 Baby Jesus in the Manger (Luke 2:7)

2433 Shepherds visited by the Angel (Luke 2:10)

2434 Wise Men and Star (Matthew 2:10)

Christmas. 400th Anniversary of the King James Bible

2011 (8 Nov.) One centre band (3242) or two phosphor bands (others). Perf 14½×14 (with one elliptical hole in each vert side)

(a) Self-adhesive

3242	**2428**	(2nd)	multicoloured	1·00	75	☐ ☐
3243	**2429**	(1st)	multicoloured	1·25	1·00	☐ ☐
3244	**2430**	(2nd Large)	multicoloured	1·50	1·25	☐ ☐
3245	**2431**	(1st Large)	multicoloured	2·00	1·50	☐ ☐
3246	**2432**	68p	multicoloured	1·70	1·70	☐ ☐
3247	**2433**	£1·10	multicoloured	2·75	2·75	☐ ☐
3248	**2434**	£1·65	multicoloured	4·00	4·00	☐ ☐
Set of 7				13·00	13·00	☐ ☐
First Day Cover					14·00	☐
Presentation Pack (P.O. Pack No. 463)				15·00		☐
PHQ Cards (set of 8) (357)				5·50	18·00	☐ ☐

(b) Ordinary gum

MS3249 116×102 mm.

| As Nos. 3242/48 | 13·00 | 13·00 | ☐ ☐ |
| First Day Cover | | 14·00 | ☐ |

The eight PHQ cards show the seven individual stamps and the miniature sheet.

The 2nd class, 1st class, 68p, £1·10 and £1·65 stamps were also issued in sheets of 20 containing eight 2nd class, eight 1st class, two 68p and two £1·10 stamps, each stamp accompanied by a se-tenant label with a verse from the King James Bible.

Separate sheets of 20 2nd, ten 1st, ten 68p and ten £1·10 were available with personal photographs.

Year Pack

2011 (8 Nov.) Comprises Nos. 3136/42, **MS**3144/52, 3154/93, 3195/3204, 3207/14, **MS**3220 and 3223/48

| CP3244a | Year Pack | £165 | ☐ |

Post Office Yearbook

2011 (8 Nov.) Comprises Nos. 3136/42, **MS**3144/52, 3154/93, 3195/3204, 3207/14, **MS**3220 and 3223/48

| YB3244a | Yearbook | £165 | ☐ |

Miniature Sheet Collection

2011 (8 Nov.) Comprises Nos. **MS**3142, **MS**3144, **MS**3172, **MS**3179/80, **MS**3193, **MS**3220, **MS**3229 and **MS**3249

| MS3244a | Miniature Sheet Collection | £130 | ☐ |

2435 Paralympic Games Emblem

2436 Olympic Games Emblem

Olympic and Paralympic Games (7th issue)

2012 (5 Jan.) Self-adhesive. Two phosphor bands. Die-cut perf 14½×14 (with one elliptical hole in each vert side)

3250	**2435**	(1st) black and orange-red	2·50	1·70	☐ ☐
3251	**2436**	(1st) black and orange-red	2·50	1·70	☐ ☐
3252	**2435**	(Worldwide up to 20g) black, bright scarlet and greenish blue	4·00	4·00	☐ ☐
3253	**2436**	(Worldwide up to 20g) black, bright scarlet and greenish blue	4·00	4·00	☐ ☐
Set of 4			12·00	11·00	☐ ☐
First Day Cover				13·00	☐
Presentation Pack (P.O. Pack No. 93)			13·50		☐
PHQ Cards (set of 4) (D32)			2·75	13·00	☐ ☐

Nos. 3250/1 were printed together in sheets of 50 (2 panes 5×5), with the two designs alternating horizontally and vertically. The upper pane had No. 3250 at top left and contained 13 of No. 3250 and 12 of No. 3251. The lower pane had No. 3251 at top left and contained 13 of No. 3251 and 12 of No. 3250.

Nos. 3250/1 were also issued in booklets of six originally sold for £2·76. The panes from this booklet exist in two versions which differ in the order of the stamps within the block of six.

Nos. 3252/3 were printed together in sheets of 25 (5×5) with the two designs alternating horizontally and vertically. There were two versions of the sheets of 25, one having No. 3252 at top left and containing 13 of No. 3252 and 12 of No. 3253, and the other having No. 3253 at top left and containing 13 of No. 3253 and 12 of No. 3252.

Nos. 3250/3 were also issued on 27 June 2012 in sheets of 20 with se-tenant labels showing Games venues, printed in lithography instead of gravure, each sheet containing eight each of Nos. 3250/1 and two each of Nos. 3252/3.

2437 Charlie and the Chocolate Factory

2438 Fantastic Mr. Fox

2439 James and the Giant Peach

2440 Matilda

2441 The Twits

2442 The Witches

Roald Dahl's Children's Stories (1st issue).
Book Illustrations by Quentin Blake

2012 (10 Jan.) 'All-over' phosphor. Perf 14

3254	**2437**	(1st) multicoloured	1·25	1·00	☐☐
3255	**2438**	66p multicoloured	1·70	1·70	☐☐
3256	**2439**	68p multicoloured	1·70	1·70	☐☐
3257	**2440**	76p multicoloured	1·90	1·90	☐☐
3258	**2441**	£1 multicoloured	2·50	2·50	☐☐
3259	**2442**	£1.10 multicoloured	2·75	2·75	☐☐
Set of 6			11·00	11·00	☐☐
First Day Cover				12·00	☐
Presentation Pack (Nos. 3254/9 and					
		MS3264)			
		(P.O. Pack No. 465)	21·00		☐
PHQ Cards (set of 11) (358)			7·50	17·00	☐☐
Set of 6 Gutter Pairs			23·00		
Traffic light Gutter Blocks of 4			45·00		☐

The complete miniature sheet is shown on one of the 11 PHQ cards with the others showing individual stamps including those from **MS**3264.

2443 The BFG carrying Sophie in his Hand

2444 The BFG wakes up the Giants

2445 Sophie sat on Buckingham Palace Window-sill

2446 The BFG and Sophie at Writing Desk

2447 Roald Dahl's The BFG

Roald Dahl's Children's Stories (2nd issue).
Book Illustrations by Quentin Blake

2012 (10 Jan.) 'All-over' phosphor. Perf 14 × 14½

3260	**2443**	(1st) multicoloured	2·00	2·00	☐☐
3261	**2444**	68p multicoloured	3·25	3·25	☐☐
3262	**2445**	76p multicoloured	3·50	3·50	☐☐
3263	**2446**	£1 multicoloured	3·75	3·75	☐☐
Set of 4			12·00	12·00	☐☐
MS3264 115×89 mm. **2447** Nos. 3260/3		12·00	12·00	☐☐
First Day Cover				13·00	☐

Nos. 3260/3 were only issued in the £11·47 'Roald Dahl, Master Storyteller' premium booklet, No.DY73 and in **MS**3264.

No. **MS**3264 commemorates the 30th Anniversary of the publication of The BFG.

2448 Edward VII (1901-10)

2449 George V (1910-36)

2450 Edward VIII (1936)

2451 George VI (1936-52)

2452 Elizabeth II (1952-)

2453 The Age of the Windsors

Kings and Queens (6th series). House of Windsor

2012 (2 Feb-6 Feb.) Two phosphor bands. Perf 14

3265	2448	(1st)	multicoloured	1·45	1·25	
3266	2449	68p	multicoloured	2·00	2·00	
3267	2450	76p	multicoloured	2·25	2·25	
3268	2451	£1	multicoloured	2·75	2·75	
3269	2452	£1·10	multicoloured	3·25	3·25	
Set of 5				10·00	10·00	
First Day Cover					11·00	
Presentation Pack (P.O. Pack No. 466)				21·00		
PHQ Cards (set of 10) (359)				6·75	14·00	
Commemorative Document (No. 3268 and £1·10 stamp from MS3229)						
(6 Feb)				11.00		
Set of 5 Gutter Pairs				19·00		
Set of 5 Traffic Light Gutter Blocks of 4			40·00			

MS3270 123×70 mm. 2453 (1st) Scott Expedition to South Pole, 1912; 68p Queen Elizabeth the Queen Mother and King George VI in bomb damaged street, c. 1940; 76p England's World Cup winning football team, 1966; £1 Channel Tunnel, 1996

	10·00	10·00
First Day Cover		11·00

The complete miniature sheet is shown on one of the ten PHQ cards with the others depicting individual stamps including those from MS3270.

2454 Diamond Jubilee

Diamond Jubilee. Miniature Sheet

2012 (6 Feb.) Two phosphor bands. Perf 14½×14 (with one elliptical hole in each vertical side)

MS3272 146×74mm. 2454 (1st)×6 Portrait from photograph by Dorothy Wilding; 1960 £1 Banknote portrait by Robert Austin; 1971 £5 Banknote portrait by Harry Eccleston; 1953 Coinage portrait by Mary Gillick; 1971 decimal coin portrait by Arnold Machin;

As No. U3271	12·00	12·00	
First Day Cover		13·00	
Presentation Pack (P.O. Pack No. 93)	14·00		
PHQ Cards (set of 7) (D33)	4·75	14·00	
Commemorative Document	14·00		

The 1st class slate-blue machin stamp from MS3272 has an iridescent overprint reading 'DIAMOND JUBILEE'.

The seven PHQ cards show the six individual stamps and the complete miniature sheet.

2455 Coventry Cathedral, 1962 (Sir Basil Spence, architect)

2456 Frederick Delius (1862-1934, composer)

2457 Orange Tree Embroidery (Mary 'May' Morris 1862-1938, designer and textile artist)

2458 Odette Hallowes (1912-95, SOE agent in occupied France)

2459 Steam Engine, 1712 (Thomas Newcomen, inventor of atmospheric steam engine)

2460 Kathleen Ferrier (1912-53, contralto)

2461 Interior of Palace of Westminster (Augustus Pugin 1812-52, Gothic revival architect and designer)

2462 Montagu Rhodes James (1862-1936 scholar and author)

2463 Bombe Code Breaking Machine (Alan Turing 1912-54, mathematician and World War II code breaker)

2464 Joan Mary Fry (1862-1955 relief worker and social reformer)

Britons of Distinction

2012 (23 Feb.) 'All-over' phosphor. Perf 14½

3273	2455	(1st)	multicoloured	1·25	1·10	
		a.	Horiz strip of 5. Nos. 3273/7	6·25	5·50	
3274	2456	(1st)	multicoloured	1·25	1·10	
3275	2457	(1st)	multicoloured	1·25	1·10	

3276	**2458**	(1st)	multicoloured	1·25	1·10
3277	**2459**	(1st)	multicoloured	1·25	1·10
3278	**2460**	(1st)	multicoloured	1·25	1·10
		a.	Horiz strip of 5.		
			Nos. 3278/82	6·25	5·50
3279	**2461**	(1st)	multicoloured	1·25	1·10
3280	**2462**	(1st)	multicoloured	1·25	1·10
3281	**2463**	(1st)	multicoloured	1·25	1·10
3282	**2464**	(1st)	multicoloured	1·25	1·10
Set of 10				12·00	10·00
First Day Cover					12·00
Presentation Pack (P.O. Pack No. 467)				14·00	
PHQ Cards (*set of* 10) (360)				6·75	18·00
Set of 2 Gutter Strips of 10				25·00	

Nos. 3273/7 and 3278/82 were each printed together, *se-tenant*, as horizontal strips of five stamps in sheets of 50 (2 panes 5×5).

2465 Classic Locomotives of Scotland

Classic Locomotives (2nd series). Scotland

2012 (8 Mar.) Sheet 180×74 mm. 'All-over' phosphor. Perf 14
MS3283 **2465** (1st) BR Class D34 Nos.
62471 *Glen Falloch* and 62496 *Glen Loy* at Ardlui, 9 May 1959; 68p BR Class D40 No. 62276 *Andrew Bain* at Macduff, July 1950; £1 *Andrew Barclay* No. 807 *Bon Accord* propelling wagons along Miller Street, Aberdeen, June 1962; £1·10 BR Class 4P No. 54767 *Clan Mackinnon* pulling fish train, Kyle of Lochalsh, October 1948 ... 8·00 ... 8·00

First Day Cover		9·50
Presentation Pack (P.O. Pack No. 468)	9·00	
PHQ Cards (*set of* 5) (361)	3·25	10·00

The five PHQ cards show the four individual stamps and the complete miniature sheet

2466 *The Dandy* and Desperate Dan

2467 *The Beano* and Dennis the Menace

2468 *Eagle* and Dan Dare

2469 *The Topper* and Beryl the Peril

2470 *Tiger* and Roy of the Rovers

2471 *Bunty* and the Four Marys

2472 *Buster* and Cartoon Character Buster

2473 *Valiant* and the Steel Claw

2474 *Twinkle* and Nurse Nancy

2475 *2000 AD* and Judge Dredd

Comics

2012 (20 Mar.) 'All-over' phosphor. Perf 14½

3284	**2466**	(1st)	multicoloured	1·25	1·25
		a.	Horiz strip of 5.		
			Nos. 3284/88	6·25	5·50
3285	**2467**	(1st)	multicoloured	1·25	1·25
3286	**2468**	(1st)	multicoloured	1·25	1·25
3287	**2469**	(1st)	multicoloured	1·25	1·25
3288	**2470**	(1st)	multicoloured	1·25	1·25
3289	**2471**	(1st)	multicoloured	1·25	1·25
		a.	Horiz strip of 5.		
			Nos. 3289/93	6·25	5·50
3290	**2472**	(1st)	multicoloured	1·25	1·25
3291	**2473**	(1st)	multicoloured	1·25	1·25
3292	**2474**	(1st)	multicoloured	1·25	1·25
3293	**2475**	(1st)	multicoloured	1·25	1·25
Set of 10				12·00	10·00
First Day Cover					12·00
Presentation Pack (P.O. Pack No. 469)				14·00	
PHQ Cards (*set of* 10) (362)				6·75	17·00
Set of 2 Gutter Strips of 5				25·00	

2476 Manchester Town Hall

2477 Narrow Water Castle, Co. Down

2488 York Minster

2489 London Zoo

UK A-Z (2nd series)

2478 Old Bailey, London

2479 Portmeirion, Wales

2012 (10 Apr.) 'All-over' phosphor. Perf 14½

3294	**2476**	(1st)	multicoloured	1·25	1·25	☐	☐
		a.	Horiz strip of 5.				
			Nos. 3294/9	7·50	6·50	☐	☐
3295	**2477**	(1st)	multicoloured	1·25	1·25	☐	☐
3296	**2478**	(1st)	multicoloured	1·25	1·25	☐	☐
3297	**2479**	(1st)	multicoloured	1·25	1·25	☐	☐
3298	**2480**	(1st)	multicoloured	1·25	1·25	☐	☐
3299	**2481**	(1st)	multicoloured	1·25	1·25	☐	☐
3300	**2482**	(1st)	multicoloured	1·25	1·25	☐	☐
		a.	Horiz strip of 5.				
			Nos. 3300/5	7·50	6·50	☐	☐
3301	**2483**	(1st)	multicoloured	1·25	1·25	☐	☐
3302	**2484**	(1st)	multicoloured	1·25	1·25	☐	☐
3303	**2485**	(1st)	multicoloured	1·25	1·25	☐	☐
3304	**2486**	(1st)	multicoloured	1·25	1·25	☐	☐
3305	**2487**	(1st)	multicoloured	1·25	1·25	☐	☐
3306	**2488**	(1st)	multicoloured	1·25	1·25	☐	☐
		a.	Horiz pair.				
			Nos. 3306/7	2·50	2·50	☐	☐
3307	**2489**	(1st)	multicoloured	1·25	1·25	☐	☐
Set of 14				14·00	12·00	☐	☐
First Day Covers (2)					14·00	☐	
Presentation Pack (P.O. Pack No. 470)				16·00		☐	
PHQ Cards (set of 14) (363)				9·50	20·00	☐	☐

2480 The Queen's College, Oxford

2481 Roman Baths, Bath

Set of 2 Gutter Strips of 12 and
1 Gutter Strip of 4   30·00   ☐

Set of 2 Traffic Light Gutter Strips of 24 and
1 Gutter Block of 8   60·00   ☐

MS3308 297×210 mm. Nos. 3230/41
and 3294/307   80·00   80·00   ☐ ☐

Nos. 3294/9 and 3300/5 were each printed together, se-tenant, as horizontal strips of six stamps in sheets of 60 (2 panes 6×5)

Nos. 3306/7 were printed together, se-tenant, as horizontal pairs in sheets of 60 (2 panes 6×5).

No. 3303 includes the 'EUROPA' emblem.

2482 Stirling Castle, Scotland

2483 Tyne Bridge, Newcastle

2484 Urquhart Castle, Scotland

2485 Victoria and Albert Museum, London

2490 Skirt Suit by Hardy Amies, late 1940s

2491 Outfit by Norman Hartnell, 1950s

2486 White Cliffs of Dover

2487 Station X, Bletchley Park, Buckinghamshire

2492 Jacket designed by John Pearce for Granny Takes a Trip Boutique, 1960s

2493 Print by Celia Birtwell for Outfit by Ossie Clark, late 1960s

2494 Suit designed for Ringo Starr by Tommy Nutter

2495 Outfit by Jean Muir, late 1970s/early 1980s

2496 'Royal' Dress by Zandra Rhodes, 1981

2497 Harlequin dress by Vivienne Westwood, 1993

2498 Suit by Paul Smith, 2003

2499 'Black Raven' by Alexander McQueen, 2009

Great British Fashion

2012 (15 May) Phosphor background. Perf 14½ × 14

3309	**2490**	(1st)	multicoloured	1·25	1·25	☐ ☐
		a.	Horiz strip of 5.			
			Nos. 3309/13	6·50	6·50	☐ ☐
3310	**2491**	(1st)	multicoloured	1·25	1·25	☐ ☐
3311	**2492**	(1st)	multicoloured	1·25	1·25	☐ ☐
3312	**2493**	(1st)	multicoloured	1·25	1·25	☐ ☐
3313	**2494**	(1st)	multicoloured	1·25	1·25	☐ ☐
3314	**2495**	(1st)	multicoloured	1·25	1·25	☐ ☐
		a.	Horiz strip of 5.			
			Nos. 3314/18	6·50	6·50	☐ ☐
3315	**2496**	(1st)	multicoloured	1·25	1·25	☐ ☐
3316	**2497**	(1st)	multicoloured	1·25	1·25	☐ ☐
3317	**2498**	(1st)	multicoloured	1·25	1·25	☐ ☐
3318	**2499**	(1st)	multicoloured	1·25	1·25	☐ ☐
Set of 10				12·00	12·00	☐
First Day Cover					14·00	☐
Presentation Pack (P.O. Pack No. 471)				15·00		☐
PHQ Cards (*set of* 10) (364)				6·75	20·00	☐ ☐
Set of 2 Gutter Strips of 10				25·00		☐
Set of 2 Traffic Light Gutter Strips of 20			50·00			☐

Nos. 3309/13 and 3314/18 were each printed together, *se-tenant*, as horizontal strips of five stamps in sheets of 50 (2 panes 5 × 5).

2500 Queen Elizabeth II at Golden Jubilee Thanksgiving Service, St. Paul's Cathedral, London, 2002

2501 Queen Elizabeth II Trooping the Colour, 1967

2502 Queen Elizabeth II inspecting 2nd Battalion Royal Welsh, Tidworth, 1 March 2007

2503 First Christmas Television Broadcast, 1957

2504 Silver Jubilee Walkabout, 1977

2505 Queen Elizabeth II in Garter Ceremony Procession, 1997

2506 Queen Elizabeth II addressing the UN General Assembly, 1957

2507 Queen Elizabeth II at Commonwealth Games, Brisbane, Australia, 1982

Diamond Jubilee (3rd issue)

2012 (31 May) 'All-over' phosphor.

(a) Sheet stamps. Ordinary gum. Gravure. Perf 14 × 14½.

A3319	**2500**	(1st)	multicoloured	1·25	1·10	☐ ☐
		a)	Horiz pair.			
			Nos. 3319/20	2·50	2·50	☐ ☐
A3320	**2501**	(1st)	black and brownish grey	1·25	1·10	☐ ☐
A3321	**2502**	77p	multicoloured	1·90	1·90	☐ ☐
		a.	Horiz pair.			
			Nos. 3321/2	3·75	3·75	☐ ☐
A3322	**2503**	77p	black and brownish grey	1·90	1·90	☐ ☐
A3323	**2504**	87p	black and brownish grey	2·25	2·25	☐ ☐
		a.	Horiz pair.			
			Nos. 3323/4	4·50	4·50	☐ ☐
A3324	**2505**	87p.	multicoloured	2·25	2·25	☐ ☐
A3325	**2506**	£1·28	black and brownish grey	3·25	3·25	☐ ☐
		a.	Horiz pair.			
			Nos. 3325/6	6·50	6·50	☐ ☐
A3326	**2507**	£1·28	multicoloured	3·25	3·25	☐ ☐
Set of 8				16·00	16·00	☐ ☐
First Day Cover					18·00	☐
Presentation Pack (P.O. Pack No. 472)			21·00			☐
PHQ Cards (*set of* 8) (365)				5·50	21·00	☐ ☐
Set of 4 Gutter Strips of 4				32·00		☐

(b) Booklet stamps. Ordinary gum. Litho. Perf 14 × 14½.

B3319	**2500**	(1st)	multicoloured	1·50	1·50	☐ ☐
B3320	**2501**	(1st)	black and brownish grey	1·50	1·50	☐ ☐
B3321	**2502**	77p	multicoloured	1·90	1·90	☐ ☐
B3322	**2503**	77p	black and brownish grey	1·90	1·90	☐ ☐
B3323	**2504**	87p	black and brownish grey	2·25	2·25	☐ ☐

B3324	**2505**	87p	multicoloured	2·25	2·25
B3325	**2506**	£1·28	black and brownish		
			grey	3·25	3·25
B3326	**2507**	£1·28	multicoloured	3·25	3·25
Set of 8				16·00	16·00

(c) Self-adhesive booklet stamp. Die-cut perf 14.

3327	**2500**	(1st) multicoloured	4·00	4·00

Nos. A3319/20, A3321/2, A3323/4 and A3325/6 were printed together, *se-tenant*, as horizontal pairs in sheets of 60 (2 panes 6×5).

Nos. B3319/26 come from the £12·77 Diamond Jubilee Prestige booklet, No. DY4.

No. 3327 was only issued in Diamond Jubilee stamp booklets, containing Nos. 3327×2 and U3271×4, originally sold for £3.60.

Diamond Jubilee (4th issue)

2012 (31 May) As No. U3271 or as Type **159** but redrawn with 1st value indicator (No. 3329). Two phosphor bands. Perf 14½×14 (with one elliptical hole in each vert side)

U3279		(1st) slate-blue	4·50	3·75
3329		(1st) light brown	4·50	3·75

Nos. U3279/3329 were issued in £12·27 Diamond Jubilee booklet, No. DY4.

Similar stamps were issued in **MS**3272.

2508 Mr. Bumble
(*Oliver Twist*)

2509 Mr. Pickwick
(*The Pickwick Papers*)

2510 The Marchioness
(*The Old Curiosity Shop*)

2511 Mrs. Gamp
(*Martin Chuzzlewit*)

2512 Captain Cuttle
(*Dombey and Son*)

2513 Mr. Micawber
(*David Copperfield*)

2514 Scenes from *Nicholas Nickleby, Bleak House, Little Dorrit* and *A Tale of Two Cities*

Birth Bicentenary of Charles Dickens

2012 (19 June) Illustrations from Character Sketches from Charles Dickens, c. 1890 by Joseph Clayton Clarke ('Kyd') (3330/5) or Book Illustrations by Hablot Knight Browne ('Phiz') (**MS**3336). One centre band (2nd) or 'all-over' phosphor (others). Perf 14 (3330/5) or 14×14½ (**MS**3336).

3330	**2508**	(2nd) multicoloured	1·00	1·00
3331	**2509**	(1st) multicoloured	1·25	1·10
3332	**2510**	77p multicoloured	1·90	1·90
3333	**2511**	87p multicoloured	2·25	2·25
3334	**2512**	£1·28 multicoloured	3·25	3·25
3335	**2513**	£1·90 multicoloured	4·75	4·75
Set of 6			13·00	13·00
First Day Cover				15·00
Presentation Pack (P.O. Pack No. 473)			22·00	
PHQ Cards (*set of 11*) (366)			7·50	20·00
Set of 6 Gutter Pairs			27·00	
Set of 6 Traffic Light Gutter Blocks of 4		55·00		

MS3336 190×67 mm. **2514** (1st)×4 Nicholas Nickleby caning headmaster Wackford Squeers (*Nicholas Nickleby*); Mrs. Bagnet is charmed with Mr. Bucket (*Bleak House*); Amy Dorrit introduces Maggy to Arthur Clennam (*Little Dorrit*); Charles Darnay arrested by French revolutionaries (*A Tale of Two Cities*)

		6·00	6·00
First Day Cover			8·00

The complete miniature sheet is shown on one of the eleven PHQ cards with the others depicting individual stamps including those from **MS**3336.

Olympic and Paralympic Games (8th series)

2012 (27 July) Designs as Nos. 3250/3. Two phosphor bands. Perf 14½×14 (with one elliptical hole in each vert side)

3337	**2436**	(1st) black and orange-red	5·00	5·00
3338	**2435**	(1st) black and orange-red	5·00	5·00
3339	**2436**	(Worldwide up to 20g) black, bright scarlet and greenish blue	12·00	12·00
3340	**2435**	(Worldwide up to 20g) black, bright scarlet and greenish blue	12·00	12·00
Set of 4			30·00	30·00
First Day Cover				32·00

Nos. 3339/40 were for use on Worldwide Mail up to 20g.

Nos. 3337/40 were only issued in the £10·71 Olympic and the Paralympic Games stamp booklet, No. DY5.

2515 Sports and London Landmarks

Welcome to London, Olympic Games

2012 (27 July) Sheet 192×75 mm. 'All-over' phosphor. Perf 14½

MS3341 **2515** (1st) Fencer and Tower Bridge; (1st) Athletes in race and Olympic Stadium; £1·28 Diver and Tate Modern; £1·28 Cyclist and London Eye

		9·50	9·50
First Day Cover			11·00
Presentation Pack (P.O. Pack No. 474)		17·00	
PHQ Cards (*set of 5*) (367)		3·50	14·00

The five PHQ cards show the four individual stamps and the complete miniature sheet.

2516 Helen Glover and Heather Stanning (rowing, women's pairs)

2517 Bradley Wiggins (cycling: road, men's time trial)

2518 Tim Baillie and Etienne Stott (canoe slalom: men's canoe double (C2))

2519 Peter Wilson (shooting: shotgun men's double trap)

2520 Philip Hindes, Chris Hoy and Jason Kenny (cycling: track men's team sprint)

2521 Katherine Grainger and Anna Watkins (rowing: women's double sculls)

2522 Steven Burke, Ed Clancy, Peter Kennaugh and Geraint Thomas (cycling: track men's team pursuit)

2523 Victoria Pendleton (cycling: track women's keirin)

2524 Alex Gregory, Tom James, Pete Reed and Andrew Triggs Hodge (rowing: men's fours)

2525 Katherine Copeland and Sophie Hosking (rowing: lightweight women's double sculls)

2526 Dani King, Joanna Rowsell and Laura Trott (cycling: track women's team pursuit)

2527 Jessica Ennis (athletics: combined women's heptathlon)

2528 Greg Rutherford (athletics: field men's long jump)

2529 Mo Farah (athletics: track men's 10,000m)

2530 Ben Ainslie (sailing: Finn men's heavyweight dinghy)

2531 Andy Murray (tennis: men's singles)

2532 Scott Brash, Peter Charles, Ben Maher and Nick Skelton (equestrian: jumping team)

2533 Jason Kenny (cycling: track men's sprint)

2534 Alistair Brownlee (men's triathlon)

2535 Laura Bechtolsheimer, Charlotte Dujardin and Carl Hester (equestrian: dressage team)

2536 Laura Trott (cycling: track women's omnium)

2537 Chris Hoy (cycling: track men's keirin)

2538 Charlotte Dujardin (equestrian: dressage individual)

2539 Nicola Adams (boxing: women's fly weight)

2540 Jade Jones (taekwondo women's under 57kg)

2541 Ed McKeever (canoe sprint: men's kayak single (K1) 200m)

2542 Mo Farah (athletics: track men's 5000m)

2543 Luke Campbell (boxing: men's bantam weight)

2544 Anthony Joshua (boxing: men's super heavy weight)

British Gold Medal Winners at London Olympic Games

2012 (2-13 Aug.) Self-adhesive. Two phosphor panels. Die-cut perf 15 × 14½

3342	**2516**	(1st)	multicoloured	2·25	2·75	
	a	Sheetlet.				
			No. 3342×6	9·50	10·50	
3343	**2517**	(1st)	multicoloured	2·25	2·75	
	a	Sheetlet.				
			No. 3343×6	9·50	10·50	
3344	**2518**	(1st)	multicoloured *(3 Aug)*	2·25	2·75	
	a	Sheetlet.				
			No. 3344×6	9·50	10·50	
3345	**2519**	(1st)	multicoloured *(3 Aug)*	2·25	2·75	
	a	Sheetlet.				
			No. 3345×6	9·50	10·50	
3346	**2520**	(1st)	multicoloured *(3 Aug)*	2·25	2·75	
	a	Sheetlet.				
			No. 3346×6	9·50	10·50	
3347	**2521**	(1st)	multicoloured *(4 Aug)*	2·25	2·75	
	a	Sheetlet.				
			No. 3347×6	9·50	10·50	
3348	**2522**	(1st)	multicoloured *(4 Aug)*	2·25	2·75	
	a	Sheetlet.				
			No. 3348×6	9·50	10·50	
3349	**2523**	(1st)	multicoloured *(4 Aug)*	2·25	2·75	
	a	Sheetlet.				
			No. 3349×6	9·50	10·50	
3350	**2524**	(1st)	multicoloured *(5 Aug)*	2·25	2·75	
	a	Sheetlet.				
			No. 3350×6	9·50	10·50	
3351	**2525**	(1st)	multicoloured *(5 Aug)*	2·25	2·75	
	a	Sheetlet.				
			No. 3351×6	9·50	10·50	
3352	**2526**	(1st)	multicoloured *(5 Aug)*	2·25	2·75	
	a	Sheetlet.				
			No. 3352×6	9·50	10·50	
3353	**2527**	(1st)	multicoloured *(5 Aug)*	2·25	2·75	
	a	Sheetlet.				
			No. 3353×6	9·50	10·50	
3354	**2528**	(1st)	multicoloured *(5 Aug)*	2·25	2·75	
	a	Sheetlet.				
			No. 3354×6	9·50	10·50	
3355	**2529**	(1st)	multicoloured *(5 Aug)*	2·25	2·75	
	a	Sheetlet.				
			No. 3355×6	9·50	10·50	
3356	**2530**	(1st)	multicoloured *(6 Aug)*	2·25	2·75	
	a	Sheetlet.				
			No. 3356×6	9·50	10·50	
3357	**2531**	(1st)	multicoloured *(6 Aug)*	2·25	2·75	
	a	Sheetlet.				
			No. 3357×6	9·50	10·50	
3358	**2532**	(1st)	multicoloured *(7 Aug)*	2·25	2·75	
	a	Sheetlet.				
			No. 3358×6	9·50	10·50	
3359	**2533**	(1st)	multicoloured *(7 Aug)*	2·25	2·75	
	a	Sheetlet.				
			No. 3359×6	9·50	10·50	
3360	**2534**	(1st)	multicoloured *(8 Aug)*	2·25	2·75	
	a	Sheetlet.				
			No. 3360×6	9·50	10·50	
3361	**2535**	(1st)	multicoloured *(8 Aug)*	2·25	2·75	
	a	Sheetlet.				
			No. 3361×6	9·50	10·50	
3362	**2536**	(1st)	multicoloured *(8 Aug)*	2·25	2·75	
	a	Sheetlet.				
			No. 3362×6	9·50	10·50	
3363	**2537**	(1st)	multicoloured *(8 Aug)*	2·25	2·75	
	a	Sheetlet.				
			No. 3363×6	9·50	10·50	
3364	**2538**	(1st)	multicoloured *(10 Aug)*	2·25	2·75	
	a	Sheetlet.				
			No. 3364×6	9·50	10·50	
3365	**2539**	(1st)	multicoloured *(10 Aug)*	2·25	2·75	
	a	Sheetlet.				
			No. 3365×6	9·50	10·50	
3366	**2540**	(1st)	multicoloured *(10 Aug)*	2·25	2·75	
	a	Sheetlet.				
			No. 3366×6	9·50	10·50	
3367	**2541**	(1st)	multicoloured *(12 Aug)*	2·25	2·75	
	a	Sheetlet.				
			No. 3367×6	9·50	10·50	
3368	**2542**	(1st)	multicoloured *(12 Aug)*	2·25	2·75	
	a	Sheetlet.				
			No. 3368×6	9·50	10·50	
3369	**2543**	(1st)	multicoloured *(12 Aug)*	2·25	2·75	

	a	Sheetlet.				
		No. 3369×6	9.50	10·50	☐	☐
3370	**2544**	(1st) multicoloured *(13 Aug)*	2·25	2·75	☐	☐
	a	Sheetlet.				
		No. 3370×6	9.50	10·50	☐	☐
Set of 29			60·00	75·00	☐	☐

First Day Covers (Sheetlets,
Nos. 3342a/70a) (29)   £350   ☐

First Day Cover (any single
gold medal stamp)   10·00   ☐

The self-adhesive base sheetlets for Nos. 3342/70 were produced by Walsall with the image, name and event of the winning athletes digitally printed by regional printers in six different locations: Attleborough, Edinburgh, London, Preston, Solihull and Swindon. Nos. 3368/70 were not produced by the Preston printer due to machinery breakdown. These sheetlets of 24 stamps were divided by roulettes into four portions of six stamps (3×2) each with either of the following inscriptions on the left margin: emblem 'TEAM GB' and Olympic rings; 'The XXX Olympiad'; barcode; Sheet number, Issue date and Printer location.

2545 Paralympic Sports and London Landmarks

Welcome to London, Paralympic Games

2012 (29 Aug.) Sheet 193×75 mm. 'All-over' phosphor. Perf 14½

MS3371 **2545** (1st) Athlete wearing running blades and Olympic Stadium; (1st) Wheelchair basketball player and Palace of Westminster; £1·28 Powerlifter, Millennium Bridge and St. Paul's Cathedral; £1·28 Cyclist and London Eye

9·50	9·50			☐	☐
First Day Cover			11·50		☐
Presentation Pack (P.O. Pack No. 475)		12·00		☐	
PHQ Cards (*set of 5*) (368)			3·50	14·00	☐ ☐

The five PHQ cards show the four individual stamps and the complete miniature sheet.

2546 Sarah Storey (cycling: track women's C5 pursuit)

2547 Jonathan Fox (swimming: men's 100m backstroke, S7)

2548 Mark Colbourne (cycling: track men's C1 pursuit)

2549 Hannah Cockroft (athletics: track women's 100m, T34)

2550 Neil Fachie and Barney Storey (cycling: men's B 1km time trial)

2551 Richard Whitehead (athletics: track men's 200m, T42)

2552 Natasha Baker (equestrian: individual championship test, grade II)

2553 Sarah Storey (cycling: track – women's C4-5 500m time trial)

2554 Ellie Simmonds (swimming: women's 400m freestyle, S6)

2555 Pamela Relph, Naomi Riches, James Roe, David Smith and Lily van den Broecke (rowing: mixed coxed four, LTAmix4+)

2556 Aled Davies (athletics: field men's discus, F42)

2557 Anthony Kappes and Craig MacLean (cycling: track men's B sprint)

2558 Jessica-Jane Applegate (swimming: women's 200m freestyle, S14)

2559 Sophie Christiansen (equestrian: individual championship test, grade 1a)

2560 David Weir (athletics: track men's 5000m, T54)

2561 Natasha Baker (equestrian: individual freestyle test, grade II)

2562 Ellie Simmonds (swimming: women's 200m individual medley, SM6)

2563 Mickey Bushell (athletics: track men's 100m, T53)

2564 Danielle Brown (archery: women's individual compound, open)

2565 Heather Frederiksen (swimming: women's 100m backstroke, S8)

2566 Sophie Christiansen (equestrian: individual freestyle test, grade 1a)

2567 David Weir (athletics: track men's 1500m, T54)

2568 Sarah Storey (cycling: road women's C5 time trial)

2569 Ollie Hynd (swimming: men's 200m individual medley, SM8)

2570 Sophie Christiansen, Deb Criddle, Lee Pearson and Sophie Wells (equestrian team, open)

2571 Helena Lucas (sailing: single-person keelboat, 2.4mR)

2572 Sarah Storey (cycling: road women's C4-5 road race)

2573 Josef Craig (swimming: men's 400m freestyle, S7)

2574 Hannah Cockroft (athletics: track women's 200m, T34)

2575 David Weir (athletics: track men's 800m, T54)

2576 Jonnie Peacock (athletics: track men's 100m, T44)

2577 Josie Pearson (athletics: field women's discus, F51/52/53)

2578 David Stone (cycling: road mixed T1-2 road race)

2579 David Weir (athletics: road men's marathon, T54)

British Gold Medal Winners at London Paralympic Games

2012 (31 Aug.-10 Sept.) Self-adhesive. Two phosphor panels. Die-cut perf 15 × 14½

3372	**2546**	(1st) multicoloured	2·00	2·00	☐	☐
	a.	Sheetlet. No. 3372 × 24·00		4·00	☐	
3373	**2547**	(1st) multicoloured (1 Sept)	2·00	2·00	☐	☐
	a.	Sheetlet. No. 3373 × 24·00		4·00	☐	
3374	**2548**	(1st) multicoloured (3 Sept)	2·00	2·00	☐	☐
	a.	Sheetlet. No. 3374 × 24·00		4·00	☐	
3375	**2549**	(1st) multicoloured (3 Sept)	2·00	2·00	☐	☐
	a.	Sheetlet. No. 3375 × 24·00		4·00	☐	
3376	**2550**	(1st) multicoloured (3 Sept)	2·00	2·00	☐	☐
	a.	Sheetlet. No. 3376 × 24·00		4·00	☐	
3377	**2551**	(1st) multicoloured (3 Sept)	2·00	2·00	☐	☐
	a.	Sheetlet. No. 3377 × 24·00		4·00	☐	
3378	**2552**	(1st) multicoloured (3 Sept)	2·00	2·00	☐	☐
	a.	Sheetlet. No. 3378 × 24·00		4·00	☐	
3379	**2553**	(1st) multicoloured (3 Sept)	2·00	2·00	☐	☐
	a.	Sheetlet. No. 3379 × 24·00		4·00	☐	
3380	**2554**	(1st) multicoloured (3 Sept)	2·00	2·00	☐	☐
	a.	Sheetlet. No. 3380 × 24·00		4·00	☐	
3381	**2555**	(1st) multicoloured (4 Sept)	2·00	2·00	☐	☐
	a.	Sheetlet. No. 3381 × 24·00		4·00	☐	
3382	**2556**	(1st) multicoloured (4 Sept)	2·00	2·00	☐	☐
	a.	Sheetlet. No. 3382 × 24·00		4·00	☐	
3383	**2557**	(1st) multicoloured (4 Sept)	2·00	2·00	☐	☐
	a.	Sheetlet. No. 3383 × 24·00		4·00	☐	
3384	**2558**	(1st) multicoloured (4 Sept)	2·00	2·00	☐	☐
	a.	Sheetlet. No. 3384 × 24·00		4·00	☐	
3385	**2559**	(1st) multicoloured (4 Sept)	2·00	2·00	☐	☐
	a.	Sheetlet. No. 3385 × 24·00		4·00	☐	
3386	**2560**	(1st) multicoloured (4 Sept)	2·00	2·00	☐	☐
	a.	Sheetlet. No. 3386 × 24·00		4·00	☐	
3387	**2561**	(1st) multicoloured (4 Sept)	2·00	2·00	☐	☐
	a.	Sheetlet. No. 3387 × 24·00		4·00	☐	
3388	**2562**	(1st) multicoloured (4 Sept)	2·00	2·00	☐	☐
	a.	Sheetlet. No. 3388 × 24·00		4·00	☐	
3389	**2563**	(1st) multicoloured (5 Sept)	2·00	2·00	☐	☐
	a.	Sheetlet. No. 3389 × 24·00		4·00	☐	
3390	**2564**	(1st) multicoloured (5 Sept)	2·00	2·00	☐	☐
	a.	Sheetlet. No. 3390 × 24·00		4·00	☐	
3391	**2565**	(1st) multicoloured (5 Sept)	2·00	2·00	☐	☐
	a.	Sheetlet. No. 3391 × 24·00		4·00	☐	
3392	**2566**	(1st) multicoloured (5 Sept)	2·00	2·00	☐	☐
	a.	Sheetlet. No. 3392 × 24·00		4·00	☐	
3393	**2567**	(1st) multicoloured (7 Sept)	4·00	4·00	☐	☐
	a.	Sheetlet. No. 3393 × 28·00		8·00	☐	
3394	**2568**	(1st) multicoloured (7 Sept)	4·00	4·00	☐	☐
	a.	Sheetlet. No. 3394 × 28·00		8·00	☐	
3395	**2569**	(1st) multicoloured (7 Sept)	4·00	4·00	☐	☐
	a.	Sheetlet. No. 3395 × 28·00		8·00	☐	
3396	**2570**	(1st) multicoloured (7 Sept)	4·00	4·00	☐	☐
	a.	Sheetlet. No. 3396 × 28·00		8·00	☐	
3397	**2571**	(1st) multicoloured (8 Sept)	2·00	2·00	☐	☐
	a.	Sheetlet No. 3397 × 2 4·00		4·00	☐	
3398	**2572**	(1st) multicoloured (8 Sept)	2·00	2·00	☐	☐
	a.	Sheetlet. No. 3398 × 24·00		4·00	☐	
3399	**2573**	(1st) multicoloured (8 Sept)	2·00	2·00	☐	☐
	a.	Sheetlet. No. 3399 × 24·00		4·00	☐	
3400	**2574**	(1st) multicoloured (8 Sept)	2·00	2·00	☐	☐
	a.	Sheetlet. No. 3400 × 24·00		4·00	☐	
3401	**2575**	(1st) multicoloured (10 Sept)	2·00	2·00	☐	☐
	a.	Sheetlet. No. 3401 × 24·00		4·00	☐	
3402	**2576**	(1st) multicoloured (10 Sept)	2·00	2·00	☐	☐
	a.	Sheetlet. No. 3402 × 24·00		4·00	☐	
3403	**2577**	(1st) multicoloured (10 Sept)	2·00	2·00	☐	☐
	a.	Sheetlet. No. 3403 × 24·00		4·00	☐	
3404	**2578**	(1st) multicoloured (10 Sept)	2·00	2·00	☐	☐
	a.	Sheetlet. No. 3404 × 24·00		4·00	☐	
3405	**2579**	(1st) multicoloured (10 Sept)	2·00	2·00	☐	☐
	a.	Sheetlet. No. 3405 × 24·00		4·00	☐	
Set of 34			70·00	70·00	☐	☐
First Day Covers (Sheetlets, Nos. 3372a/405a) (34)				£190	☐	
First Day Cover (any single gold medal stamp)				10·00	☐	

The self-adhesive base sheetlets for Nos. 3372/3405 were produced by Walsall with the image, name and event of the winning athletes digitally printed by regional printers in six different locations: Attleborough, Edinburgh, London, Preston, Solihull and Swindon. These sheetlets of 16 stamps were divided by roulettes into eight panes of two stamps (1 × 2). The left margins were inscribed as follows (reading downwards): emblem and 'ParalympicsGB'; 'London 2012 Paralymic Games'; barcode; Sheet number, Issue date and Printer location.

Nos. 3372, 3373 and 3405 were each printed in separate sheetlets of 16 stamps. Nos. 3374/7, 3381/4, 3385/8, 3389/92, 3393/6, 3397/3400 and 3401/4 were printed in sheetlets of 16 containing four stamps of each design. The sheetlets of 16 containing Nos. 3378/80 contained four each of Nos. 3378/9 and eight of No. 3380.

2580 Scenes from Olympic and Paralympic Games

Memories of London 2012 Olympic and Paralympic Games

2012 (27 Sept.) Sheet 192 × 75 mm. 'All-over' phosphor. Perf 14½

MS3406 **2580** (1st) Procession of athletes, Paralympic Games; (1st) Games makers and Olympic Stadium; £1·28 Opening ceremony of Paralympic Games; £1·28 Olympic Games closing ceremony and handover to Rio	9·50	9·50	☐	☐
First Day Cover		11·00	☐	
Presentation Pack (P.O. Pack No. 476)	22·00		☐	
PHQ Cards (set of 5) (369)	3·50	14·00	☐	☐

The five PHQ cards show the four individual stamps and the complete miniature sheet.

2581 BR Class D34 Nos. 62471 *Glen Falloch* and 62496 *Glen Loy* at Ardlui, 9 May 1959

Classic Locomotives of Scotland. Booklet stamp

2012 (27 Sept.) Design as 1st class stamp within **MS**3283 but printed in gravure. Self-adhesive. 'All-over' phosphor. Die-cut perf 14

3407	**2581**	(1st) multicoloured	4·50	4·50	☐	☐

No. 3407 was only issued in booklets containing No. 3407×2 and U3271×4, originally sold for £3·60.

2582 Sun and Particles ejected from Solar Surface seen from SOHO Observatory

2583 Venus with Clouds in Southern Hemisphere seen from Venus Express

2584 Ice in Martian Impact Crater seen from Mars Express

2585 Surface of Asteroid Lutetia seen from Rosetta Probe

2586 Saturn and its Rings seen from Cassini Satellite

2587 Titan (Saturn's largest moon) seen from Huygens Probe

Space Science

2012 (16 Oct.) 'All-over' phosphor. Perf 14

3408	**2582**	(1st) multicoloured	1·25	1·10	☐	☐
3409	**2583**	(1st) multicoloured	1·25	1·10	☐	☐
3410	**2584**	77p multicoloured	1·90	1·90	☐	☐
3411	**2585**	77p black	1·90	1·90	☐	☐
3412	**2586**	£1.28 multicoloured	3·25	3·25	☐	☐
3413	**2587**	£1.28 multicoloured	3·25	3·25	☐	☐
Set of 6			11·50	11·50	☐	☐
First Day Cover				13·00		☐
Presentation Pack (P.O. Pack No. 477)			13·00			☐
PHQ Cards (*set of 6*)(370)			5·00	14·00	☐	☐
Set of 6 Gutter Pairs			24·00			☐

2588 Six Poppies on Barbed Wire Stems

'Lest We Forget' (4th series)

2012 (23 Oct.) Self-adhesive. Two phosphor bands. Perf 14½×14 (with one elliptical hole in each vert side)

3414	**2588**	(1st) multicoloured	3·50	3·50	☐ ☐

For Type **2588** with ordinary gum, see No. 3717

2589 Reindeer with Decorated Antlers

2590 Santa with Robin

2591 Reindeer with Decorated Antlers

2592 Snowman and Penguin

2593 Santa with Robin

2594 Robin with Star Decoration in Beak

2595 Cat and Mouse decorating Christmas Tree

Christmas. Illustrations by Axel Scheffler

2012 (6 Nov.) One centre band (3415) or two phosphor bands (others). Perf 14½×14 (with one elliptical hole in each vert side)

(a) Self-adhesive

3415	**2589**	(2nd) multicoloured	1·00	90	☐	☐
3416	**2590**	(1st) multicoloured	1·25	1·10	☐	☐
3417	**2591**	(2nd Large) multicoloured	1·50	1·50	☐	☐
3418	**2592**	87p. multicoloured	2·25	2·25	☐	☐
3419	**2593**	(1st Large) multicoloured	2·00	2·00	☐	☐
3420	**2594**	£1.28 multicoloured	3·25	3·25	☐	☐
3421	**2595**	£1.90 multicoloured	4·75	4·75	☐	☐
Set of 7			14·00	14·00	☐	
First Day Cover				16·00		☐
Presentation Pack (P.O. Pack No. 478)			16·00			☐
PHQ Cards (*set of 8*)(371)			5·50	18·00	☐	☐

(b) Ordinary gum.

MS3422 115×102 mm. As Nos. 3415/21	14·00	14·00	☐ ☐
First Day Cover		16·00	☐

Year Pack

2012 (6 Nov.) Comprises Nos. 3254/9, **MS**3264/70, **MS**3272/307, 3309/18, A3319/26, 3330/6, **MS**3341, **MS**3371, **MS**3406, 3408/13 and 3415/21

CP3422a Year Pack	£210	☐

Post Office Yearbook

2012 (6 Nov.) Comprises Nos. 3254/9, **MS**3264/70, **MS**3272/307, 3309/18, A3319/26, 3330/6, **MS**3341, **MS**3371, **MS**3406, 3408/13 and 3415/21

YB3422a Yearbook	£340	☐

Miniature Sheet Collection

2012 (6 Nov.) Comprises Nos. **MS**3264, **MS**3270, **MS**3272, **MS**3283, **MS**3336, **MS**3341, **MS**3371, **MS**3406 and **MS**3422

MS3422a Miniature Sheet Collection	60·00	☐

2596 Steam Locomotive on Metropolitan Railway, 1863

2597 Navvies excavating 'Deep Cut' Tube Tunnel, 1898

2598 Commuters in Carriage, 1911

2599 Boston Manor Art Deco Station, 1934

2600 Train on Deep Cut Line, 1938

2601 Canary Wharf Station, 1999

2602 Classic London Underground Posters

150th Anniversary of the London Underground

2013 (9 Jan.) One centre band (2nd) or 'all-over' phosphor (others)

(a) Ordinary gum. Perf 14½

3423	**2596**	(2nd)	multicoloured	1·00	90	☐ ☐
3424	**2597**	(2nd)	multicoloured	1·00	90	☐ ☐
3425	**2598**	(1st)	multicoloured	1·25	1·10	☐ ☐
3426	**2599**	(1st)	multicoloured	1·25	1·10	☐ ☐
3427	**2600**	£1·28	multicoloured	2·75	2·50	☐ ☐
3428	**2601**	£1·28	multicoloured	2·75	2·50	☐ ☐
Set of 6				10·00	9·00	☐
First Day Cover					11·00	☐
Presentation Pack (Nos. 3423/**MS**3429)						
(P.O. Pack No. 480)			18·00			☐
PHQ Cards (*set of* 11) (372)			7·50	17·00		☐ ☐
Set of 6 Gutter Pairs			20·00			☐

MS3429 184×74 mm. **2602** (1st) Golders Green, 1908, By Underground to fresh air (Maxwell Armfield), 1915 and Summer Sales (Mary Koop), 1925; 77p For the Zoo (Charles Paine), 1921, Power (Edward McKnight-Kauffer), 1931 and The Seen (James Fitton), 1948; 87p A train every 90 seconds (Abram Games), 1937, Thanks to the Underground (Zero (Hans Schleger), 1935 and Cut travelling time, Victoria Line (Tom Eckersley), 1969; £1·28 The London Transport Collection (Tom Eckersley), 1975, London Zoo (Abram Games), 1976 and The Tate Gallery by

Tube (David Booth), 1987		7·00	7·00	☐ ☐
First Day Cover			9·00	☐ ☐

(b) Self-adhesive. Die-cut perf 14½

3430	**2599**	(1st)	multicoloured	7·00	7·00	☐ ☐

No. 3430 was issued in stamp booklets containing No. 3430×2 and 4×1st vermilion, each booklet originally sold for £3·60.

The complete miniature sheet is shown on one of the eleven PHQ cards with the others depicting individual stamps, including those from **MS**3429.

2603 Elinor and Marianne Dashwood (*Sense and Sensibility*)

2604 Elizabeth Bennet and Portrait of Mr. Darcy (*Pride and Prejudice*)

2605 Fanny Price (*Mansfield Park*)

2606 Emma Woodhouse and Mr. Knightley (*Emma*)

2607 Catherine Morland (*Northanger Abbey*)

2608 Anne Elliot and Captain Wentworth (*Persuasion*)

Bicentenary of the Publication of Jane Austen's *Pride and Prejudice*

2013 (21 Feb.) 'All-over' phosphor. Perf 14

3431	**2603**	(1st)	multicoloured	1·25	1·10	☐ ☐
3432	**2604**	(1st)	multicoloured	1·25	1·10	☐ ☐
3433	**2605**	77p	multicoloured	1·75	1·75	☐ ☐
3434	**2606**	77p	multicoloured	1·75	1·75	☐ ☐
3435	**2607**	£1·28	multicoloured	2·75	2·50	☐ ☐
3436	**2608**	£1·28	multicoloured	2·75	2·50	☐ ☐
Set of 6				11·00	10·00	☐
First Day Cover					12·00	☐
Presentation Pack (P.O. Pack No. 481)			13·00			☐
PHQ Cards (*set of* 6) (373)			4·00	16·00		☐ ☐
Set of 6 Gutter Pairs			23·00			☐
Set of 6 Traffic Light Gutter Pairs			26·00			☐

2609 The Eleventh Doctor (Matt Smith, 2010-14)

2610 The Tenth Doctor (David Tennant, 2005-10)

2611 The Ninth Doctor (Christopher Eccleston, 2005)

2612 The Eighth Doctor (Paul McGann, 1996)

2613 The Seventh Doctor (Sylvester McCoy, 1987-9)

2614 The Sixth Doctor (Colin Baker, 1984-6)

2615 The Fifth Doctor (Peter Davison, 1982-4)

2616 The Fourth Doctor (Tom Baker, 1974-81)

2617 The Third Doctor (Jon Pertwee, 1970-4)

2618 The Second Doctor (Patrick Troughton, 1966-9)

2619 The First Doctor (William Hartnell, 1963-6)

2620 TARDIS

2621 Dr. Who 1963-2013

**50th Anniversary of Doctor Who
(TV programme) (1st issue)**

2013 (26 Mar.) 'All-over' phosphor

				(a) Ordinary gum. 'All-over' phosphor. Perf 14		
3437	**2609**	(1st)	multicoloured		1·25	1·10	
		a·	Horiz strip of 3.			
			Nos. 3437/9		3·75	3·25	
3438	**2610**	(1st)	multicoloured		1·25	1·10	
3439	**2611**	(1st)	multicoloured		1·25	1·10	
3440	**2612**	(1st)	multicoloured		1·25	1·10	
		a.	Horiz strip of 4.			
			Nos. 3440/3		5·00	4·25	
3441	**2613**	(1st)	multicoloured		1·25	1·10	
3442	**2614**	(1st)	multicoloured		1·25	1·10	
3443	**2615**	(1st)	multicoloured		1·25	1·10	
3444	**2616**	(1st)	multicoloured		1·25	1·10	
		a.	Horiz strip of 4.			
			Nos. 3444/7		5·00	4·25	
3445	**2617**	(1st)	multicoloured		1·25	1·10	
3446	**2618**	(1st)	multicoloured		1·25	1·10	
3447	**2619**	(1st)	multicoloured		1·25	1·10	
Set of 11					12·00	11·00	
First Day Covers (2)						13·00	
Presentation Pack (P.O. Pack No. 482)					19·00		
PHQ Cards (set of 17) (374)					11·00	25·00	
Set of 1 Gutter Strip of 6 and						
			2 Gutter Strips of 8		25·00		

(b) Self-adhesive. One centre band (2nd) or two bands (others). Die-cut perf 14½ × 14 (with one elliptical hole in each vert side) (3449) or 14½ (others)

3448	**2609**	(1st)	multicoloured	7·00	7·00	
3449	**2620**	(1st)	multicoloured	2·50	2·00	
3450	**2619**	(1st)	multicoloured	7·00	7·00	

MS3451 115 × 89 mm· **2621** (2nd) Dalek; (2nd) The Ood; (2nd) Weeping Angel; (2nd) Cyberman; (1st) TARDIS   6·00   6·00

First Day Cover   7·25

Nos. 3437/9 were printed together, se-tenant, as horizontal strips of three stamps in sheets of 48 (2 panes 6 × 4)

Nos. 3440/3 and 3444/7 were each printed together, se-tenant, as horizontal strips of four stamps in sheets of 60 (2 panes 4 × 6)

Nos. 3448/50 were issued in stamp booklets, each booklet containing Nos. 3448, 3449 × 4 and 3450 and originally sold for £3·60.

A 1st class TARDIS stamp perforated 15 all round comes from the £13·37 Dr. Who premium booklet, No. DY6.

The design area of No. 3449 measures 17½ × 21 mm, slightly smaller than the same TARDIS design (Type **2620**) from the miniature sheet and premium booklet pane which measures 18 × 22 mm (all are 20 × 24 mm measured perf to perf edge).

The complete miniature sheet is shown on one of the seventeen PHQ cards with the others depicting individual stamps including those from the miniature sheet.

No. 3449 was also issued in sheets of 20 with se-tenant labels, printed in lithography instead of gravure.

**50th Anniversary of Doctor Who
(TV programme) (2nd issue)**

2013 (26 Mar.) As No. 3449 but ordinary gum
3452	**2620**	(1st)	multicoloured	3·50	3·00	

No. 3452 only comes from the £13·37 Dr. Who premium booklet, No. DY6.

2622 Norman Parkinson (1913-90, portrait and fashion photographer)

2623 Vivien Leigh (1913-67, actress)

2624 Peter Cushing (1913-94, actor)

2625 David Lloyd George (1863-1945, Prime Minister 1916-22)

2626 Elizabeth David (1913-92, cookery writer)

2627 John Archer (1863-1932, politician and civil rights campaigner)

2628 Benjamin Britten (1913-76, composer and pianist)

2629 Mary Leakey (1913-96, archaeologist and anthropologist)

2630 Bill Shankly (1913-81, football player and manager)

2631 Richard Dimbleby (1913-65, journalist and broadcaster)

Great Britons

2013 (16 Apr.) 'All-over' phosphor. Perf 14½

3453	**2622**	(1st)	multicoloured	1·25	1·10	☐ ☐
		a.	Horiz strip of 5.			
			Nos. 3453/7	6·25	5·50	☐ ☐
3454	**2623**	(1st)	multicoloured	1·25	1·10	☐ ☐
3455	**2624**	(1st)	multicoloured	1·25	1·10	☐ ☐
3456	**2625**	(1st)	multicoloured	1·25	1·10	☐ ☐
3457	**2626**	(1st)	multicoloured	1·25	1·10	☐ ☐
3458	**2627**	(1st)	multicoloured	1·25	1·10	☐ ☐
		a.	Horiz strip of 5.			
			Nos. 3458/62	6·25	5·50	☐ ☐
3459	**2628**	(1st)	multicoloured	1·25	1·10	☐ ☐
3460	**2629**	(1st)	multicoloured	1·25	1·10	☐ ☐
3461	**2630**	(1st)	multicoloured	1·25	1·10	☐ ☐

3462	**2631**	(1st) multicoloured	1·25	1·10	☐ ☐
	Set of 10		11·00	10·00	☐ ☐
	First Day Cover			12·00	☐
	Presentation Pack (P.O. Pack No. 483)		12·00		☐
	PHQ Cards (set of 10) (375)		7·00	18·00	☐ ☐
	Set of 2 Gutter Strips of 10		23·00		

Nos. 3453/7 and 3458/62 were each printed together, se-tenant, as horizontal strips of five stamps in sheets of 50 (2 panes 5×5).

2632 Jimmy Greaves (England)

2633 John Charles (Wales)

2634 Gordon Banks (England)

2635 George Best (Northern Ireland)

2636 John Barnes (England)

2637 Kevin Keegan (England)

2638 Denis Law (Scotland)

2639 Bobby Moore (England)

2640 Bryan Robson (England)

2641 Dave Mackay (Scotland)

2642 Bobby Charlton (England)

Football Heroes (1st issue)

2013 (9 May)–**14** 'All-over' phosphor

(a) Ordinary paper. Perf 14½

3463	**2632**	(1st) multicoloured	1·50	1·40	☐ ☐
		a. Horiz strip of 5.			
		Nos. 3463/7	7·50	7·00	☐ ☐
3464	**2633**	(1st) multicoloured	1·50	1·40	☐ ☐
3465	**2634**	(1st) multicoloured	1·50	1·40	☐ ☐
3466	**2635**	(1st) multicoloured	1·50	1·40	☐ ☐
3467	**2636**	(1st) multicoloured	1·50	1·40	☐ ☐
3468	**2637**	(1st) multicoloured	1·50	1·40	☐ ☐
		a. Horiz strip of 6.			
		Nos. 3468/73	9·00	8·25	☐ ☐
3469	**2638**	(1st) multicoloured	1·50	1·40	☐ ☐
3470	**2639**	(1st) multicoloured	1·50	1·40	☐ ☐
3471	**2640**	(1st) multicoloured	1·50	1·40	☐ ☐
3472	**2641**	(1st) multicoloured	1·50	1·40	☐ ☐
3473	**2642**	(1st) multicoloured	1·50	1·40	☐ ☐
Set of 11			15·00	14·00	☐
First Day Cover				15·00	☐
Presentation Pack (P.O. Pack No. 484)			16·00		☐
PHQ Cards (*set of 12*) (376)			8·00	20·00	☐ ☐
Set of 1 Gutter Strip of 12 and					
1 Gutter Strip of 10			32·00		☐
MS3474 192×74 mm. Nos. 3463/73			15·00	15·00	☐ ☐
First Day Cover				16·00	☐

(b) Self-adhesive. Gravure Walsall. Die-cut perf 14½

3475	**2635**	(1st) multicoloured	4·00	3·25	☐ ☐
3476	**2639**	(1st) multicoloured	4·00	3·25	☐ ☐
3477	**2633**	(1st) multicoloured *(20.2.14)*	4·00	3·25	☐ ☐
3478	**2641**	(1st) multicoloured *(20.2.14)*	4·00	3·25	☐ ☐

Nos. 3463/7 were printed together, *se-tenant*, as horizontal strips of five stamps in sheets of 30 (5×6).

Nos. 3468/73 were printed together, *se-tenant*, as horizontal strips of six stamps in sheets of 30 (6×5).

Nos. 3475/6 were issued in booklets, each containing Nos. 3475/6 and 4×1st vermilion and originally sold for £3·60.

Nos. 3463/87 commemorate the 150th anniversary of the Football Association and the 140th Anniversary of the Scottish Football Association.

The twelve PHQ cards depict the eleven individual stamps and the complete miniature sheet.

Football Heroes (2nd issue)

2013 (9 May) Self-adhesive. Litho. 'All-over' phosphor. Die-cut perf 14½×14

3479	**2632**	(1st) multicoloured	2·75	2·75	☐ ☐
3480	**2633**	(1st) multicoloured	2·75	2·75	☐ ☐
3481	**2634**	(1st) multicoloured	2·75	2·75	☐ ☐
3482	**2635**	(1st) multicoloured	2·75	2·75	☐ ☐
3483	**2636**	(1st) multicoloured	2·75	2·75	☐ ☐
3484	**2637**	(1st) multicoloured	2·75	2·75	☐ ☐
3485	**2638**	(1st) multicoloured	2·75	2·75	☐ ☐
3486	**2639**	(1st) multicoloured	2·75	2·75	☐ ☐
3487	**2640**	(1st) multicoloured	2·75	2·75	☐ ☐
3488	**2641**	(1st) multicoloured	2·75	2·75	☐ ☐
3489	**2642**	(1st) multicoloured	2·75	2·75	☐ ☐
Set of 11			28·00	28·00	☐ ☐

Nos. 3479/89 were only issued in the £11·11 Football Heroes premium booklet No. DY7.

No.3490 is vacant

2646 Preliminary Oil Sketch for The Coronation of Queen Elizabeth II (Terence Cuneo), 1953

2647 Queen Elizabeth II in Garter Robes (Nicky Philipps), 2012

2648 Portrait by Andrew Festing, 1999

2649 Portrait by Pietro Annigoni, 1955

2650 Portrait by Sergei Pavlenko, 2000

2651 Her Majesty Queen Elizabeth II (Richard Stone), 1992

60th Anniversary of the Coronation.
Six Decades of Royal Portraits

2013 (30 May) Phosphor band at left (2nd) or 'all-over' phosphor (others). Perf 14

3491	**2646**	(2nd) multicoloured	1·00	90	☐ ☐
3492	**2647**	(1st) multicoloured	1·25	1·10	☐ ☐
3493	**2648**	78p multicoloured	1·75	1·75	☐ ☐
3494	**2649**	88p multicoloured	2·00	2·00	☐ ☐
3495	**2650**	£1·28 multicoloured	2·75	2·50	☐ ☐
3496	**2651**	£1·88 multicoloured	3·75	3·75	☐ ☐
Set of 6			11·50	11·00	☐
First Day Cover				13·00	☐
Presentation Pack (P.O. Pack No. 485)			13·00		☐
PHQ Cards (*set of 6*) (377)			4·00	15·00	☐ ☐
Commemorative Document					
(Nos. 3491/2) *(2 June)*			15·00		☐
Set of 6 Gutter Pairs			24·00		☐
Set of 6 Traffic Light Gutter Blocks of 4			50·00		☐

2652 UTA W No. 103

2653 Classic Locomotives of Northern Ireland

Classic Locomotives (3rd series).
Northern Ireland

2013 (18 June) 'All-over' phosphor

(a) Self-adhesive. Die-cut perf 14

3497	**2652**	(1st) black, grey and gold	4·25	4·25	☐ ☐

b) Ordinary gum. Sheet 180×74 mm. Perf 14
MS3498 **2653** (1st) As Type **2652**; 78p
  UTA SG3 No. 35; 88p Peckett No. 2;
  £1·28 CDRJC Class 5 No. 4   8·00   8·00
First Day Cover   9·00
Presentation Pack (P.O. Pack No. 486)   8·50
PHQ Cards (set of 5) (378)   3·50   10·00

No. 3497 was issued in booklets, each containing No. 3497×2 and 4×1st vermilion and sold for £3·60.

The five PHQ cards show the four individual stamps and the complete miniature sheet.

2654 Comma
(*Polygonia c-album*)

2655 Orange-tip (*Anthocharis cardamines*)

2656 Small Copper
(*Lycaena phlaeas*)

2657 Chalkhill Blue
(*Polyommatus coridon*)

2658 Swallowtail
(*Papilio machaon*)

2659 Purple Emperor
(*Apatura iris*)

2660 Marsh Fritillary
(*Euphydrygus awinea*)

2661 Brimstone
(*Gonepteryx rhamni*)

2662 Red Admiral
(*Vanessa atalanta*)

2663 Marbled White
(*Melanargia galathea*)

Butterflies

2013 (11 July) 'All-over' phosphor

(a) Ordinary paper. Perf 14×14½
3499 **2654** (1st) multicoloured   1·25   1·10

				a. Horiz strip of 5.		
				Nos. 3499/3503	6·00	5·25
3500	**2655**	(1st)	multicoloured		1·25	1·10
3501	**2656**	(1st)	multicoloured		1·25	1·10
3502	**2657**	(1st)	multicoloured		1·25	1·10
3503	**2658**	(1st)	multicoloured		1·25	1·10
3504	**2659**	(1st)	multicoloured		1·25	1·10
				a. Horiz strip of 5.		
				Nos. 3504/8	6·00	5·25
3505	**2660**	(1st)	multicoloured		1·25	1·10
3506	**2661**	(1st)	multicoloured		1·25	1·10
3507	**2662**	(1st)	multicoloured		1·25	1·10
3508	**2663**	(1st)	multicoloured		1·25	1·10

Set of 10   11·00   10·00
First Day Cover   12·00
Presentation Pack (P.O. Pack No. 487)   13·00
PHQ Cards (set of 10) (379)   6·75   18·00
Set of 2 Gutter Strips of 10   23·00

(b) Self-adhesive. Die-cut perf 14×14½
3509 **2657** (1st) multicoloured   3·75   4·00
3510 **2654** (1st) multicoloured   3·75   4·00

Nos. 3499/503 and 3504/8 were each printed together, se-tenant, as horizontal strips of five stamps in sheets of 50 (2 panes 5×5)

Nos. 3509/10 were issued in stamp booklets, each containing Nos. 3509/10 and 4×1st vermilion and sold for £3·60.

2664 Andy Murray's Wimbledon Victory

Andy Murray, Men's Singles Champion, Wimbledon

2013 (8 Aug.) Sheet 192×75 mm. Multicoloured. 'All-over' phosphor. Perf 14½
MS3511 **2664** (1st) Andy Murray kissing
  Wimbledon Trophy; (1st) Andy
  Murray serving; £1·28 In action;
  £1·28 Holding Trophy   8·50   8·50
First Day Cover   9·00
Presentation Pack (P.O. Pack No. M21)   10·00

2665 Jaguar E-Type, 1961

2666 Rolls-Royce Silver Shadow, 1965

2667 Aston Martin DB5, 1963

2668 MG MGB, 1962

2669 Morgan Plus 8, 1968

2670 Lotus Esprit, 1976

2671 The Workhorses

British Auto Legends

2013 (13 Aug.) 'All-over' phosphor. Perf 13½ (3512/17) or 14 (**MS**3518)

3512	**2665**	(1st)	multicoloured	1·25	1·10	☐☐
	a.	Horiz strip of 3.				
		Nos. 3512/14		3·50	3·25	☐☐
3513	**2666**	(1st)	multicoloured	1·25	1·10	☐☐
3514	**2667**	(1st)	multicoloured	1·25	1·10	☐☐
3515	**2668**	£1·28	multicoloured	2·75	2·50	☐☐
	a.	Horiz strip of 3.				
		Nos. 3515/17		8·00	7·25	☐☐
3516	**2669**	£1·28	multicoloured	2·75	2·50	☐☐
3517	**2670**	£1·28	multicoloured	2·75	2·50	☐☐
Set of 6				11·00	10·00	
First Day Cover					12·00	☐
Presentation Pack (P.O. Pack No. 488)				17·00		☐
PHQ Cards (set of 11) (380)				7·50	18·00	☐☐
Set of 2 Gutter Strips of 6				24·00		☐

MS3518 180×74 mm. **2671** (1st) ×4 Morris Minor Royal Mail van (1953-71); Austin FX4 (1958-97) London taxi; Ford Anglia 105E (1959-67) police car; Coastguard Land Rover Defender 110 (from 1990) 6·00 6·00 ☐☐
First Day Cover 7·00 ☐

The complete miniature sheet is shown on one of the eleven PHQ cards with the others depicting individual stamps including those from the miniature sheet.
The 1st value from **MS**3518 is inscribed "EUROPA"

2672 East Indiaman *Atlas*, 1813

2673 Royal Mail Ship *Britannia*, 1840

2674 Tea Clipper *Cutty Sark*, 1870

2675 Cargo Liner *Clan Matheson*, 1919

2676 Royal Mail Ship *Queen Elizabeth*, 1940

2677 Bulk Carrier *Lord Hinton*, 1986

Merchant Navy (1st issue)

2013 (19 Sept.) 'All-over' phosphor. Perf 14

3519	**2672**	(1st)	multicoloured	1·25	1·10	☐☐
3520	**2673**	(1st)	multicoloured	1·25	1·10	☐☐
3521	**2674**	(1st)	multicoloured	1·25	1·10	☐☐
3522	**2675**	£1·28	multicoloured	2·75	2·50	☐☐
3523	**2676**	£1·28	multicoloured	2·75	2·50	☐☐
3524	**2677**	£1·28	multicoloured	2·75	2·50	☐☐
Set of 6				11·00	10·00	
First Day Cover					12·00	☐
Presentation Pack (P.O. Pack No. 489)				17·00		☐
PHQ Cards (set of 11) (381)				6·75	18·00	☐☐
Set of 6 Gutter Pairs				23·00		☐

The complete miniature sheet is shown on one of the eleven PHQ cards with the others depicting individual stamps including those from **MS**3529.

2678 Destroyer HMS *Vanoc* escorting Atlantic Convoy

2679 Merchant Ship passing the Naval Control Base in the Thames Estuary

2680 Sailors clearing Ice from the Decks of HMS *King George V* in Arctic Waters

2681 Naval Convoy of 24 Merchant Ships in the North Sea

2682 Second World War Atlantic and Arctic Convoys

Merchant Navy (2nd issue)

2013 (19 Sept.) 'All-over' phosphor. Perf 14

3525	**2678**	(1st)	multicoloured	2·00	2·00	☐ ☐
3526	**2679**	(1st)	multicoloured	2·00	2·00	☐ ☐
3527	**2680**	(1st)	multicoloured	2·00	2·00	☐ ☐
3528	**2681**	(1st)	multicoloured	2·00	2·00	☐ ☐
Set of 4				7·50	7·50	☐ ☐
MS3529 115×89 mm **2682**. Nos. 3525/8				7·50	7·50	☐ ☐
First Day Cover					8·00	☐

Nos. 3525/8 were only issued in the £11·19 Merchant Navy premium booklet, No. DY8 and in **MS**3529.

2683 Royal Mail Van

Royal Mail Transport: By Land and Sea

2013 (19 Sept.) Self-adhesive booklet stamps. Die-cut perf 14

3530	**2683**	(1st)	multicoloured	9·00	9·00	☐ ☐
3531	**2673**	(1st)	multicoloured	9·00	9·00	☐ ☐

The design of No. 3530 is as the Royal Mail van stamp within **MS**3518.

Nos. 3530/1 were only issued in booklets, each containing Nos. 3530/1 and 4 × 1st vermilion and sold for £3·60.

No. 3530 includes the 'EUROPA' emblem.

2684 Polacanthus

2685 Ichthyosaurus

2686 Iguanodon

2687 Ornithocheirus

2688 Baryonyx

2689 Dimorphodon

2690 Hypsilophodon

2691 Cetiosaurus

2692 Megalosaurus

2693 Plesiosaurus

Dinosaurs

2013 (10 Oct.) Self-adhesive. 'All-over' phosphor. Die-cut perf 13½ × 14 (with no teeth around protruding parts at top or foot of the designs)

3532	**2684**	(1st)	multicoloured	1·25	1·10	☐ ☐
		a.	Horiz strip of 5.			
			Nos. 3532/6	6·00		☐
3533	**2685**	(1st)	multicoloured	1·25	1·10	☐ ☐
3534	**2686**	(1st)	multicoloured	1·25	1·10	☐ ☐
3535	**2687**	(1st)	multicoloured	1·25	1·10	☐ ☐
3536	**2688**	(1st)	multicoloured	1·25	1·10	☐ ☐
3537	**2689**	(1st)	multicoloured	1·25	1·10	☐ ☐
		a.	Horiz strip of 5.			
			Nos. 3537/41	6·00		☐
3538	**2690**	(1st)	multicoloured	1·25	1·10	☐ ☐
3539	**2691**	(1st)	multicoloured	1·25	1·10	☐ ☐
3540	**2692**	(1st)	multicoloured	1·25	1·10	☐ ☐
3541	**2693**	(1st)	multicoloured	1·25	1·10	☐ ☐
Set of 10				11·00	10·00	☐ ☐
First Day Cover					12·00	☐
Presentation Pack (P.O. Pack No. 490)				15·00		☐
PHQ Cards (set of 10) (382)				6·75	15·00	☐ ☐

Nos. 3532/6 and 3537/41 were each printed together as horizontal strips of five stamps in sheets of 50 (2 panes 5 × 5).

2694 Madonna and Child (Francesco Granacci)

2695 Virgin and Child with the Young St. John the Baptist (detail) (Antoniazzo Romano)

2696 Madonna and Child (Francesco Granacci)

2697 St. Roch Praying to the Virgin for an End to the Plague (detail) (Jacques-Louis David)

2698 Virgin and Child with the Young St. John the Baptist (detail) (Antoniazzo Romano)

2699 La Vierge au Lys (William-Adolphe Bouguereau)

2700 Theotokos, Mother of God (Fadi Mikhail)

Christmas. Madonna and Child Paintings

2013 (5 Nov.) One centre band (3542) or two bands (others). Perf 14½ × 15

(a) Self-adhesive

3542	**2694** (2nd) multicoloured	1·00	90	☐	☐
3543	**2695** (1st) multicoloured	1·25	1·10	☐	☐
3544	**2696** (2nd Large) multicoloured	1·50	1·50	☐	☐
3545	**2697** 88p· multicoloured	2·00	2·00	☐	☐
3546	**2698** (1st Large) multicoloured	2·00	2·00	☐	☐
3547	**2699** £1·28 multicoloured	2·75	2·50	☐	☐
3548	**2700** £1·88 multicoloured	3·75	3·75	☐	☐
Set of 7		13·00	12·00	☐	
First Day Cover			14·00		☐
Presentation Pack (P.O. Pack No. 491)		15·00		☐	
PHQ Cards (*set of* 8) (383)		5·50	18·00	☐	☐

(b) Ordinary gum

MS3549 146 × 74 mm. As Nos. 3542/8	14·00	14·00	☐	☐
First Day Cover		14·50		☐

The eight PHQ cards show the seven individual stamps and the complete miniature sheet.

The 2nd class, 1st class, 88p, £1·28 and £1·88 stamps were also issued in sheets of 20 containing eight 2nd class, eight 1st class, two 88p, one £1·28 and one £1·88 stamps , each stamp accompanied by a *se-tenant* label.

Separate sheets of 20 2nd, ten 1st, ten 88p and ten £1·28 were available with personal photographs.

2701 Angels (Rosie Hargreaves)

2702 Santa (Molly Robson)

Children's Christmas

2013 (5 Nov.) One phosphor band at right (2nd) or two phosphor bands (1st). Self-adhesive. Die-cut perf 14½

3550	**2701** (2nd)	multicoloured	3·50	3·25	☐	☐
3551	**2702** (1st)	multicoloured	4·25	4·25	☐	☐
First Day Cover				9·00		☐
Presentation Pack (P.O. Pack No. M22)			9·00		☐	

Year Pack

2013 (5 Nov.) Comprises Nos. 3423/9, 3431/47, **MS**3451, 3453/73, 3491/6, **MS**3498/508, **MS**3511/24, **MS**3529 and 3532/48

CP3551a Year Pack	£175	☐

Post Office Yearbook

2013 (5 Nov.) Comprises Nos. 3423/9, 3431/47, **MS**3451, 3453/73, 3491/6, **MS**3498/3508, **MS**3511/24, **MS**3529, 3532/48 and 3550/1

YB3551a Yearbook	£180	☐

Miniature Sheet Collection

2013 (5 Nov.) Comprises Nos. **MS**3429, **MS**3451, **MS**3474, **MS**3498, **MS**3511, **MS**3518, **MS**3529 and **MS**3549

MS3551a Miniature Sheet Collection	50.00	☐

2703 Andy Pandy

2704 Ivor the Engine

2705 Dougal (*The Magic Roundabout*)

2706 Windy Miller (*Camberwick Green*)

2707 Mr. Benn

2708 Great Uncle Bulgaria (*The Wombles*)

2709 Bagpuss

2710 Paddington Bear

2711 Postman Pat

2712 Bob the Builder

2713 Peppa Pig

2714 Shaun the Sheep

Classic Children's TV

2014 (7 Jan.) 'All-over phosphor'. Self-adhesive. Die-cut perf 15

3552	**2703**	(1st)	multicoloured	1·25	1·10	☐ ☐
	a.	Horiz strip of 6.				
		Nos. 3552/7		7·25		☐
3553	**2704**	(1st)	multicoloured	1·25	1·10	☐ ☐
3554	**2705**	(1st)	multicoloured	1·25	1·10	☐ ☐
3555	**2706**	(1st)	multicoloured	1·25	1·10	☐ ☐
3556	**2707**	(1st)	multicoloured	1·25	1·10	☐ ☐
3557	**2708**	(1st)	multicoloured	1·25	1·10	☐ ☐
3558	**2709**	(1st)	multicoloured	1·25	1·10	☐ ☐
	a.	Horiz strip of 6.				
		Nos. 3558/63		7·25		☐
3559	**2710**	(1st)	multicoloured	1·25	1·10	☐ ☐
3560	**2711**	(1st)	multicoloured	1·25	1·10	☐ ☐
3561	**2712**	(1st)	multicoloured	1·25	1·10	☐ ☐
3562	**2713**	(1st)	multicoloured	1·25	1·10	☐ ☐
3563	**2714**	(1st)	multicoloured	1·25	1·10	☐ ☐
Set of 12				13·00	12·00	☐ ☐
First Day Cover					14·00	☐
Presentation Pack (P.O. Pack No. 493)				15·00		☐
PHQ Cards (*set of* 12) (384)				8·00	20·00	☐ ☐
Set of 2 Gutter Strips of 12				27·00		☐

Nos. 3552/7 and 3558/63 were each printed together *se-tenant* in horizontal strips of six stamps in sheets of 60 (6×10).

2715 Riding for the Disabled Association

2716 The King's Troop Ceremonial Horses

2717 Dray Horses

2718 Royal Mews Carriage Horses

2719 Police Horses

2720 Forestry Horse

Working Horses

2014 (4 Feb.) 'All-over' phosphor. Perf 14

3564	**2715**	(1st)	multicoloured	1·25	1·10	☐ ☐
3565	**2716**	(1st)	multicoloured	1·25	1·10	☐ ☐
3566	**2717**	88p	multicoloured	2·00	2·00	☐ ☐
3567	**2718**	88p	multicoloured	2·00	2·00	☐ ☐
3568	**2719**	£1·28	multicoloured	2·75	2·50	☐ ☐
3569	**2720**	£1·28	multicoloured	2·75	2·50	☐ ☐
Set of 6				11·00	10·00	☐ ☐
First Day Cover					12·00	☐
Presentation Pack (P.O. Pack No. 494)				13·00		☐
PHQ Cards (*set of* 6) (385)				4·00	16·00	☐ ☐
Set of 6 Gutter Pairs				23·00		☐

2721 BR Dean Goods No. 2532

2722 BR D34 Nos. 62471 & 62496

2723 UTA Class W No. 103 *Thomas Somerset* with Belfast Express, Downhill, near Castlerock, c.1950

2724 LMS No. 7720

2725 Peckett R2 *Thor*

2726 BR D40 No. 62276

2727 UTA SG3 No. 35

2728 Hunslet No. 589 *Blanche*

2729 Classic Locomotives of Wales

Classic Locomotives (4th and 5th series). Wales (MS3578) and United Kingdom (booklet)

2014 (20 Feb.) 'All-over' phosphor. Perf 14

3570	**2721**	(1st)	multicoloured	2.25	2.25	
3571	**2722**	(1st)	multicoloured	2.25	2.25	
3572	**2723**	(1st)	multicoloured	2.25	2.25	
3573	**2724**	(1st)	multicoloured	2.25	2.25	
3574	**2725**	60p	multicoloured	2.50	2·50	
3575	**2726**	68p	multicoloured	2.50	2·50	
3576	**2727**	78p	multicoloured	2·50	2·50	
3577	**2728**	78p	multicoloured	2·50	2·50	
Set of 8				17·00	17·00	

MS3578 180×74 mm. **2729** No. 3573;
No. 3577; 88p W&LLR No. 822 *The
Earl*; £1·28 BR 5600 No. 5652   11.00   11.00

First Day Cover		18.00
Presentation Pack (P.O. Pack No. 495)	18·00	
PHQ Cards (*set of* 5) (386)	3·50	20·00

Nos. 3570/7 were issued only in the £13·97 Classic Locomotives booklet, No. DY9 or also in **MS**3578 (Nos. 3573 and 3577). The five PHQ cards show the four individual stamps in the miniature sheet and the complete miniature sheet.

For the self-adhesive version of No. 3573, see No. 3634.

2730 Roy Plomley (1914-85, broadcaster and writer)

2731 Barbara Ward (1914-81, economist and broadcaster)

2732 Joe Mercer (1914-90, football player and manager)

2733 Kenneth More (1914-82, stage and screen actor)

2734 Dylan Thomas (1914-53, poet and writer)

2735 Sir Alec Guinness (1914-2000, stage and screen actor)

2736 Noorunissa Inayat Khan (1914-44, SOE agent in occupied France)

2737 Max Perutz (1914-2002, molecular biologist and Nobel laureate)

2738 Joan Littlewood (1914-2002, theatre director and writer)

2739 Abram Games (1914-96, graphic designer)

Remarkable Lives

2014 (25 Mar.) 'All-over' phosphor. Perf 14½

3579	**2730**	(1st)	multicoloured	1·25	1·10	
		a.	Horiz strip of 5.			
			Nos.· 3579/83	6·00	5·25	
3580	**2731**	(1st)	multicoloured	1·25	1·10	
3581	**2732**	(1st)	multicoloured	1·25	1·10	
3582	**2733**	(1st)	multicoloured	1·25	1·10	
3583	**2734**	(1st)	multicoloured	1·25	1·10	
3584	**2735**	(1st)	multicoloured	1·25	1·10	
		a.	Horiz strip of 5.			
			Nos. 3584/8	6·00	5·25	
3585	**2736**	(1st)	multicoloured	1·25	1·10	
3586	**2737**	(1st)	multicoloured	1·25	1·10	
3587	**2738**	(1st)	multicoloured	1·25	1·10	
3588	**2739**	(1st)	multicoloured	1·25	1·10	
Set of 10				11·00	10·00	
First Day Cover					12·00	
Presentation Pack (P.O. Pack No. 496)				13·00		
PHQ Cards (*set of* 10) (387)				6·75	20·00	
Set of 2 Gutter Strips of 10				23·00		

Nos. 3579/83 and 3584/8 were each printed together, *se-tenant*, as horizontal strips of five stamps in sheets of 50 (2 panes 5×5).

2740 Buckingham Palace, 2014

2741 Buckingham Palace, c. 1862

2742 Buckingham Palace, 1846

2743 Buckingham House, 1819

2744 Buckingham House, 1714

2745 Buckingham House, c. 1700

2746 The Grand Staircase   **2747** The Throne Room

Buckingham Palace, London (1st issue)

2014 (15 Apr.) 'All-over phosphor' Ordinary gum. Perf 14½

3589	**2740**	(1st)	multicoloured		1·25	1·10	☐ ☐
		a.	Horiz strip of 3.				
			Nos. 3589/91		3·50	3·00	☐ ☐
		b.	Perf 14×13½.		1·50	1·50	☐ ☐
3590	**2741**	(1st)	multicoloured		1·25	1·10	☐ ☐
		b.	Perf 14×13½.		1·50	1·50	☐ ☐
3591	**2742**	(1st)	multicoloured		1·25	1·10	☐ ☐
		b.	Perf 14×13½.		1·50	1·50	☐ ☐
3592	**2743**	(1st)	multicoloured		1·25	1·10	☐ ☐
		a.	Horiz strip of 3.				
			Nos. 3592/4		3·50	3·00	☐ ☐
		b.	Perf 14×13½.		1·50	1·50	☐ ☐
3593	**2744**	(1st)	multicoloured		1·25	1·10	☐ ☐
		b.	Perf 14×13½.		1·50	1·50	☐ ☐
3594	**2745**	(1st)	multicoloured		1·25	1·10	☐ ☐
		b.	Perf 14×13½.		1·50	1·50	☐ ☐
Set of 6					7·00	6·00	☐ ☐
First Day Cover						8·00	☐
Presentation Pack (Nos. 3589/44 and							
			MS3601)				
			(P.O. Pack No. 497)	14·00			☐
PHQ Cards (set of 11)				7·50	15·00		☐ ☐
Set of 2 Gutter Strips of 6				15·00			☐
			(b) Self-adhesive. Die-cut perf 14				
3595	**2746**	(1st)	multicoloured		4·50	4·50	☐ ☐

3596	**2747**	(1st)	multicoloured	4·50	4·50	☐ ☐

Nos. 3589/91 and 3592/4 were each printed together, se-tenant, as horizontal strips of three stamps in sheets of 36 (2 panes 3×6).

Nos. 3589b/94b come from £11·39 premium booklets, No. DY10.

Nos. 3595/6 were only issued in stamp booklets, each containing Nos. 3595/6 and 4×1st vermilion and originally sold for £3·72.

The complete miniature sheet is shown on one of the 11 PHQ cards with the others depicting individual stamps including those from **MS**3601.

2748 The Blue Drawing Room   **2749** The Green Drawing Room

2750 Buckingham Palace

Buckingham Palace, London (2nd issue)

2014 (15 Apr.) 'All-over' phosphor. Perf 14

3597	**2747**	(1st)	multicoloured	1·50	1·50	☐ ☐
3598	**2746**	(1st)	multicoloured	1·50	1·50	☐ ☐
3599	**2748**	(1st)	multicoloured	1·50	1·50	☐ ☐
3600	**2749**	(1st)	multicoloured	1·50	1·50	☐ ☐
Set of 4				5·50	5·50	☐ ☐
MS3601 146×74 mm. **2750**						
	Nos. 3597/3600			5·50	5·50	☐ ☐
First Day Cover					7·00	☐

Nos. 3597/3600 were only issued in the £11·39 Buckingham Palace premium booklet No. DY10, and in **MS**3601.

2751 A Matter of Life and Death (1946)

2752 Lawrence of Arabia (1962)

2753 *2001 A Space Odyssey* (1968)

2754 *Chariots of Fire* (1981)

2755 *Secrets and Lies* (1996)

2756 *Bend It Like Beckham* (2002)

2757 Films by GPO Film Unit

Great British Films

2014 (13 May) 'All-over' phosphor. Perf 14½ (3602/7) or 14 (**MS**3608).

3602	**2751**	(1st)	multicoloured	1·25	1·10	☐ ☐
		a.	Horiz strip of 3· Nos· 3602/4	3·50	3·00	☐ ☐
3603	**2752**	(1st)	multicoloured	1·25	1·10	☐ ☐
3604	**2753**	(1st)	multicoloured	1·25	1·10	☐ ☐
3605	**2754**	£1·28	multicoloured	2·75	2·50	☐ ☐
		a.	Horiz strip of 3. Nos. 3605/7	8·00	7·25	☐ ☐
3606	**2755**	£1·28	multicoloured	2·75	2·50	☐ ☐
3607	**2756**	£1·28	multicoloured	2·75	2·50	☐ ☐
Set of 6				11·00	9·50	☐
First Day Cover					11·00	☐
Presentation Pack (P.O. Pack No. 498)				17·00		☐
PHQ Cards (*set of* 11) (389)				7·50	19·00	☐ ☐

Set of 2 Gutter Strips of 6		23·00	☐

MS3608 115×89 mm. **2757** (1st)×4 *Night Mail* (1936) directed by Harry Watt and Basil Wright; *Love on the Wing* (1938) directed by Norman McLaren; *A Colour Box* (1935) directed by Len Lye; *Spare Time* (1939) directed by Humphrey Jennings   5·50   5·50   ☐ ☐
First Day Cover   7·00   ☐

Nos. 3602/4 and 3605/7 were each printed together, *se-tenant*, as horizontal strips of three stamps in sheets of 36 (2 panes 3×6).

The complete miniature sheet is shown on one of the eleven PHQ cards with the others depicting individual stamps including those from **MS**3608.

2758 Herring

2759 Red Gurnard

2760 Dab

2761 Pouting

2762 Cornish Sardine

2763 Common Skate

2764 Spiny Dogfish

2765 Wolffish

2766 Sturgeon

2767 Conger Eel

Sustainable Fish (Nos. 3609/13) and Threatened Fish (Nos. 3614/18)

2014 (5 June) 'All-over' phosphor. Perf 14×14½

3609	**2758**	(1st)	multicoloured	1·25	1·10	☐ ☐
		a.	Horiz strip of 5.			

					Nos. 3609/13	6·00	5·25		
3610	**2759**	(1st)	multicoloured			1·25	1·10	☐	☐
3611	**2760**	(1st)	multicoloured			1·25	1·10	☐	☐
3612	**2761**	(1st)	multicoloured			1·25	1·10	☐	☐
3613	**2762**	(1st)	multicoloured			1·25	1·10	☐	☐
3614	**2763**	(1st)	multicoloured			1·25	1·10	☐	☐
		a.	Horiz strip of 5.						
			Nos. 3614/18			6·00	5·25		
3615	**2764**	(1st)	multicoloured			1·25	1·10	☐	☐
3616	**2765**	(1st)	multicoloured			1·25	1·10	☐	☐
3617	**2766**	(1st)	multicoloured			1·25	1·10	☐	☐
3618	**2767**	(1st)	multicoloured			1·25	1·10	☐	☐
Set of 10						11·00	9·50		
First Day Cover							11·00	☐	
Presentation Pack (P.O. Pack No. 499)						13·00		☐	
PHQ Cards (*set of* 10)						6·75	19·00	☐	☐
Set of 2 Gutter Strips of 10						23·00		☐	

Nos. 3609/13 and 3614/18 were each printed together, *se-tenant*, as horizontal strips of five in sheets of 50 (2 panes 5×5).

2768 Judo

2770 Marathon

2771 Squash

2772 Netball

2773 Para-athlete Cycling

Commonwealth Games, Glasgow

2014 (17 July) One phosphor band (3619) or two bands (others)

(a) Ordinary gum. Perf 14×14½

3619	**2768**	(2nd)	multicoloured	1·00	90	☐	☐
3620	**2769**	(1st)	multicoloured	1·25	1·10	☐	☐
3621	**2770**	97p	multicoloured	2·00	2·00	☐	☐
3622	**2771**£1·28		multicoloured	2·75	2·50	☐	☐
3623	**2772**£1·47		multicoloured	3·25	3·25	☐	☐
3624	**2773**£2·15		multicoloured	4·25	4·25	☐	☐
Set of 6				13·00	13·00		
First Day Cover					15·00	☐	
Presentation Pack (P.O. Pack No. 500)			15·00		☐	
PHQ Cards (*set of* 6) (391)				4·00	17·00	☐	☐
Set of 6 Gutter Pairs				28·00		☐	

(b) Self-adhesive. Die-cut perf 14×14½.

3625	**2769**	(1st)	multicoloured	6·00	6·00	☐	☐

The phosphor band on No. 3619 is at centre right of the stamps.
No. 3625 was only issued in stamp booklets, each containing No. 3625×2 and 4×1st vermilion and originally sold for £3·72.

2774 *Poppy*
(Fiona Strickland)

2775 Lines from *For the Fallen*
(Laurence Binyon)

2776 Private William Cecil Tickle

2777 *A Star Shell* (C. R. W. Nevinson)

2778 *The Response* (sculpture by William Goscombe John)

2779 Princess Mary's Gift Box Fund

Centenary of the First World War (1st issue)

2014 (28 July) 'All-over' phosphor (3627, 3629) or two bands (others). Perf 14½.

3626	**2774**	(1st)	multicoloured	1·25	1·10	☐	☐
		a.	'All-over' phosphor	1·50	1·50	☐	☐
3627	**2775**	(1st)	multicoloured	1·25	1·10	☐	☐
3628	**2776**	(1st)	multicoloured	1·25	1·10	☐	☐
		a.	'All-over' phosphor	1·50	1·50	☐	☐
3629	**2777**£1·47		multicoloured	3·25	3·25	☐	☐
3630	**2778**£1·47		multicoloured	3·25	3·25	☐	☐
		a.	'All-over' phosphor	3·50	3·50	☐	☐
3631	**2779**£1·47		multicoloured	3·25	3·25	☐	☐
		a.	'All-over' phosphor	3·50	3·50	☐	☐
Set of 6				12·00	12·00	☐	☐
First Day Cover					14·00	☐	
Presentation Pack (P.O. Pack No. 501)			13·50		☐	
PHQ Cards (*set of* 6) (392)				4·00	18·00	☐	☐
Set of 6 Gutter Pairs				25·00		☐	

Nos. 3626a, 3628a, 2630a and 3631a only come from the £11·30 Centenary of the First World War booklet, No. DY11.

Sustainable Fish and Threatened Fish (2nd issue)

2014 (18 Aug.) Designs as Nos. 3613/14. Self-adhesive. Die-cut perf 14×14½

3632	**2763**	(1st)	multicoloured	6·00	6·00	☐	☐
3633	**2762**	(1st)	multicoloured	6·00	6·00	☐	☐

Nos. 3632/3 were only issued in stamp booklets, each containing Nos. 3632/3 and 4×1st vermilion and originally sold for £3·72.

Classic Locomotives of Wales

2014 (18 Sept.) Booklet stamp as T **2724**. 'All-over' phosphor. Self-adhesive. Die-cut perf 14

3634	**2724**	(1st)	multicoloured	6·00	6·00	☐	☐

No. 3634 was only issued in stamp booklets, containing No. 3634×2 and 4×1st vermilion and originally sold for £3·72.

2780 Eastbourne Bandstand

2781 Tinside Lido, Plymouth

2787 Margaret Thatcher

2788 Harold Wilson

2782 Bangor Pier

2783 Southwold Lighthouse

2789 Clement Attlee

2790 Winston Churchill

2784 Blackpool Pleasure Beach

2785 Bexhill-on-Sea Shelter

2791 William Gladstone

2792 Robert Peel

2786 British Piers

2793 Charles Grey

2794 William Pitt the Younger

Seaside Architecture

2014 (18 Sept.) Two bands (3635/40) or 'All-over' phosphor (**MS**3641). Perf 14

3635	**2780**	(1st)	multicoloured	1·25	1·10	☐☐
3636	**2781**	(1st)	multicoloured	1·25	1·10	☐☐
3637	**2782**	97p	multicoloured	2·00	2·00	☐☐
3638	**2783**	97p	multicoloured	2·00	2·00	☐☐
3639	**2784**	£1·28	multicoloured	2·75	2·50	☐☐
3640	**2785**	£1·28	multicoloured	2·75	2·50	☐☐
Set of 6				11·00	10·00	☐
First Day Cover					12·00	☐
Presentation Pack (P.O. Pack No. 502)				13·00		☐
PHQ Cards (set of 11) (393)				7·50	19·00	☐☐
Set of 6 Gutter Pairs				23·00		☐

MS3641 125×89 mm. **2786** (1st) Llandudno Pier; (1st) Worthing Pier; £1·28 Dunoon Pier; £1·28 Brighton Pier

	8·00	8·00	☐☐
First Day Cover		10·00	☐

No. 3635 includes the 'EUROPA' emblem.

The complete miniature sheet is shown on one of the 11 PHQ cards with the others depicting individual stamps including those from the miniature sheet.

Prime Ministers

2014 (14 Oct.) 'All-over' phosphor. Perf 14½

3642	**2787**	(1st)	multicoloured	1.25	1.10	☐☐
		a.	Horiz strip of 4.			
			Nos. 3642/5	5.00	4.25	☐☐
3643	**2788**	(1st)	multicoloured	1.25	1.10	☐☐
3644	**2789**	(1st)	multicoloured	1.25	1.10	☐☐
3645	**2790**	(1st)	multicoloured	1.25	1.10	☐☐
3646	**2791**	97p	multicoloured	2.00	2.00	☐☐
		a.	Horiz strip of 4.			
			Nos. 3646/9	8.00	8.00	☐☐
3647	**2792**	97p	multicoloured	2.00	2.00	☐☐
3648	**2793**	97p	multicoloured	2.00	2.00	☐☐
3649	**2794**	97p	multicoloured	2.00	2.00	☐☐
Set of 8				12.00	12.00	☐
First Day Cover					14.00	☐
Presentation Pack (P.O. Pack No. 503)				14.00		☐
PHQ Cards (set of 8) (394)				5.50	19.00	☐☐
Set of 2 Gutter strips of 8				25·00		☐

Nos. 3642/5 and 3646/9 were each printed together, *se-tenant*, as horizontal strips of four stamps in sheets of 48 (2 panes 4×6).

2795 Collecting the Christmas Tree

2796 Posting Christmas Cards

2797 Collecting the Christmas Tree

2798 Posting Christmas Cards

2799 Building a Snowman

2800 Carol Singing

2801 Ice Skating

Christmas. Illustrations by Andrew Bannecker

2014 (4 Nov.) One centre band (3650) or two bands (others). Perf 14½ × 15

(a) Self-adhesive

3650	**2795**(2nd) multicoloured	1.00	90	
3651	**2796** (1st) multicoloured	1.25	1.10	
3652	**2797** (2nd Large) multicoloured	1.50	1.50	
3653	**2798** (1st Large) multicoloured	2.00	2.00	
3654	**2799**£1·28 multicoloured	2·75	2·50	
3655	**2800**£1·47 multicoloured	3·25	3·25	
3656	**2801**£2·15 multicoloured	4.25	4.25	
Set of 7		15.00	15.50	
First Day Cover			17.00	
Presentation Pack (P.O. Pack No. 504)		16.00		
PHQ Cards (*set of* 8) (395)		5.25	18.00	

(b) Ordinary gum

MS3657 146×74 mm. As Nos. 3650/6	15.00	15.00		
First Day Cover		17.00		

The eight PHQ cards show the seven individual stamps and the complete miniature sheet.

The 2nd class, 1st class, £1·28 and £1·47 stamps were also issued in sheets of 20 containing eight 2nd class, eight 1st class, two £1·28 and two £1·47 stamps, each stamp accompanied by a *se-tenant* label.

Separate sheets of 20 2nd, 20 1st, 10 1st, 10 £1·28 and ten £1·47 were available with personal photographs.

Year Pack

2014 (4 Nov.) Comprises Nos. 3552/69, **MS**3578/94, **MS**3601/24, 3626/31, 3635/56

CP3657a Year Pack	£150	

Post Office Yearbook

2014 (4 Nov.) Comprises Nos. 3552/69, **MS**3578/94, **MS**3601/24, 3626/31, 3635/56

YB3657a Yearbook	£175	

Miniature Sheet Collection

2014 (4 Nov.) Comprises Nos. **MS**3578, **MS**3601, **MS**3608, **MS**3641 and **MS**3657 **MS**3657a

MS3657a Miniature Sheet Collection	35·00	

2802 The White Rabbit

2803 Down the Rabbit Hole

2804 Drink Me

2805 The White Rabbit's House

2806 The Cheshire-Cat

2807 A Mad Tea-Party

2808 The Queen of Hearts

2809 The Game of Croquet

2810 Alice's Evidence

2811 A Pack of Cards

Alice in Wonderland

2015 (6 Jan.) One phosphor band at right (2nd) or two bands (others)

(a) Ordinary gum. Litho. Perf 14½

3658	**2802**	(2nd) multicoloured	1·10	90	
		a. Vert pair. Nos. 3658/9	2·25	1·75	
3659	**2803**	(2nd) multicoloured	1·10	90	
3660	**2804**	(1st) multicoloured	1·40	1·10	
		a. Vert pair. Nos. 3660/1	2·75	2·25	
3661	**2805**	(1st) multicoloured	1·40	1·10	
3662	**2806**	81p. multicoloured	1·90	1·50	
		a. Vert pair. Nos. 3662/3	3·75	3·50	
3663	**2807**	81p. multicoloured	1·90	1·50	
3664	**2808**	£1·28 multicoloured	3·00	2·50	
		a. Vert pair. Nos. 3664/5	6·00	5·00	
3665	**2809**	£1·28 multicoloured	3·00	2·50	

3666 **2810** £1·47 multicoloured	3·50	3·25		
a. Vert pair.				
Nos. 3666/7	7·00	6·50		
3667 **2811** £1·47 multicoloured	3·50	3·25		
Set of 10	20·00	18·00		
First Day Cover		21·00		
Presentation Pack (P.O. Pack No. 506)	23·00			
PHQ Cards (*set of* 10) (396)	6·75	23·00		
Set of 5 Gutter Strips of 4	42·00			

(b) Self-adhesive. Gravure. Die-cut perf 14½

3668 **2804** (1st) multicoloured	8·00	8·00	
3669 **2805** (1st) multicoloured	8·00	8·00	

Nos. 3658/9, 3660/1, 3662/3, 3664/5 and 3666/7 were each printed together, *se-tenant*, as vertical pairs in sheets of 60 (2 panes 5×6).

Nos. 3658/67 commemorate the 150th anniversary of the Publication of *Alice's Adventures in Wonderland* by Lewis Carroll.

Nos. 3668/9 were issued in stamp booklets, each containing Nos. 3668/9 and 4×1st vermilion and originally sold for £3.72.

2812 Happy Birthday **2813** Well Done **2814** Wedding

2815 Love **2816** Mum **2817** New Baby

2818 Grandparent **2819** Dad

Smilers (5th series). Booklet stamps

2015 (20 Jan.) Two phosphor bands.

(a) Self-adhesive. Gravure. Die-cut perf 14½×14 (with one elliptical hole in each vert side).

3670 **2812** (1st) multicoloured	2·75	2·75		
a. Booklet pane.				
Nos. 3670×2, 3671,				
3672/3 each×2,				
3674, 3675×2				
and 3676/7	24·00			
3671 **2813** (1st) multicoloured	2·75	2·75		
3672 **2814** (1st) multicoloured	2·75	2·75		
3673 **2815** (1st) multicoloured	2·75	2·75		
3674 **2816** (1st) multicoloured	2·75	2·75		
3675 **2817** (1st) multicoloured	2·75	2·75		
3676 **2818** (1st) multicoloured	2·75	2·75		
3677 **2819** (1st) multicoloured	2·75	2·75		
Set of 8	20·00	20·00		

(b) Ordinary gum. Litho. Perf 14½×14 (with one elliptical hole in each vert side).

MS3678 134×70 mm. As Nos. 3670/7	10·00	10·00	
First Day Cover		13·00	
Presentation Pack (Pack No. M23)	12·00		
PHQ Cards (*set of* 9) (D34)	6·75	17·00	

Nos. 3670/7 were issued in booklets of 12 originally sold for £7·44.

Nos. 3670/7 were also issued in sheets of 20 with *se-tenant* greetings labels printed in lithography.

The complete miniature sheet is shown on one of the nine PHQ cards with the others depicting individual stamps.

2820 Colossus – world's first electronic digital computer **2821** World Wide Web – revolutionary global communications system

2822 Catseyes – light-reflecting road safety innovation **2823** Fibre Optics – pioneering rapid-data-transfer technology

2824 Stainless Steel – non-corrosive, versatile, 100% recyclable alloy **2825** Carbon Fibre – high-strength, lightweight, composite material

2826 DNA Sequencing – revolution in understanding the genome **2827** i-LIMB – bionic hand with individually powered digits

Inventive Britain

2015 (19 Feb.) Two phosphor bands. Perf 14½

3679 **2820** (1st) multicoloured	1·25	1·10		
a. Horiz pair.				
Nos. 3679/80	2·50	2·25		
3680 **2821** (1st) multicoloured	1·25	1·10		
3681 **2822** 81p. multicoloured	1·75	1·50		
a. Horiz pair.				
Nos. 3681/2	3·50	3·00		
3682 **2823** 81p. multicoloured	1·75	1·50		
3683 **2824** £1·28 multicoloured	2·75	2·50		
a. Horiz pair.				
Nos. 3683/4	5·50	5·00		
3684 **2825** £1·28 multicoloured	2·75	2·50		
3685 **2826** £1·47 multicoloured	3·25	3·25		
a. Horiz pair.				
Nos. 3685/6	6·50	6·50		
3686 **2827** £1·47 multicoloured	3·25	3·25		
Set of 8	16·00	15·00		
First Day Cover		17·00		
Presentation Pack (P.O. Pack No. 507)	18·00			
PHQ Cards (*set of* 8) (397)	5·25	23·00		
Set of 4 Gutter Blocks of 4	35·00			

Nos. 3679/80, 3681/2, 3683/4 and 3685/6 were each printed together, *se-tenant*, as horizontal pairs in sheets of 60 (2 panes 6×5).

2828 Tarr Steps, River Barle

2829 Row Bridge, Mosedale Beck

2830 Pulteney Bridge, River Avon

2831 Craigellachie Bridge, River Spey

2832 Menai Suspension Bridge, Menai Strait

2833 High Level Bridge, River Tyne

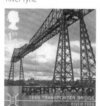

2834 Royal Border Bridge, River Tweed

2835 Tees Transporter Bridge, River Tees

2836 Humber Bridge, River Humber

2837 Peace Bridge, River Foyle

Bridges

2015 (5 Mar.) Two phosphor bands. Perf 14½ × 14.

3687	**2828**	(1st)	multicoloured	1·40	1·10	☐ ☐
	a.	Horiz strip of 5.				
		Nos. 3687/91		7·00	5·50	☐ ☐
3688	**2829**	(1st)	multicoloured	1·40	1·10	☐ ☐
3689	**2830**	(1st)	multicoloured	1·40	1·10	☐ ☐
3690	**2831**	(1st)	multicoloured	1·40	1·10	☐ ☐
3691	**2832**	(1st)	multicoloured	1·40	1·10	☐ ☐
3692	**2833**	(1st)	multicoloured	1·40	1·10	☐ ☐
	a.	Horiz strip of 5.				
		Nos. 3692/6		7·00	5·50	☐ ☐
3693	**2834**	(1st)	multicoloured	1·40	1·10	☐ ☐
3694	**2835**	(1st)	multicoloured	1·40	1·10	☐ ☐
3695	**2836**	(1st)	multicoloured	1·40	1·10	☐ ☐
3696	**2837**	(1st)	multicoloured	1·40	1·10	☐ ☐
Set of 10				12·00	10·00	☐ ☐

First Day Cover		12·00	☐
Presentation Pack (P.O. Pack No. 508)	15·00		☐
PHQ Cards (set of 10) (398)	6·75	15·00	☐ ☐
Set of 2 Gutter Strips of 10	26·00		
Set of 2 Traffic Light Gutter Strips of 10	28·00		☐

Nos. 3687/91 and 3692/6 were each printed together, se-tenant, as horizontal strips of five stamps in sheets of 50 (2 panes 5×5).

2838 Spike Milligan

2839 The Two Ronnies

2840 Billy Connolly

2841 Morecambe and Wise

2842 Norman Wisdom

2843 Lenny Henry

2844 Peter Cook and Dudley Moore

2845 Monty Python

2846 French and Saunders

2847 Victoria Wood

Comedy Greats

2015 (1 Apr.) Two phosphor bands

(a) Ordinary gum. Litho. Perf 14

3697	**2838**	(1st)	multicoloured	1·25	1·10	☐ ☐
	a.	Horiz strip of 5.				
		Nos. 3697/3701		6·25	5·50	☐ ☐
3698	**2839**	(1st)	multicoloured	1·25	1·10	☐ ☐
3699	**2840**	(1st)	multicoloured	1·25	1·10	☐ ☐
3700	**2841**	(1st)	multicoloured	1·25	1·10	☐ ☐
3701	**2842**	(1st)	multicoloured	1·25	1·10	☐ ☐
3702	**2843**	(1st)	multicoloured	1·25	1·10	☐ ☐
	a.	Horiz strip of 5.				
		Nos. 3702/6		6·25	5·50	☐ ☐
3703	**2844**	(1st)	multicoloured	1·25	1·10	☐ ☐
3704	**2845**	(1st)	multicoloured	1·25	1·10	☐ ☐
3705	**2846**	(1st)	multicoloured	1·25	1·10	☐ ☐
3706	**2847**	(1st)	multicoloured	1·25	1·10	☐ ☐
Set of 10				11·50	10·00	☐ ☐
First Day Cover					12·00	☐
Presentation Pack (P.O. Pack No. 509)			13·00			☐

PHQ Cards (set of 10) (399)	6·75	15·00	☐ ☐	
Set of 2 Gutter Strips of 10		24·00	☐	

(b) Self-adhesive. Gravure. Die-cut perf 14

3707	**2842**	(1st)	multicoloured	6·00	6·00	☐ ☐
3708	**2841**	(1st)	multicoloured	6·00	6·00	☐ ☐

Nos. 3697/701 and 3702/6 were each printed together, *se-tenant*, as horizontal strips of five stamps in sheets of 50 (2 panes 5×5).

Nos. 3707/8 were issued in stamp booklets, each containing Nos. 3707/8 and 4×1st vermilion and originally sold for £3.72.

2848 Penny Black

2849 'Penny Black' and 1840 2d. blue

175th Anniversary of the Penny Black

2015 (6 May) Two phosphor bands.

(a) Self-adhesive booklet stamps. Gravure.
Die-cut perf 14½×14 (with one elliptical hole in each vert side)

3709	**2848**	(1st)	black and gold	3·00	3·00	☐ ☐

(b) Ordinary gum. Litho. Perf 14½×14
(with one elliptical hole in each vert side)

MS3710	156×74 mm.	**2849**	(1st)	
Penny Black×2; (1st) 1840 2d. blue×2		6·00	☐ ☐	
First Day Cover		7·00	☐	
Presentation Pack (P.O. Pack No. 510)	7·00		☐	
PHQ Cards (set of 3) (400)	2·00	7·50	☐ ☐	

No. 3709 was issued in booklets of six.

The three PHQ cards show the two individual stamps and the complete miniature sheet.

Designs as No. 3709 and (1st) Twopenny Blue as within **MS**3710 but self-adhesive were also issued in sheets of 20, printed in lithography, containing ten 1st class Penny Black and ten 1st class Twopenny Blue, each stamp accompanied by a *se-tenant* label.

Sheets of ten or 20 1st Penny Black were available with personal photographs.

2850 *Poppies* (Howard Hodgkin)

2851 *All the Hills and Vales Along* (Charles Hamilton Sorley)

2852 Rifleman Kulbir Thapa

2853 *The Kensingtons at Laventie* (Eric Kennington)

2854 *'A British Soldier visits his Comrade's Grave on the Cliffs near Cape Helles'*, Gallipoli (posed photo by Ernest Brooks)

2855 London Irish Rifles' Football from Loos

Centenary of the First World War (2nd issue)

2015 (14 May) Two phosphor bands. Perf 14½

3711	**2850**	(1st)	multicoloured	1·25	1·10	☐ ☐
3712	**2851**	(1st)	multicoloured	1·25	1·10	☐ ☐
3713	**2852**	(1st)	multicoloured	1·25	1·10	☐ ☐
3714	**2853**	£1·52	multicoloured	3·25	3·25	☐ ☐
3715	**2854**	£1·52	multicoloured	3·25	3·25	☐ ☐
3716	**2855**	£1·52	multicoloured	3·25	3·25	☐ ☐
Set of 6				12·00	12·00	☐
First Day Cover					14·00	☐
Presentation Pack (P.O. Pack No. 511)			14·00		☐
PHQ Cards (set of 6) (401)			4·00	16·00	☐
Set of 6 Gutter Pairs				25·00		☐

2015 (14 May)–**2017** Premium Booklet stamp. As No. 3414 but ordinary gum. Two phosphor bands. Perf 14½×14 (with one elliptical hole in each vertical side)

3717	**2588**	(1st)	multicoloured	3·00	3·00	☐ ☐

No. 3717 comes from the Centenary of the First World War premium booklets (2nd, 3rd and 4th issues), Nos. DY13, DY18 and DY22.

2856 Magna Carta, 1215

2857 Simon de Montfort's Parliament, 1265

2858 Bill of Rights, 1689

2859 American Bill of Rights, 1791

2860 Universal Declaration of Human Rights, 1948

2861 Charter of the Commonwealth, 2013

800th Anniversary of Magna Carta

2015 (2 June) Two phosphor bands. Perf 14½

3718	**2856**	(1st)	multicoloured	1·25	1·10	
3719	**2857**	(1st)	multicoloured	1·25	1·10	
3720	**2858**	£1·33	multicoloured	2·75	2·50	
3721	**2859**	£1·33	multicoloured	2·75	2·50	
3722	**2860**	£1·52	multicoloured	3·25	3·25	
3723	**2861**	£1·52	multicoloured	3·25	3·25	
Set of 6				13·00	13·00	
First Day Cover					15·00	
Presentation Pack (P.O. Pack No. 512)				15·00		
PHQ Cards (set of 6) (402)				4·00	17·00	
Set of 6 Gutter Pairs				27·00		

2862 The Defence of Hougoumont

2863 The Scots Greys during the Charge of the Union Brigade

2864 The French Cavalry's Assault on Allied Defensive Squares

2865 The Defence of La Haye Sainte by the King's German Legion

2866 The Capture of Plancenoit by the Prussians

2867 The French Imperial Guard's Final Assault

Bicentenary of the Battle of Waterloo (1st issue)

2015 (18 June) Two phosphor bands. Perf 14½

3724	**2862**	(1st)	multicoloured	1·25	1·10	
3725	**2863**	(1st)	multicoloured	1·25	1·10	
3726	**2864**	£1	multicoloured	2·25	2·00	
3727	**2865**	£1	multicoloured	2·25	2·00	
3728	**2866**	£1·52	multicoloured	3·25	3·25	
3729	**2867**	£1·52	multicoloured	3·25	3·25	
Set of 6				12·50	12·00	
First Day Cover					14·00	
Presentation Pack (P.O. Pack No. 513)				15·00		
PHQ Cards (set of 11) (403)				7·50	20·00	
Set of 6 Gutter Pairs				27·00		

The 11 PHQ cards depict the individual stamps, including those from **MS**3734, and the complete miniature sheet.

2868 15th Infantry Regiment, IV Corps, Prussian Army

2869 Light Infantry, King's German Legion, Anglo-Allied Army

2870 92nd Gordon Highlanders, Anglo-Allied Army

2871 Grenadiers, Imperial Guard, French Army

2872 Soldiers and Battle of Waterloo Map

Bicentenary of the Battle of Waterloo (2nd issue)

2015 (18 June) Two phosphor bands. Perf 14

3730	**2868**	(1st)	multicoloured	1·50	1·50	☐ ☐
3731	**2869**	(1st)	multicoloured	1·50	1·50	☐ ☐
3732	**2870**	£1·33	multicoloured	3·00	3·00	☐ ☐
3733	**2871**	£1·33	multicoloured	3·00	3·00	☐ ☐
MS3734	156×74 mm.	**2872**	Nos. 3730/38.00		8·00	☐ ☐
First Day Cover					9·50	☐

Nos. 3730/3 come from £14·47 Bicentenary of the Battle of Waterloo premium booklet, No. DY14, and **MS**3734.

2873 Battle of Britain

75th Anniversary of the Battle of Britain.

2015 (16 July) 'All-over' phosphor. Perf 14

MS3735	**2873**	190×74 mm. (1st) Pilots scramble to their Hurricanes; (1st) Supermarine Spitfires of 610 Squadron, Biggin Hill, on patrol; (1st) Armourer Fred Roberts replaces ammunition boxes on Supermarine Spitfire; £1·33 Spotters of the Auxiliary Territorial Service looking for enemy aircraft; £1·33 Operations Room at Bentley Priory; £1·33 Pilots of 32 Squadron await orders, RAF Hawkinge, Kent	12·00	12·00	☐ ☐
First Day Cover			13·00	☐
Presentation Pack (P.O. Pack No. 514)		13·00		☐
PHQ Cards (set of 7) (404)		4·75	17·00	☐ ☐

The seven PHQ cards show the six individual stamps and the complete miniature sheet.

2874 Scabious Bee (*Andrena hattorfiana*) on Field Scabious (*Knautia arvensis*)

2875 Great Yellow Bumblebee (*Bombus distinguendus*) on Bird's-foot Trefoil (*Lotus corniculatus*)

2876 Northern Colletes Bee (*Colletes floralis*) on Wild Carrot (*Daucus carota*)

2877 Bilberry Bumblebee (*Bombus monticola*) on Bilberry (*Vaccinium myrtillus*)

2878 Large Mason Bee (*Osmia xanthomelana*) on Horseshoe Vetch (*Hippocrepis comosa*)

2879 Potter Flower Bee (*Anthophora retusa*) on Ground Ivy (*Glechoma hederacea*)

2880 The Honeybee

Bees

2015 (18 Aug.) Bees.

(a) Ordinary gum. Litho. One centre band (3736), two phosphor bands (3737/41) or phosphor background (MS3742). Perf 14×14½

3736	**2874**	(2nd)	multicoloured	1·00	90	☐ ☐
3737	**2875**	(1st)	multicoloured	1·25	1·10	☐ ☐
3738	**2876**	£1	multicoloured	2·25	2·00	☐ ☐
3739	**2877**	£1·33	multicoloured	2·75	2·50	☐ ☐
3740	**2878**	£1·52	multicoloured	3·25	3·25	☐ ☐
3741	**2879**	£2·25	multicoloured	4·50	4·50	☐ ☐
Set of 6				13·50	12·50	☐ ☐
First Day Cover					14·00	☐
Presentation Pack (P.O. Pack No. 515)			23·00		☐
PHQ Cards (set of 7) (405)			7·50	21·00	☐ ☐
Set of 6 Gutter Pairs				29·00		☐
MS3742	191×74 mm. **2880** (1st) Waggle dance; (1st) Pollination; £1·33 Making honey; £1·33 Tending young			5·50	5·50	☐ ☐
First Day Cover					9·00	☐

(b) Self-adhesive. Gravure. Two phosphor bands. Die-cut perf 14×14½

3743	**2875**	(1st)	multicoloured	5·50	5·50	☐ ☐

No. 3743 was issued in stamp booklets, each containing No. 3743×2 and 4×1st vermilion and originally sold for £3·78.

The seven PHQ cards depict the six individual stamps and the complete miniature sheet.

2881 'Long to Reign Over Us'

Long to Reign Over Us

2015 (9 Sept.) Two phosphor bands. Perf 14½ × 14 (with one elliptical hole in each vertical side) (Machin) or 14 (others)

MS3747 194×75 mm. **2881** (1st) William Wyon's City Medal depicting Queen Victoria; (1st) Portrait of Queen Elizabeth II from photo by Dorothy Wilding; As No. U3744; £1·52 Badge of the House of Windsor depicting Round Tower of Windsor Castle; £1·52 Device from

The Queen's Personal Flag	10·00	10·00	☐	☐
First Day Cover		11·00		☐
Presentation Pack (P.O. Pack No. 516)	11·00		☐	
PHQ Cards (set of 6) (406)	4·00	14·00	☐	☐

Stamps from **MS**3747 all have an iridescent overprint reading 'LONG TO REIGN OVER US'.

The PHQ cards depict the five individual stamps and the complete miniature sheet.

2882 Tackle

2883 Scrum

2884 Try

2885 Conversion

2886 Pass

2887 Drop Goal

2888 Ruck

2889 Line-Out

Rugby World Cup

2015 (18 Sept.) Two phosphor bands

(a) Ordinary gum. Litho. Perf 14						
3748	**2882**	(2nd)	multicoloured	1·00	90	☐ ☐
		a.	Horiz pair.			
			Nos. 3748/9	2·00	1·75	☐ ☐
3749	**2883**	(2nd)	multicoloured	1·00	90	☐ ☐
3750	**2884**	(1st)	multicoloured	1·25	1·10	☐ ☐
		a.	Horiz pair.			
			Nos. 3750/1	2·50	2·25	☐ ☐
3751	**2885**	(1st)	multicoloured	1·25	1·10	☐ ☐
3752	**2886**	£1	multicoloured	2·25	2·00	☐ ☐
		a.	Horiz pair.			
			Nos. 3752/3	4·50	4·00	☐ ☐
3753	**2887**	£1	multicoloured	2·25	2·00	☐ ☐
3754	**2888**	£1·52	multicoloured	3·25	3·25	☐ ☐
		a.	Horiz pair.			
			Nos. 3754/5	6·50	6·50	☐ ☐
3755	**2889**	£1·52	multicoloured	3·25	3·25	☐ ☐
Set of 8				14·00	13·00	☐ ☐
First Day Cover					15·00	☐
Presentation Pack (P.O. Pack No. 517)				16·00		☐
PHQ Cards (set of 8) (407)				5·50	19·00	☐
Set of 4 Gutter Blocks of 4				30·00		☐
(b) Self-adhesive. Gravure. Die-cut perf 14						
3756	**2884**	(1st)	multicoloured	4·50	4·50	☐ ☐
3757	**2885**	(1st)	multicoloured	4·50	4·50	☐ ☐

Nos. 3748/9, 3750/1, 3752/3 and 3754/5 were each printed together, se-tenant, as horizontal pairs in sheets of 60 (2 panes 6×5).

Nos. 3756/7 were issued in stamp booklets, each containing Nos. 3756/7 and 4×1st vermilion and originally sold for £3·78.

2890 Darth Vader

2891 Yoda

2892 Obi-Wan Kenobi

2893 Stormtrooper

2894 Han Solo

2895 Rey

2896 Princess Leia

2897 The Emperor

2898 Luke Skywalker

2899 Boba Fett

2900 Finn

2901 Kylo Ren

2902 Star Wars

Star Wars

2015 (20 Oct.) Two phosphor bands (3758/69) or 'All-over' phosphor (**MS**3770)

		(a) Ordinary gum. Perf 14½				
3758	**2890**	(1st) multicoloured	1·25	1·10		
	a.	Horiz strip of 6.				
		Nos. 3758/63	7·50	6·50		
3759	**2891**	(1st) multicoloured	1·25	1·10		
3760	**2892**	(1st) multicoloured	1·25	1·10		
3761	**2893**	(1st) multicoloured	1·25	1·10		
3762	**2894**	(1st) multicoloured	1·25	1·10		
3763	**2895**	(1st) multicoloured	1·25	1·10		
3764	**2896**	(1st) multicoloured	1·25	1·10		
	a.	Horiz strip of 6.				
		Nos. 3764/9	7·50	6·50		
3765	**2897**	(1st) multicoloured	1·25	1·10		
3766	**2898**	(1st) multicoloured	1·25	1·10		
3767	**2899**	(1st) multicoloured	1·25	1·10		
3768	**2900**	(1st) multicoloured	1·25	1·10		
3769	**2901**	(1st) multicoloured	1·25	1·10		
Set of 12			13·50	12·00		
First Day Cover				14·00		
Presentation Pack (P.O. Pack No. 518)			23·00			
PHQ Cards (*set of* 19) (408)			13·00	28·00		
Souvenir Folder (containing 3758/69)			30·00			
Set of 2 Gutter Strips of 12			30·00			

(b) Self-adhesive
MS3770   204×75 mm. **2902** (1st)
  X-wing Starfighter (60×21 mm,
  Perf 14½×14); (1st) TIE fighters
  (35×36 mm, Perf 14); (1st) X-wing
  Starfighters (60×21 mm, Perf
  14½×14); (1st) AT-AT Walkers
  (41×30 mm, Perf 14); (1st) TIE
  fighters (27×37 mm, Perf 14); (1st)
  Millennium Falcon (60×30 mm,
  P 14½)   7·50   7·50
First Day Cover   8·50
Nos. 3758/63 and 3764/9 were each printed together, *se-tenant*, as horizontal strips of six stamps in sheets of 60 (2 panes 6×5).
  The 19 PHQ cards depict the individual stamps including those from **MS**3770 and the complete miniature sheet.
  Designs as Nos. 3758/9 and 3761/2 but self-adhesive were issued in sheets of ten with *se-tenant* labels, each sheet containing Nos. 3758/9, each×3, and Nos. 3761/2, each×2.
  The four designs were available in separate sheets of ten with personal photographs.

2903 The Journey to Bethlehem

2904 The Nativity

2905 The Journey to Bethlehem

2906 The Nativity

2907 The Animals of the Nativity

2908 The Shepherds

2909 The Three Wise Men

2910 The Annunciation

Christmas

2015 (3 Nov.) One centre band (3771) or two bands (others). Perf 14½×15

		(a) Self-adhesive				
3771	**2903**	(2nd) multicoloured	1·00	90		
3772	**2904**	(1st) multicoloured	1·25	1·10		
3773	**2905**	(2nd Large) multicoloured	1·50	1·50		
3774	**2906**	(1st Large) multicoloured	2·00	2·00		
3775	**2907**	£1·00 multicoloured	2·25	2·00		
3776	**2908**	£1·33 multicoloured	2·75	2·50		
3777	**2909**	£1·52 multicoloured	3·25	3·25		
3778	**2910**	£2·25 multicoloured	4·50	4·50		
Set of 8			17·00	16·00		
First Day Cover				18·00		
Presentation Pack (P.O. Pack No. 519)			19·00			
PHQ Cards (*set of* 9) (409)			6·00	23·00		

(b) Ordinary gum
MS3779 190×74 mm. As Nos. 3771/8 17·00   17·00
First Day Cover   19·00
The nine PHQ cards show the eight individual stamps and the complete miniature sheet.
  The 2nd class, 1st class, £1, £1·33, £1·52 and £2·25 stamps were also issued in sheets of 20, printed in lithography instead of gravure and containing eight 2nd class, eight 1st class and one each of £1, £1·33, £1·52 and £2·25 stamps, each stamp accompanied by a *se-tenant* label with a verse from the King James Bible.

Year Pack

2015 (3 Nov.) Comprises Nos. 3658/67, **MS**3678/3706, **MS**3710/16, 3718/29, **MS**3734, **MS**3735/42, **MS**3747/55 and 3758/78

CP3779a Year Pack   £175   ☐

Post Office Yearbook

2015 (3 Nov.) Comprises Nos. 3658/67, **MS**3678/3706, **MS**3710/29, **MS**3734, **MS**3735/42, **MS**3747/55 and 3758/78

YB3779a Yearbook   £200   ☐

Miniature Sheet Collection

2015 (3 Nov.) Comprises Nos. **MS**3678, **MS**3710, **MS**3734, **MS**3735, **MS**3742, **MS**3747, **MS**3770 and **MS**3779

MS3779a Miniature Sheet Collection   60·00   ☐

2911 X-wing Starfighter

2912 AT-AT Walkers

2913 TIE fighters   **2914** TIE fighters

2915 X-wing Starfighters

2916 Millennium Falcon

Star Wars (2nd issue)

2015 (17 Dec.) Self-adhesive. 'All-over' phosphor. Die-cut perf 14½ × 14 (3780, 3784), 14 (3781/3) or 14½ (3785)

3780	**2911**	(1st)	multicoloured	2.00	2.00	☐ ☐
3781	**2912**	(1st)	multicoloured	2.00	2.00	☐ ☐
3783	**2914**	(1st)	multicoloured	2.00	2.00	☐ ☐
3784	**2915**	(1st)	multicoloured	2.00	2.00	☐ ☐
3785	**2916**	(1st)	multicoloured	2.00	2.00	☐ ☐
Set of 6				11.00	11.00	☐ ☐

Nos. 3780/5 were only issued in £16.99 Star Wars premium booklets or **MS**3770.

2917 Union Flag

Star Wars (3rd issue)

2015 (17 Dec.) As No. 2570 but ordinary gum. Two phosphor bands. Perf 14½ × 14 (with one elliptical hole in each vert side)

3786 **2917** (1st) multicoloured   3·00   3·00   ☐ ☐

No. 3786 comes from booklet pane No. U3014ab from the £16.99 Star Wars premium booklet.

2918 Entering the Antarctic Ice, December 1914   **2919** *Endurance* Frozen in Pack Ice, January 1915

2920 Striving to Free *Endurance*, February 1915   **2921** Trapped in a Pressure Crack, October 1915

2922 Patience Camp, December 1915 – April 1916   **2923** Safe Arrival at Elephant Island, April 1916

2924 Setting out for South Georgia, April 1916   **2925** Rescue of *Endurance* Crew, August 1916

Shackleton and the *Endurance* Expedition

2016 (7 Jan.) Two phosphor bands. Perf 14 × 14½.

3787	**2918**	(1st)	bluish grey, grey and black	1.25	1.10	☐ ☐
		a.	Horiz pair. Nos. 3787/88	2.50	2.25	☐ ☐
3788	**2919**	(1st)	bluish grey, grey and black	1.25	1.10	☐ ☐
3789	**2920**	£1	bluish grey, grey and black	2.25	2.00	☐ ☐
		a.	Horiz pair. Nos. 3789/90	4.50	4.00	☐ ☐

3790 **2921**	£1	bluish grey, grey and black	2·25	2·00	☐ ☐
3791 **2922**	£1·33	bluish grey, grey and black	2·75	2·50	☐ ☐
	a.	Horiz pair. Nos· 3791/2	5·50	5·00	☐ ☐
3792 **2923**	£1·33	bluish grey, grey and black	2·75	2·50	☐ ☐
3793 **2924**	£1·52	bluish grey, grey and black	3·25	3·25	☐ ☐
	a.	Horiz pair. Nos· 3793/4	6·50	6·50	☐ ☐
3794 **2925**	£1·52	bluish grey, grey and black	3·25	3·25	☐ ☐
Set of 8			19·00	17·50	☐ ☐
First Day Cover				21·00	☐
Presentation Pack (P.O. Pack 521)			20.00		☐
PHQ Cards (*set of 8*) (410)			5·50	25·00	☐ ☐
Set of 4 Gutter Blocks of 4			40·00		☐ ☐

Nos. 3787/8, 3789/90, 3791/2 and 3793/4 were each printed together, *se-tenant*, as horizontal pairs in sheets of 60 (2 panes 6×5).

2926 Sir Brian Tuke, Master of the Posts

2927 Mail Packet off Eastbourne (Capt. Victor Howes)

2928 Penfold Pillar Box

2929 River Post

2930 Mail Coach

2931 Medway Mail Centre

2932 Classic GPO Posters

Royal Mail 500 (1st issue)

2016 (17 Feb.) Two phosphor bands. Perf 14½ × 14 (3795/800) or 14 (**MS**3801)

3795 **2926**	(1st)	multicoloured	1·25	1·10	☐ ☐
3796 **2927**	(1st)	multicoloured	1·25	1·10	☐ ☐
3797 **2928**	(1st)	multicoloured	1·25	1·10	☐ ☐

3798 **2929**	£1·52	multicoloured	3·25	3·25	☐ ☐
3799 **2930**	£1·52	multicoloured	3·25	3·25	☐ ☐
3800 **2931**	£1·52	multicoloured	3·25	3·25	☐ ☐
Set of 6			13·00	12·50	☐ ☐
First Day Cover				15·00	☐
Presentation Pack (P.O. Pack No. 522)			22·00		☐
PHQ Cards (*set of 11*) (411)			7·50	21·00	☐
Set of 6 Gutter Pairs			27·00		☐
Set of 6 Traffic Light Gutter Pairs			29.00		
(2 stamps only in each pair)					☐

MS3801 125×89 mm. (1st) 'QUICKEST WAY BY AIR MAIL' (Edward McKnight Kauffer, 1935); (1st) 'ADDRESS your letters PLAINLY' (Hans Schleger, 1942); £1·33 'pack your parcels carefully' (Hans Unger, 1950); £1·33 'STAMPS IN BOOKS SAVE TIME' (Harry Stevens, 1960)   8·00   8·00   ☐ ☐

First Day Cover   9·00   ☐

Nos. 3795/**MS**3801 commemorate 500 years of a regular, organised postal service.

The complete miniature sheet is shown on one of the eleven PHQ cards with the others depicting individual stamps including those from the miniature sheet.

2933 'Quickest way by Air Mail' (Edward McKnight Kauffer, 1935)

2934 'address your letters plainly' (Hans Schleger, 1942)

2935 'stamps in books save time' (Harry Stevens, 1960)

2936 'pack your parcels carefully' (Hans Unger, 1950)

Royal Mail 500 (2nd issue)

2016 (17 Feb.) Two phosphor bands. Perf 14

3802 **2933**	(1st)	multicoloured	1·50	1·50	☐ ☐
3803 **2934**	(1st)	multicoloured	1·50	1·50	☐ ☐
3804 **2935**	£1·33	multicoloured	3·00	3·00	☐ ☐
3805 **2936**	£1·33	multicoloured	3·00	3·00	☐ ☐
Set of 4			9·00	9·00	☐ ☐

Nos. 3802/5 come from No. **MS**3801 and £16.36 500 Years of Royal Mail premium booklets which were issued on 18 February 2016.

2937 Penny Red

175th Anniversary of the Penny Red

2016 (18 Feb).Two phosphor bands. Self-adhesive. Gravure. Die-cut perf 14½ × 14 (with one elliptical hole in each vert side)

No. 3806 was issued in booklets of six stamps.

No. 3806 was also issued printed in lithography in sheets of 20 with attached labels showing the 'Rainbow Trials' from which the Penny Red evolved.

Sheets of ten or 20 of these Penny Red stamps were available from Royal Mail with personal photographs on the labels.

2938 Twopenny Blue

Royal Mail 500 (3rd issue)

2016 (18 Feb.) Two phosphor bands. Litho. Perf 14½ × 14 (with one elliptical hole in each vert side)

3807 **2848**	(1st)	multicoloured	2·75	2·75
3808 **2937**	(1st)	multicoloured	2·75	2·75
3809 **2938**	(1st)	multicoloured	2·75	2·75

Nos. 3807/9 come from £16·36 500 Years of Royal Mail premium booklets.

2939 Nicholas Winton (1909-2015)   2940 Sue Ryder (1924-2000)

2941 John Boyd Orr (1880-1971)   2942 Eglantyne Jebb (1876-1928)

2943 Joseph Rowntree (1836-1925)   2944 Josephine Butler (1828-1906)

British Humanitarians

2016 (15 Mar.) Two phosphor bands. Perf 14½.

3810 **2939**	(1st)	black	1·25	1·10	
	a. Horiz strip of 3.				
	Nos. 3810/12		3·75	3·25	
3811 **2940**	(1st)	black	1·25	1·10	
3812 **2941**	(1st)	black	1·25	1·10	
3813 **2942**	£1·33	black	2·75	2·50	
	a. Horiz strip of 3.				
	Nos. 3813/15		8·25	7·50	
3814 **2943**	£1·33	black	2·75	2·50	
3815 **2944**	£1·33	black	2·75	2·50	
Set of 6			11·50	10·50	
First Day Cover				13·00	
Presentation Pack (P.O. Pack No. 523)			12·50		
PHQ Cards (set of 6) (412)			4·00	15·00	
Set of 2 Gutter Strips of 6			23·00		

Nos. 3810/12 and 3813/15 were each printed together, se-tenant, as horizontal strips of three stamps in sheets of 60 (2 panes 6 × 5).

2945 'to thine own self be true' (Hamlet)

2946 'cowards die many times before their deaths. the valiant never taste of death but once.' (Julius Caesar)

2947 'Love is a smoke made with the fume of sighs' (Romeo and Juliet)

2948 'the fool doth think he is wise, but the wise man knows himself to be a fool.' (As You Like It)

2949 'there was a star danced, and under that was I born. (Much Ado About Nothing)

2950 'but if the while I think on thee, dear friend, all losses are restored and sorrows end.' (Sonnet 30)

2951 'Love comforteth like sunshine after rain' (Venus and Adonis)

2952 'we are such stuff as dreams are made on; and our little life is rounded with a sleep.' (The Tempest)

2953 'Life's but a walking shadow, a poor player That struts and frets his hour upon the stage' (Macbeth)

2954 'I wasted time, and now doth time waste me' (Richard II)

400th Death Anniversary of William Shakespeare (playwright)

2016 (5 Apr.) Two phosphor bands. Perf 14½.

3816	**2945**	(1st)	carmine, pale grey-brown and black	1·25	1·10	☐	☐
		a.	Horiz strip of 5. Nos. 3816/20	6·25	6·25	☐	☐
3817	**2946**	(1st)	carmine, pale grey-brown and black	1·25	1·10	☐	☐
3818	**2947**	(1st)	carmine, pale grey-brown and black	1·25	1·10	☐	☐
3819	**2948**	(1st)	carmine, pale grey-brown and black	1·25	1·10	☐	☐
3820	**2949**	(1st)	carmine, pale grey-brown and black	1·25	1·10	☐	☐
3821	**2950**	(1st)	carmine, pale grey-brown and black	1·25	1·10	☐	☐
		a.	Horiz strip of 5. Nos. 3821/5	6·25	6·25	☐	☐
3822	**2951**	(1st)	carmine, pale grey-brown and black	1·25	1·10	☐	☐
3823	**2952**	(1st)	carmine, pale grey-brown and black	1·25	1·10	☐	☐
3824	**2953**	(1st)	carmine, pale grey-brown and black	1·25	1·10	☐	☐
3825	**2954**	(1st)	carmine, pale grey-brown and black	1·25	1·10	☐	☐
Set of 10				12·50	12·50	☐	☐
First Day Cover					14·50		☐
Presentation Pack (P.O. Pack No. 524)				14·50		☐	
PHQ Cards (*set of* 10)(413)				6·75	19·00	☐	☐
Set of 2 Gutter Strips of 10				25·00		☐	

Nos. 3816/20 and 3821/5 were each printed together, se-tenant, as horizontal strips of five stamps in sheets of 50 (2 panes 5×5).

2955 Princess Elizabeth and her Father, the Duke of York (later King George VI), c. 1930

2956 Queen Elizabeth II at State Opening of Parliament, 2012

2957 Queen Elizabeth II with Prince Charles and Princess Anne, 1952

2958 Queen Elizabeth II on Visit to New Zealand, 1977

2959 Queen Elizabeth II and Duke of Edinburgh, 1957

2960 Queen Elizabeth II with Nelson Mandela, 1996

2961 Prince Charles, Queen Elizabeth II, Prince George and Prince William

2962 Prince Charles

2963 Queen Elizabeth II

2964 Prince George

2965 Prince William

90th Birthday of Queen Elizabeth II

2016 (21 Apr–9 June). Two phosphor bands (3826/31) or 'all-over' phosphor (**MS**3832, 3833/6)

(a) Ordinary gum. Litho.
Perf 14 × 14½ (3826/31)or 14 (**MS**3832)

3826	**2955**	(1st)	multicoloured	1·50	1·40	☐	☐
		a.	Horiz strip of 3. Nos. 3826/8	4·50	4·25	☐	☐
3827	**2956**	(1st)	multicoloured	1·50	1·40	☐	☐
3828	**2957**	(1st)	multicoloured	1·50	1·40	☐	☐
3829	**2958**	£1·52	multicoloured	3·75	3·75	☐	☐
		a.	Horiz strip of 3. Nos. 3829/31	11·00	11·00	☐	☐
3830	**2959**	£1·52	multicoloured	3·75	3·75	☐	☐
3831	**2960**	£1·52	multicoloured	3·75	3·75	☐	☐
Set of 6				14·00	13·50	☐	☐
First Day Cover					14·50		☐
Presentation Pack (P.O. Pack No. 525)				35·00		☐	
PHQ Cards (*set of* 11) (414)				10·00	30·00	☐	☐
Set of 2 Gutter Strips of 6				29·00		☐	

MS3832 189×75 mm. **2961** (1st) multi-coloured; (1st) multicoloured; (1st) multicoloured; (1st) multicoloured 20·00 20·00 ☐ ☐

First Day Cover 20·00 ☐

(b) Self-adhesive. Gravure. Die-cut perf 14.

3833	**2962**	(1st)	multicoloured	4·50	4·50	☐	☐
3834	**2963**	(1st)	multicoloured	4·50	4·50	☐	☐
3835	**2964**	(1st)	multicoloured (9.6.16)	4·50	4·50	☐	☐
3836	**2965**	(1st)	multicoloured (9.6.16)	4·50	4·50	☐	☐
Set of 4				16·00	16·00	☐	☐

Nos. 3833/6 were issued in stamp booklets containing either Nos. 3833/4 or 3835/6 and 4×1st bright lilac, each booklet originally sold for £3.84.

2966 Animail

Animail

2016 (17 May). 'All-over' phosphor. Die-cut and die-cut perf 14
Multicoloured
MS3837 **2966** 203×74 mm. (1st)

Woodpecker; (1st) Snake; £1·05			
Chimpanzee; £1·05 Bat; £1·33			
Orangutan; £1·33 Koala	14·50	14·50	
First Day Cover		15·00	
Presentation Pack (P.O. Pack No. 526)	16·00		
PHQ Cards (set of 7) (415)	6·25	21·00	

The seven PHQ cards show the six individual stamps and the
complete miniature sheet.

2967 Battlefield Poppy
(Giles Revell)

2968 Your battle wounds are scars
upon my heart
(poem To My Brother, Vera Brittain)

2969 Munitions Worker Lottie
Meade

2970 Travoys arriving with wounded
at a Dressing-Station at Smol,
Macedonia, September 1916
(Stanley Spencer)

2971 Thiepval Memorial, Somme,
France

2972 Captain A. C. Green's Battle of
Jutland Commemorative Medal

Centenary of the First World War (3rd issue)

2016 (21 June) Two phosphor bands. Perf 14½.

3838	**2967**	(1st)	multicoloured	1·50	1·40
3839	**2968**	(1st)	multicoloured	1·50	1·40
3840	**2969**	(1st)	multicoloured	1·50	1·40
3841	**2970**	£1·52	multicoloured	3·75	3·75
3842	**2971**	£1·52	multicoloured	3·75	3·75
3843	**2972**	£1·52	multicoloured	3·75	3·75
Set of 6				14·00	14·00
First Day Cover					14·50
Presentation Pack (P.O. Pack No. 527)				25·00	
PHQ Cards (set of 11) (416)				10·00	32·00

Set of 6 Gutter Pairs	29·00	

No. **MS**3848 is shown on one of the eleven PHQ cards with
the others depicting individual stamps including those from
MS3848.

2973 The Post Office Rifles

2974 Writing a Letter from the
Western Front

2975 Delivering the Mail on the
Home Front

2976 Home Depot at Regent's
Park, London

2977 The Post Office at War, 1914-18

Centenary of the First World War (3rd issue)

2016 (21 June) Two phosphor bands. Perf 14.

3844	**2973**	(1st)	multicoloured	1·50	1·50
3845	**2974**	(1st)	multicoloured	1·50	1·50
3846	**2975**	£1·33	multicoloured	3·25	3·25
3847	**2976**	£1·33	multicoloured	3·25	3·25
Set of 4				9·50	9·50
MS3848 156×74 mm. 2977 Nos. 3844/7			9·50	9·50	
First Day Cover				10·00	

Nos. 3844/7 were issued in £16·49 Centenary of the First World
War (3rd issue, No. DY18) premium booklets and in **MS**3848.

2978 The Piper at the Gates of Dawn
(1967)

2979 Atom Heart Mother (1970)

2980 The Dark Side of the Moon
(1973)

2981 Animals (1977)

2982 *Wish You Were Here* (1975)

2983 *The Endless River* (2014)

2989 Tom Kitten

2984 Pink Floyd on Stage

Pink Floyd

2016 (7 July).

(a) Album Covers. Self-adhesive. Gravure. Two phosphor bands. Die-cut perf 14½.

3849	**2978**	(1st)	multicoloured	1·50	1·40	☐ ☐
3850	**2979**	(1st)	multicoloured	1·50	1·40	☐ ☐
3851	**2980**	(1st)	multicoloured	1·50	1·40	☐ ☐
3852	**2981**	£1·52	multicoloured	3·75	3·75	☐ ☐
3853	**2982**	£1·52	multicoloured	3·75	3·75	☐ ☐
3854	**2983**	£1·52	multicoloured	3·75	3·75	☐ ☐
Set of 6				14·00	14·00	☐ ☐
First Day Cover					15·00	☐
Presentation Pack (P.O. Pack No. 528)				24·00		☐
PHQ Cards (*set of* 11) (417)				10·00	32·00	☐ ☐

(b) Pink Floyd on Stage. Ordinary gum. Litho. Phosphor frame. Perf 14½.

MS3855 202×74 mm. **2984** (1st) UFO Club, 1966; (1st) *The Dark Side of the Moon* Tour, 1973; £1·52 *The Wall* Tour, 1981; £1·52 *The Division Bell* Tour, 1994   9·00   9·00   ☐ ☐

First Day Cover   9·50   ☐

The right-hand edges of Nos. 3849/54 are all cut around to show the vinyl disc protruding from the open edge of the album cover.

A *Dark Side of the Moon* maxi sheet containing No. 3851×10 was sold at £12·95, a premium of £6·55 over face value.

The eleven PHQ cards depict the individual stamps including those from **MS**3855 and the complete miniature sheet.

2990 Benjamin Bunny

150th Birth Anniversary of Beatrix Potter (writer, illustrator and conservationist) (1st issue)

2016 (28 July) Two phosphor bands.

(a) Ordinary gum. Litho. Perf 14½×14.

3856	**2985**	(1st)	multicoloured	1·50	1·40	☐ ☐
		a. Horiz pair.				
		Nos. 3856/7		3·00	2·75	☐ ☐
3857	**2986**	(1st)	multicoloured	1·50	1·40	☐ ☐
3858	**2987**	£1·33	multicoloured	3·25	3·25	☐ ☐
		a. Horiz pair.				
		Nos. 3858/9		6·50	6·50	☐ ☐
3859	**2988**	£1·33	multicoloured	3·25	3·25	☐ ☐
3860	**2989**	£1·52	multicoloured	3·75	3·75	☐ ☐
		a. Horiz pair.				
		Nos. 3860/1		7·50	7·50	☐ ☐
3861	**2990**	£1·52	multicoloured	3·75	3·75	☐ ☐
3856/61 *Set of 6*				15·00	15·00	☐ ☐
First Day Cover					16·00	☐
Presentation Pack (P.O. Pack No. 529)				26·00		☐
PHQ Cards (*set of* 11) (418)				10·00	35·00	☐ ☐
Set of 3 Gutter Pairs (2 stamps only in each pair)				16·00		☐
Set of 3 Traffic Light Gutter Pairs (2 stamps only in each pair)				18·00		☐

(b) Self-adhesive. Gravure. Die-cut perf 14½×14.

3862	**2985**	(1st)	multicoloured	4·50	4·50	☐ ☐
3863	**2986**	(1st)	multicoloured	4·50	4·50	☐ ☐

Nos. 3856/7, 3858/9 and 3860/1 were printed together, *se-tenant*, as horizontal pairs in sheets of 60 (2 panes 6×5)

Nos. 3862/3 were issued in stamp booklets, each containing Nos. 3862/3 and 4×1st bright lilac and originally sold for £3·84.

The eleven PHQ cards depict the ten individual stamps including those from **MS**3868 and the complete miniature sheet.

2985 Peter Rabbit

2986 Mrs. Tiggywinkle

2987 Squirrel Nutkin

2988 Jemima Puddle-Duck

2991 'Now run along, and don't get into mischief.'

2992 'And then, feeling rather sick, he went to look for some parsley.'

2993 'But Peter, who was very naughty, ran straight away to Mr. McGregor's garden, and squeezed under the gate!'

2994 'He slipped underneath the gate, and was safe at last….'

2995 Illustrations from *The Tale of Peter Rabbit*

150th Birth Anniversary of Beatrix Potter (writer, illustrator and conservationist) (2nd issue)

2016 (28 July) Two phosphor bands. Perf 14½.

3864	**2991**	(1st)	multicoloured	1·90	1·90	☐ ☐
3865	**2992**	(1st)	multicoloured	1·90	1·90	☐ ☐
3866	**2993**	£1·33	multicoloured	4·25	4·25	☐ ☐
3867	**2994**	£1·33	multicoloured	4·25	4·25	☐ ☐

Set of 4   12·00   12·00   ☐ ☐

MS3868 125×89 mm. **2995** (1st) multicoloured; (1st) multicoloured; £1·33 multicoloured; £1·33 multicoloured   12·50   12·50   ☐ ☐

First Day Cover   13·00   ☐

Nos. 3864/7 were issued in £15·37 The Tale of Beatrix Potter premium booklets and in **MS**3868.

2996 Blenheim Palace

2997 Longleat

2998 Compton Verney

2999 Highclere Castle

3000 Alnwick Castle

3001 Berrington Hall

3002 Stowe

3003 Croome Park

Landscape Gardens

2016 (16 Aug.) One centre band (2nd) or two phosphor bands (others)

(a) Ordinary gum. Perf 14.

3869	**2996**	(2nd)	multicoloured	1·25	1·10	☐ ☐
	a.	Horiz pair. Nos. 3869/70		2·50	2·25	☐ ☐
3870	**2997**	(2nd)	multicoloured	1·25	1·10	☐ ☐
3871	**2998**	(1st)	multicoloured	1·50	1·40	☐ ☐
	a.	Horiz pair. Nos. 3871/2		3·00	2·75	☐ ☐
3872	**2999**	(1st)	multicoloured	1·50	1·40	☐ ☐
3873	**3000**	£1·05	multicoloured	2·50	2·50	☐ ☐
	a.	Horiz pair. Nos. 3873/4		5·00	5·00	☐ ☐
3874	**3001**	£1·05	multicoloured	2·50	2·50	☐ ☐
3875	**3002**	£1·33	multicoloured	3·25	3·25	☐ ☐
	a.	Horiz pair. Nos. 3875/6		6·50	6·50	☐ ☐
3876	**3003**	£1·33	multicoloured	3·25	3·25	☐ ☐

Set of 8   15·00   15·00   ☐ ☐
First Day Cover   16·00   ☐
Presentation Pack (P.O. Pack No. 530)   16·00   ☐
PHQ Cards (set of 8) (419)   7·25   23·00   ☐ ☐
Set of 4 Gutter Blocks of 4   32·00   ☐

(b) Self-adhesive. Die-cut perf 14.

3877	**2998**	(1st)	multicoloured	4·50	4·50	☐ ☐
3878	**2999**	(1st)	multicoloured	4·50	4·50	☐ ☐

Nos. 3869/78 commemorate the 300th birth anniversary of Capability Brown and show his landscape gardens.

Nos. 3869/70, 3871/2, 3873/4 and 3875/6 were each printed together, *se-tenant*, as horizontal pairs in sheets of 60 (2 panes 6×5)

Nos. 3877/8 were issued in stamp booklets containing Nos. 3877/8 and 4×1st bright lilac, originally sold for £3·84.

3004 Fire Breaks Out in Bakery on Pudding Lane, and Thomas Farriner and his Daughter escape through a Window, Sunday 2nd September 1666

3005 The Fire Spreads Rapidly, and Many People Flee to the River with Their Possessions, Sunday 2nd September 1666

3006 Houses are Pulled Down to Create Breaks and Prevent the Fire from Spreading, Monday 3rd September 1666

3007 As the Fire reaches St. Paul's Citizens witness the Cathedral's Destruction as Belongings stored inside Fuel the Flames, Tuesday 4th September 1666

3008 The Fire Dies Out, Many Gather at Moorfields and Temporary Food Markets are set up across London, Wednesday 5th September 1666

3009 Christopher Wren develops Plans for the Regeneration of the City and presents them to the King, Tuesday 11th September 1666

3014 *The Body in the Library*

350th Anniversary of the Great Fire of London

2016 (2 Sept).Two phosphor bands. Perf 14½.

3879	**3004**	(1st)	multicoloured	1·50	1·40	☐	☐
	a.	Horiz pair. Nos. 3879/80		3·00	2·75	☐	☐
3880	**3005**	(1st)	multicoloured	1·50	1·40	☐	☐
3881	**3006**	£1·05	multicoloured	2·50	2·50	☐	☐
	a.	Horiz pair. Nos. 3881/2		5·00	5·00	☐	☐
3882	**3007**	£1·05	multicoloured	2·50	2·50	☐	☐
3883	**3008**	£1·52	multicoloured	3·75	3·75	☐	☐
	a.	Horiz pair. Nos. 3883/4		7·50	7·50	☐	☐
3884	**3009**	£1·52	multicoloured	3·75	3·75	☐	☐
Set of 6				14·00	14·00	☐	☐
First Day Cover					14·50		☐
Presentation Pack (P.O. Pack No. 531)				15·00		☐	
PHQ Cards (*set of 6*) (420)				5·50	20·00	☐	☐
Set of 3 Gutter Blocks of 4				29·00		☐	

Nos. 3879/80, 3881/2 and 3883/4 were each printed together, *se-tenant*, as horizontal pairs in sheets of 60 (2 panes 6×5).

3010 *Murder on the Orient Express*

3011 *And Then There Were None*

3012 *The Mysterious Affair at Styles*

3013 *The Murder of Roger Ackroyd*

3015 *A Murder is Announced*

40th Death Anniversary of Agatha Christie (writer)

2016 (15 Sept.) Two phosphor bands. Perf 14½

3885	**3010**	(1st)	multicoloured	1·50	1·40	☐	☐
	a.	Vert pair. Nos. 3885/6		3·00	2·75	☐	☐
3886	**3011**	(1st)	multicoloured	1·50	1·40	☐	☐
3887	**3012**	£1·33	vermilion, turquoise-green and black	3·25	3·25	☐	☐
	a.	Vert pair. Nos. 3887/8		6·50	6·50	☐	☐
3888	**3013**	£1·33	vermilion, turquoise-green and black	3·25	3·25	☐	☐
3889	**3014**	£1·52	bright magenta, new blue and black	3·75	3·75	☐	☐
	a.	Vert pair. Nos. 3889/90		7·50	7·50	☐	☐
3890	**3015**	£1·52	bright magenta, new blue and black	3·75	3·75	☐	☐
3885/90 *Set of 6*				15·00	15·00	☐	☐
First Day Cover					16·00		☐
Presentation Pack (P.O. Pack No. 532)				16·00		☐	
PHQ Cards (*set of 6*) (421)				5·50	20·00	☐	☐
Set of 3 Gutter Pairs (only 2 stamps in each gutter pair)				16·00		☐	

Nos. 3885/6, 3887/8 and 3889/90 were each printed together, *se-tenant*, as vertical pairs in sheets of 48 (2 panes 4×6).

3016 *Mr. Happy*

3017 *Little Miss Naughty*

3018 *Mr. Bump*

3019 *Little Miss Sunshine*

MR. TICKLE
By Roger Hargreaves

MR. GRUMPY
By Roger Hargreaves

3020 *Mr. Tickle*   **3021** *Mr. Grumpy*

LITTLE MISS
PRINCESS
Roger Hargreaves

MR. STRONG
By Roger Hargreaves

3022 *Little Miss Princess*   **3023** *Mr. Strong*

LITTLE MISS
CHRISTMAS
Roger Hargreaves

MR. MESSY
By Roger Hargreaves

3024 *Little Miss Christmas*   **3025** *Mr. Messy*

Mr. Men and *Little Miss*
(children's books by Roger Hargreaves)

2016 (20 Oct.) Two phosphor bands

(a) Ordinary gum. Litho. Perf 14½

3891	**3016**	(1st)	multicoloured	1·50	1·40
	a. Horiz strip of 5.				
	Nos. 3891/5			7·50	7·00
3892	**3017**	(1st)	multicoloured	1·50	1·40
3893	**3018**	(1st)	multicoloured	1·50	1·40
3894	**3019**	(1st)	multicoloured	1·50	1·40
3895	**3020**	(1st)	multicoloured	1·50	1·40
3896	**3021**	(1st)	multicoloured	1·50	1·40
	a. Horiz strip of 5.				
	Nos. 3896/900			7·50	7·00
3897	**3022**	(1st)	multicoloured	1·50	1·40
3898	**3023**	(1st)	multicoloured	1·50	1·40
3899	**3024**	(1st)	multicoloured	1·50	1·40
3900	**3025**	(1st)	multicoloured	1·50	1·40
Set of 10				13·50	12·50
First Day Cover					14·00
Presentation Pack (P.O. Pack No. 533)			14·50		
PHQ Cards (*set of* 10) (422)			9·00	23·00	
Set of 2 Gutter Strips of 5			28·00		

(b) Self-adhesive. Gravure. Die-cut perf 14½

3901	**3016**	(1st)	multicoloured	4·50	4·50
3902	**3020**	(1st)	multicoloured	4·50	4·50

Nos. 3901/2 were issued in stamp booklets containing Nos. 3901/2 and 4×1st vermilion, originally sold for £3·84.

Designs as Nos. 3891/900 but self-adhesive were issued in sheets of 20 with *se-tenant* labels.

Designs as Nos. 3891, 3893/4, 3896/7 and 3900 were also available in sheets of ten with personal photographs on the labels.

3026 Snowman

3027 Robin

3028 Snowman

3029 Robin

3030 Christmas Tree

3031 Lantern

3032 Stocking

3033 Christmas Pudding

Christmas

2016 (8 Nov.) One centre band (3903) or two bands (others). Perf 14½×15

(a) Self-adhesive

3903	**3026**	(2nd)	multicoloured	1·25	1·10
3904	**3027**	(1st)	multicoloured	1·50	1·40
3905	**3028**	(2nd Large)	multicoloured	1·75	1·75
3906	**3029**	(1st Large)	multicoloured	2·25	2·25
3907	**3030**	£1·05	multicoloured	2·50	2·50
3908	**3031**	£1·33	multicoloured	3·25	3·25
3909	**3032**	£1·52	multicoloured	3·75	3·75
3910	**3033**	£2·25	multicoloured	5·50	5·50
3903/10 *Set of* 8				20·00	19·00
First Day Cover					21·00
Presentation Pack (P.O. Pack No. 534)			21·00		
PHQ Cards (*set of* 9)(423)			8·00	35·00	

(b) Ordinary gum

MS3911 189×74 mm. As Nos. 3903/10	22·00	22·00	
First Day Cover		23·00	

The nine PHQ cards show the eight individual stamps and the complete miniature sheet.

The 2nd class and 1st class values were also issued in sheets of 20 with *se-tenant* labels 'Celebrating 50 Years of Christmas Stamps'.

The 2nd class, 1st class, £1·05, £1·33, £1·52 and £2·25 values were also issued in sheets of 20 containing eight 2nd class, eight 1st class and one each of the £1·05, £1·33, £1·52 and £2·25 stamps, each stamp accompanied by a *se-tenant* label.

Separate sheets of 20 2nd, 20 1st, ten 1st, ten £1·05, ten £1·33 and ten £1·52 were available with personal photographs on the labels.

Year Pack

2016 (8 Nov.) Comprises Nos. 3787/**MS**3801, 3810/**MS**3832, **MS**3837/43, **MS**3848/61, **MS**3868/76, 3879/900, 3903/10

CP3911a Year Pack	£225	

Post Office Yearbook

2016 (8 Nov.) Comprises Nos. 3787/**MS**3801, 3810/**MS**3832, **MS**3837/43, **MS**3848/61, **MS**3868/76, 3879/900, 3903/10

YB3911a Yearbook	£275	

Miniature Sheet Collection

2016 (8 Nov.) Comprises Nos. **MS**3801, **MS**3832, **MS**3837, **MS**3848, **MS**3855, **MS**3868 and **MS**3911

MS3911a Miniature Sheet Collection	70.00	

3034 Battersea Shield, London, 350-50 BC

3035 Skara Brae Village, Orkney Islands, 3100-2500 BC

3036 Star Carr Headdress, Yorkshire, 9000 BC

3037 Maiden Castle Hill Fort, Dorset, 400 BC

3038 Avebury Stone Circles, Wiltshire, 2500 BC

3039 Drumbest Horns, County Antrim, 800 BC

3040 Grime's Graves Flint Mines, Norfolk, 2500 BC

3041 Mold Cape, Flintshire, 1900-1600 BC

Ancient Britain

2017 (17 Jan). Two phosphor bands. Perf 14

3912	**3034**	(1st)	multicoloured	1·50	1·40	☐☐
		a.	Horiz pair. Nos. 3912/13	3·00	2·75	☐☐
3913	**3035**	(1st)	multicoloured	1·50	1·40	☐☐
3914	**3036**	£1·05	multicoloured	2·50	2·50	☐☐
		a.	Horiz pair. Nos. 3914/15	5·00	5·00	☐☐
3915	**3037**	£1·05	multicoloured	2·50	2·50	☐☐
3916	**3038**	£1·33	multicoloured	3·25	3·25	☐☐
		a.	Horiz pair. Nos. 3916/17	6·50	6·50	☐☐
3917	**3039**	£1·33	multicoloured	3·25	3·25	☐☐
3918	**3040**	£1·52	multicoloured	3·75	3·75	☐☐
		a.	Horiz pair. Nos. 3918/19	7·50	7·50	☐☐
3919	**3041**	£1·52	multicoloured	3·75	3·75	☐☐
Set of 8				20·00	20·00	☐
First Day Cover					23·00	☐
Presentation Pack (P.O.Pack No. 536)				22·00		☐
PHQ Cards (set of 8) (424)				8·00	30·00	☐
Set of 4 Gutter Blocks of 4				40·00		☐

Nos. 3912/13, 3914/15, 3916/17 and 3918/19 were each printed together, se-tenant, as horizontal pairs in sheets of 60 (2 panes 6×5).

3042 The Long Walk

3043 The Round Tower

3044 The Norman Gate

3045 St. George's Hall

3046 The Queen's Ballroom

3047 The Waterloo Chamber

3048 St. George's Chapel Nave: Sir Reginald Bray Roof Boss

3049 St. George's Chapel Nave: Fan-vaulted Roof

Windsor Castle (1st issue)

2017 (15 Feb). Two phosphor bands.

(a) Ordinary gum. Litho. Perf 14½

3920	**3042**	(1st)	multicoloured	1·50	1·40	☐☐
		a.	Horiz strip of 3. Nos. 3920/2	4·50	4·25	☐☐

245

3921	**3043**	(1st)	multicoloured	1·50	1·40	
3922	**3044**	(1st)	multicoloured	1·50	1·40	
3923	**3045**	£1·52	multicoloured	3·75	3·75	
		a.	Horiz strip of 3.			
			Nos. 3923/5	11·00	11·00	
3924	**3046**	£1·52	multicoloured	3·75	3·75	
3925	**3047**	£1·52	multicoloured	3·75	3·75	
Set of 6				14·00	14·00	
First Day Cover					17·00	
Presentation Pack (P.O. Pack No. 537)						
(Nos. 3920/5 and **MS**3932)				24·00		
PHQ Cards (*set of* 11) (425)				10·00	38·00	
Set of 2 Gutter Strips of 3				28·00		

(b) Self-adhesive. Gravure. Die-cut perf 14½

3926	**3048**	(1st)	multicoloured	4·50	4·50	
3927	**3049**	(1st)	multicoloured	4·50	4·50	

Nos. 3920/2 and 3923/5 were each printed together, *se-tenant*, as horizontal strips of three stamps in sheets of 60 (2 panes 6×5).

Nos. 3926/7 were issued in stamp booklets containing Nos. 3926/7 and 4×1st bright scarlet, originally sold for £3·84.

3051 St. George's Chapel Quire: St. George's Cross Roof Boss

3050 St. George's Chapel Quire: Garter Banners

3052 St. George's Chapel

Windsor Castle (2nd issue)

2017 (15 Feb). Two phosphor bands. Litho. Perf 14½

3928		(1st)	As No. 3926	1·50	1·50	
3929		(1st)	As No. 3927	1·50	1·50	
3930	**3050**	£1·33	multicoloured	3·25	3·25	
3931	**3051**	£1·33	multicoloured	3·25	3·25	
Set of 4				9·50	9·50	
MS3932 125×89mm. **3052** Nos. 3928/31				9·50	9·50	
First Day Cover					10·50	

Nos. 3928/31 come from **MS**3932 and £14·58 Windsor Castle premium booklets.

3053 Hunky Dory

3054 Aladdin Sane

3055 Heroes

3056 Let's Dance

3057 Earthling

3058 Blackstar

3059 David Bowie Live

David Bowie (1947-2016, singer, songwriter and actor) Commemoration

2017 (14 Mar). Two phosphor bands

(a) Self-adhesive. Gravure. Die-cut perf 14½

3933	**3053**	(1st)	multicoloured	1·50	1·40	
3934	**3054**	(1st)	multicoloured	1·50	1·40	
3935	**3055**	(1st)	multicoloured	1·50	1·40	
3936	**3056**	£1·52	multicoloured	3·75	3·75	
3937	**3057**	£1·52	multicoloured	3·75	3·75	
3938	**3058**	£1·52	multicoloured	3·75	3·75	
Set of 6				15·00	15·00	
First Day Cover					16·00	
Presentation Pack (P.O. Pack No. 538)						
(Nos. 3933/8 and **MS**3939)				27·00		
PHQ Cards (*set of* 11) (426)				10·00	26·00	

(b) Ordinary gum. Litho. Perf 14½

MS3939 126×89mm. **3059** (1st) The Ziggy Stardust Tour, 1973; (1st) The Serious Moonlight Tour, 1983; £1·52 The Stage Tour, 1978; £1·52 A Reality Tour, 2004	10·00	10·00	
First Day Cover		11·50	

Nos. 3933/8 were printed in separate sheets of 50 (2 panes 5×5).

Nos. 3934/5 were also issued in booklets containing Nos. 3934/5 and 4×1st bright scarlet, originally sold for £3·84.

The right-hand edges of Nos. 3933/8 are all cut around to show the vinyl disc protruding from the open edge of the album cover.

The eleven PHQ cards show the individual stamps, including those from **MS**3959, and the complete miniature sheet.

Four 'fan' sheets, comprising the complete set, Types **3053/58**, Type **3053**×5 and Type **3055**×5, all printed on ordinary gummed paper, were available from Royal Mail at premium prices.

3060 Frankel

3061 Red Rum

3062 Shergar

3063 Kauto Star

3064 Desert Orchid

3065 Brigadier Gerard

3066 Arkle

3067 Estimate

Racehorse Legends

2017 (6 Apr). Two phosphor bands. Perf 14

3940	**3060**	(1st)	multicoloured	1·50	1·40
3941	**3061**	(1st)	multicoloured	1·50	1·40
3942	**3062**	£1·17	multicoloured	2·75	2·75
3943	**3063**	£1·17	multicoloured	2·75	2·75
3944	**3064**	£1·40	multicoloured	3·25	3·25
3945	**3065**	£1·40	multicoloured	3·25	3·25
3946	**3066**	£1·57	multicoloured	3·75	3·75
3947	**3067**	£1·57	multicoloured	3·75	3·75
Set of 8				20·00	20·00
First Day Cover					23·00
Presentation Pack (P.O. Pack No. 539)				22·00	
PHQ Cards (*set of* 8) (427)				8·00	30·00
Set of 8 Gutter Pairs				40·00	

3068 Great Tit
(*Parus major*)

3069 Wren
(*Troglodytes troglodytes*)

3070 Willow Warbler
(*Phylloscopus trochilus*)

3071 Goldcrest
(*Regulus regulus*)

3072 Skylark (*Alauda arvensis*)

3073 Blackcap (*Sylvia atricapilla*)

3074 Song Thrush
(*Turdus philomelos*)

3075 Nightingale (*Luscinia megarhynchos*)

3076 Cuckoo
(*Cuculus canorus*)

3077 Yellowhammer
(*Emberiza citrinella*)

Songbirds

2017 (4 May). Two phosphor bands. Perf 14½

3948	**3068**	(1st)	multicoloured	1·50	1·40
		a.	Horiz strip of 5.		
			Nos. 3948/52	7·50	7·00
3949	**3069**	(1st)	multicoloured	1·50	1·40
3950	**3070**	(1st)	multicoloured	1·50	1·40
3951	**3071**	(1st)	multicoloured	1·50	1·40
3952	**3072**	(1st)	multicoloured	1·50	1·40
3953	**3073**	(1st)	multicoloured	1·50	1·40
		a.	Horiz strip of 5.		
			Nos. 3953/7	7·50	7·00
3954	**3074**	(1st)	multicoloured	1·50	1·40
3955	**3075**	(1st)	multicoloured	1·50	1·40
3956	**3076**	(1st)	multicoloured	1·50	1·40
3957	**3077**	(1st)	multicoloured	1·50	1·40
Set of 10				14·00	14·00
First Day Cover					16·00
Presentation Pack (P.O.Pack No. 540)				16·00	
PHQ Cards (*set of* 10) (428)				11·00	25·00
Set of 2 Gutter Strips of 5				30·00	

Nos. 3948/52 and 3953/7 were each printed together, *se-tenant*, as horizontal strips of five in sheets of 50 (2 panes 5 × 5).

3078 Preliminary Sketch by Arnold Machin based on the Penny Black, January 1966

3079 Preparatory Work by Arnold Machin using Photograph of his Coin Mould, February 1966

3080 Essay with Coinage Head surrounded by Country Symbols, April/May 1966

3081 Essay of Coinage Head cropped and simplified, with Only the Denomination, October 1966

3082 Photo by John Hedgecoe with Queen Elizabeth II wearing the Diadem, August 1966

3083 Essay of the First Plaster Cast of the Diadem Head, without Corsage, October 1966

3084 The Machin Definitive 50 Years of a Design Icon

3085 The Machin Definitive Golden Anniversary Celebration

3086 £1 gold foil Machin

50th Anniversary of the Machin Definitive (1st issue)

2017 (5 June). Two phosphor bands. Gravure and embossed.
Perf 14 × 15

3958	**3078**	(1st)	multicoloured	1·50	1·40	☐☐
3959	**3079**	(1st)	multicoloured	1·50	1·40	☐☐
3960	**3080**	(1st)	multicoloured	1·50	1·40	☐☐
3961	**3081**	(1st)	multicoloured	1·50	1·40	☐☐
3962	**3082**	(1st)	multicoloured	1·50	1·40	☐☐

3963	**3083**	(1st) multicoloured	1·50	1·40	☐☐
Set of 6			8·00	7·50	☐☐

MS3964 202×74 mm. **3084** (1st) One of many preliminary sketches by Arnold Machin based on the Penny Black, January 1966; (1st) Preparatory work by Arnold Machin using a photograph of his coin mould, February 1966; (1st) One of many essays with the 'Coinage' head surrounded by Country Symbols, April/May 1966; (1st) Essay of the 'Coinage' head cropped and simplified, with only the denomination, October 1966; (1st) Photograph by John Hedgecoe with Queen Elizabeth II wearing the diadem, August 1966; (1st) Essay of the first plaster cast of the 'Diadem' head, without corsage, October 1966   8·00   8·00   ☐☐

MS3965 202×74 mm. **3085** No. X866; No. 1470; As Type **1116**; No. 2124; No. 2651; As No. U3003 (but 'MMIL' code); Type **3086**   8·00   8·00   ☐☐

First Day Cover (**MS**3964)		9·00	☐
First Day Cover (**MS**3965)		9·00	☐
Presentation Pack (**MS**3964/5)			
(P.O.Pack No. 541)	17·00		☐
PHQ Cards (set of 11) (429)	10·00	26·00	☐☐

Nos. 3958/63 were issued in £15·14 50th Anniv of the Machin Definitive premium booklets and in **MS**3964. Stamps from **MS**3964 have a darker background colour.
On **MS**3965 only the £1 gold foil stamp is embossed.

3087 Nutley Windmill, East Sussex

3088 New Abbey Corn Mill, Dumfries and Galloway

3089 Ballycopeland Windmill, County Down

3090 Cheddleton Flint Mill, Staffordshire

3091 Woodchurch Windmill, Kent

3092 Felin Cochwillan Mill, Gwynedd

Windmills and Watermills

2017 (20 June). Two phosphor bands. Perf 14½ × 14

3967	**3087**	(1st) multicoloured	1·50	1·40	
		a. Vert pair.			
		Nos. 3967/8	3·00	2·75	
3968	**3088**	(1st) multicoloured	1·50	1·40	
3969	**3089**	£1·40 multicoloured	3·25	3·25	
		a. Vert pair.			
		Nos. 3969/70	6·50	6·50	
3970	**3090**	£1·40 multicoloured	3·25	3·25	
3971	**3091**	£1·57 multicoloured	3·75	3·75	
		a. Vert pair.			
		Nos. 3971/2	7·50	7·50	
3972	**3092**	£1·57 multicoloured	3·75	3·75	
Set of 6			15·00	15·00	
First Day Cover				16·00	
Presentation Pack (P.O.Pack No. 542)			16·00		
PHQ Cards (set of 6) (430)			6·00	18·00	
Set of 3 Gutter Blocks of 4			30·00		

Nos. 3967/68, 3969/70 and 3971/72 were each printed together, *se-tenant*, as vertical pairs in sheets of 60 (2 panes 5×6).

3093 Aquatics Centre, Queen Elizabeth Olympic Park, London

3094 Library of Birmingham

3095 SEC Armadillo (formerly Clyde Auditorium), Glasgow

3096 Scottish Parliament, Edinburgh

3097 Giant's Causeway Visitor Centre, Co. Antrim

3098 National Assembly for Wales, Cardiff

3099 Eden Project, St. Austell

3100 Everyman Theatre, Liverpool

3101 IWM (Imperial War Musuem) North, Manchester

3102 Switch House, Tate Modern, London

Landmark Buildings

2017 (13 July). Two phosphor bands. Perf 14½

3973	**3093**	(1st) multicoloured	1·50	1·50	
		a. Horiz strip of 5.			
		Nos. 3973/7	7·50	7·00	
3974	**3094**	(1st) multicoloured	1·50	1·40	
3975	**3095**	(1st) multicoloured	1·50	1·40	
3976	**3096**	(1st) multicoloured	1·50	1·40	
3977	**3097**	(1st) multicoloured	1·50	1·40	
3978	**3098**	(1st) multicoloured	1·50	1·40	
		a. Horiz strip of 5.			
		+Nos. 3978/82	7·50	7·00	
3979	**3099**	(1st) multicoloured	1·50	1·40	
3980	**3100**	(1st) multicoloured	1·50	1·40	
3981	**3101**	(1st) multicoloured	1·50	1·40	
3982	**3102**	(1st) multicoloured	1·50	1·40	
Set of 10			15·00	14·00	
First Day Cover				15·00	
Presentation Pack (P.O.Pack No. 543)			16·00		
PHQ Cards (set of 10) (430)			9·00	23·00	
Set of 2 Gutter Strips of 5			28·00		

Nos. 3973/7 and 3978/82 were each printed together, *se-tenant*, as horizontal strips of five stamps in sheets of 50 (2 panes 5×5).

3103 *Shattered Poppy* (John Ross)

3104 *Dead Man's Dump* (Isaac Rosenberg)

3105 Nurses Elsie Knocker and Mairi Chisholm

3106 *Dry Docked for Sealing and Painting* (Edward Wadsworth)

3107 Tyne Cot Cemetery, Zonnebeke, Ypres Salient Battlefields, Belgium

3108 Private Lemuel Thomas Rees's Life-saving Bible

Centenary of the First World War (4th issue)

2017 (31 July). Two phosphor bands. Perf 14½

3983	**3103**	(1st)	multicoloured	1·50	1·40	☐☐
3984	**3104**	(1st)	multicoloured	1·50	1·40	☐☐
3985	**3105**	(1st)	multicoloured	1·50	1·40	☐☐
3986	**3106**	£1·57	multicoloured	3·75	3·75	☐☐
3987	**3107**	£1·57	multicoloured	3·75	3·75	☐☐
3988	**3108**	£1·57	multicoloured	3·75	3·75	☐☐
Set of 6				14·00	14·00	☐
First Day Cover					15·00	☐
Presentation Pack (P.O.Pack No. 544)				15·00		☐
PHQ Cards (*set of 6*) (431)				6·00	20·00	☐
Set of 6 Gutter Pairs				28·00		☐

3109 The Merrythought Bear

3110 Cindy Weekender Doll

3111 Spirograph

3112 Stickle Bricks
Super Set House

3113 Herald Trojan Warriors

3114 Spacehopper

3115 Fuzzy-Felt Farm Set

3116 Meccano Ferris Wheel

3117 Action Man
Red Devil Parachutist

3118 Hornby Dublo Electric Train
and TPO Mail Van

Classic Toys

2017 (22 Aug). Two phosphor bands. Perf 14½

3989	**3109**	(1st)	multicoloured	1·50	1·40	☐☐

		a. Horiz strip of 5.				
		Nos. 3989/93		7·50	7·00	☐☐
3990	**3110**	(1st)	multicoloured	1·50	1·40	☐☐
3991	**3111**	(1st)	multicoloured	1·50	1·40	☐☐
3992	**3112**	(1st)	multicoloured	1·50	1·40	☐☐
3993	**3113**	(1st)	multicoloured	1·50	1·40	☐☐
3994	**3114**	(1st)	multicoloured	1·50	1·40	☐☐
		a. Horiz strip of 5.				
		Nos. 3994/8		7·50	7·00	☐☐
3995	**3115**	(1st)	multicoloured	1·50	1·40	☐☐
3996	**3116**	(1st)	multicoloured	1·50	1·40	☐☐
3997	**3117**	(1st)	multicoloured	1·50	1·40	☐☐
3998	**3118**	(1st)	multicoloured	1·50	1·40	☐☐
Set of 10				14·00	14·00	☐
First Day Cover					15·00	☐
Presentation Pack (P.O.Pack No. 545)				16·00		☐
PHQ Cards (*set of 10*) (432)				9·00	23·00	☐
Set of 2 Gutter Strips of 5				28·00		☐

Nos. 3989/93 and 3994/8 were each printed together, *se-tenant*, as horizontal strips of five stamps in sheets of 50 (2 panes 5×5).

3119 The Story of Nelson,
The Story of the First Queen Elizabeth
and Florence Nightingale
(Adventures from History)

3120 The Gingerbread Boy,
Cinderella and The Elves and
the Shoemaker
(Well-loved Tales)

3121 We have fun, Look at this and
Things we do (Key Words Reading
Scheme)

3122 Piggly Plays Truant, Tootles the
Taxi and Other Rhymes and Smoke
and Fluff (Early Tales and Rhymes)

3123 The Ladybird Book of Things to
Make, How it works: The Telephone
and Tricks and Magic
(Hobbies and How it Works)

3124 The Nurse, The Postman and
The Fireman
(People at Work)

3125 The Ladybird Book of British
Wild Flowers, Wild Life in Britain and
Garden Flowers
(Nature and Conservation)

3126 The Story of Ships,
The Story of the Motor Car and
The Story of Metals
(Achievements)

Ladybird Books

2017 (14 Sept). One centre band (Nos. 3999/4000) or two bands (others). Perf 14

3999	**3119**	(2nd)	multicoloured	1·25	1·10	☐☐
		a. Horiz pair.				
		Nos. 3999/4000		2·50	2·25	☐☐

4000	**3120**	(2nd)	multicoloured	1·25	1·10	☐☐
4001	**3121**	(1st)	multicoloured	1·50	1·40	☐☐
		a.	Horiz pair.			
			Nos. 4001/2	3·00	2·75	☐☐
4002	**3122**	(1st)	multicoloured	1·50	1·40	☐☐
4003	**3123**	£1·40	multicoloured	3·25	3·25	☐☐
		a. Horiz pair. Nos. 4003/4		6·50	6·50	☐☐
4004	**3124**	£1·40	multicoloured	3·25	3·25	☐☐
4005	**3125**	£1·57	multicoloured	3·75	3·75	☐☐
		a.	Horiz pair.			
			Nos. 4005/6	7·50	7·50	☐☐
4006	**3126**	£1·57	multicoloured	3·75	3·75	☐☐
Set of 8				18·00	18·00	☐
First Day Cover					19·00	☐
Presentation Pack (P.O.Pack No. 546)				19.00		☐
PHQ Cards (*set of* 8) (433)				8·00	30·00	☐☐
Set of 4 Gutter Blocks of 4				36·00		

Nos. 3999/4000, 4001/02, 4003/04 and 4005/06 were each printed together, *se-tenant*, as horizontal pairs in sheets of 60 (2 panes 6×5).

3127 Maz Kanata   **3128** Chewbacca

3129 Supreme Leader Snoke   **3130** Porg

3131 BB-8   **3132** R2-D2

3133 C-3PO   **3134** K-2SO

Star Wars (4th issue). Aliens and Droids.

2017 (12 Oct). Two phosphor bands

(a) Ordinary gum. Litho. Perf 14½

4007	**3127**	(1st)	multicoloured	1·50	1·40	☐☐
		a.	Horiz strip of 4.			
			Nos. 4007/10	6·00	5·50	☐☐
4008	**3128**	(1st)	multicoloured	1·50	1·40	☐☐
4009	**3129**	(1st)	multicoloured	1·50	1·40	☐☐
4010	**3130**	(1st)	multicoloured	1·50	1·40	☐☐
4011	**3131**	(1st)	multicoloured	1·50	1·40	☐☐

		a.	Horiz strip of 4.			
			Nos. 4011/14	6·00	5·50	☐☐
4012	**3132**	(1st)	multicoloured	1·50	1·40	☐☐
4013	**3133**	(1st)	multicoloured	1·50	1·40	☐☐
4014	**3134**	(1st)	multicoloured	1·50	1·40	☐☐
Set of 8				11·00	10·00	☐
First Day Cover					11·00	☐
Presentation Pack (P.O.Pack No. 547)				12·00		☐
PHQ Cards (*set of* 8) (434)				8·00	20·00	☐☐
Set of 2 Gutter Strips of 4				22·00		

(b) Self-adhesive. Gravure. Die-cut perf 14½

4015	**3127**	(1st)	multicoloured	4·50	4·50	☐☐
4016	**3128**	(1st)	multicoloured	4·50	4·50	☐☐
4017	**3131**	(1st)	multicoloured	4·50	4·50	☐☐
4018	**3132**	(1st)	multicoloured	4·50	4·50	☐☐

Nos. 4007/10 and 4011/14 were each printed together, *se-tenant*, as horizontal strips of four stamps in sheets of 48 (2 panes 4×6).

Nos. 4015/16 and 4017/18 were each issued in stamp booklets with 4×1st bright scarlet stamps, originally sold for £3·90 each.

3135 *Virgin and Child* (attr. Gerard David)   **3136** *The Madonna and Child* (William Dyce)

3137 *Virgin and Child* (attr. Gerard David)   **3138** *The Madonna and Child* (William Dyce)

3139 *Virgin Mary with Child* (attr. Quinten Massys)   **3140** *The Small Cowper Madonna* (Raphael)

3141 *The Sleep of the Infant Jesus* (Giovanni Battista Sassoferrato)   **3142** *St. Luke painting the Virgin* (detail) (Eduard Jakob von Steinle)

Christmas. Madonna and Child

2017 (7 Nov). One phosphor band (No. 4019) or two bands

(a) Self-adhesive. Gravure. Die-cut perf 14½×15

4019	**3135**	(2nd)	multicoloured	1·25	1·10	☐☐
4020	**3136**	(1st)	multicoloured	1·50	1·40	☐☐
4021	**3137**	(2nd Large)	multicoloured	1·75	1·75	☐☐
4022	**3138**	(1st Large)	multicoloured	2·25	2·25	☐☐
4023	**3139**	£1·17	multicoloured	2·75	2·75	☐☐
4024	**3140**	£1·40	multicoloured	3·25	3·25	☐☐
4025	**3141**	£1·57	multicoloured	3·75	3·75	☐☐
4026	**3142**	£2·27	multicoloured	5·50	5·50	☐☐
Set of 8				26·00	25·00	☐☐
First Day Cover(Nos. 4019/26 and						
		4028/31)			26·00	☐

Presentation Pack (P.O.Pack No. 548)	27·00			☐
PHQ Cards (*set of* 13) (435)	12·00	40·00		☐☐

The 13 PHQ cards show the 12 individual stamps and **MS**4027.

The 2nd class (No. 4019), 2nd class (No. 4020), £1·17, £1·40, £1·57 and £2·27 values were also issued in sheets of 20 containing eight 2nd class , eight 1st class and one each of the £1·17, £1·40, £1·57 and £2·27 values, each stamp accompanied by a *se-tenant* label.

(b) Ordinary gum. Litho. Perf 14½ × 15

MS4027 189×74 mm As Nos. 4019/26 22·00	22·00		☐☐
First Day Cover	25·00		☐

Arwen Wilson, age 9

3143 Snow Family (Arwen Wilson)

Ted Lewis-Clark, age 10

3144 Santa Claus on his sleigh on a starry night (Ted Lewis-Clark)

Arwen Wilson, age 9

3145 Snow Family (Arwen Wilson)

Ted Lewis-Clark, age 10

3146 Santa Claus on his sleigh on a starry night (Ted Lewis-Clark)

Children's Christmas

2017 (7 Nov). One phosphor band (No. 4028) or two bands. Self-adhesive. Die-cut perf 14½ × 15

4028	**3143**	(2nd)	multicoloured	1·25	1·10	☐☐
4029	**3144**	(1st)	multicoloured	1·50	1·40	☐☐
4030	**3145**	(2nd Large) multicoloured	1·75	1·75	☐☐
4031	**3146**	(1st Large) multicoloured	2·25	2·25	☐☐

3147 Platinum Anniversary

Royal Platinum Wedding Anniversary of Queen Elizabeth II and Duke of Edinburgh

2017 (20 Nov). Two Phosphor Bands Litho. Perf 14½

MS4032   190×67 mm   **3147**   (1st) Engagement of Princess Elizabeth and Lt. Philip Mountbatten; (1st) Princess Elizabeth and Duke of Edinburgh after their wedding at Westminster Abbey; (1st) Princess Elizabeth and Duke of Edinburgh looking at wedding photographs during their honeymoon; £1·57 Engagement photograph; £1·57 Princess Elizabeth and Duke of Edinburgh on their wedding day; £1·57 Princess Elizabeth and Duke of Edinburgh on honeymoon

at Broadlands	15·00	15·00	☐☐
First Day Cover		17·00	☐☐

Presentation Pack (P.O.Pack No. 548)	17·00		☐
PHQ Cards (*set of* 7) (436)	7·00	24·00	☐☐
Souvenir Pack	25·00		☐

Collectors Pack

2017 (20 Nov). Comprises Nos. 3912/25, **MS**3932/3957, **MS**3964/5, 3967/4014, 4019/29 and **MS**4032

CP4031aCollectors Pack	£250	☐

Post Office Yearbook

2017 (20 Nov). Comprises Nos. 3912/25, **MS**3932/3957, **MS**3964/5, 3967/4014, 4019/31 and **MS**4032

YB4031aYearbook	£325	☐

Miniature Sheet Collection

2017 (20 Nov). Comprises Nos. **MS**3932, **MS**3939, **MS**3964/5, **MS**4027 and **MS**4032

Miniature Sheet Collection	85·00	☐

REGIONAL ISSUES

PERFORATION AND WATERMARK. All the following Regional stamps are perforated 15 × 14, unless otherwise stated.

For the listing of First Day Covers see the end of this section.

> **'Emblem' Regional Colours:** The colour descriptions of the 'Emblem' Regionals have been altered in many cases to show the perceived colours of the stamp, rather than the colours in which they are printed. Where the Queen's head has been printed in a black screen this appears as grey, which is the colour given in the description.

1 England

EN **1** Three Lions EN **2** Crowned Lion with Shield of St. George EN **3** Oak Tree EN **4** Tudor Rose

2001 (23 Apr.)–**02** Printed in gravure by De La Rue or Questa (Nos. EN1/2), De La Rue (others). One centre phosphor band (2nd) or two phosphor bands (others). Perf 15 × 14 (with one elliptical hole in each vertical side)

EN1	EN **1**	(2nd)	slate-green and silver	1·25	1·00	☐	☐
EN2	EN **2**	(1st)	lake-brown and silver	1·50	1·00	☐	☐
EN3	EN **3**	(E)	olive-green and silver	2·25	2·25	☐	☐
EN4	EN **4**	65p	deep reddish lilac and silver	3·00	3·00	☐	☐
EN5		68p	deep reddish lilac and silver *(4.7.02)*	3·00	3·00	☐	☐

Presentation Pack (P.O. Pack No. 54) (Nos. EN1/4)		8·50	☐
PHQ Cards (*set of* 4) (Nos. EN1/4) (D20)	8·00	14·00	☐ ☐

Nos. EN1/3 were initially sold at 19p, 27p and 36p, the latter representing the basic European airmail rate.

Combined Presentation Packs for England, Northern Ireland, Scotland and Wales

Presentation Pack (P.O. Pack No. 59) (contains 68p from England, Northern Ireland, Scotland and Wales (Nos. EN5, NI93, S99, W88)) 12·00 ☐

Presentation Pack (P.O. Pack No. 68) (contains 40p from England, Northern Ireland, Scotland and Wales (Nos. EN9, NI97, S112, W101)) 10·00 ☐

Presentation Pack (P.O. Pack No. 70) (contains 42p from England, Northern Ireland, Scotland and Wales (Nos. EN10, NI98, S113, W102)) 8·00 ☐

Presentation Pack (P.O. Pack No. 73) (contains 44p and 72p from England, Northern Ireland, Scotland and Wales (Nos. EN11, EN17, NI99, NI102, S114, S120, W103 and W109)) 12·00 ☐

Presentation Pack (P.O. Pack No. 76) (contains 48p and 78p from England, Northern Ireland, Scotland and Wales (Nos. EN12, EN18, NI124, NI128, S115, S121, W104 and W110)) 12·50 ☐

Presentation Pack (P.O. Pack No. 79) (contains 50p and 81p from England, Northern Ireland, Scotland and Wales (Nos. EN13, EN19, NI125, NI129, S116, S122, W105 and W111)) 11·50 ☐

Presentation Pack (P.O. Pack No. 81) (contains 2nd, 1st, 50p and 81p from England, Northern Ireland, Scotland and Wales (Nos. EN6/7, EN13, EN19, NI122/3, NI125, NI129, S109/10, S116, S122, W98/9, W105 and W111)) 48·00 ☐

Presentation Pack (P.O. Pack No. 85) (contains 56p and 90p from England, Northern Ireland, Scotland and Wales (Nos. EN14, EN120, NI126, NI130, S117, S123, W106 and W112)) 14·00 ☐

Presentation Pack (P.O. Pack No. 87) (contains 60p and 97p from England, Northern Ireland, Scotland and Wales (Nos. EN15, EN21, NI127, NI131, S118, S124, W107 and W113)) 20·00 ☐

Presentation Pack (P.O. Pack No. 91) (contains 68p and £1·10 from England, Northern Ireland, Scotland and Wales (Nos. EN31, EN41, NI100, NI111, S132, S138, W123 and W129)) 19·00 ☐

Presentation Pack (P.O. Pack No. 95) (contains 87p and £1·28 from England, Northern Ireland, Scotland and Wales (Nos. EN32, EN43, NI103, NI113, S133, S143, W124 and W134)) 24·00 ☐

Presentation Pack (P.O. Pack No. 98) (contains 88p from England, Northern Ireland, Scotland and Wales (Nos. EN33, NI104, S134, and W125)) 10·00 ☐

Presentation Pack (P.O. Pack No 100) (contains 97p. from England, Northern Ireland, Scotland and Wales (Nos. EN 34, NI105, S135 and W126) 10·00 ☐

Presentation Pack (P.O. Pack No 102) (contains £1 and £1·33 from England, Northern Ireland, Scotland and Wales (Nos. EN35, EN44, NI106, NI114, S136, S144, W127 and W135)), 24·00 ☐

Presentation Pack (P.O. Pack No 104) (contains £1·05 from England, Northern Ireland, Scotland and Wales (Nos. EN36, NI107, S137 and W128)) 10·00 ☐

Presentation Pack (P.O. Pack No 107) (contains £1·17 and £1·40 from England, Northern Ireland, Scotland and Wales (Nos. EN42, EN45, NI112, NI115, S139, S145, W130 and W136)) 25·00 ☐

2003 (14 Oct.)–**17** As Nos. EN1/3 and EN5 but with white borders. One centre phosphor band (2nd) or two phosphor bands (others). Perf 15 × 14 (with one elliptical hole in each vertical side)

(a) Printed in gravure by Walsall or De La Rue (2nd), 40p, 42p) or De La Rue (others)

EN6	EN **1**	(2nd)	slate-green and silver	1·50	60	☐	☐
EN7	EN **2**	(1st)	lake-brown and silver	1·75	75	☐	☐
EN8	EN **3**	(E)	olive-green and silver	2·40	2·40	☐	☐
EN9		40p	olive-green and silver *(11.5.04)*	1·50	1·50	☐	☐
EN10		42p	olive-green and silver *(5.4.05)*	2·25	2·25	☐	☐
EN11		44p	olive-green and silver *(28.3.06)*	1·50	1·50	☐	☐
EN12		48p	olive-green and silver *(27.3.07)*	1·25	1·25	☐	☐

EN13		50p	olive-green and silver *(1.4.08)*	1·50	1·25	☐ ☐
EN14		56p	olive-green and silver *(31.3.09)*	1·50	1·25	☐ ☐
EN15		60p	olive-green and silver *(31.3.10)*	1·50	1·40	☐ ☐
EN16	EN **4**	68p	deep reddish lilac and silver	2·50	2·50	☐ ☐
EN17		72p	deep reddish lilac and silver *(28.3.06)*	2·50	2·50	☐ ☐
EN18		78p	deep reddish lilac and silver *(27.3.07)*	2·50	2·50	☐ ☐
EN19		81p	deep reddish lilac and silver *(1.4.08)*	2·25	2·25	☐ ☐
EN20		90p	deep reddish lilac and silver *(31.3.09)*	2·25	2·25	☐ ☐
EN21		97p	deep reddish lilac and silver *(31.3.10)*	2·75	2·75	☐ ☐

(b) Printed in lithography by Enschedé (booklets) (1st) or Cartor (sheets) (1st) or Cartor (others)

EN29	EN **1**	(2nd)	slate-green and grey *(1.2013)*	1·50	1·00	☐ ☐
EN30	EN **2**	(1st)	lake-brown and silver *(20.9.07)*	1·75	1·25	☐ ☐
EN30b		(1st)	lake-brown and grey	1·75	1·25	☐ ☐
EN31	EN **3**	68p	olive-green and silver *(29.3.11)*	2·00	2·00	☐ ☐
EN32		87p	olive-green and silver *(25.4.12)*	2·50	2·50	☐ ☐
EN33		88p	olive-green and silver *(27.3.13)*	2·25	2·00	☐ ☐
EN34		97p	olive-green and silver *(26.3.14)*	2·50	2·25	☐ ☐
EN35		£1·00	olive-green and silver *(24.3.15)*	2·40	2·40	☐ ☐
EN36		£1·05	olive-green and grey *(22.1.16)*	2·40	2·00	☐ ☐
EN41	EN **4**	£1·10	deep reddish lilac and silver *(29.3.11)*	2·75	2·75	☐ ☐
EN42	EN **3**	£1·17	olive-green and grey *(21.3.17)*	2·75	2·75	☐ ☐
EN43	EN **4**	£1·28	deep reddish lilac and silver *(25.4.12)*	3·25	3·25	☐ ☐
EN44		£1·33	deep reddish lilac and silver *(24.3.15)*	3·25	3·25	☐ ☐
EN45		£1·40	deep reddish lilac and grey *(21.3.17)*	3·25	3·25	☐ ☐
Presentation Pack (P.O. Pack No. 63) (Nos. EN6/8, EN16)				6·00		☐
PHQ Cards (*set of* 4) (Nos. EN6/8, EN16) (D24)				2·00	12·00	☐ ☐

Nos. EN6/8 were initially sold at 20p, 28p and 38p, the latter representing the basic European airmail rate.

Stamps as No. EN30 but self-adhesive were issued on 23 April 2007 in sheets of 20 with *se-tenant* labels. These sheets were printed in lithography by Cartor and perforated 15 × 14 without the elliptical holes. The labels show either English scenes or personal photographs.

No. EN30 was first issued in £7·66 'British Army Uniforms' stamp booklet, No. DX40, but was issued in sheets in January 2013.

Stamps as Nos. EN30, NI95, S131 and W122 but self-adhesive were issued on 29 September 2008 in sheets of 20 containing five of each design with *se-tenant* labels. These sheets were printed in lithograhy by Cartor and perforated 15 × 14 with one elliptical hole in each vertical side.

EN **5**

Celebrating England

2007 (23 Apr.) Sheet 123 × 70 mm. Printed in gravure by De La Rue. Two phosphor bands. Perf 15 × 14 (with one elliptical hole in each vertical side) (1st) or 15 × 14½ (78p)

MSEN50 EN **5** (1st) No. EN7; (1st) St. George's flag; 78p St. George; 78p Houses of Parliament, London	9·00	9·00	☐ ☐
First Day Cover		10·00	☐
Presentation Pack (P.O. Pack No. M15)	11·00		☐
PHQ Cards (*set of* 5) (CGB2)	4·00	15·00	☐ ☐

MSEN50 was on sale at post offices throughout the UK.

The five PHQ cards show the four individual stamps and the complete miniature sheet.

Stamps as the 1st class St. George's flag stamp within **MS**EN50 but self-adhesive were issued on 23 April 2009 in sheets of 20 with *se-tenant* labels showing English castles. These sheets were printed in lithography by Cartor.

EN **6** St. George's Flag

England Flag

2013 (9 May) **-14**. Printed in lithography by Cartor or Enschedé. Two phosphor bands. Perf 14½ × 14 (with one elliptical hole in each vert side)

EN51	EN **6**	(1st) multicoloured	4·50	4·50	☐ ☐
		a. Grey Queen's head	4·50	4·50	☐ ☐

No. EN51 silver Queen's head was issued in £11·11 Football Heroes, DY 7 and £16·49 Centenary of the First World War (3rd issue) DY18 booklets. No. EN51a was issued in the £13·97 Classic Locomotives booklets, No. DY9.

2 Northern Ireland

N **1** N **2** N **3** N **4**

1958–67 Wmk **179**

NI1	N **1**	3d	lilac *(18.8.58)*	15	15	☐ ☐
		p.	One centre phosphor band *(9.6.67)*	25	25	☐ ☐
NI2		4d	blue *(7.2.66)*	15	15	☐ ☐
		p.	Two phosphor bands *(10.67)*	15	15	☐ ☐
NI3	N **2**	6d	purple *(29.9.58)*	50	50	☐ ☐
NI4		9d	bronze-green (2 phosphor bands) *(1.3.67)*	30	70	☐ ☐

NI5	N **3**	1s3d	green *(29.9.58)*	40	80	☐☐
NI6		1s6d	blue (2 phosphor bands) *(1.3.67)*	40	80	☐☐

1968–69 One centre phosphor band (Nos. NI8/9) or two phosphor bands (others). No wmk

NI7	N **1**	4d	blue *(27.6.68)*	25	25	☐☐
NI8		4d	sepia *(4.9.68)*	25	25	☐☐
NI9		4d	vermilion *(26.2.69)*	30	30	☐☐
NI10		5d	blue *(4.9.68)*	40	40	☐☐
NI11	N **3**	1s6d	blue *(20.5.69)*	2·50	2·75	☐☐
Presentation Pack (P.O. Pack No. 25)						
(comprises Nos. NI1p, NI4/6, NI8/10) 3·50						☐

Decimal Currency

1971–93 Type N **4**. No wmk

(a) Printed in photogravure with phosphor bands

NI12	2½p	bright magenta (1 centre band)	70	60	☐☐
NI13	3p	ultramarine (2 bands)	30	30	☐☐
NI14	3p	ultramarine (1 centre band) *(23.1.74)*	30	30	☐☐
NI15	3½p	olive-grey (2 bands) *(23.1.74)*	20	25	☐☐
NI16	3½p	olive-grey (1 centre band) *(6.11.74)*	45	45	☐☐
NI17	4½p	grey-blue (2 bands) *(6.11.74)*	30	35	☐☐
NI18	5p	reddish violet (2 bands)	1·40	1·40	☐☐
NI19	5½p	violet (2 bands) *(23.1.74)*	25	25	☐☐
NI20	5½p	violet (1 centre band) *(21.5.75)*	25	30	☐☐
NI21	6½p	greenish blue (1 centre band) *(14.1.76)*	20	20	☐☐
NI22	7p	purple-brown (1 centre band) *(18.1.78)*	35	25	☐☐
NI23	7½p	chestnut (2 bands)	1·75	1·75	☐☐
NI24	8p	rosine (2 bands) *(23.1.74)*	65	65	☐☐
NI25	8½p	yellow-green (2 bands) *(14.1.76)*	55	55	☐☐
NI26	9p	deep violet (2 bands) *(18.1.78)*	55	55	☐☐
NI27	10p	orange-brown (2 bands) *(20.10.76)*	40	50	☐☐
NI28	10p	orange-brown (1 centre band) *(23.7.80)*	50	50	☐☐
NI29	10½p	steel-blue (2 bands) *(18.1.78)*	90	1·00	☐☐
NI30	11p	scarlet (2 bands) *(20.10.76)*	70	80	☐☐

(b) Printed in photogravure on phosphorised paper

NI31	12p	yellowish green *(23.7.80)*	50	60	☐☐
NI32	13½p	purple-brown *(23.7.80)*	90	1·00	☐☐
NI33	15p	ultramarine *(23.7.80)*	60	70	☐☐

(c) Printed in lithography. Perf 14 (11½p, 12½p, 14p (No. NI38), 15½p, 16p, 18p, (No. NI45), 19½p, 20½p, 22p (No. NI53), 26p (No. NI60), 28p (No. NI62)) or 15 × 14 (others)

NI34	11½p	drab (1 side band) *(8.4.81)*	85	85	☐☐
NI35	12p	bright emerald (1 side band) *(7.1.86)*	90	90	☐☐
NI36	12½p	light emerald (1 side band) *(24.2.82)*	60	60	☐☐
		a. Perf 15 × 14 *(28.2.84)*	5·25	5·25	☐☐
NI37	13p	pale chestnut (1 side band) *(23.10.84)*	80	75	☐☐
NI38	14p	grey-blue (phosphorised paper) *(8.4.81)*	75	75	☐☐
NI39	14p	deep blue (1 centre band) *(8.11.88)*	75	60	☐☐

NI40	15p	bright blue (1 centre band) *(28.11.89)*	90	60	☐☐
NI41	15½p	pale violet (phosphorised paper) *(24.2.82)*	80	80	☐☐
NI42	16p	drab (phosphorised paper) *(27.4.83)*	1·25	1·25	☐☐
		a. Perf 15 × 14 *(28.2.84)*	8·25	8·50	☐☐
NI43	17p	grey-blue (phosphorised paper) *(23.10.84)*	90	95	☐☐
NI44	17p	deep blue (1 centre band) *(4.12.90)*	1·00	80	☐☐
NI45	18p	deep violet (phosphorised paper) *(8.4.81)*	1·00	1·00	☐☐
NI46	18p	deep olive-grey (phosphorised paper) *(6.1.87)*	1·00	90	☐☐
NI47	18p	bright green (1 centre band) *(3.12.91)*	1·00	95	☐☐
		a. Perf 14 *(31.12.92)**	7·50	7·50	☐☐
NI48	18p	bright green (1 side band) *(10.8.93)*	2·25	2·25	☐☐
NI49	19p	bright orange-red (phosphorised paper) *(8.11.88)*	1·00	1·00	☐☐
NI50	19½p	olive-grey (phosphorised paper) *(24.2.82)*	2·00	2·00	☐☐
NI51	20p	brownish black (phosphorised paper) *(28.11.89)*	1·00	80	☐☐
NI52	20½p	ultramarine (phosphorised paper) *(27.4.83)*	4·50	4·25	☐☐
NI53	22p	blue (phosphorised paper) *(8.4.81)*	1·40	1·40	☐☐
NI54	22p	yellow-green (phosphorised paper) *(23.10.84)*	1·25	1·25	☐☐
NI55	22p	bright orange-red (phosphorised paper) *(4.12.90)*	1·25	90	☐☐
NI56	23p	bright green (phosphorised paper) *(8.11.88)*	1·25	1·10	☐☐
NI57	24p	Indian red (phosphorised paper) *(28.11.89)*	1·25	1·25	☐☐
NI58	24p	chestnut (phosphorised paper) *(3.12.91)*	1·10	90	☐☐
NI59	24p	chestnut (2 bands) *(10.8.93)*	2·50	2·75	☐☐
NI60	26p	rosine (phosphorised paper) *(24.2.82)*	1·25	1·25	☐☐
		a. Perf 15 × 14 *(27.1.87)*	3·00	3·25	☐☐
NI61	26p	drab (phosphorised paper) *(4.12.90)*	1·75	1·75	☐☐
NI62	28p	deep violet-blue (phosphorised paper) *(27.4.83)*	1·50	1·50	☐☐
		a. Perf 15 × 14 *(27.1.87)*	1·25	1·25	☐☐
NI63	28p	deep bluish grey (phosphorised paper) *(3.12.91)*	1·50	1·50	☐☐
NI64	31p	bright purple (phosphorised paper) *(23.10.84)*	1·75	2·00	☐☐
NI65	32p	greenish blue (phosphorised paper) *(8.11.88)*	1·75	1·75	☐☐
NI66	34p	deep bluish grey (phosphorised paper) *(28.11.89)*	1·75	1·75	☐☐
NI67	37p	rosine (phosphorised paper) *(4.12.90)*	2·00	2·50	☐☐

NI68   39p   bright mauve
                (phosphorised
                paper) *(3.12.91)*   2·00   2·25   ▢ ▢

* Earliest known date of use.
Nos. NI48 and NI59 were only issued in stamp booklets.

Presentation Pack (P.O. Pack No. 29) (contains
    2½p (NI12), 3p (NI13), 5p (NI18), 7½p
    (NI23))   3·50   ▢
Presentation Pack (P.O. Pack No. 61) (contains
    3p (NI14), 3½p (NI15), 5½p (NI19), 8p (NI24)
    later with 4½p (NI17) added)   3·75   ▢
Presentation Pack (P.O. Pack No. 84) (contains
    6½p (NI21), 8½p (NI25), 10p (NI27),
    11p (NI30))   2·00   ▢
Presentation Pack (P.O. Pack No. 129d)
    (contains 7p (NI22), 9p (NI26), 10½p (NI29),
    11½p (NI34), 12p (NI31), 13½p (NI32), 14p
    (NI38), 15p (NI33), 18p (NI45), 22p (NI53))   9·00   ▢
Presentation Pack (P.O. Pack No. 4) (contains
    10p (NI28), 12½p (NI36), 16p (NI42), 20½p
    (NI52), 26p (NI60), 28p (NI62))   18·00   ▢
Presentation Pack (P.O. Pack No. 8) (contains
    10p (NI28), 13p (NI37), 16p (NI42a), 17p
    (NI43), 22p (NI54), 26p (NI60), 28p (NI62),
    31p (NI64))   18·00   ▢
Presentation Pack (P.O. Pack No. 12) (contains
    12p (NI35), 13p (NI37), 17p (NI43),
    18p (NI46), 22p (NI54), 26p (NI60a),
    28p (NI62a), 31p (NI64))   20·00   ▢

Combined Presentation Packs for Northern Ireland, Scotland and Wales

Presentation Pack (P.O. Pack No. 17) (contains
    14p, 19p, 23p, 32p from Northern Ireland,
    Scotland and Wales (Nos. NI39, NI49, NI56,
    NI65,   S54,   S62,   S67,   S77,   W40,
    W50, W57, W66))   17·00   ▢
Presentation Pack (P.O. Pack No. 20) (contains
    15p, 20p, 24p, 34p from Northern Ireland,
    Scotland and Wales (Nos. NI40, NI5l, NI57,
    NI66,   S56,   S64,   S69,   S78,   W41,
    W52, W58, W67))   16·00   ▢
Presentation Pack (P.O. Pack No. 23) (contains
    17p, 22p, 26p, 37p from Northern Ireland,
    Scotland and Wales (Nos. NI44, NI55, NI6l,
    NI67,   S58,   S66,   S73,   S79,   W45,
    W56, W62, W68))   16·00   ▢
Presentation Pack (P.O. Pack No. 26) (contains
    18p, 24p, 28p, 39p from Northern Ireland,
    Scotland and Wales (Nos. NI47, NI58,
    NI63, NI68, S60, S70, S75, S80, W48,
    W59, W64, W69))   16·00   ▢

1993 (7 Dec.)–2000

(a) Printed in lithography by Questa. Perf 15 × 14 (with one
    elliptical hole in each vertical side)

NI69   N 4   19p   bistre (1 centre band)   90   80   ▢ ▢
NI70   19p   bistre (1 side band)
                   (26.7.94)   1·25 1·75 ▢ ▢
NI71   20p   bright green (1 centre
                   band) *(23.7.96)*   1·50 1·50 ▢ ▢
NI72   25p   red (2 bands)   75   75   ▢ ▢
NI73   26p   red-brown (2 bands)
                   (23.7.96)   1·75 1·75 ▢ ▢
NI74   30p   deep olive-grey
                   (2 bands)   1·25 1·25 ▢ ▢
NI75   37p   bright mauve
                   (2 bands) *(23.7.96)*   2·75 3·00 ▢ ▢
NI76   41p   grey-brown (2 bands)   1·50 1·75 ▢ ▢
NI77   63p   light emerald
                   (2 bands) *(23.7.96)*   5·00 5·00 ▢ ▢

(b) Printed in photogravure by Walsall (19p, 20p, 26p
    (No. NI81b), 38p, 40p, 63p, 64p, 65p), Harrison or Walsall
    (26p (No. NI81), 37p). Perf 14 (No. NI80) or 15 × 14 (others)
    (both with one elliptical hole in each vertical side)

NI78   N 4   19p   bistre (1 centre
                   band) *(8.6.99)*   3·00 3·00 ▢ ▢
NI79   20p   bright green (1 centre
                   band) *(1.7.97)*   1·90 80   ▢ ▢
NI80   20p   bright green (1 side
                   band) *(13.10.98)*   4·00 4·00 ▢ ▢
NI81   26p   chestnut (2 bands)
                   (1.7.97)   1·75 1·50 ▢ ▢
             b.   Perf 14 *(13.10.98)*   4·00 4·00 ▢ ▢
NI82   37p   bright mauve
                   (2 bands) *(1.7.97)*   3·50 3·50 ▢ ▢
NI83   38p   ultramarine
                   (2 bands) *(8.6.99)*   8·00 8·00 ▢ ▢
NI84   40p   deep azure (2 bands)
                   (25.4.00)   3·50 3·50 ▢ ▢
NI85   63p   light emerald
                   (2 bands) *(1.7.97)*   5·00 5·00 ▢ ▢
NI86   64p   turquoise-green
                   (2 bands) *(8.6.99)*   9·00 9·00 ▢ ▢
NI87   65p   greenish blue
                   (2 bands) *(25.4.00)*   4·00 4·00 ▢ ▢

Nos. NI70, NI80 and NI81b were only issued in stamp booklets.
No. NI70 exists with the phosphor band at the left or right of
the stamp.

Presentation Pack (P.O. Pack No. 47)
    (contains 19p, 26p, 38p, 64p (Nos. NI78,
    NI81, NI83 NI86))   17·00   ▢
Presentation Pack (P.O. Pack No. 52)
    (contains 1st, 40p, 65p (Nos. NI84,
    NI87, NI88b))   18·00   ▢

Combined Presentation Packs for Northern Ireland, Scotland and Wales

Presentation Pack (P.O. Pack No. 31) (contains
    19p, 25p, 30p, 41p from Northern Ireland,
    Scotland and Wales (Nos. NI69, NI72, NI74,
    NI76,   S81,   S84,   S86,   S88,   W70,
    W73, W75, W77))   16·00   ▢
Presentation Pack (P.O. Pack No. 36) (contains
    20p, 26p, 37p, 63p from Northern Ireland,
    Scotland and Wales (Nos. NI71, NI73, NI75,
    NI77,   S83,   S85,   S87,   S89,   W72,
    W74 W76, W78))   26·00   ▢
Presentation Pack (P.O. Pack No. 42) (contains
    20p (1 centre band), 26p, 37p, 63p from
    Northern Ireland, Scotland and Wales
    (Nos. NI79, NI81/2, NI85, S90/3, W79/82))   26·00   ▢

N **5**

2000 (15 Feb.–25 Apr.) Type N **4** redrawn with '1st' face value as
Type N **5**. Two phosphor bands. Perf 14 (with one elliptical hole
in each vertical side)

NI88   N 5   (1st)   bright orange-red   3·00   3·00   ▢ ▢
             b.   Perf 15 × 14 *(25 Apr.)* 11·00 10·00 ▢ ▢

No. NI88 was only issued in £7·50 'Special by Design' stamp
booklets. No. NI88b was issued in sheets on 25 April.

N **6** Basalt Columns, Giant's Causeway

N **7** Aerial View of Patchwork Fields

N **8** Linen Pattern

N **9** Vase Pattern from Belleck

2001 (6 Mar.)–02 Printed in lithography by De La Rue (68p), De La Rue or Walsall (E), Walsall or Enschedé (2nd) or Walsall (others). One centre phosphor band (2nd) or two phosphor bands (others). Perf 15 × 14 (with one elliptical hole in each vertical side)

NI89	N **6**	(2nd)	black, slate and drab	1·50	75	☐☐
NI90	N **7**	(1st)	black, bright green, and greenish black	1·75	1·20	☐☐
NI91	N **8**	(E)	olive-grey and black	2·25	1·60	☐☐
NI92	N **9**	65p	olive-bistre and black	3·25	3·25	☐☐
NI93		68p	olive-bistre and black (4.7.02)	3·25	3·25	☐☐
Presentation Pack (P.O. Pack No. 53) (Nos. NI89/92)				8·00		☐
PHQ Cards (set of 4) (Nos. NI89/92)(D19)				8·00	14·00	☐☐

Nos. NI89, NI90 and NI91 were initially sold at 19p, 27p and 36p, the latter representing the basic European airmail rate.

For combined presentation packs for all four Regions, see under England.

2003 (14 Oct.)–17 As Nos. NI89/91 and NI93 but with white borders. One centre phosphor band (2nd) or two phosphor bands (others). Perf 15 × 14 (with one elliptical hole in each vertical side)

(a) Printed in lithography by Walsall (NI98), De La Rue, Enschedé or Cartor/ISP Cartor (NI95), Cartor (NI101, NI106/7, NI112, NI114) or De La Rue (others)

NI94	N **6**	(2nd)	black, slate and drab	1·50	1·00	☐☐
NI95	N **7**	(1st)	black, bright green, and greenish black	1·75	1·00	☐☐
NI96	N **8**	(E)	olive-grey and black	2·50	2·50	☐☐
NI97		40p	olive-grey and black (11.5.04)	1·75	1·75	☐☐
NI98		42p	bluish grey and black (5.4.05)	2·25	1·75	☐☐
NI99		44p	olive-grey and black (28.3.06)	1·50	1·00	☐☐
NI100	N **9**	68p	olive-bistre and black	2·75	2·75	☐☐
NI101	N **8**	68p	olive-grey and black (29.3.11)	1·75	1·50	☐☐
NI102	N **9**	72p	olive-bistre and black (28.3.06)	2·75	2·50	☐☐
NI103	N **8**	87p	olive-grey and black (25.4.12)	2·50	2·50	☐☐
NI104		88p	olive-grey and black (27.3.13)	2·50	2·00	☐☐
NI105		97p	olive-grey and black (26.3.14)	2·50	2·25	☐☐
NI106		£1	olive-grey and black (24.3.15)	2·40	2·40	☐☐
NI107		£1·05	olive-grey and black (22.3.16)	2·40	2·40	☐☐
NI111	N **9** £1·10		olive-bistre and black (29.3.11)	2·75	2·75	☐☐
NI112	N **8** £1·17		olive-grey and black (21.3.17)	2·50	2·50	☐☐
NI113	N **9** £1·28		olive-bistre and black (25.4.12)	3·25	3·25	☐☐
NI114		£1·33	olive-bistre and black (24.3.15)	3·25	3·25	☐☐
NI115		£1·40	olive-bistre and black (21.3.17)	3·25	3·25	☐☐

(b) Printed in gravure by De La Rue

NI122	N **6**	(2nd)	black, slate and drab (20.9.07)	1·50	60	☐☐
NI123	N **7**	(1st)	black, bright green, and greenish black (20.9.07)	1·75	75	☐☐
NI124	N **8**	48p	olive-grey and black (27.3.07)	1·20	1·20	☐☐
NI125		50p	olive-grey and black (1.4.08)	1·20	1·20	☐☐
NI126		56p	olive-grey and black (31.3.09)	1·50	1·25	☐☐
NI127		60p	olive-grey and black (30.3.10)	1·75	1·40	☐☐
NI128	N **9**	78p	olive-bistre and black (27.3.07)	2·00	2·00	☐☐
NI129		81p	olive-bistre and black (1.4.08)	2·00	2·00	☐☐
NI130		90p	olive-bistre and black (31.3.09)	2·25	2·25	☐☐
NI131		97p	olive-bistre and black (30.3.10)	2·40	2·40	☐☐
Presentation Pack (P.O. Pack No. 66) (Nos. NI94/6, NI100)				7·50		☐
PHQ Cards (set of 4) (Nos. NI94/6, NI100) (D27)				7·50	10·00	☐☐

Nos. NI94/6 were initially sold at 20p, 28p and 38p, the latter representing the basic European airmail rate.

The Enschedé printing of No. NI95 comes from £7·66 'British Army Uniforms' stamp booklet, No. DX40.

Stamps as NI95 but self-adhesive were issued on 11 March 2008 in sheets of 20 with se-tenant labels. These sheets were printed in lithography by Cartor and perforated 15 × 14 without the ellipitcal holes. The labels show either Northern Ireland scenes or personal photographs.

Stamps as No. NI95 but self-adhesive were issued again on 17 March 2009 in sheets of 20 with se-tenant labels showing Northern Ireland castles. These sheets were printed in lithography by Cartor.

Stamps as Nos. EN30, NI95, S131 and W122 but self-adhesive were issued on 29 September 2008 in sheets of 20 containing five of each design with se-tenant labels.

N **10**

Celebrating Northern Ireland

2008 (11 Mar.) Sheet 123 × 70 mm. Printed in lithography by De La Rue. Two phosphor bands. Perf 15 × 14½ (with one elliptical hole in each vertical side) (1st) or 15 × 14½ (78p)

MSNI152 N **10**	(1st)	Carrickfergus Castle; (1st) Giant's Causeway; 78p St. Patrick; 78p Queen's Bridge and 'Angel of Thanksgiving' sculpture, Belfast	7·00	7·00	☐☐
First Day Cover				8·00	☐
Presentation Pack (P.O. Pack No. 410)			9·00		☐
PHQ Cards (set of 5) (CGB3)			4·00	17·00	☐☐

MSNI152 was on sale at post offices throughout the UK.

The five PHQ cards depict the complete miniature sheet and the four stamps within it.

N **11**

50th Anniversary of the Country Definitives (1st issue)

2008 (29 Sept.) Sheet 124×70 mm, containing designs as Nos. NI1, NI3, NI5, S1, S3, S5, W1, W3 and W5 (regional definitives of 1958) but inscribed 1st and printed in gravure by De La Rue on pale cream. Two phosphor bands. Perf 15×14 (with one elliptical hole in each vertical side)

MSNI153	N **11**	(1st) As No. W1; (1st) As					
		No. S1; (1st) As No. W5; (1st) As No. S5;					
		(1st) As No. NI1; (1st) As No. W3; (1st)					
		As No. S3; (1st) As No. NI3; (1st) As No.					
		NI5		13·00	13·00	☐	☐
First Day Cover					14·00		☐
Presentation Pack (P.O. Pack No. 80)				15·00		☐	
PHQ Cards (*set of* 10) (D29)				15·00	20·00	☐	☐

MSNI153 was on sale at post offices throughout the UK.

The ten PHQ cards show the nine individual stamps and the complete sheet.

50th Anniversary of the Country Definitives (2nd issue)

2008 (29 Sept.) As Nos. NI1, NI3 and NI5 (definitives of 1958) but inscribed 1st and printed in lithography by De La Rue. Two phosphor bands. Perf 15×14½ (with one elliptical hole in each vertical side)

NI154	N **1**	(1st)	deep lilac	3·00	3·00	☐ ☐
NI155	N **3**	(1st)	green	3·00	3·00	☐ ☐
NI156	N **2**	(1st)	deep claret	3·00	3·00	☐ ☐
Set of 3				8·00	8·00	☐ ☐

Nos. NI154/6 were only issued in the £9·72 'The Regional Definitives' booklet.

3 Scotland

S **1**　　　　S **2**　　　　S **3**　　　　S **4**

1958–67 Wmk **179**

S1	S **1**	3d	lilac *(18.8.58)*	15	15	☐ ☐
		p.	Two phosphor bands *(21.9.63)*	13·00	4·00	☐ ☐
		pa.	One side band *(30.4.65)*	20	25	☐ ☐
		pd.	One centre phosphor band *(9.11.67)*	15	15	☐ ☐
S2		4d	blue *(7.7.66)*	20	20	☐ ☐
		p.	Two phosphor bands	20	20	☐ ☐
S3	S **2**	6d	purple *(29.9.58)*	25	25	☐ ☐
		p.	Two phosphor bands *(29.1.63)*	25	25	☐ ☐
S4		9d	bronze-green (2 phosphor bands) *(1.3.67)*	35	40	☐ ☐

S5	S **3**	1s3d	green *(29.9.58)*	40	40	☐ ☐
		p.	Two phosphor bands *(29.1.63)*	50	50	☐ ☐
S6		1s6d	blue (2 phosphor bands) *(1.3.67)*	60	60	☐ ☐

No. S1pa exists with the phosphor band at the left or right of the stamp.

1967–70 One centre phosphor band (Nos. S7, S9/10) or two phosphor bands (others). No wmk

S7	S **1**	3d	lilac *(16.5.68)*	15	15	☐ ☐
S8		4d	blue *(28.11.67)*	30	30	☐ ☐
S9		4d	sepia *(4.9.68)*	15	10	☐ ☐
S10		4d	vermilion *(26.2.69)*	15	10	☐ ☐
S11		5d	blue *(4.9.68)*	25	15	☐ ☐
S12	S **2**	9d	bronze-green *(28.9.70)*	6·00	6·00	☐ ☐
S13	S **3**	1s6d	blue *(12.12.68)*	1·75	1·50	☐ ☐
Presentation Pack (containing Nos. S3, S5p, S7, S9/13) (P.O. Pack No. 23)				8·00		☐	

Decimal Currency

1971(7 July)–**93** Type S **4**. No wmk

(a) Printed in gravure by Harrison and Sons with phosphor bands. Perf 15×14

S14		2½p	bright magenta (1 centre band)	25	20	☐ ☐
S15		3p	ultramarine (2 bands)	35	15	☐ ☐
S16		3p	ultramarine (1 centre band) *(23.1.74)*	35	30	☐ ☐
S17		3½p	olive-grey (2 bands) *(23.1.74)*	20	25	☐ ☐
S18		3½p	olive-grey (1 centre band) *(6.11.74)*	20	25	☐ ☐
S19		4½p	grey-blue (2 bands) *(6.11.74)*	40	45	☐ ☐
S20		5p	reddish violet (2 bands)	1·00	1·25	☐ ☐
S21		5½p	violet (2 bands) *(23.1.74)*	30	35	☐ ☐
S22		5½p	violet (1 centre band) *(21.5.75)*	20	25	☐ ☐
S23		6½p	greenish blue (1 centre band) *(14.1.76)*	20	25	☐ ☐
S24		7p	purple-brown (1 centre band) *(18.11.78)*	30	30	☐ ☐
S25		7½p	chestnut (2 bands)	1·25	1·40	☐ ☐
S26		8p	rosine (2 bands) *(23.1.74)*	60	45	☐ ☐
S27		8½p	yellow-green (2 bands) *(14.1.76)*	40	40	☐ ☐
S28		9p	deep violet (2 bands) *(18.1.78)*	40	40	☐ ☐
S29		10p	orange-brown (2 bands) *(20.10.76)*	45	50	☐ ☐
S30		10p	orange-brown (1 centre band) *(23.7.80)*	40	50	☐ ☐
S31		10½p	steel-blue (2 bands) *(18.1.78)*	90	1·00	☐ ☐
S32		11p	scarlet (2 bands) *(20.10.76)*	55	60	☐ ☐

(b) Printed in gravure by Harrison and Sons on phosphorised paper. Perf 15×14

S33		12p	yellowish green *(23.7.80)*	50	60	☐ ☐
S34		13½p	purple-brown *(23.7.80)*	1·00	1·10	☐ ☐
S35		15p	ultramarine *(23.7.80)*	60	70	☐ ☐

(c) Printed in lithography by John Waddington. One side phosphor band (11½p, 12p, 12½p, 13p) or phosphorised paper (others). Perf 14

S36		11½p	drab *(8.4.81)*	80	80	☐ ☐
S37		12p	bright emerald *(7.1.86)*	2·00	2·00	☐ ☐
S38		12½p	light emerald *(24.2.82)*	60	70	☐ ☐
S39		13p	pale chestnut *(23.10.84)*	85	75	☐ ☐
S40		14p	grey-blue *(8.4.81)*	75	75	☐ ☐

S41	15½p pale violet *(24.2.82)*	80	80	☐ ☐
S42	16p drab *(27.4.83)*	80	85	☐ ☐
S43	17p grey-blue *(23.10.84)*	1·50	1·50	☐ ☐
S44	18p deep violet *(8.4.81)*	80	80	☐ ☐
S45	19½p olive-grey *(24.2.82)*	1·75	1·75	☐ ☐
S46	20½p ultramarine *(27.4.83)*	3·50	3·50	☐ ☐
S47	22p blue *(8.4.81)*	1·00	1·10	☐ ☐
S48	22p yellow-green *(23.10.84)*	4·25	4·25	☐ ☐
S49	26p rosine	1·25	1·25	☐ ☐
S50	28p deep violet-blue	1·25	1·25	☐ ☐
S51	31p bright purple	2·50	2·50	☐ ☐

(d) Printed in lithography by Questa. Perf 15 × 14

S52	12p bright emerald (1 side band) *(29.4.86)*	2·25	2·50	☐ ☐
S53	13p pale chestnut (1 side band) *(4.11.86)*	70	75	☐ ☐
S54	14p deep blue (1 centre band) *(8.11.88)*	60	70	☐ ☐
S55	14p deep blue (1 side band) *(21.3.89)*	80	90	☐ ☐
S56	15p bright blue (1 centre band) *(28.11.89)*	1·00	1·00	☐ ☐
S57	17p grey-blue (phosphorised paper) *(29.4.86)*	4·00	4·00	☐ ☐
S58	17p deep blue (1 centre band) *(4.12.90)*	1·00	1·10	☐ ☐
S59	18p deep olive-grey (phosphorised paper) *(6.1.87)*	1·10	85	☐ ☐
S60	18p bright green (1 centre band) *(3.12.91)*	1·25	90	☐ ☐
	a. Perf 14 *(26.9.92)**	1·00	1·25	☐ ☐
S61	18p bright green (1 side band) *(10.8.93)*	2·75	3·00	☐ ☐
S62	19p bright orange-red (phosphorised paper) *(8.11.88)*	70	70	☐ ☐
S63	19p bright orange-red (2 bands) *(21.3.89)*	2·40	2·40	☐ ☐
S64	20p brownish black (phosphorised paper) *(28.11.89)*	95	95	☐ ☐
S65	22p yellow-green (phosphorised paper) *(27.1.87)*	1·25	1·50	☐ ☐
S66	22p bright orange-red (phosphorised paper) *(4.12.90)*	1·25	90	☐ ☐
S67	23p bright green (phosphorised paper) *(8.11.88)*	1·25	1·10	☐ ☐
S68	23p bright green (2 bands) *(21.3.89)*	12·00	12·00	☐ ☐
S69	24p Indian red (phosphorised paper) *(28.11.89)*	1·25	1·25	☐ ☐
S70	24p chestnut (phosphorised paper) *(3.12.91)*	1·40	1·25	☐ ☐
	a. Perf 14 *(10.92)**	8·00	8·00	☐ ☐
S71	24p chestnut (2 bands) *(10.8.93)*	2·75	3·00	☐ ☐
S72	26p rosine (phosphorised paper) *(27.1.87)*	3·75	4·00	☐ ☐
S73	26p drab (phosphorised paper) *(4.12.90)*	1·25	1·25	☐ ☐
S74	28p deep violet-blue (phosphorised paper) *(27.1.87)*	1·25	1·25	☐ ☐
S75	28p deep bluish grey (phosphorised paper) *(3.12.91)*	1·25	1·50	☐ ☐
	a. Perf 14 *(18.12.93)**	9·00	9·00	☐ ☐

S76	31p bright purple (phosphorised paper) *(29.4.86)*	2·25	2·25	☐ ☐
S77	32p greenish blue (phosphorised paper) *(8.11.88)*	1·75	2·00	☐ ☐
S78	34p deep bluish grey (phosphorised paper) *(28.11.89)*	1·75	1·75	☐ ☐
S79	37p rosine (phosphorised paper) *(4.12.90)*	2·00	2·25	☐ ☐
S80	39p bright mauve (phosphorised paper) *(3.12.91)*	2·00	2·25	☐ ☐
	a. Perf 14 *(11.92)*	15·00	15·00	☐ ☐

* Earliest known date of use.

Nos. S55, S61, S63, S68 and S71 were only issued in stamp booklets.

Presentation Pack (P.O. Pack No. 27) (contains 2½p (S14), 3p (S15), 5p (S20), 7½p (S25))	3·50	☐
Presentation Pack (P.O. Pack No. 62) (contains 3p (S16), 3½p (S17), 5½p (S21), 8p (S26), later with 4½p (S19) added)	3·00	☐
Presentation Pack (P.O. Pack No. 85) (contains 6½p (S23), 8½p (S27), 10p (S29), 11p (S32))	2·50	☐
Presentation Pack (P.O. Pack No. 129b) (contains 7p (S24), 9p (S28), 10½p (S31), 11½p (S36), 12p (S33), 13½p (S34), 14p (S40), 15p (S35), 18p (S44), 22p (S47))	9·00	☐
Presentation Pack (P.O. Pack No. 2) (contains 10p (S30), 12½p (S38), 16p (S42), 20½p (S46), 26p (S49), 28p (S50))	18·00	☐
Presentation Pack (P.O. Pack No. 6) (contains 10p (S30), 13p (S39), 16p (S42), 17p (S43), 22p (S48), 26p (S49), 28p (S50), 31p (S51))	17·00	☐
Presentation Pack (P.O. Pack No. 10) (contains 12p (S52), 13p (S53), 17p (S57), 18p (S59), 22p (S65), 26p (S72), 28p (S74), 31p (S76))	20·00	☐

For combined packs containing values from all three Regions see under Northern Ireland.

1993 (7 Dec.)–**98**

(a) Printed in lithography by Questa. Perf 15 × 14 (with one elliptical hole in each vertical side)

S81	S **4**	19p bistre (1 centre band)	80	70	☐ ☐
S82		19p bistre (1 side band) *(25.4.95)*	3·00	3·25	☐ ☐
S83		20p bright green (1 centre band) *(23.7.96)*	1·50	1·50	☐ ☐
S84		25p red (2 bands)	1·10	1·00	☐ ☐
S85		26p red-brown (2 bands) *(23.7.96)*	1·75	2·00	☐ ☐
S86		30p deep olive-grey (2 bands)	1·25	1·25	☐ ☐
S87		37p bright mauve (2 bands) *(23.7.96)*	2·75	3·00	☐ ☐
S88		41p grey-brown (2 bands)	2·00	2·25	☐ ☐
S89		63p light emerald (2 bands) *(23.7.96)*	4·50	4·75	☐ ☐

(b) Printed in gravure by Walsall (20p, 26p (No. S91a), 63p), Harrison or Walsall (26p (No. S91), 37p). Perf 14 (No. S90a) or 15 × 14 (others) (both with one elliptical hole in each vertical side)

S90	S **4**	20p bright green (1 centre band) *(1.7.97)*	1·50	1·10	☐ ☐
S90a		20p bright green (1 side band) *(13.10.98)*	4·00	4·00	☐ ☐
S91		26p chestnut (2 bands) *(1.7.97)*	1·40	1·20	☐ ☐
		a. Perf 14 *(13.10.98)*	4·00	4·00	☐ ☐
S92		37p bright mauve (2 bands) *(1.7.97)*	2·00	2·25	☐ ☐
S93		63p light emerald (2 bands) *(1.7.97)*	4·25	4·50	☐ ☐

Nos. S82, S90a and S91a were only issued in stamp booklets.
For combined presentation packs for all three Regions, see under Northern Ireland.

S 5 Scottish Flag

S 6 Scottish Lion

S 7 Thistle

S 8 Tartan

1999 (8 June)–**2002** Printed in gravure by De La Rue (68p), De La Rue, Questa or Walsall (2nd, 1st) or Walsall (others). One centre phosphor band (2nd) or two phosphor bands (others). Perf 15 × 14 (with one elliptical hole in each vertical side)

S94	S 5	(2nd)	new blue, blue and silver	1·50	75	
S95	S 6	(1st)	yellow, deep rose-red, rose-red and silver	1·75	1·00	
S96	S 7	(E)	bright lilac, deep lilac and silver	2·50	2·00	
S97	S 8	64p	greenish yellow, bright magenta, new blue, grey-black and silver	9·00	9·00	
S98		65p	greenish yellow, bright magenta, new blue, grey-black and silver (25.4.00)	3·00	3·25	
S99		68p	greenish yellow, bright magenta, new blue, grey-black and silver (4.7.02)	3·25	3·25	

Presentation Pack (P.O. Pack No. 45) (contains 2nd, 1st, E, 64p, (Nos. S94/7)	14·00	
Presentation Pack (P.O. Pack No. 50) (contains 65p) (No. S98))	11·00	
Presentation Pack (P.O. Pack No. 55) (contains 2nd, 1st, E, 65p (Nos. S94/6, S98)	15·00	
PHQ Cards (Nos. S94/7) (D12)	8·00	14·00	

Nos. S94, S95 and S96 were initially sold at 19p, 26p and 30p, the latter representing the basic European airmail rate.
For combined presentation packs for all four Regions, see under England.

S 9

2000 (15 Feb.) Type S 4 redrawn with '1st' face value as Type S 9. Two phosphor bands. Perf 14 (with one elliptical hole in each vertical side)

| S108 | S 9 | (1st) | bright orange-red | 3·00 | 3·25 | |

No. S108 was only issued in £7·50 'Special by Design' stamp booklets.

2003 (14 Oct.)–**16** As Nos. S94/6 and S99 but with white borders. One centre phosphor band (2nd) or two phosphor bands (others). Perf 15 × 14 (with one elliptical hole in each vertical side)

(a) Printed in gravure by Walsall or De La Rue (42p) or De La Rue (others)

S109	S 5	(2nd)	new blue, blue and silver	1·50	60	
S110	S 6	(1st)	yellow, deep rose-red and silver	1·50	85	
S111	S 7	(E)	bright lilac, deep lilac and silver	2·50	2·50	

S112		40p	bright lilac, deep lilac and silver (11.5.04)	1·75	1·75	
S113		42p	bright lilac, deep lilac and silver (5.4.05)	1·75	1·75	
S114		44p	bright lilac, deep lilac and silver (28.3.06)	1·50	1·50	
S115		48p	bright lilac, deep lilac and silver (27.3.07)	1·25	90	
S116		50p	bright lilac, deep lilac and silver (1.4.08)	1·25	75	
S117		56p	bright lilac, deep lilac and silver (31.3.09)	1·25	1·25	
S118		60p	bright lilac, deep lilac and silver (30.3.10)	1·50	1·40	
S119	S 8	68p	bright magenta, greenish yellow, new blue, grey-black and silver	2·00	2·00	
S120		72p	bright magenta, greenish yellow, new blue, grey-black and silver (28.3.06)	2·00	2·00	
S121		78p	bright magenta, greenish yellow, new blue, grey-black and silver (27.3.07)	2·00	2·00	
S122		81p	bright magenta, greenish yellow, new blue, grey-black and silver (1.4.08)	2·25	2·00	
S123		90p	bright magenta, greenish yellow, new blue, grey-black and silver (31.3.09)	2·25	2·25	
S124		97p	bright magenta, greenish yellow, new blue, grey-black and silver (30.3.10)	2·40	2·40	

(b) Printed in lithography by Enschedé or Cartor (1st) or Cartor (others)

S130	S 5	(2nd)	new blue, blue and silver (27.6.12)	1·25	1·00	
S130a		(2nd)	new blue, blue and grey (5.16)	1·50	1·00	
S131	S 6	(1st)	yellow, deep rose-red, rose-red and silver (20.9.07)	1·75	1·25	
S131a		(1st)	yellow, deep rose-red, rose-red and grey (5.16)	1·75	1·25	
S132	S 7	68p	bright lilac, deep lilac and silver (29.3.11)	2·00	1·50	
S133		87p	bright lilac, deep lilac and silver (25.4.12)	2·50	2·50	
S134		88p	bright lilac, deep lilac and silver (27.3.13)	2·50	2·00	
S135		97p	bright lilac, deep lilac and silver (26.3.14)	2·75	2·25	
S136		£1	bright lilac, deep lilac and silver (24.3.15)	2·40	2·40	
S137		£1·05	bright lilac, deep lilac and grey (22.3.16)	2·40	2·40	
S138	S 8	£1·10	silver, greenish yellow, bright magenta, new blue and black (29.3.11)	2·75	2·75	
S139	S 7	£1·17	bright lilac, deep lilac and grey (21.3.17)	2·75	2·75	
S143	S 8	£1·28	silver, greenish yellow, bright magenta, new blue and black (25.4.12)	3·25	3·25	
S144		£1·33	silver, greenish yellow, bright magenta, new blue and black (24.3.15)	3·25	3·25	
S145		£1·40	silver, greenish yellow, bright magenta, new blue and black (21.3.17)	3·25	3·25	

Presentation Pack (P.O. Pack No. 64)
   (Nos. S109/11, S119)   7·00   ☐

PHQ Cards (set of 4) (Nos. S109/11,
   S119) (D25)   2·00   10·00 ☐ ☐

Nos. S109/11 were initially sold at 20p, 28p and 38p, the latter representing the basic European airmail rate.

No. S131 was issued in £7·66 'British Army Uniforms' stamp booklet, No. DX40, printed by Enschedé and also on 27 June 2012 in sheets.

Stamps as No. S131 but self-adhesive were issued on 30 November 2007 in sheets of 20 with se-tenant labels. These sheets were printed by Cartor in lithography, and perforated 15×14 without the elliptical holes. The labels show either Scottish scenes or personal photographs.

Stamps as Nos. EN30, NI95, S131 and W122 but self-adhesive were issued on 29 September 2008 in sheets of 20 containing five of each design with se-tenant labels.

S 9a

Opening of New Scottish Parliament Building

2004 (5 Oct.) Sheet 123×70 mm. Printed in gravure by De La Rue. One centre phosphor band (2nd) or two phosphor bands (others). Perf 15×14 (with one elliptical hole in each vertical side)

MSS152 S **9a** Nos. S109, S110×2
   and S112×2   7·00   7·00 ☐ ☐
First Day Cover   8·00   ☐

S 10

Celebrating Scotland

2006 (30 Nov.) Sheet 124×71 mm. Printed in photogravure by De La Rue. Two phosphor bands. Perf 15×14 (with one elliptical hole in each vertical side) (1st) or 14×14 (72p)

MSS153 S **10** (1st) As No. S110;
   (1st) Scottish Flag; 72p St. Andrew;
   72p Edinburgh Castle   7·00   7·00 ☐ ☐
First Day Cover   8·00   ☐
Presentation Pack (P.O. Pack No. M14) 8·00   ☐
PHQ Cards (set of 5) (CGB1)   7·50   17·00 ☐ ☐

MSS153 was on sale at post offices throughout the UK.

The five PHQ cards depict the complete miniature sheet and the four stamps within it.

Stamps as the 1st class Scottish flag stamp within **MS**S153 but self-adhesive were issued on 30 November 2009 in sheets

of 20 with se-tenant labels showing Scottish castles. These sheets were printed in lithography by Cartor.

50th Anniversary of the Country Definitives

2008 (29 Sept.) As Nos. S1, S3 and S5 (definitives of 1958) but inscribed 1st and printed in lithography by De La Rue. Two phosphor bands. Perf 15×14½ (with one elliptical hole in each vertical side)

S154	S **1**	(1st)	deep lilac	3·00	3·00	☐ ☐
S155	S **3**	(1st)	green	3·00	3·00	☐ ☐
S156	S **2**	(1st)	deep claret	3·00	3·00	☐ ☐

Nos. S154/6 come from £9·72 'The Regional Definitives' stamp booklets.

S 11

250th Birth Anniversary of Robert Burns (Scottish poet)

2009 (22 Jan.) Sheet 145×74 mm. Printed in gravure by Enschedé. One centre band (2nd) or two phosphor bands (others). Perf 14½ (size 34×34 mm) or 15×14 (with one elliptical hole in each vertical side) (others).

MSS157 (2nd) No. S109; (1st) 'A Man's
   a Man for a' that' and Burns
   ploughing (detail) (James Sargent
   Storer) (34×34 mm); (1st) No. S110;
   (1st) Portrait of Burns (Alexander
   Nasmyth) (34×34 mm); 50p
   No. S116; 81p No. S122   9·00   9·00 ☐ ☐
First Day Cover   10·00   ☐
Presentation Pack (P.O. Pack No. 422) 11·00   ☐
PHQ Cards (set of 3) (319)   3·50   12·00 ☐ ☐

MSS157 was on sale at post offices throughout the UK.

The three PHQ cards show the two 34×34 mm Robert Burns stamps and the complete miniature sheet.

S 12 Saltire

Scotland Flag

2013 (9 May) **-14.** Printed in lithography by Cartor or Enschedé. Two phosphor bands. Perf 14½×14 (with one elliptical hole in each vert side)

S158   S **12** (1st) multicoloured   5·00   5·00 ☐ ☐

No. S158 was only issued in £11·11 Football Heroes and £13·97 Classic Locomotives booklets, Nos. DY7 and DY9.

4 Wales

W **1**   W **2**   W **3**

1958–67 Wmk 179

W1	W **1**	3d	lilac *(18.8.58)*	15	15	☐☐
		p.	One centre phosphor band *(16.5.67)*	20	15	☐☐
W2		4d	blue *(7.2.66)*	20	15	☐☐
		p.	Two phosphor bands *(10.67)*	20	25	☐☐
W3	W **2**	6d	purple *(29.9.58)*	35	40	☐☐
W4		9d	bronze-green (two phosphor bands) *(1.3.67)*	40	50	☐☐
W5	W **3**	1s3d	green *(29.9.58)*	40	55	☐☐
W6		1s6d	blue (two phosphor bands) *(1.3.67)*	45	55	☐☐

1967–69 One centre phosphor band (Nos. W7, W9/10) or two phosphor bands (others). No wmk

W7	W **1**	3d	lilac *(6.12.67)*	15	20	☐☐
W8		4d	blue *(21.6.68)*	15	20	☐☐
W9		4d	sepia *(4.9.68)*	15	20	☐☐
W10		4d	vermilion *(26.2.69)*	15	20	☐☐
W11		5d	blue *(4.9.68)*	15	30	☐☐
W12	W **3**	1s6d	blue *(1.8.69)*	3·50	3·50	☐☐

Presentation Pack (P.O. Pack No. 24)

(comprises Nos. W4, W6/7, W9/11)   4·00   ☐

W **4** With 'p'   W **5** Without 'p'

Decimal Currency

1971–92 Type W **4**. No wmk

(a) Printed in photogravure with phosphor bands

W13	2½p	bright magenta (1 centre band)	20	20	☐☐
W14	3p	ultramarine (2 bands)	25	20	☐☐
W15	3p	ultramarine (1 centre band) *(23.1.74)*	30	35	☐☐
W16	3½p	olive-grey (2 bands) *(23.1.74)*	20	30	☐☐
W17	3½p	olive-grey (1 centre band) *(6.11.74)*	20	30	☐☐
W18	4½p	grey-blue (2 bands) *(6.11.74)*	40	45	☐☐
W19	5p	reddish violet (2 bands)	1·25	1·25	☐☐
W20	5½p	violet (2 bands) *(23.1.74)*	30	40	☐☐
W21	5½p	violet (1 centre band) *(21.5.75)*	30	40	☐☐
W22	6½p	greenish blue (1 centre band) *(14.1.76)*	20	20	☐☐
W23	7p	purple-brown (1 centre band) *(18.1.78)*	25	25	☐☐
W24	7½p	chestnut (2 bands)	1·75	1·75	☐☐
W25	8p	rosine (2 bands) *(23.1.74)*	50	60	☐☐
W26	8½p	yellow-green (2 bands) *(14.1.76)*	40	50	☐☐
W27	9p	deep violet (2 bands) *(18.1.78)*	40	40	☐☐

W28	10p	orange-brown (2 bands) *(20.10.76)*	45	55	☐☐
W29	10p	orange-brown (1 centre band) *(23.7.80)*	40	40	☐☐
W30	10½p	steel-blue (2 bands) *(18.1.78)*	1·00	1·10	☐☐
W31	11p	scarlet (2 bands) *(20.10.76)*	45	55	☐☐

(b) Printed in photogravure on phosphorised paper

W32	12p	yellowish-green *(27.3.80)*	50	60	☐☐
W33	13½p	purple-brown *(27.3.80)*	1·00	1·10	☐☐
W34	15p	ultramarine *(27.3.80)*	70	80	☐☐

(c) Printed in lithography. Perf 14 (11½p, 12½p, 14p (No. W39), 15½p. 16p, 18p (No. W46), 19½p, 20½p, 22p (No. W54), 26p (No. W61), 28p (No. W63)) or 15 × 14 (others)

W35	11½p	drab (1 side band) *(8.4.81)*	90	1·00	☐☐
W36	12p	bright emerald (1 side band) *(7.1.86)*	2·00	2·00	☐☐
W37	12½p	light emerald (1 side band) *(24.2.82)*	70	70	☐☐
		a. Perf 15 × 14 *(10.1.84)*	4·75	4·25	☐☐
W38	13p	pale chestnut (1 side band) *(23.10.84)*	60	60	☐☐
W39	14p	grey-blue (phosphorised paper) *(8.4.81)*	70	70	☐☐
W40	14p	deep blue (1 centre band) *(8.11.88)*	75	75	☐☐
W41	15p	bright blue (1 centre band) *(28.11.89)*	80	75	☐☐
W42	15½p	pale violet (phosphorised paper) *(24.2.82)*	75	75	☐☐
W43	16p	drab (phosphorised paper) *(27.4.83)*	1·75	1·75	☐☐
		a. Perf 15 × 14 *(10.1.84)*	1·75	1·75	☐☐
W44	17p	grey-blue (phosphorised paper) *(23.10.84)*	90	1·00	☐☐
W45	17p	deep blue (1 centre band) *(4.12.90)*	90	80	☐☐
W46	18p	deep violet (phosphorised paper) *(8.4.81)*	1·00	95	☐☐
W47	18p	deep olive-grey (phosphorised paper) *(6.1.87)*	95	90	☐☐
W48	18p	bright green (1 centre band) *(3.12.91)*	75	75	☐☐
		b. Perf 14 *(12.1.93)**	7·50	7·50	☐☐
W49	18p	bright green (1 side band) *(25.2.92)*	2·25	2·25	☐☐
W50	19p	bright orange-red (phosphorised paper) *(8.11.88)*	1·00	1·10	☐☐
W51	19½p	olive-grey (phosphorised paper) *(24.2.82)*	2·00	2·25	☐☐
W52	20p	brownish black (phosphorised paper) *(28.11.89)*	90	90	☐☐
W53	20½p	ultramarine (phosphorised paper) *(27.4.83)*	3·75	3·75	☐☐
W54	22p	blue (phosphorised paper) *(8.4.81)*	1·20	1·30	☐☐
W55	22p	yellow-green (phosphorised paper) *(23.10.84)*	1·10	1·25	☐☐
W56	22p	bright orange-red (phosphorised paper) *(4.12.90)*	1·00	1·10	☐☐
W57	23p	bright green (phosphorised paper) *(8.11.88)*	1·00	1·10	☐☐
W58	24p	Indian red (phosphorised paper) *(28.11.89)*	1·40	1·40	☐☐

W59	24p	chestnut (phosphorised paper) *(3.12.91)*	75	75	☐ ☐
	b.	Perf 14 *(14.9.92)**	7·50	7·50	☐ ☐
W60	24p	chestnut (2 bands) *(25.2.92)*	2·50	2·75	☐ ☐
W61	26p	rosine (phosphorised paper) *(24.2.82)*	1·10	1·10	☐ ☐
	a.	Perf 15×14 *(27.1.87)*	5·75	6·00	☐ ☐
W62	26p	drab (phosphorised paper) *(4.12.90)*	1·75	1·75	☐ ☐
W63	28p	deep violet-blue (phosphorised paper) *(27.4.83)*	1·50	1·50	☐ ☐
	a.	Perf 15×14 *(27.1.87)*	1·50	1·50	☐ ☐
W64	28p	deep bluish grey (phosphorised paper) *(3.12.91)*	1·50	1·50	☐ ☐
W65	31p	bright purple (phosphorised paper) *(23.10.84)*	1·75	1·75	☐ ☐
W66	32p	greenish blue (phosphorised paper) *(8.11.88)*	1·75	1·75	☐ ☐
W67	34p	deep bluish grey (phosphorised paper) *(28.11.89)*	1·75	1·75	☐ ☐
W68	37p	rosine (phosphorised paper) *(4.12.90)*	2·25	2·25	☐ ☐
W69	39p	bright mauve (phosphorised paper) *(3.12.91)*	2·25	2·25	☐ ☐

* Earliest known date of use.

Nos. W49 and W60 were only issued in stamp booklets. The former exists with the phosphor band at the left or right of the stamp.

Presentation Pack (P.O. Pack No. 28) (contains 2½p (W13), 3p (W14), 5p (W19), 7½p (W24)) 3·50 ☐

Presentation Pack (P.O. Pack No. 63) (contains 3p (W15), 3½p (W16), 5½p (W20), 8p (W25), later with 4½p (W18) added) 3·00 ☐

Presentation Pack (P.O. Pack No. 86) (contains 6½p (W22), 8½p (W26), 10p (W28), 11p (W31)) 2·00 ☐

Presentation Pack (P.O. Pack No. 129c) (contains 7p (W23), 9p (W27), 10½p (W30), 11½p (W35), 12p (W32), 13½p (W33), 14p (W39), 15p (W34), 18p (W46), 22p (W54)) 9·00 ☐

Presentation Pack (P.O. Pack No. 3) (contains 10p (W29), 12½p (W37), 16p (W43), 20½p (W53), 26p (W61), 28p (W63)) 20·00 ☐

Presentation Pack (P.O. Pack No. 7) (contains 10p (W29), 13p (W38), 16p (W43a), 17p (W44), 22p (W55), 26p (W61), 28p (W63), 31p (W65)) 17·00 ☐

Presentation Pack (P.O. Pack No. 11) (contains 12p (W36), 13p (W38), 17p (W44), 18p (W47), 22p (W55), 26p (W61a), 28p (W63a), 31p (W65)) 20·00 ☐

For combined packs containing values from all three Regions see under Northern Ireland.

1993 (7 Dec.)–**96** Printed in lithography by Questa. Perf 15×14 (with one elliptical hole in each vertical side)

W70	W **4**	19p	bistre (1 centre band)	80	70	☐ ☐
W71		19p	bistre (1 side band) *(25.4.95)*	3·75	4·00	☐ ☐
W72		20p	bright green (1 centre band) *(23.7.96)*	1·75	2·00	☐ ☐
W73		25p	red (2 bands)	1·25	1·00	☐ ☐
W74		26p	red-brown (2 bands) *(23.7.96)*	2·00	2·25	☐ ☐
W75		30p	deep olive-grey (2 bands)	1·25	1·40	☐ ☐
W76		37p	bright mauve (2 bands) *(23.7.96)*	2·75	3·00	☐ ☐

| W77 | 41p | grey-brown (2 bands) | 2·00 | 2·00 | ☐ ☐ |
| W78 | 63p | light emerald (2 bands) *(23.7.96)* | 4·50 | 4·75 | ☐ ☐ |

No. W71 was only issued in stamp booklets.

For combined presentation packs for all three Regions see under Northern Ireland.

1997 (1 July)–**98** Printed in photogravure by Walsall (20p, 26p (No. W80a), 63p), Harrison or Walsall (26p (No. W80), 37p) Perf 14 (No. W79a) or 15×14 (others) (both with one elliptical hole in each vertical side)

W79	W **5**	20p	bright green (1 centre band)	1·25	1·25	☐ ☐
W79a		20p	bright green (1 side band) *(13.10.98)*	4·00	4·00	☐ ☐
W80		26p	chestnut (2 bands)	1·50	1·50	☐ ☐
		a.	Perf 14 *(13.10.98)*	4·00	4·00	☐ ☐
W81		37p	bright mauve (2 bands)	3·50	3·50	☐ ☐
W82		63p	light emerald (2 bands)	5·50	5·50	☐ ☐

Presentation Pack (P.O. Pack No. 39) (Nos. W79 and W80/2) 15·00 ☐

Nos. W79a and W80a were only issued in stamp booklets.

W **6** Leek   W **7** Welsh Dragon   W **8** Daffodil   W **9** Prince of Wales Feathers

1999 (8 June)–**2002** Printed in gravure by De La Rue (68p), Walsall or De La Rue (1st), (2nd), (No.W83) or Walsall (others). One phosphor band (2nd) or two phosphor bands (others). Perf 14 (No. W83a) or 15×14 (others) (both with one elliptical hole in each vertical side)

W83	W **6**	(2nd)	orange-brown, yellow-orange and black (1 centre band)	1·50	1·00	☐ ☐
W83a		(2nd)	orange-brown, yellow-orange and black (1 side band) *(18.9.00)*	4·00	4·00	☐ ☐
W84	W **7**	(1st)	blue-green, greenish yellow, silver and black	1·75	1·00	☐ ☐
W85	W **8**	(E)	greenish blue, deep greenish blue and grey-black	2·25	1·90	☐ ☐
W86	W **9**	64p	violet, gold, silver and black	9·00	9·00	☐ ☐
W87		65p	violet, gold, silver and black *(25.4.00)*	3·25	3·25	☐ ☐
W88		68p	violet, gold, silver and black *(4.7.02)*	3·25	3·25	☐ ☐

Presentation Pack (P.O. Pack No. 46) (contains 2nd, 1st, E, 64p) (Nos. W83, W84/6) 14·00 ☐

Presentation Pack (P.O. Pack No. 51) (contains 65p) (No. W87) 12·00 ☐

Presentation Pack (P.O. Pack No. 56) (contains 2nd, 1st, E, 65p) (Nos. W83, W84/5, W87) 18·00 ☐

PHQ Cards (Nos. W83, W84/6) (D13) 8·00 14·00 ☐ ☐

Nos. W83, W84 and W85 were initially sold at 19p, 26p and 30p, the latter representing the basic European airmail rate.

No. W83a was only issued in the £7 'Treasury of Trees' stamp booklet, No. DX26

For combined presentation packs for all four Regions, see under England.

W **10**

2000 (15 Feb.) Type W **4** redrawn with '1af/st' face value as Type W **10**. Two phosphor bands. Perf 14 (with one elliptical hole in each vertical side)
W97 W **10** (1st) bright orange-red   3·00   3·00 ☐☐
No. W97 was only issued in £7·50 'Special by Design' stamp booklets.

2003 (14 Oct.)–**16** As Nos. W83, W84/5 and W88, but with white borders. One centre phosphor band (2nd) or two phosphor bands (others). Perf 15 × 14 (with one elliptical hole in each vertical side)

(a) Printed in gravure by Walsall or De La Rue (42p)
     or De La Rue (others)

W98	W **6**	(2nd)	orange-brown, deep orange-brown and black	1·50	75	☐☐
W99	W **7**	(1st)	blue-green, greenish yellow, silver and black	1·75	75	☐☐
W100	W **8**	(E)	greenish blue, deep greenish blue and grey-black	2·50	2·50	☐☐
W101		40p	greenish blue, deep greenish blue and grey-black (11.5.04)	1·50	1·50	☐☐
W102		42p	greenish blue, deep greenish blue and grey-black (5.4.05)	2·00	1·50	☐☐
W103		44p	greenish blue, deep greenish blue and grey-black (28.3.06)	1·75	1·50	☐☐
W104		48p	greenish blue, deep greenish blue and grey-black (27.3.07)	1·25	90	☐☐
W105		50p	greenish blue, deep greenish blue and grey-black (1.4.08)	1·50	1·00	☐☐
W106		56p	greenish blue, deep greenish blue and grey-black (31.3.09)	1·50	1·25	☐☐
W107		60p	greenish blue, deep greenish blue and grey-black (30.3.10)	1·75	1·40	☐☐
W108	W **9**	68p	violet, gold, silver and black	2·25	2·25	☐☐
W109		72p	violet, gold, silver and black (28.3.06)	2·00	2·00	☐☐
W110		78p	violet, gold, silver and black (27.3.07)	2·25	2·00	☐☐
W111		81p	violet, gold, silver and black (1.4.08)	2·25	2·00	☐☐
W112		90p	violet, gold, silver and black (31.3.09)	2·50	2·25	☐☐
W113		97p	violet, gold, silver and black (30.3.10)	2·75	2·40	☐☐

(b) Printed in lithography by Enschedé or Cartor (W122 1st) or
     Cartor (others)

W121	W **6**	(2nd)	orange-brown, deep orange-brown and black (1.2013)	1·50	1·00	☐☐
W122	W **7**	(1st)	blue-green, greenish yellow and black (20.9.07)	1·75	1·25	☐☐

W123	W **8**	68p	greenish blue, deep greenish blue and black (29.3.11)	2·00	1·50	☐☐
W124		87p	greenish blue, deep greenish blue and black (25.4.12)	2·75	2·50	☐☐
W125		88p	greenish blue, deep greenish blue and black (27.3.13)	2·50	2·00	☐☐
W126		97p	greenish blue, deep greenish blue and black (26.3.14)	2·50	2·25	☐☐
W127		£1	greenish blue, deep greenish blue and black (24.3.15)	2·75	2·75	☐☐
W128		£1·05	greenish blue, deep greenish blue and black (22.3.16)	2·40	2·40	☐☐
W129	W **9**	£1·10	violet, gold, silver and black (29.3.11)	2·75	2·75	☐☐
W130	W **8**	£1·17	greenish blue, deep greenish blue and black (21.3.17)	2·75	2·75	☐☐
W134	W **9**	£1·28	violet, gold, silver and black (25.4.12)	3·25	3·25	☐☐
W135		£1·33	violet, gold, silver and black (24.3.15)	3·25	3·25	☐☐
W136		£1·40	violet, gold, silver and black (21.3.17)	3·25	3·25	☐☐
Presentation Pack (P.O. Pack No. 65) (Nos. W98/100, W108)				7·00		☐
PHQ Cards (set of 4) (Nos. W98/100, W108) (D26)				7·50	10·00	☐☐

Nos. W98/100 were initially sold at 20p, 28p and 38p, the latter representing the basic European airmail rate.

No. W122 was first issued in the £7·66 'British Army Uniforms' stamp booklets, No. DX40, and **MS**W125. It was issued in sheets in January 2013.

Stamps as W**122** but self-adhesive were issued on 1 March 2007 in sheets of 20 with se-tenant labels. These sheets were printed in lithography and perforated 15 × 14 without the elliptical holes. The labels show either Welsh scenes or personal photographs.

Stamps as Nos. EN30, NI95, S131 and W122 but self-adhesive were issued on 29 September 2008 in sheets of 20 containing five of each design with se-tenant labels.

Type W **10a**

Opening of New Welsh Assembly Building, Cardiff

2006 (1 Mar.) Sheet 123 × 70 mm. Printed in gravure by De La Rue. One centre phosphor band (2nd) or two phosphor bands (others). Perf 15 × 14 (with one elliptical hole on each vertical side

MSW143 W **10a** Nos. W98, W99 × 2 and W108 × 2		7·50	7·50	☐☐
First Day Cover			9·00	☐

50th Anniversary of the Country Definitives

2008 (29 Sept.) As Nos. W1, W3 and W5 (definitives of 1958) but inscribed 1st and printed in lithography by De La Rue. Two phosphor bands. Perf 15 × 14½ (with one elliptical hole on each vertical side)

W144	W **1**	(1st)	deep lilac	3·00	3·00	☐ ☐
W145	W **3**	(1st)	green	3·00	3·00	☐ ☐
W146	W **2**	(1st)	deep claret	3·00	3·00	☐ ☐
Set of 3				8.00	8.00	☐ ☐

Nos. W144/6 were only issued in the £9·72 'The Regional Definitives' stamp booklet.

W **11**

Celebrating Wales miniature sheet

2009 (26 Feb.) Sheet 123 × 70 mm. Printed in lithography by De La Rue. Two phosphor bands. Perf 15 × 14 (with one elliptical hole on each vertical side (1st) or 14½ × 14 (81p)

MSW147 (1st) Red dragon; (1st) No.

W120; 81p St. David; 81p National Assembly for Wales, Cardiff	7·50	7·50	☐ ☐
First Day Cover		9·00	☐
Presentation Pack (P.O. Pack No. 424)	9·00		☐
PHQ Cards (*set of 5*) (CGB4)	6·00	17·00	☐ ☐

MSW125 was on sale at post offices throughout the UK.

The five PHQ cards show the four individual stamps and the complete miniature sheet.

Stamps as the 1st class red dragon stamp from **MS**W147 but self-adhesive were issued on 1 March 2010 in sheets of 20 with *se-tenant* labels showing Welsh castles. These sheets were printed in lithography by Cartor.

W **12** Red Dragon

Welsh Flag

2013 (9 May) **–14.** Printed in lithography by Cartor or Enschedé. Two phosphor bands. Perf 14½ × 14 (with one elliptical hole in each vert side)

W148	W **12**	(1st)	multicoloured	5·50	5·50	☐ ☐

No. W148 was only issued in the £11·11 Football Heroes and £13·97 Classic Locomotives booklets Nos. DY7 and DY9.

5 Isle of Man

Regional Issues

1 **2** **3**

1958–67 Wmk **179**. Perf 15 × 14

1	**1**	2½d	red *(8.6.64)*		90	1·75	☐ ☐
2	**2**	3d	lilac *(18.8.58)*		50	20	☐ ☐
		p.	One centre phosphor band *(27.6.68)*		20	50	☐ ☐
3		4d	blue *(7.2.66)*		1·50	2·00	☐ ☐
		p.	Two phosphor bands *(5.7.67)*		30	40	☐ ☐

1968–69 One centre phosphor band (Nos. 5/6) or two phosphor bands (others). No wmk

4	**2**	4d	blue *(24.6.68)*	25	30	☐ ☐
5		4d	sepia *(4.9.68)*	25	30	☐ ☐
6		4d	vermilion *(26.2.69)*	45	75	☐ ☐
7		5d	blue *(4.9.68)*	45	75	☐ ☐

Decimal Currency

1971 (7 July) One centre phosphor band (2½p) or two phosphor bands (others). No wmk

8	**3**	2½p	magenta	30	30	☐ ☐
9		3p	ultramarine	30	30	☐ ☐
10		5p	violet	1·10	1·10	☐ ☐
11		7½p	chestnut	1·50	1·50	☐ ☐
Presentation Pack (P.O. Pack No. 30)				3·50		☐

For comprehensive listings of the Independent Administration issues of the Isle of Man, see Stanley Gibbons *Collect Channel Islands and Isle of Man Stamps.*

6 Channel Islands General Issue

C **1** Gathering Vraic   C **2** Islanders gathering Vraic

Third Anniversary of Liberation

1948 (10 May) Wmk Type **127**. Perf 15 × 14

C1	C **1**	1d	red	25	55	☐ ☐
C2	C **2**	2½d	blue	25	60	☐ ☐
First Day Cover					35·00	☐

7 Guernsey

(a) War Occupation Issues

Stamps issued under British authority during the German Occupation.

| 1 | 2 | 3 |

1941–44 Rouletted

(a) White paper. No wmk

1d	**1**	½d	green	4·00	2·00	☐ ☐
2		1d	red	3·25	2·00	☐ ☐
3a		2½d	blue	15·00	12·00	☐ ☐

(b) Dark bluish French bank-note paper. Wmk loops

| 4 | **1** | ½d | green | 32·00 | 25·00 | ☐ ☐ |
| 5 | | 1d | red | 18·00 | 25·00 | ☐ ☐ |

(b) Regional Issues

1958–67 Wmk **179**. Perf 15 × 14

6	**2**	2½d	red *(8.6.64)*	40	50	☐ ☐
7	**3**	3d	lilac *(18.8.58)*	30	40	☐ ☐
		p.	One centre phosphor band *(24.5.67)*	20	30	☐ ☐
8		4d	blue	40	50	☐ ☐
		p.	Two phosphor bands *(24.10.67)*	15	25	☐ ☐

1968–69 One centre phosphor band (Nos. 10/11) or two phosphor bands (others). No wmk

9	**3**	4d	blue *(16.4.68)*	10	20	☐ ☐
10		4d	sepia *(4.9.68)*	10	15	☐ ☐
11		4d	vermilion *(26.2.69)*	20	25	☐ ☐
12		5d	blue *(4.9.68)*	30	40	☐ ☐

For comprehensive listings of the Independent Postal Administration issues of Guernsey, see Stanley Gibbons *Collect Channel Islands and Isle of Man Stamps*.

8 Jersey

(a) War Occupation Issues

Stamps issued under British authority during the German Occupation.

5

6 Old Jersey Farm   **7** Portelet Bay

8 Corbière Lighthouse   **9** Elizabeth Castle

10 Mont Orgueil Castle   **11** Gathering Vraic (seaweed)

1941–42 White paper. No wmk. Perf 11

| 1 | **5** | ½d | green | 8·00 | 6·00 | ☐ ☐ |
| 2 | | 1d | red | 8·00 | 5·00 | ☐ ☐ |

1943 No wmk. Perf 13½

3	**6**	½d	green	12·00	12·00	☐ ☐
4	**7**	1d	red	3·00	50	☐ ☐
5	**8**	1½d	brown	8·00	5·75	☐ ☐
6	**9**	2d	orange	7·50	2·00	☐ ☐
7a	**10**	2½d	blue	1·00	1·75	☐ ☐
8	**11**	3d	violet	3·00	2·75	☐ ☐
Set of 6				30·00	21·00	☐ ☐

(b) Regional Issues

| 12 | 13 |

1958–67 Wmk **179**. Perf 15 × 14

9	**12**	2½d	red *(8.6.64)*	75	1·00	☐ ☐
10	**13**	3d	lilac *(18.8.58)*	30	40	☐ ☐
		p.	One centre phosphor band *(9.6.67)*	15	25	☐ ☐
11		4d	blue *(7.2.66)*	25	30	☐ ☐
		p.	Two phosphor bands *(5.9.67)*	15	25	☐ ☐

1968–69 One centre phosphor band (4d values) or two phosphor bands (5d). No wmk

12	**13**	4d	sepia *(4.9.68)*	15	25	☐ ☐
13		4d	vermilion *(26.2.69)*	15	25	☐ ☐
14		5d	blue *(4.9.68)*	15	50	☐ ☐

For comprehensive listings of the Independent Postal Adminstration issues of Jersey, see Stanley Gibbons *Collect Channel Islands and Isle of Man Stamps*.

REGIONAL FIRST DAY COVERS

PRICES for First Day Covers listed below are for stamps, as indicated, used on illustrated envelopes and postmarked with operational cancellations (before 1964) or with special First Day of Issue cancellations (1964 onwards). First Day postmarks of 8 June 1964 and 7 February 1966 were of the machine cancellation 'envelope' type.

£sd Issues

18 Aug. 1958

Guernsey 3d (No. 7)	20·00	☐
Isle of Man 3d (No. 2)	32·00	☐
Jersey 3d (No. 10)	20·00	☐
Northern Ireland 3d (No. NI1)	30·00	☐
Scotland 3d (No. S1)	17·00	☐
Wales 3d (No. W1)	12·00	☐

29 Sept. 1958

Northern Ireland 6d, 1s3d (Nos. NI3, NI5)	35·00	☐
Scotland 6d, 1s3d (Nos. S3, S5)	25·00	☐
Wales 6d, 1s3d (Nos. W3, W5)	25·00	☐

8 June 1964

Guernsey 2½d (No. 6)	30·00	☐
Isle of Man 2½d (No. 1)	45·00	☐
Jersey 2½d (No. 9)	30·00	☐

7 Feb. 1966

Guernsey 4d (No. 8)	8·00	☐
Isle of Man 4d (No. 3)	15·00	☐
Jersey 4d (No. 11)	10·00	☐
Northern Ireland 4d (No. NI2)	7·00	☐
Scotland 4d (No. S2)	7·00	☐
Wales 4d (No. W2)	7·00	☐

1 Mar. 1967

Northern Ireland 9d, 1s6d		
(Nos. NI4, NI6)	4·00	☐
Scotland 9d, 1s6d (Nos. S4, S6)	6·00	☐
Wales 9d, 1s6d (Nos. W4, W6)	4·00	☐

4 Sept. 1968

Guernsey 4d, 5d (Nos. 10, 12)	3·00	☐
Isle of Man 4d, 5d (Nos. 5, 7)	4·00	☐
Jersey 4d, 5d (Nos. 12, 14)	3·00	☐
Northern Ireland 4d, 5d		
(Nos. NI8, NI10)	3·00	☐
Scotland 4d, 5d (Nos. S9, S11)	3·00	☐
Wales 4d, 5d (Nos. W9, W11)	3·00	☐

Decimal Issues

7 July 1971

Isle of Man 2½p, 3p, 5p, 7½p		
(Nos. 8/11)	3·00	☐
Northern Ireland 2½p, 3p, 5p, 7½p		
(Nos. NI12/13, NI18, NI23)	3·50	☐
Scotland 2½p, 3p, 5p, 7½p		
(Nos. S14/15, S20, S25)	3·00	☐
Wales 2½p, 3p, 5p, 7½p		
(Nos.W13/14, W19, W24)	3·00	☐

23 Jan. 1974

Northern Ireland 3p, 3½p, 5½p, 8p		
(Nos. NI14/15, NI19, NI24)	2·40	☐
Scotland 3p, 3½p, 5½p, 8p		
(Nos. S16/17, S21, S26)	2·50	☐
Wales 3p, 3½p, 5½p, 8p		
(Nos. W15/16, W20, W25)	2·50	☐

6 Nov. 1974

Northern Ireland 4½p (No. NI17)	1·50	☐
Scotland 4½p (No. S19)	1·50	☐
Wales 4½p (No. W18)	1·50	☐

14 Jan. 1976

Northern Ireland 6½p, 8½p		
(Nos. NI21, NI25)	1·50	☐
Scotland 6½p, 8½p		
(Nos. S23, S27)	1·50	☐
Wales 6½p, 8½p		
(Nos. W22, W26)	1·50	☐

20 Oct. 1976

Northern Ireland 10p, 11p		
(Nos. NI27, NI30)	1·75	☐
Scotland 10p, 11p (Nos. S29, S32)	1·50	☐
Wales 10p, 11p (Nos. W28, W31)	1·50	☐

18 Jan. 1978

Northern Ireland 7p, 9p, 10½p		
(Nos. NI22, NI26, NI29)	1·75	☐
Scotland 7p, 9p, 10½p		
(Nos. S24, S28, S31)	1·75	☐
Wales 7p, 9p, 10½p		
(Nos. W23, W27, W30)	1·75	☐

23 July 1980

Northern Ireland 12p, 13½p, 15p		
(Nos. NI31/3)	3·00	☐
Scotland 12p, 13½p, 15p		
(Nos. S33/5)	2·75	☐
Wales 12p, 13½p, 15p		
(Nos. W32/4)	3·00	☐

8 April 1981

Northern Ireland 11½p, 14p, 18p, 22p		
(Nos. NI34, NI38, NI45, NI53)	2·50	☐
Scotland 11½p, 14p, 18p, 22p		
(Nos. S36, S40, S44, S47)	2·50	☐
Wales 11½p, 14p, 18p, 22p		
(Nos. W35, W39, W46, W54)	2·50	☐

24 Feb. 1982

Northern Ireland 12½p, 15½p, 19½p,		
26p (Nos. NI36, NI41, NI50, NI60)	4·00	☐
Scotland 12½p, 15½p, 19½p, 26p		
(Nos. S38, S41, S45, S49)	3·50	☐
Wales 12½p, 15½p, 19½p, 26p		
(Nos. W37, W42, W51, W61)	3·50	☐

27 April 1983

Northern Ireland 16p, 20½p, 28p		
(Nos. NI42, NI52, NI62)	4·00	☐
Scotland 16p, 20½p, 28p		
(Nos. S42, S46, S50)	4·00	☐
Wales 16p, 20½p, 28p		
(Nos. W43, W53, W63)	3·50	☐

23 Oct. 1984

Northern Ireland 13p, 17p, 22p, 31p		
(Nos. NI37, NI43, NI54, NI64)	4·75	☐
Scotland 13p, 17p, 22p, 31p		
(Nos. S39, S43, S48, S51)	4·00	☐
Wales 13p, 17p, 22p, 31p		
(Nos. W38, W44, W55, W65)	4·25	☐

7 Jan. 1986

Northern Ireland 12p (No. NI35)	2·00	☐
Scotland 12p (No. S37)	2·00	☐
Wales 12p (No. W36)	2·00	☐

6 Jan. 1987

Northern Ireland 18p (No. NI46)	2·00	☐
Scotland 18p (No. S59)	1·80	☐
Wales 18p (No. W47)	2·00	☐

8 Nov. 1988

Northern Ireland 14p, 19p, 23p, 32p		
(Nos. NI39, NI49, NI56, NI65)	4·25	☐
Scotland 14p, 19p, 23p, 32p		
(Nos. S54, S62, S67, S77)	4·25	☐
Wales 14p, 19p, 23p, 32p		
(Nos. W40, W50, W57, W66)	4·50	☐

28 Nov. 1989

Northern Ireland 15p, 20p, 24p, 34p		
(Nos. NI40, NI51, NI57, NI66)	5·00	☐
Scotland 15p, 20p, 24p, 34p		
(Nos. S56, S64, S69, S78)	5·00	☐
Wales 15p, 20p, 24p, 34p		
(Nos. W41, W52, W58, W67)	5·00	☐

4 Dec. 1990

Northern Ireland 17p, 22p, 26p, 37p		
(Nos. NI44, NI55, NI61, NI67)	5·00	☐
Scotland 17p, 22p, 26p, 37p		
(Nos. S58, S66, S73, S79)	5·00	☐
Wales 17p, 22p, 26p, 37p		
(Nos.W45, W56, W62, W68)	5·00	☐

3 Dec. 1991

Northern Ireland 18p, 24p, 28p, 39p		
(Nos. NI47, NI58, NI63, NI68)	5·50	☐
Scotland 18p, 24p, 28p, 39p		
(Nos. S60, S70, S75, S80)	5·50	☐
Wales 18p, 24p, 28p, 39p		
(Nos. W48, W59, W64, W69)	5·50	☐

7 Dec. 1993

Northern Ireland 19p, 25p, 30p, 41p		
(Nos. NI69, NI72, NI74, NI76)	6·00	☐
Scotland 19p, 25p, 30p, 41p		

(Nos. S81, S84, S86, S88)	6·00	☐
Wales 19p, 25p, 30p, 41p		
(Nos. W70, W73, W75, W77)	6·00	☐

23 July 1996

Northern Ireland 20p (1 centre band), 26p, 37p, 63p (Nos. NI71, NI73, NI75, NI77)	8·75	☐
Scotland 20p (1 centre band), 26p, 37p, 63p (Nos. S83, S85, S87, S89)	8·75	☐
Wales 20p, 26p, 37p, 63p (Nos. W72, W74, W76, W78)	7·00	☐

1 July 1997

Wales 20p (1 centre band), 26p, 37p, 63p (Nos. W79 and W80/2)	6·00	☐

8 June 1999

Northern Ireland 38p, 64p (Nos. NI83, NI86)	4·00	☐
Scotland 2nd, 1st, E, 64p (Nos S94/7)	6·00	☐
Wales 2nd, 1st, E, 64p (Nos. W83, W84/6)	6·00	☐

25 Apr. 2000

Northern Ireland 1st, 40p, 65p (Nos. NI84, NI87, NI88b)	7·00	☐
Scotland 65p (No. S98)	3·00	☐
Wales 65p (No. W87)	3·00	☐

6 Mar. 2001

Northern Ireland 2nd, 1st, E, 65p (Nos. NI89/92)	4·50	☐

23 Apr. 2001

England 2nd, 1st, E, 65p (Nos. EN1/4)	3·25	☐

4 July 2002

England 68p (No. EN5)	3·50	☐
Northern Ireland 68p (No. NI93)	2·50	☐
Scotland 68p (No. S99)	1·75	☐
Wales 68p (No. W88)	1·75	☐

14 Oct. 2003

England 2nd, 1st, E, 68p (Nos. EN6/8, EN16)	3·25	☐
Northern Ireland 2nd, 1st, E, 68p (Nos. NI94/6, NI100)	3·25	☐
Scotland 2nd, 1st, E, 68p (Nos. S109/11, S119)	3·25	☐
Wales 2nd, 1st, E, 68p (Nos. W98/100, W108)	3·25	☐

11 May 2004

England 40p (No. EN9)	2·75	☐
Northern Ireland 40p (No. NI97)	2·75	☐
Scotland 40p (No. S112)	2·75	☐
Wales 40p (No. W101)	2·75	☐

5 Apr. 2005

England 42p (No. EN10)	1·40	☐
Northern Ireland 42p (No. NI98)	1·40	☐
Scotland 42p (No. S113)	1·40	☐
Wales 42p (No. W102)	1·40	☐

28 Mar. 2006

England 44p, 72p (Nos. EN11, EN17)	2·75	☐
Northern Ireland 44p, 72p (Nos. NI99, NI102)	2·75	☐
Scotland 44p, 72p (Nos. S114, S120)	2·75	☐
Wales 44p, 72p (Nos. W103, W109)	2·75	☐

27 Mar. 2007

England 48p, 78p (Nos. EN12, EN18)	4·00	☐
Northern Ireland 48p, 78p (Nos. NI124, NI128)	4·00	☐
Scotland 48p, 78p (Nos. S115, S121)	4·00	☐
Wales 48p, 78p (Nos. W104, W110)	3·50	☐

1 Apr. 2008

England 50p, 81p (Nos. EN13, EN19)	4·00	☐
Northern Ireland 50p, 81p (Nos. NI125, NI129)	4·00	☐
Scotland 50p, 81p (Nos. S116, S122)	4·00	☐
Wales 50p, 81p (Nos. W105, W111)	4·00	☐

31 Mar. 2009

England 56p, 90p (Nos. EN14, EN20)	4·75	☐
Northern Ireland 56p, 90p (Nos. NI126, NI130)	4·75	☐
Scotland 56p, 90p (Nos. S117, S123)	4·75	☐
Wales 56p, 90p (Nos. W106, W112)	4·75	☐

31 Mar. 2010

England 60p, 97p (Nos. EN15, EN21)	4·00	☐
Northern Ireland 60p, 97p (Nos. NI127, NI131)	4·00	☐
Scotland 60p, 97p (Nos. S118, S124)	4·00	☐
Wales 60p, 97p (Nos. W107, W113)	4·00	☐

29 Mar. 2011

England 68p, £1·10 (Nos. EN31, EN41)	6·00	☐
Northern Ireland 68p, £1·10 (Nos. NI100, NI111)	6·00	☐
Scotland 68p, £1·10 (Nos. S132, S138)	6·00	☐
Wales 68p, £1·10 (Nos. W123, W129)	6·00	☐

25 Apr. 2012

England 87p, £1·28 (Nos. EN32, EN43)	7·25	☐
Northern Ireland 87p, £1·28 (Nos. NI103, NI113)	7·25	☐
Scotland 87p, £1·28 (Nos. S133, S143)	7·25	☐
Wales 87p, £1·28 (Nos. W124, W134)	7·25	☐

27 Mar. 2013

England 88p (No. EN33,)	3·00	
Northern Ireland 88p, (No. NI104)	3·00	
Scotland 88p, (Nos. S134)	3·00	
Wales 88p, (No. W125)	3·00	

26 Mar. 2014

England 97p (No. EN34,)	3·50	
Northern Ireland 97p, (No. NI105)	3·50	
Scotland 97p, (Nos. S135)	3·50	
Wales 97p, (No. W126)	3·50	

24 Mar. 2015

England £1, £1·33 (Nos. EN35, EN44)	7.75	
Northern Ireland £1, £1·33 (Nos. NI106, NI114)	7·75	
Scotland £1, £1·33 (Nos. S136, S144)	7·75	
Wales £1, £1·33 (Nos. W127, W135)	7·75	

22 Mar. 2016

England £1·05 (No. EN36)	3.50	
Northern Ireland £1·05 (No. NI107)	3·50	
Scotland £1·05 (No. S137)	3·50	
Wales £1·05 (No. W128)	3·50	

21 Mar. 2017

England £1·17, £1·40 (No. EN36, EN45)	8·00	
Northern Ireland £1·17, £1·40 (No. NI112, NI115)	8·00	
Scotland £1·17, £1·40 (No. S139, S145)	8·00	
Wales £1·17, £1·40 (No. W130, W136)	8·00	

POSTAGE DUE STAMPS

PERFORATION. All postage due stamps to No. D101 are perf 14×15.

D **1**

D **2**

1914–22 Wmk Type **100** (Royal Cypher ('Simple')) sideways

D1	D **1**	½d	green	50	25	
D2		1d	red	50	25	
D3		1½d	brown	48·00	20·00	
D4		2d	black	50	25	
D5		3d	violet	5·00	75	
D6wi		4d	green	40·00	5·00	
D7		5d	brown	7·00	3·50	
D8		1s	blue	40·00	5·00	
Set of 8				£130	32·00	

1924–31 Wmk Type **111** (Block G V R) sideways

D10	D **1**	½d	green	1·25	75	
D11		1d	red	60	25	
D12		1½d	brown	48·00	22·00	
D13		2d	black	1·00	25	
D14		3d	violet	1·50	25	
D15		4d	green	15·00	4·25	
D16		5d	brown	65·00	45·00	
D17		1s	blue	8·50	50	
D18	D **2**	2s6d	purple/yellow	85·00	1·75	
Set of 9				£200	70·00	

1936–37 Wmk Type **125** (E 8 R) sideways

D19	D **1**	½d	green	15·00	10·50	
D20		1d	red	2·00	1·75	
D21		2d	black	15·00	12·00	
D22		3d	violet	2·00	2·00	
D23		4d	green	65·00	35·00	
D24a		5d	brown	40·00	28·00	
D25		1s	blue	25·00	8·50	
D26	D **2**	2s6d	purple/yellow	£325	12·00	
Set of 8				£450	£100	

1937–38 Wmk Type **127** (G VI R) sideways

D27	D **1**	½d	green	13·00	3·75	
D28		1d	red	3·00	50	
D29		2d	black	11·00	30	
D30		3d	violet	1·00	30	
D31		4d	green	£110	10·00	
D32		5d	brown	17·00	75	
D33		1s	blue	80·00	75	
D34	D **2**	2s6d	purple/yellow	85·00	1·25	
Set of 8				£290	16·00	

1951–52 Colours changed and new value (1½d). Wmk Type **127** (G VI R) sideways

D35	D **1**	½d	orange	3·50	3·50	
D36		1d	blue	1·50	75	
D37		1½d	green	2·00	2·00	
D38		4d	blue	50·00	22·00	
D39		1s	brown	28·00	5·25	
Set of 5				75·00	30·00	

1954–55 Wmk Type **153** (Mult Tudor Crown and E 2 R) sideways

D40	D **1**	½d	orange	7·00	5·25	
D41		2d	black	26·00	23·00	
D42		3d	violet	75·00	60·00	

D43		4d	blue	26·00	32·00	
D44		5d	brown	20·00	20·00	
D45	D **2**	2s6d	purple/yellow	£150	5·75	
Set of 6				£250	£130	

1955–57 Wmk Type **165** (Mult St Edward's Crown and E 2 R) sideways

D46	D **1**	½d	orange	2·75	3·25	
D47		1d	blue	5·00	1·50	
D48		1½d	green	8·50	7·00	
D49		2d	black	45·00	3·50	
D50		3d	violet	6·00	1·50	
D51		4d	blue	25·00	6·00	
D52		5d	brown	26·00	20·00	
D53		1s	brown	65·00	2·25	
D54	D **2**	2s6d	purple/yellow	£200	8·25	
D55		5s	red/yellow	£150	32·00	
Set of 10				£475	75·00	

1959–63 Wmk Type **179** (Mult St Edward's Crown) sideways

D56	D **1**	½d	orange	15	1·25	
D57		1d	blue	15	50	
D58		1½d	green	2·50	2·50	
D59		2d	black	1·10	50	
D60		3d	violet	30	30	
D61		4d	blue	30	30	
D62		5d	brown	45	60	
D63		6d	purple	50	30	
D64		1s	brown	90	30	
D65	D **2**	2s6d	purple/yellow	3·00	50	
D66		5s	red/yellow	8·25	1·00	
D67		10s	blue/yellow	12·00	6·00	
D68		£1	black/yellow	45·00	8·00	
Set of 13				65·00	20·00	

1968–69 Design size 22½ × 19 mm. No wmk

D69	D **1**	2d	black	75	1·00	
D70		3d	violet	1·00	1·00	
D71		4d	blue	1·00	1·00	
D72		5d	orange-brown	8·00	11·00	
D73		6d	purple	2·25	1·75	
D74		1s	brown	4·00	2·50	
Set of 6				15·00	16·00	

1968–69 Design size 21½ × 17½ mm. No wmk

D75	D **1**	4d	blue	7·00	6·50	
D76		8d	red	50	1·00	

D **3**

D **4**

Decimal Currency

1970–75 No wmk

D77	D **3**	½p	turquoise-blue	15	2·50	
D78		1p	reddish purple	15	15	
D79		2p	myrtle-green	20	15	
D80		3p	ultramarine	20	15	
D81		4p	yellow-brown	25	15	
D82		5p	violet	25	15	
D83		7p	red-brown	35	1·00	
D84	D **4**	10p	red	30	30	
D85		11p	green	50	1·00	
D86		20p	brown	60	25	
D87		50p	ultramarine	2·00	1·25	
D88		£1	black	4·00	1·00	
D89		£5	orange-yellow and black	36·00	1·50	
Set of 13				40·00	8·00	
Presentation Pack (P.O. Pack No. 36)						
(Nos. D77/82, D84, D86/8)			35·00			

Presentation Pack (P.O. Pack No. 93)
(Nos. D77/88)   18·00   ☐

D 5   D 6   D 7

1982 No wmk

D90	D 5	1p lake	10	30	☐☐
D91		2p bright blue	30	30	☐☐
D92		3p deep mauve	15	30	☐☐
D93		4p deep blue	15	25	☐☐
D94		5p sepia	20	25	☐☐
D95	D 6	10p light brown	30	40	☐☐
D96		20p olive-green	50	60	☐☐
D97		25p deep greenish blue	80	90	☐☐
D98		50p grey-black	1·75	1·75	☐☐
D99		£1 red	3·25	1·25	☐☐
D100		£2 turquoise-blue	7·00	4·25	☐☐
D101		£5 dull orange	14·00	2·25	☐☐
Set of 12			24·00	10·00	☐☐
Set of 12 Gutter Pairs			55·00		☐
Presentation Pack (P.O. Pack No. 135)			40·00		☐

1994 (15 Feb.) Perf 15×14 (with one elliptical hole on each vertical side)

D102	D 7	1p red, yellow and black	10	75	☐☐
D103		2p magenta, purple and black	10	75	☐☐
D104		5p yellow, red-brown and black	15	50	☐☐
D105		10p yellow, emerald and black	30	75	☐☐
D106		20p blue-green, violet and black	75	1·50	☐☐
D107		25p cerise, rosine and black	1·50	2·00	☐☐
D108		£1 violet, magenta and black	7·00	10·00	☐☐
D109		£1·20 greenish blue, blue-green and black	8·00	12·00	☐☐
D110		£5 greenish black, blue-green and black	30·00	20·00	☐☐
Set of 9			45·00	45·00	☐☐
First Day Cover				45·00	☐
Presentation Pack (P.O. Pack No. 32)			50·00		☐

ROYAL MAIL POSTAGE LABELS

These imperforate labels were issued as an experiment by the Post Office. Special microprocessor-controlled machines were installed at post offices in Cambridge, London, Shirley (Southampton) and Windsor to provide an after-hours sales service to the public. The machines printed and dispensed the labels according to the coins inserted and the buttons operated by the customer. Values were initially available in ½p steps to 16p and in addition, the labels were sold at philatelic counters in two packs containing either three values (3½, 12½, 16p) or 32 values (½p to 16p).

From 28 August 1984 the machines were adjusted to provide values up to 17p. After 31 December 1984 labels including ½p values were withdrawn. The machines were taken out of service on 30 April 1985.

Machine postage-paid impression in red on phosphorised paper with grey-green background design. No watermark. Imperforate.

1984 (1 May–28 Aug.)

Set of 32 (½p to 16p)	15·00	22·00	☐☐
Set of 3 (3½p, 12½p, 16p)	2·50	3·00	☐☐
Set of 3 on First Day Cover (1 May)		6·50	☐
Set of 2 (16½p, 17p) (28 August)	4·00	3·00	☐☐

ROYAL MAIL POST & GO STAMPS

FT **2** Blue Tit

Following trials of a number of self-service machines capable of dispensing postage labels, Royal Mail began installing "Post and Go" machines in larger post offices in October 2008. In addition to postage labels, the machines dispense stamps with a pre-printed background and an inkjet printed indicator of the service required, together with a four-part code.

The first machines were sited at the Galleries post office in Bristol and came into use on 8 October 2008. They dispensed five different stamps, dependent on the service; the code at the foot of the stamp referring to the branch in which the machine is sited, the machine number within the branch, and the session and transaction numbers.

The five original stamps were later complemented by values for 40g., 60g. and 100g. Unused stocks of earlier designs, such as Birds and Farmyard Animals also began to appear carrying the new service indicators and those seen have now been listed, although the set prices shown are generally for the values available at the time each design was released.

By the end of 2016 Post & Go machines could be found in most large post offices, nationwide.

Collectors should note that the listings are for the different *values* available from Post & Go machines, not the different designs provided in the special packs available from Tallents House. These packs are listed as separate items below each set.

FT **1**

2008 (8 Oct.)–**12** Type FT **1**. Olive-brown background. Self-adhesive. Two phosphor bands. Gravure Walsall, thermally printed service indicator Two phosphor bands. Perf 14 × 14½

FS1a	(1st Class up to 100g)	3.25	3.25	☐	☐
FS2a	(1st Large up to 100g)	3.50	3.50	☐	☐
FS3a	(Europe up to 20g)	4.00	4.00	☐	☐
FS3cb	(Euro 20g World 10g)	5.50	5.50	☐	☐
FS3dc	(Europe up to 60g)	8.50	8.50	☐	☐
FS3ea	(Europe up to 100g)	8.50	8.50	☐	☐
FS4a	(Worldwide up to 10g)	6.00	6.00	☐	☐
FS5a	(Worldwide up to 20g)	4.75	4.75	☐	☐
FS5e	(Worldwide up to 40g)	13.00	13.00	☐	☐
FS5fc	(Worldwide up to 60g)	9.25	9.25	☐	☐
FS5ga	(Worldwide up to 100g)	9.25	9.25	☐	☐
FS1a/3a, 4a,5a, 5e Set of 6		32.00	32.00	☐	☐
Special Pack (Nos. FS1/5) *(31.3.09)*		100.00		☐	

The special pack contains separate stamps. These are reproductions of the first "Post and Go" stamps printed at the Galleries Post Offices, Bristol. They differ from machine printed stamps in having the service indicator and branch code printed in gravure.

It is possible to obtain *se-tenant* strips of mixed values from "Post and Go" machines but we do not list these.

See also Nos. FS77a/84b

Birds of Britain (1st series)

2010 (17 Sept.) Multicoloured. Self-adhesive. Two phosphor bands. Designs printed in gravure by Walsall, thermally printed service indicator. Perf 14 × 14½

FS6	(1st Class up to 100g)	9.00	9.00	☐	☐
FS7	(1st Large up to 100g)	9.50	9.50	☐	☐
FS8	(Europe up to 20g)	9.50	9.50	☐	☐
FS8a	(Europe up to 60g)	90.00	90.00	☐	☐
FS9	(Worldwide up to 10g)	18.00	18.00	☐	☐
FS10	(Worldwide up to 20g)	13.00	13.00	☐	☐
FS10a	(Worldwide up to 40g)	60.00	60.00	☐	☐
FS10b	(Worldwide up to 60g)	90.00	90.00	☐	☐
FS6/10 *Set of 5*		55.00	55.00	☐	☐
First Day Cover (No. FS6 in 6 designs)			20.00		☐
Special Pack (No. FS6 in sheetlet of					
6 gravure designs)		24.00		☐	

Nos. FS6/10b were each available in six different designs: Type FT **2**, Goldfinch, Wood Pigeon, Robin, House Sparrow and Starling.

Nos. FS6/10 were available from Post and Go terminals in 30 post offices.

Stamps from the special pack and first day cover sold by Tallents House differ from machine printed stamps in having the service indicator and branch code printed in gravure.

Nos. FS8a, FS10a and FS10b resulted from the late use of old stock.

FT **3** Blackbird

FT **5** Puffin

Birds of Britain (2nd series)

2011 (24 Jan.) Multicoloured. Self-adhesive. Two phosphor bands. Designs printed in gravure by Walsall, thermally printed service indicator. Perf 14 × 14½

FS11	(1st class up to 100g)	4·00	4·00	☐	☐
FS12	(1st Large up to 100g)	4·25	4·25	☐	☐
FS13	(Europe up to 20g)	4·25	4·25	☐	☐
FS13a	(Europe up to 60g)	26·00	26·00	☐	☐
FS14	(Worldwide up to 10g)	9·00	9·00	☐	☐
FS15	(Worldwide up to 20g)	4·75	4·75	☐	☐
FS15a	(Worldwide up to 40g)	32·00	32·00	☐	☐
FS15b	(Worldwide up to 60g)	27·00	27·00	☐	☐
FS11/13, 14, 15 Set of 5		24·00	24·00	☐	☐
First Day Cover (No. FS11 in 6 designs)			20·00		☐
Special Pack (No. FS11 in sheetlet of					
	6 gravure designs)		45·00		☐

Nos. FS11/15b were each available in 6 different designs: FT **3**, two Magpies, Long-tailed Tit, Chaffinch, Collared Dove and Greenfinch.

Stamps from the special pack and first day cover sold by Tallents House differ from machine printed stamps in having the service indicator and branch code printed in gravure.

No. FS13a, FS15a and FS15b resulted from the late use of old stock

FT **4** Mallard

Birds of Britain (3rd series)

2011 (19 May) Multicoloured. Self-adhesive. Two phosphor bands. Designs printed in gravure by Walsall, thermally printed service indicator. Perf 14 × 14½

FS16	(1st Class up to 100g)	3·50	3·50	☐	☐
FS17	(1st Large up to 100g)	4·00	4·00	☐	☐
FS18	(Europe up to 20g)	4·00	4·00	☐	☐
FS18a	(Europe up to 60g)	40·00	40·00	☐	☐
FS19	(Worldwide up to 10g)	6·00	6·00	☐	☐
FS20	(Worldwide up to 20g)	4·50	4·50	☐	☐
FS20a	(Worldwide up to 40g)	14·00	14·00	☐	☐
FS20b	(Worldwide up to 60g)	40·00	40·00	☐	☐
FS16/18,19, 20 Set of 5		20·00	20·00	☐	☐
First Day Cover (No. FS16 in 6 designs)			8·75		☐
Special Pack (No. FS16 in sheetlet of					
	6 gravure designs)		10·00		☐

Nos. FS16/20b were each available in six different designs: , FT **4**, Greylag Goose, Kingfisher, Moorhen, Mute Swan, and Great Crested Grebe.

Stamps from the special pack sold by Tallents House differ from machine printed stamps in having the service indicator and branch code printed in gravure.

Nos. FS18a, FS20a and FS20b resulted from the late use of old stock.

Birds of Britain (4th series)

2011 (16 Sept.) Multicoloured. Self-adhesive. Two phosphor bands. Designs printed in gravure by Walsall, thermally printed service indicator. Perf 14 × 14½

FS21	(1st class up to 100g)	2·75	2·75	☐	☐
FS22	(1st Large up to 100g)	3·25	3·25	☐	☐
FS23	(Europe up to 20g)	3·25	3·25	☐	☐
FS23a	(Europe up to 60g)	12·00	12·00	☐	☐
FS24	(Worldwide up to 10g)	5·25	5·25	☐	☐
FS25	(Worldwide up to 20g)	4·00	4·00	☐	☐
FS26	(Worldwide up to 40g)	11·00	11·00	☐	☐
FS26a	(Worldwide up to 60g)	13·00	13·00	☐	☐
FS21/3, 24/6 Set of 6		26·00	26·00	☐	☐
First Day Cover (FS21 in 6 designs)			7·25		☐
Special Pack (No. FS21 in sheetlet of					
	6 gravure designs)		10·00		☐

Nos. FS21/26a were each available in six different designs: Type FT **5**, Gannet, Oystercatcher, Ringed Plover, Cormorant and Arctic Tern.

Stamps from the special pack sold by Tallents House differ from machine printed stamps in having the service indicator and branch code printed in gravure.

Nos. FS23a, and FS26a resulted from the late use of old stock.

FT **6** Welsh Mountain Badger Face

British Farm Animals (1st series). Sheep

2012 (24 Feb.) Multicoloured. Self-adhesive Two phosphor bands. Designs printed in gravure by Walsall, thermally printed service indicator. Perf 14 × 14½.

FS27	(1st Class up to 100g)	2·75	2·75	☐	☐
FS28	(1st Large up to 100g)	3·25	3·25	☐	☐
FS29	(Europe up to 20g)	3·25	3·25	☐	☐
FS29a	(Euro 20g World 10g)	10·00	10·00	☐	☐
FS29b	(Europe up to 60g)	12·00	12·00	☐	☐
FS30	(Worldwide up to 10g)	5·25	5·25	☐	☐
FS31	(Worldwide up to 20g)	4·00	4·00	☐	☐
FS32	(Worldwide up to 40g)	5·75	5·75	☐	☐
FS32b	(Worldwide up to 60g)	13·00	13·00	☐	☐
FS27/9, 30/2 Set of 6		22·00	22·00	☐	☐
First Day Cover (FS27 in 6 designs)			8·75		☐
Special Pack (FS27 in strip of 6 designs)					
	(P&G 6)		10·00		☐

Nos. FS27/32b were each available in six different designs: FT **6**; Dalesbred; Jacob; Suffolk; Soay; Leicester Longwool.

Nos. FS29a, FS29b and FS32b resulted from the late use of old stock.

FT **7** Berkshire

FT **9** Irish Moiled

British Farm Animals (2nd series). Pigs

2012 (24 Apr.) Multicoloured. Self-adhesive. Two phosphor bands. Designs printed in gravure by Walsall, thermally printed service indicator. Perf 14 × 14½.

FS33	(1st class up to 100g)	2·75	2·75	☐ ☐
FS34	(1st Large up to 100g)	3·25	3·25	☐ ☐
FS35	(Europe up to 20g)	3·25	3·25	☐ ☐
FS35a	(Euro20g World 10g)	8·75	8·75	☐ ☐
FS35b	(Europe up to 60g)	13·00	13·00	☐ ☐
FS36	(Worldwide up to 10g)	5·25	5·25	☐ ☐
FS37	(Worldwide up to 20g)	4·00	4·00	☐ ☐
FS38	(Worldwide up to 40g)	5·75	5·75	☐ ☐
FS38b	(Worldwide up to 60g)	13·00	13·00	☐ ☐
FS33/5, 36/8 Set of 6		22·00	22·00	☐
First Day Cover (No. FS33 in 6 designs)			8·50	☐
Special Pack (FS33 in strip of 6 designs)				
(P&G 7)			10·00	☐

Nos. FS33/38b were each available in six different designs: FT **7**; Gloucestershire Old Spot; Oxford Sandy and Black; Welsh; Tamworth; British Saddleback.

Nos. FS35a, FS35b and FS38b resulted from the late use of old stock.

FT **8** Union Flag

Union Flag

2012 (21 May) Type FT **8**. Multicoloured. Self-adhesive. Two phosphor bands. Designs printed in gravure by Walsall, thermally printed service indicator. Perf 14 × 14½

FS39	(1st Class up to 100g)	2·75	2·75	☐ ☐
FS40	(1st Large up to 100g)	3·25	3·25	☐ ☐
FS41	(Europe up to 20g)	3·50	3·50	☐ ☐
FS41a	(Euro20g World 10g)	3·50	3·50	☐ ☐
FS41b	(Europe up to 60g)	9·75	9·75	☐ ☐
FS41c	(Europe up to 100g)	9·50	9·50	☐ ☐
FS42	(Worldwide up to 10g)	5·25	5·25	☐ ☐
FS43	(Worldwide up to 20g)	4·50	4·50	☐ ☐
FS44	(Worldwide up to 40g)	6·00	6·00	☐ ☐
FS44b	(Worldwide up to 60g)	10·50	10·50	☐ ☐
FS44c	(Worldwide up to 100g)	10·50	10·50	☐ ☐
FS39/41, 42/44 Set of 6		23·00	23·00	☐
First Day Cover (No. FS39 only)			2·50	☐
Special Pack (No. FS39 only) (P&G 8)		3·00		☐

British Farm Animals (3rd series). Cattle

2012 (28 Sept.) Multicoloured. Self-adhesive. Two phosphor bands. Designs printed in gravure by Walsall, thermally printed service indicator. Perf 14 × 14½

FS45	(1st Class up to 100g)	4·00	4·00	☐ ☐
FS46	(1st Large up to 100g)	4·75	4·75	☐ ☐
FS47	(Europe up to 20g)	5·00	5·00	☐ ☐
FS47a	(Euro 20g World 10g)	10·00	10·00	☐ ☐
FS47b	(Europe up to 60g)	12·00	12·00	☐ ☐
FS48	(Worldwide up to 10g)	6·00	6·00	☐ ☐
FS49	(Worldwide up to 20g)	5·25	5·25	☐ ☐
FS50	(Worldwide up to 40g)	7·00	7·00	☐ ☐
FS50b	(Worldwide up to 60g)	13·00	13·00	☐ ☐
FS45/7, 48/50 Set of 6		29·00	29·00	☐ ☐
First Day Cover (No. FS45 in 6 designs)			8·50	☐
Special Pack (FS45 in strip of 6 designs)				
(P&G 9)			10·00	☐

Nos. FS45/50b were each available in six different designs: FT**9**; Welsh Black; Highland; White Park; Red Poll; Aberdeen Angus.

Nos. FS47a, FS47b and FS50b resulted from the late use of old stock.

FT **10** Robin

Christmas Robin

2012 (6 Nov.) Type FT **10**. With date code in background. Multicoloured. Self-adhesive. Two phosphor bands. Designs printed in gravure by Walsall, thermally printed service indicator. Perf 14 × 14½

FS51	(1st Class up to 100g)	2·75	2·75	☐ ☐
FS52	(1st Large up to 100g)	3·25	3·25	☐ ☐
FS53	(Europe up to 20g)	3·50	3·50	☐ ☐
FS53c	(Euro 20g World 10g)	5·00	5·00	☐ ☐
FS53da	(Europe up to 60g)	9·00	9·00	☐ ☐
FS53e	(Europe up to 100g)	13·00	13·00	☐ ☐
FS54	(Worldwide up to 10g)	4·00	4·00	☐ ☐
FS55	(Worldwide up to 20g)	4·50	4·50	☐ ☐
FS56	(Worldwide up to 40g)	5·75	5·75	☐ ☐
FS56da	(Worldwide up to 60g)	9·75	9·75	☐ ☐
FS56e	(Worldwide up to 100g)	14·00	14·00	☐ ☐
FS51/53, 54/56 Set of 6		22·00	22·00	☐ ☐

Nos. FS53ca, FS53da, FS53e, FS56da and FS56e resulted from the late use of old stock.

Nos. FS57 and FS58 are vacant.

FT **11** Lesser Silver Water Beetle

FT **13** Minnow

Freshwater Life (1st series). Ponds

2013 (22 Feb.) Multicoloured. Self-adhesive. Two phosphor bands. Designs printed in gravure by Walsall, thermally printed service indicator. Perf 14 × 14½

FS59	(1st Class up to 100g)	3·50	3·50	☐	☐
FS60	(1st Large up to 100g)	3·75	3·75	☐	☐
FS61	(Europe up to 20g)	4·00	4·00	☐	☐
FS61a	(Euro 20g World 10g)	10·00	10·00	☐	☐
FS61b	(Europe up to 60g)	11·00	11·00	☐	☐
FS62	(Worldwide up to 10g)	5·00	5·00	☐	☐
FS63	(Worldwide up to 20g)	4·25	4·25	☐	☐
FS64	(Worldwide up to 40g)	6·00	6·00	☐	☐
FS64b	(Worldwide up to 60g)	12·00	12·00	☐	☐
FS59/61, 62/4 Set of 6		24·00	24·00	☐	☐
First Day Cover (FS59 in 6 designs)			9·50		☐
Special Pack (FS59 in strip of 6 designs)					
	(P&G 11)		10·00		☐

Nos. FS59/64b were each available in six different designs: Type FT **11**, Three-spined Stickleback, Smooth Newt, Fairy Shrimp, Emperor Dragonfly and Glutinous Snail.

Nos. FS61a, FS61b and FS64b resulted from the late use of old stock.

FT **12** Perch

Freshwater Life (2nd series). Lakes

2013 (25 June) Multicoloured. Self-adhesive. Two phosphor bands. Designs printed in gravure by Walsall, thermally printed service indicator. Perf 14 × 14½

FS65	(1st Class up to 100g)	4·00	4·00	☐	☐
FS66	(1st Large up to 100g)	4·75	4·75	☐	☐
FS67	(Europe up to 20g)	5·00	5·00	☐	☐
FS67a	(Euro 20g World 10g)	9·00	9·00	☐	☐
FS67b	(Europe up to 60g)	12·00	12·00	☐	☐
FS68	(Worldwide up to 10g)	6·00	6·00	☐	☐
FS69	(Worldwide up to 20g)	5·25	5·25	☐	☐
FS70	(Worldwide up to 40g)	7·00	7·00	☐	☐
FS70b	(Worldwide up to 60g)	13·00	13·00	☐	☐
FS65/7, 68/70 Set of 6		29·00	29·00	☐	☐
First Day Cover (FS65 in 6 designs)			9·50		☐
Special Pack (FS65 in strip of 6 designs)					
	(P&G 12)		11·00		☐

Nos. FS65/70b were each available in six different designs: Type FT **12**, European Eel, Crucian Carp, Caddis Fly Larva, Arctic Char and Common Toad.

Nos. FS67a, FS67b and FS70b resulted from the late use of old stock.

Freshwater Life (3rd series). Rivers

2013 (20 Sept.) Multicoloured. Self-adhesive. Two phosphor bands. Designs printed in gravure by Walsall, thermally printed service indicator. Perf 14 × 14½

FS71	(1st Class up to 100g)	3·25	3·25	☐	☐
FS72	(1st Large up to 100g)	3·50	3·50	☐	☐
FS73	(Europe up to 20g)	3·75	3·75	☐	☐
FS73a	(Euro 20g World 10g)	9·00	9·00	☐	☐
FS73b	(Europe up to 60g)	10·50	10·50	☐	☐
FS74	(Worldwide up to 10g)	5·75	5·75	☐	☐
FS75	(Worldwide up to 20g)	4·50	4·50	☐	☐
FS76	(Worldwide up to 40g)	6·25	6·25	☐	☐
FS76b	(Worldwide up to 60g)	11·50	11·50	☐	☐
FS71/73, 74/76 Set of 6		24·00	24·00	☐	☐
First Day Cover (FS71 in 6 designs)			9·50		☐
Special Pack (FS71 in strip of 6 designs)		10·00		☐	
	(P&G 13)				

Nos. FS71/76b were each available in six different designs: Type FT **13**, Atlantic Salmon, White-clawed Crayfish, River Lamprey, Blue-winged Olive Mayfly Larva and Brown Trout.

Nos. FS73a, FS73b and FS76b resulted from the late use of old stock.

NOTE: From FS77 onwards all Post & Go stamps incorporated a date code, unless otherwise stated.

2013 (19 Nov.) Type FT **1** with date code in background. Olive-brown background, Self-adhesive. Two phosphor bands. Designs printed in gravure by Walsall, thermally printed service indicator. Perf 14 × 14½

FS77a	(1st Class up to 100g)	2·50	2·50	☐	☐
FS78a	(1st Large up to 100g)	3·00	3·00	☐	☐
FS79	(Europe up to 20g)	5·50	5·50	☐	☐
FS79ba	(Euro 20g World 10g)	3·25	3·25	☐	☐
FS80a	(Europe up to 60g)	6·00	6·00	☐	☐
FS80c	(Europe up to 100g)	4·25	4·25	☐	☐
FS81a	(Worldwide up to 10g)	—		☐	☐
FS82a	(Worldwide up to 20g)	3·75	3·75	☐	☐
FS83a	(Worldwide up to 40g)	—		☐	☐
FS84a	(Worldwide up to 60g)	7·00	7·00	☐	☐
FS84c	(Worldwide up to 100g)	5·75	5·75	☐	☐
FS77a, 78a, 79ba, 80c, 82a, 84c Set of 6		20·00	20·00	☐	☐

2013 (17 Nov.) Union Flag Type FT **8** with date code in background. Multicoloured. Self-adhesive. Two phosphor bands. Designs printed in gravure by Walsall; thermally printed service indicator. Perf 14 × 14½

FS85a	(1st Class up to 100g)	4·00	4·00	☐	☐
FS86a	(1st Large up to 100g)	4·25	4·25	☐	☐
FS87	(Europe up to 20g)	-	-	☐	☐
FS87a	(Euro 20g World 10g)	4·50	4·50	☐	☐
FS88	(Europe up to 60g)	20·00	20·00	☐	☐
FS88a	(Europe up to 100g)	5·50	5·50	☐	☐
FS89	(Worldwide up to 10g)	-	-	☐	☐
FS90a	(Worldwide up to 20g)	4·75	4·75	☐	☐
FS91	(Worldwide up to 40g)	-	-	☐	☐
FS92	(Worldwide up to 60g)	21·00	21·00	☐	☐
FS92a	(Worldwide up to 100g)	6·75	6·75	☐	☐
FS85a, 86a, 87a, 88a, 90a, 92a *Set of 6*		27·00	27·00	☐	☐

FT **14**

2013 (20 Nov.) Type FT **14** with date code in background. New blue background. Self-adhesive. One phosphor band (over the Queen's head). Designs printed in gravure by Walsall; thermally printed service indicator. Perf 14 × 14½

FS93a	(2nd Class up to 100g)	2.50	2.50	☐	☐
FS94a	(2nd Large up to 100g)	2·75	2·75	☐	☐
Special Pack (FS93/94) *(20.02.13)*		10·00		☐	
(P&G 10)					

Post & Go stamps as Type FT **14** were issued by Tallents House on 20 February 2013 in packs and on first day covers (price £7 per pack or £3 per first day cover.) They were also sold at Spring Stampex 2013 from machines, but were not made available through post offices until November 2013.

FT **15** Primrose

British Flora (1st series). Spring Blooms

2014 (19 Feb.) Multicoloured. Self-adhesive. Two phosphor bands. Designs printed in gravure by ISP Walsall; thermally printed service indicator. Perf 14 × 14½

FS95	(1st Class up to 100g)	4·50	4·50	☐	☐
FS96	(1st Large up to 100g)	5·25	5·25	☐	☐
FS97	(Europe up to 20g)	5·50	5·50	☐	☐
FS97b	(Euro 20g World 10g)	6·00	6·00	☐	☐
FS98a	(Europe up to 60g)	7·50	7·50	☐	☐
FS98b	(Europe up to 100g)	11·50	11·50	☐	☐
FS99	(Worldwide up to 10g)	6·50	6·50	☐	☐
FS100	(Worldwide up to 20g)	5·75	5·75	☐	☐
FS101	(Worldwide up to 40g)	7·50	7·50	☐	☐
FS102a	(Worldwide up to 60g)	8·50	8·50	☐	☐
FS102b	(Worldwide up to 100g)	12·50	12·50	☐	☐
FS95/7, FS99/101 *Set of 6*		32·00	32·00	☐	☐
First Day Cover (FS95 in 6 designs)			9·50		☐
Special Pack (FS95 in strip of 6 designs)					
(P&G 14)		10·00		☐	

Nos. FS95/102b were each available in six different designs: Type FT **15**, Snowdrop, Lesser Celandine, Dog Violet, Wild Daffodil and Blackthorn.

OPEN VALUE LABELS In February 2014, "Open Value labels", previously dispensed from Post & Go machines printed on white self-adhesive paper began to appear on the same illustrated background designs as Post & Go stamps. These show a service indicator "1L" (1st Letter), "2SP" (2nd Small Parcel), etc and the price. These are outside the scope of this catalogue, but on 7 July 2014 Royal Mail released a special pack (P&G 15) containing five such labels in the Machin Head design, as Types FT **1** and FT **14** (Price £8).

FT **16** Forget-me-not

British Flora (2nd series). Symbolic Flowers

2014 (17 Sept.) Multicoloured. Self-adhesive. Two phosphor bands. Designs printed in gravure by ISP Walsall, thermally printed service indicator. Perf 14 × 14½

FS103	(1st Class up to 100g)	3·00	3·00	☐	☐
FS104	(1st Large up to 100g)	3·25	3·25	☐	☐
FS104b	(Europe up to 20g)	25·00	25·00	☐	☐
FS105	(Euro 20g World 10g)	3·50	3·50	☐	☐
FS106	(Europe up to 60g)	6·75	6·75	☐	☐
FS106b	(Europe up to 100g)	10·00	10·00	☐	☐
FS107	(Worldwide up to 20g)	4·50	4·50	☐	☐
FS108	(Worldwide up to 60g)	7·25	7·25	☐	☐
FS108b	(Worldwide up to 100g)	11·00	11·00	☐	☐
FS103/8 *Set of 6*		26·00	26·00	☐	☐
First Day Cover (FS103 in 6 designs)			9·50		☐
Special Pack (FS103 in strip of 6 designs)					
(P&G 16)		10·00		☐	

Nos. FS103/108b were each available in six different designs: Type FT **16**, Common Poppy, Dog Rose, Spear Thistle, Heather and Cultivated Flax.

The Poppy design was released as a single design roll in the run-up to Remembrance Sunday in October 2014, October 2015, October 2016 and October 2017.

FT **17** Common Ivy

British Flora (3rd series). Winter Greenery

2014 (13 Nov.) Multicoloured. Self-adhesive. One phosphor band (FS109/10) or two phosphor bands (others). Designs printed in gravure by ISP Walsall, thermally printed service indicator. Perf 14 × 14½

FS109	(2nd Class up to 100g)	3·50	3·50	☐	☐
FS110	(2nd Large up to 100g)	4·00	4·00	☐	☐
FS111	(1st Class up to 100g)	3·50	3·50	☐	☐
FS112	(1st Large up to 100g)	4·00	4·00	☐	☐
FS113	(Euro 20g World 10g)	4·00	4·00	☐	☐
FS113c	(Europe up to 20g)	25·00	25·00	☐	☐
FS114	(Europe up to 60g)	4·50	4·50	☐	☐
FS114c	(Europe up to 100g)	10·00	10·00	☐	☐
FS115	(Worldwide up to 20g)	4·25	4·25	☐	☐

FS116 (Worldwide up to 60g)	5·75	5·75	☐	☐
FS116c (Worldwide up to 100g)	11·00	11·00	☐	☐
FS109/16 *Set of 8*	30·00	30·00	☐	☐
First Day Cover (FS109/12 in 4 designs)		9·50	☐	
Special Pack (FS109/12 in 4 designs) (P&G 17)	8·00		☐	

Nos. FS109/110 were each available as Type FT **17** or Mistletoe. Nos. FS111/116c were all available as Butcher's Broom and Holly.

FT **18** *Falcon*

Working Sail

2015 (18 Feb.) Multicoloured. Self-adhesive. Two phosphor bands. Designs printed in gravure by ISP Walsall, thermally printed service indicator. Perf 14 × 14½

FS117 (1st Class up to 100g)	3·75	3·75	☐	☐
FS118 (1st Large up to 100g)	4·25	4·25	☐	☐
FS119 (Euro 20g World 10g)	4·50	4·50	☐	☐
FS120 (Europe up to 60g)	7·50	7·50	☐	☐
FS121 (Europe up to 100g)	14·00	14·00	☐	☐
FS122 (Worldwide up to 20g)	5·25	5·25	☐	☐
FS123 (Worldwide up to 60g)	8·25	8·25	☐	☐
FS124 (Worldwide up to 100g)	15·00	15·00	☐	☐
FS117/20, 122, 123 *Set of 6*	30·00	30·00	☐	☐
First Day Cover (FS117 in 6 designs)		9·50	☐	
Special Pack (FS117 in strip of 6 designs) (P&G 18)	8·00		☐	

Nos. FS117/124 were each available in six different designs: Type FT **18**; *Briar, Harry, Margaret, Stag* and *Nell Morgan*.

FT **19** Lion

Heraldic Beasts

2015 (13 May) Multicoloured. Self-adhesive. Two phosphor bands. Designs printed in gravure by ISP Walsall, thermally printed service indicator. Perf 14 × 14½

FS125 (1st Class up to 100g)	3·75	3·75	☐	☐
FS126 (1st Large up to 100g)	4·25	4·25	☐	☐
FS127 (Euro 20g World 10g)	4·50	4·50	☐	☐
FS128 (Europe up to 100g)	5·50	5·50	☐	☐
FS129 (Worldwide up to 20g)	5·25	5·25	☐	☐
FS130 (Worldwide up to 100g)	6·75	6·75	☐	☐
FS125/130, *Set of 6*	27·00	27·00	☐	☐
First Day Cover (FS125 in 6 designs)		9·50	☐	
Special Pack (FS125 in strip of 6 designs) (P&G 19)	8·00		☐	

Nos. FS125/130 were each available in six different designs: Type FT **19**; Unicorn, Yale, Dragon, Falcon and Griffin.

FT **20** Dover

Sea Travel

2015 (16 Sept.) Multicoloured. Self-adhesive. Two phosphor bands. Designs printed in gravure by ISP Walsall, thermally printed service indicator. Perf 14 × 14½

FS131 (1st Class up to 100g)	3·75	3·75	☐	☐
FS132 (1st Large up to 100g)	4·25	4·25	☐	☐
FS133 (Euro 20g World 10g)	4·50	4·50	☐	☐
FS134 (Europe up to 100g)	5·50	5·50	☐	☐
FS135 (Worldwide up to 20g)	5·25	5·25	☐	☐
FS136 (Worldwide up to 100g)	6·75	6·75	☐	☐
FS131/136, *Set of 6*	27·00	27·00	☐	☐
First Day Cover (FS131 in 6 designs)		9·50	☐	
Special Pack (FS131 in strip of 6 designs) (P&G 20)	8·00		☐	

Nos. FS131/136 were each available in six different designs: Type FT **20**; Hong Kong, Sydney, Ha Long Bay, New York City and Venice.

Nos. FS137/42, Poppies, are omitted from this listing as they fall outside the scope of Collect British Stamps, A full listing will be found in the *Great Britain Concise Catalogue*.

FT **22** Mountain Hare

Winter Fur and Feathers

2015 (16 Nov.) Multicoloured. Self-adhesive. One phosphor band (FS143/4) or two phosphor bands (others). Designs printed in gravure by ISP Walsall, thermally printed service indicator. Perf 14 × 14½

FS143 (2nd Class up to 100g)	2·25	2·25	☐	☐
FS144 (2nd Large up to 100g)	3·00	3·00	☐	☐
FS145 (1st Class up to 100g)	3·75	3·75	☐	☐
FS146 (1st Large up to 100g)	4·25	4·25	☐	☐
FS147 (Euro 20g World 10g)	4·50	4·50	☐	☐
FS148 (Europe up to 100g)	5·50	5·50	☐	☐
FS149 (Worldwide up to 20g)	5·25	5·25	☐	☐
FS150 (Worldwide up to 100g)	6·75	6·75	☐	☐
FS143/50, *Set of 8*	28·00	28·00	☐	☐
First Day Cover (FS143/6 in 4 designs)		8·00	☐	
Special Pack (FS143/6 in 4 designs) (P&G 21)	7·00		☐	

Nos. FS143/4 were each available as Type FT **22** or Redwing. Nos. FS145/6 were all available as Red Fox or Red Squirrel.

FT **23** Post boy, 1640s

Royal Mail Heritage: Transport

2016 (17 Feb.) Multicoloured. Self-adhesive. Two phosphor bands. Designs printed in gravure by ISP Walsall, thermally printed service indicator. Perf 14 × 14½

FS151 (1st Class up to 100g)	2·50	2·50
FS152 (1st Large up to 100g)	2·75	2·75
FS153 (Euro 20g World 10g)	2·75	2·75
FS154 (Europe up to 100g)	4·00	4·00
FS155 (Worldwide up to 20g)	3·75	3·75
FS156 (Worldwide up to 100g)	5·75	5·75
FS151/6 Set of 6	20·00	20·00
First Day Cover (FS151 in 6 designs)		9·50
Special Pack (FS151 in strip of 6 designs)		
(P&G 22)	8·00	

Nos. FS151/6 were each available in six different designs: Type FT **23**; Mail Coach, 1790s; Falmouth Packet, 1820s; Travelling Post Office, 1890s; Airmail, 1930s and Royal Mail Minivan, 1970s.

2016 (5 Aug.) As Type FT **14** with background text reading, alternately, '2ND CLASS' in large lettering and 'ROYALMAIL' in small lettering, with date code. New blue background. Self-adhesive. One phosphor band (over the Queen's head). Designs printed in gravure by Walsall, thermally printed service indicator. Perf 14 × 14½

FS157 (2nd Class up to 100g)	2·50	2·50
FS158 (2nd Large up to 100g)	2·75	2·75

FT **24** Seven-spot Ladybird

Ladybirds

2016 (14 Sept.) Multicoloured. Self-adhesive. Two phosphor bands. Designs printed in gravure by ISP Walsall, thermally printed service indicator. Perf 14 × 14½

FS159 (1st Class up to 100g)	2·50	2·50
FS160 (1st Large up to 100g)	2·75	2·75
FS161 (Euro 20g World 10g)	2·75	2·75
FS162 (Europe up to 100g)	4·00	4·00
FS163 (Worldwide up to 20g)	3·75	3·75
FS164 (Worldwide up to 100g)	5·75	5·75
FS159/64 Set of 6	20·00	20·00
First Day Cover (FS159 in 6 designs)		9·50
Special Pack (FS159 in strip of 6 designs)		
(P&G 23)	6·50	

Nos. 159/64 were each available in six different designs: Type FT **24**; Fourteen-spot Ladybird; Orange Ladybird; Heather Ladybird; Striped Ladybird and Water Ladybird.

FT **25** Hedgehog

Hibernating Animals

2016 (14 Nov.) Multicoloured. Self-adhesive. One phosphor band (FS163/4) or two phosphor bands (others). Designs printed in gravure by ISP Walsall, thermally printed service indicator. Perf 14 × 14½

FS165 (2nd Class up to 100g)	2·50	2·50
FS166 (2nd Large up to 100g)	2·75	2·75
FS167 (1st Class up to 100g)	2·50	2·50
FS168 (1st Large up to 100g)	2·75	2·75
FS169 (Euro 20g World 10g)	2·75	2·75
FS170 (Europe up to 100g)	4·00	4·00
FS171 (Worldwide up to 20g)	3·75	3·75
FS172 (Worldwide up to 100g)	5·75	5·75
FS165/72 Set of 8	23·00	23·00
First Day Cover (FS165/8 in 4 designs)		8·00
Special Pack (FS165/8 in 4 designs)		
(P&G 24)	6·50	

Nos. FS165/6 were each available as Type FT **25** or Grass Snake. Nos. FS167/72 were all available as Dormouse or Brown Long-eared Bat.

1st Class up to 100g

FT **26** Travelling Post Office: bag exchange

Royal Mail Heritage: Mail by Rail

2017 (15 Feb.) Multicoloured. Self-adhesive. Two phosphor bands. Designs printed in gravure by ISP Walsall, thermally printed service indicator. Perf 14 × 14½

FS173 (1st Class up to 100g)	2·50	2·50
FS174 (1st Large up to 100g)	2·75	2·75
FS175 (Euro 20g World 10g)	3·00	3·00
FS176 (Europe up to 100g)	3·75	3·75
FS177 (Worldwide up to 20g)	3·50	3·50
FS178 (Worldwide up to 100g)	5·75	5·75
FS173/78 Set of 6	20·00	20·00
First Day Cover (FS173 in 6 designs)		9·50
Special Pack (FS173 in strip of 6 designs)		
(P&G 25)	6·50	

Nos. FS173/8 were each available in six different designs: Type FT **26**; Post Office (London) Railway; Night Mail: Poster; Travelling Post Office: Loading; Travelling Post Office: sorting and Travelling Post Office: on the move.

FT 27 Machin Commemorative Head

Machin Anniversary 1967-2017

2017 (5 Jun.) Self-adhesive. Two phosphor bands. Designs printed in gravure by ISP Walsall, thermally printed service indicator. Perf 14 × 14½

FS179 (1st Class up to 100g)	2·50	2·50	☐	☐
FS180 (1st Large up to 100g)	2·75	2·75	☐	☐
FS181 (Euro 20g World 10g)	3·00	3·00	☐	☐
FS182 (Europe up to 100g)	3·75	3·75	☐	☐
FS183 (Worldwide up to 20g)	3·50	3·50	☐	☐
FS184 (Worldwide up to 100g)	5·75	5·75	☐	☐
FS179/84 *Set of* 6	20·00	20·00	☐	☐
First Day Cover (FS179 in 6 designs)		9·50		☐
Special Pack (FS179 in strip of 6 designs) (P&G 26)		6·50	☐	

Nos. FS179/8 were each available in six different colours: orange-brown, light olive, violet, deep sepia, bright emerald and drab.

FT 28 First UK Aerial Mail, 1911

Royal Mail Heritage: Mail by Air

2017 (13 Sept.) Multicoloured. Self-adhesive. Two phosphor bands. Designs printed in gravure by ISP Walsall, thermally printed service indicator. Perf 14 × 14½

FS185 (1st Class up to 100g)	2·50	2·50	☐	☐
FS186 (1st Large up to 100g)	2·75	2·75	☐	☐
FS187 (Euro 20g World 10g)	3·00	3·00	☐	☐
FS188 (Europe up to 100g)	3·75	3·75	☐	☐
FS189 (Worldwide up to 20g)	3·50	3·50	☐	☐
FS190 (Worldwide up to 100g)	5·75	5·75	☐	☐
FS185/90 *Set of* 6	20·00	20·00	☐	☐
First Day Cover (FS185 in 6 designs)		9·50		☐
Special Pack (FS185 in strip of 6 designs) (P&G 27)	6·50		☐	

Nos. FS185/90 were each available in six different designs: Type FT **28**; Military Mail Flight, 1919; International Airmail, 1933; Domestic Airmail, 1934; Flying Boat Airmail, 1937 and Datapost Service, 1980s.

OFFICIAL STAMPS

Various stamps of Queen Victoria and King Edward VII overprinted in Black.

I.R.	**I. R.**	**O.W.**
OFFICIAL	**OFFICIAL**	**OFFICIAL**
(O **1**)	(O **2**)	(O **3**)

ARMY	**ARMY**	**GOVT**
		PARCELS
OFFICIAL	**OFFICIAL**	**GOVT PARCELS**
(O **4**)	(O **5**)	(O **7**)

BOARD	**R.H.**	**ADMIRALTY**
OF		
EDUCATION	**OFFICIAL**	**OFFICIAL**
(O **8**)	(O **9**)	(O **10**)

1 Inland Revenue
Overprinted with Types O **1** or O **2** (5s, 10s, £1)

1882–1901 Queen Victoria

O2	52	½d green	90·00	40·00	☐	☐
O5		½d blue	85·00	35·00	☐	☐
O13	71	½d vermilion	15·00	7·00	☐	☐
O17		½d green	20·00	15·00	☐	☐
O3	57	1d lilac (Die II)	8·00	6·00	☐	☐
O6	64	2½d lilac	£525	£180	☐	☐
O14	74	2½d purple on blue	£175	30·00	☐	☐
O4	43	6d grey (Plate 18)	£575	£140	☐	☐
O18	79	6d purple on red	£500	£150	☐	☐
O7	65	1s green	£6000	£1900	☐	☐
O15	82	1s green	£1000	£375	☐	☐
O19		1s green and red	£4250	£1800	☐	☐
O9	59	5s red	£12000	£2500	☐	☐
O10	60	10s blue	£11500	£3750	☐	☐
O11	61	£1 brown (Wmk Crowns)	£75000	£30000	☐	☐
O12		£1 brown (Wmk Orbs)	£100000	£40000	☐	☐
O16		£1 green	£12500	£2500	☐	☐

1902–04 King Edward VII

O20	83	½d blue-green	32·00	4·50	☐	☐
O21		1d red	22·00	3·00	☐	☐
O22	86	2½d blue	£1000	£275	☐	☐
O23	83	6d purple	£500000	£300000	☐	☐
O24	93	1s green and red	£3750	£900	☐	☐
O25	95	5s red	£45000	£11000	☐	☐
O26	96	10s blue	£100000	£48000	☐	☐
O27	97	£1 green	£62500	£25000	☐	☐

2 Office of Works
Overprinted with Type O **3**

1896–1902 Queen Victoria

O31	71	½d vermilion	£350	£150	☐	☐
O32		½d green	£475	£225	☐	☐
O33	57	1d lilac (Die II)	£500	£150	☐	☐
O34	78	5d dull purple and blue	£4000	£1400	☐	☐
O35	81	10d dull purple and red	£7250	£2250	☐	☐

1902–03 King Edward VII

O36	83	½d blue-green	£575	£180	☐	☐
O37		1d red	£575	£180	☐	☐
O38	85	2d green and red	£2000	£450	☐	☐
O39	86	2½d blue	£3500	£675	☐	☐
O40	92	10d purple and red	£47500	£7000	☐	☐

3 Army
Overprinted with Types O **4** (½d, 1d) or O **5** (2½d, 6d)

1896–1901 Queen Victoria

O41	71	½d vermilion	8·00	3·00	☐	☐
O42		½d green	10·00	15·00	☐	☐
O43	57	1d lilac (Die II)	8·00	7·00	☐	☐
O44	74	2½d purple on blue	50·00	35·00	☐	☐
O45	79	6d purple on red	£110	60·00	☐	☐

Overprinted with Type O **4**

1902 King Edward VII

O48	83	½d blue-green	5·50	2·25	☐	☐
O49		1d red	5·50	2·25	☐	☐
O50		6d purple	£175	80·00	☐	☐

4 Government Parcels
Overprinted with Type O **7**

1883–1900 Queen Victoria

O69	57	1d lilac (Die II)	£100	30·00	☐	☐
O61	62	1½d lilac	£400	£100	☐	☐
O65	72	1½d purple and green	£160	28·00	☐	☐
O70	73	2d green and red	£250	50·00	☐	☐
O71	77	4½d green and red	£400	£275	☐	☐
O62	63	6d green	£3500	£1400	☐	☐
O66	79	6d purple on red	£275	75·00	☐	☐
O63	64	9d green	£2750	£1200	☐	☐
O67	80	9d purple and blue	£425	£120	☐	☐
O64	44	1s brown (Plate 13)	£1750	£300	☐	☐
O64c		1s brown (Plate 14)	£3500	£600	☐	☐
O68	82	1s green	£700	£275	☐	☐
O72		1s green and red	£650	£275	☐	☐

1902 King Edward VII

O74	83	1d red	75·00	22·00	☐	☐
O75	85	2d green and red	£225	60·00	☐	☐
O76	83	6d purple	£275	60·00	☐	☐
O77	91	9d purple and blue	£650	£175	☐	☐
O78	93	1s green and red	£1350	£300	☐	☐

5 Board of Education
Overprinted with Type O **8**

1902 Queen Victoria

O81	**78**	5d	dull purple and blue	£5750	£1500	☐	☐
O82	**82**	1s	green and red	£12000	£6000	☐	☐

1902–04 King Edward VII

O83	**83**	½d	blue-green	£180	40·00	☐	☐
O84		1d	red	£180	40·00	☐	☐
O85	**86**	2½d	blue	£4850	£450	☐	☐
O86	**89**	5d	purple and blue	£35000	£10000	☐	☐
O87	**93**	1s	green and red	£200000		☐	

6 Royal Household
Overprinted with Type O **9**

1902 King Edward VII

O91	**83**	½d	blue-green	£375	£200	☐	☐
O92		1d	red	£325	£175	☐	☐

7 Admiralty
Overprinted with Type O **10**

1903 King Edward VII

O101	**83**	½d	blue-green	30·00	15·00	☐	☐
O102		1d	red	20·00	8·00	☐	☐
O103	**84**	1½d	purple and green	£325	£150	☐	☐
O104	**85**	2d	green and red	£350	£160	☐	☐
O105	**86**	2½d	blue	£475	£150	☐	☐
O106	**87**	3d	purple on yellow	£425	£160	☐	☐

Prestige and Sponsored Booklets
– a Simplified listing

On 1 December 1969 a new style of large-size booklet was issued, entitled "Stamps for Cooks", sponsored by the Milk Marketing Board and containing recipes and stamps to a value of £1. The booklet contained one pane in a *se-tenant* combination that was not available from any other source, ensuring that sales to stamp collectors were high, even if those to cooks were probably rather limited!

In spite of this success, however, it was 1972 before a second sponsored booklet, "The Story of Wedgwood" was issued, providing the only source of the ½p Machin definitive with one phosphor band at left. Nearly eight years were to pass before the same company sponsored a second "Story of Wedgwood" booklet, followed two years later by Stanley Gibbons with "Story of Stanley Gibbons".

From then on, sponsored large-size booklets became an annual event, generally containing at least one stamp which was not available from any other source. In 1989 Royal Mail themselves became the "sponsors" of each new booklet, which were by then widely known among collectors simply as "Prestige Booklets". Their frequency of issue increased steadily, until in 2009 four such booklets were issued.

In 2011, with the issue of the "Morris & Co" booklet, Royal Mail introduced an additional charge, over and above the face value of the stamps contained in them to cover the costs of manufacturing these booklets and with this change the Stanley Gibbons catalogue number prefix was altered from "DX" to "DY".

This simplified checklist provides a complete listing of the Prestige and Sponsored booklets issued to the end of 2017.

DX**3**

ZP1a	£1	Stamps for Cooks *1.2.69*	13·00	☐
DX1	£1	The Story of Wedgwood *24.5.72*	75·00	☐
DX2	£3	The Story of Wedgwood *16.4.80*	8·00	☐
DX3	£4	Story of Stanley Gibbons *19.5.82*	11·00	☐
DX4	£4	Story of the Royal Mint *14.9.83*	11·00	☐
DX5	£4	The Story of our Christian Heritage *4.9.84*	25·00	☐
DX6	£5	The Story of The Times *8.1.85*	20·00	☐
DX7	£5	The Story of British Rail *18.3.86*	25·00	☐
DX8	£5	The Story of P&O *3.3.87*	25·00	☐
DX9	£5	The Story of The Financial Times *9.2.88*	32·00	☐
DX10	£5	The Scots Connection *21.3.89*	22·00	☐

DX11	£5	London Life 20.3.90	28·00	☐	
DX12	£6	Alias Agatha Christie 19.3.91	20·00	☐	
DX13	£6	Cymru-Wales 25.2.92	20·00	☐	
DX14	£6	Tolkien, the Centenary 27.10.92	20·00	☐	
DX15	£5·64	The Story of Beatrix Potter 10.8.93	22·00	☐	
DX16	£6·04	Northern Ireland 26.7.94	25·00	☐	
DX17	£6	The National Trust 25.4.95	25·00	☐	
DX18	£6·48	European Football Championship 14.5.96	20·00	☐	
DX19	£6·15	Celebrating 75 years of the BBC 23.9.97	22·00	☐	
DX20	£7·49	The Wilding Definitives 10.3.98	26·00	☐	
DX21	£6·16	Breaking Barriers 13.10.98	35·00	☐	
DX22	£7·54	Profile on Print 16.2.99	45·00	☐	
DX23	£6·99	World Changers 21.9.99	30·00	☐	
DX24	£7·50	Special by Design 15.2.00	42·00	☐	
DX25	£7·03	The Life of the Century 4.8.00	32·00	☐	
DX26	£7·00	A Treasury of Trees 18.9.00	35·00	☐	
DX27	£6·76	Unseen & Unheard 22.10.01	40·00	☐	
DX28	£7·29	A Gracious Ascension 6.2.02	45·00	☐	
DX29	£6·83	Across the Universe 24.9.02	35·00	☐	
DX30	£6·99	Microcosmos 25.2.03	38·00	☐	
DX31	£7·46	A Perfect Coronation 2.6.03	70·00	☐	
DX32	£7·44	Letters by Night 16.3.04	30·00	☐	
DX33	£7·23	The Glory of the Garden 25.5.04	40·00	☐	
DX34	£7·43	The Brontë Sisters 24.2.05	28·00	☐	
DX35	£7·26	Battle of Trafalgar 18.10.05	28·00	☐	
DX36	£7·40	Isambard Kingdom Brunel 23.2.06	26·00	☐	
DX37	£7·44	Victoria Cross 21.9.06	35·00	☐	
DX38	£7·49	World of Invention 1.3.07	24·00	☐	
DX39	£7·66	The Machin, the Making of a Masterpiece 5.6.07	24·00	☐	
DX40	£7·66	British Army Uniforms 20.9.07	26·00	☐	
DX41	£7·40	Ian Fleming's James Bond 8.1.08	30·00	☐	
DX42	£7·15	Pilot to Plane, RAF Uniforms 18.9.08	25·00	☐	
DX43	£9·72	50th Anniversary of Country Definitives 29.9.08	32·00	☐	
DX44	£7·68	British Design Classics 13.1.09	38·00	☐	
DX45	£7·75	Charles Darwin 12.2.09	50·00	☐	
DX46	£8·18	Treasures of the Archive 18.8.09	24·00	☐	
DX47	£7·93	Royal Navy Uniforms 17.9.09	20·00	☐	
DX48	£8·06	Classic Album Covers 7.1.10	35·00	☐	
DX49	£7·72	The Royal Society 25.2.10	20·00	☐	
DX50	£11·15	King George V 8.5.10	25·00	☐	
DX51	£9·76	Britain Alone 13.5.10	22·00	☐	
DX52	£9·05	WWF, For a Living Planet 22.3.11	21·00	☐	
DY1	£9·99	Morris & Co 5.5.11	23·00	☐	
DY2	£9·97	First United Kingdom Aerial Post 9.9.11	45·00	☐	

DY3	£11·47	Roald Dahl 10.1.12	26·00	☐	
DY4	£12·77	The Diamond Jubilee 31.5.12	28·00	☐	
DY5	£10·71	Olympic and Paralympic Games 27.7.12	50·00	☐	
DY6	£13·77	50 Years of Doctor Who 26.3.13	30·00	☐	
DY7	£11·11	Football Heroes 9.5.13	35·00	☐	
DY8	£11·19	Merchant Navy 19.9.13	24·00	☐	
DY9	£13·97	Classic Locomotives 20.2.14	32·00	☐	
DY10	£11·39	Buckingham Palace 15.4.14	29·00	☐	
DY11	£11·30	Centenary of the First World War 28.7.14	26·00	☐	
DY12	£14·50	Inventive Britain 19.2.15	32·00	☐	
DY13	£13·96	Centenary of the First World War (2nd issue) 14.5.15	30·00	☐	
DY14	£14·47	Bicentenary of the Battle of Waterloo 18.6.15	32·00	☐	
DY15	£16·99	The Making of Star Wars The British Story (17.12.15)	38·00	☐	
DY16	£16·36	500 Years of Royal Mail (18.2.16)	35·00	☐	
DY17	£15·11	90th Birthday of Queen Elizabeth II (21.4.16)	35·00	☐	
DY18	£16·49	Centenary of the First World War (3rd issue) (21.6.16)	35·00	☐	
DY19	£15·37	The Tale of Beatrix Potter (28.7.16)	35·00	☐	
DY20	£14·58	Windsor Castle (15.2.17)	32·00		
DY21	£15·14	50th Anniversary of the Machin Definitive (5.6.17)	35·00	☐	
DY22	£15·41	Centenary of the First World War (4th issue) (31.7.17)	35·00		
DY23	£15·99	Star Wars. The Making of the Droids, Aliens and Creatures (14.12.17)	35·00	☐	

Philatelic, Numismatic and Philatelic Medallic Covers

On 2 June 1993 Royal Mail and the Royal Mint prepared a commemorative cover to celebrate the 40th anniversary of the Coronation of Her Majesty The Queen. The cover bore the Royal Mint's Coronation Anniversary Crown and the £10 'Britannia' stamp, issued on 2 March 1993 (No. 1658).

On 1 March 1994 a similar cover was produced for the 25th Anniversary of the Investiture of HRH The Prince of Wales. The cover bore the set of five stamps issued on that date (Nos. 1810/14), showing paintings by Prince Charles, and a commemorative medal struck by the Royal Mint.

So began a series of Philatelic Numismatic Covers (PNC) and Philatelic Medallic Covers (PMC) produced by Royal Mail and the Royal Mint.

This listing comprises only those jointly produced covers sold by the Philatelic Bureau. Privately sponsored covers incorporating coins or medals including those sponsored by the Royal Mint alone, are outside its scope.

No.	Date	Issue	Stamps	Coin/Medal	Price
RMC1	2.6.93	Coronation 40th Anniversary	1658	£5 Coin	28·00
RMC2	1.3.94	Prince of Wales Investiture 25th Anniversary	1810/14	Medal	22·00
RMC3	27.7.94	Bank of England 300th Anniversary	1666×4 + label	£2 Coin	20·00
RMC4	20.5.95	R. J. Mitchell Birth Centenary	1666×4 + label	Medal	20·00
RMC5	15.8.95	End of Second World War 50th Anniversary	1873, 1875	£2 Coin	20·00
RMC6	29.10.95	William Wyon Birth Bicentenary	Y1725	Medal	20·00
RMC7	21.4.96	Queen's 70th Birthday	1666×4 + label	£5 Coin	24·00
RMC8	14.5.96	European Football Championship	1925/9	£2 Coin	20·00
RMC9	1.10./3.11.96	Classic Sports Cars	1945/9	Medal	20·00
RMC10	28.1.97	King Henry VIII 450th Death Anniversary	1965/71	£1 Coin	20·00
RMC11	30.6.97	Transfer of Hong Kong to Chinese Rule	1671×4 + label	Hong Kong $5 Coin	22·00
RMC12	23.8.97	British Aircraft Designers	1984/8	£2 Coin	20·00
RMC13	20.11.97	Royal Golden Wedding	2011/14	£5 Coin	24·00
RMC14	24.2.98	Order of the Garter 650th Anniversary	2026/30	£1 Coin	£100
RMC15	5.7.98	NHS 50th Anniversary	2046/9	50p Coin	20·00
RMC16	25.8.98	Notting Hill Carnival	2055/8	50p Coin	20·00
RMC17	14.11.98	HRH Prince of Wales 50th Birthday	1666×4 + label	£5 Coin	24·00
RMC18	12.5.99	Berlin Airlift 50th Anniversary	1666×4 + label	Medal	20·00
RMC19	1.7.99	New Scottish Parliament Building	S94/7	£1 Coin	60·00
RMC20	1.10.99	Rugby World Cup, Wales	1664a×4 + label	£2 Coin	20·00
RMC21	31.12.99	Millennium	**MS**2123	£5 Coin	24·00
RMC22	4.4.00	National Botanic Garden of Wales	2124×4 + label	£1 Coin	20·00
RMC23	14.8.00	150 Years of Public Libraries	2116, 2121, 2100	50p Coin	20·00
RMC24	4.8.00	Queen Mother's 100th Birthday	**MS**2161	£5 Coin	24·00
RMC25	1.1.01	Archers Radio Programme 50th Anniversary	2107/8, 2110	Medal	20·00
RMC26	24.5.01	RN Submarine Service Centenary	2202/5	Medal	20·00
RMC27	20.6.01	Queen Victoria Death Centenary	2133 + label	£5 Coin	24·00
RMC28	2.10.01	Northern Ireland	NI89/92	£1 Coin	15·00
RMC29	6.2.02	Golden Jubilee	2253/7	£5 Coin	24·00
RMC29a	6.2.02	Golden Jubilee	2258/9	£5 Coin and £5 note	28·00
RMC30	31.5.02	World Cup Football, Japan & Korea	5×1st from **MS**2292	£1 Coin	20·00
RMC31	16.7.02	17th Commonwealth Games, Manchester	2299/303	4×£2 Coins	£100
RMC32	11.12.02	Queen Mother Commemoration	2280/3	£5 Coin	24·00
RMC33	25.2.03	Discovery of DNA 50th Anniversary	2343/7	£2 Coin	21·00
RMC34	2.6.03	Coronation 50th Anniversary	2368/77	£5 Coin	24·00
RMC35	27.8.03	Extreme Endeavours	2360/5	£1 Coin	20·00
RMC36	7.10.03	British Museum 250th Anniversary	2404/9	Medal	20·00
RMC37	13.1.04	Classic Locomotives	2417/22	£2 Coin	21·00
RMC38	6.4.04	Entente Cordiale Centenary	2446/7 + France 50c, 75c	£5 Coin	25·00
RMC39	13.4.04	Ocean Liners	2448/53	Medal	22·00
RMC40	25.5.04	RHS Bicentenary	2456/61	Medal	21·00
RMC41	30.11.04	Scotland Definitive	S109/10, S112/13	£1 Coin	25·00
RMC42	24.2.05	Charlotte Brontë 150th Death Anniversary	2518/23	50p Coin	20·00
RMC43	1.3.05	Wales Definitive	W98/9, W101/2	£1 Coin	20·00
RMC44	21.4.05	World Heritage Sites	2532/5 + Australia 2×50c. & 2×$1	50p Coin + Australia 50c.	40·00
RMC45	5.7.05	End of the War 60th Anniversary	**MS**2547	Medal and £2 Coin	24·00
RMC46	18.10.05	Battle of Trafalgar Bicentenary	2574/9	2×£5 Coins	37·00
RMC47	23.2.06	Brunel Birth Bicentenary	2607/12	2×£2 Coins	24·00

No.	Date	Issue	Stamps	Coin/Medal	Price
RMC48	17.3.06	Northern Ireland Definitive	NI94/5, NI98, NI100	£1 Coin	20·00
RMC49	21.4.06	Queen's 80th Birthday	2620/7	£5 Coin	27·00
RMC50	6.6.06	World Cup Football	2628/33	Medal	22·00
RMC51	18.7.06	National Portrait Gallery 150th Anniversary	2640/9	Medal	22·00
RMC52	21.9.06	Victoria Cross 150th Anniversary	2657/62	2×50p Coins	23·00
RMC53	16.1.07	Act of Union 300th Anniversary	6×1st as 2570 but litho	£2 Coin	23·00
RMC54	13.2.07	'The Sky at Night' 50th Anniversary	2709/14	Medal	22·00
RMC55	22.3.07	Abolition of the Slave Trade Bicentenary	2728/33	£2 Coin	35·00
RMC56	23.4.07	England Definitive	EN6/8, EN12, EN15	£1 Coin	25·00
RMC57	5.6.07	First Machin Stamps 40th Anniversary	Type **1984**	Medal	22·00
RMC58	3.7.07	British Motor Racing	2744/9	Medal	22·00
RMC59	26.7.07	Scouting Centenary	2758/63	50p Coin	23·00
RMC60	20.11.07	Diamond Wedding	2780/6	£5 Coin	35·00
RMC61	1.4.08	Territorial Army Centenary	2774/6	Medal	22·00
RMC62	13.5.08	St. Paul's Cathedral 300th Anniversary	**MS**2847	Medal	22·00
RMC63	5.6.08	First Machin Coin 40th Anniversary	Type **1984**	Medal	22·00
RMC64	17.7.08	Farnborough 'A Celebration of Aviation'	2885/60	Medal	22·00
RMC65	24.7.08	1908 Olympic Games, London Centenary	4×1st	£2 Coin	30·00
RMC66	29.9.08	Country Definitives 50th Anniversary and £1 Coin 25th Anniversary	**MS**NI111	£1 Coin	20·00
RMC67	6.11.08	Armistice 90th Anniversary	2883/5	Medal	22·00
RMC68	13.1.09	Mini car 50th Anniversary	2889×2	Medal	22·00
RMC69	22.1.09	Robert Burns 250th Birth Anniversary	**MS**S137	£2 Coin	35·00
RMC70	12.2.09	Charles Darwin Birth Bicentenary	2898/903	£2 Coin	35·00
RMC71	2.3.09	First Concorde Test Flight 40th Anniversary	2891×2	Medal	22·00
RMC72	23.4.09	Accession of Henry VIII 500th Anniversary and Accession of Elizabeth I 450th Anniversary	2925, 2929 2×£5	Coins	35·00
RMC73	19.5.09	Royal Botanic Gardens, Kew 250th Anniversary	**MS**2941	50p Coin	£250
RMC74	1.9.09	Fire and Rescue Service	2958/63	Medal	22·00
RMC75	18.9.09	Big Ben 150th Anniversary	Type **1517** + label	Medal	22·00
RMC76	22.10.09	Countdown to London 2012 Olympic Games I The countdown begins...	2981/90	£5 Coin	26·00
RMC77	1.12.09	High value Security Definitives	U2913/16	£1 Coin	24·00
RMC78	2.2.10	Girlguiding Centenary	**MS**3025	50p Coin	23·00
RMC79	25.2.10	Royal Society 350th Anniversary	3026/35	Medal	22·00
RMC80	11.3.10	Battersea Cats and Dogs Home 150th Anniversary	3036/45	Medal	22·00
RMC81	21.4.10	City of London	As 1st St. George's flag stamp from **MS**EN19 but self-adhesive+label	£1 Coin	30·00
RMC82	13.5.10	Dunkirk	**MS**3086	Medal	22·00
RMC83	27.7.10	Countdown to London 2012 Olympic Games II The Games spring to life...	3097/106	£5 Coin	26·00
RMC84	1.8.10	Florence Nightingale	2570 + label	£2 Coin	35·00
RMC85	12.10.10	Olympic and Paralympic Sports I. Athletics – Track	2983	50p Coin	15·00
RMC86	12.10.10	Olympic and Paralympic Sports II Cycling	3101	50p Coin	15·00
RMC87	30.11.10	Olympic and Paralympic Sports III Football	3104	50p Coin	15·00
RMC88	30.11.10	Olympic and Paralympic Sports IV Boccia	2985	50p Coin	15·00
RMC89	11.1.11	'F.A.B. The Genius of Gerry Anderson'	**MS**3142	Medal	22·00
RMC90	1.2.11	Olympic and Paralympic Sports V Weightlifting	2989	50p Coin	15·00
RMC91	1.2.11	Olympic and Paralympic Sports VI Hockey	3103	50p Coin	15·00
RMC92	17.3.11	City of Belfast	NI103	£1 Coin	30·00
RMC93	22.3.11	WWF 50th Anniversary	**MS**3172	50p Coin	24·00
RMC94	24.3.11	Olympic and Paralympic Sports VII Shooting	3098	50p Coin	15·00
RMC95	24.3.11	Olympic and Paralympic Sports VIII Goalball	3105	50p Coin	15·00
RMC96	21.4.11	Royal Wedding	**MS**3180	£5 Coin	35·00
RMC97	26.5.11	Olympic and Paralympic Sports IX Taekwondo	3100	50p Coin	15·00
RMC98	26.5.11	Olympic and Paralympic Sports X Boxing	3106	50p Coin	15·00
RMC99	14.6.11	Thomas the Tank Engine	3187/92	Medal	22·00
RMC100	27.7.11	Countdown to London 2012 Olympic Games IV The final push to the line	3195/204	£5 Coin	26·00
RMC101	27.7.11	Olympic and Paralympic Sports XI Wrestling	3199	50p Coin	15·00
RMC102	27.7.11	Olympic and Paralympic Sports XII Handball	3204	50p Coin	15·00
RMC103	23.8.11	Restoration of the Monarchy	3207/14	£5 Coin	23·00
RMC104	22.9.11	Olympic and Paralympic Sports XIII Basketball	2990	50p Coin	15·00
RMC105	22.9.11	Olympic and Paralympic Sports XIV Modern Pentathlon	3099	50p Coin	15·00
RMC106	6.10.11	500th Anniversary of Launch of Mary Rose	2925 and Mary Rose stamp from **MS**2930	£2 Coin	60·00

No.	Date	Issue	Stamps	Coin/Medal	Price
RMC107	8.11.11	Christmas 400th Anniversary of the King James Bible	3237/43	£2 coin	60·00
RMC108	29.11.11	Olympic and Paralympic Sports XV Canoeing	2981	50p coin	15·00
RMC109	29.11.11	Olympic and Paralympic Sports XVI Archery	2982	50p coin	15·00
RMC110	30.11.11	City of Edinburgh	S110 + label	£1 coin	24·00
RMC111	5.1.12	Olympic and Paralympic Games	3250/3	£2 coin	26·00
RMC112	12.1.12	Olympic and Paralympic Sports XVII Aquatics	2984	50p coin	15·00
RMC113	12.1.12	Olympic and Paralympic Sports XVIII Rowing	3097	50p coin	15·00
RMC114	28.2.12	Olympic and Paralympic Sports XIX Sailing	3195	50p coin	15·00
RMC115	28.2.12	Olympic and Paralympic Sports XX Badminton	2988	50p coin	15·00
RMC116	1.3.12	City of Cardiff	W99+label	£1 coin	24·00
RMC117	1.4.12	Olympic and Paralympic Sports XXI Judo	2986	50p coin	15·00
RMC118	1.4.12	Olympic and Paralympic Sports XXII Triathlon	3203	50p coin	15·00
RMC119	6.5.12	Olympic and Paralympic Sports XXIII Wheelchair rugby	3198	50p coin	15·00
RMC120	6.5.12	Olympic and Paralympic Sports XXIV Volleyball	3197	50p coin	15·00
RMC121	31.5.12	Diamond Jubilee	3319/26	£5 coin	26·00
RMC122	12.6.12	Olympic and Paralympic Sports XXV Equestrian	2987	50p coin	15·00
RMC123	12.6.12	Olympic and Paralympic Sports XXVI Table Tennis	3102	50p coin	15·00
RMC124	19.6.12	Charles Dickens Birth Bicentenary	3330/5	£2 coin	32·00
RMC125	27.7.12	Olympic and Paralympic Sports XXVII Wheelchair Tennis	3200	50p coin	15·00
RMC126	27.7.12	Olympic and Paralympic Sports XXVIII Fencing	3201	50p coin	15·00
RMC127	27.7.12	Countdown to London 2012 Olympic Games IV. Crossing the Finishing Line	MS3341	£5 coin and £5 silver proof coin	26·00
RMC128	28.8.12	Olympic and Paralympic Sports XXIX Gymnastics	3202	50p coin	15·00
RMC129	28.8.12	Olympic and Paralympic Sports XXX Athletics – Field	3196	50p coin	15·00
RMC130	9.1.13	150th Anniversary of the London Underground	3423/8	2×£2 Coins	40·00
RMC131	30.5.13	60th Anniversary of the Coronation. Six Decades of Royal Portraits	3491/6	£2 Coin	30·00
RMC132	22.11.13	Birth Centenary of Benjamin Britten	3459	50p. Coin	40·00
RMC133	7.1.14	Classic Children's TV	3552/63	Medal	30·00
RMC134	15.4.14	Buckingham Palace	3589/94	Medal	22·00
RMC135	17.7.14	Commonwealth Games, Glasgow	3619/24	50p. coin	26·00
RMC136	28.7.14	Centenary of the First World War	3626/31	£2 coin	26·00
RMC137	23.9.14	Ryder Cup, Gleneagles	S158	Medal	22·00
RMC138	18.9.14	500th Anniversary of Trinity House	3638	£2 coin	24·00
RMC139	24.1.15	50th Death Anniversary of Winston Churchill	3645	£5 Coin	26·00
RMC140	5.3.15	Alice in Wonderland	3658/67	Medal	22·00
RMC141	6.5.15	175th Anniversary of the Penny Black	MS3710	Medal	22·00
RMC142	14.5.15	Centenary of the First World War (2nd issue)	3711/16	£2 Coin	26·00
RMC143	2.6.15	800th Anniversary of the Magna Carta	3718/23	£2 coin	24·00
RMC144	18.6.15	Centenary of the Battle of Waterloo (1st issue)	3724/9	£5 Coin	26·00
RMC145	9.9.15	Long to Reign Over Us	MS3747	£5 Coin	26·00
RMC146	15.9.15	75th Anniversary of the Battle of Britain	MS3735	50p. Coin	32·00
RMC147	20.10.15	Star Wars. Battles	3758/62, 3764/7	Medal	23·00
RMC148	20.10.15	Star Wars. Vehicles	MS3770	Medal	23·00
RMC149	17.12.15	Star Wars. Characters	3758/69	Medal	23·00
RMC150	5.4.16	400th Death Anniversary of William Shakespeare	3816/25	3×£2 Coins	45·00
RMC151	21.4.16	90th Birthday of Queen Elizabeth II	MS3832	£5 Coin	30·00
RMC152	21.6.16	Centenary of the First World War (3rd issue)	3838/43	£2 Coin	26·00
RMC153	28.7.16	The Tale of Peter Rabbit	MS3868	50p. Coin	32·00
RMC154	2.9.16	350th Anniversary of the Great Fire of London	3879/84	£2 Coin	32·00
RMC155	14.10.16	950th Anniversary of the Battle of Hastings	EN5	1×4+label 50p. Coin	24·00
RMC156	15.2.17	Windsor Castle	3920/5	Medal	23·00
RMC157	6.4.17	Racehorse Legends	3940/7	Medal	23·00
RMC158	5.6.17	50th Anniversary of the Machin definitive	MS3964	Medal	23·00
RMC159	31.7.17	Centenary of the First World War (4th issue)	3983/8	Coin	23·00
RMC160	12.10.17	Star Wars. BB 8	4007/14	Medal	23·00
RMC161	12.10.17	Star Wars. R2-D2	4007/14	Medal	23·00
RMC162	20.11.17	Royal Platinum Wedding Anniversary	MS4031	Coin	23·00
RMC163	14.12.17	Star Wars. C3-PO	4007/14	Medal	23·00

Stanley Gibbons
Stamp Catalogues

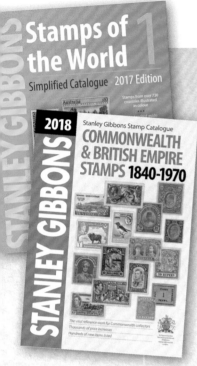

Stamps of the World 1
Simplified Catalogue — **2017 Edition**
Stamps from over 730 countries illustrated in colour

2018
Stanley Gibbons Stamp Catalogue
COMMONWEALTH & BRITISH EMPIRE STAMPS 1840-1970

STANLEY GIBBONS

The vital reference work for Commonwealth collector
Thousands of price increases
Hundreds of new items listed

e have catalogues
suit every aspect of
mp collecting

r catalogues cover stamps issued
n across the globe - from the
ny Black to the latest issues.
ether you're a specialist in a
tain reign or a thematic collector,
should have something to suit
r needs. All catalogues include
famous SG numbering system,
king it as easy as possible to find
stamp you're looking for.

**Commonwealth & British Empire Stamps
1840–1970** (120th edition, 2018)

Commonwealth Country Catalogues

Australia & Dependencies
(10th Edition, 2016)
Bangladesh, Pakistan & Sri Lanka
(3rd edition, 2015)
Belize, Guyana, Trinidad & Tobago
(2nd edition, 2013)
Brunei, Malaysia & Singapore
(5th edition, 2017)
Canada (6th edition, 2016)
Cyprus, Gibraltar & Malta
(4th edition, 2014)
East Africa with Egypt & Sudan
(3rd edition, 2014)
Eastern Pacific (3rd edition, 2015)
Falkland Islands (7th edition, 2016)
Hong Kong (5th edition, 2015)
**India (including Convention &
Feudatory States)** (4th edition, 2013)
Indian Ocean (3rd edition, 2016)
Ireland (6th edition, 2015)
Leeward Islands (3rd edition, 2017)
New Zealand (6th edition, 2016)
Northern Caribbean, Bahamas & Bermuda
(4th edition, 2016)
St. Helena & Dependencies
(6th edition, 2017)
Southern & Central Africa
(2nd edition, 2014)
West Africa (2nd edition, 2012)
Western Pacific (4th edition, 2017)
Windward Islands & Barbados
(3rd edition, 2015)

Stamps of the World 2018

Volume 1	Abu Dhabi – Charkhari
Volume 2	Chile – Georgia
Volume 3	German Commands – Jasdan
Volume 4	Jersey – New Republic
Volume 5	New South Wales – Singapore
Volume 6	Sirmoor – Zululand

Great Britain Catalogues

2018 Collect British Stamps
(69th edition, 2018)

Collect Channel Islands & Isle of Man
(30th edition, 2016)
Great Britain Concise Stamp Catalogue
(32nd edition, 2017)

Great Britain Specialised

Volume 1	Queen Victoria
	(16th edition, 2012)
Volume 2	King Edward VII to
	King George VI
	(14th edition, 2015)
Volume 3*	Queen Elizabeth II
	Pre-decimal issues
	(12th edition, 2011)
Volume 4*	Queen Elizabeth II Decimal
	Definitive Issues – Part 1
	(10th edition, 2008)

**Queen Elizabeth II Decimal Definitive
Issues – Part 2*** (10th edition, 2010)

Foreign Countries

Antarctica (2nd edition, 2012)
Arabia (1st edition, 2016)
Belgium & Luxembourg
(1st edition, 2015)
Central America (3rd edition, 2007)
China (11th edition, 2015)
Czech Republic and Slovakia
(1st edition, 2017)
Finland and Sweden
(1st edition, 2017)
France, Andorra and Monaco
(1st edition, 2015)
French Colonies (1st edition, 2016)
Germany (11th edition, 2014)
Japan & Korea (5th edition, 2008)
Netherlands & Colonies
(1st edition, 2017)
Poland (1st edition, 2015)
Russia (7th edition, 2014)
South-East Asia (5th edition, 2012)
United States of America
(8th edition, 2015)

*Currently out of stock.

APPOINTMENT TO
MAJESTY THE QUEEN
PHILATELISTS
STANLEY GIBBONS LTD
LONDON

STANLEY GIBBONS
LONDON 1856

399 Strand, WC2R 0LX, London
Phone: +44 1425 472 363 | Email: support@stanleygibbons.com
www.stanleygibbons.com

STANLEY GIBBONS
LONDON 1856

399 Strand, WC2R 0LX, London
Phone: **+44 1425 472 363** | Email: **support@stanleygibbons.com**
www.stanleygibbons.com

One Country Albums

Ideal for the straightforward single country
collection, the Stanley Gibbons, One Country range
comes complete with 130gsm white acid free leaves
and SG numbers for easy identification.
Page dimensions: 222 x 276mm.
Album colour: ●

Great Britain Albums (4-Ring binders)

	Album		Leaves	
Vol. 1 Album (1840-1970)	R5250MAR	£49.95	R5274	£39.95
Vol. 2 Album (1971-1990)	R5252MAR	£49.95	R5275	£39.95
Vol. 3 Album (1991-1999)	R5254MAR	£49.95	R5276	£39.95
Vol. 4 Album (2000-2008)	R5255MAR	£49.95	R5246	£39.95
Vol. 5 Album (2009-2011)	R5238MAR	£49.95	R5236	£39.95
Vol. 6 Album (2012-2014)	R5149MAR	£49.95	R5149	£39.95
Vol. 7 Album (2015-2016)	R5150MAR	£49.95	R5150	£39.95
Complete Set (1840-2016)	R5250(SO)	£290 SAVE £59.65		

These ring-fitting albums follow
the Collect British Stamps
catalogue.

British Islands Albums (22-Ring binders)
Available individually or as a special four volume set.

	Album		Leaves	
Guernsey Vol. 1 (1941-1994)	R5524MAR	£49.95	R5524	£39.95
Guernsey Vol. 2 (1995-2004)	R5526MAR	£49.95	R5526	£39.95
Guernsey Vol. 3 (2005-2011)	R5529MAR	£49.95	R5528	£39.95
Guernsey Vol. 4 (2012-2014)	R5153MAR	£49.95	R5133	£39.95
Alderney Vol. 1 (1983-2016)	R5130MAR	£49.95	R5130	£39.95
Guernsey & Alderney 5 Vol. Set (1941-2016)	R5524(SO)	£200 SAVE £49.75		
Jersey Vol. 1 (1941-1994)	R5525MAR	£49.95	R5525	£39.95
Jersey Vol. 2 (1995-2004)	R5527MAR	£49.95	R5527	£39.95
Jersey Vol. 3 (2005-2011)	R5528MAR	£49.95	R5529	£39.95
Jersey Vol. 4 (2012-2016)	R5157MAR	£49.95	R5157	£39.95
Jersey 4 Vol. Set (1941-2016)	R5525(SO)	£170 SAVE £29.80		
Isle of Man Vol. 1 (1958-1994)	R5256MAR	£49.95	R5277	£39.95
Isle of Man Vol. 2 (1995-2004)	R5257MAR	£49.95	R5279	£39.95
Isle of Man Vol. 3 (2005-2012)	R5265MAR	£49.95	R5235	£39.95
Isle of Man Vol. 4 (2013-2016)	R5161MAR	£49.95	R5161	£39.95
Isle of Man 3 Vol. Set (1958-2016)	R5256(SO)	£170 SAVE £29.80		

Prices correct at time of printing.

Come and Visit us at 399 Strand

56   1896   1936   1976   2017

Get advice from our experienced and knowledgeable staff

See first hand our superb range of top quality stamps, albums and accessories

Get insider tips on how to enhance and expand your collection

Ask for guidance on techniques for care and storage of your stamps and covers

View our specialist material

All Stanley Gibbons stamps come with a lifetime guarantee of authenticity from our stamp specialists.

Everything for the stamp collector.

Collect British Stamps Order Form

YOUR ORDER

Stanley Gibbons account number ☐ ☐ ☐ ☐ ☐ ☐

Condition (mint/UM/ used)	Country	SG No.	Description	Price	Office use only
			POSTAGE & PACKING	£3.60	
			TOTAL		

The lowest price charged for individual stamps or sets purchased from Stanley Gibbons Ltd, is £1.

Payment & address details

Name ....

Address (We cannot deliver to PO Boxes) ....

....

.... Postcode ....

Tel No. ....

Email ....

PLEASE NOTE Overseas customers MUST quote a telephone number or the order cannot be dispatched. Please complete ALL sections of this form to allow us to process the order.

☐ Cheque (made payable to Stanley Gibbons)

☐ I authorise you to charge my

☐ Mastercard ☐ Visa ☐ Diners ☐ Amex ☐ Maestro

Card No. ☐☐☐☐ ☐☐☐☐ ☐☐☐☐ ☐☐☐☐ (Maestro only)

Valid from ☐☐☐☐ Expiry date ☐☐☐☐ Issue No. (Maestro only) ☐☐ CVC No. (4 if Amex) ☐☐☐☐

CVC No. is the last three digits on the back of your card (4 if Amex)

Signature _____ Date _____

4 EASY WAYS TO ORDER

Post to
Mark Pegg,
Stamp Mail Order
Department, Stanley
Gibbons Ltd, 399
Strand, London,
WC2R 0LX, England

Call
020 7836 8444
+44 (0)20 7836 844

Fax
020 7557 4499
+44 (0)20 7557 449

Click
lmourne@
stanleygibbons.com

Delivering Your Dream Collection...
...can cost less than you think

MY favourite stamp is probably the same as my wife's – the GB PUC £1. Just take a look at the design / engraving – and in single monochrome – utterly magnificent. Strictly speaking I should say the 1d black – it's iconic and an amazing work of design/art in the first place as this stamp represents in communication terms the 'Apple i-phone' of its time – also barring damage to the actual paper – the 1d black is virtually indestructible … the colour is so 'fast' that you can soak a 1d black in a 1/10 part solution of 'milton/water' (nappy bleach) … the paper will turn white but the black will remain unaffected. This is the reason why you sometimes see a magnificent used 1d black but the paper is too white – simply it has been left too long in bleach … over-white paper will actually lower value … as with most things it is a question of degree …

Reader: That's all very interesting Andrew, but where is this going ..?

When I was, theoretically, growing up (in my teens) you could ask me the retail price of virtually any British commemorative set (think 'special issue' for the indoctrinated) and I would know it as black is to white. But nowadays, in value terms, what is black and what is white? – courtesy perhaps more than anything of the internet … so much is 'grey' and blurred around the edges … that 'retail' price depends more than ever upon the quality of what is being retailed and no longer does one price fit all … Just search on-line for an 'Agatha Christie' booklet – don't look at what sellers wish for – look at reality – click 'completed' – far fewer do … actual 'sold' prices can be 50% of each other

… now look at fixed retail prices, consider the postally valid 'face value' and finally the 'catalogue' value … you could be forgiven for throwing your arms up in the air. The point is making sense of it all … not just for 'bog standard' commodity price items but for stamps with character – generally pre-QEII and pre 1950 / 1940 classic stamps of which they're not making any more (excepting on-line auction offers of modern fakes/reproductions) … so it follows that if you can be confident of just _**four**_ things:
1. the supplier is real and reputable (and internet ratings only tell part of the story), 2. the quality is as described, 3. the price is realistic against comparison, 4. You have a reliable guarantee … then that's the way for you to go …

But to realise your dream maybe there's another way for you to go so that ...

1st
£55
FREE WINNINGS

Continued overleaf ☞